AMERICAN BAR ASSOCIATION
Defending Liberty
Pursuing Justice



# Performance Bond Manual

## Of the 50 States, District of Columbia, Puerto Rico, and Federal Jurisdictions

Lawrence Lerner
Theodore M. Baum

Editors



TORT TRIAL INSURANCE

Tort Trial & Insurance Practice
Fidelity and Surety Law Committee

Cover design by ABA Publishing.



Printed in the United States of America.

10 09 08 07 06 5 4 3 2 1

Library of Congress Cataloging –in-Publication

Performance Bond / Lawrence Lerner, Theodore M. Baum, editors
p.cm.
ISBN: 1-59031- 648-7

Discounts are available for books ordered in bulk. Special condsideration is given to state bars, CLE programs, and other bar-related organizations. Inquire at Publication, Planning & Marketing, American Bar Association, 321 North Clark Street, Chicago, Illinois 60610.

# CONTENTS

# CONTRIBUTORS

Phillip G. Alber
Alber Crafton, PSC
Troy, Michigan

Samuel J. Arena, Jr.
Stradley, Ronon, Stevens & Young, LLP
Philadelphia, Pennsylvania

Mark Aronson
Anderson, McPharlin & Conners LLP
Los Angeles, California

Randy L. Arthur
Bullivant Houser Bailey PC
Portland, Oregon

Daniel J. Auerbach
Browning, Kaleczyc, Berry & Hoven, P.C.
Helena, Montana

Brian J. Babcock
Babcock Scott & Babcock, PC
Salt Lake City, Utah

Dennis J. Bartlett
Kerr Brosseau Bartlett O'Brien, LLC
Denver, Colorado

Theodore M. Baum
Ernstrom & Dreste, LLP
Rochester, New York

Richard R. Beretta
Adler Pollock & Sheehan P.C.
Providence, Rhode Island

Stacy Blakeley
Kleiman Lawrence Baskind Fitzgerald LLP
Dallas, Texas

Jeffrey M. Boldt
Locke Reynolds, LLP
Indianapolis, Indiana

Cline I. Boone
Levy and Craig, A Professional Corporation
Kansas City, Missouri

Shannon J. Briglia
Wickwire Gavin, P.C.
Vienna, Virginia

David M. Burkholder
Stradley, Ronon, Stevens & Young, LLP
Philadelphia, Pennsylvania

Robert T. Carlton, Jr.
Wolff & Samson, P.C.
Philadelphia, Pennsylvania

Bradford R. Carver
Hinshaw & Culbertson LLP
Boston, Massachusetts

Gary M. Case
Wolf, Horowitz, Etlinger & Case, L.L.C.
Hartford, Connecticut

Ann M. Conway
Miller Stratvert P.A.
Albuquerque, New Mexico

Victor E. Covalt
Ballew Schneider Covalt Gaines & Engdahl, PC, LLO
Lincoln, Nebraska

Thomas E. Crafton
Alber Crafton, PSC
Louisville, Kentucky
(Troy, Michigan and Columbus, Ohio)

Shashauna M. Dermody
Krebs, Farley & Pelleteri, L.L.C.
New Orleans, Louisiana

J. Scott Dickens
Starnes & Atchison, LLP
Birmingham, Alabama
(and Mobile, Alabama)

Brian A. Dodd
Starnes & Atchison, LLP
Birmingham, Alabama
(and Mobile, Alabama)

Cynthia R. Estrella
Mann, Berens & Wisner, LLP
Phoenix, Arizona

Mark D. Etchart
Browning, Kaleczyc, Berry & Hoven, P.C.
Helena, Montana

Edward Etcheverry
Etcheverry Harrison LLP
Ft. Lauderdale, Florida

Charles G. Evans
Law Office of Charles G. Evans
Anchorage, Alaska

Kurt C. Faux
Faux & Associates
Las Vegas, Nevada

Amy L. Fischer
The Cunningham Law Firm, P.A.
West Palm Beach, Florida

Alexander Friedrich
Yusen & Friedrich
Seattle, Washington

William P. Fuller
Woods, Fuller, Shultz & Smith P.C.
Sioux Falls, South Dakota

Evan B. Gatewood
Hayes Magrini & Gatewood
Oklahoma City, Oklahoma

Joseph T. Getz
Less, Getz & Lipman, LLC
Memphis, Tennessee

C. Allen Gibson, Jr.
Buist Moore Smythe McGee P.A.
Charleston, South Carolina

John P. Giffune
Verrill Dana LLP
Portland, Maine

Douglas W. Gigler
Nilles, Ilvedson, Stroup, Plambeck & Selbo, Ltd.
Fargo, North Dakota

Jason Glasgow
Wolf, Horowitz, Etlinger & Case, L.L.C.
Hartford, Connecticut

David A. Grace
Hardin & Grace, a Professional Association
North Little Rock, Arkansas

Daniel R. Hansen
Shumaker, Loop & Kendrick, LLP
Charlotte, North Carolina

Omar J. Harb
Alber Crafton, PSC
Troy, Michigan

Dan Hendy
Frost Brown Todd LLC
Cincinnati, Ohio

Eric M. Hurwitz
Stradley, Ronon, Stevens & Young, LLP
Philadelphia, Pennsylvania

Vivian Katsantonis
Watt, Tieder, Hoffar & Fitzgerald, L.L.P.
McLean, Virginia

Cheryl Kniffen
Thompson Slagle & Hannan, LLC
Duluth, Georgia

David J. Krebs
Krebs, Farley & Pelleteri, L.L.C.
New Orleans, Louisiana

James H. Lawhn
Oliver, Lau, Lawhn, Ogawa and Nakamura
Honolulu, Hawaii

Laird E. Lawrence
Kleiman Lawrence Baskind Fitzgerald LLP
Dallas, Texas

Lawrence Lerner
Levy and Craig, A Professional Corporation
Kansas City, Missouri

Eric H. Loeffler
Hinshaw & Culbertson LLP
Boston, Massachusetts

Robert G. Lovett, Jr.
Dickie, McCamey & Chilcote, P.C.
Pittsburgh, Pennsylvania

Geoffrey W. Millsom
Adler Pollock & Sheehan P.C.
Providence, Rhode Island

Brian W. Mullins
Wickwire Gavin, P.C.
Madison, Wisconsin

Bryan A. Nickels
Hall, Farley, Oberrecht & Blanton, P.A.
Boise, Idaho

Patrick J. O'Connor
Faegre & Benson LLP
Minneapolis, Minnesota

Kevin M. O'Shea
Sulloway & Hollis, P.L.L.C.
Concord, New Hampshire

Phillip S. Oberrecht
Hall, Farley, Oberrecht & Blanton, P.A.
Boise, Idaho

David Olson
Frost Brown Todd LLC
Cincinnati, Ohio

James E. Owers
Sulloway & Hollis, P.L.L.C.
Concord, New Hampshire

Raymond Peréz-Brayfield, CPCU
Etcheverry Harrison LLP
Ft. Lauderdale, Florida

Loren D. Podwill
Bullivant Houser Bailey PC
Portland, Oregon

Cynthia E. Rodgers-Waire
Whiteford, Taylor & Preston L.L.P.
Baltimore, Maryland

A. Robert Ruesch
Verrill Dana LLP
Portland, Maine

Kevin J. Russell
Lindabury, McCormick & Estabrook, P.A.
Westfield, New Jersey

Bryan M. Seifert
Leo & Weber, P.C.
Chicago, Illinois

Dawn C. Stewart
The Stewart Law Firm, PLLC
Washington, D.C.

L. Graves Stiff, III
Starnes & Atchison, LLP
Birmingham, Alabama
(and Mobile, Alabama)

Steven J. Strawbridge
Locke Reynolds, LLP
Indianapolis, Indiana

William H. Sturges
Shumaker, Loop & Kendrick, LLP
Charlotte, North Carolina

DeWitte Thompson
Thompson Slagle & Hannan, LLC
Duluth, Georgia

W. Alan Torrance, Jr.
Dickie, McCamey & Chilcote, P.C.
Pittsburgh, Pennsylvania

Benjamin B. Ullem
Whitfield & Eddy, P.L.C.
Des Moines, Iowa

Sara K. Van Norman
Faegre & Benson LLP
Minneapolis, Minnesota

Nichole Velasquez
Whiteford, Taylor & Preston L.L.P.
Baltimore, Maryland

Robert G. Watt
Watt, Tieder, Hoffar & Fitzgerald, L.L.P.
McLean, Virginia

Michael J. Weber
Leo & Weber, P.C.
Chicago, Illinois

Ron A. Yarbrough
Brunini, Grantham, Grower & Hewes, PLLC
Jackson, Mississippi

Gene F. Zipperle, Jr.
Alber Crafton, PSC
Louisville, Kentucky
(Troy, Michigan and Columbus, Ohio)

# INTRODUCTION

Performance bonds can be mystical creatures, their beauty beheld in different ways. Some, including some bond obligees, believe that properly handled, a surety performance bond can be used to spin flax into gold. Others, primarily bond principals and underwriters, believe performance bonds are like reflections in a pond, whose countenances will disappear the moment the water's surface is disturbed. Of course, these are just fairy tale images.

In reality, performance bonds are three-party contracts which attach to an underlying two-party agreement. The typical example arises in the context of a construction project. The underlying agreement is the construction contract itself, by which the primary obligor, the contractor, agrees to deliver construction materials, labor, and services to the obligee, usually an owner. The performance bond adds a third party to the relationship, a surety. The surety agrees that in the event of the principal's default, it will perform the principal's work obligations to the obligee, provided that the obligee has fulfilled its own obligations under the contract and bond.

The ABA-TTIPS Fidelity and Surety Law Committee has published numerous excellent scholarly works which examine in a broad fashion the theory of surety bond rights, liabilities, and defenses, as well as the concepts of indemnity and subrogation. This Performance Bond Manual examines the statutes and case law concerning performance bonds for 53 jurisdictions. The Performance Bond Manual contains a section for each of the 50 United States, plus the territory of Puerto Rico, the District of Columbia, and federal Miller Act performance bonds. Each section provides the reader with an overview of the particular jurisdiction, and is laid out in a standardized format. The intent is to provide the reader, in a consistent presentation style, with a brief useful description of the statutes and case law of each such jurisdiction, and how such statutes and case law impact the rights and liabilities of sureties in that particular jurisdiction. For the surety claims handler and practitioner alike, the Performance Bond Manual is intended to provide a broad brush understanding of the law of performance bonds in a particular jurisdiction. As such, each section is not necessarily intended to be an exhaustive work, but rather to provide some basic tools for consideration in the initial evaluation of a performance bond claim and developing a strategy to respond and fulfill the surety's obligations under the bond.

This work would not have been possible without the thoughtful contributions of the authors of each section. With a reward no greater than mere attribution, these authors generously provided their time and their knowledge, and distilled the barrels of raw information on performance bonds in each jurisdiction into a small glass, so that it may be enjoyed one sip at a time.

The editors wish to express their gratitude for the efforts of Sharon K. Curry. Her tireless and accurate review, her suggestions, her organization, and her professional input and support are responsible for the ultimate assembly of this entire work in every way.

Lawrence Lerner
Levy and Craig, A Professional Corporation
Kansas City, Missouri
Editor

Theodore M. Baum
Ernstrom & Dreste, LLP
Rochester, New York
Editor

Michael A. Jankowski
Chair
Fidelity and Surety Law Committee

# FOREWORD

The intent of this publication is to permit the reader to quickly review the general rules, applicable statutes, and significant case law concerning performance bonds in each jurisdiction. For ease of reference, each section was prepared in a uniform fashion. The standard format is illustrated below in a fashion similar to the guidelines provided by the editors to the authors of each section.

**STATE**
**Author(s)**

**1. Requirement for Bond**

*Sets out the statutes governing the requirement for performance bonds, including bond amounts and projects to which applicable.*

*Addresses the **statutory provisions for projects that are:***

**Public**
**Private**
**Department of Transportation**

*Sets forth **case law rules that might generally apply***

**2. Damages Covered**

*As may be **set forth in any statutes and/or case law***
***Obligations of surety to perform and/or pay***
***Whether failure to provide insurance transfers burden to surety***

*Sets forth any **limitations on damages;** for example, no punitive damages, no delay damages, etc.*

***Whether obligee may set off bonded contract funds against other principal-obligee debts or obligations***

***Incorporation of specific contract terms by reference***

**3. Penal Sum Variations**

***Limitations per statute***

***Effect of changes in work upon penal sum, if at all***

***Statutory or case law protections or dangers to penal sum.*** *For example, does performance without an agreement "to limit damages to the penal sum" mean that undertaking performance removes the penal sum protection?*

**4. Parties Covered**

*Provisions in statutes and/or case law as to whether only obligees are covered; can others make a claim on the performance bond?*

***Coverage for:***

**Third-party beneficiaries**
**Assignees**
**Dual obligees**

**5. Notice or Filing Required**

***Statutory provisions***

***Case law rules concerning condition precedent notice***

**6. Time for Suit**

*Includes a discussion of* ***statutes of limitation particular to performance bonds and other applicable statutes of limitation***

*Includes* ***case law statements about enforceability of limitations contained in bonds***

***Varying statutes of limitation by agreement in bond or contract?*** *For example, any statutory or case law rules that parties may (or may not) contract to shorten the time within which to commence an action on the bond.*

**7. Procedure**

***Statutory or procedural rules that may affect handling or administration of lawsuits*** *(unrelated to notice or time limitations that are covered above)*

***Venue requirements and jurisdictional limitations***
***Court rules***
***Particular agency regulations/rules***
***Arbitration requirements and application***

**8. Attorney's Fees**

***Statutes and/or case law limiting or permitting recovery of attorney's fees***

***What fees are recoverable, if any***

**9. Special Provisions**

*This is intended to be a catchall for other statutory peculiarities.*

**10. Remarks**

*Catchall for common law or case law peculiarities.*

*Catchall for author comments, if any, not covered in above or in case law below.*

**11. Case Annotations**

*Shows one/two sentences and then case name/cite.*

***Interpretation of AIA bond forms***
***Cases in which surety steps into shoes of obligee***

# ALABAMA

L. Graves Stiff, III, J. Scott Dickens, and Brian A. Dodd[1]

## 1. Requirement for Bond

***Statutory provisions for projects that are:***

**Public** – Ala. Code § 39-1-1 (1975) requires bonds for persons or entities contracting for public works. The code section states:

> Any person entering into a contract with an awarding authority in this state for the prosecution of any public work shall, before commencing the work, execute a performance bond, with penalty equal to 100 percent of the amount of the contract price.

**Private** – Alabama law does not require performance bonds on private projects.

1 L. Graves Stiff, III and J. Scott Dickens are members and Brian A. Dodd is an associate of:
Starnes & Atchison, LLP
P. O. Box 598512
100 Brookwood Place, 7th Floor
Birmingham, Alabama 35259
(205) 858-6000
and
63 South Royal Street, Suite 1106
Mobile, Alabama 36602

**Department of Transportation** – Section 103.05 of the Standard Specifications for the Alabama Department of Transportation states:

> The bidder to whom the award is made shall, within 10 days after the prescribed forms have been presented to him for signature (i.e. after date of award), furnish and file with the State Highway Director an acceptable surety bond on the form included in the proposal in an amount equal to 100 percent of the contract bid price of the contract as awarded. Said bond shall be furnished by a surety company qualified and authorized to make such bond in the State of Alabama, and countersigned by an authorized agent resident in the State who is qualified to execute such instruments. The bond shall have attached thereto power of attorney of the signing official unless such power of attorney is already on file in the office of the Department.

***Case law rules that might generally apply***

Bonds issued pursuant to the Alabama Public Works Act will be deemed subject to the terms and conditions of the statute, notwithstanding inconsistent provisions of the bond form. *Universal Elec. Constr. Co. v. Robbins*, 239 Ala. 105, 194 So. 194 (1940); *American Cas. Co. v. Devine*, 275 Ala. 628, 157 So. 2d 661 (1963).

The Public Works Act applies only to bonds furnished by a general contractor to the State of Alabama or a division thereof. Bonds which may be furnished by subcontractors in favor of general contractors are not subject to provisions of the Act, nor are bonds which may be issued in favor of industrial development boards and other quasi-governmental entities. *See George A. Fuller Co. v. Vulcan Materials*, 301 So. 2d 74 (Ala. 1974).

## 2. Damages Covered

***Set forth in any statutes and/or case law***

ALDOT § 103.05(a) – In case of default on the part of the Contractor, all expense incident to ascertaining and collecting losses suffered by the State under the bond, including engineering, direct administration, and legal services, shall be charged against the contract bond for performance of work.

ALDOT § 108.10 – Should the Contractor, or in case of default, the surety, fail to complete the work within the time stipulated in the contract or the adjusted time as granted under the provisions of Article 108.09, a deduction for each calendar day or work day that any work shall remain uncompleted, an amount indicated by the Liquidated Damages Schedule shown in Article 108.11 or provided in the contract documents shall be deducted from any monies due the Contractor on monthly estimates. Any adjustments due to approved time extensions or overruns in the contract amount will be made on the monthly, semi-final or final estimate as may be appropriate.

***Obligations of surety to perform and/or pay*** – Not applicable.

***Whether failure to provide insurance transfers burden to surety*** – Not applicable.

***Limitations on damages***

Generally, the liability of a surety is coextensive with that of its principal. *Federal Ins. Co. v. I. Kruger, Inc.*, 829 So. 2d 732 (Ala. 2002); *A. G. Gaston Const. Co. v. Hicks*, 674 So. 2d 545 (Ala. Civ. App. 1995). A principal's liability is the limit of and a necessary element of the surety's liability. *American Cas. Co. of Reading, Pa. v. Divine*, 157 So. 2d 661(Ala. 1963).

A surety may make any defense, not personal to the principal, that the principal may make. *Alabama Surface Mining Reclamation Comm'n v. Commercial Standard Ins. Co.*, 469 So. 2d 619 (Ala. Civ. App. 1985).

Because a surety's liability arises out of contract, a surety cannot be held liable for an amount greater than the penal amount of the bond. *Victore Ins. Co. v. Ross Neely Systems, Inc.*, 757 So. 2d 473 (Ala. Civ. App. 2000).

Under Alabama's Public Works Act, attorney's fees are allowable to claimants under labor and material payment bonds, but not to the obligee of a performance bond. *Cincinnati Ins. Co. v. City of Talladega*, 342 So. 2d 331 (Ala. 1977). A surety is not liable for attorney's fees incurred by an obligee unless there is a statute or express provision in the contract or bond binding the principal to that effect. *Mason v. City of Albertville*, 158 So. 2d 924 (Ala. 1963).

***Whether obligee may set off bonded contract funds against other principal-obligee debts or obligations*** – Not applicable.

***Incorporation of specific contract terms by reference***

Where the bond references and incorporates the terms of the bonded contract, those terms will typically be read into the bond. *Pacific Ins. Co. v. Wilbanks*, 214 So. 2d 279 (Ala. 1968). *See also, Maryland Casualty Co. v. Cunningham*, 173 So. 2d 506 (Ala. 1937).

## 3. Penal Sum Variations

***Limitations per statute***

Ala. Code § 39-1-1(a) (1975) requires the issuance of a performance bond for all public works projects in an amount equal to the contract price:

> Any person entering into a contract with an awarding authority in this state for the prosecution of any public work shall, before commencing the work, execute a performance bond, with penalty equal to 100 percent of the amount of the contract price.

***Effect of changes in work upon penal sum, if at all***

Under Alabama law, a material change in the scope of work may result in the discharge of the performance bond.

"It is the settled rule in this state that before a surety may take advantage of any change in the obligation that this change in the contract must be material and must in order to discharge the surety prejudice the surety." *United Bonding Ins. Co. v. W. S. Newell, Inc.*, 232 So. 2d 616, 625 (Ala. 1969).

"It is the well recognized rule that '[a]n alteration or change in the contract or obligation must be material in order for a compensated or corporate surety to be discharged from liability thereby...." *Maryland Cas. Co. v. First Nat'l Bank of Eufaula*, 165 So. 2d 359, 360 (Ala. 1964).

***Statutory case law protections or dangers to penal sum***

Because the liability of a surety arises out of a contract, it is axiomatic that a surety cannot be held liable for an amount greater than the amount named in its bond. *Victore Ins. Co. v. Ross Neely Systems,*

*Inc.*, 757 So. 2d 473 (Ala. Civ. App. 2000) (*citing* 74 AM. JUR. 2D, *Suretyship* § 24 (1974)).

The appellate courts of Alabama have not addressed or recognized a tort claim for bad faith against performance bond sureties.

## 4. Parties Covered

***Statutes and/or case law as to whether only obligees are covered***

A surety is not liable to third parties for the consequences of acts of negligence by its principal resulting in bodily injury or property damage; such exposures are typically covered by policies of general liability insurance, but are not properly the subject of payment or performance bond claims. This is true even if the obligee characterizes its claim in terms of negligence in the performance of a bonded contract. *Water Works, Gas & Sewer Bd. of City of Oneonta v. P. A. Buchanan Contracting Co.*, 318 So. 2d 267 (Ala. 1975).

***Coverage for:***

**Third-party beneficiaries** – A performance bond does not entitle the principal's subcontractors, as third party beneficiaries under the bond, to recover from the surety for their work, labor and materials furnished under the construction contract. *Bill White Roofing & Specialty Co., Inc. v. Cedric's, Inc.*, 387 So. 2d 189 (Ala. 1980).

Additionally, in *Hinkle Metals & Supply Co., Inc. v. Ohio Cas. Ins. Co.*, 2005 WL 628885 (Ala. Civ. App. March 18, 2005), a material supplier filed suit seeking recovery for non-payment under the license bond after the bonded heating and air conditioning contractor became insolvent. In affirming the entry of judgment in favor of the license bond surety, the Court of Civil Appeals held that the license bond was not intended to cover claims for non-payment by material suppliers of licensed heating and air conditioning contractors. Rather, the bond was issued to guarantee performance and "to protect the public with regard to the installation, service, and repair of heating and cooling systems." Therefore, the surety was not found liable to the supplier as a third-party beneficiary under the bond. *Hinkle Metals*, 2005 WL 628885 at *3.

**Assignees** – Not applicable.

**Dual obligees** – Not applicable.

## 5. Notice or Filing Required

***Statutory provisions*** – There are no statutory provisions in Alabama establishing notice requirements as a condition precedent to the commencement of an action against a performance bond.

***Case law rules concerning condition precedent notice***

Under Alabama law, no obligation of a surety under a performance bond arises unless and until the principal has been declared to be in default by the obligee. Notice to the surety must be conveyed in clear, direct and unequivocal language. A mere threat to declare a principal in default is insufficient to trigger the obligations of a performance bond surety.

"A declaration of default sufficient to invoke the surety's obligations under the bond must be made in clear, direct, and unequivocal language. The declaration must inform the surety that the principal has committed a material breach or series of material breaches of the subcontract, that the obligee regards the subcontract as terminated, and that the surety must immediately commence performing under the terms of its bond." *Bank of Brewton, Inc. v. International Fid. Ins. Co.*, 827 So. 2d 747, 754 (Ala. 2002) (quoting *L & A Contracting Co. v. Southern Concrete Services., Inc.*, 17 F.3d 106, 111 (5th Cir. 1994).

## 6. Time for Suit

***Statutes of limitation particular to performance bonds and other applicable statutes of limitation***

There are no statutory provisions in Alabama that specifically establish a statute of limitation for claims against a performance bond.

Ala. Code § 6-2-34 (1975) establishes a six-year statute of limitation for actions based upon a contract.

Ala. Code § 6-2-33 (1975) establishes a 10-year statute of limitation for actions based upon any contract or writing under seal.

Ala. Code § 6-5-221 (1975) establishes a two-year statute of limitations for all civil actions in tort, contract, or otherwise against licensed general contractors, architects and engineers.

Any claim or cause of action against a licensed general contractor, architect or engineers which accrues or would have accrued more than 13 years after the substantial completion of construction of the improvement on or to the real property is barred as a matter of law. Ala. Code § 6-5-221 (1975).

***Case law statements about enforceability of limitations contained in bonds***

Under Alabama law, it is well-settled that a surety may avail itself of any defense not personal its principal, including the statute of limitations. *Commercial Standard Ins. Co. v. Alabama Surface Mining Reclamation Comm'n*, 443 So. 2d 1245, 1249 (Ala. Civ. App. 1983). Given this fact, a performance bond surety can arguably assert the two-year statute of limitation available to its principal under Ala. Code § 6-5-221 (1975). This issue is currently on appeal before the Alabama Supreme Court in *Housing Auth. of the City of Huntsville v. Hartford Accident & Indem. Co.* (Appeal No. 1040885).

***Varying statutes of limitation by agreement in bond or contract***

Ala. Code § 6-2-15 (1975):

> Except as may be otherwise provided by the Uniform Commercial Code, any agreement or stipulation, verbal or written, whereby the time for the commencement of any action is limited to a time less than that prescribed by law for the commencement of such action is void.

## 7. Procedure

***Statutory or procedural rules that may affect handling or administration of lawsuits*** – Not applicable.

### *Venue requirements and jurisdictional limitations*

Ala. Code § 6-3-7 (1975) establishes venue limitations for actions against foreign and domestic corporations. It provides as follows:

> (a) All civil actions against corporations may be brought in any of the following counties:
>
> (1) In the county in which a substantial part of the events or omissions giving rise to the claim occurred, or a substantial part of real property that is the subject of the action is situated; or
>
> (2) In the county of the corporation's principal office in this state; or
>
> (3) In the county in which the plaintiff resided, or if the plaintiff is an entity other than an individual, where the plaintiff had its principal office in this state, at the time of the accrual of the cause of action, if such corporation does business by agent in the county of the plaintiff's residence; or
>
> (4) If subdivisions (1), (2), or (3) do not apply, in any county in which the corporation was doing business by agent at the time of the accrual of the cause of action.

Ala. Code § 12-11-30(a) (1975) establishes general jurisdictional limitations for civil claims:

> The circuit court shall have exclusive original jurisdiction of all civil actions in which the matter in controversy exceeds $10,000 exclusive of interest and costs, and shall exercise original jurisdiction concurrent with the district court in all civil actions in which the matter in controversy exceeds $3,000 exclusive of interest and costs.

***Court rules*** – Not applicable.

***Particular agency regulations/rules*** – Not applicable.

### *Arbitration requirements and application*

Ala. Code § 8-1-41(3) (1975) prohibits the enforcement of contracts requiring the resolution of disputes by arbitration as a matter of public policy.

Notwithstanding this provision, a pre-dispute arbitration clause can still be enforced if the contract involves a transaction affecting interstate commerce within the meaning of the *Federal Arbitration Act*, 9 U.S.C. § 1.

"A party seeking to compel arbitration has the burden of proving the existence of a contract calling for arbitration and proving that that contract involves a transaction affecting interstate commerce within the meaning of the Federal Arbitration Act, 9 U.S.C. § 1. This is so, because the FAA makes specifically enforceable a 'written provision in any ... contract evidencing a transaction involving commerce to settle by arbitration a controversy...arising out of such contract or transaction.' 9 U.S.C. § 2. [T]he term 'involving commerce' in the FAA [is] the functional equivalent of the ... familiar term 'affecting commerce' - words of art that ordinarily signal the broadest permissible exercise of Congress' Commerce Clause power. Congress' Commerce Clause power 'may be exercised in individual cases without showing any specific effect upon interstate commerce' if in the aggregate the economic activity in question would represent 'a general practice ... subject to federal control.' Nevertheless, '[t]he party moving for arbitration must produce some evidence which tends to establish its claim that the transaction involved interstate commerce.' " *Adcock v. Adams Homes, LLC*, 2005 WL 78766 *3-4 (Ala. Jan. 24, 2005) (Internal citations omitted).

## 8. Attorney's Fees

***Statutes and/or case law limiting or permitting recovery of attorney's fees***

Although Ala. Code § 39-1-1 (1975) provides for the recovery of attorney's fees under a payment bond, there are no statutes in Alabama that specifically limit or permit the recovery of attorney's fees under a performance bond. Alabama case law does, however, address this issue, and provides that a surety may be held liable for attorney's fees under a performance bond when there is an express provision in the contract or bond binding the principal. *Mason v. City of Albertville*, 158 So. 2d 924 (Ala. 1963).

***What fees are recoverable, if any***

In Alabama reasonable attorney's fees are recoverable, and the determination of whether an attorney fee is reasonable is within the discretion of the trial court. *Lunceford v. Monumental Life Ins. Co.*, 641 So. 2d 244 (Ala. 1994); *City of Birmingham v. Horn*, 810 So. 2d 667, 681-82 (Ala. 2001).

"A trial court should consider several factors when awarding attorney fees: '(1) the nature and value of the subject matter of the employment; (2) the learning, skill, and labor requisite to its proper discharge; (3) the time consumed; (4) the professional experience and reputation of the attorney; (5) the weight of his responsibilities; (6) the measure of success achieved; (7) the reasonable expenses incurred; (8) whether a fee is fixed or contingent; (9) the nature and length of a professional relationship; (10) the fee customarily charged in the locality for similar legal services; (11) the likelihood that a particular employment may preclude other employment; and (12) the limitations imposed by the client or by the circumstances.' " *Haar v. Glover*, 897 So. 2d 364 (Ala. Civ. App. 2004) (quoting *Anderson v. Lee*, 621 So. 2d 1305, 1307 (Ala. 1993)).

These criteria are for purposes of evaluating whether an attorney fee is reasonable; they are not an exhaustive list of specific criteria that must all be met. *Beal Bank, SSB v. Schilleci,* 896 So. 2d 395 (Ala. 2004) (citing *Graddick v. First Farmers & Merchants Nat'l Bank of Troy,* 453 So. 2d 1305 (Ala. 1984).

## 9. Special Provisions

Several Alabama decisions have noted that the Public Works Act is patterned after the Miller Act and the construction to federal statute is applicable to any performance bond issues which arise under the Alabama Act. *See State ex rel. Wadsworth v. Southern Surety Co.*, 127 So. 805 (Ala. 1930) *National Surety Corp. v. Wunderlich*, 111 F. 622 (8th Cir. 1940); *Price v. H. L. Cobble Const. Co.*, 317 F. 2d 312 (5th Cir. 1963).

## 10. Remarks

In a 1997 amendment to the Public Works Act, the Alabama legislature expressly prohibited the designation of a particular surety or insurance company by any officer or employee of an awarding authority. *See* Ala. Code 39-1-4 (1975).

## 11. Case Annotations

The contractor's performance bond and any bond issued in accordance with the Public Works Act should be liberally construed to effect the purpose of the statute. *State ex rel. Wadsworth v. Southern Surety Co.*, 127 So. 805 (Ala. 1930).

***Interpretation of AIA bond forms*** – No Alabama case has construed a particular AIA bond form.

***Cases in which surety steps into shoes of obligee***

Upon default of the contractor and completion of performance obligations by surety, all remaining sums due under the contract, up to the amount expended by surety, are owed by the governmental entity to the surety and not to the contractor, which has no property or right to property in these contract funds upon which any tax lien, federal or state, can attach. *See Alabama ex rel. Gallion v. Bessemer Materials, Inc.*, 224 F. Supp. 182 (N.D. Ala. 1963).

# ALASKA

Charles G. Evans [1]

## 1. Requirement for Bond

***Statutory provisions for construction projects:***

**Public** – A.S. 36.25.010 - 025, Alaska's Little Miller Act, requires for public construction contracts exceeding $100,000 a performance bond furnished to the state or political subdivision of the state in graduated amounts depending upon the amount payable under the contract. Contracts of greater than $100,000 but not more than $1,000,000 require a performance bond in the amount of one-half of the contract payable. Contracts exceeding $1,000,000 but less than $5,000,000 require a performance bond of 40 percent of the amount payable. For contracts greater than $5,000,000 the performance bond shall be $2,500,000.

A.S. 36.95.010(6) defines "state or political subdivision of the state" as any state department, state agency, state university, borough, city, village, school district, or other state subdivision.

A.S. 36.95.010(3) defines "public construction" or "public works" as the on site field surveying, erection, rehabilitation, extension or repair, including painting or redecorating of buildings, highways, or other

---

1 Charles G. Evans is with:
Law Office of Charles G. Evans
1351 Huffman Road, Suite 201
Anchorage, Alaska 99515
(907) 278-4691

improvements to real property under contract for the state, a political subdivision, or a regional school board.

A.S. 36.25.025 allows municipalities, by ordinance, to exempt contractors from compliance with furnishing a performance bond required by A.S. 36.25.010(a), if the estimated cost of the project does not exceed $400,000 and the contractor provides other required evidence of credit worthiness.

A.S. 18.55.996(h) provides that 16 regional native housing authorities, quasi-public corporations chartered by the State of Alaska, shall comply with the performance bond requirements of Alaska's Little Miller Act.

**Private** – No statutes in Alaska require performance bonds on private projects. However, the Alaska Supreme Court addressed a private commercial construction performance bond in *Loyal Order of Moose v. International Fidelity Ins. Co.*, 797 P.2d 622 (Alaska 1990).

**Department of Transportation** – The Alaska Department of Transportation construction contracts are covered by the Alaska Little Miller Act.

***Case law rules that might generally apply***

Alaska generally follows federal case law interpretations of the Miller Act. "Alaska's statute is substantially similar to 40 U.S.C. § 270(a) *et seq.*, the 'Miller Act'." *Hyundai Construction Co. Ltd. v. Kalmbach, Inc.*, 502 P.2d 856, n.1 (Alaska 1972). The opinion in *State ex rel. Palmer Supply Co. v. Walsh & Co.*, 575 P.2d 1213 (Alaska 1978) states, "... we will give more weight to principles derived from federal case law interpreting the Miller Act than to general common law principles governing debtor-creditor relations." *Id.* 575 P.2d at 1218. *See also*, *McGee Steel Co. v. McDonald Industries Alaska*, 723 P.2d 611, 617, fn. 11 (Alaska 1986).

## 2. Damages Covered

***Set forth in any statues and/or case law*** – There are no Alaska statutes or case law interpreting the damages covered by a performance bond.

***Obligations of surety to perform and/or pay*** – Not applicable.

***Whether failure to provide insurance transfers burden to surety*** – Not applicable.

***Limitations on damages*** – There are no Alaska cases addressing limitations on damages on performance bonds.

***Whether obligee may set off bonded contract funds against other principal-obligee debts or obligations*** – There are no cases in Alaska addressing an obligee's set off rights.

***Incorporation of specific contract terms by reference***

In *Loyal Order of Moose Lodge v. International Fidelity Ins. Co.*, 797 P.2d 622 (Alaska 1990), the Alaska Supreme Court recognized an expressed incorporation in the bond of an arbitration clause in the underlying construction contract. 797 P.2d at 629.

## 3. Penal Sum Variations

***Limitations per statute*** – Alaska does not have statutory limitations on performance bond penal sums.

***Effect of changes in work upon penal sum, if at all***

Alaska has no case law interpreting such changes in work, but typically the language of the performance bonds include specific incorporation of the contract and may specifically waive any surety objections to increases in the contract sum.

***Statutory or case law protections or dangers to penal sum*** – Alaska does not have statutory or case law protections of the penal sum.

## 4. Parties Covered

***Statutes and/or case law as to whether only obligees are covered*** – Alaska does not have statutes or cases concerning the parties covered by performance bonds.

***Coverage for:***

**Third-party beneficiaries** – Not applicable.

**Assignees** – Not applicable.

**Dual obligees** – Not applicable.

## 5. Notice or Filing Required

***Statutory provisions*** – Alaska does not have a statutory provision requiring any notice prior to enforcement of a surety's performance bond obligations.

***Case law rules concerning conditions precedent notice*** – Alaska has no case law addressing notice as a condition precedent.

## 6. Time for Suit

***Statutes of limitation particular to performance bonds and other applicable statutes of limitation***

A.S. 36.25.020(c) of the Alaska Little Miller Act provides, "a suit may not be started after the expiration of one year after the date of final settlement of the contract." This language comes from the Heard Act, the predecessor of the Miller Act. When Congress amended the Miller Act statute of limitations to specify an action must be filed within one year after final work on the project, Alaska did not follow suit to amend its original Heard Act language. In *Safeco Ins. Co. of America v. Honeywell, Inc.*, 639 P.2d 996 (Alaska 1981), the Alaska Supreme Court held "final settlement" means not only that a contract has been completed but there has been, "... a specific administrative act authorizing payment." 639 P.2d at 1002. As a practical matter, especially with state or federally funded highway projects, final payment may lag a number of years after completion of the project. Rarely are claims untimely pursuant to the one year statute of limitation expressed in A.S. 36.25.020(c).

For private bonds, A.S. 09.10.050 establishes a three year statute of limitations upon a contract or liability, expressed or implied. This provision may be waived by the terms of the contract.

***Case law statements about enforceability of limitations contained in bonds***

In *Alaska Energy Authority v. Fairmont Insurance Company*, 845 P.2d 420 (Alaska 1993) the performance bond required suit to be filed before the expiration of two years from the date on which final payment under the contract became due. However, the court reasoned its prior decision in *Estes v. Alaska Ins. Guar. Ass'n*, 774 P.2d 1315 (Alaska 1989) held contractual time limitations to bring suit will not be enforced without a showing of prejudice. "A requirement that suit be filed while the process of investigation is proceeding will not be enforced without a showing of prejudice." 845 P.2d at 423-424.

***Varying statutes of limitation by agreement in bond or contract*** – Private performance bonds required by contract may contain terms waiving the three year statute of limitations applicable in A.S. 09.10.050.

**7. Procedure**

***Statutory or procedural rules that may affect handling or administration of lawsuits***

A.S. 21.09.180 requires insurers to appoint the Director of the Division of Insurance of the State of Alaska as its agent to receive service of process issued against it in the State of Alaska. Pursuant to A.S. 21.09.180(b) service of process against a foreign or alien insurer shall be made only upon the director. Rule 12 of the Alaska Rules of Civil Procedure provides a non-governmental party shall serve an answer 40 days after service upon an officer of the state appointed to receive service pursuant to statute. Insurance companies served with process through the director have 40 days to answer, rather than the 20 days typically specified in the summons.

***Venue requirements and jurisdictional limitations***

In Alaska, civil trial court jurisdiction is divided between district dourt and superior court. Civil appeals lie from the district court to the superior court and from the superior court directly to the Alaska Supreme Court. Civil jurisdiction in district court is limited to cases seeking damages of less than $100,000. Superior court jurisdiction extends to all claims exceeding $100,000.

A.S. 22.10.030 provides venue for all actions shall be set under rules adopted by the Alaska Supreme Court. Rule 3(c) of the Alaska Rules of Civil Procedure provides civil actions may be commenced either in the judicial district in which the claim arose or in the judicial district in which the defendant may be personally served.

***Court rules*** – Not applicable.

***Particular agency regulations/rules*** – Not applicable.

***Arbitration requirements and application***

Alaska has adopted the Revised Uniform Arbitration Act as A.S. 09.43.300-595.

In *Loyal Order of Moose Lodge v. International Fidelity Ins. Co.*, 797 P.2d 622 (Alaska 1990), where the private performance bond expressly incorporated the arbitration clause of the construction contract, the Alaska Supreme Court enforced an obligee's duty to arbitrate all disputed questions of fact relative to the principal's or the obligee's compliance with the terms of the construction contract. The court observed, "Such arbitration, pursuant to and limited to the underlying contract, will bind the surety as well as the principal and beneficiary." 797 P.2d at 629 (footnote omitted).

## 8. Attorney's Fees

***Statute and/or case law limiting or permitting recovery of attorney's fees***

Pursuant to its constitutional rule making authority, the Alaska Supreme Court adopted Rule 82 of the Alaska Rules of Civil Procedure, providing for the award of attorney fees to the prevailing party. Civil Rule 82 provides for the recovery of partial attorney fees incurred by the prevailing party. If a money judgment is recovered, a schedule in Civil Rule 82 sets forth the presumptive recovery of attorney fees between 1 percent and 20 percent based upon the amount of the money judgment and whether the case was resolved with or without trial. Where a prevailing party recovers no money judgment the award of attorney fees falls between 20 and 30 percent of the prevailing party's reasonable actual attorney fees, necessarily incurred.

***What fees are recoverable, if any*** – Not applicable.

**9. Special Provisions** – Not applicable.

**10. Remarks**

In *Loyal Order of Moose Lodge v. International Fidelity Ins. Co.*, 797 P.2d 622 (Alaska 1990) the Alaska Supreme Court concluded an implied covenant of good faith and fair dealing exists between a surety and its obligee on performance bonds. Failure by a surety minimally to investigate its principal's alleged default may constitute bad faith if that investigation would confirm the obligee's allegations in material part. The surety may satisfy its duty of good faith to an obligee by acting reasonably in response to a claim by its obligee.

In *McGee Steel Co. v. McDonald Industries Alaska*, 723 P.2d 611 (Alaska 1986) the Alaska Supreme Court held an Alaska Little Miller Act surety is liable for rental of a crane only for the time the crane was actually used or "substantially consumed" on the bonded project. *Id.*, 723 P.2d at 617. Moreover, following federal Miller Act precedents, the court held that damage to the crane caused by negligence was not an expense to be borne by the surety. *Id.*, 723 P.2d at 618.

In *SKW/Eskimos v. Sentry Auto. Sprinkler*, 723 P.2d 1293, the Alaska Supreme Court held " ... that a surety can not be held liable beyond the scope of the principal's duty...." The court rejected claims for materials by a subcontractor where the principal's contract was to provide only labor.

## 11. Case Annotations

***Interpretation of AIA bond forms*** – Alaska has no cases or statutes on this issue.

***Cases in which surety steps into shoes of obligee***

The scenario in *Alaska State Bank v. General Insurance Company*, 579 P.2d 1362 (Alaska 1978) examined the classic situation of the competing rights of a surety with those of a bank holding a perfected security interest in contract receivables. The dispute contested earned progress payments on a state road construction project. The principal defaulted and the surety completed the contract and paid numerous claimants. After the default, the state issued progress payments in the amount of $169,895 payable to the surety. Alaska State Bank sued to recover the payments based upon its perfected security interest to all contract rights of the contractor. The bank argued that the UCC required the surety to perfect, or lose, its assignment of its principal's contract rights found in the General Indemnity Agreement. The surety asserted its rights of equitable subrogation, independent of the contractual assignment found in the General Indemnity Agreement, primed the perfected UCC assignment of the bank.

The Alaska Supreme Court found, "that the majority of American jurisdictions which have considered the question have accepted the theory of equitable subrogation as the rule in situations such as the one before us." 579 P.2d at 1366. Further the court held, "that a surety's rights to earned progress payments does not qualify as an interest in personal property subject to the filing provisions of the Alaska Uniform Commercial Code since the surety has the right to complete the job it has bonded and apply any earned funds against its costs." 579 P.2d at 1368.

The supreme court held the surety's right to earned progress payments does not qualify as an interest in personal property subject to the recording provisions of the Alaska Uniform Commercial Code. A surety which completes a bonded job has the right by equitable subrogation to apply any earned payments against its costs. In Alaska, equitable subrogation trumps the rights of a secured creditor to contract proceeds.

# ARIZONA

Cynthia R. Estrella [1]

## 1. Requirement for Bond

***Statutory provisions for projects that are:***

**Public** – There are several Arizona statutes that require performance bonds for public building or improvement projects.

A.R.S. § 34-222 requires contractors that contract with any county, city, town, or tax levying public improvement districts, and county or city improvement districts *for the construction, alteration, or repair of any public building, a public work or improvement*, to furnish a performance bond in an amount equal to the full contract amount. The specific language required in these statutory bonds is contained at A.R.S. § 34-222(F).

A.R.S. § 34-608(A)(1)(a) requires that any person or firm that contracts for *job-order-contracting construction services* to furnish a performance bond in an amount equal to the full amount of construction under the job-order-contracting construction services contract, but shall not include any design services, pre-construction services, finance

1 Cynthia R. Estrella is a partner of:
Mann, Berens & Wisner, LLP
2929 North Central Avenue, Suite 1600
Phoenix, Arizona 85012
(602) 258-6200
Ms. Estrella expresses her thanks to Daniel Gebremeskal, an associate at Mann, Berens & Wisner, for his assistance in preparing this chapter.

services, maintenance services, operations services or other related services included in the contract. The specific language required in these statutory bonds is contained in A.R.S. § 34-608(G).

A.R.S. § 34-608(A)(1)(b) requires that any person or firm that contracts for *construction-manager-at-risk construction services and design-build construction services* to furnish a performance bond in an amount equal to the price of construction and shall not include the cost of any design services, pre-construction services, finance services, maintenance services, operations services or any other related services included in the contract. The specific language required in these statutory bonds is contained in A.R.S. § 34-608(G).

A.R.S. § 41-2574(1) requires that for *every expenditure of public monies*, including federal assistance monies by this state, *for building, altering, repairing, improving or demolishing any public structure or other public improvements of any kind to any public real property*, the contractor must provide a performance bond in an amount equal to 100 percent of the contract price. Performance bonds for these construction contracts are issued in accordance with A.R.S. § 34-222, *supra.*

A.R.S. § 41-2574(1)(a)-(b) require that for every expenditure of public monies, including federal assistance monies by this state, for construction services, which includes job-order-contracting construction services, construction-manager-at-risk construction services and design-build construction services, the contractor must provide a performance bond in an amount equal to 100 percent of the price specified in the contract but shall not include any design services, pre-construction services, finance services, maintenance services, operations services or other related services included in the contract. Performance bonds for these service contracts are issued in accordance with A.R.S. § 34-608, *supra.*

A.R.S. § 15-213 requires contractors that contract with a *school district* for the *construction, alteration, or repair of any project* to provide a performance bond in an amount equal to the full contract amount for the protection of the school district.

A.R.S. § 15-213 requires contractors that contract with a *school district* for *job-order-contracting construction services* to furnish a performance bond in an amount equal to the full amount of construction under the job-order-contracting construction services contract, but shall not include any design services, pre-construction services, finance services, maintenance services, operations services or other related services included in the contract.

A.R.S. § 15-213 requires contractors that contract with a *school district* for *construction-manager-at-risk construction services and design-build construction services* to furnish a performance bond in an amount equal to the price of construction and shall not include the cost of any design services, pre-construction services, finance services, maintenance services, operations services or any other related services included in the contract.

A.R.S. § 11-806.01 requires contractors that contract with any *county board of supervisors* to post a performance bond as may be appropriate and necessary to assure the installation of required street, sewer, electric and water utilities, drainage, flood control and improvements.

A.R.S. § 48-925 requires that any contractor that contracts with any *county improvement district,* including domestic wastewater improvement districts, for the construction, reconstruction and repair of any street, sewer or waterworks shall provide a performance bond in accordance with A.R.S. § 34-222, *supra*.

A.R.S. § 9-463.01 requires contractors that contract with any *unincorporated city or town* to post a performance bond as may be appropriate and necessary to assure the installation of required *street, sewer, electric and water utilities, drainage, flood control and improvements.*

A.R.S. § 48-2055 requires that any contractor that contracts with a *sanitary district* for the construction, reconstruction and repair of all or part of the improvements and maintenance of sewers, pipelines and channels for sanitary or drainage purposes, treatment works, effluent disposal facilities and other appurtenances in, under, over or through any street shall provide a performance bond in accordance with A.R.S. § 34-222, *supra*.

A.R.S. § 48-587 requires that any contractor who contracts with a *public improvement district* formed to provide public service within the district including such services as public safety, fire protection, refuse collection, street or sidewalk cleaning or landscape maintenance in public areas, shall provide a performance bond in accordance with A.R.S. § 34-222, supra.

A.R.S. § 48-2665 requires that any person to whom a contract is awarded for the *construction, maintenance, operation and repair works necessary for drainage purposes* to provide a performance bond in an amount equal to the full contract amount in accordance with A.R.S. § 34-222, *supra.*

A.R.S. § 48-2665 requires that any person or persons to whom a contract is awarded for the *purchase of materials for the construction, maintenance, operation and repair works necessary for drainage purposes* shall provide a performance bond in an amount equal to the full contract amount in accordance with A.R.S. § 34-222, *supra.*

A.R.S. § 48-2986 requires that any person or firm to whom a contract is awarded a contract to *construct, maintain and keep in repair levees* for the protection of lands included therein from overflow shall provide a performance bond in an amount equal to the full contract amount in accordance with A.R.S. § 34-222, *supra.*

A.R.S. § 48-4857(E) requires that any person or firm to whom a contract is awarded a contract with an *active management area water district for the construction or maintenance of district facilities* shall provide a performance bond in an amount equal to the full contract amount in accordance with A.R.S. § 34-222, *supra.*

**Private** – The State of Arizona does not have a statute that requires performance bonds to be furnished on private work.

**Department of Transportation** – A.R.S. § 28-6713 requires that any contractor that contracts with a county for the construction or reconstruction of county and other legal subdivision highways to provide a performance bond in an amount equal to the full contract amount in favor of the Arizona Department of Transportation.

A.R.S. § 28-6748 requires that any contractor that contracts with a county for the construction or improvement of public highways to provide a performance bond in an amount equal to the full contract amount in favor of the Arizona Department of Transportation.

A.R.S. § 28-6923 requires that for all items of construction or reconstruction of department facilities involving an expenditure of $50,000 or more, a contractor provide a performance bond in an amount equal to the full contract amount in favor of the Arizona Department of Transportation.

A.R.S. § 28-7363 requires that for any design-build method of delivery of highway construction projects, involving an expenditure of $50,000 or more, a contractor provide a performance bond in an amount equal to the full contract amount in favor of the Arizona Department of Transportation.

A.R.S. § 28-7366 requires that a contractor to whom a contract for construction-manager-at-risk construction services and job-order-contracting construction services is awarded to provide a performance bond in an amount equal to the full contract amount in favor of the Arizona Department of Transportation.

***Case law rules that might generally apply***

A.R.S. § 34-222 is read into those contracts for which a performance bond is required for the construction of public buildings. *Paul Schoonover, Inc. v. Ram Constr., Inc.*, 129 Ariz. 204, 630 P.2d 27 (1981).

Suretyship contracts are construed according to the same rules applicable to other contracts. *Western Sur. Co. v. Horrall*, 111 Ariz. 486, 533 P.2d 543 (1975); *Cushman v. National Sur. Corp. of New York*, 4 Ariz. App. 24, 417 P.2d 537 (1966).

A completing performance bond surety confers a benefit on the government. The purpose of a performance bond is to insure the proper completion of the public works project so as to avoid the necessity of spending the citizens' money to fulfill the contractor's responsibilities. *Hartford Accident & Indem. Co. v. Arizona Dep't of Transp.*, 172 Ariz. 564, 568, 838 P.2d 1325, 1328 (Ct. App. 1992), citing *Norton v. First Fed. Sav.*, 128 Ariz. 176, 624 P.2d 854 (1981).

When a bond has been issued pursuant to a statute, the terms of the statute control the surety's liability even when the terms of the bond are more expansive than the terms of the statute. *Paul Schoonover, Inc. v. Ram Constr., Inc.*, 129 Ariz. 204, 206, 630 P.2d 27, 29 (1981); *Norton v. First Fed. Sav.*, 128 Ariz. 176, 178, 624 P.2d 854, 856 (1981); *Porter v. Eyer*, 80 Ariz. 169, 172, 294 P.2d 661, 663 (1956); *Hartford Accident & Indem. Co. v. Arizona Dep't of Transp.*, 172 Ariz. 564, 566, 838 P.2d 1325, 1327 (Ct. App. 1992); *Brown Wholesale Elec. v. Merchants Mut. Bond.*, 148 Ariz. 90, 95, 713 P.2d 291, 296 (Ct. App. 1984).

Surety bonds will be construed most strongly against the surety and in favor of the obligees. *Massachusetts Bonding & Ins. Co. v. Lentz*, 40 Ariz. 46, 9 P.2d 408 (1932); *New York Indem. Co. v. May*, 295 P. 314 (Ariz. 1931).

A performance bond indemnifies the obligee for the principal's failure to fully perform the contracted work. *American Cas. Co. of Reading, Pa. v. D.L. Withers Constr.*, 204 Ariz. 382, 384, 64 P.3d 210, 212 (Ct. App. 2003).

A breach by the bond principal rendered surety liable and the obligee was entitled to be placed in position he would have been in had the principal performed. *Sorensen v. Robert N. Ewing, General Contractor*, 8 Ariz. App. 540, 542, 448 P.2d 110, 112 (1968).

## 2. Damages Covered

### *Set forth in any statutes and/or case law*

A.R.S. § 48-586 allows the governing *municipal public improvement districts* to prescribe in the form of the contract, an amount, not as a forfeit or penalty, but as *liquidated damages*, per calendar day to be paid by the contractor if the contractor fails to complete the work within the time fixed in the contract or as the time for completion of the work may have been extended by the superintendent with the consent of the governing body.

### *Limitations on damages*

Surety's liability is strictly limited to that assumed by its terms. *Cushman v. National Sur. Corp. of New York*, 4 Ariz. App. 24, 417 P.2d 537 (1966).

Where contract was shown to have been performed at least in part under a joint venture agreement involving a party other than surety's principal, surety, which had issued performance bond and labor and material bond, could not be held liable to obligee. *Mead, Samuel & Co. v. U.S. Fid. & Guar. Co.*, 125 Ariz. 525, 528, 611 P.2d 112, 115 (Ct. App. 1980).

Where in a contract for the construction of a road, the county reserved the right to make changes in the scope of work, including the right to reduce the scope of work, contractor may not recover damages for "anticipated profits" - the benefits or the gains that would have accrued to the contractor had the contract remained unchanged. *Johnson v. Gila County*, 21 Ariz. 136, 185 P. 929 (1919).

"The 'cost of repair' rule relates to the general rule of damages applicable to breach of construction contracts, that is, damages are awarded based upon the reasonable cost of construction and completion in accordance with the contract." *Maricopa County v. Walsh & Oberg Architects, Inc.*, 16 Ariz. App. 439, 441, 494 P.2d 44, 46 (1972).

Where obligee retained a portion of the contract price, obligee's measure of damages for breach of contract was reasonable cost of completing the contract and repairing the principal's defective performance, less the part of the contract price still unpaid. *Sorensen v. Robert N. Ewing, General Contractor*, 8 Ariz. App. 540, 542, 448 P.2d 110, 112 (1968).

**Interest** – A.R.S. § 44-1201(A) provides that interest on any loan, indebtedness, judgment or other obligation shall be at the rate of 10 percent per annum, unless a different rate is contracted for in writing, in which event any rate of interest may be agreed to.

The rule in Arizona is that a performance bond is liable for interest calculated from the date the sums became due, rather than when demand is made upon the surety for payment. *Webb v. Crane Co.*, 52 Ariz. 299, 80 P.2d 698 (1938); *L. M. White Contracting Co. v. St. Joseph Structural Steel Co.*, 15 Ariz. App. 260, 265, 488 P.2d 196, 201 (1971).

**Taxes** – Performance bond surety on road construction contract was liable for its principal's unpaid unemployment insurance taxes incurred in connection with bonded project. Both the terms of bond and the statute under which bond was issued required that bond guarantee full performance of all conditions of contract, one of which was principal's obligation to pay unemployment taxes. *Hartford Accident & Indem. Co. v. Arizona Dep't of Transp.*, 172 Ariz. 564, 569-70, 838 P.2d 1325, 1330 (Ct. App. 1992).

**Bad faith damages** – A surety will incur tort liability "if it either knows that its position is groundless or when it fails to undertake an investigation adequate to determine whether its position is tenable." In other words, a surety must have intended the alleged "act or omission," while lacking a "founded belief that such conduct was permitted by the policy." *Dodge Fidelity & Deposit Co. of Md.*, 161 Ariz. 344, 347, 778 P.2d 1240, 1243 (1989). As long as a surety acts reasonably in response to a claim made by its obligee, the surety does not risk bad faith tort liability. *Dodge*, 161 Ariz. at 347, 778 P.2d at 1243 citing *Noble v. National Am. Life Ins. Co.*, 128 Ariz. 188, 190, 624 P.2d 866, 868 (1981) ("The tort of bad faith arises when the insurance company intentionally denies, fails to process or pay a claim without a reasonable basis for such action.").

### 3. Penal Sum Variations

#### *Limitations per statute*

A.R.S. § 48-924(E) provides that if the board of directors of any *county improvement district* finds that the contractor is unable to continue with the work or to perform the work according to the contract or has not performed the work according to the contract, the board of directors shall hold the contractor in default and make demand on the surety to act in accordance with the contract and terms and conditions of the performance bond. *The demand may not exceed the penal sum of the performance bond.*

A.R.S. § 48-586(F) provides that if the governing *municipal public improvement district* finds that the contractor is unable to continue with the work or to perform the work according to the contract, the governing body shall hold the contractor in default and make demand upon the surety to act in accordance with the contract and terms and conditions of the performance bond. *The demand may not exceed the penal sum of the performance bond.*

A.R.S. § 48-2054(E) provides that if any *sanitary district and sewer construction board* finds that the contractor is unable to continue with the work or to perform the work according to the contract, the board shall hold the contractor in default and make demand on the surety to act according to the contract and the terms and conditions of the performance bond. *The demand may not exceed the penal sum of the performance bond.*

#### *Effect of changes in work upon penal sum, if at all*

Where the performance bond incorporates the construction contract, and the construction contract allows for additions and or deductions from the contract amount, the bond contemplates that such changes might be made. *Massachusetts Bonding & Ins. Co. v. Lentz*, 40 Ariz. 46, 9 P.2d 408 (1932).

***Statutory or case law protections or dangers to penal sum*** – See above.

## 4. Parties Covered

***Statutes and/or case law as to whether only obligees are covered***

The classification of a bond as either a "performance" bond or a "payment" bond does not determine who may make a claim against the bond. *American Cas. Co. of Reading, Pa. v. D.L. Withers Constr.*, 204 Ariz. 382, 384, 64 P.3d 210, 212 (Ct. App. 2003).

If a company agrees to be a surety for a particular principal, the contract is understood to be only for that named principal. Any material change in the obligation not assented to by the surety as one of the parties to the contract will discharge the surety from liability. This rule is applicable when there is a change of principals. *Western Sur. Co. v. Horrall*, 111 Ariz. 486, 533 P.2d 543 (1975).

***Coverage for:***

**Third-party beneficiaries generally** – The Arizona rule is that in order for a person to recover as a third-party beneficiary of a contract, an intention to benefit that person must be indicated in the contract itself. The contemplated benefit must be both intentional and direct, and it must definitely appear that the parties intend to recognize the third party as the primary party in interest. *Norton v. First Fed. Sav.*, 128 Ariz. 176, 178, 624 P.2d 854, 856 (1981); *Irwin v. Murphey*, 81 Ariz. 148, 154, 302 P.2d 534, 538 (1956); *Basurto v. Utah Constr. & Mining Co.*, 15 Ariz. App. 35, 485 P.2d 859 (1971).

**Third-party beneficiaries and A.R.S. § 34-222** – A.R.S. § 34-222(A) provides that a performance "bond shall be *solely* for the protection of the state or the public body awarding the contract, as the case may be."

There are several Arizona cases holding that incidental third-party beneficiaries are not entitled to recover under the bond. *Norton v. First Fed. Sav.*, 128 Ariz. 176, 180, 624 P.2d 854, 858 (1981); *Irwin v.*

*Murphey*, 81 Ariz. 148, 302 P.2d 534 (1956); *Tanner Companies v. Insurance Mktg. Svcs., Inc.*, 154 Ariz. 442, 445-46, 743 P.2d 951, 954-55 (App. 1987); *Basurto v. Utah Constr. & Mining Co.*, 15 Ariz. App. 35, 485 P.2d 859 (1971).

**Assignees** – There are no Arizona cases that address the enforceability of a provision that prohibits assignment of a performance bond. Generally, however, Arizona courts will enforce a valid contractual provision that precludes assignment. *Hanigan v. Wheeler*, 19 Ariz. App. 49, 504 P.2d 972 (1972).

**Dual obligees** – Not applicable.

## 5. Notice or Filing Required

***Statutory provisions*** – Not applicable.

***Case law rules concerning condition precedent notice***

Although there are no reported Arizona decisions involving surety bonds, Arizona courts will only construe a contractual provision as a condition precedent when such construction is plainly and unambiguously required by the language of the contract. *Watson Constr. Co. v. Reppel Steel & Supply Co.*, 123 Ariz. 138, 140, 598 P.2d 116, 118 (Ct. App. 1979).

## 6. Time for Suit:

***Statutes of limitation particular to performance bonds and other applicable statutes of limitation***

In the absence of a contractual provision limiting the time for suit, A.R.S. § 12-548 requires that an action on a written contract shall be commenced and prosecuted within six years after the cause of action accrues, and not afterward.

***Case law statements about enforceability of limitations contained in bonds***

The time for filing an action under a performance bond is prescribed by the terms of the bond. Such limitation clauses are enforceable. *Decca Design Build, Inc. v. American Auto. Ins. Co.*, 206 Ariz. 301, 77 P.3d 1251 (Ct. App. 2003) (enforcing AIA bond provision limiting the time to bring suit to two years from when payment became due).

***Varying statutes of limitation by agreement in bond or contract***

*Zuckerman v. Transamerica Ins. Co.*, 133 Ariz. 139, 142-43, 650 P.2d 441, 444-45 (1982) (upholding an insurance policy's one-year limitations period, which was significantly shorter than the six-year statutory period applicable to written contracts).

## 7. Procedure

***Statutory or procedural rules that may affect handling of administration of lawsuits***

A.R.S. § 48-586(F) provides that if any municipal public improvement district governing body finds that the contractor is unable to continue with the work or to perform the work according to the contract, the governing body shall hold the contractor in default and make demand upon the surety to act in accordance with the contract and terms and conditions of the performance bond. If the surety fails to act within 60 days from written notice, the governing body may order that bids be received from other contractors to complete the work. After receiving bids, the governing body may award the contract to the lowest responsible bidder. If, after receiving the new bids, the cost of completion exceeds the monies or bonds available for payment, the governing body shall make a demand upon the defaulting contractor's bondsman for payment of the differential within 20 days of the mailing of the notice. If the bondsman is represented by an attorney-in-fact, the demand may be served upon the attorney-in-fact or at the bondsman's principal office within this state.

A.R.S. § 48-924(D) provides that if the work is not prosecuted with diligence, the county improvement district board of directors, after a hearing upon notice mailed or personally served upon the contractor, the contractor's surety and all persons shown as the owners of property affected by the assessments as their names and addresses appear on the last certified property tax roll, may prescribe such terms and conditions as it deems proper before permitting the contractor to continue with the work if the board of directors determines that the contractor is capable of continuing the work.

A.R.S. § 48-924(E) provides that if the contractor is unable to continue with the work or has not performed the work according to the contract, the county improvement district board of directors shall hold the contractor in default and make demand on the surety to act in accordance with the contract and the performance bond. If the surety fails to act within 60 days from receiving written notice, the board of directors may order that bids be received from other contractors to complete the work. After receiving bids, the board of directors may award the contract to the lowest responsible bidder. If, after receiving the new bids, the cost of completion exceeds the monies or bonds available for payment, the board of directors shall make a demand on the defaulting contractor's surety for payment of the difference within 20 days of the mailing of the notice. If the surety is represented by an attorney-in-fact, the demand may be served on the attorney-in-fact or at the surety's principal office within this state. If the surety has no attorney-in-fact and no principal office within this state, the demand shall be served upon the director of insurance.

A.R.S. § 48-2054(E) provides that if any sanitary district and/or sewer construction board finds that the contractor is unable to continue with the work or to perform the work according to the contract, the board shall hold the contractor in default and make demand on the surety to act according to the contract and the terms and conditions of the performance bond. If the surety fails to act within 60 days from the date of the written notice, the board may order that bids be received from other contractors to complete the work. After receiving bids, the board may award the contract to the lowest responsible bidder. If, after receiving the new bids, the cost of completion exceeds the monies or bonds available for payment, the board shall make a demand on the defaulting contractor's surety for payment of the difference within 20 days of the mailing of the notice. If the surety is represented by an attorney-in-fact, the demand may be served on the attorney-in-fact or at the surety's principal office in this state. If the surety has no attorney-in-fact and no principal office in this state, the demand shall be served on the director of insurance.

***Venue requirements and jurisdictional limitations***

A.R.S. § 20-1532 provides that any surety insurer may be sued in respect of any surety bond issued by it in the county where the bond, recognizance, stipulation or undertaking was made or guaranteed, or in the county where the principal office of the insurer in this state is located, and for the purposes hereof, it shall be treated as made or guaranteed in the county in which such office is located or in which it is filed, or in the county in which the principal resided when it was made or guaranteed.

***Court rules***

**Case law statements about procedure** – Ordinarily, the principal obligor on a surety bond must be joined in any action against the surety. The rule has an exception permitting actions against a surety without joinder of the principal obligor "when the latter resides beyond the limits of the state, or in such a part of the state that he cannot be reached by ordinary process of law." Once the principal is shown to be within an exception to Ariz. R. Civ. P. 17(f), the plaintiff may proceed against the surety alone. *Smith Plumbing Co. v. Aetna Cas. & Sur. Co.*, 149 Ariz. 524, 527-28, 720 P.2d 499, 502-03 (1986), citing Ariz. R. Civ. P. 17(f); see also *First Nat'l Bank of Albuquerque v. Standard Accident Ins. Co.*, 38 Ariz. 77, 81-82, 297 P. 864, 866 (1931).

**Time for answer after suit** – A.R.S. § 20-222 provides that where a surety is served with process through the Arizona Department of Insurance, the surety has 40 days to file an answer or other responsive pleading.

***Particular agency regulations/rules***

**Transportation and roadway construction** – A.R.S. § 28-7703 provides that if there is a material and continuing default in the performance of the private entity's construction duties or contractual obligations or if construction has not begun within two years of the date of the agreement authorized by this article or after final clearance of all necessary government approvals and authorizations, whichever is later, the board, after a hearing in which the private entity has notice and an opportunity to participate, may (1) revoke the agreement; (2) declare a default in the construction or lease of the transportation facility; (3) make the appropriate claims under any completion or performance bond; or (4) take other action determined appropriate by the board under the circumstances.

**Suits against municipalities** – A.R.S. § 12-821 provides that all actions against any public entity or public employee shall be brought within one year after the cause of action accrues and not afterward.

**Suits against public entities** – A.R.S. § 12-821.01 requires that all persons who have claims against a public entity or a public employee shall file claims with the person or persons authorized to accept service for the public entity or public employee as set forth in the Arizona Rules of Civil Procedure within 180 days (180 days - *not* six months) after the cause of action accrues. The notice of claim shall contain facts sufficient to permit the public entity or public employee to understand the basis upon which liability is claimed, a specific amount for which the claim can be settled and the facts supporting that amount. Any claim which is not filed within 180 days after the cause of action accrues is barred and no action may be maintained thereon. A cause of action accrues when the damaged party realizes he or she has been damaged and knows or reasonably should know the cause, source, act, event, instrumentality or condition which caused or contributed to the damage.

### *Arbitration requirements and application*

A.R.S. § 12-1501 provides that "a written agreement to submit any existing controversy to arbitration or a provision in a written contract to submit to arbitration any controversy thereafter arising between the parties is valid, enforceable and irrevocable, save upon such grounds as exist at law or in equity for the revocation of any contract."

Arizona has enacted legislation relating to the enforceability of arbitration provisions (A.R.S. §§ 12-1501, 12-1502) and Arizona case law provides the framework to analyze the enforceability of an arbitration agreement, which limits the scope of judicial inquiry into the merits of a contract dispute to whether or not there exists an arbitration clause governing the controversy. *Stevens/Leinweber/Sullens, Inc. v. Holm Dev. & Mgmt., Inc.*, 165 Ariz. 25, 28, 795 P.2d 1308, 1311 (Ct. App. 1990); *New Pueblo Constructors, Inc. v. Lake Patagonia*, 12 Ariz. App. 13, 16, 467 P.2d 88, 91 (1970)("[A] arbitration clause[s] should be construed liberally and any doubts as to whether or not the matter in question is subject to arbitration should be resolved in favor of arbitration.")

## 8. Attorney's Fees

***Statutes and/or case law limiting or permitting recovery of attorney's fees***

A.R.S. § 12-341.01(A) provides that reasonable attorney's fees may be awarded at discretion of the trial court but only in an action "arising out of contract." An action arises out of contract if it could not exist but for the contract. In the surety context, since a performance bond is considered a contract, attorney's fees are recoverable in actions against a performance bond. *Sparks v. Republic Nat'l Life Ins. Co.*, 132 Ariz. 529, 543, 647 P.2d 1127, 1141, *cert. denied*, 459 U.S. 1070, 103 S. Ct. 490 (1982).

The award of attorney's fees is within the sole discretion of the trial court. *State Farm Mut. Auto. Ins. Co. v. Arrington*, 192 Ariz. 255, 963 P.2d 334 (Ct. App. 1998).

**Public buildings and improvement contracts** – If a performance bond is issued in accordance with A.R.S. § 34-222, then pursuant to subsection G, the performance bond must include the following provision:

> The prevailing party in a suit on this bond shall recover as part of the judgment reasonable attorney fees that may be fixed by a judge of the court.

**Procurement of service contracts with public monies** – If a performance bond is issued pursuant to A.R.S. § 34-608 or A.R.S. § 41-2574, for construction services, which includes construction-manager-at-risk, design-build and job-order-contracting construction services, then the performance bond must include a provision allowing the prevailing party in a suit on the bond to recover as a part of the judgment any reasonable attorney fees as may be fixed by the court.

**Bad faith actions** – An action alleging insurer's bad faith is one "arising out of a contract" within the meaning of A.R.S § 12-341.01. *Sparks v. Republic Nat'l Life Ins. Co.*, 132 Ariz. 529, 544, 647 P.2d 1127, 1142, *cert. denied,* 459 U. S. 1070, 103 S. Ct. 490 (1982).

## 9. Special Provisions

A.R.S. § 34-222 requires that, notwithstanding any other statute, each such surety bond issued in accordance with this section, shall be executed solely by a surety company or companies holding a certificate of authority to transact surety business in this state issued by the director of the department of insurance pursuant to Title 20, Chapter 2, Article 1. The bonds shall *not* be executed by an individual surety or sureties.

The administrative regulations that correspond to the statutes that govern the procurement and construction of the state and county agencies provide that acceptable performance bonds must be executed solely by a surety company or companies holding a certificate of authority to transact surety business in Arizona issued by the Director of the Department of Insurance pursuant to A.R.S. Title 20, Chapter 2, Article 1. *See e.g.*, Ariz. Admin. Code R2-7-356 (procurement of material and service contracts); Ariz. Admin. Code R2-7-503, R2-7-504 (procurement of construction services); Ariz. Admin. Code R7-2-1033, R7-2-1111, R7-2-1112 (state board of education procurement of construction services).

**Statutory requirement to negotiate delay claims** – A.R.S. § 34-221(F) requires that a contract for the procurement of construction shall include a provision which provides for negotiations between the agent and the contractor for the recovery of damages related to expenses incurred by the contractor for a delay for which the agent is responsible, which is unreasonable under the circumstances and which was not within the contemplation of the parties to the contract. The section shall not be construed to void any provision in the contract which requires notice of delays, provides for arbitration or other procedure for settlement or provides for liquidated damages.

A.R.S. § 15-213(D) requires that a contract for the procurement of construction or construction services shall include a provision which provides for negotiations between the school district and the contractor for the recovery of damages related to expenses incurred by the contractor for a delay for which the school district is responsible, which is unreasonable under the circumstances and which was not within the contemplation of the parties to the contract. The section shall not be construed to void any provision in the contract which requires notice of delays, provides for arbitration or other procedure for settlement or provides for liquidated damages.

A.R.S. § 48-586(E) provides that if the work is not prosecuted with diligence, the body governing any general public improvements, after a hearing upon notice served upon the contractor and his bondsmen, may prescribe such terms and conditions as it deems proper before permitting the contractor to continue with the work.

A.R.S. § 48-2054(D) provides that if the work is not performed with diligence, any sanitary district and/or sewer construction board, after a hearing and service of notice on the contractor and his surety, may prescribe such terms and conditions as it deems proper before permitting the contractor to continue with the work.

**Jurisdiction over sureties** – A.R.S. § 12-401 provides that no person shall be sued out of the county in which such person resides, but contains an exception that suits against insurance companies may be brought in any county in which the cause of action, or a part thereof, arose, or in the county in which defendant has an agent or representative, owns property or conducts any business.

**Subrogation of surety to rights of judgment creditor** – A.R.S. § 12-1643(A) provides that "When a person who is surety on an undertaking is compelled to pay a judgment or part thereof, or makes a payment upon a judgment by reason of suretyship, such judgment shall not be discharged by such payment but shall remain in force for the use of the surety and shall be considered as assigned to the surety together with all rights of the creditor thereunder to the extent of the payment made by the surety, and interest thereon."

**10. Remarks** – Not applicable.

## 11. Case Annotations

***Interpretation of AIA bond forms*** – Not applicable.

***Cases in which surety steps into shoes of obligee***

**Surety liability co-extensive with principal** – In the absence of limitations in the contract, the liability of a surety on a performance bond is co-extensive with that of its principal. *Paul Schoonover, Inc. v. Ram Constr., Inc.*, 129 Ariz. 204, 630 P.2d 27 (1981); *Sorensen v. Robert N. Ewing, General Contractor*, 8 Ariz. App. 540, 542, 448 P.2d 110, 112 (1968).

A surety is not liable on a bond unless the principal is liable and the surety may set up any defense available to the principal. An exception to this rule exists where the principal takes advantage of a personal defense - of such a character that the principal, as he chooses, may insist upon them or not - or where the extinction of the principal's obligation arises from a cause which originates in the law. *Smith Plumbing Co. v. Aetna Cas. & Sur. Co.*, 149 Ariz. 524, 527, 720 P.2d 499, 502 (1986); *see also Spear v. Industrial Comm'n.*, 114 Ariz. 601, 562 P.2d 1099 (Ct. App. 1977).

Where an Indian tribe, as principal, had the power either to insist upon or to waive its sovereign immunity, that immunity is considered a personal defense not available to the tribe's surety. *Smith Plumbing Co. v. Aetna Cas. & Sur. Co.*, 149 Ariz. 524, 527, 720 P.2d 499, 502 (1986).

**Surety Bad Faith Applicable in Arizona** – Surety has a duty to act in good faith in responding to its obligee's claims that principal has defaulted; breach of that duty entitles obligee to maintain tort action and recover tort damages. Dodge v. Fidelity & Deposit Co. of Md., 161 Ariz. 344, 348, 778 P.2d 1240, 1244 (1989). The court reasoned that "a surety who in bad faith refuses to pay a valid claim by deliberately refusing to pay an obligation arising from the performance bond deprives the insured of the protection he sought by purchasing insurance." Id. at 346, 778 P.2d at 1242.

A surety will incur tort liability "if it either knows that its position is groundless or when it fails to undertake an investigation adequate to determine whether its position is tenable." In other words, a surety must have intended the alleged "act or omission," while lacking a "founded belief that such conduct was permitted by the policy." As long as a surety acts reasonably in response to a claim made by its obligee, the surety does not risk bad faith tort liability. *Dodge v. Fidelity & Deposit Co. of Md.*, 161 Ariz. 344, 347, 778 P.2d 1240, 1243 (1989).

**Third-party beneficiaries and bad faith** – Arizona courts have held that third-party beneficiaries may sue for bad faith, but the courts have yet to develop this in the commercial surety context. *Rowland v. Great States Ins. Co.*, 199 Ariz. 577, 582, 20 P.3d 1158, 1163 (Ct. App. 2001); *Nahom v. Blue Cross & Blue Shield of Arizona, Inc.*, 180 Ariz. 548, 553, 885 P.2d 1113, 1118 (Ct. App. 1994).

**Subrogation** – Arizona cases have adopted the general rule that a completing surety under a performance bond becomes equitably subrogated both to the contractor's rights to receive the retained contract funds and to the government's right to use those funds to complete the contract. *Hartford Accident & Indem. Co. v. Arizona Dep't of Transp.*, 172 Ariz. 564, 568, 838 P.2d 1325, 1328 (Ct. App. 1992), *citing Pearlman v. Reliance Ins. Co.,* 371 U.S. 132, 83 S. Ct. 232 (1962).

A surety's equitable subrogation right arises out of the equitable doctrine that when one, pursuant to a legal obligation and not as a volunteer, fulfills the duty of another he is entitled to assert the rights of that other against third parties. *General Acrylics v. U.S. Fid. & Guar.*, 128 Ariz. 50, 623 P.2d 839 (Ct. App. 1981).

The general rule is that a person having an interest in property who pays off an encumbrance in order to protect his interest is subrogated to the rights and limitations of the person paid. Upon the general principles of equity he should have every right to enforce his claim which the original party had, but upon the same principles he is not entitled to any new or additional rights. *Mosher v. Conway*, 45 Ariz. 463, 472, 46 P.2d 110, 114 (1935).

# ARKANSAS

David A. Grace[1]

## 1. Requirement for Bond

***Statutory provisions for projects that are:***

**Public** – No contract in any sum exceeding $20,000 providing for the repair, alteration or erection of any public building, public structure or public improvement shall be entered into by the State of Arkansas or any subdivision thereof, or by any county, municipality, school district or other local taxing unit, or by any agency of any of the foregoing, unless the contractor shall furnish to the party letting the contract a bond in a sum equal to the amount of the contract. A.C.A. § 18-44-503.

**Religious or Charitable Organizations** – No contract in any sum exceeding $1,000 providing for the repair, alteration or erection of any building, structure or improvement shall be entered into by any church, religious organization, charitable institution, or by any agency of the foregoing, unless the contractor shall furnish to the party letting the contract a bond in a sum equal to the amount of the contract. A.C.A. § 18-44-504.

---

[1] David A. Grace is a shareholder of:
Hardin & Grace, a Professional Association
500 Main Street, Suite A
P.O. Box 5851
North Little Rock, Arkansas 72119-5851
(501) 378-7900

**Private** – Any person, firm, corporation or association entering into a contract for the repair, alteration or erection of any building, structure or improvement may, at his or her or its option, require the contractor to furnish a bond in a sum equal to the amount of the contract. A.C.A. § 18-44-505.

**Arkansas Highway and Transportation Department** – Every contractor for work in excess of $1,000 shall be required to furnish a bond to be approved by a majority of the state highway commission in an amount at least equal to the amount of the contract, conditioned as the Commission may require. A.C.A. § 27-65-131(b); *see also,* § 103.05(a), Standard Specifications for Highway Construction (1996 Ed.).

***Case law rules that might generally apply***

The requirement that a contractor be bonded when a public authority enters into a contract to repair, alter or erect a public building, structure or improvement is not applicable where the public authority entered into a contract to purchase public housing units after the units were constructed. *Raywick Manufacturing Co., Inc. v. Talisman, Inc.*, 17 Ark. App. 202, 706 S.W.2d 194 (1986).

The [bond] liability imposed by A.C.A. § 22-9-401 on any bond furnished by a public works contractor shall be deemed an integral part of the bond, whether or not the liability is explicitly set out or assumed therein. A.C.A. § 22-9-403; *see also, Detroit Fidelity & Surety Co. v. Yaffe Iron and Metal Co.*, 184 Ark. 1095, 44 S.W. 2d 1085 (1932).

The bond required or authorized in A.C.A. § 18-44-501, *et seq.*, shall in itself be in full compliance with all other statutes of this state in effect relating to bond requirements or contracts for the repair, alteration or erection of any building, structure or improvement, public or private, it being the intention of this subchapter to provide a uniform bonding procedure in conjunction with such contracts. A.C.A. § 18-44-501; *see also, River Valley, Inc. v. American States Insurance Co.*, 287 Ark. 386, 699 S.W.2d 745 (1985).

## 2. Damages Covered

### *Set forth in any statutes and/or case law*

In all cases in which loss occurs and the ... surety ... liable therefor shall fail to pay the losses within the time specified in the policy after demand is made, the [surety] shall be liable to pay the holder of the policy or his or her assigns, in addition to the amount of the loss, 12 percent damages upon the amount of the loss, together with all reasonable attorney's fees for the prosecution and collection of the loss. A.C.A. § 23-79-208(a)(1).

Recovery of less than the amount demanded by the person entitled to recover under the policy shall not defeat the right to the 12 percent damages and attorney's fees provided for in this section if the amount recovered for the loss is within 20 percent of the amount demanded or which is sought in the suit. A.C.A. § 23-79-208(d).

The parties to any contract, whether the contract is under seal or not, may agree in writing for the payment of interest not exceeding the applicable rate set forth in Arkansas Constitution, Article 19, Section 13, on money due or to become due. A.C.A. § 4-57-104. Pre-judgment interest is recoverable in all cases where there is a method of determination of the value of the claim at the time of the injury. *Lovell v. Marianna Federal Savings & Loan Association*, 267 Ark. 164, 589 S.W.2d 577 (1979). What has to be ascertainable is the initial measure of damages, which is to be distinguished from the precise amount sought in the complaint or the amount which is ultimately awarded by the fact finder. *Wooten v. McClendon*, 272 Ark. 61, 612 S.W.2d 105 (1981). In contract actions, pre-judgment interest is "almost automatically awarded" by Arkansas courts. Brill, *Law of Damages* (5th Ed.), § 10.1.

### *Obligations of surety to perform and/or pay*

The duty of an issuer of a performance bond is established by the language of the bond. *Angelo Iafrate Construction, LLC v. Potashnick Construction, Inc.*, 370 F.3d 715 (8th Cir. 2004) (interpreting Arkansas law); *see also, New Amsterdam Casualty Co. v. Detroit Fidelity & Surety Co.*, 187 Ark. 97, 58 S.W.2d 418 (1933).

Where the sureties of a building contractor, upon his default, assume to carry out his contracts, they are estopped to deny the terms of his contract with a subcontractor. *Beckley v. Miller*, 96 Ark. 379, 131 S.W. 876 (1910).

A surety contracting with the state relegates any relief based on a breach of the contract into the hands of the legislative branch. *Travelers Casualty & Surety Co. of America v. Arkansas State Highway Commission*, 353 Ark. 721, 120 S.W.3d 50 (2003).

A performance bond surety may have a duty to indemnify the Arkansas Highway and Transportation Commission for claims for personal injury and property damage caused by the work performed under its principal's contract pursuant to § 107.14 of the Standard Specifications for Highway Construction. *See Angelo Iafrate Construction, LLC v. Potashnick Construction, Inc.*, 370 F.3d 715 (8th Cir. 2004).

***Whether failure to provide insurance transfers burden to surety***

Where a contract between an owner and a contractor specifically required the contractor to obtain a builder's risk policy and the performance bond guaranteed performance by the contractor, but the builder's risk policy had not been procured when the owner sustained a loss of an insurable interest, this was a breach of the contract, and the surety was not released from its obligations contained in the performance bond. Therefore, the owner was entitled to recover from the surety. *Carroll-Boone Water District v. M & P Equipment Co.*, 280 Ark. 560, 661 S.W.2d 345 (1983).

***Limitations on damages***

Bonds are construed as if the law was written into them and a court will not make implications against sureties not clearly embraced within the language used. *Merchants Bonding Co. v. Starkey*, 337 Ark. 229, 987 S.W.2d 717 (1999).

The liability of a surety in a performance bond is derivative and ordinarily does not exceed that of the principal. *Travelers Casualty & Surety Co. of America v. Arkansas State Highway Commission, supra.*

Where a contractor was not liable for damages for delay in completion of a contract for construction of a sewer treatment pond and five sewage pump stations, there was no basis for a judgment against the surety on the contractor's bond. *City of Whitehall v. Southern Mechanical Contracting, Inc.*, 269 Ark. 563, 599 S.W.2d 430 (1980).

The surety on a road contractor's bond which was bound to indemnify the obligee against loss from the contractor's negligence in prosecuting the work and failing to pay bills and to complete the work within the time specified, is not liable for money overpaid the contractor through the fraud or gross mistake of the engineer. *Gage & Spencer v. Road Improvement District No. 3 of Newton County*, 159 Ark. 642, 252 S.W. 922 (1923).

A bond obligee may not increase the surety's risk or undermine the surety's subrogation rights. A surety bond embodies the principle that any material change in the bonded contract that increases the surety's risk or obligation without the surety's consent affects the surety relationship. *Pennsylvania National Mutual Casualty Insurance Co. v. City of Pine Bluff*, 354 F.3d 945 (8th Cir. 2004) (interpreting Arkansas law).

It is not necessary for a surety to prove bad faith or fraudulent misrepresentation in showing that a creditor has breached a duty to disclose facts which materially increase the surety's risks. The surety only has to prove the elements set forth in Restatement of Security § 124(1) defining a creditor's duty to disclose. *Camp v. First Financial Federal Savings & Loan Association*, 299 Ark. 455, 772 S.W.2d 602 (1989).

Where a building contract provided that the owner should maintain insurance on the building as it progressed, the owner's failure to so maintain insurance does not, where no loss results, discharge a surety on the contractor's bond. *Rowland v. Lindsey*, 104 Ark. 49, 146 S.W. 115 (1912).

An alteration of a performance bond contract is not "material" unless the surety is placed in the position of doing more than the undertaking contained in the performance bonds. *Carroll-Boone Water District v. M & P Equipment Co., supra.*

A failure to do an act required to be done by a surety's agreement is a breach of the contract rather than a material alteration. *Carroll-Boone Water District v. M & P Equipment Co., supra*. If the breach of contract causes damages to the surety, it may assert a claim for such damages, or may assert a set off against a claim against it. *Vogel v. Simmons First National Bank of Pine Bluff*, 15 Ark. App. 69, 679 S.W.2d 576 (1985).

A judgment against a principal for breach of an obligation, without fraud, is only *prima facie* evidence in an action against the surety, so that in an action on the bond of a mutual company, conditioned for prompt payment over of assessments, the surety could show that the assessments were promptly paid, notwithstanding a judgment against the company. *Ingle v. Batesville Grocery Co.*, 89 Ark. 378, 117 S.W. 241 (1909); *see also, Aetna Casualty & Surety Co. v. Henslee*, 163 Ark. 492, 260 S.W. 414 (1924).

***Whether obligee may set off bonded contract funds against other principal-obligee debts or obligations***

There are no reported cases in Arkansas which are directly on point with this issue. *C.f. Fidelity & Deposit Co. v. Merchants & Farmers Bank*, 120 Ark. 519, 179 S.W. 1019 (1915).

***Incorporation of specific contract terms by reference***

The terms of a contract in which a surety promises performance must be read into its own contract. The principal's contract and the bond or undertaking of the surety are to be construed together as one instrument. *Matson, Inc. v. Lamb & Associates Packaging, Inc.*, 328 Ark. 705, 947 S.W.2d 324 (1997).

In suretyship, the principal's contract and the surety's undertaking or bond are to be construed together as one instrument. *F & M Building Partnership v. Farmers & Merchants Bank*, 316 Ark. 60, 871 S.W.2d 338 (1994).

## 3. Penal Sum Variations

***Limitations per statute***

Applicable Arkansas statutes do not expressly limit the amount of a performance bond's penal sum, although such statutes require that the penal sum of the performance bond equal the amount of the contract. *See* § 1, *supra*.

***Effect of changes in work upon penal sum, if at all*** – There are no reported cases in Arkansas which are directly on point with this issue.

***Statutory or case law protections or dangers to penal sum*** – There are no reported cases in Arkansas which are directly on point with this issue.

## 4. Parties Covered

***Statutes and/or case law as to whether only obligees are covered***

A performance bond protects the owner or obligee, insuring project completion if the general contractor defaults. *Pennsylvania National Mutual Casualty Insurance Co. v. City of Pine Bluff, supra*.

No right of action exists in favor of a materialman against the surety on a private contractor's bond conditioned merely to indemnify and save harmless the owner from any pecuniary loss resulting from the breach of any terms of the contract between the owner and the contractor, since such bond is not intended for the benefit or protection of the third parties, but merely to indemnify the owner. *Employers Liability Assurance Corp. v. A.W. Johnson Co.*, 234 Ark. 806, 354 S.W.2d 733 (1962).

***Coverage for:***

**Third-party beneficiaries** – In general, a surety is liable to a third person only when its obligations to the principal obligor contain a promise which may be reasonably and clearly interpreted for the third person's benefit. Any liability of a surety to a third person must be measured by a reasonable interpretation of its obligation under the terms of the bond. *Tri-State Insurance Co. v. United States*, 340 F.2d 542 (8th Cir. 1965).

The issuer of a performance bond to a grading contractor related to a highway project owed no duty to advise the obligee or a third-party contractor responsible for surface paving that the grading contractor had financial problems, where the bonds only required that the issuer give notice of its own finances. *Angelo Iafrate Construction, LLC v. Potashnick Construction, Inc., supra*.

It is a general rule under Arkansas contract law that a contract will not be construed as having been made for the benefit of a third party unless it clearly appears that such was the intention of the parties. .... The performance obligations due under a performance bond are commonly owed solely to the obligee. *Angelo Iafrate Construction, LLC v. Potashnick Construction, Inc.*, *supra*.

The requirement under applicable statutes that a contractor engaged in a public work shall execute a bond conditioned to pay for labor and materials furnished in the construction of such works inures to the benefit of those furnishing labor and materials and they may sue thereon. *Aetna Casualty & Surety Co. v. Henslee*, *supra*.

**Assignees** – There are no reported cases in Arkansas which are directly on point with this issue.

**Dual obligees** – A contractor's dual obligation bond was reformed on the basis of a mutual mistake to conform to the terms of a previously issued performance and payment bond which had been voided because a bank's financing agreement required that it be named as an obligee in the bond despite the apparent acceptance of the second bond by subcontractors and materialmen. *River Valley, Inc. v. American States Insurance Co.*, *supra*.

## 5. Notice or Filing Required

***Statutory provisions***

Before any work is performed under [a contract required to be secured by a bond], the bond shall be filed with the clerk of the circuit court of the county in which the repairs, alterations or erections of any building, structure or improvements are made. A.C.A. § 18-44-507.

A public contractor's bond is statutory notwithstanding the failure to file the bond with the circuit court clerk. *Benton County Lumber Co. v. National Surety Co. of New York*, 179 Ark. 941, 18 S.W.2d 1017 (1929) (decided under a prior statute).

If the bond is not filed as provided in A.C.A. § 18-44-504(b)(1), any person performing labor or furnishing material, except the principal contractor, shall have a lien upon the property for the unpaid amount of the claim. A.C.A. § 18-44-504(b)(3).

***Case law rules concerning condition precedent notice***

A covenant to notify a surety of the default of its principal "immediately" is not performed by mailing a notice 11 days after the known default. *National Surety Co. v. Long*, 125 F. 887 (8th Cir. 1903); *see also, National Surety Co. v. Long*, 79 Ark. 523, 96 S.W. 745 (1906).

If surety had knowledge or was chargeable with knowledge of principal's default, failure to give notice in form required by construction bond would not relieve surety from liability. *Jack v. Craighead Rice Mill Co.*, 167 F.2d 96 (8th Cir. 1948) (interpreting Arkansas law).

Surety is not discharged from further liability, generally, upon failure of obligee to notify him of his principal's default where the suretyship contract contains no stipulation that such notice shall be given. *Gazette Publishing Co. v. Stephens*, 199 Ark. 641, 135 S.W.2d 313 (1940); *United States Fidelity & Guaranty Co. v. Lyons and Carnahan*, 188 Ark. 1078, 70 S.W.2d 552 (1934).

In dicta, the Supreme Court of Arkansas has suggested that an obligee might lose its claim against a performance bond surety for completion costs and liquidated damages where the obligee failed to give notice to surety as required by the express terms of the bond, thereby failing "to afford the surety the opportunity to complete any remaining work under the contract." *City of Whitehall v. Southern Mechanical Contracting, Inc., supra.*

## 6. Time for Suit

***Statutes of limitation particular to performance bonds and other applicable statutes of limitation***

A surety bond guaranteeing workmanship and materials is a common law obligation, not a bond required by statute, and the applicable statute of limitations bars actions after five years. *City of Hot Springs v. National Surety Co.*, 258 Ark. 1009, 531 S.W.2d 8 (1975); *see also,* A.C.A. § 16-56-111.

***Case law statements about enforceability of limitations contained in bonds***

A claim against a surety does not arise until the obligee suffers actual damage. *Arkansas State Highway Commission v. Union Indemnity Insurance Co. of New York*, 295 Ark. 273, 748 S.W.2d 338 (1988).

Where an equipment company's cause of action was actually based upon a surety's assumption of responsibility for completion of a public construction job, not upon the original contract of suretyship, the date of final payment on the contract was not controlling in determining whether an action had been timely brought. *Argonot Insurance Co. v. M & P Equipment Co.*, 269 Ark. 302, 601 S.W.2d 824 (1980).

An action by an improvement district on a performance bond was not subject to dismissal due to a two-year limitation period, notwithstanding claim that contractor had ceased work, where contractor's obligation to work continued and contractor had received extension of time to continue work after performance of other work by a third party. *Grady-Gould Watershed Imp. Dist. of Jefferson, Lincoln & Desha Counties, Ark. v. Transamerica Ins. Co.*, 570 F.2d 720 (8th Cir. 1978) (interpreting Arkansas law).

***Varying statutes of limitation by agreement in bond or contract***

An owner's acceptance of a surety bond can be presumed from the owner's retention of the bond, coupled with the owner having permitted the contractor to enter upon the performance of his contract without objecting to the bond tendered by him, and by bringing suit on the bond the owner, by necessary implication, treated the bond as acceptable and ratified it. The parties to a surety bond are free to contract for a limitation of time within which actions may be brought on the contractual undertaking which is shorter than is prescribed by the applicable statute of limitations as long as the stipulated time is not unreasonably short and the agreement does not contravene some statutory requirement or rule based upon public policy. A two-year limitation in a surety bond in which an owner could bring an action on a contractual undertaking is a condition precedent to an action thereon and there is no statutory prohibition against such a requirement. *City of Hot Springs v. National Surety Co., supra.*

## 7. Procedure

***Statutory or procedural rules that may affect handling or administration of lawsuits***

Contractors are proper but not necessary parties to suits on their bonds for public works construction projects. *R. J. Bob Jones Excavating Contractor, Inc. v. Fireman's Fund Insurance Co. of Newark, New Jersey*, 324 Ark. 282, 920 S.W.2d 483 (1996).

A performance bond surety may not file suit for declaratory judgment against the Arkansas Highway and Transportation Department to determine whether its principal is in breach of its contract. *Travelers Casualty & Surety Co. of America v. Arkansas State Highway Commission, supra.*

***Venue requirements and jurisdictional limitations***

An action brought in the State of Arkansas by or in behalf of an insured or beneficiary against a domestic or foreign surety on a contractor's payment or performance bond may be brought in either:

(1) The county in which the loss occurred,
(2) The county of the insured's residence at the time of the loss, or
(3) The county of the beneficiary's residence at the time of the loss.

A.C.A. § 16-60-115.

***Court rules*** – Not applicable.

***Particular agency regulations/rules***

The form of statutory performance bond used by the Arkansas State Highway and Transportation Department provides that "if the responsible surety fails to actively respond to the Resumption Order within 30 days and to secure immediate completion/closing of the project, then no future bonds will be accepted from the surety until the matter is resolved to the Department's satisfaction." *See also,* § 103.05 of the Standard Specifications for Highway Construction (1996 Ed.).

***Arbitration requirements and application***

Arkansas has adopted the Uniform Arbitration Act. *See* A.C.A. § 16-108-201, *et seq.*

Where a surety bond upon which an obligee brought suit incorporated an agreement to the effect that questions of breach and performance were subject to arbitration, the Uniform Arbitration Act as adopted in Arkansas does not prohibit the enforcement of that provision. *Matson, Inc. v. Lamb & Associates Packaging, Inc., supra.*

## 8. Attorney's Fees

***Statutes and/or case law limiting or permitting recovery of attorney's fees***

A performance bond claimant is entitled to recover a 12 percent penalty, plus reasonable attorney's fees in the event that it recovers at least 80 percent of its demand against a surety. *See* § 2, *supra.*

A surety paying a claim against its bond principal before final adjudication of the principal's liability, over the principal's objection, cannot recover from the principal without showing that it made a good faith effort to protect the principal against the adverse claim. *Fireman's Fund Insurance Co. v. Clark*, 253 Ark. 1025, 490 S.W.2d 447 (1973). The Arkansas Supreme Court has stated, *in dicta*, that it might be inappropriate to penalize a surety pursuant to A.C.A. § 23-79-208 when its principal has not been held liable or unable to pay and is asserting a good faith defense, where the surety does not contest the claim, but acknowledges its liability is contingent upon a finding that the principal is liable. *Verne Barnett Construction Co. v. J.A. Hadley Construction Co.*, 254 Ark. 866, 496 S.W.2d 446 (1973). The Arkansas Supreme Court has held that A.C.A. § 23-79-208 is not applicable to a surety which withheld payment of a claim which was being litigated by its principal in an action to which the surety was not a party. *R. J. Bob Jones Excavating Contractor, Inc. v. Fireman's Fund Insurance Co. of Newark, New Jersey, supra.*

***What fees are recoverable, if any***

An allowance for an attorney fee should not be speculative or contingent, but should be such a fee as would be reasonable for a litigant to pay his attorney for prosecuting such a case, however, the amount which the beneficiary receives is an element to be considered along with the difficulty of the issues. *Equitable Life Assurance Society v. Rummell*, 257 Ark. 90, 514 S.W.2d 224 (1974).

The award of an attorney's fee is a matter for the sound discretion of the trial court, and in the absence of abuse, its judgment will be sustained on appeal. *Southall v. Farm Bureau Mutual Insurance Co.*, 283 Ark. 335, 676 S.W.2d 228 (1984).

**9. Special Provisions** – Not applicable.

**10. Remarks** – As stated above.

**11. Case Annotations**

***Interpretation of AIA bond forms*** – Arkansas cases have not specifically addressed AIA forms of bonds A311 and A312.

***Cases in which surety steps into shoes of obligee***

Where a contractor defaulted in performance of a construction contract which provided that the owner would pay the contractor in monthly installments as work progressed, the contractor's surety had a duty to pay the debts of the contractor and to complete the contract, and upon doing so was entitled, under doctrine of equitable subrogation, to the amount of monthly installments retained by the owner. *Exchange Bank & Trust Co. v. Texarkana School District No. 7, Miller County*, 227 Ark. 759, 301 S.W.2d 453 (1957).

A surety on a building contract, which completed the work on the contractor's default, is entitled to recover from the owner of the building payments made by the owner to the contractor in violation of the contract, whether those payments are characterized as loans or advances against future performance. Surety did not waive its right of recovery by completing performance of its principal's contract with knowledge of such payments because it expressly reserved the right to seek such recovery. *Fidelity & Deposit Co. v. Merchants & Farmers Bank*, 120 Ark. 519, 179 S.W. 1019 (1915).

# CALIFORNIA

Mark Aronson[1]

## 1. Requirement for Bond

The State of California has numerous statutes that requires performance bonds to be furnished on public work, with many, cities, counties and state agencies requiring such bonds as part of the procurement process. California Code of Civil Procedure § 995.311. provides:

> (a) Notwithstanding any other provision of law, any bond required on a public works contract, as defined in § 1101 of the Public Contract Code, shall be executed by an admitted surety insurer. A public agency approving the bond on a public works contract shall have a duty to verify that the bond is being executed by an admitted surety insurer.
>
> (b) A public agency may fulfill its duty under subdivision (a) by verifying the status of the party executing the bond in one of the following ways:
>
> (1) Printing out information from the website of the Department of Insurance confirming the surety is an admitted surety insurer and attaching it to the bond.

---

1 Mark Aronson is a senior partner and was assisted by senior associate Steven Huff at:
Anderson, McPharlin & Conners LLP
444 S. Flower Street, Suite 3100
Los Angeles, California 90071
(213) 688-0080

(2) Obtaining a certificate from the county clerk that confirms the surety is an admitted insurer and attaching it to the bond.

***Statutory provisions for projects that are:***

**Public** – Public Contracts Code § 10221 requires every contractor must file a performance bond for all contracts entered into with any state agency. Under Public Contracts Code § 10222, the amount of the bond must be at least one-half of the contract price unless the contract is over $250,000 and if so, then the amount of the bond must be either one-half of the contract price or $500,000, whichever is less.

**Private** – No statute in California requires performance bonds on private projects.

**California State University Projects** – Public Contracts Code § 10821 provides "[E]very contract shall provide for the filing of separate performance and payment bonds by the contractor executed by an admitted surety insurer, subject to the approval of the trustees." Section 10822 requires that the amount of the bond must be at least one-half of the contract price.

**Counties** – Public Contracts Code § 20129 (b) requires that every person who contracts with any county must provide a bond for the faithful performance of the contract.

**School Districts** – Government Code § 17250.30(b) requires a performance bond in a form approved by the Department of General Services.

**Local Agencies** – Local agencies including cities may set the requirements for performance bonds under a form developed by the agency. Public Contracts Code § 20175.1(d)(2).

**Public Improvements** – Government Code § 66462 requires every developer must provide security identified in Government Code § 66499 for every agreement entered into with a city, county or city and county for public improvements including street work and utilities to be installed on land to be used for public or private streets, highways, ways, and easements as are necessary for the general use of the lot owners in the subdivision and local neighborhood traffic and drainage needs as a condition precedent to the approval and acceptance of the final map as well as any other specific improvements or types of improvements, the installation of which, either by the subdivider, by public agencies, by private utilities, by any other entity approved by the local agency or by a combination thereof, is necessary to ensure consistency with, or implementation of, the general plan or any applicable specific plan.

Government Code § 66499 (c) – identifies bond or bonds by one or more duly authorized corporate sureties as one form of security a local agency can require.

Government Code § 66499.1 – prescribes the form required for the performance bond.

Government Code § 66499.3 – the performance bond must be determined by the legislative body not less than 50 percent nor more than 100 percent of the total estimated cost of the improvement or of the act to be performed conditioned upon the faithful performance of the act or agreement.

Government Code § 66499.9 – limits liability to (a) the performance of the work covered by the agreement between the subdivider and the legislative body or the performance of the required act; (b) the performance of any changes or alterations in such work; provided, that all such changes or alterations do not exceed 10 percent of the original estimated cost of the improvement; (c) the guarantee and warranty of the work, for a period of one year following completion and acceptance thereof, against any defective work or labor done or defective materials furnished, in the performance of the agreement with the legislative body or the performance of the act; and, (d) costs and reasonable expenses and fees, including reasonable attorney's fees.

**State Park System Properties** – Public Resources Code § 5080.18 – All concessionaires who occupy any portion of the state park system for a period of more than two years must provide a performance bond.

***Case law rules that might generally apply***

"Performance bonds, like all contracts of surety, are construed with reference to the same rules that govern interpretation of other types of contracts." California Civil Code § 2837. *Cates Construction, Inc. v. Talbot Partners,* 21 Cal. 4th 28 (1999).

"[T]he extent of the surety's liability must be gathered from the language used, when read in light of the circumstances attending the transaction." *Verdugo Highlands, Inc. v. Security Ins. Co.* 240 Cal. App. 2d 527, 531 (1966).

## 2. Damages Covered

***Set forth in any statutes and/or case law***

"Where a surety bond is given pursuant to the requirements of a particular statute, the statutory provisions are incorporated into the bond." *Bank of America v. Dowdy,* 186 Cal. App. 2d 690, 692-693 (1960); *Krebs v. Travelers Indem. Co.*, 192 Cal. App. 2d 83, 85.

**Liquidated Damages** – If the construction contract is incorporated into the performance bond and contains an enforceable liquidated damage clause, the general rule is that the performance bond surety will be liable for liquidated damages in the event that the principal, without excuse, delays the completion of the project. *Cates Construction, Inc. v. Talbot Partners*, 21 Cal. 4th 28 (1999). California Civil Code 1671 provides:

> (a) This section does not apply in any case where another statute expressly applicable to the contract prescribes the rules or standard for determining the validity of a provision in the contract liquidating the damages for the breach of the contract.
>
> (b) Except as provided in subdivision (c), a provision in a contract liquidating the damages for the breach of the contract is valid unless the party seeking to invalidate the provision establishes that the provision was unreasonable under the circumstances existing at the time the contract was made.
>
> (c) The validity of a liquidated damages provision shall be determined under subdivision (d) and not under subdivision (b) where the liquidated damages are sought to be recovered from either:
>
> > (1) A party to a contract for the retail purchase, or rental, by such party of personal property or services, primarily for the party's personal, family, or household purposes; or
> >
> > (2) A party to a lease of real property for use as a dwelling by the party or those dependent upon the party for support.

> (d) In the cases described in subdivision (c), a provision in a contract liquidating damages for the breach of the contract is void except that the parties to such a contract may agree therein upon an amount which shall be presumed to be the amount of damage sustained by a breach thereof, when, from the nature of the case, it would be impracticable or extremely difficult to fix the actual damage.

We find no authority supporting the proposition that the giving of a performance bond ipso facto subjects the completing surety to liability for liquidated damages provided for in the contract between the contractor and the obligee. To determine whether the completing surety is liable in such a case, the court must look to the contract and to the bond. If the bond expressly referred to the contract between principal and the obligee, incorporated that contract by reference, the surety is bound by the provisions in the contract for liquidated damages. *Pacific Employers Ins. Co. v. City of Berkeley*, 158 Cal. App. 3d 145, 150 (1984).

**Delay damages** – Government Code § 53069.85. provides:

> The legislative body of a city, county, or district may include or cause to be included in contracts for public projects a provision establishing the time within which the whole or any specified portion of the work contemplated shall be completed. The legislative body may provide that for each day completion is delayed beyond the specified time, the contractor shall forfeit and pay to the agency involved a specified sum of money, which may be deducted from any payments due or to become due to the contractor. The sum so specified is valid as liquidated damages unless manifestly unreasonable under the circumstances existing at the time the contract was made. A contract for such a project may also provide for the payment of extra compensation to the contractor, as a bonus for completion prior to the specified time. These provisions, if used, shall be included in the specifications upon which proposals or bids are received, which specifications shall clearly set forth the liquidated damages provisions.
>
> For purposes of this section, "public project" shall include the erection, construction, alteration, repair, or improvement of any structure, building, road, railway, or other improvement, and the procurement of any other goods or services that are manufactured specifically, designed specifically, or produced specifically, pursuant to a contract with a public agency.

California Public Contracts Code § 7102 provides:

> Contract provisions in construction contracts of public agencies and subcontracts thereunder which limit the contractee's liability to an extension of time for delay for which the contractee is responsible and which delay is unreasonable under the circumstances involved, and not within the contemplation of the parties, shall not be construed to preclude the recovery of damages by the contractor or subcontractor.
>
> No public agency may require the waiver, alteration, or limitation of the applicability of this section. Any such waiver, alteration, or limitation is void. This section shall not be construed to void any provision in a construction contract which requires notice of delays, provides for arbitration or other procedure for settlement, or provides for liquidated damages.

> As a general rule, a contract performance bond will be read with the contract. Since the express purpose of the contract performance bond is to secure the performance of the specified contract, it is obvious that the bond and the contract ... should be construed together – this for the obvious reason that when a party enters into a contract to do certain work on certain terms, and procures a surety to guarantee the faithful performance of the work, the surety necessarily contracts with reference to the contract as made; otherwise it would not know what obligation it was assuming. And this is particularly so where the bond expressly declares that the contract is made a part of the bond and the terms of the contract are incorporated into the bond. Otherwise stated, the liability of a surety on a contractor's performance bond does not rest solely on the terms of the bond, but grows out of and is dependent upon the terms of the contractor's contract, for the obvious reason that there can be no obligation on the part of the surety unless there has been a default by the contractor on his contract. However, it does not follow from the fact that the contract and bond should be construed together that a performance bond necessarily guarantees performance of all covenants and agreements contained in the contract. *Pacific Employers Ins. Co. v. City of Berkeley*, 158 Cal. App. 3d 145, 151 (1984).

### *Obligations of surety to perform and/or pay*

"A bond which is given for the faithful performance of a contract, to which it refers, binds the surety for labor performed and materials furnished thereunder as completely as though the surety were a party to the contract." *Continental Cas. Co. v. Hartford Acc. & Indem. Co.*, 243 Cal. App. 2d 565 (1966).

"Upon breach by the principal, the surety is, unless otherwise specifically provided in the contract, free to rest upon the contract of suretyship and if it does it cannot be held beyond the limit of its bond and it may invoke any defense open to it as surety. If, however, upon breach by the principal it elects to and is permitted under the contract or by permission obtained after breach to step into the place of its principal and perform that principal's contract, it then makes itself subject to the principal's liabilities." *Caron v. Andrew*, 133 Cal. App. 2d 402, 411 (1955).

***Whether failure to provide insurance transfers burden to surety*** – Statutes do not transfer the burden to surety.

***Limitations on damages***

California Civil Code § 3287 provides:

> (a) Every person who is entitled to recover damages certain, or capable of being made certain by calculation, and the right to recover which is vested in him upon a particular day, is entitled also to recover interest thereon from that day, except during such time as the debtor is prevented by law, or by the act of the creditor from paying the debt. This section is applicable to recovery of damages and interest from any such debtor, including the state or any county, city, city and county, municipal corporation, public district, public agency, or any political subdivision of the state.
>
> (b) Every person who is entitled under any judgment to receive damages based upon a cause of action in contract where the claim was unliquidated, may also recover interest thereon from a date prior to the entry of judgment as the court may, in its discretion, fix, but in no event earlier than the date the action was filed.

"Obligee of a construction performance bond may not recover punitive damages for the surety's breach of the implied covenant of good faith and fair dealing." *Cates Construction, Inc. v. Talbot Partners*, 21 Cal. 4th 28 (1999).

***Whether obligee may set off bonded contract funds against other principal-obligee debts or obligations*** – Not applicable.

***Incorporation of specific contract terms by reference***

"As a general rule, a contract performance bond will be read with the contract." *Pacific Employers Ins. Co. v. City of Berkeley*, 158 Cal. App. 3d 145 (1984).

"Where contractor's bond referred to contract and was by its terms executed to comply with statute relating to mechanic's liens, and condition of bond was that work contracted for be faithfully performed and claims paid in full, bond incorporated contract by reference, and contract provisions became provisions of bond as a performance bond." *Culbertson v. Cizek*, 225 Cal. App. 2d 451, 467 (1964).

"It is not necessary that bond contain recitals that it is given pursuant to statute in order that it be determined to be a bond contemplated by statute for limitation purposes, and it is not necessary that bond contain words of statute if its substance and legal effect are same as prescribed by statute." *Winick Corp. v. General Ins. Co.*, 187 Cal. App. 3d 142 (1986).

"Performance bonds given in connection with public works of improvement are intended to provide a substitute for the mechanics' lien rights (see Civ. Code, § 3110 *et seq.*) available to those persons who provide labor for or furnish materials or equipment to a private work of improvement because the mechanic's lien provisions of Civil Code § 3110 are inapplicable to any public work of improvement. (Civ. Code, § 3109; *John A. Artukovich Sons, Inc. v. American Fidelity Fire Ins. Co.*, 72 Cal. App. 3d 940, 946 (1977).

## 3. Penal Sum Variations

***Limitations per statute*** – California does not have statutory limitation on performance bond penal sums.

***Effect of changes in work upon penal sum, if at all*** – Monies advanced under a financing arrangement do not, in the absence of the written agreement of the obligee, lessen a surety's obligation pursuant to the performance bond. *Caron v. Andrew,* 133 Cal. App. 2d 402 (1955).

***Statutory or case law protections or dangers to penal sum*** – There are no cases that require a variation in the penal sum.

## 4. Parties Covered

***Statutes and/or case law as to whether only obligees are covered***

"It may be stated that if the subcontractor's bond is conditioned for the indemnification of the contractor for any claim or damage for which the principal contractor may be held liable and for the payment of which the subcontractor is primarily liable, liability exists on the part of the surety on the bond of the subcontractor to indemnify the principal contractor against any liability which may be imposed upon him, or to reimburse him for any payment he may be required to make, in respect of labor and materials furnished to the subcontractor. This conclusion is a fortiori true where payment for labor and materials furnished to the subcontractor is expressly made a condition of the bond of the subcontractor, or has that effect by reference in the bond to the provisions of the subcontract as to payment for materials and labor furnished to the subcontractor." *Continental Casualty Co. v. Hartford Acc. & Indem. Co.*, 243 Cal. App. 2d 565, 570 (1966).

"The faithful performance of an agreement with the subcontractor for the supplying of labor and materials for a structure is not a pledge for the sole benefit of [the general contractor], but inures to the benefit of any person who performs labor or furnishes materials which are used in the structure, pursuant to the provisions of the subcontract. [Citations.]" *C. O. Sparks, Inc. v. Pacific Coast Paving Co.*, 159 Cal. App. 2d 513,518 (1958).

***Coverage for:***

**Third-party beneficiaries** – The obligee alone is entitled to institute legal action to collect on the faithful performance bond but is not entitled to treat as a windfall the proceeds of a faithful performance bond realized as a consequence of work not performed. *Berman v. Aetna Cas. & Surety Co.*, 40 Cal. App. 3d 908, 911 (1974).

**Assignees** – There are no California cases discussing assignment of obligee's right to make a claim against a performance bond.

**Dual obligees** – "Where a mortgagee has made a loan or an advance for the construction of improvements on the mortgaged property and, in order to strengthen his security, has required a surety bond guaranteeing completion of the improvements, in an action for breach of the bond, recovery is limited to the injury to the mortgagee's security interest which is measured by the difference between the value of the property with and without the completed improvements. [Citations omitted]. The rule is a sound one because, as we have explained, the bargained-for contractual benefit of which the mortgagee has been deprived is the value which the improvements would have added to the security." *Glendale Fed. Sav. & Loan Assn. v. Marina View Heights Dev. Co.*, 66 Cal. App. 3d 101, 125 (1977).

## 5. Notice or Filing Required

***Statutory provisions*** – California statutes do not provide for any unusual notice requirements for suit under a performance bond.

***Case law rules concerning condition precedent notice*** – Not applicable.

## 6. Time for Suit

***Statutes of limitation particular to performance bonds and other applicable statutes of limitation***

California Code of Civil Procedure § 337, subdivision 1 states that an action upon an obligation in writing must be commenced within four years from the time it accrues. "Section 337 applies to the obligation of a surety or guarantor." *County of Los Angeles v. Security Ins. Co.*, 52 Cal. App. 3d 808, 817 (1975).

***Case law statements about enforceability of limitations contained in bonds*** – Limitation of actions provision contained within the bond have generally been upheld. *Fageol T. & C. Co. v. Pacific Indemnity Co.*, 18 Cal. 2d 748, 753 (1941).

***Varying statutes of limitation by agreement in bond or contract***

"Bonds must be construed most strongly against the surety, and contractual stipulations limiting the right to sue to a period shorter than granted by a statute are looked on with disfavor and should be strictly construed." *Lewis v. Hopper*, 140 Cal. App. 2d 365, 367 (1956).

"While the general rule is correct, it should not be used to destroy the effect of the words of the contract itself. Furthermore, this general rule should not be used to destroy the effect of a more specific rule of law on the subject of third-party beneficiaries. When plaintiff seeks to secure benefits under a contract as to which he is a third-party beneficiary, he must take that contract as he finds it. As the rules above stated make clear, the third party cannot select the parts favorable to him and reject those unfavorable to him." *Sanders v. American Casualty Co.*, 269 Cal. App. 2d 306 (1969).

## 7. Procedure

***Statutory or procedural rules that may affect handling or administration of lawsuits***

California Civil Code § 2845 provides:

> A surety may require the creditor, subject to Section 996.440 of the Code of Civil Procedure, to proceed against the principal, or to pursue any other remedy in the creditor's power which the surety cannot pursue, and which would lighten the surety's burden; and if the creditor neglects to do so, the surety is exonerated to the extent to which the surety is thereby prejudiced.

California Code of Civil Procedure 410.42 provides:

> The following provisions of a contract between the contractor and a subcontractor with principal offices in this state, for the construction of a public or private work of improvement in this state, shall be void and unenforceable:
>
> (a) A provision which purports to require any dispute between the parties to be litigated, arbitrated, or otherwise determined outside this state.

(b) A provision which purports to preclude a party from commencing such a proceeding or obtaining a judgment or other resolution in this state or the courts of this state.

For purposes of this section, "construction" means any work or services performed on, or materials provided for, a work of improvement, as defined in Section 3106 of the Civil Code, and for which a lien may be claimed pursuant to Section 3110 of the Civil Code (whether or not a lien is in fact claimed) or for which such a lien could be claimed but for Section 3109.

***Venue requirements and jurisdictional limitations*** – Not applicable.

***Court rules*** – Not applicable.

***Particular agency regulations/rules*** – Not applicable.

***Arbitration requirements and application***

A party can be compelled to submit a dispute to arbitration only where he has agreed in writing to do so. *Berman v. Renart Sportswear Corp.,* 222 Cal. App 2d 385, 388 (1963).

By virtue of the provision in its performance bond incorporating the contract, the surety agreed to be bound by the arbitration provision of the contract. *Boys Club of San Fernando Valley, Inc. v. Fidelity and Deposit Co.,* 6 Cal. App. 4th 1266, 1274 (1992).

## 8. Attorney's Fees

***Statutes and/or case law limiting or permitting recovery of attorney's fees***

California Civil Code § 2808 provides:

> Where one assumes liability as a surety upon a conditional obligation, his liability is commensurate with that of the principal, and he is not entitled to notice of the default of the principal, unless he is unable, by the exercise of reasonable diligence, to acquire information of such default.

Civil Code § 2808 does not distinguish between subcontractors and owners, or between payment and performance bonds. It flatly provides that a surety's liability is commensurate with the liability of its principal. *T & R Painting Construction, Inc. v. St. Paul Fire & Marine Ins. Co.*, 23 Cal. App. 4th 738, 746.

***What fees are recoverable, if any***

California Civil Code § 1717 provides:

> (a) In any action on a contract, where the contract specifically provides that attorney's fees and costs, which are incurred to enforce that contract, shall be awarded either to one of the parties or to the prevailing party, then the party who is determined to be the party prevailing on the contract, whether he or she is the party specified in the contract or not, shall be entitled to reasonable attorney's fees in addition to other costs. Reasonable attorney's fees shall be fixed by the court, and shall be an element of the costs of suit.

9. **Special Provisions** – Not applicable.

10. **Remarks** – As stated above.

11. **Case Annotations**

***Interpretation of AIA bond forms*** – California cases have not specifically addressed AIA forms of bonds A311 and A312.

***Cases in which surety steps into shoes of obligee*** – Not applicable.

# COLORADO

Dennis J. Bartlett[1]

## 1. Requirement for Bond

The State of Colorado does require bonding or other security for all public works projects. There are two levels of bonding requirements. For cities, counties, municipalities, school districts, or other political subdivisions, any contract in excess of $50,000 must be bonded. For state projects, any contract in excess of $100,000 must be bonded. The bond must be issued in an amount equal to at least 50 percent of the contract awarded. Public owners have the right to require bonding for smaller projects.

***Statutory provisions for projects that are:***

**Public** – Bonding is mandated by Colorado's Public Works Act, C.R.S. § 38-26-106 and the Colorado Procurement Code, C.R.S. § 24-105-202(A).

**Private** – There is no statute in Colorado requiring bonding on private contracts.

---

[1] Dennis J. Bartlett is a member of:
Kerr Brosseau Bartlett O'Brien, LLC
1600 Broadway, Suite 1600
Denver, Colorado 80202
(303) 812-1200

**Department of Transportation** – The Colorado Department of Transportation ("CDOT") requires a performance bond executed by a surety and on a form agreeable to CDOT in a penal sum "equal to the nearest integral $100 in excess of the original bid items plus all forced account items specified." See, Colorado Department of Transportation, Standard Specifications for Road and Bridge Construction, § 103.03 (2005 Ed).

***Case law rules that might generally apply***

There is no right of action by an aggrieved party for the state, city, county or political subdivision's failure to require the requisite bond be issued in a public works contract. *School Dist. No. 28 v. Denver Pressed Brick Co.,* 14 P.2d 487 (Colo. 1932).

If bonds issued provide greater coverage or rights than as required by the statute, the terms of the bond will control. *Montezuma Plumbing & Heating, Inc. v. Housing Authority,* 651 P.2d 426 (Colo. Ct. App. 1982).

The purpose of a performance bond is to guaranty to the obligee that the principal's contract will be performed. *General Ins. Co. v. Colorado Springs,* 638 P.2d 752 (Colo. 1981).

Colorado law holds a surety's obligations are contractual in nature and are defined by the terms of the bond. *People v. National Surety Company,* 176 P. 948 (Colo. 1918).

A surety contract is construed according to the plain meaning of its terms. *Fuqua Homes, Inc. v. Western Surety Company,* 616 P.2d 163 (Colo. Ct. App. 1980).

A performance bond surety is subject to bad faith liability to the obligee. The standard is whether the surety's conduct was knowingly unreasonable or whether the surety acted with reckless disregard of the fact that its conduct was unreasonable. *See Transamerica Premier Insurance Co. v. Brighton Sch. Dist., 27J,* 940 P.2d 348 (Colo. 1997).

## 2. Damages Covered

***Set forth in any statutes and/or case law***

By statute, public works performance bonds must be conditioned upon:

> [t]he faithful performance of the contract and, in addition, shall provide that, if the contractor or his subcontractor fails to duly pay for any labor, materials, team hire, sustenance, provisions, provender, or other supplies used or consumed by such contractor or his subcontractor in performance of the work contracted to be done, or fails to pay any person who supplies laborers, rental machinery, tolls, or equipment, all amounts due as the result of the use of laborers, rental machinery, tools, or equipment, in the prosecution of the work, the surety will pay the same in an amount not exceeding the sum specified in the bond together with interest at the rate of eight percent per annum.

C.R.S. § 38-26-106. Note, a separate section of the public works act, C.R.S. § 38-26-105, governs the payment bond requirements.

Generally, the surety's liability is co-extensive with the principal except the surety's liability is capped by the penal sum of its bond. *General Ins. Co. v. Colorado Springs,* 638 P.2d 752 , 757 (Colo. 1981); *Riva Ridge Apartments v. Robert G. Fisher Co.,* 745 P.2d 1034 (Colo. Ct. App. 1987).

Interest is recoverable from the surety and runs from the date of demand until payment and may exceed the penal sum of the bond. *Autocon Industries, Inc. v. Western States Constr. Co.,* 728 P.2d 374 (Colo. Ct. App. 1986).

***Obligations of surety to perform and/or pay***

The statute does not define the surety's rights upon the principal's default and the surety's options and rights upon the principal's default will be determined by the language of the performance bond it issued and the indemnity agreement it has with its principal.

***Whether failure to provide insurance transfers burden to surety*** – The applicable statutes do not transfer this burden to the performance bond surety. Whether the bonded contract transfers this obligation requires a fact-specific analysis.

***Limitations on damages***

Contractual limitations on the recovery of damages are enforced in Colorado unless the result would be unconscionable. *Jefferson County Bank v. Armored Motors Service,* 366 P.2d 134 (Colo. 1961); *University*

*Hills Beauty Academy v. Mountain States Tel. & Tel. Co.,* 554 P.2d 723, 726 (Colo. Ct. App. 1976).

The enforceability of exculpatory provisions, which insulate a party from liability is determined by consideration of various factors - whether there is a duty to the public, the nature of the service performed, whether the contract was fairly entered into, and whether the intention of the parties is expressed in clear and unambiguous language. *Jones v. Dressel,* 623 P.2d 370, 376 (Colo. 1981).

Extra-contractual damages are available for the surety's bad faith breach of its obligations. *See Transamerica Premier Insurance Co. v. Brighton Sch. Dist., 27J,* 940 P.2d 348 (Colo. 1997). The amount awarded is generally limited to the amount of actual damages except in special circumstances the court may increase the award to three times actual damages. C.R.S. § 13-21-102.

No damage for delay clauses in a contract will be enforced absent fraud, bad faith or coercion. *W.C. James, Inc. v. Phillips Petroleum Co.,* 347 F. Supp. 381, 385 (D. Colo. 1972).

***Whether obligee may set off bonded contract funds against other principal-obligee debts or obligations***

The obligee's and surety's rights to contract funds on public works projects is codified in the Colorado Procurement Code, C.R.S. § 24-91-104, which does not, per se, allow the obligee to set off against funds owed on one bonded project to cover losses it incurred on another project.

***Incorporation of specific contract terms by reference***

When a bond refers to other instruments, the court should look to those instruments and the bond to determine the party's intent in construing the bond. *See Western Sur. Co. v. Smith,* 914 P.2d 451 (Colo. Ct. App. 1995), *cert. denied* (Colo. 1996) and *Edmonds v. Western Sur. Co.,* 962 P.2d 323 (Colo. Ct. App. 1998). When a bonded contract references a statute, courts properly look to the terms and requirements of the statute to interpret the bond obligations. *CPS Distribut., Inc. v. Federal Ins. Co.,* 685 P.2d 783 (Colo. Ct. App. 1994) overruled on other grounds by *Colorado Crane & Hauling, Inc. v. Robert E. McKee, Inc.,* 761 P.2d (Colo. Ct. App. 1988).

### 3. Penal Sum Variations

***Limitations per statute***

The statute requires the performance bond be in an amount at least equal to one half of the contract price. C.R.S. § 38-26-106(1) and § 24-105-202(1)(a). CDOT requires the bond penal sum be equal to the contract price plus all force account allowance items in the bid. Colorado Department of Transportation, Standard Specifications for Road and Bridge Construction, § 103.03 (2005 Ed). Private projects have no limitations.

***Effect of changes in work upon penal sum, if at all***

In *United States ex rel. B&M Roofing v. AKM Assocs., Inc.*, 961 F. Supp. 1441 (D. Colo. 1997) (applying the federal common law) the court considered whether the penal sum of a Miller Act payment bond increased automatically with the contract delivery orders under an indefinite delivery, indefinite quantity contract and concluded the surety's liability for both payment and performance bonds is calculated "by adding the total value of the delivery orders that have been placed." 961 F. Supp. at 1444. While there are no cases interpreting Colorado's Public Works Act and there are certainly good reasons as to why *B&M* should be limited to its facts it must be acknowledged that it is an open question as to whether Colorado courts would interpret bond penal sums as increasing with change orders.

***Statutory or case law protections or dangers to penal sum***

While the author is not aware of any Colorado cases on point the author's experience is that at least some state agencies will not sign a takeover agreement if the surety tries to limit its exposure to the penal sum so that at least with those agencies a surety exercising its performance option arguably removes the penal sum protection.

## 4. Parties Covered

***Statutes and/or case law as to whether only obligees are covered*** – This is an open question under Colorado law.

***Coverage for:***

**Third-party beneficiaries** – Under Colorado law, mere incidental beneficiaries of a contract cannot maintain an action on the contract. *E.B. Roberts Constr. Co. v. Concrete Contractors, Inc.*, 704 P.2d 859, 865 (Colo. 1985). In *National Union Fire Ins. Co. v. Denver Brick & Pipe Co.*, 427 P.2d 861 (Colo. 1967), the surety issued only a "Contract Bond." In that case, the construction contract was incorporated into the bond by reference. The court analyzed the contract and determined unpaid lien claimants could claim against the bond. 427 P.2d at 866. See also, *South-Way Constr. Co. v. Adams City Service*, 458 P.2d 250 (Colo. 1969) and *Rocky Mountain Assoc. of Credit Management v. Marshall*, 615 P.2d 68 (Colo. Ct. App. 1980), which have been, in the author's opinion, incorrectly cited for the proposition that third parties can assert a payment bond claim against a public works performance bond. Neither case dealt with the situation where separate performance and payment bonds had been issued to satisfy the conditions of the Public Works Act.

**Assignees** – No statutes or reported Colorado cases deal with an assignee's ability to assert a claim on a performance bond.

**Dual obligees** – No statutes or reported Colorado cases deal with dual obligees.

## 5. Notice or Filing Required

***Statutory provisions*** – Unlike payment bond claimants who have a limited time period to assert their claims, performance bond obligees have no statutory notice requirements.

***Case law rules concerning condition precedent notice***

Of course, it seems obvious that there must be a declared default termination to proceed against the performance bond. While the author is not aware of any reported Colorado cases holding a declared default termination is a condition precedent, at the trial court level, courts readily accept that a clear and unequivocal default is a condition precedent to a claim on a performance bond and prejudice to the surety is presumed where the obligee takes over without allowing the surety to exercise its options to arrange completion. *See, e.g., School Bd. v. TIG Premier Ins. Co.*, 110 F. Supp. 2d 1351, 1353-54 (N.D. Fla. 2000).

## 6. Time for Suit

***Statutes of limitation particular to performance bonds and other applicable statutes of limitation***

On public works projects payment bond claimants have the later of six months from substantial completion or 90 days from the advertised final settlement of the project to file suit against the surety. C.R.S. §§ 38-26-105 & 107 and *Rocky Mountain Assoc. of Credit Management v. Marshall,* 615 P.2d 68 (Colo. Ct. App. 1980).

The statute of limitation on breach of contract actions is three years. C.R.S. § 13-80-101(a). The statute of limitations on written instruments securing payment or evidencing a debt is six years. C.R.S. § 13-90-103.5(a). There is a special two year statute of limitation on claims against contractors, including claims for breach of contract. C.R.S. § 13-80-104(1)(a).

***Case law statements about enforceability of limitations contained in bonds***

In Colorado a contractual limitation on the time to sue, if reasonable, will be enforced. *Regents of the Univ. of Colo. v. Harbert Constr. Co.,* 51 P.3d 1037 (Colo. Ct. App. 2001) (not a bond case).

***Varying statutes of limitation by agreement in bond or contract***

While a surety may give a party longer time to sue than required by statute, the surety may not shorten the time limit to less than required by the statute. *Montezuma Plumbing & Heating Inc. v. Housing Auth.,* 651 P.2d 426 (Colo. Ct. App. 1982).

## 7. Procedure

***Statutory or procedural rules that may affect handling or administration of lawsuits*** – Colorado's rules of civil procedure are similar to the federal rules including the requirements of voluntary disclosures.

***Venue requirements and jurisdictional limitations***

Colorado Rule of Civil Procedure 98(c) provides contract actions shall be tried in the county where any defendant resides, where plaintiff resides when service is made on defendants in that county, or where the contract was to be performed. Colorado's district courts are courts of general jurisdiction and have unlimited jurisdiction.

***Court rules*** – Not applicable.

***Particular agency regulations/rules*** – Not applicable.

***Arbitration requirements and application*** – The extent to which a surety is bound by an arbitration award against its principal is an open question under Colorado law.

## 8. Attorney's Fees:

***Statutes and/or case law limiting or permitting recovery of attorney's fees***

The public works statute does not provide for recovery of attorney fees against the surety and absent an enforceable contract provision attorney's fees are not recoverable against the surety. *Cement Asbestos Products Co. v. Hartford Accid. & Indem. Co.,* 592 F.2d 1144 (10th Cir. 1979).

## 9. Special Provisions:

On Colorado Public Works Act projects, any unpaid subcontractor or supplier may file a verified statement of claim with the project owner prior to advertised final settlement date. This lien on funds is in addition to the unpaid person's rights against the contractor's bond. The effect of this is to require the public entity to withhold from payment to the contractor an amount sufficient to cover all such verified claims so long as an action is commenced within 90 days of the date fixed for final settlement and a *lis pendens* is filed with the public owner. C.R.S. § 38-26-107. By statute, this lien on funds is prior to and superior to the surety's interest in either earned and unpaid or unearned and unpaid contract balances. C.R.S. § 24-91-104. Any person who knowingly files an overstated verified statement of claim or asserts a claim against a principal or surety for an amount greater than due forfeits all rights to the amount claimed and is liable to the contractor and/or surety for reasonable attorney's fees incurred in responding to that overstated claim. C.R.S. § 38-26-110.

Colorado's Public Works Act allows for the bonding around of verified statements of claim which have been filed. See, C.R.S. § 38-26-108.

Colorado's Public Works Act has specific trust fund requirements which require the contractor and its subcontractors to hold all funds disbursed to them in trust for the payment of labor, materials, etc. used or consumed on the job. C.R.S. § 38-26-109.

## 10. Remarks

A surety paying payment bond claims on Colorado Public Works projects should always take an assignment of the claimant's rights under C.R.S. § 38-26-107. In addition, if enough verified claims have been filed, it may not be necessary for a surety to issue a stop payment notice to protect unpaid contract funds in the case of a troubled principal.

## 11. Case Annotations

***Interpretation of AIA bond forms*** – No cases found.

***Cases in which surety steps into shoes of obligee***

While no cases were found specifically discussing this rule, in Colorado indemnity agreements are valid and enforceable as written. *Wilson & Co. v. Walsenburg Sand & Gravel Co.,* 779 P.2d 1386 (Colo. Ct. App. 1989).

# CONNECTICUT

Gary M. Case and Jason Glasgow[1]

## 1. Requirement for Bond

The State of Connecticut does not have a statute mandating that performance bonds be furnished for public works projects. However, state agencies and cities often require such bonds as part of the procurement process. In addition, there are several statutes which indirectly address the requirements for performance bonds.

***Statutory provisions for projects that are***

**Public** – Connecticut General Statutes § 49-41(a) (eff. October 1, 2005) provides that, for all public work projects exceeding $100,000 a payment bond must be provided. Connecticut General Statutes § 49-41(b) further provides:

> (b) Nothing in this section or sections 49-41a to 49-43, inclusive, shall be construed to limit the authority of any contracting officer to require a performance bond or other security in addition to the bond referred to in subsection (a) of this section, except that no such officer shall require a performance bond in relation to any general bid in which the total estimated cost of labor and materials under the contract with respect to

---

1 Gary M. Case is a member of and Jason Glasgow is an associate of:
Wolf, Horowitz, Etlinger & Case, L.L.C.
99 Pratt Street Suite 401
Hartford, Connecticut 06103
(860) 724-6667

> which such general bid is submitted is less than $25,000 or in relation to any sub-bid in which the total estimated cost of labor and materials under the contract with respect to which such sub-bid is submitted is less than $50,000.

Connecticut General Statutes § 4b-91 addresses the prequalification requirements for public building projects. Subsection (b) of the statute provides:

> If the general bidder selected as the general contractor fails to perform the general contractor's agreement to execute a contract in accordance with the terms of the general contractor's general bid and furnish a performance bond and also a labor and materials or payment bond to the amount specified in the general bid form, an award shall be made to the next lowest responsible and qualified general bidder.

Connecticut General Statutes § 8-25 gives municipalities the authority to require a performance bond in connection with the performance of improvements on subdivisions. Section 8-25(a) provides that the municipality "may accept a bond in an amount and with surety and conditions satisfactory to it securing to the municipality the actual construction, maintenance and installation of such improvements and utilities within a period specified in the bond."

**Private** – Connecticut General Statutes § 10-411(b) provides that the owner of any historic structure or landmark provide a performance bond in connection with the performance of any preservation work.

***Case law rules that might generally apply***

The "liabilities of sureties [under performance bonds] is to be determined by the specified conditions of the bond ... [W]hen a bond is required by statute, a court will read the statute into the contract between the principal, surety and obligee ... A contractor's bond, given for the full and faithful performance of a contract for a public improvement, will be construed with reference to the statute pursuant to which it is given, and such statutory provisions will be read into the bond...." *Town of Southington v. Commercial Union Insurance Company*, 757 A.2d 549, 556 (Conn. 2000)

"A performance bond guarantees that the contractor will perform the contract, and usually provides that, if the contractor defaults and fails to complete the contract, the surety can itself complete the contract or pay damages up to the limit of the bond." *Groton Development Association v. International Fidelity Insurance Company*, No. 517864, 1995 WL 645921 (Conn. Super., Oct. 27, 1995).

## 2. Damages Covered

***Set forth in any statutes and/or case law***

"In an action for breach of contract, the general rule is that the award of damages is designed to place the injured party, so far as can be done by money, in the same position as that he would have been in had the contract been performed." The obligee's attempt to recover under the performance bond was rejected by the court where the evidence showed that the obligee had not paid more than the original contract price to complete the project. *Groton Development Association v. International Fidelity Insurance Company*, No. 517864, 1995 WL 645921 (Conn. Super., Oct. 27, 1995).

***Obligations of surety to perform and/or pay***

"Under a performance and completion bond, a surety generally has two options upon its principal's default. First, the surety may undertake to complete the principal's work itself; this obligation may be satisfied by the surety funding the principal to complete its work. Second, the surety has the option of paying the obligee's under the bond its damages, essentially, the obligee's cost of completion." *Balfour Beatty Construction v. Colonial Ornamental Ironworks*, 986 F. Supp. 82, 87 (D. Conn. 1997) *citing Granite Computer Leasing Company v. The Travelers Indemnity Company*, 894 F.2d 547 (2d Cir. 1990).

***Whether failure to provide insurance transfers burden to surety*** – Statutes do not transfer burden to surety.

### *Limitations on damages*

"It is a fundamental precept of suretyship law that the liability of the surety is conditioned on accrual of some obligation on the part of the principal; the surety will not be liable on the surety contract if the principal has not incurred liability on the primary contract... In the absence of limitations or restrictions contained in the (surety) contract, the liability of the surety is coextensive with that of the principal ... The surety's promise is in the same terms as that of the principal and the consequent duty similar and primary...." *Star Contracting Corp. v. Manway Construction Corp.*, 337 A.2d 669, 670-71 (Conn. Super. 1973).

Obligee's decision to reject lowest bid for completion work, in favor of next-lowest bid, did not under the circumstances constitute a breach of the obligee's duty to mitigate damages, nor was it a breach of the performance bond. Obligee was entitled to take into account factors other than price in weighing the bids. *Town of Newington v. General Sanitation Service Company*, 491 A.2d 363, 364 (Conn. 1985).

### *Whether obligee may set off bonded contract funds against other principal-obligee debts or obligations*

"Once the [obligee] has made demand on the surety according to the terms of the bond and the surety has fulfilled its obligations, the doctrine of equitable subrogation allows the surety to make a claim for reimbursement from the defaulting party for funds expended in fulfillment of the bond obligations ... The surety, standing in the shoes of the obligee, has the same rights against the defaulting party as had the obligee." *Nationwide Mutual Insurance Company v. R & S Associates*, CV92-0451559S, 1992 WL 257777 (Conn. Super., Sept. 18, 1992) (holding that surety on subdivision bond was subrogated to the rights of the obligee to assert claim for reimbursement from defaulting principal, but subrogation rights did not allow the surety to assert an equitable lien against the subject property, since the obligee never had such a lien).

### *Incorporation of specific contract terms by reference*

The "liabilities of sureties [under performance bonds] is to be determined by the specified conditions of the bond ... [W]hen a bond is required by statute, a court will read the statute into the contract between the principal, surety and obligee ... A contractor's bond, given for the full and faithful performance of a contract for a public improvement, will be construed with reference to the statute pursuant to which it is given, and such statutory provisions will be read into the bond ..." *Town of Southington v. Commercial Union Insurance Company*, 757 A.2d 549, 556 (Conn. 2000) (subdivision performance bond).

## 3. Penal Sum Variations

***Limitations per statute*** – Connecticut does not have any statutory limitations on performance bond penal sums.

***Effect of changes in work upon penal sum, if at all***

Although Connecticut courts do not specifically refer to the Cardinal Change Doctrine, Connecticut does recognize the similar doctrines of abandonment of contract and substantial alteration.

The issue of substantiality, a determination of whether the enumerated differences in the final plans were substantial, is a question of fact which depends on a consideration of the circumstances. The factual issue includes in this case the total undertaking covered by the writing, the amount of work affected by the alterations and the net change in the cost of performance. In dealing with contract provisions allowing alterations or modifications, an appropriate standard for substantiality is whether such changes unreasonably alter the character of the work or unduly increase its costs, or effect such a material change as to constitute a radical departure from the original contract. *Naek Constr. Co., Inc. v. PAG Charles St. Ltd. P-ship*, CV 02-0080135S, 2004 Conn. Super. LEXIS 3185 (J.D. Tolland, Nov. 3, 2004) *citing Randolph Constr. Co. v. Kings East Corp.*, 165 Conn. 269, 274, 334 A.2d 464 (1973).

This is substantially similar to a "cardinal change" as discussed in two U.S. Court of Claims cases cited in the *Naek* case:

> A cardinal change is a breach. It occurs when the government effects an alteration in the work so drastic that it effectively requires the contractor to perform duties material (sic) different from those originally bargained for. By definition, then a cardinal change is so profound that it is not redressable under the contract, and thus renders the government in breach....The touchstone of the doctrine is that

> Government actions subsequent to the contract so alter the contractor's duties and rights that wholesale reformation of the contract occurs.

*Naek Constr. Co., Inc. v. PAG Charles St. Ltd. P-ship*, CV 02-0080135S, 2004 Conn. Super. LEXIS 3185 (J.D. Tolland, Nov. 3, 2004) *citing Allied Materials & Equip. Co., Inc. v. United States*, 215 Ct. Cl. 406, 569 F.2d 562, 563-64 (U.S. Court Claims 1978) and *Paragon Energy Corp. v. United States*, 229 Ct. Cl. 524 (1981).

No Connecticut case law discusses these issues in the context of a performance bond.

***Statutory or case law protections or dangers to penal sum***

In the case of a performance bond for subdivision improvements, it has been established in Connecticut that the measure of damages is limited to the cost of completion of the improvements. *Brookfield v. Greenridge, Inc.*, 177 Conn. 527, 537, 418 A.2d 907 (1979).

Connecticut General Statutes § 52-238 limits the liability to a surety to the penalty of the bond plus interest. This was confirmed in *New Haven v. Eastern Brick Co.*, 78 Conn. 689, 63 A. 517 (1906).

There is no Connecticut case law addressing the issue of whether a surety is exposed to liability in excess of the penal sum of the bond for allegations of bad faith.

## 4. Parties Covered

***Statutes and/or case law as to whether only obligees are covered***

There are no Connecticut cases directly addressing whether only obligees are covered. In the context of a payment bond suit, a tavern which cashed checks of the subcontractor's employees in a public school construction project was not an assignee of the payment bond rights of the subcontractor. *Dysart Corp. v. Seaboard Surety Co.*, 240 Conn. 10, 688 A.2d 306 (1997). In that case a tavern located near the project and frequented by employees of the subcontractor often cashed the checks of the employees. When it attempted to deposit the checks, the subcontractor had insufficient funds to cover them. The tavern thereafter submitted a claim under the payment bond.

The court held that the endorsement of a check by a subcontractor's employee did not constitute an equitable assignment of any rights in an underlying payment bond. The court did not address how this may apply to performance bonds. However, the court reasoned that "[w]e see no reason to invoke equity and expand the effect of an endorsement of a check beyond what the statutes explicitly provide for, especially in the present context, where...policy concerns mandate circumscribing the class of potential payment bond claimants." *Id.* at 312-13.

***Coverage for:***

**Third-party beneficiaries** – A warehouse subcontractor to a trucking company could not recover as a third-party beneficiary under a performance bond because the performance bond was not intended for the benefit of third parties. *C&M Warehouse, Inc. v. Eastern Trucking*, No. CV 93-0521412S, CV93-0521412S, 1994 WL 551238 (Conn. Super., Sept. 26, 1994). In this case the issue was whether the surety had issued a payment bond for the trucking contract or a performance bond. The court cited the statutory definition of a performance bond as:

> Performance bond means a bond conditioned upon the completion by the principal of a contract in accordance with its terms.

Conn. Gen. Stat. § 32-55a(2). Then the court looked to the Restatement of the Law, Surety to juxtapose a performance bond with a payment bond:

> § 165. Where a surety for a contractor on a construction contract agrees in terms with the owner that the contractor will pay for labor and materials, or guarantees to the owner the promise of the contractor to pay for labor and materials, those furnishing labor and materials have a right against the surety as third party beneficiaries of the surety's contract, unless the surety's contract in terms disclaims liability to such persons.
>
> § 166. Where the surety guarantees the performance of a contract by a contractor who does not promise to pay those furnishing labor or materials but agrees to complete the work free of liens or to furnish labor and material, laborers and materialmen (sic) have no rights against the surety.

Thus, the court reasoned that the very essence of a payment bond is that it is intended and conditioned on benefiting third parties such as subcontractors, laborers and those who provide material. The court held the language of the bond to be that of a performance bond, and therefore the third party warehouse did not have standing to bring suit under the bond.

**Assignees** – A successor developer was not precluded from calling a performance bond even where it was in effect the principal and the obligee on the bond. *Town of Southington v. Commercial Union Ins. Co.*, 71 Conn. App. 715, 805 A.2d 76 (2002). In that case, a developer's sole shareholder executed a bond with the surety on a town-approved construction contract. The shareholder subsequently purchased the land on which the subdivision was to be built. The developer failed to complete the work as required under the terms of the bond, filed bankruptcy, and the town purchased the land at auction. The issue was whether the town, as the effective principal and obligee, could call the bond.

The court held it could call the performance bond because the language of the bond allowed it. The bond bound the surety to complete the project in the event the developer did not finish within two years. The developer did not complete, and the performance bond surety was obligated to finish the job, as the bond contained no limitation on the surety's obligation to the obligee.

**Dual obligees** – There are no Connecticut cases discussing a performance bond surety's obligation to dual obligees.

## 5. Notice or Filing Required

***Statutory provisions*** – Connecticut does not provide for any unusual notice requirements for suit under a performance bond.

***Case law rules concerning condition precedent notice***

In order to trigger the surety's liability under the performance bond, "two conditions had to be met. First, [the principal] had to be "in default" under the subcontract agreement, and second, [the obligee] had to "declare[] [the principal] to be in default" under the subcontract agreement. Such a declaration of default had to be made to [the surety] in precise terms... " *Elm Haven Construction Limited Partnership v. Neri Construction, LLC*, 376 F.3d 96, 100 (2d Cir. 2004) *affirming* 281 F. Supp. 2d 406, 2003 U.S. Dist. LEXIS 15956 (D. Conn., 2003) (obligee breached the performance bond by hiring completion contractors before declaring the principal in default and before giving the surety the opportunity to cure the default).

"[C]onstruction surety law recognizes a difference between a mere technical breach and a material breach which may constitute a default... Not every breach of contract constitutes a default sufficient to require a surety to step in and remedy it ... A legal default requires a material breach or series of material breaches such that the obligee is justified in terminating the contract.... A material breach ... is not enough, however; it only justifies the obligee's action in the next step of the process which is a declaration of default ... Thus, there is a distinction in the concepts of 'breach' and 'default' that is to be recognized in construction suretyship law." *Crystal Lake Condominium Association v. Colonial Surety Company*, 2005 Conn. Super LEXIS 1062 (2005).

## 6. Time for Suit

***Statutes of limitation particular to performance bonds and other applicable statutes of limitation***

Connecticut General Statutes § 38a-290 states:

> No insurance company doing business in this state shall limit the time within which any suit shall be brought against it or any claim shall be submitted to arbitration on .... (b) a construction performance bond to a period less than three years from the date on which the principal last performed work under the contract[.]

Connecticut General Statutes § 52-576 states:

> No action for an account, or on any simple or implied contract, or on any contract in writing, shall be brought but within six years after the right of action accrues[.]

***Case law statements about enforceability of limitations contained in bonds***

Connecticut General Statutes § 38a-290 states:

> No insurance company doing business in this state shall limit the time within which any suit shall be brought against it or any claim shall be submitted to arbitration on .... (b) a construction performance bond to a period less than three years from the date on which the principal last performed work under the contract[.]

***Varying statute of limitations by agreement in bond or contract***

Connecticut General Statutes § 38a-290 states:

> No insurance company doing business in this state shall limit the time within which any suit shall be brought against it or any claim shall be submitted to arbitration on .... (b) a construction performance bond to a period less than three years from the date on which the principal last performed work under the contract[.]

## 7. Procedure

***Statutory or procedural rules that may affect handling or administration of lawsuits***

Connecticut General Statutes §§ 42-158i through 42-158r provide for special rules pertaining to private construction contracts for work performed in Connecticut. For example, § 42-158m states:

> Any provision in a construction contract for the performance of work on a construction site located in this state that purports to require that any dispute arising under the construction contract be adjudicated in or under the laws of a state other than Connecticut shall be void and of no effect, regardless of whether the construction contract was executed in this state.

In addition, §§ 42-158o provides for the surety's obligations under private construction contracts as follows:

> No surety shall be obligated to include in the payment of a bond issued by such surety any interest, costs, penalties or attorney's fees imposed on the principal of such bond under any provision of sections 42-158i to 42-158o, inclusive, 49-33 or subsection (a) of section 52-249, unless the terms of the bond expressly reference said sections and subsection and state that such surety is obligated to pay such interest, costs, penalties or attorney's fees.

***Venue requirements and jurisdictional limitations***

Connecticut General Statutes §§ 52-45a, et. seq. provide the rules pertaining to the service of process and the required time for return, necessary parties and the pleading procedures.

The Connecticut venue statutes are located at Conn. Gen. Stat. § 51-345.

***Court rules*** – Not applicable.

***Particular agency regulations/rules*** – Not applicable.

***Arbitration requirements and application***

A performance bond surety was not bound by an arbitration clause in the contract between the principal and the obligee in *Peerless Ins. Co. v. Structural Preservations Systems, Inc.*, No. CV 99-0175067, Conn. Super. LEXIS 2150 (J.D. of Stamford, Aug. 16, 2000). The plaintiff there was the successor and assignee of a performance bond issued on behalf of the defendant's subcontractor. The defendant filed a demand for arbitration pursuant to an arbitration clause in its contract with its subcontractor. The plaintiff objected and filed for a temporary injunction against the arbitration. The court held the plaintiff was not bound by the arbitration clause in the subcontract. While a nonsignatory to an agreement to arbitrate may be obliged to arbitrate if the guaranty "explicitly" incorporates the arbitration agreement, the court found that the performance bond, while referring to the subcontract, did not make specific reference to the agreement to arbitrate.

Connecticut General Statutes § 4-61(b) allows a party to submit for arbitration a dispute against the state for highway or other public works projects. Findings of fact and the decision made shall be final and conclusive and not subject to review by any court or government agency for errors of fact or law. Any awards are final and binding and subject to modification, confirmation or vacation.

## 8. Attorney's Fees

***Statutes and/or case law limiting or permitting recovery of attorney's fees***

The common law rule in Connecticut, also known as the American Rule, is that attorney's fees and costs are not allowed to the successful party absent statutory authority or a contractual provision. *Ames v. Commissioner of Motor Vehicles*, 267 Conn. 524, 839 A.2d 1250 (2004).

***What fees are recoverable, if any***

Connecticut General Statutes § 37-3a allows the recovery of interest in civil actions as damages for the detention of money after it becomes payable. We have construed the statute to make the allowance of interest depend upon "whether the detention of the money is or is not wrongful under the circumstances." *Cecio Bros., Inc. v. Feldmann*, 161 Conn. 265, 275, 287 A.2d 374 (1971). "The allowance of interest as an element of damages is, thus, primarily an equitable determination and a matter lying within the discretion of the trial court." *Bertozzi v. McCarthy*, 164 Conn. 463, 467, 323 A.2d 553 (1973).

## 9. Special Provisions – Not applicable.

## 10. Remarks – As stated above.

## 11. Case Annotations

***Interpretation of AIA bond forms*** – Connecticut cases have not specifically addressed AIA bond forms A311 and A312.

***Cases in which surety steps into shoes of obligee***

Once the surety has fulfilled its obligations pursuant to the terms of the bond, the doctrine of equitable subrogation allows the surety to step into the shoes of the obligee to make a claim for reimbursement from the defaulting party. *Balboa Insurance Co. v. Bank of Boston Connecticut*, 702 F. Sup. 34, 36 (D. Conn. 1988). The surety, standing in the shoes of the obligee, has the same rights against the defaulting party as had the obligee. *Id.* at 37.

# DELAWARE

Samuel J. Arena, Jr. and David M. Burkholder[1]

## 1. Requirement for Bond

The bonding requirements for Delaware public works projects are set forth in the Delaware Public Works Contracting Laws (the "Public Works Law"), 29 Del. C. §§ 6961-6962, which is a part of Delaware's State Procurement Code, 29 Del. C. §§ 6901-6986.

29 Del. C. § 6902(21) defines "Public works contract" as "construction, reconstruction, demolition, alteration and repair work and maintenance work paid for, in whole or in part, with public funds."

29 Del. C. § 6961(a) ("Small public works contracts procedures") provides that "[a]ny State contract for which an Agency is a party and for which the probable cost is less than or equal to the threshold amount(s) set by the Contracting and Purchasing Advisory Council pursuant to § 913 of this Act for small public works contracts shall be subject to the provisions of this Section" (i.e., subject to the requirements of bid and performance bonds as set forth in § 6961 of the Public Works Law).[2]

---

1 Samuel J. Arena, Jr. is a partner and David M. Burkholder is an associate with:
Stradley, Ronon, Stevens & Young, LLP
2600 One Commerce Square
Philadelphia, Pennsylvania 19103-7098
(215) 564-8000

2 According to the Delaware Department of Administrative Services' website and effective November 1, 1996, the Contracting and Purchasing Advisory Council - pursuant to its authority under § 6913 - established $50,000 as the threshold for large public works contracts in Delaware. (*See* Delaware

29 Del. C. § 6962(a) ("Large public works contracts procedures") provides that "[a]ny State contract for which an Agency is a party and for which the probable cost is greater than the amount set by the Contracting and Purchasing Advisory Council pursuant to § 6913 of this Act for small public works contracts shall be subject to the provisions of this Section" (i.e., subject to the requirements of bid and performance bonds as set forth in § 6962 of the Public Works Law).

29 Del. C. § 6962(d)(9) ("Performance Bonding Requirements") provides that "[s]imultaneous with the execution of the formal contract, the successful bidder shall also execute a good and sufficient bond to the contracting Agency for the benefit of the Agency, with corporate surety authorized to do business in this State, in a sum equal to 100 percent of the contract price."

29 Del. C. § 6962(d)(9)(a) provides that "the bond form used shall be the standard form issued by the Office of Management and Budget."[3]

29 Del. C. § 6902(1) defines "Agency" as "every board, department, burcau, commission, person or group of persons or other authority which directly receives monies under any budget appropriation act or supplemental appropriation act and which was created and now exists or hereafter is created to:

---

Department of Administrative Services: Division of Facilities Management, http://www2.state.de.us/dfm/construc/papwp.asp at September 5, 2005.)

3 As of June 30, 2005, the 143rd Delaware General Assembly approved a resolution amending those pertinent sections of the Public Works Law as follows:

> by striking all references to the Department of Administrative Services and the Secretary thereof, whether such references appear as "Department of Administrative Services", "Secretary of the Department of Administrative Services", or "Secretary of Administrative Services", or any variation thereof in any grammatical form wherever they may appear in each section, and by substituting in lieu thereof the appropriate grammatical form of "Office of Management and Budget" or "Director of the Office of Management and Budget" as appropriate in context ....

Prior versions of the Public Works Law statute, therefore, will refer to the Department of Administrative Services rather than the Office of Management and Budget.

a. Execute, supervise, control and/or administer governmental functions under the laws of this State; and/or

b. To perform such governmental functions under the laws of this State, or to perform such other duties as may be prescribed; and/or

c. To collect and/or use any taxes, fees, licenses, permits or other receipts for service or otherwise for the performance of any function or related to or supported in whole or in part by the laws of this State; and/or

d. To administer any laws providing for the collection of taxes, fees, permits, licenses or other forms of receipts from any sources whatsoever for the use of the State or any agency of the State."

29 Del. C. § 6902(1) also defines "Agency" to include the Delaware Technical and Community College and the Delaware State University, but the term "Agency" shall not include "any local government unit or agency receiving only grants-in-aid appropriations from the State and no other appropriations, as described herein, the University of Delaware, volunteer ambulance/rescue companies, volunteer fire departments and the Delaware Transit Corporation." 29 Del. C. § 6902(1).

**Private** – No statutes in Delaware require performance bonds on private projects.

**Department of Transportation** – The Delaware Department of Transportation is considered an "agency" pursuant to 29 Del. C. § 6902(1)(a) and (b) of the Public Works Law. *See also Daisy Concrete, Inc. v. Dep't of Trans.*, Civ. A. No. 8764, 1987 WL 7958, at *3 (Del. Ch. Ct. Mar. 17, 1987) (referring to Department of Transportation in the context of public works contracts as a "state agency.").

29 Del. C. § 6962(d)(9)(h) provides that the construction contracts "may contain a waiver of the bond requirement, provided, however, that the successful bidder post with the contracting Agency an irrevocable letter of credit or other suitable or readily collectible financial security for the project," which "shall be subject to the terms and conditions of the contracting Agency."

***Case law rules that might generally apply***

Bonds executed pursuant to the Public Works Law will be construed to provide at least the minimum coverage required by the statute. *Certain-Teed Prod. Corp. v. United Pac. Ins. Co.*, 389 A.2d 777, 779 (Del. Super. Ct. 1978).

Parties executing the performance bond may contract for broader coverage than required by the statute. *Id.*

Where the claimant has no opportunity to negotiate the terms and conditions of the contract of suretyship, the bonds are liberally construed in favor of the claimant. *Del. State College v. Fidelity and Dep. Co. of Md.*, 194 A.2d 858, 861 (Del. 1963). This rule of construction, however, does not extend a surety's liability beyond the terms for which it has contracted. *Id.*

Conditions placed in a bond inconsistent with the language or purpose of the Public Works Law "may be disregarded and treated as surplusage." *Id.* at 862.

## 2. Damages Covered

***Obligations of surety to perform and/or pay***

Generally, the liability of the surety on the statutory bond "is coextensive with the liability of the general contractor." *Quality Elec. Co., Inc. v. Eastern States Constr. Serv., Inc.*, 663 A.2d 488 (Del. Super. Ct. 1995).

***Whether failure to provide insurance transfers burden to surety*** – No statutes in Delaware provide that a surety has the burden of insurance coverage for a public works project where the principal has failed to acquire insurance coverage.

***Limitations on damages***

Generally, damages for breach of a performance bond are limited to the non-breaching party's expectation interest. *Int'l Fidelity Ins. Co. v. Delmarva Systems Corp.*, No. 99C-10-065 WCC, 2001 WL 541469, *2 (Del. Super. Ct. 2001, May 9, 2001).

**Bad faith damages** – In 2001, the Superior of Court of Delaware recognized a claim of bad faith against a surety. *See Int'l Fidelity Ins. Co. v. Delmarva Systems Corp.*, No. 99C-10-065 WCC, 2001 WL 541469, *2 (Del. Super. Ct. 2001, May 9, 2001). The court analyzed conflicting opinions from other jurisdictions to determine whether Delaware law should recognize claims of bad faith against sureties. The court reasoned that, *inter alia*, the "presence of sureties in the insurance statutes [of Delaware] is reflective of the Legislature's intent and deserves merit." *Id.* at *8. Further, the court determined that "the purpose of the construction performance bond is not for a commercial advantage but to protect the obligee from calamity that may result if the principal defaults on the contract." *Id.* at *9. The court concluded, therefore, that an obligee needs "insurance that the project can be completed." *Id.* By allowing a bad faith claim, which permits the aggrieved party to recover punitive damages, in the surety context, sureties would be deterred from intentionally delaying or purposely manipulating payment to their benefit. *Id.* The court acknowledged that parties in the suretyship context are on "more equal footing than that of a normal insurance contract," but it did not find that merely risking the recovery of the contract amount "sufficiently remedies the potentially catastrophic losses related to the surety's bad faith delay." *Id.* Accordingly, by recognizing this cause of action against a surety, tort damages, including punitive damages, are available against a surety for bad faith breach of a performance bond. *Id.* at *9-10.

***Whether obligee may set off bonded contract funds against other principal-obligee debts or obligations*** – There are no statutes or cases concerning this topic.

***Incorporation of specific contract terms by reference*** – There are no statutes or cases concerning this topic for performance bonds.

### 3. Penal Sum Variations:

***Limitations per statute*** – 29 Del. C. § 6962(a) provides that a performance bond is required on all public works contracts in excess of $50,000. *See also* n.2, *supra*.

***Effect of changes in work upon penal sum, if at all*** – There are no statutes or cases concerning this topic.

***Statutory or case law protections or dangers to penal sum*** – There are no statutes or cases concerning this topic.

## 4. Parties Covered

***Statutes and/or case law as to whether only obligees are covered***

29 Del. C. § 6962(d)(9)(d) provides that the contracting agency and "every firm furnishing materiel or performing labor under the contract for which the successful bidder is liable may maintain an action on the bond for its own use in the name of the Agency in any court of competent jurisdiction for the recovery of such sum or sums as may be due such firm from the successful bidder."

***Coverage for:***

**Third-party beneficiaries** – A supplier to a subcontractor generally cannot maintain an action against a general contractor and its surety under the Public Works Law. *Quality Elec. Co., Inc. v Eastern States Constr. Serv., Inc.*, 663 A.2d 488 (Del. Super. Ct. 1995) (relying on the limitation in 29 Del. C. § 6962(d)(9)(d) above). Absent that express limitation language, however, a supplier to the bonded principal can bring an action against the surety for reimbursement of materials supplied for the bonded project. *Id.*

**Assignees** – There are no statutes or cases concerning this topic.

**Dual obligees** – The statutes do not contain any provision for dual obligees.

## 5. Notice or Filing Required

Delaware has no statutory provisions regarding notice or filing requirements for a performance bond claim other than the below referenced statute of limitations.

## 6. Time for Suit

***Statutes of limitation particular to performance bonds and other applicable statutes of limitations***

29 Del. C. § 6962(d)(9)(d) provides that, if the performance bond so provides, no suit shall be commenced after the expiration of one year following the date on which the successful bidder ceased work on the contract. Otherwise, suits pursuant to the performance bond may be commenced at any time within three years following the date the last work was done on the contract.

***Case law statements about enforceability of limitations contained in bonds***

Statute permits one-year limitation in performance bonds; however, where no such limitation exists, suit must be commenced within three years. *Rumsey Elec. Co. v. Univ. of Del.*, 334 A.2d 226, 230 (Del. Super. Ct. 1975) (construing identical limitation language under predecessor section to 29 Del. C. § 6962(d)(9)(d)).

***Varying statute of limitations by agreement in bond or contract***

*See* 29 Del. C. § 6962(d)(9)(d) (permitting one-year limitation in performance bonds but providing for three-year period of limitations where no such limitation exists in the bond).

**Bad faith claims** – The statute of limitations for a cause of action for bad faith under Delaware law is three years. *See Hostetter v. Hartford Ins. Co.*, C.A. No. 85C-06-28, 1992 WL 179423, *3-4 (Del. Super. Ct. July 13, 1992); *see also* 10 Del. C. § 8106 ("no action based on a promise ... to recover damages caused by an injury unaccompanied with force" shall be brought within three years "from the accruing of the cause of such action").

A cause of action for bad faith refusal to pay a claim accrues "when the party seeking to bring the action knows facts which would put a reasonable person on notice of the possible existence" of the bad faith. *Hostetter*, 1992 WL 179423 at *4.

## 7. Procedure

***Statutory or procedural rules that may affect handling or administration of lawsuits*** – There is no special statutory procedure for an action against a performance bond surety.

***Venue requirements and jurisdictional limitations*** – Not applicable.

***Court rules*** – Delaware has one set of rules of civil procedure governing its courts. The United States District Court for Delaware has its own local rules of civil procedure.

***Particular agency regulations/rules*** – There are no agency regulations or rules applicable to performance bonds that may affect the handling or administration of lawsuits under performance bonds in Delaware.

***Arbitration requirements and application***

In Delaware, cases where the amount in controversy - exclusive of interest does not exceed $50,000 shall be heard in the Delaware Court of Common Pleas. 10 Del. C. § 1322. Cases with an amount in controversy exceeding $50,000 shall be heard in the superior court. *Id.*

## 8. Attorney's Fees

***Statutes/case law limiting or permitting recovery of attorney's fees***

No statute in Delaware permits the recovery of attorney's fees on performance bonds provided for public works contracts.

Generally, under Delaware law, "a court may not order the payment of attorney's fees as part of the costs to be paid by the losing party unless the payment of such fees is authorized by some provision of a statute or of the bond sued upon." *Great Am. Indem. Co. v. State,* 88 A.2d 426, 428 (Del. Ch. Ct. 1952).

## 9. Special Provisions

There are no special provisions in the Public Works Law or the Procurement Code beyond the plain language of the statutes, which require bonds for 100 percent of the contract price and conditioned upon the principal's faithful performance of the contract.

**10. Remarks** – As stated above.

## 11. Case Annotations

***Interpretation of AIA bond forms*** – There are no statutes or cases concerning this topic.

***Cases in which surety steps into shoes of obligee*** – There are no statutes or cases concerning this topic.

# DISTRICT OF COLUMBIA

Dawn C. Stewart[1]

## 1. Requirement for Bond

***Statutory provisions for projects that are:***

**Public** – D.C. Code Ann. § 2-305.03 – The District of Columbia requires performance bonds, or the cash equivalent, on all construction contracts estimated to exceed $100,000.

D.C. Code Ann. § 2-201.01 ("Little Miller Act") – Performance bonds are required before any contract, exceeding $25,000 in amount, for the construction, alteration or repair of any public building or public work of the District of Columbia is awarded.

D.C. Code Ann. § 2-303.22 – Performance bonds are required for all contracts for energy conservation measures.

D.C. Code Ann. § 34-1256.05 – Performance bonds are required for cable television franchise operators, to ensure the operation of the cable system continues uninterrupted.

**Private** – No statutes in the District of Columbia require performance bonds on private projects.

---

1 Dawn C. Stewart is a member of:
The Stewart Law Firm, PLLC
1050 Connecticut Ave., NW; Tenth Floor
Washington, D.C. 20036
(202) 772-1080

**Department of Transportation** – Not applicable.

***Case law rules that might generally apply***

"Under the law of the District of Columbia, a surety's obligations must be measured by the conditions stated in the bond." *Goldberg. Marchesan. Kohlman. Inc., v. Old Republic Sur. Co.*, 727 A.2d 858, 860-61 (D.C. 1999).

## 2. Damages Covered

***Set forth in any statutes and/or case law*** – See below.

***Obligations of surety to perform and/or pay*** – When examining the surety's options upon the principal's default, the best reference is the terms of the bond at issue.

***Whether failure to provide insurance transfers burden to surety*** – Statutes do not transfer the burden to surety.

***Limitations on damages***

Judgment against the surety cannot exceed the penal sum of the bond. *In re Estate of Spinner*, 717 A.2d 362, 366 (D.C. 1998) (judgment against personal representative's surety, Old Republic Insurance Company, was reduced to the penal sum of the bond.)

"A surety's obligation must be measured by the condition stated in the bond, and when the condition is ... merely to indemnify the owner against loss or damage by reason of the failure of the contractor to perform, such condition cannot be construed to go further than its terms and give rights to others not mentioned either expressly or by intendment." *Bevard v. New Amsterdam Casualty Co.*, 132 A.2d 157, 159 (D.C. 1957).

A nominal bond is intended to secure only the payment of the estate's unsecured debts, and will not be extended to cover losses caused by the malfeasance of the personal representative. *In re Estate of Dickson*, 736 A.2d 1007, 1009 (D.C. 1999).

***Whether obligee may set off bonded contract funds against other principal-obligee debts or obligations***

Obligee's right against principal to set off excess costs on an unbonded job on which the principal also defaulted, was ineffective against the surety. Surety's subrogation rights relate back to the date of issuance of the bond. *Glassman Construction Co. v. Fidelity and Casualty Co. of New York*, 356 F.2d 340, 343 (D.C. 1966).

***Incorporation of specific contract terms by reference***

When a contract with the district is incorporated into a bond by reference, it becomes a part of the bond as much as if set forth verbatim. *U.S. to the use of District of Columbia v. Bayly*, 39 App. D.C. 105, 108 (1912). *See also*, *Peake v. U.S.*, 16 App. D.C. 415 (1900).

"[a] valid contract can be spelled out in multiple papers, some unsigned, if they are referred to in a signed document and thus become incorporated by reference." *Superior Oil v. Udall*, 409 F.2d 1115, 1120 (D.C. 1969).

However, papers left out of a sealed bid, although purported to be incorporated, cannot be used to remedy deficiencies in the sealed bid itself. *Id.*

Incorporation of the contract, by reference, into the surety bond, does not turn the surety into a co-principal. *Gunnell Construction Co., Inc. v. Hartford Accident and Indemnity Co.*, 374 F.2d 278, 280 (D.C. 1967).

## 3. Penal Sum Variations

***Limitations per statute*** – The District of Columbia does not have statutory limitations on performance bond penal sums.

***Effect of changes in work upon penal sum, if at all*** – None found.

***Statutory or case law protections or dangers to penal sum***

D.C. Code Ann. § 28-2502 – Damages to be recovered from the surety, may not exceed the penal sum of a bond containing an avoidance condition.

"Interest in excess of the maximum penalty of the undertaking may become due from the surety, but only because of the surety's own default." *Cunningham v. Cunningham,* 157 F.2d 859, 861, 81 U.S. App. D.C. 300, 302 (D.C. Cir. 1946).

## 4. Parties Covered

***Statutes and/or case law as to whether only obligees are covered*** – Not applicable.

***Coverage for:***

**Third-party beneficiaries** – Essential to recovery by materialmen and subcontractors, is some indication of intention either in the bond or relevant statute ... to benefit them. There must be some indication the bond is intended to benefit someone other than the obligee. *Bevard v. New Amsterdam Casualty Co.*, 132 A.2d 157, 159 (D.C. 1957).

**Assignees** – There are no District of Columbia cases discussing assignment of obligee's right to make a claim against a performance bond.

**Dual obligees** – One of two joint obligees under a contract, could not bring an action at law without the other, but could bring a suit in equity. *Cochran v. Burdick*, 70 F.2d 754, 755 (D.C. 1934).

## 5. Notice or Filing Required

***Statutory provisions*** – District of Columbia statutes do not provide for any unusual notice requirements for suit under a performance bond.

***Case law rules concerning condition precedent notice***

"By almost universal custom fidelity bonds as now written require notice of default within a limited period of time, and that provision the courts enforce according to its strict terms. And in such a case it is immaterial whether the surety is able to show it was prejudiced by failure to receive notice, for the contract is enforced in accordance with its terms, and the question of prejudice does not affect the result. Notice is of the essence of the contract, and compliance with its terms is indispensable to fix liability." *U.S. Shipping Board Merchant Fleet Corp. v. Aetna Casualty & Surety Company*, 98 F.2d 238, 242 (D.C. 1938).

## 6. Time for Suit

***Statutes of limitation particular to performance bonds and other applicable statutes of limitation***

D.C. Code Ann. § 12-301(6) – action may not be brought on an executor or administrator's bond more than five years after the cause of action accrues.

D.C. Code Ann. § 12-301(6) – action may not be brought on any other type of bond, or single bill, covenant, or other instrument under seal, more than 12 years after the cause of action accrues.

D.C. Code Ann. § 12-301(7) – action may not be brought on a simple contract, express or implied, more than three years after the cause of action accrues.

***Case law statements about enforceability of limitations contained in bonds.***

A cause of action under a personal representative bond accrues when the final accounting is filed and approved by the court. *In re Estate of Green*, 816 A.2d 14, 20 (D.C. 2003).

***Varying statute of limitations by agreement in bond or contract*** – The District of Columbia permits parties to alter, by contract, the period within which suit may be filed for a breach of contract. *See, e.g., Roumel v. Niagara Fire Ins. Co.*, 225 A.2d 658 (D.C. 1967).

## 7. Procedure

***Statutory or procedural rules that may affect handling or administration of lawsuits*** – Not applicable.

***Venue requirements and jurisdictional limitations***

D.C. Code Ann. § 13-423(a) – a District of Columbia Court may exercise personal jurisdiction over a person as to a claim arising from the person's ...: (1) transacting any business in the District of Columbia.

The "transacting business" standard for conferring long arm jurisdiction is co-extensive with the minimum contacts needed to establish personal jurisdiction under the Due Process Clause. *Digital Broadcast Corp. v. Rosenman & Colin, LLP*, 847 A.2d 384, 390 (D.C. 2004); or

D.C. Code Ann. § 13-423(a)(2) – contracting to supply services in the District of Columbia; or

D.C. Code Ann. § 13-423(a)(5) – having an interest in, using, or possessing real property in the District of Columbia; or

D.C. Code Ann. § 13-423(a)(6) – contracting to insure or act as surety for or on any person, property, or risk, contract, obligation, or agreement located, executed, or to be performed within the District of Columbia at the time of contracting, unless the parties otherwise provide in writing.

***Court rules*** – Not applicable.

***Particular agency regulations/rules*** – Not applicable.

***Arbitration requirements and application***

In general, D.C. Code Ann. § 16-4301, et. seq.

Under District of Columbia law, arbitration is predicated upon the consent of the parties to the dispute. A determination of whether the parties have given consent, is to be determined based on the contracts between the parties. *Bailey v. Nat. Mortg. Ass'n*, 209 F.3d 740, 746 (D.C. Cir. 2000).

"In *Cole,* the D.C. Circuit concluded that an arbitration agreement was enforceable so long as it '(1) provides for neutral arbitrators, (2)

provides for more than minimal discovery, (3) requires a written award, (4) provides for all of the types of relief that would otherwise be available in court, and (5) does not require employees to pay either unreasonable costs *or* any arbitrators′ fees or expenses as a condition of access to the arbitration forum.′ Thus, one requirement for an enforceable arbitration agreement is that 'more than minimal' discovery be permitted." *Booker v. Robert Half Intern, Inc.*, 315 F. Supp. 2d 94, 102 (D.D.C. 2004), quoting, *Cole v. Burns Intern. Sec. Services*, 105 F.3d 1465, 1482 (D.C. Cir. 1997).

## 8. Attorney's Fees

***Statutes and/or case law limiting or permitting recovery of attorney's fees***

The District of Columbia does not address the issue of whether attorney's fees can be awarded against a surety either by statute or in the case law.

The U.S. District Court for the District of Columbia has refused to carve out an exception to the American Rule that each side bears its own attorney's fees, in the insurance context, given the absence of any local guidance. *Harris v. Howard University, Inc.*, 48 F. Supp. 2d 43, 46 (D.D.C. 1999).

***What fees are recoverable, if any*** – Not applicable.

## 9. Special Provisions – Not applicable.

## 10. Remarks – Not applicable.

## 11. Case Annotations

***Interpretation of AIA bond forms*** – District of Columbia cases have not specifically addressed AIA forms of bonds A311 and A312.

***Cases in which surety steps into shoes of obligee***

Where the only claimants to monies held by a government agency are the surety and the defaulting contractor, the surety who has performed, in full satisfaction of its obligation, under a public works performance bond agreement, is subrogated to all rights and remedies the government may have had against the principal had the government been required to complete the project, including the right to set off. *District of Columbia v. Aetna Ins. Co.*, 462 A.2d 428 (1983).

# FEDERAL

Robert G. Watt and Vivian Katsantonis[1]

## 1. Requirement for Bond

***Statutory provisions for projects that are:***

Federal Acquisition Regulations (FAR) 28.102-1, pursuant to the Miller Act, 40 U.S.C. §§ 3131-3143, requires a performance bond for any construction contract exceeding $100,000 awarded by the United States government. A surety who issues a Miller Act performance bond guarantees full and complete performance of the prime contract should its bonded prime contractor default. *Transamerica Ins. Co. v. United States*, 31 Fed. Cl. 532 (Fed. Cl. 1994).

The FAR's requirement for bond may be waived (1) under the Miller Act; or (2) as authorized by the contracting officer (CO) where the work is to be performed in a foreign country and the CO determines that it would be impracticable for the contractor to furnish a performance bond.

FAR 28.103-2 states that the government may also require performance bonds "for contracts exceeding the simplified acquisition threshold when necessary to protect the Government's interest," and lists the following situations as those that may warrant a performance bond:

---

1 Robert G. Watt and Vivian Katsantonis are partners with:
Watt, Tieder, Hoffar & Fitzgerald, L.L.P.
8405 Greensboro Drive, Suite 100
McLean, Virginia 22102
(703) 749-1080

"(1) Government property or funds are to be provided to the contractor for use in performing the contract or as partial compensation (as in retention of salvaged material). (2) A contractor sells assets to or merges with another concern, and the Government, after recognizing the latter concern as the successor in interest, desires assurance that it is financially capable. (3) Substantial progress payments are made before delivery of end items starts. (4) Contracts are for dismantling, demolition, or removal of improvements."

***Case law rules that might generally apply***

The government may terminate a contractor for default if the contractor fails to provide a payment or performance bond. *Appeal of Pacific Sunset B, Inc.*, ASBCA 39312, 93-3 ¶ BCA 25935 (1993).

**Equitable Subrogation** – "A surety can sue the Government in the Court of Federal Claims under the non-contractual doctrine of equitable subrogation." *Admiralty Constr. by National Am. Ins. Co. v. Dalton*, 156 F.3d 1217, 1221 (Fed. Cir. 1998). See also *Balboa Ins. Co. v. United States*, 775 F.2d 1158, 1161 (Fed. Cir. 1985) ("the traditional means of asserting a surety's claim is under the equitable doctrine of subrogation").

"A subrogee, after stepping into the shoes of a government contractor, may rely on the waiver of sovereign immunity in the Tucker Act and bring suit against the United States" in the Court of Federal Claims. *Ins. Co. of the West v. United States*, 243 F.3d 1367, 1375 (Fed. Cir. 2001).

FAR 32.800 *et seq*. and the Assignment of Claims of Act, 31 U.S.C. 15 and 41 U.S.C. § 15, prohibit the contractor from assigning its claims under a federal government contract to a third party other than "a bank, trust company, or other financing institution, including any federal lending agency." Because a surety does not fit within the statutory definition of a lending agency, a contractor may not assign to a surety its claims, such as for changes or delays, against the government. Accordingly, a surety's subrogation right is limited to claims on the contract balance. *Appeal of United Pac. Ins. Co.*, ASBCA No. 52419 (2001). See also *Transamerica Ins. Co. v. United States*, 31 Fed. Cl. 532 (1994) (allowing a subrogated surety to challenge the assessment of liquidated damages from the unpaid contract balance); *Universal Sur. Co. v. United States*, 10 Cl. Ct. 794, 800 (1986) (denying a surety's claim for damages resulting from five change orders and the additional expenses incurred, stating that under equitable subrogation, a surety is limited to traditional equitable relief; "namely, for losses incurred by the surety on its bonds to the extent of the contract balance held by the government/owner.").

**Takeover Agreements** – FAR 49.404(d) "There may be conflicting demands for the defaulting contractor's assets, including unpaid prior earnings (retained percentages and unpaid progress estimates). Therefore, the surety may include a "takeover" agreement in its proposal, fixing the surety's rights to payment from those funds. The contracting officer may (but not before the effective date of termination) enter into a written agreement with the surety. The contracting officer should consider using a tripartite agreement among the Government, the surety, and the defaulting contractor to resolve the defaulting contractor's residual rights, including assertions to unpaid prior earnings."

A takeover agreement provides the surety standing to sue the government. However, the surety's ability to bring a claim that arose before the takeover may depend on the specificity of the takeover agreement and on the forum in which the surety seeks relief.

The Court of Federal Claims has exercised jurisdiction over pre-takeover claims where "the takeover agreement... encompassed the prior contract's rights and obligations." *Employers Ins. of Wausau v. United States*, 23 Cl. Ct. 579 (1991), 10 FPD ¶ 91. See also *Intercargo Ins. Co. v. United States*, 41 Fed. Cl. 449, 460 (1998) (allowing the surety to challenge the propriety of the government's decision to default terminate); *Roxco, Ltd. v. United States*, 60 Fed. Cl. 39 (2004) 46 GC ¶ 156 (exercising jurisdiction over a suit brought by the contractor for pre-takeover claims where the surety completed the project without signing a takeover agreement).

A takeover agreement conveying general contract rights to the surety is an insufficient basis to establish jurisdiction over pre-default claims in a board of contract appeals. "[F]or the Board to have jurisdiction under the Contract Disputes Act, over a claim by a surety that entered into a takeover agreement with the United States, the claim must "arise under" a contract the surety had with the government prior to that agreement." *United Pac. Ins. Co. v. Roche*, 380 F.3d 1352, 1356 (Fed. Cir. 2004) (restating and following the holding of *Fireman's Fund Ins. Co. v. England*, 313 F.3d 1344 (Fed. Cir. 2002)). In *United Pacific*, a general provision in the takeover agreement stating "SURETY expressly reserves all prior rights including but not limited to the Government's overpayment" to the contractor did not give the board jurisdiction over a pre-default claim brought by the surety. *Id.* The court stated, "The Board's jurisdiction is defined by the Contract Disputes Act. Parties cannot, by agreement, confer upon a tribunal jurisdiction that it otherwise would not have." *Id.* at 1356-57.

## 2. Damages Covered

### *Set forth in any statutes and/or case law*

Under general principles of law, the obligation of a bond is to be measured by the penalty named in the bond itself. *Bill Curphy Co. v. Elliot*, 207 F.2d 103, 106 (5th Cir. 1953); *Aetna Cas. & Sur. Co. v. Butte-Meade Sanitary Water Dist.*, 500 F. Supp. 193 (D.S.D. 1980).

FAR 28.001(6) provides that the penal sum of the bond is the maximum payment for which the surety is obligated.

FAR 49.406 states:"The contract provides that the contractor and the surety are liable to the Government for resultant damages. The contracting officer shall use all retained percentages of progress payments previously made to the contractor and any progress payments due for work completed before the termination to liquidate the contractor's and surety's liability to the Government. If the retained and unpaid amounts are insufficient, the contracting officer shall take steps to recover the additional sum from the contractor and the surety."

"[A] surety cannot be taxed with interest on the principal's debt until demand is made upon the surety for payment of the principal's obligation." *United States v. Reul*, 959 F.2d 1572, 1579 (Fed. Cir. 1992).

A surety may be liable for accrued interest in excess of the penal sum resulting in the surety's failure to timely make payment. 951 F.2d 1244 (Fed. Cir. 1991) 651 N.Y.S.2d 58 (App. Div. 1996).

"Sureties, if answerable at all for interest beyond the amount of the penalty of the bond given by their principal, can only be held for such an amount as accrued from their own default in unjustly withholding payment after being notified of the default of their principal." *United States v. USF&G Co.*, 236 U.S. 512, 530-31 (1915).

***Obligations of surety to perform and/or pay***

"A performance bond generally gives the surety the option of taking over and completing performance or of assuming liability for the government's costs in completing the contract which are in excess of the contract price...[or of providing] funds to an insolvent contractor to complete performance..." *Ins. Co. of the West v. United States*, 243 F.3d 1367, 1370 (Fed. Cir. 2001).

"[T]here is no requirement that a performing surety must assume 'the primary responsibility for the completion of the work,'" rather, the performing surety may "take over the project and contract for its completion." *Aetna Cas. & Surety Co. v. United States*, 845 F.2d 971, 975 (Fed. Cir. 1988).

FAR 49.404(c) provides: "The contracting officer should permit surety offers to complete the contract, unless the contracting officer believes that the persons or firms proposed by the surety to complete the work are not competent and qualified or the proposal is not in the best interest of the government."

***Whether failure to provide insurance transfers burden to surety*** – Statutes do not transfer the burden to the surety.

***Limitations on damages*** – FAR 49.404(e)(2) states: "The surety is bound by contract terms governing liquidated damages for delays in completion of the work, unless the delays are excusable under the contract."

***Whether obligee may set off bonded contract funds against other principal-obligee debts or obligations***

A surety is entitled to recover from any remaining contract proceeds the costs it has incurred for completion of the work without set off from any competing claim. See *Aetna Cas. Ins. & Sur. Co. v. United States*, 845 F.2d 971, 974 (Fed. Cir. 1988).

"A surety that pays on a performance bond in order to complete the subject contract has priority over the United States to the retainages in its hands. A surety that pays on its payment bond, however, does not have priority when the United States is asserting a tax or other obligation owed by the prime contractor." *United States Fidelity & Guar. Co. v. United States*, 475 F.2d 1377, 1383 (Ct. Cl. 1973).

***Incorporation of specific contract terms by reference***

A takeover agreement may incorporate by reference certain clauses of the original construction contract between the contractor and the government. See *United Pac. Ins. Co. v. Roche*, 380 F.3d 1352, 1357-58 (Fed. Cir. 2004) (incorporating by reference into the takeover agreement FAR 52.232-5(h), regarding presentation of release of all claims against the government, before the surety can be entitled to the balance due on the construction contract).

**3. Penal Sum Variations**

***Limitations per statute***

FAR 28.001(6) provides that the "'[p]enal sum' or 'penal amount' means the amount of money specified in a bond (or a percentage of the bid price in a bid bond) as the maximum payment for which the surety is obligated or the amount of security required to be pledged to the Government in lieu of a corporate or individual surety for the bond."

***Effect of changes in work upon penal sum, if at all***

FAR 28.106-5 states that upon modification of any contract, the CO "shall obtain the consent of the surety if (1) an additional bond is obtained from other than the original surety; (2) No additional bond is required and (i) The modification is for new work beyond the scope of the original contract; or (ii) The modification does not change the contract price (upward or downward) by more than 25 percent or $50,000; or (3) Consent of surety is required for a novation agreement."

FAR 28.102-2(b) provides that the penal amount of performance bonds for contracts exceeding $100,000 must equal 100 percent of the original contract price, unless the CO determines that a lesser amount provides adequate protection of the government. If there is an increase in the original contract price, the penal amount of the performance bond must increase by an equal amount.

FAR 28.102-2(a) states that "[o]riginal contract price means the award price of the contract; or, for requirements contracts, the price payable for the estimated total quantity; or, for indefinite-quantity contracts, the price payable for the specified minimum quantity. Original contract price does not include the price of any options, except those options exercised at the time of the contract award."

***Statutory or case law protections or dangers to penal sum***

FAR 49.404(c) provies: "Any takeover agreement must require the surety to complete the contract and the Government to pay the surety's costs and expenses up to the balance of the contract price unpaid at the time of default." This rule is subject to four conditions: (1) "any unpaid earnings of the defaulting contractor...must be subject to debts due the Government by the contractor, except to the extent that the unpaid earnings may be used to pay the completing surety its actual costs..."; (2) the surety is "bound by contract terms governing liquidated damages for delays in completion of the work..."; (3) "if the contract proceeds have been assigned to a financing institution, the surety must not be paid from unpaid earnings..."; and (4) the CO "must not pay the surety more than the amount it expended completing the work and discharging its liability under the defaulting contractor's payment bond."

## 4. Parties Covered

***Statutes and/or case law as to whether only obligees are covered*** – Not applicable.

***Coverage for:***

**Third-party beneficiaries** – "A surety bond creates a three-party relationship, in which the surety becomes liable for the principal's debt or duty to the third party obligee. If the surety fails to perform, the obligee can sue it on the bond. There is no contractual relationship between the surety and the third party obligee." *Ins. Co. of the West v. United States*, 243 F.3d 1367, 1370 (2001). See also *Admiralty Constr., Inc. v. Dalton*, 156 F.3d 1217, (Fed. Cir. 1998); *Balboa Ins. Co. v. United States*, 775 F.2d 1158 (Fed. Cir. 1985).

Upon a general contractor's default termination on a federal project for which there is a Miller Act performance bond, the federal government becomes a claimant under the bond. Such bonds provide no rights to subcontractors or suppliers. "The Miller Act did not contemplate that the subcontractor would become entitled to a performance bond. That was solely a right running to the United States. The subcontractor could only be protected for the labor and materials supplied by him or them." *United States use of Lichter v. Henke Const. Co.*, 35 F. Supp. 388, 389 (D. Mo. 1940). See also *Transamerica Premier Ins. Co. v. Ober*, 894 F. Supp. 471 (D. Me. 1995) (holding that the Miller Act did not provide for recovery under the performance bond by subcontractors and that permitting both the U.S. and subcontractors to claim against the performance bond penal sum could result in a depletion of the funds available).

"The Miller Act provides for two bonds - a 'performance bond' for the protection of the United States and a 'payment bond' for the protection of the suppliers of labor and material....It is well settled that suppliers of material and labor do not have a lien against property of the United States for the amounts due them under the contract. Their right of recovery is against the surety on the payment bond. ...[S]uppliers of material and labor are limited to recovery under the payment bond." *Sun Ins. Co. of New York v. Diversified Engineers, Inc.*, 240 F. Supp. 606, 608-09 (D. Mont. 1965). See also *United States ex rel. James E. Simon Co., Inc. v. Ardelt-Horn Constr. Co.*, 316 F. Supp. 254, 261-62 (D. Neb. 1970) ("Nothing in the wording of the act gives to the one who furnished labor or material any right to sue on the performance bond...[A] subcontractor who furnished labor and material is not entitled to recover on a Miller Act performance bond....").

**Assignees** – 41 U.S.C. § 15, the Anti-Assignment Act, states that "[n]o contract or order...shall be transferred by the party to whom such contract or order is given to any other party, and any such transfer shall cause the annulment of the contract or order transferred, so far as the United States is concerned. All rights of action, however, for any breach of such contract by the contracting parties, are reserved to the United States...The [above] provisions...shall not apply in any case in which the moneys due or to become due from the United States or from any agency or department thereof, under a contract providing for payments aggregating $1,000 or more, are assigned to a bank, trust company, or other financing institution, including any Federal lending agency, provided: (1) That, in the case of any contract entered into after October 9, 1940, no claim shall be assigned if it arises under a contract which forbids such assignment. (2) That, unless otherwise expressly permitted by such contract, any such assignment shall cover all amounts payable under such contract and not already paid, shall not be made to more than one party, and shall not be subject to further assignment, except that any such assignment may be made to one party as agent or trustee for two or more parties participating in such financing. (3) That, in the event of any such assignment, the assignee thereof shall file written notice of the assignment together with a true copy of the instrument of the assignment with (A) the contracting officer or the head of his department or agency; (B) the surety or sureties upon the bond or bonds, if any, in connection with such contract; and (C) the disbursing officer, if any, designated in such contract to make payment."

31 U.S.C. § 3727, the Assignment of Claims Act, provides in relevant part:

> (a) In this section, "assignment" means (1) a transfer or assignment of any part of a claim against the United States Government or of an interest in the claim; or (2) the authorization to receive payment for any part of the claim.
>
> (b) An assignment may be made only after a claim is allowed, the amount of the claim is decided, and a warrant for payment of the claim has been issued. The assignment shall specify the warrant, must be made freely, and must be attested to by 2 witnesses. The person making the assignment shall acknowledge it before an official who may acknowledge a deed, and the official shall certify the assignment. The certificate shall state that the official completely explained the assignment when it was acknowledged. An assignment under this subsection is valid for any purpose.
>
> (c) Subsection (b) of this section does not apply to an assignment to a financing institution of money due or to become due under a contract providing for payments totaling at least $1,000 when (1) the contract does not forbid an assignment; (2) unless the contract expressly provides otherwise, the assignment (A) is for the entire amount not already paid; (B) is made to only one party, except that it may be made to a party as agent or trustee for more than one party participating in the financing; and (C) may not be reassigned; and (3) the assignee files a written notice of the assignment and a copy of the

> assignment with the contracting official or the head of the agency, the surety on a bond on the contract, and any disbursing official for the contract....
>
> (e) (1) An assignee under this section does not have to make restitution of, refund, or repay the amount received because of the liability of the assignor to the Government that arises from or is independent of the contract. (2) The Government may not collect or reclaim money paid to a person receiving an amount under an assignment or allotment of pay or allowances authorized by law when liability may exist because of the death of the person making the assignment or allotment.

"Notwithstanding the strict provisions of the claims act, it has long been held that the Government may recognize an assignment." *Appeal of Sec. Ins. Co. of Hartford and Nat'l Amer. Ins. Co.*, ASBCA No. 51,813 (2001) (citing *Mafia v. United States*, 163 F. Supp. 859 (Ct. Cl. 1958). "The precise actions which constitute recognition are unclear, but where 'the Government's course of conduct, its statements to the parties and its dealings with the assignee indicate it acknowledges the assignee as the contractor, recognition has been found.'" *Id.* at 156,089 (citing *Tuftco Corp. v. United States*, 614 F. 2d 740, 745 (Ct. Cl. 1980)).

**Dual obligees** – Not applicable.

## 5. Notice or Filing Required

### *Statutory provisions*

FAR 49.102(b) provides that upon termination for convenience or for default of a contract by the government, the CO "shall simultaneously send the termination notice to the contractor, and a copy to the contract administration office and to any known assignee, guarantor, or surety of the contractor."

### *Case law rules concerning condition precedent notice*

Subdivisions (a)(1)(ii) and (a)(1)(iii) of FAR's default clause, located at FAR 52.249(8)-(10), provide that the government is entitled to default termination when the contractor fails to perform certain provisions of the contract (such as not furnishing a required performance bond). Where termination is predicated on such a failure, FAR 49.402-3(d) requires the contracting officer to give the contractor written notice specifying the failure and providing a period of 10 days (or a longer period as necessary) in which to cure the failure.

If the government fails to provide notice to the surety of the contractor's default, the surety is not necessarily discharged. See *Rowe, Inc. v. Gen. Servs. Admin*, GSBCA No. 14,211 (2001) (failure to notify surety of default on a fixed price delivery contract did not invalidate an otherwise justified default termination).

## 6. Time for Suit

***Statutes of limitation particular to performance bonds and other applicable statutes of limitation***

FAR 33.206 states: "Contractor claims shall be submitted, in writing, to the contracting officer for a decision within 6 years after accrual of a claim, unless the contracting parties agreed to a shorter time period. This 6-year time period does not apply to contracts awarded prior to October 1, 1995. The contracting officer shall document the contract file with evidence of the date of receipt of any submission from the contractor deemed to be a claim by a contracting officer."

FAR 33.211, the Contract Disputes Act, states that an aggrieved contractor has the right to appeal a contracting officer's decision to an agency Board of Contract Appeals within 90 days from the date of receipt of a contracting officer's decision.

FAR 33.211 gives the contractor the right to bring a de novo action in the Court of Federal Claims. This action is in lieu of an appeal to the agency and it must be brought within one year from the date of receipt of the contracting officer's decision.

***Case law statements about enforceability of limitations contained in bonds***

The limitations periods in the Court of Federal Claims and under the Contract Disputes Act are considered jurisdictional requirements attached by Congress as a condition of the government's waiver of sovereign immunity. As such, they must be strictly construed. *See Hopland Band of Pomo Indians v. United States*, 855 F.2d 1573, 1576-77

(Fed. Cir. 1988) (strictly construing six year limitations period in the Claims Court); *Hamza v. United States*, 36 Fed. Cl. 10 (Fed. Cl. 1996) ("Statutes of limitations, such as contained in the CDA, are waiver[s] of sovereign immunity and thus must be strictly construed.") (internal citations omitted).

***Varying statutes of limitation by agreement in bond or contract*** – Not applicable.

**7. Procedure**

***Statutory or procedural rules that may affect handling or administration of lawsuits***

A surety asserting a claim under its right of equitable subrogation and/or the pre-default claims of the contractor should proceed in the Court of Federal Claims under the Tucker Act.

A surety that has entered into a takeover agreement with the government is deemed a "contractor" under the Contract Disputes Act and therefore can proceed in a Board of Contract Appeals for claims arising thereunder.

***Venue requirements and jurisdictional limitations***

FAR 33.211 states that a contractor, after receiving a decision from the CO may either "bring an action directly in the United States Court of Federal Claims," or that the contractor may appeal "to the agency board of contract appeals."

***Court rules*** – Both the Court of Federal Claims and the Armed Services Board of Contract Appeals (ASBCA) each have codified procedural rules.

***Particular agency regulations/rules*** – See court rules above.

***Arbitration requirements and application***

FAR 33.214(c) provides: "ADR procedures may be used at any time that the contracting officer has authority to resolve the issue in controversy. If a claim has been submitted, ADR procedures may be applied to all or a portion of the claim."

## 8. Attorney's Fees

***Statutes and/or case law limiting or permitting recovery of attorney's fees***

5 U.S.C.S. § 504 (2005), the Equal Access to Justice Act, provides that "[a]n agency that conducts an adversary adjudication shall award, to a prevailing party other than the United States, fees and other expenses incurred by that party in connection with that proceeding, unless the adjudicative officer of the agency finds that the position of the agency was substantially justified or that special circumstances make an award unjust. Whether or not the position of the agency was substantially justified shall be determined on the basis of the administrative record, as a whole, which is made in the adversary adjudication for which fees and other expenses are sought."

**9. Special Provisions** – Not applicable.

## 10. Remarks

FAR 52.233(1) defines a claim for the purposes of the Contract Disputes Act (CDA) as a "written demand or written assertion by one of the contracting parties seeking, as a matter of right, the payment of money in a sum certain, the adjustment or interpretation of contract terms, or other relief arising under or relating to [the] contract."

In a recent decision, the ASBCA dismissed an appeal for delay damages for failure to state a claim for a "sum certain." The CDA claim submitted to the CO, and appealed to the ASBCA, demanded payment for delay damages in an amount "no less than $1,072,957.05." The board followed ASBCA precedent in finding that "no less than" does not state a sum certain for CDA purposes. *Appeal of Sandoval Plumbing Repair, Inc.*, ASBCA No. 54,640 (Sept. 14, 2005).

## 11. Case Annotations

***Interpretation of AIA bond forms*** – Not applicable.

***Cases in which surety steps into shoes of obligee***

"Numerous ... decisions by the Federal Circuit ... have clarified that while, under the typical arrangement, the surety owes certain obligations to the government and *vice-versa,* those obligations are not directly contractual in nature, but arise either because the government is a third-party beneficiary of the guaranty between the surety and the primary obligor, or when the surety steps into the shoes either of the contractor or the government under some permutation of the doctrine of equitable subrogation." *American Ins. Co. v. United States*, 62 Fed. Cl. 161, 155 n. 3 (2004).

"[A] performance bond surety is in a favored position when it completes performance of the contract. It steps into the shoes not only of the defaulting contractor but also into the shoes of the Government. In other words, it is equitably subrogated to the rights of the Government to the retained funds. The retained funds are intended to assure completion of the contract. The Government has the right to apply those funds to the completion of the contract and thus, through the equitable subrogation, so does the completing surety." *Appeal of Home Ins. Co.*, 81-1 BCA ¶ 14,884, ASBCA No. 22,898 (1980).

"A surety can establish a right of subrogation in either of two ways: by completing the contract pursuant to its obligation under the performance bond or by paying off materialmen's claims brought under the payment bond. In the first situation - where the surety completes the contract - it steps into the shoes of the Government." *Transamerica Premier Ins. Co. v. United States*, 32 Fed. Cl. 308 (1994).

# FLORIDA

Amy L. Fischer[1]

## 1. Requirement for Bond

***Statutory provisions for projects that are:***

**Public** – Florida has statutes requiring public performance bonds, as well as sessions laws creating limited exemptions from bonding requirements for specific types of projects:

*Florida's "Little Miller Act"* – Fla. Stat. § 255.05 (1)(a) requires the posting of payment and performance bonds for the construction of public projects. State contracts for work for less than $100,000 require no bonds. *Id.* At the discretion of the official board awarding contracts for work done for any county, city, political subdivision or public authority, any person entering into a contract for less than $200,000 may be exempted from executing payment and performance bonds. *Id.* When the work is done for the state, the Secretary of Department of Management Services may delegate to the state agencies the authority to exempt contractors entering into contracts amounting to more than $100,000, but less than $200,000 from the obligation to post payment and performance bonds. *Id.* If the exemption is granted, officers or officials are expressly

1 Amy L. Fischer is a member of:
The Cunningham Law Firm, P.A.
400 Australian Avenue South
West Palm Beach, Florida 33401
(561) 833-6400

exempted from personal liability to a person suffering loss because of granting the exemptions. *Id.*

In lieu of a bond, the contractor may file with the political authority "an alternative form of security in the form of cash, a money order, a certified check, a cashier's check, an irrevocable letter of credit or a security of the type listed in part II of chapter 625." Fla. Stat. § 255.05 (7).

Florida has a permissive statutory bond form. Fla. Stat. § 255.05 (3). The payment bond, however, must specifically reference the statutory notice and time limitations. Fla. Stat. § 255.05 (6). Bond language that conflicts with statutory requirements is disregarded unless the language affords coverage greater than that required by statute. If the bond offers greater coverage than required by statute, the more expansive language of the bond controls. *National Fire Ins. Co. of Hartford v. L.J. Clark Constr. Co., Inc.*, 579 So. 2d 743 (Fla. Dist. Ct. App. 1991).

A bond that provides coverage greater than that required by statute becomes a common law bond, subject to a five year statute of limitations period, as opposed to the one year limitation specified in Fla. Stat. § 255.05. *Florida Keys Cmty. Coll. v. Insurance Co. of N. Am.*, 456 So. 2d 1250 (Fla. Dist. Ct. App. 1984).

In resolving issues of first impression in interpreting § 255.05, Florida courts will look to federal court's interpretation of the Miller Act for guidance. *Board of Pub. Instruction, Broward County, Fla. v. Rood Const. Co.,* 166 So. 2d 701, 702 (Fla. Dist. Ct. App. 1964) (Florida's "Little Miller Act" is based on federal Miller Act).

*Other Public Works Bonds* – Fla. Stat. § 153.79 requires a bond for the "full and faithful performance" of a contract for "the construction, reconstruction or acquisition or improvement of a *water system or a sewer system* both or any part thereof…." (emphasis added). Contracts under $1,000 need not be publicly bid. *Id.*

Fla. Stat. § 157.04 specifies that the board of county commissioners contracting for the construction of any *ditch, drain or canal* shall require a bond payable to the governor for the construction and completion of the work according to the terms of the contract.

Fla. Stat. § 157.21 and .22 provide that the person whose bid is accepted for a contract entered into by a board of county commissioners to *enlarge or deepen any drain* shall post "a good an sufficient bond for the faithful performance of said contract…" and for contracts to *repair any public drain*, the contractor shall post "a sufficient bond…for the faithful performance of said work…"

Fla. Stat. § 180.24(1) requires the posting of bonds for contracts issued by a municipality for the construction of *utilities*.

Fla. Stat. § 1010.07(2) requires that "*Contractors paid from school district, community college, or university funds* shall give bond for the faithful performance of their contracts in such amount and for such purposes as prescribed by s. 255.05 or by the rule of the State Board of Education…. It shall be the duty of the school board to require from every contractor a bond adequate to protect the school and school funds involved." (emphasis added)

Fla. Stat. § 1037.47 requires contractors building *educational facilities* to furnish the school board with payment and performance bonds as set forth in Fla. Stat. § 255.05.

Fla. Stat. § 489.145(5)(c), Florida's "Guaranteed Energy Performance Savings Contracting Act," provides that for contracts entered into by the state, a municipality, or a political subdivision for the "evaluation, recommendation, and implementation of *energy conservation measures*," (emphasis added) the contractor shall provide "a 100-percent public construction bond to the agency for its faithful performance, as required by Fla. Stat. § 255.05."

*Acceptable Sureties for Public Bonds* – Fla. Stat. § 287.0935 provides that when a project does not exceed $500,000 and public funds are used, the person or political entity shall not reject bonds issued by a surety satisfying five criteria: (1) the surety is licensed to do business in state; (2) the surety holds a certificate authorizing it to write bonds in state; (3) the surety has twice the minimum surplus and capital required by the Florida Insurance Code when the invitation to bid is issued; (4) the surety otherwise complies with the Florida Insurance Code; and (5) the surety holds a certificate of authority issued by the U.S. Department of Treasury.

*Limited Exemptions* – Hillsborough County may waive the bond requirements for public works costing less than $500,000 awarded pursuant to "a race and gender neutral economic development program for encouraging local small businesses" that has been adopted by county ordinance or resolution. H.B. 785 Ch. No. 414, Laws of 2004 (effective Oct. 1, 2004, and expiring on Sept. 30, 2009).

*Waiver of Sovereign Immunity for Lack of Bonds* – A governmental entity's failure to procure the required bonds for a public works project may render the public entity liable for losses due to the lack of a statutory bond. *See, e.g., Palm Beach Co. v. Trinity Indus., Inc.* 661 So. 2d 942 (Fla. Dist. Ct. App. 1995) (county that failed to require contractor to obtain statutory payment bond was liable to unpaid subcontractor upon contractor's insolvency); *Warren v. Glen Falls Indem. Co. of Glen Falls, N.Y.*, 66 So. 2d 54 (Fla. 1953) (school board members had mandatory statutory duty to confirm that required statutory bond was posted and failure to do so resulted in individual liability for board members).

**Quasi-Public** – Fla. Stat. § 944.712 requires that if any bidder submits a proposal to the Department of Corrections for a contract that involves the construction of a "*private correctional facility*" and "if the state is required to make payments for construction prior to the completion of construction, the contract shall contain a construction performance bond...."

**Private** – No statutes in Florida require performance bonds on private projects; however, Fla. Stat. § 713.24 allows for the transfer of liens on private projects to a bond.

**Department of Transportation** – Fla. Stat. *§* 337.18 requires bonds for *transportation projects*, with all bonds "payable to the department and conditioned for the prompt, faithful, and efficient performance of the contract according to plans and specifications, and for the prompt payment of all persons defined in s. 713.01 furnishing labor, material, equipment and supplies for the work...." Fla. Stat. *§* 337.18(1)(a). The Florida Department of Transportation can waive the bond requirement for contracts of $150,000 or less if it determines "the project is of a noncritical nature and nonperformance will not endanger public health, safety, or property." *Id.* The department may require alternative means of security if a surety bond is waived. If the contract is $25,000 or less, the bidder may at its discretion post security in the form of a cashier's check, bank money order or state national bank or postal money order.

Fla. Stat. § 337.105(2) provides:

> For any *contractual service*, except a contractual service provided to the department under s. 287.055, the department [of transportation]

> may require a performance bond equal to the full contract value if such requirement is deemed to be in the best interest of the state. (emphasis added)

***Case law rules that might generally apply***

"A surety on a bond does not undertake to do more than that expressed in the bond, and has the right to stand upon the strict terms of the obligation as to his liability hereon." *American Home Assurance Co. v. Larkin Gen. Hosp., Ltd.*, 593 So. 2d 195, 198 (Fla. 1992) (citing *Crabtree v. Aetna Cas. & Sur. Co.,* 438 So. 2d 102, 105 (Fla. Dist. Ct. App. 1983)).

Statutes control the scope regardless of language in the bond which purports to limit the surety's liability or expand its performance options beyond what is permitted by the express terms of the statute. *Florida Keys Comm. Coll. v. Ins. Co. of North America,* 456 So. 2d 1250 (Fla. Dist. Ct. App. 1984).

When a surety executes a bond in compliance with or for the purpose of fulfilling statutory bond requirement, the surety will be liable for conditions provided by statute. *W.F. Thompson Const. Co. v. Southeastern Palm Beach County Hosp. Dist.,* 174 So. 2d 410 (Fla. Dist. Ct. App. 1965).

The words used in an insurance contract should be given their common meaning. *Deni Assoc. of Florida v. State Farm Fire & Cas. Co.,* 711 So. 2d 1135 (Fla. 1998). Likewise, words used in a bond should be given their common, literal meaning. *Daubmyre v. Hunter,* 144 So. 2d 408 (Fla. 1932).

The party against whom a bond is construed depends on whether the surety was compensated:

> The rule of construction of a contract of suretyship depends on whether the surety is acting gratuitously or for hire. In the former case, the surety is entitled to a strict construction of the contract in his favor, as a surety is "a favorite of the law."... The rule is otherwise as to sureties who receive compensation;... their contracts are regarded as analogous to contracts of insurance, and are to be *strictly construed against the surety and in favor of the obligee....* (emphasis added)

28 Fla. Jur. 2d § 62 "Guaranty and Suretyship," at p.291.

"The maximum that sureties are favored in the law has no application to contracts of suretyship made by licensed surety companies in the business of suretyship for hire." 28 Fla. Jur. 2d § 62, citing *Tapping v. McIntosh*, 104 Fla. 715, 140 So. 2d 773 (1932); *Ruwitch v. First Nat. Bank of Miami*, 291 So. 2d 650 (Fla. Dist. Ct. App. 1974), appeal after remand , 327 So. 2d 833 (Fla. Dist. Ct. App. 1976); *Phoenix Indem. Co. v. Board of Public Instruction of Alachua County*, 114 So. 2d 478 (Fla. Dist. Ct. App. 1959).

"Florida's policy is to construe any ambiguity in a bond 'in favor of granting the broadest possible coverage to those intended to be benefited by the protection of the bond.'" *School Board of Broward County, Florida v. The Great American Ins. Co.,* 807 So. 2d 750, 752 (Fla. Dist. Ct. App. 2002) (citing *National Fire Ins. Co. of Hartford v. L.J. Clark Constr. Co., Inc.*, 579 So. 2d 743, 745 (Fla. Dist. Ct. App. 1991) and *General Ins. Co. of America v. Sentry Indem. Co.*, 384 So. 2d 1305, 1306 (Fla. Dist. Ct. App. 1980)).

Under Florida law, contracts of compensated sureties, like insurance contracts, are strictly construed against the insurer/surety and in favor of the obligee. *Gulf Power Co. v. Ins. Co. of North* America, 445 So. 2d 1141 (Fla. Dist. Ct. App. 1984); *Travelers Indemn. Co. v. R.B. Mercer*, 250 So. 2d 283 (Fla. Dist. Ct. App. 1971).

## 2. Damages Covered

***Set forth in any statutes and/or case law***

**Delay Damages** – A surety may be liable for consequential damages by virtue of its failure to perform according to the terms of its performance bond; however, a surety will not be liable for consequential damages arising solely from the principal's default, where the surety assumes no such obligation under the express terms of the bond. *American Home Assurance Co. v. Larkin Gen. Hosp. Ltd.*, 593 So. 2d 195 (Fla. 1992). Thus, if the bond does not expressly state that the surety shall be liable for delay damages, the court shall not expand the liability of the surety to encompass such types of damages. *Id.; see also Mycon Constr. Corp. v. Board of Regents of the State,* 755 So. 2d 154 (Fla. Dist. Ct. App. 2000) (surety was not liable under its bond for damages associated with relocating students during repairs to defectively constructed dormitories as bond made surety liable only for cost of completion less balance of contract sum and contained no provision for delay damages).

An obligee cannot recover liquidated damages for delays for which it was solely responsible. *Mid-State Hauling Co. v. Watson,* 172 So. 2d 262 (Fla. Dist. Ct. App. 1965). Where both the obligee and the principal have contributed to the delays in the construction, the obligee is not entitled to recover liquidated damages, but retains the right to recover its actual delay damages. *Id.*

Assuming the bond expressly covers delay or liquidated damages, the claim may still be subject to challenge based on the unenforceability of the underlying provision. Parties to a contract may stipulate in advance an amount of damages to be paid in the event of a breach by the other party. *See, e.g., Lefemine v. Baron*, 573 So. 2d 326 (Fla. 1991). Generally, a liquidated damage provision in a contract will be enforceable if two conditions are met: (1) the extent of damages flowing from a breach must be difficult or impossible to ascertain at the time the contract was entered into; and (2) the stipulated sum must bear a reasonable relationship to damages that might reasonably be expected to flow from the breach of contract and not intended to be a penalty. *Hyman v. Cohen,* 73 So. 2d 393 (Fla. 1954).

**Latent Defects** – Claims for latent defects are considered part of the bond obligations of the surety. *Federal Ins. Co. v. Southwest Retirement Ctr., Inc.*, 707 So. 2d 1129 (Fla. 1998) (declining to extend *Larkin* to latent defect claims). The statute of limitations for latent defects is five years, beginning to accrue on the date of acceptance of the project. *Id.*

**Bad Faith** – By recent amendment to Florida's Insurance Code, sureties were removed as potential defendants to statutory bad faith actions:

> A surety issuing a payment or performance bond on the construction or maintenance of a building or roadway project is not an insurer for purposes of subsection (1).

Fla. Stat. *§* 624.155(9); Laws 2005, c. 2005-218, § 2, eff. June 14, 2005.

***Obligations of surety to perform and/or pay***

The surety's performance options are strictly limited to those specified in the bond. Thus, if a bond does not specify tender as an option, the surety is obligated to perform:

> [Surety's] tender of a new contractor did not "correct" [the contractor's] default under the performance bond. The interpretation of the bond language urged by [the surety] would narrow the scope of coverage by allowing it to substitute a new contractor and surety for full performance under the contract. To accept [the surety's] tender, the [obligee] would have had to give up its right to insist on performance by [the surety] under the bond. The condition of the bond was [the contractor's] *full* performance.... [The surety] did not "correct" [the contractor's default] by tendering only a new deal.

*School Board of Broward County, Florida v. The Great American Ins. Co.,* 807 So. 2d 750, 751-2 (Fla. Dist. Ct. App. 2002) (emphasis in original).

***Whether failure to provide insurance transfers burden to surety*** – Statutes do not transfer the burden to surety.

***Limitations on damages***

"Florida courts have long recognized that the liability of a surety should not be extended by implication beyond the terms of the contract, i.e., the performance bond.... ' [a] surety on a bond does not undertake to do more than that expressed in the bond, and has the right to stand upon the strict terms of the obligation as to his liability hereon.'" *American Home Assurance Co. v. Larkin Gen. Hosp., Ltd.*, 593 So. 2d 195, 198 (Fla. 1992) (citing *Crabtree v. Aetna Cas. & Sur. Co.,* 438 So. 2d 102, 105 (Fla. Dist. Ct. App. 1983)).

"If the creditor releases the debtor from performance of his obligation, the surety is also released, although this may not have been the creditor's intention." *Baker v. Peddie*, 467 So. 2d 821, 823 (Fla. 1st DCA 1985).

"The liability of the surety is ordinarily measured by the liability of the principal ... and generally the surety is not liable if the principal is not liable." *Cincinnati Ins. Co. v. Putnam*, 335 So. 2d 855, 856 (Fla. 4th DCA 1976).

***Whether obligee may set off bonded contract funds against other principal-obligee debts or obligations***

To the extent an indemnity agreement assigns contract funds on bonded and unbonded contracts, sureties have recovered contract funds from the contract on which they did not have a loss by invoking their assignment rights. *Logan v. Aetna Cas. & Sur. Co.*, 208 So. 2d 131 (Fla. 1968).

***Incorporation of specific contract terms by reference***

Certain types of provisions in a general contract will be deemed incorporated by reference into the performance bond, and others not.

*Provisions Not Incorporated* – A liquidated damages for delay provision will not be read into the bond. *American Home Assurance Co. v. Larkin Gen. Hosp., Ltd.*, 593 So. 2d 195 (Fla. 1992).

*Provisions that May be Incorporated* – Warranties for the work are deemed incorporated by reference. *Federal Ins. Co. v. Southwest Fla. Retirement Ctr., Inc.*, 707 So. 2d 1119 (Fla. 1998). Arbitration provisions in the underlying general contract are also read as part of the bond. *St. Paul Fire & Marine Ins. Co. v. Woolley/Sweeney Hotel No. 5*, 545 So. 2d 958 (Fla. Dist. Ct. App. 1989). A prevailing party attorney's fees provision may be deemed incorporated into the bond. *Merchants Bonding Co. v. City of Melbourne*, 832 So. 2d 184, 186 (Fla. Dist. Ct. App. 2002) (acknowledging incorporation of fee provision from underlying contract, but denying surety's fee claim as both contracting parties were at fault, and thus court awarded no party fees; however, city failed to preserve objection to incorporation of fees as issue for appeal).

### 3. Penal Sum Variations

***Limitations per statute*** – Florida does not have statutory limitations on performance bond penal sums for public works or private projects.[2]

***Effect of changes in work upon penal sum, if at all***

The surety is afforded a *pro tanto* discharge of liability to the extent that its security is compromised. *Gibbs v. Hartford Acc. & Indem. Co.*, 62 So. 2d 599 (Fla. 1953). Thus, if the obligee overpays for the work in place so as to reduce the contract balance remaining on the primary obligation, the surety may be prejudiced to the extent of the overpayment and concomitant reduction in its collateral, the contract balance remaining.

***Statutory or case law protections or dangers to penal sum***

The general rule is that recovery on a bond is limited by the amount of the bond with interest from date of breach; however, an exception to the general rule, limiting recovery arises in those instances where the bond or statute pursuant to which the bond is issued indicates its intention to extend liability of the bond beyond the penal sum. *Travelers Indem. Co. v. Askew*, 280 So. 2d 469 (Fla. Dist. Ct. App. 1973).

While ordinarily a surety's liability may not exceed the penal sum of the bond, where a surety's own misconduct causes damages to exceed the bond amount, the surety may be liable for such excess amounts. *Nichols v. Preferred Nat'l Ins. Co.*, 704 So. 2d 1371 (Fla. 1997).

A surety may be held liable for attorney's fees in excess of the penal sum of the bond, even absent a showing of misconduct. *David Boland, Inc. v. Trans Coastal Roofing Co.*, 851 So. 2d 724 (Fla. 2003).[3]

---

2 Licensing bonds that counties may require in conjunction with regulating different construction disciplines are limited by statute; however, this topic is beyond the scope of this paper.

3 The Florida Supreme Court answered the following certified question, an issue of first impression, in the affirmative:

> Does Florida Statute § 627.428 authorize recovery of attorney's fees in excess of a performance bond's face amount from a

## 4. Parties Covered

### ***Statutes and/or case law as to whether only obligees are covered***

*Common Law Bonds* – Who is entitled to recover under a common law bond is a function of the language of the bond. A common law bond provided on a public works project in Florida provides expanded coverage for claimants on public works projects beyond the coverage specified by Fla. Stat. § 255.05. Its purpose is to provide protection that exceeds the minimum obligations imposed by statute. As parties have the ability to contract freely, the issue of which parties are protected by a common law bond will depend upon the intention of the parties and which parties are expressly included in the language of the bond.

### ***Coverage for:***

**Third-party beneficiaries** – Claimants other than the named obligee have asserted a right of action against the bond as third-party beneficiary, or as assignees or subrogees of the obligee. In general, such claims have met with limited success when the performance bond disclaims any benefit to third-parties. *Aetna Ins. Co. v. Estero Mfg. & Bldg Supply, Inc.* 174 So. 2d 747 (Fla. Dist. Ct. App. 1965).

Generally, a surety has no liability to the owner of the construction project by virtue of issuing a subcontract performance bond as such bonds typically contain clauses limiting the right to recovery to the named obligee or its successors. *Pierce Assocs. v. Nemours Found.,* 865 F. 2d 530 (3d Cir. 1988). Florida, however, has allowed such claims for intended beneficiaries. *Crabtree v. Aetna Cas. & Sur. Co.,* 438 So. 2d 102 (Fla. Dist. Ct. App. 1983).

A performance bond surety of a defaulted principal is equitably subrogated to its principal's claims against subcontractor's performance bonds. *Argonaut Ins. Co. v. Commercial Standard Ins. Co.*, 380 So. 2d 1066 (Fla. Dist. Ct. App. 1980)

---

subcontractor's surety, when the fees claimant has not shown independent misconduct on the party of the surety?

*Id.* at 725.

**Assignees** – A successor owner cannot be the third-party beneficiary of a performance bond if the successor entity did not exist at the time the construction contract was executed and bond secured. *Beachpoint Condo. Ass'n v. Beachpoint Corp.* 480 So. 2d 239 (Fla. Dist. Ct. App. 1985) (condominium association was not third party beneficiary on bond secured by general contractor in favor of original owner-developer of condominium, even if association's creation may have been foreseen, it appears that the association was not even in existence at the time the construction contract was executed and the bond secured).

**Dual obligees** – The insertion of additional obligees should not alter the basic principles of suretyship; in the absence of a default by the principal, the surety will have no obligation to the dual obligee. *Atlantic Nat'l Bank v. Modular Age, Inc.,* 363 So. 2d 1152 (Fla. Dist. Ct. App. 1978).

## 5. Notice or Filing Required

***Statutory provisions*** – Florida statutes do not provide for any unusual notice requirements for suit under a performance bond.

***Case law rules concerning condition precedent notice***

Actual damage resulting from failure to give notice must be pleaded and proved as a defense, and failure to give a compensated surety notice of a principal's default as required in the bond does not relieve surety where failure results in no loss to it. *Carnival Cruise Lines, Inc. v. Financial Indem. Co.*, 347 So. 2d 825 (Fla. Dist. Ct. App. 1977); *American Fire & Cas. Co. v. Collura*, 163 So. 2d 784 (Fla. Dist. Ct. App. 1964); *Maule Indus., Inc. v. Gaines Constr. Co.*, 157 So. 2d 835 (Fla. Dist. Ct. App. 1963).

The failure to give the bond-specified notices before proceeding to correct the defective work may prejudice the surety by denying the surety the opportunity to investigate the claim and cure the default. *See, e.g., Insurance Co. of North America v. Metropolitan Dade County, Florida*, 705 So. 2d 33 (Fla. Dist. Ct. App. 1998) (public owner's failure to comply with common law bond notice requirements "stripped" surety of its bargained for right to notice and thus relieved surety of all liability under performance bond); *School Board of Escambia County, Inc. v. TIG*

*Premier Ins.* Co., 110 F. Supp. 2d 1351 (N.D. Fla. 2000) (granting motion for summary judgment in favor of surety based upon obligee's failure to give notice to surety and its unilateral completion of bonded contracts).

The obligation to terminate the contractor will not be construed as a condition precedent to the surety's obligation to perform unless his condition is set forth as a condition in the bond. *See DCC Constructors, Inc. v. Randall Mech., Inc.,* 791 So. 2d 575 (Fla. Dist. Ct. App. 2001) (summary judgment for surety reversed as bond did not require termination as condition precedent and underlying contract specified termination as one option upon default).

### 6. Time for Suit

***Statutes of limitation particular to performance bonds and other applicable statutes of limitation***

Fla. Stat. § 255.05 provides that for a statutory form of bond "no action shall be instituted against the contractor or the surety on the payment bond or the payment provisions of a combined payment and performance bond after one year from the performance of the labor or completion of delivery of the materials or supplies."

On non-public projects, *Fla. St.* § 713.23(e) provides "no action shall be instituted or prosecuted against the contractor or against the surety on the bond under this section after one year from the performance of the labor or completion of delivery of materials and supplies." The one year statute of limitations for actions against the surety bond begins when a certificate of substantial completion is issued and the owner accepts the constructed building.

The suit limitation applicable to common law bonds is the statute of limitations applicable to breach of contract claims, *i.e.,* the five year period under Fla. Stat. § 95.11(2)(b), with the statute of limitations starting to run from the date the project was accepted. *Federal Ins. Co. v. Southwest Retirement Ctr.*, 707 So. 2d 1119 (Fla. 1998).

An action against a surety for breach of the performance bond accrues when the construction project is completed and accepted; thus, the period for bringing a performance bond claim is not extended by couching the claim in terms of an action for indemnification. *Clark Constr. Group, Inc. v. Wentworth Plastering of Boca Raton, Inc.*, 840 So.

2d 357 (Fla. Dist. Ct. App. 2003). In *Clark Construction,* the contractor asserted that the subcontractor's performance bond was one for indemnity and that the statute of limitations did not begin to run until it was sued by the owner for defects in the subcontractor's work. In rejecting this argument, the *Clark Construction* court reasoned that even if "the language of the bond and the subcontract impose separate and distinct indemnity obligations, this did not alter the fact that the [general contractor's] claim against [the subcontractor's performance bond] is still one for breach of a performance bond" that is subject to a five year statute of limitations running from the date of the completion of the work. *Id.* at 359.

***Case law statements about enforceability of limitations contained in bonds***

Statutory bonds for contracts with public authorities for the construction of public buildings limit the time within which to bring an action against the surety to one year from the performance of the labor or completion of delivery of the materials or supplies. Fla. Stat. § 255.05(2). Provided the bond does not expand the payment provisions or class of claimants protected, a surety may rely on this shorter statutory limitation. *National Fire Ins. v. L.J. Clark Constr. Co., Inc.*, 579 So. 2d 743, 745-46 (Fla. Dist. Ct. App. 1991). Where the bond has coverage that is more expansive than that specified in the statute, however, it becomes a common law bond governed by the five year statute of limitations. *Id.*

A contractor's performance bond would remain in effect for one year after the effective date of completion of the construction contract, where the one year statute of limitations applied to contractor's surety under Fla. Stat. § 255.05. *Logan v. Aetna Cas. & Sur. Co.,* 208 So. 2d 131 (Fla. Dist. Ct. App. 1968).

***Varying statute of limitations by agreement in bond or contract*** – Contract provisions shorting statutes of limitation are void. Fla. Stat. §95.03.

## 7. Procedure

***Statutory or procedural rules that may affect handling or administration of lawsuits***

**Default Judgments or Awards** – Judgments or arbitration awards entered by default are generally regarded as having little probative value as to whether or not the principal breached the bond condition. Thus, the imposition or extent of the preclusive effect of a default adjudication against the principal is restricted to the *prima facie* or rebuttable presumption level. *Heritage Ins. Co. of Am. v. Foster Elec. Co.,* 393 So. 2d 28 (Fla. Dist. Ct. App. 1981).

***Venue requirements and jurisdictional limitations***

Any actions under a public works bond may be brought in the county in which the public building or public work is being constructed or repaired. Fla. Stat. § 255.05(5).

Motion to dismiss for *forum non conveniens* should be supported by affidavit or other evidence offered under oath; the "only exception would be where the complaint itself shows on its face that a *forum non conveniens* transfer is warranted." *Ground Improv. Tech. v. Merchants Bonding*, 707 So. 2d 1138, 1139 (Fla. Dist. Ct. App. 1998).

"Under the *forum non conveniens* statute [Fla. Stat. § 47.11], a plaintiff's forum selection is presumptively correct and the burden is on the defendant to show either substantial inconvenience or that the undue expense requires change for the convenience of the parties or witnesses." *Eggers v. Eggers*, 776 So. 2d 1096, 1098 (Fla. Dist. Ct. App. 2001).

***Court rules*** – Not applicable.

***Particular agency regulations/rules*** – Not applicable.

***Arbitration requirements and application*** – In general, Fla. Stat. Ch. 682, the Florida Arbitration Code.

**Surety's Obligation to Arbitrate** – Florida has a strong public policy favoring arbitration. *Roe v. Amica Mut. Ins. Co.,* 533 So. 2d 279 (Fla. 1988). Thus, sureties have been compelled to arbitrate when the contract of the principal that is incorporated by reference into the bond requires arbitration. *St. Paul Fire & Marine Ins. Co. v. Woolley/Sweeney Hotel No. 5*, 545 So. 2d 958 (Fla. Dist. Ct. App. 1989). By issuing a performance bond which incorporates a contract with an arbitration clause, the surety is deemed to have voluntarily agreed to arbitrate disputes consistent with that incorporated clause. Conversely, the surety can compel the obligee to arbitrate. *Henderson Inv. Corp. v. International Fid. Ins. Co.*, 575 So. 2d 770 (Fla. Dist. Ct. App. 1991).

**Determination of Attorney's Fees Incurred in Arbitration** – "Unless otherwise provided in the agreement or provision for arbitration, the arbitrators' and umpire's expenses and fees, together with other expenses, not including counsel fees, incurred in the conduct of the arbitration, shall be paid as provided in the award." Fla. Stat. § 682.11

Fla. Stat. § 682.11 has been read as designating the court as vested with jurisdiction to award attorney's fees. Neither entitlement to attorney's fees nor amount are issues that an arbitrator may decide without the agreement of the parties. *A-1 Duran Roofing, Inc. v. Select Contracting, Inc.*, 865 So. 2d 601 (Fla. Dist. Ct. App. 2004) (if arbitrator fails to state basis for award or record is insufficient to determine basis upon which party prevailed, trial court should remand matter back to arbitrator for explanation of basis for recovery). The circuit court, which would otherwise be the court of proper jurisdiction pursuant to Fla. Stat.§§ 34.01(c) and 26.012(2)(a), is deemed the proper forum to determine fees and costs incurred in an arbitration and determines the fee issue in accord with the findings of the arbitrators as to the claim. *Moser v. Barron Chase Sec., Inc.*, 783 So. 2d 231 (Fla. 2001).

Parties are not required to prepare separate written agreement explicitly waiving right to have the circuit court determine attorney fees in connection with arbitration proceedings; parties may, by their actions, filings, and submissions, expressly waive their right to insist that only a court decide the issue of fees. *Cassedy v. Merrill, Lynch, Pierce, Fenner & Smith, Inc.*, 751 So. 2d 143 (Fla. Dist. Ct. App. 2000); *see also Robert Gay Const. Co. v. CECO Bldg. Systems,* 680 So. 2d 1124 (Fla. Dist. Ct. App. 1996) (submission of prevailing party issue to arbitrator waived right to have prevailing party determined by circuit court and therefore deprived circuit court of authority to award attorney fees to supplier in confirming arbitration award).

The court has exclusive jurisdiction to resolve factual issue of whether parties to arbitration have waived their statutory right to have the circuit court decide the issue of attorney's fees. *Dean Witter Reynolds, Inc. v. Wood*, 676 So. 2d 464 (Fla. Dist. Ct. App. 1996).

**Determination of Coverage** – The existence of insurance coverage is a question for the court, not one for arbitration. *State Farm Fire & Cas. Co. v. Glass,* 421 So. 2d 759, 760 (Fla. Dist. Ct. App. 1982); *see also State Farm Fire and Cas. Co. v. Licea*, 685 So. 2d 1285, 1287-88 (Fla. 1996) (when insurance policy provides for appraisal procedure, only "defense" that remains for insurer is no coverage under policy for loss as whole or violation of usual policy conditions such as fraud, lack of notice, and failure to cooperate; coverage is "exclusively a *judicial question...")* (emphasis added). Under the Florida Insurance Code, an "insurer" includes a "surety." Fla. Stat. § 624.03; *David Boland, Inc. v. Trans Coastal Roofing Co.*, 851 So. 2d 724, 726 n. 1 (Fla. 2003). Thus, this "insurance coverage exception" to arbitration could be read to extend to bond coverage disputes.

**Preclusive Effect of Arbitration** – For preclusion purposes, courts generally treat confirmed arbitration awards as they would any other court judgment and apply the same preclusion analysis as would be applied to judgments, according arbitration awards the same binding effect as judgments. In *Von Egg's Co. v. R. W. Roberts Const. Co.*, 457 So. 2d 1080, 1082 (Fla. Dist. Ct. App. 1984), the court bound the surety to an arbitration award in favor of a payment bond claimant and against the principal because "when a surety has notice of a suit against the principal and is afforded an opportunity to appear and defend, a judgment...is conclusive against the surety as to all material questions therein determined." If the surety did not have notice and an opportunity to defend, a judgment against the principal would constitute only *prima facie* evidence of the surety's liability. *Id.*

## 8. Attorney's Fees

***Statutes and/or case law limiting or permitting recovery of attorney's fees***

Attorney's fees are recoverable by a successful claimant against a surety pursuant to *Fla Stat.* § 627.428, which permits recovery of attorney's fees by any party prevailing against an insurance company.

A surety may be entitled to the award of prevailing party's attorney's fees if the underlying contract provides for such an award and the principal prevails in the underlying action; however, if the surety prevails based on a suretyship defense, "then its surety status as to [the contractor] would have vanished along with any right to claim under its principal's contract with the [obligee]." *Merchants Bonding Co. v. City of Melbourne*, 832 So. 2d 184, 186 (Fla. Dist. Ct. App. 2002).

Fla. Stat.§ 255.05(2)(a) also provides for the recovery of attorney's fees by the prevailing party in an action on the payment bond.

Fla. Stat.§ 337.18(1) (d) provides for the recovery of reasonable attorney's fees for trial and appeal or arbitration by the prevailing party on a payment bond action involving a contract with the Department of Transportation.

A claimant may recover attorney's fees in excess of the penal sum of the bond as Fla. Stat. § 627.428 does not limit the recovery of fees to the penal sum. *David Boland, Inc. v. Trans Coastal Roofing Co.*, 851 So. 2d 724 (Fla. 2003).

Florida's "prevailing party" test does not apply to the award of statutory fees against an insurer/surety:

> Under [Fla. Stat. § 627.428 and 627.756], an insured or beneficiary who prevails is entitled to attorney's fees. The statute offers no similar prospect to the surety, nor does the statute say that the fees will be unavailable if the surety prevails on some but not all of the issues .... [t]he trial court, in determining the fee award, may take into account the fact that the insured or beneficiary has not prevailed on all issues and the degree to which this has extended the litigation or increased its costs. Likewise, ... a "prevailing insured or beneficiary" is one who has obtained a judgment greater than any offer of settlement previously tendered by the insurer.... Absent that, the insured or beneficiary is entitled to no fee award.

*Danis Industries Corp. v. Ground Improvement Technologies, Inc.*, 645 So. 2d 420, 421 (Fla. 1994).

***What fees are recoverable, if any***

An offer of settlement in excess of recovery cuts off the accrual of fees under Fla. Stat. § 627.428, but does not preclude the recovery of fees up to the offer. *Scottsdale Ins. Co. v. DeSalvo*, 748 So. 2d 941 (Fla. 1999) ("the failure to recover more than an offer of settlement does not mean that an insured that is awarded some recovery is precluded from being awarded any portion of their attorney's fees and costs."):

> [T]he trial judge is to determine reasonable attorney fees, costs and prejudgment interest through the date of the first offer of settlement which exceeds the recovery amount, including the damage award and the attorney fees, costs, and interest the insured would have received if the insured had accepted that offer of settlement on the date it was made. The insured would be then entitled to a judgment which would include the insurance or surety amount determined in the trial to be owed by the insurer plus the attorney fees, costs, and prejudgment interest determined to have been incurred through the date of the first offer of settlement which exceeds the recovery amount.

*Id.* at 943.[4]

---

[4] By way of illustration, the Florida Supreme Court offered a hypothetical:

(1) The period for settling claims made upon a policy or bond expires August 1.
(2) Insurer serves offer of settlement in the amount of $20,000 on December 1, and the offer is rejected.
(3) On February 1, a judicial determination is made that the insurer owes $10,000 on the policy or bond.
(4) The trial judge is then to calculate the attorney fees, costs, and prejudgment interest which had accrued as of December 1, the date of the offer of settlement.
(5) If the sum of (4) above plus the $10,000 determined to be owed in (3) and (4) exceeds $20,000, then the insured is entitled to the sum of (3) and (4) plus attorney fees, costs and prejudgment interest through the date judgment is entered following the determination of the amount determined in (3).

*Id.* at 943 n. 3.

**9. Special Provisions** – Not applicable.

**10. Remarks** – Not applicable.

**11. Case Annotations**

***Interpretation of AIA bond forms***

AIA Document A311 requires that suit be brought within two years after the contractor defaults, ceases working, or within two years after the surety refuses or fails to perform its obligations under the bond, whichever occurs first. Florida is among the many states that nullify such provisions. Any provision in a contract that shortens the applicable statute of limitations is void. Fla. Stat. § 95.03; *see also National Fire Ins. v. L.J. Clark Constr. Co., Inc.*, 579 So. 2d 743 (Fla. Dist. Ct. App. 1991). The applicable statute of limitations in Florida for a common law bond is the five year limitation in § 95.11(2)(b).

***Cases in which surety steps into shoes of obligee***

A surety is subrogated to all the rights of its principal under principles of equitable subrogation. *TransAmerica Ins. Co. v. Barnett Bank of Marion Co.,* 540 So. 2d 113 (Fla. 1989).

The liability of the surety is coextensive with that of its principal. *A.M. Crabtree v. Aetna Casualty & Surety Co.*, 438 So. 2d 102 (Fla. Dist. Ct. App. 1983). However, a "surety on a bond does not undertake to do more than that expressed in the bond, and has the right to stand upon the strict terms of the obligation as to his liability hereon." *American Home Assurance Co. v. Larkin Gen. Hosp., Ltd.*, 593 So. 2d 195, 198 (Fla. 1992).

The surety stands in the shoes of the general contractor and can assert any defense available to the contractor. *C.A. Oakes Const. Co., Inc. v. Ajax Paving Indust., Inc.,* 652 So. 2d 914, 916 (Fla. Dist. Ct. App. 1995).[5]

---

[5] Not all of the contractor's defenses are available to the surety. For example, a surety cannot avail itself of a paid-when-paid-clause as a defense to a payment bond claim unless the payment bond itself conditions payment on payment by the owner. *OBS Co., Inc. v. Pace Constr. Corp., Inc.,* 404 So.

2d 558 (Fla. 1990). Fla. Stat. § 713.245 dictates the required form for a "conditional payment" bond.

# GEORGIA

DeWitte Thompson and Cheryl Kniffen[1]

## 1. Requirement for Bond

***Statutory provisions for projects that are:***

**Public** – The pertinent statutory provisions for performance bonds issued in Georgia as required under the "Little Miller Act" include:

O.C.G.A. § 13-10-40 requires performance bonds on all public projects in excess of $100,000 and allows the state to require a performance bond on any contract regardless of the contract amount. The performance bond must be in the contract amount and must be increased if the contract is increased.

O.C.G.A. § 13-10-42 provides that *only an obligee* may maintain a cause of action under the performance bond and any such action must be *instituted within one year* from the completion of the contract and the acceptance of the public work by the state.

**Private** – Georgia law does not require that contractors furnish bonds on private projects.

---

1 DeWitte Thompson is a partner and Cheryl Kniffen is associated with:
Thompson Slagle & Hannan, LLC
12000 Findley Road
Suite 250
Duluth, Georgia 30097
(770) 662-5999

**Department of Transportation** – O.C.G.A. § 32-2-70 requires that a performance bond that complies with the dictates of Chapter 10 of Title 13 (see above) must be posted for any project in which the contract exceeds $50,000.

**Other** – Georgia law of suretyship is codified at O.C.G.A. § 10-7-1 *et seq*. The liability and obligation of the surety is generally coextensive with that of its principal and is one of contract.

***Case law rules that might generally apply***

Both compensated and uncompensated sureties may utilize the procedure outlined in O.C.G.A. § 10-7-24 and at any time a surety become liable on a debt, the surety may give notice to the person controlling the debt to proceed to collect the debt from its principal, and if the creditor refuses to commence the action within three months the surety is discharged. *Morrison Assurance Co. v. Preston Carroll Co., Inc.*, 254 Ga. 608, 331 S.E.2d 520 (1985); *Balboa v. Kellos*, 247 Ga. 393, 276 S.E.2d 599 (1981).

*Commercial Casualty Ins. Co. v. Carothers Construction Co.*, Civil Action No. 91-227-2-MAC(DF) (M.D. Ga., January 21, 1992). Obligee initiated arbitration with principal on contract bond, but did not make surety a party. Obligee did, however, notify surety of proceedings and that obligee would consider surety bound by result. Surety filed declaratory judgment action seeking determination that adverse award against principal would not be conclusive as to surety. District court agreed that, under Georgia law, a judgment against a principal on a contract bond would not be conclusive as to the surety's liability.

"In contrast to the general rule that policies of insurance are construed strictly against the insurer, the obligation of a surety is construed strictly in the surety's favor." *R. J. Griffin & Co. v. Continental Ins. Co.*, 230 Ga. App. 822, 823, 497 S.E.2d 586, 98 FCDR 830 (1998) (citing *Arnold v. Indcon, L. P.*, 219 Ga. App. 813 (1), 466 S.E.2d 684 (1996); *Johns v. Leaseway of Ga.*, 166 Ga. App. 472, 304 S.E.2d 555 (1983)).

The obligation of a surety is construed strictly in the surety's favor. Commercial Cas. Ins. Co. of Georgia v. Maritime Trade Center Builders, 257 Ga. App. 779, 572 S.E.2d 319 (2002), reconsideration denied, (Oct. 9, 2002).

Extremely protective statutes governing suretyship do not govern compensated sureties, which are conducting business for profit and therefore have no greater claim for favored status than other businesses and which, moreover, are in the insurance business. *Houston General Ins. Co. v. Brock Const. Co., Inc.*, 241 Ga. 460, 246 S.E.2d 316 (1978). While this decision has not been overturned, its holding was called into question by *Morrison Assur. Co. v. Preston Carroll Co., Inc.*, 254 Ga. 608, 331 S.E.2d 520 (1985).

One-year statute of limitations for action on performance and payment bond began to run when the work was completed by general contractor and accepted by Department of Transportation, and not when Department of Transportation had completed its audit and checked contract items and request for payments. *United States Fidelity & Guaranty Co. v. Rome Concrete Pipe Co., Inc.*, 256 Ga. 661, 353 S.E.2d 15 (1987).

No construction of surety bond is required or even permissible when language employed by parties in contract is plain, unambiguous, and capable of only one reasonable interpretation. *R.J. Griffin & Co. v. Continental Ins. Co.*, 230 Ga. App. 822, 497 S.E.2d 586 (1998).

## 2. Damages Covered

***As set forth in any statutes and/or case law***

O.C.G.A. § 10-7-30 – Surety bad faith provides that if a corporate surety does not pay a performance claim made upon a bond within 60 days after demand, the obligee may assert a bad faith claim against the surety and upon a showing of bad faith refusal to pay by the surety, the obligee shall be entitled to recover in addition to the loss a 25 percent penalty and all reasonable attorney's fees. There is no independent tort action available against the surety for bad faith refusal to settle. *Ayers Enterprises, Ltd. v. Exterior Designing, Inc.,* 829 F. Supp. 1330 (N. D. Ga. 1993).

O.C.G.A. § 13-6-2 – Breach of Contract Damages – Generally the measure of damages available in a breach of contract action is the amount that would compensate the injured party for the loss which fulfillment of the contract would have prevented.

O.C.G.A. § 13-6-6 – Nominal Damages – Upon a showing of breach of contract, the party proving the breach is entitled to recover at a minimum nominal damages sufficient to cover the costs of bringing the action.

O.C.G.A. § 13-6-9 – Expenses Necessary for Compliance with Contract – A party has a right to recover upon a showing of breach, any expenditures incurred in preparation for performance.

O.C.G.A. § 13-6-7 – Liquidated Damages – Liquidated damages are allowed in Georgia, but for a clause to meet the statutory requirements of Georgia law, three conditions must be met: (1) injury caused by the breach must be difficult or impossible to estimate; (2) the parties must intend to provide for such damages; and (3) the sum stipulated must be a reasonable pre-estimate of the probable loss. *Oasis Goodtime Emporium I, Inc. v. Cambridge Capital Group, Inc.*, 234 Ga. App. 641, 507 S.E. 2d 823 (1998).

O.C.G.A. § 7-4-15 – Prejudgment Interest – Under Georgia law, prejudgment interest does not accrue on contract claims unless and until all contractual conditions are satisfied, because, until then, no payment is due. The prejudgment interest rate is 7 percent. O.C.G.A. § 7-4-2.

O.C.G.A. § 7-4-12 – Post-Judgment Interest – For all actions filed after July 1, 2003, post judgment interest will be calculated using the rate of prime plus 3 percent on the date that judgment is entered. For any action filed prior to July 1, 2003, the prior statutory post judgment interest rate was 12 percent.

***Obligations of surety to perform and/or pay***

O.C.G.A. § 10-7-30 – Surety bad faith provides that if a corporate surety does not pay a performance claim made upon a bond within 60 days after demand, the obligee may file a bad faith claim against the surety and upon a showing of bad faith refusal to pay by the surety, the obligee shall be entitled to recover in addition to the loss a 25 percent penalty and reasonable attorney's fees.

O.C.G.A. § 10-7-24 provides that at any time a surety become liable on a debt, it may give notice to the person controlling the debt to proceed to collect the debt from its principal, and if the creditor refuses to commence the action within three months the surety is discharged.

The provisions of O.C.G.A. § 10-7-24 apply to both compensated and uncompensated sureties. *Morrison Assurance Co. v. Preston Carroll Co., Inc.*, 254 Ga. 608, 331 S.E.2d 520 (1985); *Balboa v. Kellos*, 247 Ga. 393, 276 S.E.2d 599 (1981).

In *American Fidelity Fire Ins. Co. v. DeKalb County*, 236 Ga. 883, 225 S.E.2d 913 (1976), the granting of a motion for interlocutory injunction seeking to compel the surety and its principal to comply with the contract terms was upheld.

In *Transamerica Ins. Co. v. H.V.A.C. Contractors, Inc.*, 857 F. Supp. 969 N.D. Ga. (1994), the court, interpreting Georgia law, rejected the indemnitors argument that the surety breached a fiduciary duty to them by paying performance and payment bond claims that were questioned by the principal finding that, even if the payments were made erroneously, because they were not made in bad faith, there was no cause of action against the surety.

***Whether failure to provide insurance transfers burden to surety*** – Not applicable.

***Limitations on damages***

No damage for delay clauses are generally enforceable in Georgia. In *Department of Transp. v. Fru-Con Constr. Corp.*, 206 Ga. App. 821, 426 S.E.2d 905 (1992), the Georgia Court of Appeals upheld such a clause in a case in which the contractor on a bridge project sought to hold the Georgia Department of Transportation could not be held vicariously liable for damages resulting from the delivery of materials to the site. However, because the nature of such clauses is exculpatory, if the party seeking to enforce them is in breach, the clause will not be enforced. *Department of Transp. v. APAC-Georgia, Inc.*, 217 Ga. App. 103, 456 S.E.2d 668 (1992) (DOT could be held liable for its failure to properly coordinate the work of various contractors); *Department of Transp. v. Arapaho Constr. Inc.*, 180 Ga. App. 341, 349 S.E.2d 196 (1986), *aff'd*, 257 Ga. 269, 357 S.E.2d 668 (1987).

Liquidated damages are a sum to be paid in lieu of performance. *Thorne v. Lee Timber Products, Inc.*, 158 Ga. App. 226, 279 S.E.2d 521 (1981).

Unless otherwise provided for by law (see O.C.G.A. § 10-7-30), only compensatory damages are available for breach of contact actions. O.C.G.A. § 13-6-10.

The injured party has a duty to mitigate damages. O.C.G.A. § 13-6-5

Damages for pain and suffering are not recoverable in breach of contract cases. *Rogers v. Georgia Ports Auth.*, 183 Ga. App. 325, 329, 358 S.E.2d 855, 859 (1987).

***Whether obligee may set off bonded contract funds against other principal debts***

While Georgia courts have not addressed this particular issue, it is likely that Georgia would adopt the position set forth in § 31 of the Restatement (Third) of Suretyship and Guaranty that such set off is not allowed, as Georgia courts have typically looked to the Restatement for guidance. *See, e.g., Lahaina Acquisitions, Inc. v. GCA Strategic Inv. Fund Ltd.*, 261 Ga. App. 800, 584 S.E.2d 51 (2003).

***Incorporation of specific contract terms by reference***

Whenever the bond incorporates the contract or subcontract by reference, the two documents must be construed together. Georgia courts will construe each document to give its plan unambiguous meaning, and read each document consistently with the other. *Commercial Cas. Ins. Co. of Georgia v. Maritime Trade Center Builders*, 257 Ga. App. 779, 572 S.E.2d 319 (2002). *R.J. Griffin & Co. v. Continental Ins. Co.,* 230 Ga. App. 822, 823, 497 S.E.2d 586 (1998). However, in construing the two documents together, the obligation of a surety is construed strictly in the surety's favor. *Tucker Materials v. Devito Contracting & Co.,* 245 Ga. App. 309, 310, 535 S.E.2d 858 (2000).

### 3. Penal Sum Variations

***Limitations per statute***

O.C.G.A. § 13-10-40 requires a performance bond that is equal to the contract amount. Although Georgia courts had consistently held that the penal limit of the bond capped the exposure for the surety, the adoption of O.C.G.A. § 10-7-30 brings that rule into question because though the performance bond claim could not exceed the penal limit, the 25 percent penalty against the surety could theoretically exceed the penal limit of the bond.

### *Effect of changes in work upon penal sum, if at all*

A surety on a bond cannot be held liable on a bond for a sum greater than the penal limit of the bond. *Long v. City of Midway*, 169 Ga. App. 72, 311 S.E.2d 508 (1983).

Because O.C.G.A. § 13-10-40 requires the performance bond to be in the contract amount, the custom and practice therefore has become in construction contracts for the obligee generally to require that any significant change to the contract, which would increase the price, mandates the contractor to obtain a substitute bond for the increased amount so that a bond for the full contract amount is in effect at all times.

### *Statutory or case law protections or dangers to penal sum*

A surety on a bond cannot be held liable on a bond for a sum greater than the penal limit of the bond. *Long v. City of Midway*, 169 Ga. App. 72, 311 S.E.2d 508 (1983).

Contract of suretyship is one of strict law, and thus, surety cannot, in law or equity, be bound further than the very terms of his contract. O.C.G.A. 10-7-3; *Roswell Festival, LLP v. Athens Intern., Inc.*, 259 Ga. App. 445, 576 S.E.2d 908 (2003) (compensated guarantor); *Avec Corp. v. Schmidt,* 207 Ga. App. 374, 375, 427 S.E.2d 850 (1993).

## 4. Parties Covered

### *Statutes and/or case law as to whether only obligees are covered*

Unless surety contractually provides for third party liability, third parties should look to liability policy rather than performance or payment bond. In that case a private property owner whose property was flooded during installation of pipe as part of a city project was held not to have standing to file a performance bond claim since the performance bond was obtained solely for the protection of the obligee city. *Long v. City of Midway*, 169 Ga. App. 72, 311 S.E.2d 508 (1983).

O.C.G.A. § 13-10-42 provides in connection with Little Miller Act performance bonds that *only an obligee* may maintain a cause of action under the performance bond and any such action must be *instituted within one year* from the completion of the contract and the acceptance of the public work by the state.

***Coverage for:***

**Third Party Beneficiaries** – Unless surety contractually provides for third party liability, third parties should look to liability policy rather than performance or payment bond. *Long v. City of Midway*, 169 Ga. App. 72, 311 S.E.2d 508 (1983).

**Assignees** – Lender for obligee on performance bond executed by construction contractor as obligor was only assignee of obligee and not its successor, and thus could not recover under bond, which expressly provided that no right of action would exist under bond for anyone other than obligee or, *inter alia*, its successors; there was no evidence of duly authorized legal succession by which lender became invested with rights and assumed burdens of obligee. *TRST Atlanta, Inc. v. 1815 Exchange, Inc.*, 220 Ga. App. 184, 469 S.E.2d 238 (1996).

**Dual obligees** – While there are no Georgia decisions on point, O.C.G.A. § 13-10-42 does not prohibit joint obligees, so as long as two obligees were named in the bond, presumably Georgia courts would uphold actions by each or both jointly. While dual obligees were not at issue in the decision in *TRST Atlanta, Inc. v. 1815 Exchange, Inc.*, 220 Ga. App. 184, 469 S.E.2d 238 (1996), the court noted that there were dual obligees.

## 5. Notice or Filing Required

***Statutory provisions***

Failure of obligee under contract of suretyship to wait 60 days after surety's receipt of notice of default or demand for payment before making claim under statute providing for penalties for bad-faith refusal of corporate surety to perform suretyship contract operates as bar against recovery of penalties, including recovery of attorney's fees. O.C.G.A. § 10-7-30.

O.C.G.A. § 10-7-24 provides, in pertinent part:

> Any surety, guarantor, or endorser, at any time after the debt on which he is liable becomes due, may give notice in writing to the creditor, his agent, or any person having possession or control of the obligation, to

> proceed to collect the debt from the principal...; and, if the creditor or holder refuses or fails to commence an action for the space of three months after such notice (the principal being within the jurisdiction of this state), the endorser, guarantor, or surety giving the notice... shall be discharged. No notice which does not state the county in which the principal resides shall be considered in compliance with the requirements of this Code Section.

***Case law rules concerning condition precedent notice***

To collect on performance bond, general contractor was not required to give surety notice of subcontractor's default before supplementing subcontractor's labor or materials, because the bond did not address the contingency of a contractor supplementing the subcontractor's work before it defaulted, subcontract allowed general contractor to supplement subcontractor's work after 48 hours notice, and terms of subcontract were incorporated into bond by reference. The default provisions of the bond (A312) were not held to be applicable in the event of supplementation of forces. *Commercial Cas. Ins. Co. of Georgia v. Maritime Trade Center Builders*, 257 Ga. App. 779, 572 S.E.2d 319 (2002).

Failure of obligee under contract of suretyship to wait 60 days after surety's receipt of notice of default or demand for payment before making claim under statute providing for penalties for bad-faith refusal of corporate surety to perform suretyship contract operates as bar against recovery of penalties, including recovery of attorney's fees. O.C.G.A. § 10-7-30; *Ayers Enterprises, Ltd. v. Exterior Designing, Inc.*, 829 F. Supp. 1330 (N.D. Ga.1993).

## 6. Time for Suit

***Statutes of limitations particular to performance bonds and other applicable statutes of limitation***

O.C.G.A. § 13-10-42 provides that *only an obligee* may maintain a cause of action under the performance bond and any such action must be *instituted within one year* from the completion of the contract and the acceptance of the public work by the state.

O.C.G.A. § 9-3-23. Actions on bond or instruments under seal – Actions upon bonds or other instruments under seal shall be brought within 20 years after the right of action has accrued. No instrument shall be considered under seal unless so recited in the body of the instrument.

***Case law statements about enforceability of limitations contained in bonds***

One-year statute of limitations for action on performance and payment bond began to run when the work was completed by general contractor and accepted by Department of Transportation, and not when Department of Transportation had completed its audit and checked contract items and request for payments. *United States Fidelity & Guaranty Co. v. Rome Concrete Pipe Co., Inc.*, 256 Ga. 661, 353 S.E.2d 15 (1987).

An obligee who files suit before the statutory 60-day waiting period has expired is barred from recovering a bad faith penalty against its surety under O.C.G.A. § 10-7-30. *Columbus Fire & Safety Equipment Co., Inc. v. American Druggist Insurance Co., Inc.*, 166 Ga. App. 509, 510-11, 304 S.E.2d 471 (1983).

Surety on construction performance bond was obligated beyond conclusion of one-year warranty period specified in construction subcontract, where subcontractor was obligated to make good any defective work discovered for a period of time as may be prescribed by law. Under those facts, the applicable statute of limitations was six years as set forth in O.C.G.A. § 9-3-24, setting forth the statute of limitations for all contract in writing. *McDevitt & Street Co. v. K-C Air Conditioning Service, Inc.*, 203 Ga. App. 640, 418 S.E.2d 87 (1992) (cert. denied).

***Varying statutes of limitation by agreement in bond or contract***

Under contractor's bond executed upon condition that written notice of particular facts showing date of any default of principal and nature of default should be given immediately to surety, giving of required notice was a condition precedent to recovery, and failure to allege compliance with condition precedent or to show legal justification for noncompliance was fatal. *Jenkins v. Gordy*, 105 Ga. App. 255, 124 S.E.2d 303 (1962).

A requirement in a contractor's bond that obligee shall give immediate notice to the surety of any default by the contractor is equivalent to a requirement of reasonable notice, and what constitutes reasonable notice in each situation is a matter for the trier of fact. *Thomason v. Keeney*, 8 Ga. App. 852, 70 S.E. 220 (1911).

It has long been a principle of Georgia law that "[t]he parties [to a contract] may fix upon a shorter period [than the statutory statute of limitations], and the stipulation violates no principle of public policy, provided the period fixed be not so unreasonable as to show imposition or undue advantage in some way." *Brown v. Savannah Mut. Ins. Co.*, 24 Ga. 97, 100 (1858).

## 7. Procedure

***Statutory or procedural rules that may affect handling or administration of lawsuits***

Pursuant to O.C.G.A. § 9-11-12 a defendant shall serve his answer within 30 days after the service of the summons and complaint upon him, unless otherwise provided by statute. A cross-claim or counterclaim shall not require an answer, unless one is required by order of the court, and shall automatically stand denied.

Pursuant to O.C.G.A. § 9-11-55 in any case, in which an answer has not been filed within the time required by this chapter, the case shall automatically become in default unless the time for filing the answer has been extended as provided by law. The default may be opened as a matter of right by the filing of such defenses within 15 days of the day of default, and upon the payment of costs. If the case is still in default after the expiration of the period of 15 days, the plaintiff at any time thereafter shall be entitled to verdict and judgment by default, in open court or in chambers, as if every item and paragraph of the complaint or other original pleading were supported by proper evidence, without the intervention of a jury, unless the action is one ex delicto or involves unliquidated damages.

Ga. Const. Art. 1, § 1, ¶ XI guarantees a right to a jury trial except that the court shall render judgment without the verdict of a jury in all civil cases where no defense is filed and where a jury is not demanded in writing by either party. Generally, a trial jury shall consist of 12 persons; but the General Assembly may prescribe any number, not less than six, to constitute a trial jury.

O.C.G.A. § 9-11-38 guarantees a right to a trial by jury as set forth in the Georgia Constitution. O.C.G.A. § 9-11-39 allows parties to waive their right to a trial by jury, and allows trial courts to order a trial by jury if it deems one proper.

Third Party claims are governed by O.C.G.A. § 9-10-34. Vouching in, although not used as often due to the availability of third party claims is authorized by O.C.G.A. § 9-10-13.

### *Venue requirements and jurisdictional limitations*

Sureties and their principals are considered joint obligors and can be sued jointly in the residence of either the principal or the surety. *See generally* Ga. Const. Art. VI, § II, ¶ IV.

Venue in actions against sureties that are governed as insurance companies in Georgia is controlled by O.C.G.A. § 33-4-1, which provides:

> Except for actions arising against unauthorized insurers or under surplus line contracts which are provided for in Chapter 5 of this title, whenever any person shall have a claim or demand on any insurer, such person may bring an action in any of the following places:
>
> (1) In the county where the principal office of the company is located;
>
> (2) In any county where the company shall have an agent or place of doing business;
>
> (3) In any county where such agent or place of doing business was located at the time the cause of action accrued or the contract was made out of which such cause of action arose; or
>
> (4) In any county where the property covered by an insurance contract upon which an action is brought is located or where the person entitled to the proceeds of an insurance contract upon which action is brought maintains his legal residence. For the purpose of this paragraph, personal property shall be deemed to be located in the county of the legal residence of the owner of such personal property, and, for the purpose of bringing an action under this paragraph, a company which has written a contract of insurance upon persons or property located in a particular county or which has become surety for the performance of an obligation in a particular county shall be deemed to be transacting business in such county and shall be deemed to be a legal resident of such county; provided, further, that any action on the bond of a sheriff or other arresting or law enforcement officer or superior court clerk or deputy clerk or clerk or deputy of any court of

> record, upon which any guaranty or surety company or fidelity insurance company is bound and obligated as surety, shall be instituted in the county of the residence of the officer and not in any other county; and the county of the residence of the officer is hereby fixed as the venue of any action on such bond; and the officer may be made a party defendant or may by intervention become a party defendant

Otherwise Georgia's general venue statute for corporate defendants is found at O.C.G.A. § 14-2-510 and provides that each domestic corporation and each foreign corporation authorized to transact business in this state shall be deemed to reside and to be subject to venue as follows:

> (1) In civil proceedings generally, in the county of this state where the corporation maintains its registered office; or if the corporation fails to maintain a registered office, it shall be deemed to reside in the county where its last named registered office or principal office, as shown by the records of the Secretary of State, was maintained;
>
> (2) In actions based on contracts, in that county in this state where the contract to be enforced was made or is to be performed, if the corporation has an office and transacts business in that county;
>
> (3) In actions for damages because of torts, wrong, or injury done, in the county where the cause of action originated, if the corporation has an office and transacts business in that county;
>
> (4) In actions for damages because of torts, wrong, or injury done, in the county where the cause of action originated. If venue is based solely on this paragraph, the defendant shall have the right to remove the action to the county in Georgia where the defendant maintains its principal place of business. A notice of removal shall be filed within 45 days of service of the summons. Upon motion by the plaintiff filed within 45 days of the removal, the court to which the case is removed may remand the case to the original court if it finds that removal is improper under the provisions of this paragraph. Upon the defendant's filing of a notice of removal, the 45-day time period for filing such notice shall be tolled until the remand, the entry of an order by the court determining that the removal is valid, or the expiration of the time period for the plaintiff to file a motion challenging the removal, whichever occurs first.

State court actions on performance bonds can be filed in either the superior courts or state courts of Georgia, which have concurrent jurisdiction over them. *See generally* Subcontractor's action against surety for breach of payment bond contract, bad faith, and attorney fees was within superior court's subject matter jurisdiction. *Harry S. Peterson Co., Inc. v. National Union Fire Ins. Co.*, 209 Ga. App. 585, 434 S.E.2d 778 (1993); Ga. Const. Art. 6, § 4, Par. 1.

***Court rules***

Actions pending in the Superior Courts of Georgia are governed by the Uniform Superior Court Rules. After those rules were adopted all local rules, with the exception of those rules relating to the drawing of jurors, expired effective December 31, 1994. Pursuant to Uniform Superior Court Rule 1.2, each superior court retained authority to make local rules as long as those rules were not inconsistent with the uniform rules or the Civil Practice Act. Except with the exceptions set forth in the Uniform State Court Rules, the Uniform Superior Court rules are applicable in both superior and state courts of the state.

***Particular agency regulations/rules*** – Not applicable.

***Arbitration requirements and application***

The Georgia Arbitration Code is codified at O.C.G.A. § 9-9-1 *et seq.* In 1988, the General Assembly revised the Georgia Arbitration Code extensively, renumbering the statute, deleting the phrase "for Construction Contracts" from its title, and extending the enforcement of arbitration provisions to all contracts in which the parties have agreed to arbitration in writing. *Choate Const. Co., Inc. v. Ideal Elec. Contractors, Inc.*, 246 Ga. App. 626, 541 S.E.2d 435 (2000).

In *Holt & Holt, Inc. v. Choate Const. Co.*, 271 Ga. App. 292, 609 S.E.2d 103 (2004), the Georgia Court of Appeals upheld a provision in a contract requiring the parties to file for arbitration within 30 days as reasonable and enforceable.

In *Conmac Corp. v. Southern Diversified Development, Inc.*, 245 Ga. App. 895, 539 S.E.2d 532 (2000), the Georgia Court of Appeals rejected the appellants argument that by the parties agreeing to be bound by the rules of the American Arbitration Association, the parties had removed their arbitration from the Georgia Arbitration Act. In that case, the court found that "[b]y its very language, [AAA] Rule 53 gives the arbitration panel the authority to interpret the AAA Rules, but does not empower it to circumvent or disregard express procedural requirements or limitations on its power that have been adopted by the Georgia Legislature."

In *Abe Engineering, Inc. v. Travelers Indem. Co.*, 210 Ga. App. 551, 436 S.E.2d 754 (1993), the Georgia Court of Appeals rejected a subcontractor's argument that it should be allowed to modify its award against the general contractor to include the general contractor's surety, as well holding that the subcontractor's failure to serve the surety with the arbitration action initially was fatal to binding it later.

While Georgia courts have not specifically addressed the question of whether a surety can be compelled to arbitrate, because Georgia appellate courts have indicated their inclination to enforce arbitration agreements, *Joja Partners, LLC v. Abrams Properties, Inc.*, 262 Ga. App. 209, 585 S.E.2d 168 (2003), and the majority of jurisdictions considering this question have held that a surety can be compelled to arbitration, it is probable Georgia courts would require the surety to arbitrate at least all underlying construction contract issues if the bond incorporated a construction contract containing a valid arbitration clause.

## 8. Attorney's Fees

Absent a contractual provision allowing for the recovery of attorneys fees, or a surety's bad faith refusal to pay a claim pursuant to O.C.G.A. § 10-7-30, attorney's fees are not recoverable against a surety as part of a performance bond claim.

### *Statutes and/or case law limiting or permitting recovery of attorney's fees*

O.C.G.A. § 10-7-30 – Surety bad faith provides that if a corporate surety does not pay a performance claim made upon a bond within 60 days after demand, the obligee may file a bad faith claim against the surety and upon a showing of bad faith refusal to pay by the surety, the obligee shall be entitled to recover in addition to the loss a 25 percent penalty and all reasonable attorney's fees.

***What fees are recoverable, if any***

For attorney's fees to be recovered, both their actual cost and their reasonableness must be shown. *Santora v. American Combustion, Inc.*, 225 Ga. App. 771, 485 S.E.2d 606 (1997); *Southern Cellular Telecom v. Banks*, 209 Ga. App. 401, 402, 433 S.E.2d 606 (1993).

In *Arford v. Blalock*, 199 Ga. App. 434, 405 S.E.2d 698 (1991), the Georgia Court of Appeals held that the party seeking attorney's fees is entitled to recover attorney's fees only for that portion of fees which are allocable to attorney's efforts to prosecute cause of action, against particular defendant, on which prayer for attorney's fees is based.

An obligee who files suit prematurely is similarly barred from recovering a bad faith penalty against its surety under § 10-7-30. *Columbus Fire & Safety Equipment Co., Inc. v. American Druggist Insurance Co., Inc.*, 166 Ga. App. 509, 510-11, 304 S.E.2d 471 (1983).

Attorney's fees are recoverable through arbitration, and contract provisions, allowing for recovery of attorney's fees, are enforceable in arbitrations. *Yates Paving & Grading Co. v. Bryan*, 265 Ga. App. 578, 594 S.E.2d 756 (2004).

## 9. Special Provisions

O.C.G.A. § 10-7-1 – there is no distinction between contracts of suretyship and guaranty.

O.C.G.A. § 13-10-41 allows the state, in any contract that is $300,000 or less, to exercise its discretion to accept an irrevocable letter of credit from a bank or a savings and loan association in lieu of a performance bond.

O.C.G.A. § 10-7-42 – if a principal has notice of pendency of an action against its surety, and the surety makes payment on the judgment, the amount of the judgment is conclusive against the principal. If no payment was made by the surety, the principal may dispute the amount of the judgment or the validity of the award.

O.C.G.A. § 10-7-50 provides that sureties are allowed to seek contribution from other co-sureties, and if a co-surety is insolvent then the solvent sureties must bear the deficiency equally.

O.C.G.A. § 9-11-13 provides for vouching in and allows any defendant that is sued, who has a remedy against a third party for the same claim to vouch in the third party by giving them notice of the pendency of the action and then any judgment is conclusive against any party vouched as to the right and amount that the plaintiff is to recover. This section has the effect of inducing a principal to come to court and present any defenses to the debt, but this procedure is not a substitution for the surety (vouchee) to prove its right to recovery against the principal.

O.C.G.A. § 9-3-24. Simple contracts in writing – All actions upon simple contracts in writing shall be brought within six years after the same become due and payable. However, this Code section shall not apply to actions for the breach of contracts for the sale of goods under Article 2 of Title 11 or to negotiable instruments under Article 3 of Title 11.

O.C.G.A. § 9-3-20. Actions upon foreign judgments – All actions upon judgments obtained outside this state, except judgments for child support or spousal support, or both, shall be brought within five years after such judgments have been obtained.

O.C.G.A. § 9-3-26. Other actions ex contractu – All other actions upon contracts express or implied not otherwise provided for shall be brought within four years from the accrual of the right of action. However, this Code section shall not apply to actions for the breach of contracts for the sale of goods under the UCC.

## 10. Remarks

The common law distinction between guarantors and sureties was abolished by the Georgia General Assembly in 1981. Therefore, most of the statutory provisions set forth in Title 10, Chapter 7 of the Code of Georgia are applicable to compensated sureties. *See* 1981 Ga. Laws 870; *Balboa Insurance Co. v. A.J. Kellos Construction Co.,* 247 Ga. 393, 276 S.E.2d 599 (1981).

An obligee who files suit prematurely is similarly barred from recovering a bad faith penalty against its surety under O.C.G.A.§ 10-7-30. *Columbus Fire & Safety Equip. Co., Inc. v. American Druggist Insurance Co., Inc.,* 166 Ga. App. 509, 510-11, 304 S.E.2d 471 (1983).

## 11. Case Annotations

In non-bonded projects, if a contractor defaults on or abandons a project, the owner may have the contract completed and charge any necessary costs of completion against the contract value. *Crowe v. Holloway Dev. Corp.*, 114 Ga. App. 856, 152 S.E.2d 913 (1966).

The statute that makes judgments against sureties conclusive against their principals as to the amount for which the surety is bound applies only if the judgment is final. *Life Ins. Co. of American v. St. Paul Fire & Marine Ins. Co.*, 278 Ga. 800, 606 S.E.2d 855 (2004).

Whether surety is liable is generally a matter of law for the courts. *Sim's Crane Service, Inc. v. Reliance Ins. Co.*, 514 F. Supp. 1033 (S.D. Ga. 1981).

Any change to the underlying contract, whether to the surety's benefit or detriment, is a novation which discharges the surety. *Upshaw v. First State Bank*, 244 Ga. 433, 260 S.E.2d 483 (1979); O.C.G.A. § 10-7-21.

Although a novation will generally release a surety from its obligations, if a surety or guarantor consents in advance to a change that would otherwise result in his discharge, the surety is still bound. *Griswold v. Whetsell*, 157 Ga. App. 800, 278 S.E.2d 753 (1981).

Suretyship may be proven by parol evidence. *Decatur Coca-Cola Bottling Co. v. Variety Vending Corp.*, 277 F. Supp. 393 (N.D. Ga. 1967); O.C.G.A. § 10-7-45.

Until a surety is called upon to perform its obligation under a payment or performance bond, the right of subrogation is an inchoate one, which becomes choate only upon the maturing and performance of the obligation to pay. *Cotton States Mut. Ins. Co. v. Citizens and Southern Nat. Bank*, 168 Ga. App. 83, 308 S.E.2d 199 (1983).

A contract of suretyship between the alleged principal and its surety can be either written or oral. *Griswold v. Wells Aluminum, Moultrie, Inc.*, 156 Ga. App. 19, 274 S.E.2d 7 (1980).

***Interpretation of AIA bond forms*** – Not applicable.

***Cases in which surety steps into shoes of obligee***

By payment of a primary obligation a surety becomes fully subrogated to all of that creditor's rights against the principal. *Hogan v. Maxey*, 121 Ga. App. 490, 174 S.E.2d 208 (1970).

Surety, who has paid the debt of his principal is subrogated, both at law and at equity, to all the rights of the creditor, and, in a controversy with other creditors, the debt is ranked as if it still belonged to the creditor. *Royal Indem. Co. v. Mayor & etc. of City of Savannah*, 209 Ga. 383, 73 S.E.2d 205 (1952).

# HAWAII

James H. Lawhn[1]

## 1. Requirement for Bond

***Statutory provisions for projects that are:***

**Public** – In Hawaii, all public works projects for the state and counties are governed by Chapter 103D of the Hawaii Revised Statutes (the "Procurement Code"). Section 103D-324 requires that a performance bond and a labor and material payment bond be provided for contracts in excess of $25,000, the penal sum of each to be 100 percent of the contract amount. The form of performance bond required on public works is specified pursuant to the Procurement Code by the policy board by procurement directive.

**Private** – Except where a private works project may be regulated by statute, such as a condominium development, the requirement for a performance bond is a matter of contract between the developer and the contractor, as is the form and penal sum of the bond.

**Department of Transportation** – No performance bond statute in Hawaii applies specifically to Department of Transportation projects.

---

1 James H. Lawhn is of counsel to:
Oliver, Lau, Lawhn, Ogawa and Nakamura
707 Richards Street, Suite 600
Honolulu, Hawaii 96813
(808) 533-3994

***Case law rules that might generally apply***

Under Hawaii law, traditional principles of contract interpretation are applied to bonds. *Island Ins. Co., Ltd v. Hawaiian Foliage & Landscape Inc.*, 288 F.3d 1161 (9th Cir. 2000).

Surety is entitled to pro tanto discharge to extent of prejudice, not complete exoneration. *Honolulu Roofing Co. v. Felix* 426 P.2d 298 (Haw. 1967).

Surety owes a duty of good faith and fair dealing. *Bd. of Dir. of AOAO Discovery Bay v. United Pacific Ins. Co.* 884 P.2d 1134 (Haw. 1994).

**2. Damages Covered.**

***Set forth in any statutes and/or case law***

There is little difference in the damages covered by performance bonds on private and public works. In Hawaii, performance bonds are construed according to traditional principles of contract interpretation, and accordingly the surety would be liable for damages within the contemplation of the parties unless the bond has specific language limiting or enlarging the scope of damages.

Since suretyship is classified as "insurance" under Hawaii's Insurance Code and since the Insurance Code prohibits insuring against punitive damages, presumably the performance bond would not cover punitive damages assessed against the principal.

Hawaii is a bad faith jurisdiction and the surety may incur extra contractual damages if it is found to have acted in bad faith in denying a claim.

***Obligations of surety to perform and/or pay*** – There are no applicable cases.

***Whether failure to provide insurance transfers burden to surety*** – There are no applicable cases.

***Limitations on damages***

Surety will not be liable for delay damages where bond so provides and obligee may not withhold delay damages from contract funds. *Mayer v. Alexander & Baldwin, Inc.*, 532 P.2d 1007 (Haw. 1975).

***Whether obligee may set off bonded contract funds against other principal-obligee debts or obligations***

Owner/obligee has common law rights of recoupment from contract funds for losses arising out of contract. *Erickson v. Volcano Stables & Transp. Co.*, 13 Haw. 428 (Haw. 1901)

***Incorporation of specific contract terms by reference*** – There are no applicable cases.

## 3. Penal Sum Variations

***Limitations per statute***

**Public Work** – Neither the Procurement Code, nor the regulations promulgated thereunder address adjustments in the penal sum of the performance bond except to provide that the penal sum may be adjusted downward during construction if the procurement officer certifies in writing that the adjustment is in the best interest of the state. The form of performance bond specified by the policy board for public works contains language waiving notice of changes by the surety as well as language providing that no alterations in work or contract terms will exonerate the surety. As a matter of practice, the penal sum is adjusted to reflect change orders to the bonded contract due, primarily, to the practice of increasing the bond premium to reflect the change orders.

**Private Work** – The majority of performance bonds written in Hawaii for private works follow the AIA format and accordingly provide for a waiver of notice of changes in the underlying bonded contract. Thus lack of the surety's consent to changes in the work will not exonerate the surety, except in the case of cardinal changes. Whether or not any particular change also increases the penal sum of the bond is an issue of fact which usually is resolved against the surety due to the adjustment in premium to reflect change orders to the bonded contract.

***Effect of changes in work upon penal sum, if at all***

Where the bonded contract allows for changes, surety is not discharged by changes unless they are of such a nature as could not reasonably supposed to have been within the contemplation of the parties at the time the contract was entered into. *Hustace v. Davis*, 23 Haw. 606 (Haw. 1917).

***Statutory or case law protections or dangers to penal sum***

Hawaii courts have not ruled upon whether a takeover agreement which does not limit the surety's obligation to the penal sum of the bond will expose the surety to liability in excess of the penal sum. The form of performance bond specified for use on public works contains express language limiting the liability of the surety to the penal sum.

## 4. Parties Covered

***Statutes and/or case law as to whether only obligees are covered***

**Public Works** – Hawaii's Procurement Code does not grant any third party rights under a public works performance bond, nor have Hawaii courts interpreted the Procurement Code to establish any such rights as yet. However, the Ninth Circuit, interpreting Hawaii law on a private works performance bond, has held that a government is an intended beneficiary under a performance bond based on the bond's incorporation by reference of the bonded subcontract containing express covenants for payment of taxes, and the bond's condition that the principal shall "duly and truly perform and complete said subcontract."

**Private Works** – Absent an additional obligee rider, or indication of legislative intent, whether or not a third party has rights under a private works performance bond is a matter to be determined in accordance with normal third party beneficiary analysis. As noted under "Public Works" above, the Ninth Circuit decision imposing liability on the surety for the principal's withholding taxes was based on a third party beneficiary analysis. In limited instances, such as condominium developments, performance bonds are required by statute and in such instances arguments have been advanced that the legislature intended purchasers to have rights under the performance bond. No Hawaii appellate court has ruled as yet on this issue. Although there is no case or statute so holding, rights of the obligee under the performance bond can probably be assigned to the extent allowed by Sec. 13 of the Restatement of Suretyship and Guaranty.

***Coverage for:***

**Third-party beneficiaries** – Governmental entities owed withholding taxes are third party beneficiaries under a performance bond incorporating a subcontract by reference that requires payment of all taxes, and is conditioned upon performance and completion of the subcontract. *Island Ins. Co., Ltd v. Hawaiian Foliage & Landscape Inc.*, 288 F.3d 1161 (9th. Cir. 2000)

**Assignees** – Except as noted above, there are no statutes or case law relating to this topic.

**Dual obligees** – Except as noted above, there are no statutes or case law relating to this topic.

## 5. Notice or Filing Required

***Statutory provisions*** – There is no statutory procedure relating to notice or filing of a claim under either a public or private works performance bond.

***Case law rules concerning condition precedent notice*** – No applicable statutes or case law.

## 6. Time for Suit

***Statutes of limitation particular to performance bonds and other applicable statutes of limitation***

Since a performance bond is a contract, an action on a performance bond may be brought within six years following the date the complaining party either knew or should have known of the breach. However, if the subject matter of the action is a defect in construction, the action must be brought within two years after the party either knew or should have known of the defect, and no action whatsoever may be brought more than 10 years following the "date of completion" of the construction as defined in Hawaii's mechanic's lien statute.

**Public Works** – There is no express authority in Hawaii's Procurement Code allowing a contracting agency to shorten the time within which suit may be brought under the performance bond, nor does the form of performance bond issued by the procurement policy office contain any such provision.

**Private Works** – Hawaii allows private parties to shorten the time within which suit may be brought under a performance bond, provided that the shortened time is reasonable, and subject to the rule that the language will be construed most strongly against the surety.

***Case law statements about enforceability of limitations contained in bonds*** – Not applicable.

***Varying statutes of limitation by agreement in bond or contract***

Parties to a bond may contract for a shortened time within which to bring suit provided the time is reasonable and provided that the language will be construed strictly against the surety. *Honolulu Roofing Co. v. Felix,* 426 P.2d 298 (Haw. 1967).

## 7. Procedure

***Statutory or procedural rules that may affect handling or administration of lawsuits*** – Not applicable.

***Venue requirements and jurisdictional limitations***

**Public Works** – Actions upon public works performance bonds lie in any court of competent jurisdiction, which in the case of the state is the circuit court in the county in which the project is located; and in the case of the various counties may be either the circuit court in the county in which the project is located or the U.S. District Court for Hawaii if diversity exists.

**Private Works** – Jurisdiction and venue is the same as with county public works performance bonds.

***Court rules*** – No special rules apply to claims against sureties.

***Particular agency regulations/rules*** – Not applicable (except as noted above).

***Arbitration requirements and application***

Hawaii law favors arbitration. If the underlying bonded contract contains an arbitration clause, arbitration between the contractor and obligee will be compelled and the arbitration award will be binding upon the surety in an action on the performance bond subject however to any special suretyship defenses. The surety has the right, but not the obligation, to participate in the arbitration.

## 8. Attorney's Fees

***Statutes and/or case law limiting or permitting recovery of attorney's fees***

The general rule in Hawaii is that absent a provision for attorney fees, no attorney fees are allowed on contract actions; provided however that since an action upon a bond is one in assumpsit, fees may be allowed according to the statutory schedule under Hawaii's assumpsit statute. In addition, since performance bonds are defined by statute to be "insurance" under Hawaii's insurance code, and since the insurance code allows for attorney fees in actions to recover benefits under a policy, arguments have been advanced that attorney fees are recoverable under

Hawaii's insurance code. To date, no Hawaii appellate court has ruled upon this issue as it may pertain to bonds.

Where the bond does not include an attorney fee clause, Hawaii's statute relating to attorney fees in assumpsit actions governs. *Honolulu Roofing Co. v. Felix*, 426 P.2d 298 (Haw. 1967).

***What fees are recoverable, if any*** – In contract actions, Hawaii allows prejudgment interest at 10 percent per annum from the date of breach.

## 9. Special Provisions

Other than as noted above, there are no unusual statutory provisions regarding public or private works performance bonds.

## 10. Remarks

In a bad faith context, the surety may withhold performance under its bond if there is a genuine dispute as to liability under the bonded obligation.

Set-aside letters from lenders are common in Hawaii and may become relevant in negotiating completion terms and conditions.

## 11. Case Annotations

***Interpretation of AIA bond forms*** – There are no applicable cases.

***Cases in which surety steps into shoes of obligee***

Surety is not entitled to set off profits from completion of one bonded job against losses on other bonded jobs where bonds contained no provision allowing such set off. *U.S. v. MidPac Lumber Co., Ltd.*, 976 F. Supp. 1310 (D. Haw. 1997).

Surety under a performance bond is subrogated to rights of both principal and obligee and may apply remaining contract funds to completion of work to same extent obligee could have notwithstanding claims of third parties to the contract funds. *Mayer v. Alexander & Baldwin, Inc.*, 532 P.2d 1007 (Haw. 1975).

# IDAHO

Phillip S. Oberrecht and Bryan A. Nickels[1]

## 1. Requirements for Bond

***Statutory provisions for projects that are:***

**Public** – There are two Idaho statutes that require public performance bonds.

Idaho Code § 54-1926 requires contractors to obtain a bond of at least 85 percent (or higher, as set by the applicable authority) of the contract amount for a contract for "the construction, alteration, or repair of any public building or public work or improvement of the state of Idaho, or of any county, city, town, municipal corporation, township, school district, public educational institution, or other political subdivision, public authority, or public instrumentality, or of any officer, board, commission, institution, or agency" thereof.

Idaho Code § 54-4512 requires contractors acting as construction managers to obtain a bond "in the amount of the total construction management contract to secure the construction manager's obligations thereunder."

---

[1] Phillip S. Oberrecht is a shareholder and Bryan A. Nickels is an associate of:

Hall, Farley, Oberrecht & Blanton, P.A.
702 West Idaho Street, Suite 700
P.O. Box 1271
Boise, Idaho 83701
(208) 395-8500

**Private (Quasi-Public)** – Idaho Code § 20-805 requires contracting entities for the construction of private prisons to obtain a bond "that is adequate and appropriate for the proposed construction or renovation contract."

**Department of Transportation** – The Department of Transportation has no separate statute(s) for performance bonds.

***Case law rules that might generally apply***

"I.C. § 54-1926 requires a bond executed by a surety authorized to do business in Idaho, and the county was not at liberty to waive that requirement in favor of some alternative form of security." *McKay Construction Co. v. Ada County Board of County Commissioners*, 99 Idaho 235, 239, 580 P.2d 412, 416 (1978).

**2. Damages Covered**

***Set forth in any statutes and/or case law***

"Simply stated the statute contemplates that if the contractor fails to perform the work contracted, for the performance of which the statute requires a bond to be given in a sum equaling the full amount of the contract price, then the surety, under the obligations of the required bond, must provide performance of the contracted work. The surety in such a case is required to step into the shoes of the contractor; the surety to perform as the contractor originally agreed to do." *Minidoka County for Use and Benefit of Deweiler*, 88 Idaho 395, 419, 399 P.2d 962, 977 (1965) (under prior statute).

***Obligations of surety to perform and/or pay*** – See above.

***Whether failure to provide insurance transfers burden to surety*** – Idaho statutes do not transfer the burden to surety.

***Limitations on damages*** – Idaho statutes do not provide an express limitation on damages.

***Whether obligee may set off bonded contract funds against other principal-obligee debts or obligations*** – Idaho case law does not address this subject.

***Incorporation of specific contract terms by reference***

"A secondary document becomes part of a contract as though recited verbatim when it is incorporated into the contract by reference *provided that the terms of the incorporated document are readily available to the other party.*" *Loomis, Inc. v. Cudahy*, 104 Idaho 106, 118-19, 656 P.2d 1359, 1371-72 (1982) (quoting *King v. Larsen Realty, Inc.*, 121 Cal. App. 3d 349, 358, 175 Cal. Rptr. 226, 231 (Ct. App. 1981) (emphasis in original)).

## 3. Penal Sum Variations

***Limitations per statute***

Idaho Code § 54-1926 does not provide a maximum penal sum. Further, the statute notes that:

> Nothing in this section shall be construed to limit the authority of the state of Idaho or other public body hereinabove mentioned to require a performance bond or other security in addition to these, or in cases other than the cases specified in this chapter.

***Effect of changes in work upon penal sum, if at all***

No specific bond language is dictated by statute, and the courts will defer to the language of the bond in determining effect of changes in the work, including, for example, a provision allowing for changes resulting in up to a 20 percent increase in contract price. *See, e.g., Minidoka County for Use and Benefit of Deweiler*, 88 Idaho 395, 419 & n.2, 399 P.2d 962, 977 & n.2 (1965) (under prior statute) ("Although specific phraseology of the performance bond is not set forth by statute, such bond ... covered all the undertakings, covenants, terms, conditions and agreements of the prime contract as well as any and all authorized modifications of said contract.")

***Statutory or case law protections or dangers to penal sum***

"Any diminution of value of the security caused by the creditor, whether by negligence or not, results in pro tanto discharge. The reason for the pro tanto discharge of the surety is the impairment of the surety's right of subrogation to enforce the security...." *Bank of Idaho v. Nesseth*, 104 Idaho 842, 845, 664 P.2d 270, 273 (1983) (quoting *National Bank of Washington v. Equity Investors*, 86 Wash. 2d 545, 546 P.2d 440, 447 (Wash. 1976).

## 4. Parties Covered

***Statutes and/or case law as to whether only obligees are covered***

"Thus, *Seubert* stands for the proposition that, where a performance or payment bond exists, a subcontractor is a third party beneficiary of the bond as a matter of law and can bring a direct action against the surety or guarantor on the bond." *Great Plains Equipment, Inc., v. Northwest Pipeline Corp.*, 132 Idaho 754, 766, 979 P.2d 627, 639 (1999) (citing *Seubert Excavators, Inc. v. Eucon Corp.*, 125 Idaho 744, 874 P.2d 555 (Ct. App. 1993), *review granted, modified on other grounds*, 125 Idaho 409, 871 P.2d 826 (1994)).

***Coverage for:***

**Third-party beneficiaries** – "Thus, *Seubert* stands for the proposition that, where a performance or payment bond exists, a subcontractor is a third party beneficiary of the bond as a matter of law and can bring a direct action against the surety or guarantor on the bond." *Great Plains Equipment, Inc., v. Northwest Pipeline Corp.*, 132 Idaho 754, 766, 979 P.2d 627, 639 (1999) (citing *Seubert Excavators, Inc. v. Eucon Corp.*, 125 Idaho 744, 874 P.2d 555 (Ct. App. 1993), *review granted, modified on other grounds*, 125 Idaho 409, 871 P.2d 826 (1994)).

"We agree with respondents' contention that premature payment of retainage, if premature, does not, ipso facto, have the effect of releasing the Surety as against third-party creditor beneficiaries." *See, e.g., Minidoka County for Use and Benefit of Deweiler*, 88 Idaho 395, 412, 399 P.2d 962, 972-73 (1965) (under prior statute)

**Assignees** – There are no Idaho cases discussing assignment of obligee's right to make a claim against a performance bond.

**Dual obligees** – There are no Idaho cases discussing dual obligees in a performance bond context.

## 5. Notice or Filing Required

***Statutory provisions*** – Idaho statutes do not provide for any unusual notice requirements for suit under a performance bond.

***Case law rules concerning condition precedent notice***

"A surety on building contractor's bond is not entitled to notice of contractor's default, unless bond specifically provides therefore." *Minidoka County for Use and Benefit of Deweiler*, 88 Idaho 395, 419, 399 P.2d 962, 977 (1965) (under prior statute) (quoting *Corporation of President of Church of Jesus Christ of Latter-Day Saints v. Hartford Acc. Etc. Co.*, 98 Utah 297, 95 P.2d 736 (1939).

## 6. Time for Suit

***Statutes of limitation particular to performance bonds and other applicable statutes of limitation***

Idaho Code § 5-216 provides the statute of limitations for written contracts:

> "ACTION ON WRITTEN CONTRACT. Within five years: An action upon any contract, obligation or liability founded upon an instrument in writing. The limitations prescribed by this section shall never apply to actions in the name or for the benefit of the state and shall never be asserted nor interposed as a defense to any action in the name or for the benefit of the state although such limitations may have become fully operative as a defense prior to the adoption of this amendment."

***Case law statements about enforceability of limitations contained in bonds*** – Idaho has no cases addressing this subject.

***Varying statutes of limitation by agreement in bond or contract***

"It is established law in Idaho that statutes of limitation may not be contractually shortened by the parties.... But where the parties agree to lengthen the statutory period within which suit can be instituted, the law will not interfere and shorten the period." *City of Weippe v. Yarno*, 94 Idaho 257, 258-59, 486 P.2d 268, 269-70 (1971).

## 7. Procedure

***Statutory or procedural rules that may affect handling or administration of lawsuits***

Idaho Code § 6-905 provides:

> FILING CLAIMS AGAINST STATE OR EMPLOYEE – TIME. All claims against the state arising under the provisions of this act and all claims against an employee of the state for any act or omission of the employee within the course or scope of his employment shall be presented to and filed with the secretary of state within 180 days from the date the claim arose or reasonably should have been discovered, whichever is later.

Idaho Code § 6-906 provides:

> FILING CLAIMS AGAINST POLITICAL SUBDIVISION OR EMPLOYEE – TIME. All claims against a political subdivision arising under the provisions of this act and all claims against an employee of a political subdivision for any act or omission of the employee within the course or scope of his employment shall be presented to and filed with the clerk or secretary of the political subdivision within 180 days from the date the claim arose or reasonably should have been discovered, whichever is later.

Idaho Code § 6-904(7) provides:

> EXCEPTIONS TO GOVERNMENTAL LIABILITY. A governmental entity and its employees while acting within the course and scope of their employment and without malice or criminal intent shall not be liable for any claim which: ... (7) Arises out of a plan or design for construction or improvement to the highways, roads, streets, bridges, or

other public property where such plan or design is prepared in substantial conformance with engineering or design standards in effect at the time of preparation of the plan or design or approved in advance of the construction by the legislative body of the governmental entity or by some other body or administrative agency, exercising discretion by authority to give such approval.

***Venue requirements and jurisdictional limitations***

"For an Idaho court to exercise personal jurisdiction over an out-of-state defendant, 'two criteria must be met; the act giving rise to the cause of action must fall within the scope of our long-arm statute and the constitutional standards of due process must be met.'" *McAnally v. Bonjac, Inc.*, 137 Idaho 488, 491, 50 P.3d 983, 986 (2002); *see also Western States Equipment Co. v. American Amex, Inc.*, 125 Idaho 155, 868 P.2d 483 (1994).

Idaho Code § 5-404 provides:

OTHER ACTIONS – VENUE DETERMINED BY RESIDENCE – EXCEPTIONS. In all other cases the action must be tried in the county in which the defendants, or some of them, reside, at the commencement of the action; or, if none of the defendants reside in the state, or, if residing in this state, the county in which they reside is unknown to the plaintiff, the same may be tried in any county which the plaintiff may designate in his complaint; and if the defendant is about to depart from the state, such action may be tried in any county where either of the parties reside, or service is had, subject, however, to the power of the court to change the place of trial, as provided in this code; provided, that all actions against life or fire insurance companies, suit or action may be commenced and tried in the county where the death occurred or the loss was sustained; and provided, further, that in all actions against any corporation organized under the laws of the state of Idaho, suit or action shall be commenced and tried in any county of this state where the defendant has its principal place of business or in the county in which the cause of action arose.

***Court rules*** – Not applicable.

***Particular agency regulations/rules*** – Not applicable.

***Arbitration requirements and application*** – Idaho has adopted the Uniform Arbitration Act. *See* Idaho Code §§ 7-901 *et seq.*

## 8. Attorney's Fees

***Statutes and/or case law limiting or permitting recovery of attorney's fees***

Idaho Code § 54-1929 provides that "In any action brought upon either of the bonds provided herein, or against the public body failing to obtain the delivery of the payment bond, the prevailing party, upon each separate cause of action, shall recover a reasonable attorney's fee to be taxed as costs."

***What fees are recoverable, if any***

Fees on appeal are not recoverable under Idaho Code § 54-1929. *See LaGrand Steel Products Co. v. A.S.C.*, 108 Idaho 817, 819, 702 P.2d 855, 857 (Ct. App. 1985).

"In an action on a contractor's bond attorney's fees are merely an incident of the judgment and not a separate cause of action." *City of Weippe v. Yarno*, 94 Idaho 257, 259, 486 P.2d 268, 270 (1971).

"[T]hat failure to grant such fees [under I.C. sec. 54-1929] is reversible error." *Interform Co. v. Mitchell*, 575 F.2d 1270, 1280 (9th Cir. 1978).

## 9. Special Provisions

Idaho has adopted a special pre-trial "evaluation" procedure for cases less than $25,000. *See generally* Idaho Code §§ 7-1501 *et seq.*

**10. Remarks** – Not applicable.

## 11. Case Annotations

***Interpretation of AIA bond forms*** – Idaho cases have not specifically addressed AIA forms of bonds A311 and A312.

***Cases in which surety steps into shoes of obligee***

"Simply stated the statute contemplates that if the contractor fails to perform the work contracted, for the performance of which the statute requires a bond to be given in a sum equaling the full amount of the contract price, then the surety, under the obligations of the required bond, must provide performance of the contracted work. The surety in such a case is required to step into the shoes of the contractor; the surety to perform as the contractor originally agreed to do." *Minidoka County for Use and Benefit of Deweiler*, 88 Idaho 395, 419, 399 P.2d 962, 977 (1965) (under prior statute).

# ILLINOIS

Michael J. Weber and Bryan M. Seifert[1]

## 1. Requirement for Bond

***Statutory provisions for projects that are:***

**Public** – 30 ILCS 550/1, the Public Construction Bond Act, requires contractors to provide a performance bond for contracts on all public works in excess of $5,000 to be performed for the State of Illinois or any political subdivision of the state. The penal sum of the performance bond shall be determined by the public officials, boards, commissions, commissioners or agents. In certain circumstances, a political subdivision may allow the contractor to provide a non-diminishing irrevocable bank letter of credit, in lieu of a bond required under 30 ILCS 550/1, on contracts under $100,000.

50 ILCS 20/19, the Public Building Commission Act, provides that any contract let for the construction, repair, alteration, or improvement of any building, its demolition or removal of debris or any other type of construction or repair work, shall contain provisions requiring the contractor undertaking such work to provide a bond for the amount of the

---

[1] Michael J. Weber is a shareholder and Bryan M. Seifert is an associate of:
Leo & Weber, P.C.
One North LaSalle Street
Suite 3600
Chicago, Illinois 60602
(312) 857-0910

contract conditioned for the faithful performance of the contract as the Board of Commissioners may determine.

70 ILCS 2605/11.13, the Metropolitan Water Reclamation District Act, requires contractors to provide a bond for all contracts relative to the construction, rehabilitation or repair of any of the works of the sanitary district to insure the timely performance of the contract and to indemnify and hold harmless the sanitary district against all liabilities, judgments, costs and expenses as a consequence of granting such contract.

310 ILCS 10/8.15, the Housing Authorities Act, provides that a Housing Authority may acquire by purchase, condemnation, or otherwise any real property, the acquisition of which is necessary for the implementation of a conservation plan for a conservation area as defined by the act. Improvements as may be required under the conservation plan to be done by the authority in excess of $1,000 shall be let by free and competitive bidding to the lowest responsible bidder upon such bond.

315 ILCS 5/15, the Blighted Areas Redevelopment Act of 1947, provides that when a Land Clearance Commission has acquired title to and possession of real property located within a redevelopment project under this act, it may let contracts for the demolition and removal of buildings under the act. Any contract entered into by the Commission under the act shall contain provisions requiring the contractor to provide a bond in an amount equal to one-third of the contractor's bid price, but in no event in excess of $25,000 conditioned for the faithful performance of the contract.

**Private** – No statutes in Illinois require performance bonds on private projects.

**Department of Transportation** – There are no Illinois statutory provisions that specifically enumerate requirements for performance bonds in connection with the Illinois Department of Transportation. Performance bonds in which the Illinois Department of Transportation appears as obligee will be governed by the Illinois Public Construction Bond Act, 30 ILCS 550/1.

***Case law rules that might generally apply***

"The liability of a surety is measured by that of its principal. Such co-extensive responsibility has been interpreted to mean that where a bond is signed by a general contractor as principal and by an insurance company as surety, no suit on the bond can be maintained against the surety unless it could have been maintained against the principal. Thus, if a principal and surety are jointly sued and the action fails as to the principal, the surety is discharged." *Village of Rosemont v. Lentin Lumber Company*, 144 Ill. App. 3d 651, 668 (Ill. App. 1986).

"Contracts of compensated suretyship are treated as contracts of insurance." *Fisher v. Fidelity and Deposit Co. of Maryland*, 125 Ill. App. 3d 632, 641 (Ill. App. 1984).

A construction bond and the contract it secures must be read as one instrument. When the bond incorporates the contract by reference, the provisions of the contract become the provisions of the bond. *Lake View Trust & Savings Bank v. Filmore Construction Company*, 74 Ill. App. 3d 755, 758 (Ill. App. 1979).

"A contract must be given a reasonable interpretation and to do so the language of the contract must be resorted to as evidence of the intention of the parties. Sureties are not bound beyond the express terms of their undertakings, but where ambiguity exists the contracts of sureties are strictly construed against them. However, the intention of the parties must be determined solely from the language used when no ambiguity exists." 39 Ill. App. 3d 255, 258-59 (Ill. App. 1976).

"A statute requiring a bond constitutes a part of the bond, and it must be assumed that the bond is executed with reference to the provisions of the statute." *Chicago Housing Authority for Use of General Bronze Corporation v. United States Fidelity and Guaranty Company*, 49 Ill. App. 2d 407, 410 (Ill. App. 1964).

## 2. Damages Covered

### *Set forth in any statutes and/or case law*

30 ILCS 550/1 provides a surety under the performance bond agrees that all the undertakings, covenants, terms, conditions and agreements of the underlying contract entered into between the principal and the state or any political subdivision will be performed and fulfilled.

215 ILCS 5/155 of the Illinois Insurance Code provides that any action by or against a company wherein there is in issue the liability of a company on a policy of insurance or the amount of the loss payable for an unreasonable delay in settling a claim, and it appears to the court that

such action or delay is vexatious and unreasonable, the court may allow as part of the taxable costs in the action reasonable attorney fees, plus an amount not to exceed any one of the following amounts: (a) 60 percent of the amount which the court or jury finds such party is entitled to recover against the company, exclusive of all costs; (b) $60,000; (c) the excess of the amount which the court or jury finds such party is entitled to recover, exclusive of costs, over the amount, if any, which the company offered to pay in settlement of the claim prior to the action.

740 ILCS 35/3, Construction Contract Indemnification for Negligence Act, states "This Act does not apply to construction bonds or insurance contracts or agreements."

815 ILCS 205/2, the Illinois Interest Act provides that creditors shall be allowed to receive at the rate of 5 percent per annum for all moneys after they become due on any bond, bill, promissory note or other instrument of writing on money due on the settlement of account and on money withheld by unreasonable and vexatious delay of payment.

"Contracts of a compensated surety are treated as contracts of insurance. Insurers have a duty of good faith and fair dealing in handling claims, but they are entitled to insist on their legal rights in a permissible way. A cause of action for vexatious and unreasonable delay must allege facts showing conduct by the surety which is willful, wanton, malicious, reckless, intentional or in bad faith. This court must consider the totality of the circumstances in determining vexatious delay. In adopting [215 ILCS 5/155] the legislature preempted the field for recovery of punitive damages for refusal to pay, barring the common law action for such remedies." *Fisher v. Fidelity and Deposit Co. of Maryland*, 125 Ill. App. 3d 632, 641-42 (Ill. App. 1984).

"Unlike an action in fraud, a bad-faith action involves insurer misconduct that is similar to unreasonable and vexatious misconduct. This court, however, has never recognized such a tort." The *Cramer* court went on to state that "we hesitate to recognize a new common law tort where the legislature has passed a statutory scheme providing a limited remedy." The *Cramer* court concluded that Section 155 does not preempt a claim of insurer misconduct based on a separate and independent tort. *Cramer v. Insurance Exchange Agency et. al.*, 174 Ill. 2d 513, 524-31 (Ill. 1997).

"No Illinois case or statute supports a cause of action for bad-faith dealing outside the area of insurance and employment law." *Chicago*

*College of Osteopathic Medicine v. George A. Fuller Company*, 719 F.2d 1335, 1349 (7th Cir. 1983).

Where there is suit upon a [performance] bond it is sufficient to show that it was a bond sued upon and that the money was due. Interest is properly allowed from the date of suit. *Fisher v. Fidelity and Deposit Co. of Maryland*, 125 Ill. App. 3d 632, 643 (Ill. App. 1984).

***Obligations of surety to perform and/or pay***

"Where a bond guarantees performance the obligations of the contractor in legal effect becomes the obligation of the surety and the obligee need not actually incur expenses or correct deficient performance of the contract in order to be entitled to recovery against the surety." *Fisher v. Fidelity and Deposit Co. of Maryland*, 125 Ill. App. 3d 632, 640 (Ill. App. 1984).

When a principal's default was caused by the owner's material breach of a construction project, the surety has a valid defense to performance. *Chicago College of Osteopathic Medicine v. George A. Fuller Co.*, 719 F.2d 1335 (7th Cir. 1983).

"If a contract that a surety has guaranteed is altered without the surety's consent, he is discharged, on the theory that he insured only the original contract. As a corollary to this rule, he is discharged if the obligee under the suretyship contract makes advance payments to the principal beyond those provided for in the contract." *Argonaut Insurance Company v. Town of Cloverdale, Indiana*, 699 F.2d 417, 420 (7th Cir. 1983).

Discharge of the surety as to unauthorized payments to the principal operates only to the extent of unauthorized payments. *Argonaut Insurance Company v. Town of Cloverdale, Indiana*, 699 F.2d 417, 420 (7th Cir. 1983).

A surety is discharged by the obligee's breach of its contractual obligations to the principal. *Chicago College of Osteopathic Medicine v. George A. Fuller Co.*, 719 F.2d 1351-52 (7th Cir. 1983).

"A compensated surety is not discharged by an extension of time for performing the underlying contract unless the extension is supported by valid and sufficient consideration." *Keene Corporation v. International Fidelity Insurance Company*, 736 F.2d 388, 392-93 (7th Cir. 1984).

A surety is discharged by the unauthorized payments to the principal only to the extent of the obligee's unauthorized payments. *Argonaut*

*Insurance Company v. Town of Cloverdale, Ind.*, 699 F.2d 417, (7th Cir. 1983).

### *Whether failure to provide insurance transfers burden to surety*

"Indemnity agreements, except in construction bonds and agreements to insure to protect the indemnitor from contractual liability, are void because the dominant aspect of these agreements is the disincentive to the exercise of care by the indemnitee which results; and indemnity agreements in construction bonds and agreements to provide liability insurance for another party to the contract, even though that party is an indemnitee, are valid because their dominant aspect is to afford a source of funds for persons tortiously injured in the work on the construction contract." *GTE North, Incorporated v. Henkels & McCoy, Inc.*, 245 Ill. App. 3d 322, 329 (Ill. App. 1993).

In interpreting the Illinois Construction Contract Indemnification for Negligence Act which barred all promises and agreements in private and public construction contracts to indemnify and hold harmless another person from that person's own negligence, the *Capua* court held that where the performance bond contains indemnity language, the surety will be liable to the obligee for damages sustained as a result of the principal's negligence. *Capua v. W.E. O'Neil Construction Company*, 67 Ill. 2d 255, 258-59 (Ill. 1977).

In a contract where the contractor was not required to provide liability insurance, where the contractor agreed to "indemnify and save harmless the district against all claims for damages to real or personal property, caused in any manner whatsoever by explosives, blasting, or handling explosives in work under the contract," and where the indemnification provisions of the underlying contract where not contingent upon the contractor's negligence, the liability of the surety under the performance bond guaranteeing performance of the contractor's obligations included all obligations of the underlying contract. *Sanitary District of Chicago v. United States Fidelity & Guaranty Company*, 392 Ill. 602, 610-11 (Ill. 1946).

The terms and conditions of a construction contract requiring the owner to purchase and maintain property insurance upon the entire work site including an all-risk policy for physical loss and damage encompassed the interests of the contractor, subcontractors and sub-subcontractors and where the owner and contractor waived all rights against each other for damages covered by the policy, the waiver provisions of the policy applied to the surety as the performance bond incorporated the terms of the underlying construction contract. *Village of Rosemont v. Lentin Lumber Company*, 144 Ill. App. 3d 651, 668 (Ill. App. 1986).

***Limitations on damages***

The surety's liability is coextensive with the liability of its principal under the contract. *Turk v. United States Fidelity & Guaranty Co.*, 361 Ill. 206 (Ill. 1935).

The liability of a surety is measured by the liability of its principal. *Village of Rosemont v. Lentin Lumber Company*, 144 Ill. App. 3d 651, 668 (Ill. App. 1986).

"No Illinois case or statute supports a cause of action for bad-faith dealing outside the area of insurance and employment law." *Chicago College of Osteopathic Medicine v. George A. Fuller Company*, 719 F.2d 1335, 1349 (7th Cir. 1983).

In adopting 215 ILCS 5/155 of the Illinois Insurance Code, the legislature preempted the field for recovery of punitive damages for refusal to pay, barring the common law action for such remedies. *Fisher v. Fidelity and Deposit Co. of Maryland*, 125 Ill. App. 3d 632, 641-42 (Ill. App. 1984).

To the extent notice of default is not given to the surety and the surety could have remedied delays and additional costs thereto, the surety is discharged to the extent of the additional costs; however, to the extent notice of default would have been futile, then failure to give notice to the surety is immaterial and the surety is liable for any delays that could not have been avoided by the surety. *Blackhawk Heating & Plumbing Co., Inc. v. Seaboard Surety Company*, 534 F. Supp. 309, 316 (N.D. Ill. 1982).

***Whether obligee may set off bonded contract funds against other principal-obligee debts or obligations***

There are no Illinois cases that directly address the issue as to whether an obligee may set off bonded contract funds against other principal-obligee debts over the performing surety's subrogation rights to bonded contract funds.

### *Incorporation of specific contract terms by reference*

30 ILCS 550/1, the Public Construction Bond Act requires the bond to incorporate by reference the terms and conditions of the construction contract stating in part "The principal and sureties on this bond agree that all the undertakings, covenants, terms, conditions and agreements of the contract or contracts entered into between the principal and the State or any political subdivision thereof will be performed ..."

"When the bond incorporates by reference the construction contract, the provisions of the contract are provisions of the bond." *Fisher v. Fidelity and Deposit Co. of Maryland*, 125 Ill. App. 3d 632, 640 (Ill. App. 1984).

"All Illinois public works payment and performance bonds are governed by the Act. Section 1 requires that every public works contractor must furnish a bond that, "among other conditions," provides for the completion of the contract, and for the payment of materials used and labor performed, whether by the subcontractor or otherwise. By the terms of the statute, each such bond is deemed to contain provisions for coverage of all just claims for labor and materials, regardless of whether the bond, by its terms, includes such coverage or not. Thus by operation of law every public construction bond is in compliance with the statute; attempts to provide less coverage are simply ineffective. Broader coverage than the minimum mandated is also permissible." *Concrete Structures of the Midwest, Inc. v. Fireman's Insurance Company of Newark, New Jersey*, 790 F.2d 41, 43 (7th Cir. 1986).

Where a surety issued a performance bond on behalf of an assignee under a subcontract and where the subcontract required the assignee to indemnify and hold harmless the prime contractor from any and all loss, expenses and attorney's fees as a result of the breach of the assignee's contractual obligations, the assignor upon payment of the assignee's obligations arising out of the contract became subrogated to the prime contractor's right to costs and attorney's fees and entitled to assert such right against the assignee and the surety. *Ruckman and Hansen Inc. v. Contracting and Material Company, Inc.*, 328 F.2d 744, 748 (7th Cir. 1964).

## 3. Penal Sum Variations

**Limitations per statute** – Illinois does not have any statutory limitations on performance bond penal sums.

***Effect of changes in work upon penal sum, if at all***

The surety's liability is limited to the terms of its undertaking. The extent of the surety's liability is limited to the penal sum of the bond even when the principal's liability is greater. *Fisher v. Fidelity and Deposit Co. of Maryland*, 125 Ill. App. 3d 632, 643 (Ill. App. 1984).

***Statutory or case law protections or dangers to penal sum***

A surety's liability is contractual and cannot exceed the amount of liability expressly assumed in the surety contract. *Simmons, Inc. v. Pinkerton's, Inc.*, 762 F.2d 591, 609 (7th Cir. 1985).

Where a surety takes over completion of a construction contract and reserves its rights and defenses to the extent of the surety's liability to the penal sum of the bond, the surety's reservation constituted a modification of the underlying contract, that was incorporated by reference into the performance bond, for which there was no consideration. *Village of Fox Lake v. Aetna Casualty & Surety Company*, 178 Ill. App. 3d 887, 908-11 (Ill. App. 1989).

"Where the liability of the principal and surety upon a bond is not co-extensive with the principal's objections under its underlying contract, payments made by the principal in satisfaction of the underlying obligation on a performance bond, which exceed the penal sum on the bond, do not serve to discharge the surety and principal from further liability." *Griffin Wellpoint Corporation v. Engelhardt, Inc.*, 92 Ill. App. 3d 252, 259 (Ill. App. 1980).

## 4. Parties Covered

***Statutes and/or case law as to whether only obligees are covered***

A board of education lacked standing to file suit on a performance bond where the bond stated that "no right of action shall accrue on this bond to or for the use of any person or corporation other than the Obligee named herein" where the board was not a named obligee under the performance bond. *Board of Education, School District No. 15, DuPage County v. Fred L. Ockerland, Jr. & Associates Inc.*, 165 Ill. App. 3d 439, 443-44 (Ill. App. 1988).

A project owner did not have standing to bring an action on a subcontract performance bond where the named obligee on the bond, who was acting in its capacity as agent and construction manager for the project owner, provided in the subcontract performance bond a no right of action clause for the use of any person or corporation other than the named obligee. *Rush Presbyterian St. Luke's Medical Center v. Safeco Insurance Company of America*, 825 F.2d 1204, 1207 (7th Cir. 1987).

***Coverage for:***

**Third-party beneficiaries** – While an obligee may be an incidental third-party beneficiary to a statutory labor and material payment bond, the definition of the statutory payment bond pursuant to 30 ILCS 550/1, clearly demonstrates that it was not entered into to guarantee the principal's performance as that was already guaranteed by the statutory performance bond. As a statutory labor and material bond is not executed for the benefit of the obligee, the obligee cannot maintain an action under a performance bond for obligations that are guaranteed under the payment bond. *See Board of Education of Community High School District No. 99, DuPage County v. Hartford Accident and Indemnity Company*, 152 Ill. App. 3d 745, 753-54 (Ill. App. 1987).

Where a subcontractor's performance bond gave only a contractor or its successor a right of action on the bond, the *Young* court dismissed a cause of action brought by a construction project's landowner against a surety, finding that the intention of the parties under the bond was clear that no action could accrue for the use of a third-party beneficiary. *Young v. General Insurance Company of America*, 33 Ill. App. 3d 119, 122-23 (Ill. App. 1975).

A subcontractor was deemed to have third party beneficiary status under a Miller Act performance bond based on the principal's violations of the Fair Labor Standards Act because the bond incorporated the prime contract by reference and the prime contract required the principal to pay all labor of mechanics and laborers. *U.S. for the Use of Edward Hines Lumber Co. v. Kalady Construction Company, Inc.*, 227 F. Supp. 1017, 1018-21 (N.D. Ill. 1964).

Material supplier was a direct third-party beneficiary to the surety's performance bond as the construction contract was incorporated by reference into the bond and the contract required the contractor to pay all laborers and material suppliers. *Neenah Foundry Company v. National Surety Corporation*, 47 Ill. App. 2d 427, 431-33 (Ill. App. 1964).

A project owner did not have standing to bring an action on a subcontract performance bond where the named obligee on the bond, who was acting in its capacity as agent and construction manager for project owner, provided in the subcontract performance bond a no right of action clause for the use of any person or corporation other than the named obligee. *Rush Presbyterian St. Luke's Medical Center v. Safeco Insurance Company of America*, 825 F.2d 1204, 1207 (7th Cir. 1987).

**Assignees** – Where a performance bond provided for no right of action as to assignees, no valid assignment could have been made under the bond without the surety's consent. *Young v. General Insurance Company of America*, 33 Ill. App. 3d 119, 742-43 (Ill. App. 1975).

**Dual obligees** – Trust company is a direct beneficiary of a performance bond as a named obligee under a dual obligee rider. *Centerre Trust Company of St. Louis v. The Continental Insurance Company*, 167 Ill. App. 3d 376, 378 (Ill App. 1988).

Trustee under a land trust as dual obligee was entitled to recovery under the bond pursuant to the express language of the bond and contract. *Lake View Trust & Savings Bank v. Filmore Construction Company*, 74 Ill. App. 3d 755, 758-59 (Ill. App. 1979).

## 5. Notice or Filing Required

***Statutory provisions***

30 ILCS 550/2, recovery on bond or letter of credit; notice of claim; limitation states:

> Every person furnishing material or performing labor, either as an individual or as a sub-contractor for any contractor, with the State, or a political subdivision thereof where bond or letter of credit shall be executed as provided in this Act, shall have the right to sue on such bond or letter of credit in the name of the State, or the political subdivision thereof entering into such contract ... however, that any

> person having a claim for labor, and material as aforesaid shall have no such right of action unless he shall have filed a verified notice of said claim with the officer, board, bureau or department awarding the contract, within 180 days after the date of the last item of work or the furnishing of the last item of materials, and shall have furnished a copy of such verified notice to the contractor within 10 days of the filing of the notice with the agency awarding the contract.

The Illinois Public Construction Bond Act further states:

> No defect in the notice herein provided for shall deprive the claimant of his right of action under this article unless it shall affirmatively appear that such defect has prejudiced the rights of an interested party asserting the same.

***Case law rules concerning condition precedent notice***

Where a performance bond states "Whenever Contractor shall be, and declared by Owner to be in default under the Contract, the Owner having performed Owner's obligations thereunder, the Surety may promptly remedy the default" the obligee must declare the contractor in default before the surety's obligations under the performance bond are triggered. *Liberty Mutual Insurance Company v. Construction Management Services, Inc.*, 2004 WL 2271811 (N.D. Ill. October 6, 2004).

Where the construction contract required the obligee to give the contractor and its surety seven days written notice prior to the termination of the contractor and where the performance bond incorporated the construction contract by reference, the obligee's failure to provide adequate notice of the contractor's termination and the hiring of a completion contractor stripped the surety of its right to limit its liability and constituted a material breach of contract which rendered the surety bonds null and void. *Dragon Construction, Inc. v. Parkway Bank & Trust*, 287 Ill. App. 3d 29, 34 (Ill. App. 1997).

To the extent notice of default is not given to the surety and the surety could have remedied delays and additional costs thereto, the surety is discharged to the extent of the additional costs; however, to the extent notice of default would have been futile, then failure to give notice to the surety is immaterial and the surety is liable for any delays that could not have been avoided by the surety. *Blackhawk Heating &*

*Plumbing Co., Inc. v. Seaboard Surety Company*, 534 F. Supp. 309, 316 (N.D. Ill. 1982).

Where a subcontract performance bond that incorporated the subcontract by reference and required the obligee to give notice of the subcontractor's default only in the event that the obligee arranged for performance of the contract, the obligee's failure to give the surety notice of default until after completion of the work, where the obligee corrected the deficiencies and default by the subcontractor, did not release the surety from liability to the obligee under the bond. *Chrysler Corporation v. The Hanover Insurance Company*, 350 F.2d 652, 656 (7th Cir. 1965).

## 6. Time for Suit

***Statutes of limitation particular to performance bonds and other applicable statutes of limitation***

735 ILCS 5/13-206, ten-year limitation, states in part "actions on bonds, promissory notes, bills of exchange, written leases, written contracts, or other evidences of indebtedness in writing, shall be commenced within 10 years next after the cause of action accrued."

***Case law statements about enforceability of limitations contained in bonds***

"Performance bonds are considered written contracts and are subject to the 10-year statute of limitations period provided for in the Code of Civil Procedure." *Board of Education of Community High School District No. 99, DuPage County v. Hartford Accident and Indemnity Company*, 152 Ill. App. 3d 745, 751 (Ill. App. 1987)

"A surety on a performance bond may not avoid liability on the sole basis a statute of limitations has barred an action against a principal and actions based upon bonds are normally subject to a 10-year statute of limitations. However, the parties may, by contract, limit the time in which a party may file an action on the bond." *People ex rel. Skinner v. Graham*, 170 Ill. App. 3d 417, 441 (Ill. . 1998).

***Varying statutes of limitation by agreement in bond or contract***

"In the absence of any prohibitory statute, the time within which a suit may be brought upon a bond may be limited by a contractual provision in the bond ... Contractual provisions shortening the period of time in which an action may be brought upon a bond to secure public as well as private construction contracts have been upheld to the extent that the period fixed is a reasonable one." *Board of Education of Community High School District No. 99, DuPage County v. Hartford Accident and Indemnity Company*, 152 Ill. App. 3d 745, 750-51 (Ill. App. 1987).

## 7. Procedure

***Statutory or procedural rules that may affect handling or administration of lawsuits***

735 ILCS 5/2-603, form of pleadings, states in part "All pleadings shall contain a plain and concise statement of the pleader's cause of action, counterclaim, defense, or reply. Each separate cause of action upon which a separate recovery might be had shall be stated in a separate count or counterclaim, as the case may be and each count, counterclaim, defense or reply, shall be separately pleaded, designated and numbered, and each shall be divided into paragraphs numbered consecutively, each paragraph containing, as nearly as may be, a separate allegation."

735 ILCS 5/2-605, verification of pleadings, states in part "Any pleading, although not required to be sworn to, may be verified by the oath of the party filing it or of any other person or persons having knowledge of the facts pleaded. Corporations may verify by the oath of any officer or agent having knowledge of the facts. If any pleading is so verified, every subsequent pleading must also be verified, unless verification is excused by the court. In pleadings which are so verified, the several matters stated shall be stated positively or upon information and belief only, according to the fact. Verified allegations do not constitute evidence except by way of admission."

735 ILCS 5/2-1105, jury demand, states in part "A plaintiff desirous of a trial by jury must file a demand therefor with the clerk at the time the action is commenced. A defendant desirous of a trial by jury must file a demand therefor not later than the filing of his or her answer. Otherwise, the party waives a jury."

***Venue requirements and jurisdictional limitations***

705 ILCS 505/8, court of claims jurisdiction, provides that the Illinois court of claims shall have exclusive jurisdiction to hear and determine all claims against the state founded upon any law of the State of Illinois or upon any regulation adopted thereunder by an executive or administrative officer or agency and all claims against the state founded upon any contract entered into with the State of Illinois.

735 ILCS 5/2-101, is the Illinois venue statute that states in part "every action must be commenced (1) in the county of residence of any defendant who is joined in good faith and with probable cause for the purpose of obtaining a judgment against him or her and not solely for the purpose of fixing venue in that county, or (2) in the county in which the transaction or some part thereof occurred out of which the cause of action arose."

***Court rules*** – Each Illinois judicial district has its own local rules regarding the procedure for that district.

***Particular agency regulations/rules*** – Not applicable.

***Arbitration requirements and application***

710 ILCS 5/1, the Illinois Arbitration Act, provides "A written agreement to submit any existing controversy to arbitration or a provision in a written contract to submit to arbitration any controversy thereafter arising between the parties is valid, enforceable and irrevocable save upon such grounds as exist for the revocation of any contract."

Where a provision of the bond incorporated the underlying terms and conditions of the contract and the underlying contract provided for arbitration of all disputes and claims, the surety had standing to assert arbitration provision as a basis for its motion to dismiss the obligee's complaint. *Bolingbrook Park District v. National-Ben Franklin Insurance Company of Illinois*, 96 Ill. App. 3d 26, 29 (Ill. App. 1981).

"The right of a contractor to arbitration does not exist in the surety on the contractor's performance bond since the surety is not a party to the contract. The surety would be entitled at most to a stay of action on its principal's bond until the owner's rights to compel arbitration of disputes arising under the contract were determined." *U.S. for the Use and Benefit of Frank A. Trucco & Sons Company v. Bergman Construction Corp.*, 256 F.2d 851, 854 (7th Cir. 1958).

"A guarantor who is not a signatory to a contract containing an arbitration clause is not bound by the arbitration clause." *Grundstad v. Ritt*, 106 F.3d 201, 204 (7th Cir. 1997).

"A subcontract with a guarantor or surety may incorporate a duty to arbitrate by reference to an arbitration clause in a general contract." *Gingiss International, Inc. v. Bormet*, 58 F.3d 328, 331-32 (7th Cir. 1995).

## 8. Attorney's Fees

***Statutes and/or case law limiting or permitting recovery of attorney's fees***

215 ILCS 5/155 of the Illinois Insurance Code provides that any action by or against a company wherein there is in issue the liability of a company on a policy of insurance or the amount of the loss payable for an unreasonable delay in settling a claim, and it appears to the court that such action or delay is vexatious and unreasonable, the court may allow as part of the taxable costs in the action reasonable attorney fees, plus an amount not to exceed any one of the following amounts: (a) 60 percent of the amount which the court or jury finds such party is entitled to recover against the company, exclusive of all costs; (b) $60,000; (c) the excess of the amount which the court or jury finds such party is entitled to recover, exclusive of costs, over the amount, if any, which the company offered to pay in settlement of the claim prior to the action.

***What fees are recoverable, if any***

Prejudgment interest as well as damages was properly allowed for the performance bond surety's unreasonable and vexatious delay pursuant to 215 ILCS 5/155 of the Illinois Insurance Code. *Fisher v. Fidelity and Deposit Co. of Maryland*, 125 Ill. App. 3d 632, 643 (Ill. App. 1984).

An obligee's failure to plead that the performance bond surety was liable for attorney's fees for vexatious and unreasonable delay pursuant to 215 ILCS 5/155 is waived if raised for the first time on appeal and an award of attorney's fees against the surety is not authorized in the absence of some statutory basis. *Community Consolidated School District No. 169, Champaign County v. Meneley Construction Company*, 86 Ill. App. 3d 1101, 1105 (Ill. App. 1980).

**9. Special Provisions** – Not applicable.

**10. Remarks** – Not applicable.

**11. Case Annotations**

See *supra* for case annotations.

***Interpretation of AIA bond forms*** – Illinois has no cases that directly interpret the terms and conditions of AIA bonds as they relate to the performing surety's obligations under the bond.

***Cases in which surety steps into shoes of obligee***

Authors' note: There are no reported Illinois cases that specifically affirm *Pearlman v. Reliance Insurance Company,* 371 U.S. 132 (1962).

Where a principal executed a general agreement of indemnity, in which the principal assigned to the surety all of the principal's rights under future contracts to the surety, and the surety issued performance bonds on behalf of the principal, the assignment granted the surety an unperfected security interest in contract proceeds until the principal was declared in default and the surety was required to perform under the bonds, subject to the IRS' superior tax lien; as completing surety, it was subrogated to the rights of the owner. *Capitol Indemnity Corporation v. U.S.*, 41 F.3d 320, 325-26 (7th Cir. 1994).

The court *In re Pyramid Industries, Inc.*, recognized the surety's subrogation rights to recover amounts paid for completion of a construction contract and pursuant to a performance bond subject to the federal government's right of setoff. The court also held that "sureties who have not performed the contract or paid the laborers and material suppliers are not entitled to receive any of the withheld contract proceeds." *In re Pyramid Industries, Inc.*, 170 B.R. 974, (N.D. Ill. 1994).

Where a performance bond states "Whenever Contractor shall be, and declared by Owner to be in default under the Contract, the Owner having performed Owner's obligations thereunder, the Surety may promptly remedy the default" the obligee must declare the contractor in default before the surety can "step into the shoes of [the contractor] and become entitled to the proceeds under the construction contract." *Liberty Mutual Insurance Company v. Construction Management Services, Inc.*, 2004 WL 2271811 (N.D. Ill. October 6, 2004).

# INDIANA

Steven J. Strawbridge and Jeffrey M. Boldt[1]

## 1. Requirement for Bond

**Public** – Indiana law divides public works projects into four distinct categories. Each category of public works project imposes different requirements regarding the provision of performance bonds. The four categories are named according to the part of the Indiana Code that addresses them: Title 4 projects, Title 5 projects, Title 8 projects and Title 36 projects.

***Title 4 projects*** involve the construction or improvement of certain state public works projects solicited by the Indiana Department of Administration after June 30, 1985. Public works means the process of altering, building, constructing, demolishing, improving, or repairing any public structure or building or other public improvement to real property owned by, or leased in the name of, the State of Indiana and includes the preparation of drawings, plans, and specifications therefor. Title 4 projects do not include the following:

---

1 Steven J. Strawbridge is a partner and Jeffrey M. Boldt is an associate of:
Locke Reynolds, LLP
201 N. Illinois Street, Suite 1000
P.O. Box 44961
Indianapolis, Indiana 46244-0961
(317) 237-3800

1. Indiana Commission for Higher Education;
2. State educational institutions;
3. Military offices and military and armory boards of the state;
4. State Fair Commission;
5. Any entity established by the general assembly as a body corporate and political having the authority and power to issue bonds to be secured and repaid solely be revenues pledged for that purpose (however, such an entity shall comply with Title 4 if the law creating the entity requires it to do so); and,
6. Indiana Department of Transportation.

Indiana Code § 4-13.6-7-7(a) provides that:

> [i]f the estimated cost of a public works project is at least $150,000, the contractor must provide a performance bond in an amount equal to 100 percent of the total contract price. The bond shall include at least the following provisions:
>
> (1) The contractor shall well and faithfully perform the contract.
>
> (2) No change, modification, omission, or addition in or to the terms or conditions of the contract, plans, specifications, drawings, or profile or any irregularity or defect in the contract or in the procedures preliminary to the letting and awarding of the contract shall affect or operate to release or discharge the surety in any way.
>
> (3) The provisions and conditions of this chapter shall be a part of the terms of the contract and bond.

Indiana Code § 4-13.6-7-7(b) allows the state to permit the bond given by the contractor to provide for incremental bonding in the form of multiple or chronological bonds that, if taken as a whole, equal the total contract price.

Indiana Code § 4-13.6-7-7(c) provides that the state may accept bonds provided on its own forms or on forms given by surety companies.

***Title 5 projects*** are those state public works projects not covered by Title 4.

Indiana Code § 5-16-5.5-4 pertains to contracts in excess of $100,000 and provides that at the time of entering into any such contract, the contractor must furnish a valid performance bond which is acceptable to the state agency involved in an amount equal to his total contract price. If it is acceptable to the state agency involved, this performance bond may provide for incremental bonding in the form of multiple or chronological bonds which, when taken as a whole, equal the total contract price. No change, modification, omission or addition in and to the terms or conditions of said contract, plans, specifications, drawings or profile or any irregularity or defect in said contract or in the proceedings preliminary to the letting and awarding thereof, shall in any way affect or operate to release or discharge the surety.

***Title 36 projects*** involve local government projects and include all public works projects performed or contracted for by a political subdivision or their agencies, regardless of whether the projects are performed on property owned or leased by the political subdivision or agency. Public work is defined as the construction, reconstruction, alteration, or renovation of a public building, airport facility, or other structure that is paid for out of a public fund or out of a special assessment. It includes construction, alteration, or repair of a highway, street, alley, bridge, sewer, drain, or other improvement that is paid for out of a public fund or out of a special assessment.

Indiana Code § 36-1-12-14(e) provides that on local government projects, all contracts in excess of $100,000 for projects other than highways, roads, streets and related contracts, the contractor must furnish a performance bond equal to the contract price. If acceptable to the board, the performance bond may provide for incremental bonding in the form of multiple or chronological bonds that, when taken as a whole, equal the contract price. The surety on the performance bond may not be released until one year after the date of the board's final settlement with the contractor. The performance bond must specify that:

> (1) a modification, omission, or addition to the terms and conditions of the public work contract, plans, specifications, drawings, or profile; (2) a defect in the public work contract; or
> (3) a defect in the proceedings preliminary to the letting and awarding of the public work contract; does not discharge the surety.

Indiana Code § 36-1-12-14(g) provides that if the contract is for more than $100,000 but less than $250,000, the contractor may substitute a letter of credit acceptable to the board, in place of the performance bond.

**Private** – The State of Indiana does not have a statute that requires performance bonds to be furnished on private work.

**Department of Transportation** – Title 8 projects involve the construction of a highway or bridge in the state highway system or the construction or repair of a building or other structure for the Department of Transportation.

Indiana Code § 8-23-9-8 provides that contractors bidding on Department of Transportation projects must submit a performance bond payable to the state. However this requirement may be waived by the state on contracts of less than $100,000.

Indiana Code § 8-23-9-12 provides the exact language which must be used on a performance bond issued in connection with work performed on behalf of the Indiana Department of Transportation.

***Case law rules that might generally apply*** – Not applicable.

## 2. Damages Covered

***Set forth in any statutes and/or case law***

Indiana Code § 8-23-9-10 provides that on a Title 8 contract, any party to whom money is due for labor or materials must, within one year after the acceptance of said labor and materials, furnish the surety with a statement of the amount owed.

Indiana Code § 8-23-9-25 provides that if a contractor fails to commence or carry forward, improperly performs, has abandoned, fails or refused to complete its contract, the commissioner may relet the work or may complete the work. The commissioner shall deduct the cost of completion from any amount due the contractor and, if that is not sufficient, the commissioner shall require the surety to pay the balance.

***Obligations of surety to perform and/or pay*** – Not applicable.

***Whether failure to provide insurance transfers burden to surety*** – Not applicable.

***Limitations on damages***

A surety's obligation under its performance bond is no greater than that of its principal's obligation to the owner. *State ex rel. Lawson v. Warren Bros. Roads, Co.*, 59 N.E.2d 912 (Ind. App. 1945). A surety's liability for the failure of the contractor to comply with the terms and conditions of its contract is limited to the extent of the obligation of the surety's bond. *Id.* A surety's liability is determined by the language of the bond (and any applicable statutes in the case of a public bond) and that liability cannot be enlarged beyond the fair import of the bond's terms. *Id.*

***Whether obligee may set off bonded contract funds against other principal-obligee debts or obligations*** – Not applicable.

***Incorporation of specific contract terms by reference*** – Not applicable.

### 3. Penal Sum Variations

***Limitations per statute*** – Indiana Code § 8-23-9-9 provides that on Title 8 projects, the amount of a performance bond is set by the commissioner but may not be less than a bidder's proposal or the contract price.

***Effect of changes in work upon penal sum, if at all*** – Not applicable.

***Statutory or case law protections or dangers to penal sum*** – Not applicable.

### 4. Parties Covered

***Statutes and/or case law as to whether only obligees are covered*** – Not applicable.

***Coverage for:***

**Third-party beneficiaries** – Generally, the only intended beneficiary of a performance bond is the named obligee and in rare instances a lender may be named a co-obligee. However, Indiana courts have determined in unique situations that unnamed third-parties may make claims against a performance bond. Such a claimant must show that the materials or labor provided bore a close relationship to the project and that specific language in the bond or underlying contract exists showing that non-privies are protected under the bond. *Garco Indust. Equipment Co., Inc. v. Mallory*, 485 N.E.2d 652, 655 (Ind. Ct. App. 1985). Such language should indicate that the contractor is bound to pay for labor or materials or that the contract can not be completed without payment to laborers and materialmen. *Id.*

**Assignees** – There are no Indiana cases or statutes discussing assignment of obligee's rights to make a claim against a performance bond.

**Dual obligees** – There are no Indiana cases or statutes discussing a dual obligee's rights to make a claim against a performance bond.

## 5. Notice or Filing Required

***Statutory provisions***

**Title 4 projects** – Indiana Code § 4-13.6-7-10(a) provides, *inter alia*, that in order to proceed against the bond of the contractor required under IC § 4-13.6-7-6, any subcontractor or supplier making a claim for payment on account of having performed any labor or having furnished any material or service in relation to a public works project must file a verified claim with the division within 60 days from the last labor performed, last material furnished, or last service rendered. The claim must state the amount due and owing to the person and shall give as much detail explaining the claim as possible.

Indiana Code § 4-13.6-7-10(b) provides that in order to proceed against the bond of the contractor required under IC § 4-13.6-7-6, the claimant must notify the surety of the contractor by sending a copy of the claim required by subsection (a) to the surety company. The claimant shall also inform the division that the surety has been notified. The division shall supply the claimant with any information the claimant requires to notify the surety.

Indiana Code § 4-13.6-7-10(c) provides that the claimant may not file suit against the contractor's surety on the contractor's bond until the expiration of 30 days after filing of the claim with the division. If the claim is not paid in full at the expiration of the 30-day period, the claimant may bring an action in a court of competent jurisdiction in the claimant's own name upon the bond.

**Title 8 projects** – Indiana Code § 8-23-9-10 provides that on Title 8 contracts, any party to whom money is due for labor or materials must, within one year after the acceptance of said labor and materials, furnish the surety with a statement of the amount owed.

Indiana Code § 8-23-9-11 provides that on Title 8 contracts, suit may not be brought against a surety on a bond until the expiration of 60 days after the furnishing of a statement under IC § 8-23-9-10. If the amount owed is not paid after the 60-day waiting period, the party may bring a suit in its own name upon the bond. The action must be commenced within 18 months from the date of final acceptance of the highway or improvement.

***Case law rules concerning condition precedent notice*** – Not applicable.

## 6. Time for Suit

***Statutes of limitation particular to performance bonds and other applicable statutes of limitation***

**Title 4 projects** – Indiana Code § 4-13.6-7-7(d) provides that on Title 4 contracts, the state shall not release sureties of a contractor until the expiration of one year after the final settlement with the contractor.

Indiana Code § 4-13.6-7-11 provides that unless the bond provides a greater period of time, all suits must be brought against a surety on a bond required by this chapter within one year after final settlement with the contractor under IC § 4-13.6-7-8. All suits against the surety after this time are barred.

**Title 5 projects** – Indiana Code § 5-16-5.5-4 provides in pertinent part that the surety on a Title 5 performance bond shall not be released for a period of one year after final settlement with the contractor.

Indiana Code § 5-16-5.5-7 provides that all suits must be brought against a surety on a Title 5 performance bond within one year after the completion of the work or service in question .

**Title 8 projects** – Indiana Code § 8-23-9-10 provides that on Title 8 contracts, any party to whom money is due for labor or materials must, within one year after the acceptance of said labor and materials, furnish the surety with a statement of the amount owed.

Indiana Code § 8-23-9-11 provides that on Title 8 contracts, suit may not be brought against a surety on a bond until the expiration of 60 days after the furnishing of a statement under IC § 8-23-9-10. If the amount owed is not paid after the 60-day waiting period, the party may bring a suit in its own name upon the bond. The action must be commenced within 18 months from the date of final acceptance of the highway or improvement.

**Title 36 projects** – Indiana Code § 36-1-12-14(g) provides that on Title 36 contracts, actions against a surety on a performance bond must be brought within one year after the date of the board's final settlement with the contractor.

**Non-governmental provisions** – *Indiana Code § 34-11-2-11* provides that an action upon contracts in writing other than those for the payment of money, and including all mortgages other than chattel mortgages, deeds of trust, judgments of courts of record, and for the recovery of the possession of real estate, must be commenced within 10 years after the cause of action accrues.

Generally, a cause of action accrues when a wrongfully inflicted injury causes damage. *C & E Corp. v. Ramco Indus.*, 717 N.E.2d 642, 644 (Ind. Ct. App. 1999). It is not necessary that the extent of the damage be known or even ascertainable, but only that some ascertainable damage has occurred. *Id.* at 644.

***Case law statements about enforceability of limitations contained in bonds***

While sureties are not "favorites of the law," gratuitous or accommodation sureties are entitled to a strict construction of the contract in their favor, so as not to impose a greater burden on them than they agreed to. This rule, however, does not apply in the case of a surety for hire. Instead, the contract of a surety for hire is viewed as analogous to an insurance contract and is construed most strictly against the surety and in favor of the person to be protected. *Knight & Jillson Co. v. Castle*, 87 N.E. 976, 981 (Ind. 1909); *Garco Indust. Equipment Co., Inc. v. Mallory*, 485 N.E.2d 652, 654 (Ind. Ct. App. 1985).

***Varying statutes of limitations by agreement in bond or contract***

A contractual provision limiting the time within which an action must be brought may be valid, *Statesman Ins. Co. v. Reibly*, 371 N.E.2d 414 (Ind. Ct. App. 1978); *Schafer v. Buckeye Union Ins. Co.*, 381 N.E.2d 519, but it is not favored, *Id.* The person asserting such a provision may waive it or be estopped to use it. *Statesman Ins. Co.*, 371 N.E.2d 414. A limitations period imposed contractually must afford a reasonable time within which to commence an action. *Schafer*, 381 N.E.2d 519.

## 7. Procedure

***Statutory or procedural rules that may affect handling or administration of lawsuits*** – Not applicable.

***Venue requirements and jurisdictional limitations***

In *Kimco Leasing, Inc. v. Ransom Junior High School*, 556 N.E.2d 1371 (Ind. Ct. App. 1990), it was held that when a trial court has subject matter jurisdiction, a party to a contract may consent to personal jurisdiction. The court found a forum selection clause to be prima facie valid and that a trial court could only disregard such a clause when the party opposing enforcement clearly shows that "enforcement would be unreasonable and unjust," or that the clause was invalid for such reason as fraud or overreaching.

To determine whether an Indiana court has personal jurisdiction, a court must proceed with a two-step analysis. *Anthem Ins. Cos., Inc. v. Tenet Healthcare Corp.*, 730 N.E.2d, 1227, 1232 (Ind. 2000); *Brockman v. Kravic*, 779 N.E.2d 1250, 1255 (Ind. Ct. App. 2002). First, the court must determine if the defendant's contacts with Indiana fall under the "long-arm statute," Ind. Trial Rule 4.4. *Anthem*, 730 N.E.2d at 1231-32. Trial Rule 4.4 enumerates eight acts which can serve as the basis for jurisdiction over non-residents. If the contacts fall under Rule 4.4, the court must then determine whether the defendant's contacts satisfy federal due process analysis. *Id.* at 1232.

Indiana Code 32-28-3-17 is part of the Indiana Mechanics' Lien Statute and provides that a provision in a contract for the improvement of real estate in Indiana is void if the provision either makes the contract subject to the laws of another state; or requires litigation, arbitration, or other dispute resolution process on the contract occur in another state.

***Court rules*** – Not applicable.

***Particular agency regulations/rules*** – Not applicable.

***Arbitration requirements and application***

*See generally*, Indiana Code § 34-57-2 through Indiana Code § 34-57-2-22, The Indiana Uniform Arbitration Act.

Indiana Code § 34-57-2-1(a) provides that "[a] written agreement to submit to arbitration is valid, and enforceable, an existing controversy or a controversy thereafter arising is valid and enforceable, except upon such grounds as exist at law or in equity for the revocation of any contract. If the parties to such an agreement stipulate in writing, the agreement may be enforced by designated third persons, who shall in such instances have the same rights as a party under this chapter."

Indiana recognizes a strong policy favoring enforcement of arbitration agreements. *Northwestern Mut. Life Ins. Co. v. Stinnett*, 698 N.E.2d 339, 343 (Ind. Ct. App. 1998). Nevertheless, because arbitration is a matter of contract, a party cannot be required to submit to arbitration unless he or she has agreed to do so. *Int'l Creative Mgmt., Inc. v. D & R Entm't Co.*, 670 N.E.2d 1305, 1311 (Ind. Ct. App. 1996), *trans. denied*; *Mid-America Surgery Center, L.L.C. v. Schooler*, 719 N.E.2d 1267 (Ind. Ct. App. 1999).

## 8. Attorney's Fees

***Statutes and/or case law limiting or permitting recovery of attorney's fees***

Indiana follows the American Rule, which ordinarily requires each party to pay his own attorney's fees. *Swartz v. Swartz*, 720 N.E.2d 1219, 1223 (Ind. Ct. App. 1999). Generally, attorney's fees are not recoverable from the opposing party as costs, damages, or otherwise, in the absence of an agreement between the parties, statutory authority, or rule to the contrary. *Id.*

Attorney's fees are not recoverable without an express contractual obligation or specific statutory authority stipulating such fees are recoverable. *Shumate v. Lycan*, 675 N.E.2d 749, 754 (Ind. App. 1997), *trans. denied.*

***What fees are recoverable, if any***

A trial court has wide discretion in awarding attorney's fees. *Mason v. Mason*, 775 N.E.2d 706, 711 (Ind. Ct. App. 2002), *trans. denied,* 792 N.E.2d 34 (Ind. 2003). The court may look at the responsibility of the parties in incurring the attorney's fees. *Id.* The judge has personal expertise he or she may use when determining reasonable attorney's fees. *Id.*

Pursuant to Ind. Professional Conduct Rule 1.5(a) these factors must be considered in determining the reasonableness of a fee:

(1) the time and labor required, the novelty and difficulty of the questions involved, and the skill requisite to perform the legal service properly;

(2) the likelihood, if apparent to the client, that the acceptance of the particular employment will preclude other employment by the lawyer;

(3) the fee customarily charged in the locality for similar services;

(4) the amount involved and the results obtained;

(5) the time limitations imposed by the client or by the circumstances;

(6) the nature and length of the professional relationship with the client;

(7) the experience, reputation, and ability of the lawyer or lawyers performing the services; and

(8) whether the fee is fixed or contingent.

***Incorporation of specific contract terms*** – Not applicable.

**9. Special Provisions** – Not applicable.

**10. Remarks**

Where a surety provided a performance bond which incorporated its principal's contract with a municipality and the municipality has fully performed, the surety cannot avoid its liability under the performance bond even if the municipality failed to follow legal formalities when letting the contract. *City of Crawfordsville v. Price*, 778 N.E.2d 495 (Ind. App. 2002).

**11. Case Annotations**

***Interpretation of AIA bond forms*** – Indiana cases have not specifically addressed AIA forms of bonds A311 and A312.

***Cases in which surety steps into shoes of obligee***

The surety's rights of subrogation relate back to the date when the bond was issued and thus entitle the surety to priority in payment over all subsequent lienholders and general creditors. *Southern Surety Co. v Merchants' and Farmers' Bank of Avilla*, 176 N.E. 146 (Ind. 1931); *Southern Railroad Co. v. Bertz*, 104 N.E. 19 (Ind. 1914); *Fidelity & Casualty Co. of New York v. Indiana National Bank*, 216 N.E.2d 857 (Ind. Ct. App. 1966).

# IOWA

Benjamin B. Ullem[1]

## 1. Requirement for Bond

***Statutory provisions for projects that are:***

**Public** – I.C.A. § 99G.23 requires a vendor who has executed a contract with the Iowa Lottery Authority to post a performance bond or letter of credit from a bank or credit provider in an amount deemed necessary by the Authority.

I.C.A. § 207.10 requires a coal mine operator to file a performance bond of not less than $10,000 before the issuance of a coal mining permit.

I.C.A. § 455B.275 permits the Department of Natural Resources to require the furnishing of a performance bond as a condition of an approval order or permit issued pursuant to a contract involving water allocation and use or flood plain control.

I.C.A. § 468.36 requires the successful bidder of a contract to construct a levee or drainage improvement in a drainage district to execute a performance bond in an amount not less than 75 percent of the contract price of the work.

---

[1] Benjamin B. Ullem is a member of:
Whitfield & Eddy, P.L.C.
317 6th Avenue, Suite 1200
Des Moines, Iowa 50309-4112
(515) 288-6041

I.C.A. § 573.2 requires a performance bond on a contract for the construction of a public improvement when the contract price equals or exceeds $25,000 and under § 573.3 this requirement may not be limited or avoided by contract.

I.C.A. § 12.44 requires state agencies to waive the requirement of a performance bond for targeted small businesses that are able to demonstrate a lack of ability to secure such a bond due to lack of experience, lack of net worth, or lack of capital.

**Private** – Iowa does not require performance bonds on private jobs. See Iowa Code Chapter 572. I.C.A. § 543C.4 requires the owner or subdivider of land outside the state that is to be sold in the state to either furnish a performance bond executed by an authorized surety or place sufficient funds in escrow.

**Department of Transportation** – Not applicable.

**Other** – I.C.A. § 9D.3 requires an application to establish a travel agency to be accompanied by a surety or cash performance bond in the principal amount of $10,000.

I.C.A. § 706A.3 permits the district court, before the determination of liability, to require the execution of a performance bond to prevent, restrain, or remedy violations constituting ongoing criminal conduct under § 706A.2 that are the subject of a civil proceeding.

I.C.A. § 809A.12 permits a court, before or after the filing of a notice of pending forfeiture of property or a complaint against an accused, and on application of the prosecutor, to require the execution of a performance bond.

## 2. Damages Covered

***Set forth in any statutes and/or case law***

I.C.A. § 9D.3 provides that the registrant of the bond shall pay any judgment recovered by a person in an Iowa court for actual damages, or for rescission, resulting from a claim involving the offer or sale of travel services. The bond is open to successive claims but the aggregate amount of damages paid may not exceed the principal amount of the bond.

I.C.A. § 207.14 provides that upon the discovery of certain violations during an inspection, the attorney general shall institute forfeiture proceedings when a coal mine operator fails to demonstrate cause as to why their permit should not be revoked. All reasonable costs and expenses may be assessed against either party.

***Obligations of surety to perform and/or pay***

"Under a performance bond, a surety generally has two options if the principal defaults: (1) undertake the completion of the principal's work itself; or (2) pay the obligee the amount of the bond." *Employers Mut. Cas. Co. v. United Fire & Cas. Co.*, 682 N.W.2d 452, 456 (Iowa App. 2004).

***Whether failure to provide insurance transfers burden to surety***

Sureties on a contractor's bond were not liable for damages caused by negligent acts of the contractor's employees when the contractor failed to obtain liability insurance and the county permitted the contract to go into effect without it. The court determined that shifting the liability to the bond would diminish the protection to those individuals for whose use and benefit the bond was required. *Schisel v. Marvill*, 198 Iowa 725, 197 N.W. 662 (1924).

***Limitations on damages***

I.C.A. § 9D.3 provides that the bond is open to successive claims but the aggregate amount of damages paid may not exceed the principal amount of the bond.

"Up to the face of a private bond the surety is liable for interest the same as the principal. For any other interest in excess of the face of the bond the surety can be held liable only for its own default." *Mechanicsville Trust & Sav. Bank v. Hawkeye-Security Ins. Co.*, 158 N.W.2d 89, 93 (Iowa 1968).

***Whether obligee may set off bonded contract funds against other principal-obligee debts or obligations***

"It was held in *Stadler Bros. & Co. v. Parmlee & Watts*, 10 Iowa 23 (1859), that if the bond was joint and several, the obligee might set off his damages against a demand in favor of one or all the obligors. But not so when the bond was joint only." *Branch of State Bank v. Morris*, 13 Iowa 136 (1862).

***Incorporation of specific contract terms by reference***

"[L]iability may not be predicated upon provisions of a statutory bond which are broader than and beyond the requirements of the statute providing for the bond, and under which the bond is given." *Ottumwa Boiler Works v. M. J. O'Meara & Son*, 206 Iowa 577, 586, 218 N.W. 920, 924 (1928).

"Having made reference in the bond to the contract and the conditions, guaranties, and agreements in the contract, and having bound itself as surety to the performance of the contract, it must be [held] to have undertaken the performance of all the agreements of the contract." *Streator Clay Mfg. Co. v. Henning-Vineyard Co.*, 176 Iowa 297, 311, 155 N.W. 1001, 1005 (1916).

"'The surety may not stand upon the strict letter of its undertaking and demand to be released therefrom for any and every variation in the terms or the performance of its principal's contract, with reference to which the surety's agreement is made, but it may insist upon the compliance with requirements, clearly expressed, which are made the condition to liability.'" *Gileman & Gindt v. Faus*, 178 Iowa 644, 658, 158 N.W. 597, 602 (1916) (quoting *Doyle v. Faust*, 153 N.W. 725 (Mich. 1915)).

## 3. Penal Sum Variations

***Limitations per statute*** – I.C.A. § 9D.3 provides that the bond is open to successive claims but the aggregate amount of damages paid may not exceed the principal amount of the bond.

***Statutory or case law protections or damages to penal sum***

"When a surety takes over performance of a contract, the surety's liability is no longer limited by the amount of the bond. We note: Ordinarily, a surety on a bond is not liable beyond the penalty named therein. However, this limitation may be varied by the contract, by bad faith on the part of the surety, or by statute; and where a surety assumes the role of the principal and completes the contract, the surety is liable to pay sums in excess of the penal sum." *Employers Mut. Cas. Co. v. United Fire & Cas. Co.*, 682 N.W.2d 452, 457 (Iowa App. 2004) (citations omitted).

## 4. Parties Covered

***Statutes and/or case law as to whether only obligees are covered***

"The liability of a surety is to be determined by the specified conditions of the bond and cannot be enlarged beyond them. It is frequently stated by courts that the intention of the parties to a contractor's bond is the controlling factor in determining the right of laborers and materialmen to recover thereon." *Bourrett v. W. M. Bride Constr. Co.*, 248 Iowa 1080, 1084, 84 N.W.2d 4, 6-7 (1957).

"The fact only the owner is named as obligee of the bond is unimportant. 'Although there are a few outside decisions to the contrary it is well settled in Iowa and is the weight of authority generally that laborers and materialmen may recover on a contractor's bond conditioned that the contractor shall pay all claims for labor and material, or shall faithfully perform a contract providing for such payment, although the owner alone is named as obligee of the bond.'" *Westinghouse Electric Corp. v. Mill & Elevator Co.*, 254 Iowa 874, 878, 118 N.W.2d 528, 530 (1962) (quoting *Bourrett v. W. M. Bride Constr. Co.*, 248 Iowa 1080, 1085, 84 N.W.2d 4, 7 (1957)).

***Coverage for:***

**Third-party beneficiaries** A subcontractor who has furnished material to a public contractor may maintain an action on the performance bond given to the public corporation:

1. When the bond by reference makes the contract a part thereof.
2. When the contract by reference makes certain instructions to bidders a part thereof.
3. When the instructions to bidders require a bond to protect subcontractors.

*Clinton Bridge Works v. Kingsley*, 188 Iowa 218 (1920).

**Assignees** – Materialman to which contractor assigned contract, thereby terminating agreement to purchase materials, held in no better position to recover from surety on contractor's bond for materials furnished than contractor would have been for his own default. *Sibley Lumber Co. v. Madsen*, 198 Iowa 880, 200 N.W. 425 (Iowa 1924).

**Dual obligees** – "At some point in the trial below, defendants raised objections to the right of the obligees in the bond to join in bringing suit thereon, insisting that, if either or any of said obligees had sustained any damage, it was individual in character, and a recovery therefor could be had only in an individual and separate action. The same question is raised in this court, and is practically the single proposition relied upon for a reversal of the judgment below. The lack of merit in the point so made is too manifest to call for any extended consideration." *Dennis v. Mantle*, 173 Iowa 450, 451 (1916).

## 5. Notice or Filing Required

Counsel should note that while Iowa Code Chapter 573 addresses the requirements for what purports to be a *performance* bond on public jobs, there are separate notice and timing provisions contained therein with respect to claims for *payment.*

***Statutory provisions***

I.C.A. § 207.14 provides that "[w]hen on the basis of an inspection, or other information available to the division, the administrator has reasonable cause to believe that the [coal mine] operator is unable to complete reclamation of all or a portion of the permit area as required by law, the administrator shall issue an order to the operator to show cause as to why all or a portion of the performance bond required by section 207.10 should not be revoked."

***Case law rules concerning condition precedent notice***

"We may also observe that the rule prevails in many jurisdictions that failure to give a paid surety any notice of the contractor's default in failing to complete the building in the time agreed upon is no defense to an action on the bond based upon default arising from unpaid claims for labor and material." *Rowe v. Stufflebeam*, 249 Iowa 985, 988-989, 89 N.W.2d 875, 877 (1958).

"[T]he condition requiring notice to the surety is one to be performed after the occurrence of the loss or damage for which recovery is sought, and is not essential to the binding force of the contract while it is running prior to any default. Conditions of this class pertain to the remedy, and, though precedent to the maintenance of an action, are not ordinarily as strictly construed by the courts as are those conditions involving the essence of the agreement." *Van Buren County v. Am. Sur. Co.*, 137 Iowa 490, 495, 115, N.W. 24, 27 (1908).

## 6. Time for Suit

***Statutes of limitation particular to performance bonds and other applicable statutes of limitation***

I.C.A. § 573.16 requires the public corporation, principal contractor, any claimant who has filed a claim, or the surety to bring an action in equity after the expiration of 30 days, and not later than 60 days, following the completion and final acceptance of the public improvement.

I.C.A. § 614.1 provides that statute of limitations for actions on a written contract is 10 years.

I.C.A. § 614.1 provides that actions "founded on the cancellation, transfer, redemption, or replacement of public bonds or obligations by an issuer, trustee, transfer agent, registrar, depository, paying agent, or other agent of the public bonds or obligations, [must be brought] within 11 years of the cancellation, transfer, redemption, or replacement of the public bonds or obligations."

***Case law statements about enforceability of limitations contained in bonds***

A provision of a bond given to secure the performance of a contract that any action thereon must be brought within six months after the breach of the contract is a reasonable one, and constitutes a complete defense by the surety to an action brought against it thereon more than six months after the alleged breach of the contract. *Marshalltown Stone Co. v. Louis Drach Constr. Co.*, 123 F. 746 (S.D. Iowa 1903). *See also*, *Douglass v. American Family Mutual Insurance Co.*, 508 N.W.2d 665, 667 (Iowa 1993). *See also, infra.*

***Varying statutes of limitation by agreement in bond or contract***

"In Iowa, the Iowa Supreme Court has consistently held that individuals may enter into 'private agreements which vary general statutes of limitations' ... Under Iowa law, a contractual limitations period is enforceable if it is reasonable under the circumstances of the particular case and sufficient to allow a plaintiff to file a claim after the alleged damage has been ascertained." *Davidson v. Wal-Mart Associates Health and Welfare Plan*, 305 F. Supp. 2d 1059, 1069-1071 (S.D. Iowa 2004) (citations omitted).

**7. Procedure**

***Statutory or procedural rules that may affect handling or administration of lawsuits*** – Not applicable.

***Venue requirements and jurisdictional limitations***

I.C.A. § 616.7 provides that "[w]hen, by its terms, a written contract is to be performed in any particular place, action for a breach thereof may, except as otherwise provided, be brought in the county wherein such place is situated."

I.C.A. § 616.5 provides that "[s]uit may be brought against any company or corporation furnishing or pretending to furnish surety, fidelity, or other bonds in this state, in any county in which the principal place of business of such company or corporation is maintained in this state, or in any county wherein is maintained its general office for the transaction of its Iowa business, or in the county where the principal resides at the time of bringing suit, or in the county where the principal did reside at the time the bond or other undertaking was executed; and in the case of bonds furnished by any such company or corporation for any building or improvement, either public or private, action may be brought in the county wherein said building or improvement, or any part thereof is located."

I.C.A. § 616.14 provides that "[w]hen a corporation, company, or individual has an office or agency in any county for the transaction of business, any actions growing out of or connected with the business of that office or agency may be brought in the county where such office or agency is located."

"Personal jurisdiction over a nonresident defendant can exist under the Due Process Clause only when 'the defendant has 'certain minimum contacts with [the forum state] such that the maintenance of the suit does not offend 'traditional notions of fair play and substantial justice''' ... We consider five factors to determine whether a nonresident defendant has sufficient minimum contacts with Iowa: (1) the quantity of the contacts; (2) the nature and quality of the contacts; (3) the source of and connection of the cause of action with those contacts; (4) the interest of the forum state; and (5) the convenience of the parties." *Ross v. Thousand Adventures*, 675 N.W.2d 812, 815-816 (Iowa 2004) (citations omitted).

***Court rules***

Iowa has adopted a uniform system of practice in state district courts which are denominated the Iowa Rules of Civil Procedure. Each Iowa Judicial District may adopt further local rules. To the extent such rules exist, they are available at http://www.judicial.state.ia.us/rules/local/.

***Particular agency regulations/rules*** – Not applicable.

***Arbitration requirements and application***

Iowa has its own version of the Uniform Arbitration Act. *See* Iowa Code Chapter 679A.

"Although arbitrability is for the courts to decide, judicial determination of arbitrability is limited to (1) whether the agreement contains a grievance procedure providing for compulsory arbitration of contractual disputes and (2) whether the grievance alleges a violation of a provision of the agreement. The court may not consider the merits of the underlying claim in analyzing arbitrability. There is a presumption of arbitrability when the agreement contains an arbitration clause unless it may be said with positive assurance that the arbitration clause is not susceptible of an interpretation that covers the asserted dispute. Doubts should be resolved in favor of coverage." *State v. State Police Officers Council*, 525 N.W.2d 834, 836 (Iowa 1994) (citations omitted).

**8. Attorney's Fees**

***Statutes and/or case law limiting or permitting recovery of attorney's fees***

I.C.A. § 9D.3 permits the recovery of reasonable attorney's fees.

I.C.A. § 207.14 permits the recovery of reasonable attorney's fees.

I.C.A. § 573.21 permits the recovery of reasonable attorney's fees for "any claimant for labor or materials who has, in whole or in part, established a claim."

***What fees are recoverable***

"'An applicant for attorney fees has the burden to prove that the services were reasonably necessary and that the charges were reasonable in amount.' The district court should consider a number of factors, including 'the time necessarily spent, the nature and extent of the service, the amount involved, the difficulty of handling and importance of the issues, the responsibility assumed and results obtained, the standing and experience of the attorney in the profession, and the customary charges for similar service.'" *GreatAmerica Leasing Corp. v. Cool Comfort Air Conditioning & Refrigeration, Inc.*, 691 N.W.2d 730, 733 (Iowa 2005) (citations omitted).

**9. Special Provisions** – Not applicable.

## 10. Remarks

"[W]here the situation is such as to require a statutory bond, and the bond given by the contractor conforms in material and essential respects to the requirements of the statute, the parties will be held to have intended to make a statutory bond, notwithstanding the omission from the bond of other conditions required by the statute, or the inclusion of stipulations contrary to the statute." *Philip Carey Co. v. Maryland Cas. Co.*, 201 Iowa 1063, 1069, 206 N.W. 808, 810 (1926).

Conversely, statutory provisions are read into statutory bond and they prevail over contrary bond provisions. *United Fire & Cas. Co. v. Acker*, 541 N.W.2d 517 (Iowa 1995).

## 11. Case Annotations

***Interpretation of AIA bond forms*** – Iowa has no statutes or cases on this issue.

***Cases in which surety steps into shoes of obligee***

"In the case of a surety, the essential prerequisite to subrogation is the payment of the obligation by the surety. When he has done this, a court of equity may, and generally should, grant subrogation, by letting the surety step into the shoes of the creditor, as to any lien or equity the creditor may have against the obligor. The right to subrogation is not a contractual right. It is one established and recognized by equity as within its plenary power to effectuate justice. The very basis and foundation of the right rests upon performance of the obligation on the part of the surety. There can be no subrogation until the surety has performed. Then, and not until then, does any right to subrogation come into being." *Leach v. Com. Sav. Bank*, 205 Iowa 1154, 1161, 213 N.W. 517, 520 (1928).

# KANSAS

Lawrence Lerner and Cline I. Boone[1]

## 1. Requirement for Bond

***Statutory provisions for projects that are:***

**Public** – There are several Kansas statutes that require public performance bonds.

K.S.A. 13-1343 requires contractors that contract with the board of park commissioners of any city for the performance of *any work* in excess of $100 to provide a performance bond equal to the contract price.

K.S.A. 68-704 requires any contractor that contracts with the board of county commissioners in any county for the improvement of *any road* to provide a performance bond for at least the amount of the contract.

K.S.A. 19-214 requires contractors that contract with the board of county commissioners for the expenditure of county moneys for the construction of *any courthouse, jail or other county building, or the construction of any bridge* in excess of $10,000 to provide a performance bond in the amount of the contract.

K.S.A. 68-521 requires contractors that contract with the board of county commissioners for the *construction, surfacing, repairing or*

[1] Lawrence Lerner is a shareholder and Cline I. Boone is a member of:
Levy and Craig, A Professional Corporation
1301 Oak Street
Kansas City, Missouri 64106
(816) 474-8181

*maintaining of any road* in excess of $10,000 to provide a performance bond in the penal sum of the amount of the contract.

K.S.A. 24-525 requires contractors that contract with the Board of Directors of *any drainage district for improvements* to provide a performance bond.

K.S.A. 24-426 requires contractors that contract with the Board of Directors of *any drainage district for any work* done under the provisions of this act to provide a performance bond in a sum sufficient to secure the proper execution of the contract and conditioned to pay all damages.

K.S.A. 42-373 requires contractors that contract with the Board of Irrigation Commissioners of any district to build *any irrigation works or any portion thereof to supply water for the purpose of irrigating the lands* of said irrigation district to provide a performance bond that is sufficient as deemed by the board.

**Private (Quasi-Public)** – K.S.A. 17-1902 allows a city to require a *telecommunications provider* to obtain a performance bond for any construction and maintenance of facilities located in a public right of way.

No statutes in Kansas require performance bonds on private projects.

**Department of Transportation** – K.S.A. 68-410 requires contractors to provide a performance and payment bond to the Secretary of Transportation for all projects which exceed $1,000 except such bond is not required when the construction contract is between the Secretary of Transportation and the various counties. Such bond must be filed with and approved by the Secretary of State. The bond amount shall be not less than the contract amount.

***Case law rules that might generally apply***

A bond is a contract, the meaning of which is to be ascertained in the same manner as the meaning of any other contract and within that meaning, the surety is bound to the extent it has agreed to be bound. *Stevens v. Farmers Elevator Mutual Ins. Co.,* 197 Kan. 74, 76, 415 P.2d 236 (1966).

When a statute requires a bond to be given, and a bondsman undertakes to furnish it, the obligation of the bond imposed by the statute is read into the terms of the bond, and the bond must be interpreted in the light of the statute. *Bartley v. Bartley,* 171 Kan. 465, 233 P.2d 735 (1951); *Ellsworth v. Hurt,* 158 Kan. 232, 233, 146 P.2d 365 (1944).

## 2. Damages Covered

***Set forth in any statutes and/or case law***

K.S.A. 40-256 states "That in all actions hereafter commenced, in which judgment is rendered against any insurance company as defined in K.S.A. 40-201, and including in addition thereto any fraternal benefit society and any reciprocal or interinsurance exchange on any policy or certificate of any type or kind of insurance, if it appear from the evidence that such company, society or exchange has refused without just cause or excuse to pay the full amount of such loss, the court in rendering such judgment shall allow the plaintiff a reasonable sum as an *attorney's fee* for services in such action, including proceeding upon appeal, to be recovered and collected as a part of the costs: *Provided, however,* That when a tender is made by such insurance company, society or exchange before the commencement of the action in which judgment is rendered and the amount recovered is not in excess of such tender no such costs shall be allowed." (emphasis added).

K.S.A. 16-201 states "Creditors shall be allowed to receive interest at the rate of 10 percent per annum, when no other rate of interest is agreed upon, for any money after it becomes due; for money lent or money due on settlement of account, from the day of liquidating the account and ascertaining the balance; for money received for the use of another and retained without the owner's knowledge of the receipt; for money due and withheld by an unreasonable and vexatious delay of payment or settlement of accounts; for all other money due and to become due for the forbearance of payment whereof an express promise to pay interest has been made; and for money due from corporations and individuals to their daily or monthly employees, from and after the end of each month, unless paid within 15 days thereafter."

K.S.A. 16-205(a) states "When a rate of interest or charges is specified in any contract, that rate shall continue until full payment is made, and any judgment rendered on any such contract shall bear the same rate of interest or charges mentioned in the contract, which rate shall be specified in the judgment; but in no case shall such rate or charges exceed the maximum rate or amount authorized by law, and any bond, note, bill, or other contract for the payment of money, which in effect provides that any interest or charges or any higher rate of interest or charges shall accrue as a penalty for any default, shall be void as to any such provision."

***Obligations of surety to perform and/or pay***

Surety may be responsible for prejudgment interest in action against performance bond by subcontractor pursuant to K.S.A. 16-201. *Blinne Contracting Co., Inc. v. Bobby Goins*, 715 F. Supp 1044 (D. Kan. 1989).

***Whether failure to provide insurance transfers burden to surety*** – Generally there are no cases addressing this.

***Limitations on damages***

Under principles of general law the obligation of a bond is to be measured by the bond itself and may not be extended by implication or enlarged by construction beyond the terms of the executed contract. *In re Conservatorship of Huerta*, 273 Kan. 97, 41 P.3d 814 (2002).

Generally, damages for breach of contract are limited to pecuniary loss sustained, and exemplary or punitive damages are not recoverable, in absence of independent tort or wrong causing additional injury. *Mabery v. Western Cas. & Sur. Co.,* 173 Kan. 586, 250 P.2d 824 (1952).

In an action for breach of a penal bond, interest on the amount of the recovery is generally recoverable as an element of damages for delay upon the part of the surety in making payment after he should have paid, even though the total sum is thus made to exceed the stated amount of the penalty of the bond, and therefore, judgment may be had for the whole penalty of the bond, and in addition thereto interest and costs, and need not be so limited that the whole recovery, including interest and costs, does not exceed the penalty; nor does an allowance of reasonable costs and legal expenses violate the general rule which limits liability on a bond to the penal sum named in the bond. *In re Conservatorship of Huerta*, 273 Kan. 97, 41 P.3d 814 (2002).

***Whether obligee may set off bonded contract funds against other principal-obligee debts or obligations***

Contractor's surety could not defeat liability on bond to owner on ground that surety was not party to action between contractor and owner, where surety refrained from participating in action, though properly notified thereof. Where surety executed contract guaranteeing contractor's faithful performance, owner could recover from surety necessary and reasonable expenses incurred in defeating contractor's laborers' and materialmen's lien claims in litigation of which surety was properly notified, but in which surety refrained from participating. *Olmstead v. Fidelity & Deposit Co. of Maryland*, 138 Kan. 825, 28 P.2d 722 (1934).

The contract right of a surety to collect premium on bond for performance of contract with drainage district given under statute is not affected by agreement between directors of district and contractor to which surety is not a party. *Fidelity & Deposit Co. of Maryland v. Callahan Bros.*, 98 Kan. 547, 158 P. 658 (1916).

***Incorporation of specific contract terms by reference***

The rule is established that the obligations of those signing a statutory contract bond are fixed by the terms of the bond, and if the bond shows an intention to guarantee compliance with the terms of the contract pursuant to which the bond is given, the surety signing the bond becomes the surety for the full performance of all the terms of the contract. *Thompson Transport Co. v. Middlestates Construction Co.*, 194 Kan. 52, 397 P.2d 368 (1964).

## 3. Penal Sum Variations

***Limitations per statute*** – Kansas does not have statutory limitations on performance bond penal sums.

***Effect of changes in work upon penal sum, if at all*** – Kansas has no case law interpreting such changes in work.

***Statutory or case law protections or dangers to penal sum***

Under principles of general law the obligation of a bond is to be measured by the bond itself and may not be extended by implication or enlarged by construction beyond the terms of the executed contract. *In re Conservatorship of Huerta*, 273 Kan. 97, 41 P.3d 814 (2002).

## 4. Parties Covered

***Statutes and/or case law as to whether only obligees are covered***

Landowner, as a supplier to a subcontractor, could not recover on a performance and payment bond issued for the sole benefit of the general contractor; the bond named the general contractor as the only obligee and explicitly excluded the possibility of any third party being able to claim that it was an intended beneficiary with a right to sue. *Dawson v. Givens Construction Co., Inc.* 27 Kan. App. 2d 1042, 11 P.3d 81 (2001).

***Coverage for:***

**Third-party beneficiaries** – Where construction contract, which was part of completion bond, required owner and contractor to pay claims for labor and materials used in construction of apartment building, claimants of liens for labor and materials so used were entitled to enforce payment of their claims from surety on the bond, notwithstanding provision of bond that no right of action should accrue thereon for use of any one other than specified obligees. Where an irreconcilable conflict exists between general provisions of a contract and particular portions written into the contract, preference is given to the latter for purpose of ascertaining the intention of the parties. *Haynes Hardware Co. v. Western Casualty & Surety Co.*, 156 Kan. 356, 133 P.2d 574 (1943).

**Assignees** – There are no Kansas cases discussing assignment of obligee's right to make a claim against a performance bond.

***Dual obligees*** – Where general contractor and apartment project owner formed joint venture for purpose of permitting 10 percent profit and risk factor to be included in total cost of apartment project, joint venture obtained performance bond, and joint venture thereafter purported to enter into subcontract with general contractor for construction of apartment project, purported subcontract between joint venture and general contractor did not relieve surety of liability on purchase order contract entered into between general contractor and plaintiff subcontractor. *Neighbors Const. Co., Inc. v. J. R. Seal-Wells Const.,* 219 Kan. 382, 548 P.2d 491 (1976).

## 5. Notice or Filing Required

### *Statutory provisions*

A public bond given by a contractor for an improvement to the state house, for the protection of workmen and materialmen, is not void as to the sureties thereon, so as to release them from liability for labor performed, because said bond was not filed in the office of the clerk of the district court, as required by the paragraph last above cited. *Evans v. Watson*, 8 Kan. App. 144, 55 P. 17 (1898).

### *Case law rules concerning condition precedent notice*

Bonding companies engaged in the business of insuring the performance of contracts of others for pay are not "favorites of the law" in the sense the term is applied to accommodation sureties; that such companies are in fact insurers; and that the failure of the obligee to give notice of the principal's default in strict compliance with the terms of the bond does not relieve the surety of liability when the failure to notify resulted in no actual loss or prejudice to the surety. The breach of a condition precedent in a bond given by an insurer for pay will not relieve the insurer from liability for any loss for which he would otherwise be liable, unless such breach contributed to the loss. *School District No. 1 of Clark County v. Massachusetts Bonding & Ins.*, 92 Kan. 53, 143 P. 1077 (1914).

## 6. Time for Suit

***Statutes of limitation particular to performance bonds and other applicable statutes of limitation***

K.S.A. 60-511 is the statute of limitations applicable to written contracts and actions on statutory bonds. It states as follows:

> The following actions shall be brought within five years:
>
> (1) An action upon any agreement, contract or promise in writing. ... (4) An action upon the official bond or undertaking of an executor, administrator, conservator, sheriff, or any other officer, or upon the bond or undertaking given in attachment, injunction, arrest, or in any case required by statute.

***Case law statements about enforceability of limitations contained in bonds***

Highway subcontractor waiting until statutory limitation for bringing action on contractor's bond conditioned for payment of all indebtedness incurred for labor and materials had passed could not sue on faithful performance bond, conditioned for faithful performance of contract, for amount still owing subcontractor from principal contractor. *Cavanaugh v. Globe Indemnity Co.*, 141 Kan. 774, 44 P.2d 216 (1935).

***Varying statutes of limitation by agreement in bond or contract*** – Kansas law permits contractual modification of the statute of limitations. *Graphic Technology, Inc. v. Pitney Bowes, Inc.,* 968 F. Supp. 602 (1997).

## 7. Procedure

***Statutory or procedural rules that may affect handling or administration of lawsuits***

K.S.A. 60-212 allows a defendant 20 days to file an answer after service of the summons. However, if a defendant is served out of state, no default judgment shall be taken until the expiration of at least 30 days. K.S.A. 60-308(a)(3).

Pursuant to K.S.A. 60-238, a party must demand a trial by jury in writing at any time after the commencement of the action and not later than 10 days after the service of the last pleading directed to such issue. Failure to make such demand constitutes a waiver.

K.S.A. 12-105b(d) states as follows:

> (d) Any person having a claim against a municipality which could give rise to an action brought under the Kansas tort claims act shall file a written notice as provided in this subsection before commencing such action. The notice shall be filed with the clerk or governing body of the municipality and shall contain the following: (1) The name and address of the claimant and the name and address of the claimant's attorney, if any; (2) a concise statement of the factual basis of the claim, including the date, time, place and circumstances of the act, omission or event complained of; (3) the name and address of any public officer or employee involved, if known; (4) a concise statement of the nature and the extent of the injury claimed to have been suffered; and (5) a statement of the amount of monetary damages that is being requested. In the filing of a notice of claim, substantial compliance with the provisions and requirements of this subsection shall constitute the valid filing of a claim. The contents of such notice shall not be admissible in any subsequent action arising out of the claim. Once notice of the claim is filed, no action shall be commenced until after the claimant has received notice from the municipality that it has denied the claim or until after 120 days has passed following the filing of the notice of claim, whichever occurs first. A claim is deemed denied if the municipality fails to approve the claim in its entirety within 120 days unless the interested parties have reached a settlement before the expiration of that period. No person may initiate an action against a municipality unless the claim has been denied in whole or part. Any action brought pursuant to the Kansas tort claims act shall be commenced within the time period provided for in the code of civil procedure or it shall be forever barred, except that, a claimant shall have no less than 90 days from the date the claim is denied or deemed denied in which to commence an action.

Further, the definition of municipality is found in K.S.A. 12-105a, which states:

> (a) "Municipality" means and includes county, township, city, school district of whatever name or nature, community junior college, municipal university, drainage district, cemetery district, fire district, and other political subdivision or taxing unit, and including their boards, bureaus, commissions, committees and other agencies, such as, but not limited to, library board, park board, recreation commission, hospital board of trustees having power to create indebtedness and make payment of the same independently of the parent unit.

### *Venue requirements and jurisdictional limitations*

K.S.A. 60-304 is the Kansas venue statute for lawsuits against corporations (foreign or domestic). It reads as follows:

> An action against a domestic corporation, or against a foreign corporation which is qualified to do business in this state, other than an action for which venue is otherwise specifically prescribed by law, may be brought in the county in which:
> (1) Its registered office is located;
> (2) the cause of action arose;
> (3) the defendant is transacting business at the time of the filing of the petition, if the plaintiff is a resident of such county at the time the cause of action arose;
> (4) there is located tangible personal property which is the subject of an action for the possession thereof if immediate possession is sought in accordance with K.S.A. 60-1005 and amendments thereto at the time of the filing of the action; or
> (5) equipment or facilities for use in the supply of transportation services, or communication services, including, without limitation, telephonic communication services, are located, where the subject of such action relates to transportation services or communication services supplied or rendered, in whole or in part, using such equipment or facilities.

In Kansas, a plaintiff may file a civil case under Chapter 60 or Chapter 61. However, the limitations behind Chapter 61 civil are as follows in K.S.A. 61-2802:

> (a) This act may be used to govern the procedure for a civil lawsuit filed in the district court which:

(1) Seeks judgment for a debt which is not secured by a lien and arises out of a contract for the providing of goods, services or money, without limitation as to the amount claimed in the lawsuit;
(2) seeks judgment for a debt which is secured by a lien and arises out of a contract for the providing of goods, services or money, where the amount claimed in the lawsuit, not counting costs, interest and fees, does not exceed $25,000; or
(3) seeks judgment where the claim does not arise out of a contract and the amount claimed in the lawsuit, not counting costs, interest and fees, does not exceed $25,000.

(b) The following types of lawsuits may not be filed under this act:
(1) Actions against any officers of the state, or any subdivisions thereof, for misconduct in office, except as authorized by the Kansas tort claims act, K.S.A. 75-6101 *et seq.*, and amendments thereto;
(2) actions for specific performance of contracts for real estate;
(3) actions in which title to real estate is sought to be recovered or in which an interest in real estate, either legal or equitable, is sought to be established, except that nothing in this paragraph shall be construed as limiting the right to bring an action for forcible detainer as provided in K.S.A. 2004 Supp. 61-3801 through 61-3808, and amendments thereto;
(4) actions to foreclose real estate mortgages or to establish and foreclose liens on real estate as provided in article 11 of chapter 60 of the Kansas Statutes Annotated, and amendments thereto;
(5) actions for divorce, separate maintenance or custody of minor children;
(6) habeas corpus;
(7) receiverships;
(8) change of name;
(9) declaratory judgments;
(10) mandamus and quo warranto;
(11) injunctions;
(12) class actions;
(13) rights of majority; and
(14) any appeal from an order or ruling of an administrative officer or body.

***Court rules*** – Each Kansas Judicial District has its own local rules regarding the procedure for that district to determine any local procedural rules.

***Particular agency regulations/rules*** – Not applicable.

***Arbitration requirements and application***

Kansas has its own Uniform Arbitration Act. See K.S.A. 5-401 *et seq*. However, Kansas law prohibits compulsory arbitration provisions in state construction contracts entered into by secretary of administration. K.S.A. 75-3741(b)(4).

Further, K.S.A. 5-401 states as follows:

> (a) A written agreement to submit any existing controversy to arbitration is valid, enforceable and irrevocable except upon such grounds as exist at law or in equity for the revocation of any contract.
>
> (b) Except as provided in subsection (c), a provision in a written contract to submit to arbitration any controversy thereafter arising between the parties is valid, enforceable and irrevocable except upon such grounds as exist at law or in equity for the revocation of any contract.
>
> (c) The provisions of subsection (b) shall not apply to: (1) Contracts of insurance, except for those contracts between insurance companies, including reinsurance contracts; (2) contracts between an employer and employees, or their respective representatives; or (3) any provision of a contract providing for arbitration of a claim in tort.

## 8. Attorney's Fees

***Statutes and/or case law limiting or permitting recovery of attorney's fees*** – See K.S.A. 40-256, *supra*.

***What fees are recoverable if any***

A reasonable attorney's fee is recoverable under K.S.A. 40-256.

The reasonableness of attorney fees rests within the sound discretion of the trial court, and it can draw on its own knowledge and expertise in determining a reasonable amount. *City of Wichita v. B G Products, Inc.*, 252 Kan. 367, Syl. ¶ 4, 845 P.2d 649 (1993).

Any litigation arising from an award of attorney fees must occur within the action or is barred by collateral estoppel. *Shughart Thomson & Kilroy, P.C. v. Max Rieke & Bros., Inc.,* 24 Kan. App. 2d 205, 209, 943 P.2d 508 (1997).

## 9. Special Provisions

Sureties on a delivery bond were included in the judgment in a former action against the debtor-property owner in the absence of fraud or collusion between the parties. The surety was not permitted to retry the issues resolved in the former action. The surety was also precluded from setting up any defenses which with reasonable diligence could have been raised in the former action. *General Motors Acceptance Corporation v. Mogge,* 181 Kan. 346, 311 P.2d 339 (1957).

## 10. Remarks

Generally, while bonds not provided for by statute and extorted by public officers under color of their office are not enforceable, the mere absence of specific statutory authority for the giving of a bond does not invalidate a bond which is given voluntarily and which is not in contravention of public policy and the bond is valid as a common-law obligation or as a contractual obligation voluntarily undertaken. *State ex rel. Hedrick v. Hartford Acc. & Indem. Co.*, 154 Kan. 79, 114 P.2d 812 (1941).

## 11. Case Annotations

A surety bond is to be construed in the light of the circumstances in which it is given, so as to effectuate its purpose. *Kendall v. Black*, 99 Kan. 101, 102, 160 P. 1015 (1916); *City of Wichita v. Home Cab Co.*, 151 Kan. 679, 687, 101 P.2d 219 (1940).

***Interpretation of AIA bond forms*** – Kansas has no cases or statutes on this issue.

### ***Cases in which surety steps into shoes of obligee***

Where a surety stands in the shoes of the entity it indemnified, the right of legal or equitable subrogation arises by operation of law and does not depend on the existence of privity of contract. *Western Sur. Co. v. Loy*, 3 Kan. App. 2d 310, 594 P.2d 257 (1979).

A city held not liable to surety of a defaulting contractor for money paid contractor's assignee, where city's agreement to pay was made before the contractor's default, notwithstanding the fact that the surety completed the contract and was thereby entitled to the entire balance of the contract price for the sewer, and to all rights of the defaulting contractor under the contract. *U.S. Fidelity & Guaranty Co. v. City of Pittsburg*, 115 Kan. 740, 225 P. 83 (1924).

# KENTUCKY

Thomas E. Crafton and Gene F. Zipperle, Jr.[1]

## 1. Requirement for Bond

***Statutory provisions for projects that are:***

**Public** – ***Chapter 45A – Kentucky Model Procurement Code***

The Kentucky Model Procurement Code ("KMPC") requires bonds on public works contracts which exceed $25,000. For smaller projects, the terms of the contract will generally govern what bonds are required.

KRS 45A.190 provides:

(1) When a construction contract is awarded in an amount in excess of $25,000 the following bonds shall be furnished to the Commonwealth, and shall be binding on the parties upon the award of the contract:

(a) A performance bond satisfactory to the Commonwealth executed by a surety company authorized to do business in the Commonwealth, or otherwise supplied, satisfactory to the Commonwealth, in an amount equal to 100 percent of the contract price as it may be increased; and

---

1 Thomas E. Crafton and Gene F. Zipperle, Jr. are shareholders of:
Alber Crafton, PSC
Hurstbourne Place, Suite 1300
9300 Shelbyville Road
Louisville, Kentucky 40222
(502) 815-5000
with offices also located in Troy, Michigan and Columbus, Ohio.

(b) A payment bond satisfactory to the Commonwealth executed by a surety company authorized to do business in the Commonwealth, or otherwise supplied, satisfactory to the Commonwealth, for the protection of all persons supplying labor and material to the contractor or his subcontractors, for all the performances of the work provided for in the contract. The bond shall be in an amount equal to 100 percent of the original contract price.

The KMPC does not contain any provisions regarding notice or other requirements for making a performance or payment bond claims, therefore, the bond must be carefully reviewed in order to determine the proper notice to the surety and other filing requirements. The KMPC does not appear to authorize the use of a "combination" type bond, the total amount of which equals 100 percent of the contract price. Since a public works bond incorporates the KMPC, it could be argued that a combination performance/payment bond with a penal sum equal to 100 percent of the contract price must be construed to be two bonds, each with penal sums equal to the contract price.

***Scope of the KMPC*** – Except for transactions between the commonwealth and political subdivisions or other governments and by statutorily recognized purchasing units, the KMPC applies "to every expenditure of public funds" by the commonwealth "under any contract or like business agreement."[2] This includes construction, which is defined as "the process of building, altering, repairing, improving, or demolishing any public structures or buildings, or other public improvements of any kind to any public real property."[3]

The KMPC also pertains to local public agencies, such as cities, counties, schools and special districts, and combinations of agencies.[4] However, regulation of local government procurement is neither mandatory nor pervasive. The KMPC merely provides that local procurement agencies may, but are not required to, adopt the portion of the Code applicable to local governments.[5] As a practical matter, few

---

2 KRS 45A.010(1).

3 KRS 45A.030(4).

4 KRS 45A.345(11).

5 KRS 45A.343. Counties are required to adopt a county administration code that includes procedures for "purchasing and award of contracts." KRS 68.005(1)(d).

local public agencies have exercised this option. There is no centralized listing identifying local government bodies that have adopted the KMPC.

***KMPC's application to Kentucky Transportation Cabinet*** – The KMPC designates the Kentucky Finance and Administration Cabinet as the central procurement and contracting agency for the Commonwealth.[6] Under separate statutes, the Kentucky Transportation Cabinet also plays a significant, independent role predominantly through the Department of Highways, a subdivision of the Transportation Cabinet.[7] Both are authorized to acquire real property needed for state use.[8]

**Private** – There are no statutory requirements for bonds on private projects.

**Department of Transportation** – See above.

**Other** – KRS 107.080 – for public construction projects upon or after acceptance of bid by governing body, that body may determine principal amount of bonds to be issued for the payment, taking into account the amount of the accepted bid(s) and all other costs of the project. Each contract shall be supported by a performance bond for the full amount of the contract with good surety to be approved by the governing body.

KRS 154A.600(5) – applies to state lottery vendors. Each vendor shall, at the execution of the contract with the (lottery) corporation post a performance bond (or letter of credit) in an amount equal to the full amount estimated to be paid annually to the vendor under the contract.

KRS 197.510 – applies to contracts for operation and management of adult correctional facilities. The provisions of the Kentucky Model Procurement Code KRS 45A also apply. Under KRS 197.510(31) any contract between the state and the private provider shall require the private provider to give a performance bond to the commonwealth as obligee, in a form satisfactory to the commonwealth, executed by a surety company authorized to do business in Kentucky and in the penal sum equal to: 20 percent multiplied by the maximum number of inmates

---

6 KRS 45A.045.

7 KRS 174.050, KRS 176.070(1) and KRS 177.020.

8 KRS 45A.045 and KRS 177.021.

to be housed in the adult correctional facility multiplied by 365 and further multiplied by the rate to be paid the private provider per inmate per day.

KRS 337.200 – except for employers doing business in the state for five years, every employer engaged in construction work, or the severance, preparation or transportation of minerals, shall furnish a performance bond to assure the payment of all wages due from the employer. Surety for the bond shall be in an amount equal to the employer's gross payroll operating at full capacity for four weeks.

KRS 350.064 – requires the applicant for a surface coal mining and reclamation permit to file, after the permit has been approved, a reclamation bond for performance payable, as appropriate to the state and conditional upon faithful performance of all the requirements of this chapter and the permit. The initial bond must cover the area of land within the permit upon which surface coal mining and reclamation will take place. As succeeding areas of land are used, additional bonds must be filed.

KRS 367.474 – pertains to a performance bond provided for the sale of any subdivision primarily directed toward recreation or retirement use. If any improvements of the subdivision are advertised but not completed, or which are completed but for which supplier of labor and material have not been paid, the subdivider shall furnish a performance bond payable to the attorney general in an amount equal to the costs of all improvements, including, but not limited to, roads, lakes, golf courses, and stables which are advertised prior to the sale of land or property. The bond shall remain in effect until the advertised improvements are made, and if these improvements are not made within a reasonable time the bond is forfeited to the Attorney General for the use and benefit of the property owners.

## 2. Damages Covered

### *Set forth in any statutes and/or case law*

The liability of a surety construction contract is generally coextensive with that of its principal. *Kentucky Ins. Guaranty Ass'n. v. Dooley Const. Co.*, 732 S.W.2d 887 (Ky. App. 1987).

***Obligations of surety to perform and/or pay***

Any material variance to the contract between the principal and the obligee that results in injury, loss or prejudice to the surety discharges the surety. Minor or trivial variations to the contract will not discharge the surety. *Ferguson Contracting Co. v. Story Const. Co.*, 417 S.W.2d 228 (Ky. 1967).

***Whether failure to provide insurance transfers burden to surety*** – No Kentucky statutes transfer the burden to the surety.

***Limitations on damages***

As a general rule the obligations of the surety are coextensive with the obligations of its principal, therefore, if a bond obligee cannot enforce a bonded contract term against the bonded principal, then likewise, the bond obligee cannot enforce that contract term against the surety.

**Liquidated Damages** – If actual damages cannot be ascertained the court will look to measure of damages fixed by contract; but generally where actual damages can be determined, the court will disregard the contract damages particularly when such damages are oppressive, and give the complaining party more damages than actually sustained. *Fidelity and Deposit Co. of Maryland v. Jones*, 75 S.W.2d 1057 (1934).

*Island Creek Corp. v. Anker Energy Corp.*, No. 91-5968, 1992 WL 159789 (6th Cir. (Ky.), July 10, 1992)) reiterated that parties to a contract can agree to liquidated damages, limitations in a reasonable amount, but that any such remedy is optional unless it is expressly stated to be the exclusive sale, remedy. A party cannot recover both actual and liquidated damages.

**Delay damages** – "No damage for delay" clauses are enforceable. *Apex Contracting, Inc. v. City of Paris*, 2004 WL 758276, Ky. App. April 29, 2004.

**Interest** – Awarded in the court's discretion. Obligation of surety is fixed when judgment rendered against principal and interest can begin to run per KRS 360.040. *Polk v. American Cas. Co.*, 816 S.W.2d 178 (Ky. 1991).

When added to the principal amount of the claim, interest will not increase the surety's liability beyond the penal sum of its bond. *Polk v. American Casualty Co.*, 816 S.W.2d 178 (Ky. 1991).

***Whether obligee may set off bonded contract funds against other principal-obligee debts or obligations***

A surety who has paid the debts of its principal, is entitled to step into the shoes of the creditor or complete the work, and assert the creditor's right of set off against the debtor to recover any payments made by the surety. *Larbar Corp. v. Kentucky Central Ins. Co.*, 177 F.3d 439 (6th Cir. 1999).

**Set-off** – See also *In re: Wallace's Bookstores, Inc.*, 2004 Bankr. LEXIS 4 (2004).

***Incorporation of specific contract terms by reference*** –

If contract is incorporated into bond, bond and underlying contract will be read together to determine intention of the parties about what is covered. *ABCO-Bramer, Inc. v. Markel Ins.*, 55 S.W. 3d 841 (2000).

### 3. Penal Sum Variations

***Limitations per statute*** – Kentucky does not have statutory limitations on performance bond penal sums.

***Effect of changes in work upon penal sum, if at all***

Under KRS 45A.190 a performance bond on a public contract will be issued in an amount equal to 100 percent of the contract as it may be increased.

***Statutory or case law protections or dangers to penal sum*** – None applicable.

## 4. Parties Covered

***Statutes and/or case law as to whether only obligees are covered***

The obligee of a bond is the only one who can enforce the liability of sureties on a bond, unless a statute, or an express provision in the bond states otherwise. *Owens v. Georgia Life Ins. Co.*, 165 Ky. 507 (1915).

***Coverage for:***

**Third-party beneficiaries** – In *Wehr Const., Inc. v. Steel Fabricators*, 769 S.W.2d 51 (Ky. App. 1988) the court stated "[t]he performance bond creates a third party beneficiary relationship between Wehr (principal) and those who contracted with Wehr's subcontractor." However, reading the case, it is apparent that the bond in question is a payment bond.

In *Dayton Lumber & Mfg. Co. v. New Capital Hotel, Inc.*, 222 Ky. 29 (1927), the court held that a materialman was not a third-party beneficiary to a bond that guaranteed faithful performance of the contract. Only the obligee was protected.

**Assignees** – There are no statutes or cases dealing directly with assignees.

**Dual obligees** – There are no statutes or cases regarding dual obligees.

## 5. Notice or Filing Required

***Statutory provisions*** – There are no statutory provisions regarding notice or filing for a performance bond.

***Case law rules concerning condition precedent notice***

Notice of default, when required must be given within the time specified in the bond, but if no definite time is stated in the bond, then within a reasonable time. However, whether the bonding company was harmed by any such delay is a question of material fact. *United Bonding Ins. Co. v. Sperry & Hutchinson Co.*, 465 S.W.2d 291 (Ky. 1971).

## 6. Time for Suit

***Statutes of limitation particular to performance bonds and other applicable statutes of limitation***

KRS 413.090(2) provides a 15-year statute of limitations after a cause of action accrues upon a bond, recognizance or written contract.

KRS 413.220 discharges sureties after seven years 1) on a judgment without the issue of execution and prosecution in good faith for collection; 2) on a bond given in the course of any judicial proceeding after the cause of action accrues, or 3) in any obligation or contract, except those in KRS 413.230, after the cause of action accrues.

***Case law statements about enforceability of limitations contained in bonds*** – Not applicable.

***Varying statutes of limitation by agreement in bond or contract***

A time limitation in an insurance contract though shorter than the statutory period is not invalid if it is not unreasonably short. *Robert F. Simmons Const. Co. v. American States Ins. Co.*, 426 S.W.2d 441 (Ky. 1968) construing a bond.

## 7. Procedure

***Statutory or procedural rules that may affect handling or administration of lawsuits*** – Not applicable.

***Venue requirements and jurisdictional limitations***

KRS 454.210; long arm statute pertains to jurisdiction over person or entity transacting any business in Kentucky, contracting to insure any person, property or risk, located in Kentucky, and provides that suit can be brought in county where plaintiff resides or cause of action or any part thereof arose.

KRS 452.450 action against corporation which has offices or place of business in Kentucky or chief officer or agent residing in Kentucky must be brought in county where office, place of business, or agent or officer located, *or* in the county in which the contract is made or to be performed.

Kentucky has adopted § 80 of the Restatement (2d) of Conflict of Laws that states that "The parties agreement as to the place of the action cannot oust a state of judicial jurisdiction, but such an agreement will be given effect unless it is unfair or unreasonable." *Prudential Resources Corp. v. Plunkett*, 583 S.W.2d 97 (Ky. App. 1979).

***Court rules*** – No special rules.

***Particular agency regulations/rules*** – No special rules.

***Arbitration requirements and application***

Surety bonds are subject to arbitration provisions of KRS 417.050. *Buck Run Baptist Church, Inc. v. Cumberland Surety Ins.*, 983 S.W.2d 501 (Ky. 1998) distinguishing between surety bond and insurance policy.

## 8. Attorney's Fees

Absent a written agreement or authorizing statute, a party to an action may not recover attorney fees from the adverse party. *Louisville Label Inc. v. Hildesheim*, 843 S.W.2d 321 (Ky. 1992), *Motorists Mut. Ins. Co. v. Glass*, 996 S.W.2d 437 (Ky. 1997).

***Statutes and/or case law limiting or permitting recovery of attorney's fees***

Kentucky statutes such as the Consumer Protection Act, provide for an award of attorney fees but these statutes are not directly applicable to bonds.

**Costs** – Ky. R. Civ. Pro. 54.04 awards costs to a prevailing party unless otherwise directed by court. But, there is an indication that a party who obtains a verdict in a lawsuit, but who is not awarded any damages has not prevailed for purposes of awarding costs. *Lewis v. Grange Mut. Cas. Co.*, 11 S.W.3d 591 (Ky. App. 2000).

## 9. Special Provisions

In *Intercargo Ins. Co., v. B.W. Farrell, Inc., et al.*, 89 S.W.3d 422 (Ky. App. 2002) signatories to a general indemnity agreement claimed that it was unenforceable because it did not comport with the requirements of KRS 371.065, a statute unique to Kentucky, which states that no guaranty of indebtedness is valid or enforceable unless it is signed by the guarantor *and* that it specifies the amount of the maximum liability and a date on which the guaranty terminates. The court first determined that a performance bond was not an "instrument" as contemplated by the statute. The court then distinguished between a guaranty which is in the nature of commercial paper or a negotiable instrument, and an indemnity agreement which is an obligation requiring a promiser to make good any loss which another has incurred while acting for the benefit of the promisor, that creates a direct, primary liability between the promisor and the promise that is independent of any other obligation. Thus, KRS 371.065 did not apply to indemnity agreements.

## 10. Remarks

The Kentucky Supreme Court recently decided *Presnell Construction Managers, Inc. v. EH Construction, LLC*, 134 S.W.3d 575 (2004) adopting the Restatement of Torts 2d § 552 allowing a contractor, and presumably its surety, to recover damages caused by the negligence of an architect or engineer notwithstanding the lack or privity or not withstanding the "Economic Loss" Doctrine.

## 11. Case Annotations

***Interpretation of AIA bond forms*** – Not applicable.

***Cases in which surety steps into shoes of obligee*** – *Davis v. Kinnard*, 271 Ky. 428 (1937).

# LOUISIANA

David J. Krebs and Shashauna M. Dermody[1]

## 1. Requirement for Bond

The State of Louisiana has three statutory schemes specifically dealing with construction projects: the Public Works Act, La. R.S. 38:2241, *et seq*.; the DOTD Public Works Act, La. R.S. 48:250, *et seq*.; and the Private Works Act, La. R.S. 9:4801, *et seq*.

***Statutory provisions for projects that are:***

**Public** – La. R.S. 38:2216(A)(1) requires that when any bid is accepted for the construction or doing of any public works, the party to whom the contract is awarded shall furnish a good and solvent bond in an amount not less than half of the amount of the contract for the faithful performance of his duties.

La. R.S. 38:2241(D) further provides "[n]othing contained herein shall in any way limit the liability on the bond for the performance of the work pursuant to the contract in question.

**Private** – A bond is not statutorily required under the Private Works Act, La. R.S. 4801, *et seq*. However, if a bond is provided, La. R.S.

---

1 David J. Krebs is a member and Shashauna M. Dermody is an associate of:
Krebs, Farley & Pelleteri, L.L.C.
400 Poydras Street, Suite 2500
New Orleans, Louisiana 76130
(504) 299-3570

9:4812(C)(2) specifically provides that a condition of the bond shall be that the surety guarantees, to the owner, the complete and timely performance of the contract unless such guarantee is expressly excluded by the terms of the bond.

**Department of Transportation (DOTD)** – La. R.S. 48:255(D)(1) requires contractors on projects headed by the DOTD to provide a performance bond to guarantee the faithful performance of the contractor's duties for contracts in excess of $50,000.

***Case law rules that might generally apply***

"Louisiana public works bonds are statutory in nature and not only guarantee performance of the construction work but also payment of laborers and materialmen." *Lambert v. Md. Cas. Co.*, 403 So. 2d 739, 753 (La. App. 4th Cir. 1981).

"The [Public Works] Act is to be strictly construed and the liability of the surety should not be expanded beyond the statute." *Metro Builders Hardware, Inc. v. Burko Constr., Inc.*, 633 So. 2d 838, 839 (La. App. 4th Cir. 1994), *writ denied*, 637 So. 2d 1049 (La. 1994).

"Consequently, La. R.S. 38:2189 is one of the statutes in the Public Works Act which should be strictly construed so as to not expand the liability of the surety beyond that set forth explicitly in the statute." *State Through Div. of Admin. v. McInnis Bros. Constr.*, 701 So. 2d 937, 944 (La. 1997).

"A bond on a private work is not a statutory bond in the sense that a bond on a public work is statutory for there is no mandatory requirement that one be furnished." *Patent Scaffolding Co. v. Ross Corp.*, 172 So. 2d 364, 367 (La. App. 4th 1965).

"The provisions of the [Private Works] Act relating to the liability of the surety (mainly R.S. 9:4812 and 4813), apply only to (1) payment bonds, and (2) bonds furnished by the general contractor in favor of the owner and all persons having a claim against the contractor arising out of the work performed. R.S. 9:4812(C)(1). The [Private Works] Act does not purport to regulate performance bonds at all. Its only mention of a performance bond is the provision that the payment bond required of the general contractor shall be deemed to include a performance condition in favor of the owner, unless the bond expressly excludes such a guarantee. R.S. 9:4812(C)(2). Surety bonds, whether for payment or performance or both, given by subcontractors to contractors, are not mentioned at all in the [Private Works] Act." *Congregation of St. Peter's Roman Catholic Church of Gueydan v. Simon*, 497 So. 2d 409, 412 (La. App. 3d Cir. 1986).

## 2. Damages Covered

### *Set forth in any statutes and/or case law*

Surety may be liable to the owner for indirect or consequential damages depending on the bond provisions, including lost rentals based upon specific language of the performance bond. *See Bossier Medical Props. v. Abbott and Williams Constr. Co. of La., Inc.*, 557 So. 2d 1131, 1134 (La. App. 2d Cir. 1990).

Contractor who completes contract on behalf of defaulted subcontractor may be entitled to recover from subcontractor's surety a profit on the additional cost incurred by it in completing contract. *E.E. Rabalais & Sons, Inc.*, 226 So. 2d 528 (La. App. 3d Cir. 1969).

"[T]he language of the bond indicates the surety contemplated potential liability for 'other costs and damages' in addition to costs of completion. We construe the language strictly in favor of protecting the obligee. Although [the surety] could have limited its liability under the provisions of the surety agreement to costs of repairs or replacement, it did not do so in the instant case. Accordingly, we find that it was error to have limited [the surety's] liability to the ... cost of repairs. The judgment is amended to reflect that [surety] is liable, in solido, with [the contractor] for the full amount of pecuniary damages assessed against [the contractor]." *Stonecipher v. Mitchell*, 655 So. 2d 1381, 1390 (La. App. 2d Cir. 1995).

"Owner's right to recover of the surety such items of expense as interest, diminution in property value, engineering fees for corrective plans and specifications, attorney's fees incurred in concursus proceedings, and damage to Owner's professional reputation allegedly resulting from Contractor's default, must be determined in the light of the bond provisions." *Calandro Dev., Inc. v. R. M. Butler Contractors, Inc.*, 249 So. 2d 254, 267 (La. App. 1st Cir. 1971).

***Obligations of surety to perform and/or pay***

"Suretyship is an accessory contract. La. C.C. art. 3035. As such, the derivative liability of a surety cannot exist unless the principal is first liable. *Pacific Lining Co. v. Algernon-Blair Construction Co.*, 812 F.2d 237 (5th Cir. 1987). Because we find that [the principal] has no liability in this matter, [the surety] can have no derivative liability under the performance bond." *Belleville Historic Dev., L.L.C. v. GCI Constr., Inc.*, 807 So. 2d 335, 339 (La. App. 4th Cir. 2002).

Performance bond providing that the surety "shall fully indemnify and save harmless" the owner from all costs and damages which it may suffer by reason of the principal's failure to do so obligates the surety to pay for all costs to complete the contract. Therefore, performance bond became actionable after arbitration award against contractor was determined and contractor failed to pay damages due. *Town of Melville v. Safeco Ins. Co. of Am.*, 651 So. 2d 404, 409 (La. App. 3d Cir. 1995).

"Under La. R.S. 48:255.2, the surety must strictly comply with the statutory obligation of presenting the DOTD with a plan to assume performance and procure completion of the project or a response for the contractor's default within 45 days of notice of contractor's default from DOTD. Failure to do so subjects the surety to statutory damages, including cost to complete the project and stipulated damages up to the total amount of the bond." *United Rentals Highway Techs., Inc. v. St. Paul Sur.*, 852 So. 2d 1200, 1204 (La. App. 2d Cir. 2003).

***Whether failure to provide insurance transfers burden to surety*** – Louisiana statutes do not transfer the burden to surety.

***Limitations on damages***

Under Louisiana law, an obligee has a duty to make reasonable efforts to mitigate its damages caused by the obligor's failure to perform. La. C.C. art. 2002.

"The surety promises to satisfy the entire obligation, unless the agreement is otherwise limited." *Stonecipher v. Mitchell*, 655 So. 2d 1381, 1389 (La. App. 2d Cir. 1995).

"Since suretyship is an accessory promise by which a person binds himself for another already bound, by its very nature the contract binds the surety to the identical performance obligation of the principal under the latter's contract with the obligee. La. C.C. arts. 3035, 3036 and 3040. If the principal breaches the performance bond the surety is liable for such breach. 13 Couch on Insurance, 2d Ed., § 47:127 (1982)." *Congregation of St. Peter's Roman Catholic Church of Gueydan v. Simon*, 497 So. 2d 409, 413 (La. App. 3d Cir. 1986).

***Whether obligee may set off bonded contract funds against other principal-obligee debts or obligations***

The United States was not entitled to set off its judgment indebtedness against the retained funds earned by performance surety after principal was placed in default by owner, where construction project, which was basis of surety's suit for retained funds, was not the one which resulted in judgment against principal. *Reliance Ins. Co. v. Dep't of Transp. and Dev., Office of Highways*, 471 So. 2d 248, 254 (La. App. 1st Cir. 1985).

***Incorporation of specific contract terms by reference***

Where bonded contract specifically provides for imposition of attorney's fees upon breach, and performance bond refers to and incorporates bonded contract, surety will be held liable for attorney's fees. *See Austin v. Parker*, 672 F.2d 508, 518 (5th Cir. 1982); *L & A Contracting Co., Inc. v. Ram Indus. Coatings, Inc.*, 762 So. 2d 1223, 1236-37(La. App. 1st Cir. 2000).

"The surety on a construction contract, is required to arbitrate a time-bar defense under its performance bond, pursuant to the bond's incorporation of the arbitration provision in the construction contract." *Jewish Fed'n of Greater New Orleans v. Fid. & Deposit Co. of Md.*, 273 F.3d 1094, 1094 (5th Cir. 2001).

## 3. Penal Sum Variations

***Limitations per statute***

**Public** – La. R.S. 38:2216(A)(1) requires a contractor awarded a contract on a public project to "furnish good and solvent bond in an amount not less than one-half of the amount of the contract, for the faithful performance of his duties."

**DOTD** – La. R.S. 48:255(D) provides that "the party to whom the contract is awarded shall furnish good and solvent bond in an amount equal to the contract bid cost for the faithful performance of his duties."

**Private** – La. R.S. 9:4812(B) provides that the amount of the bond:

> shall not be less than the following amounts or percentages of the price of the work stipulated or estimated in the contract:
>
> (1) If the price is not more than $10,000 the amount of the bond shall be 100 percent of the price.
>
> (2) If the price is more than $10,000 but not more than $100,000 the amount of the bond shall be 50 percent of the price, but not less than $10,000.
>
> (3) If the price is more than $100,000 but not more than $1,000,000 the amount of the bond shall be 33⅓ percent of the price, but not less than $50,000.
>
> (4) If the price is more than $1,000,000 the amount of the bond shall be 25 percent of the price, but not less than $333,333.

***Effect of changes in work upon penal sum, if at all***

The penal sum of a performance bond does not automatically increase to accommodate the approved change orders, although it may increase the base price of the contract. *See U.S. Pollution Control, Inc. v. Nat'l Am. Ins. Co.*, 663 So. 2d 119, 120-21 (La. App. 3d Cir. 1995).

***Statutory or case law protections or dangers to penal sum***

"The sureties could not be held liable for an amount greater than the amount of the bond, but are liable to the amount of the bond." *Arcadia Lumber Co. v. Austin*, 131 So. 601, 603 (La. App. 2d Cir. 1930).

However, in *L&A Contracting Co. v. Ram Industrial Coatings, Inc.*, 762 So. 2d 1223 (La. App. 1st Cir. 2000), the court held that the liability of a surety on a conventional bond could exceed the penal sum of the bond. The *L&A* court further went on to state "[j]urisprudence has held that a surety that obligates itself to fulfill all the obligations of its principal is thereby bound to pay all sums adjudged, even if they are found to be in excess of the actual bond amount." *L & A Contracting Co.*, 762 So. 2d at 1238 (La. App. 1st Cir. 2000) (citing *Hershell Corp. v. Fireman's Fund Ins. Co.*, 743 So. 2d 698, 705-706 (La. App. 3rd Cir. 1999) (holding that a surety on a release of lien bond could be held liable for interest and penalties in excess of the penal sum).

## 4. Parties Covered

***Statutes and/or case law as to whether only obligees are covered***

**Public Works** – "A bond issued pursuant to [the Public Works Act] shall not create, nor shall such bond be construed to create, any cause of action in favor of the public entity, or any third party, for personal injury or property damages sustained by any third party during the effective period of the bond. Nothing contained herein shall in any way limit the liability on the bond for the performance of the work pursuant to the contract in question; however, to the extent that the public contract in question should contain any provisions for a hold harmless or indemnity agreement, or both, by the contractor, in favor of the public entity, for personal injury or property damages sustained by third parties, the hold harmless or indemnity agreement, or both, shall not be deemed or construed to be secured by the bond, conditioned upon the concurrence of the contract." La. R.S. 38:2241(D).

"Any provisions of a bond issued pursuant to this Section which are contrary to Subsection D hereof are hereby declared to be contrary to the public policy of the state of Louisiana and are null and void." La. R.S. 38:2241(E).

**DOTD** – "The performance bond described by this Section shall inure solely to the benefit of the department and its successors or assigns, and no other person shall have any right of action based thereon." La. R.S. 48:255(D)(5).

**Private Works** – "It is axiomatic that there are no rights of action on a private works performance bond other than those rights reposed in the obligees named in the bond." *Nat'l Am. Bank of New Orleans v. Southcoast Contractors, Inc.*, 276 So. 2d 777, 781 (La. App. 1st Cir. 1973); *see also Jimco, Inc. v. Gentilly Terrace Apartments*, 230 So. 2d 281 (La. App. 4th Cir. 1971); *Fireman's Fund Ins. Cas. v. Milstid*, 253 So. 2d 571 (La. App. 1st Cir. 1971).

***Coverage for:***

**Third-party beneficiaries** – Language of subcontractor's conventional performance bond making contractor sole obligee did not give third persons, such as allegedly unpaid lessor of barges to subcontractor, right of action on bond. *Gateway Barge Line, Inc. v. R. B. Tyler Co.*, 175 So. 2d 867, 870 (La. App. 1st Cir. 1965).

**Assignees** – An assignee "has no independent or individual right of action against the surety on the performance bond; that its rights are derivative under the assignment from the owner, and any defenses available to the surety against the owner in an action on the bond can as well be asserted against the [assignee]." *Nat'l Am. Bank of New Orleans v. Southcoast Contractors, Inc.*, 276 So. 2d 777, 781 (La. App. 1st Cir. 1973).

**Dual obligees** – "An obligation is solidary for the obligees when it gives each obligee the right to demand the whole performance from the common obligor." La. C.C. art. 1790.

### 5. Notice or Filing Required

***Statutory provisions***

Louisiana statutes do not provide for any unusual notice requirements for suit under a performance bond. Rather, La. R.S.

9:4813(C) provides "[t]he liability of the surety is not extinguished by a deficiency in the amount of the bond, the failure to attach the bond to the notice of contract, or the failure to file the notice as required in R.S. 9:4811."

***Case law rules concerning condition precedent notice***

"Given the consequences that follow a declaration of default, it is *vital* that the declaration be made in terms sufficiently clear, direct and unequivocal to inform the breaching party that it has defaulted on its obligations.... If deprived of this clear notice of default, parties would be reluctant to enter into otherwise profitable contracts. Nothing in the record before this court indicates that the parties intended such an impractical result." *Cent. La. Elec. Co., Inc. v. Dolet Hills Mining Venture*, 116 F. Supp. 2d 726, 738 (W.D. La. 2000) (citing *L & A Contracting Co. v. S. Concrete Servs, Inc.*, 17 F.3d 106, 110-11 (5th Cir. 1994).

## 6. Time for Suit

***Statutes of limitation particular to performance bonds and other applicable statutes of limitation***

**Public Works** – La. R.S. 38:2189 provides "[a]ny action against the contractor on the contract or on the bond, or against the contractor or the surety or both on the bond furnished by the contractor, all in connection with the construction, alteration, or repair of any public works let by the state or any of its agencies, boards or subdivisions shall prescribe 5 years from the substantial completion, as defined in R.S. 38:2241.1, or acceptance of such work, whichever occurs first, or of notice of default of the contractor unless otherwise limited in this Chapter."

**DOTD** – La. R.S. 48:251.2 provides "[a]ny action against a contractor on a contract or on the bond furnished by the contractor, or against a contractor or the surety or both on the bond furnished by the contractor, all in connection with the construction or maintenance of any public works let by the department shall prescribe five years from recordation of the acceptance of such work, or of notice of default of the contractor, whichever occurs first."

**Private Works** – La. R.S. 9:4813(E) provides "[t]he surety's liability, except as to the owner, is extinguished as to all persons who fail to institute an action asserting their claims or rights against the owner, the contractor, or the surety within one year after the expiration of the time specified in R.S. 9:4822 for claimants to file their statement of claim or privilege."

**Louisiana General Statutes Applicable to Contractors** – "An action against a contractor or an architect on account of defects of construction, renovation, or repair of buildings and other works is subject to a liberative prescription of 10 years." La. C.C. art. 3500.

La. R.S. 9:2772(A) provides a five-year peremptive period for actions involving deficiencies in surveying, design, supervision, or construction of immovables or improvements thereon.

***Case law statements about enforceability of limitations contained in bonds***

"The interruption of prescription against one solidary obligor is effective against all solidary obligors and their heirs." La. C.C. art. 1799.

The five-year statute of limitations for bringing action against public works contractor or its surety on contract or bond, La. R.S. 38:2189 is "peremptive," not prescriptive, so the five-year period is not susceptible to interruption, suspension or renunciation. *State Through Div. of Admin. v. McInnis Bros. Constr.*, 701 So. 2d 937, 948 (La. 1997); *see also Orleans Parish School Bd. v. Scheyd, Inc.*, 737 So. 2d 954, 956-957 (La. App. 4th Cir. 1999).

***Varying statutes of limitation by agreement in bond or contract***

"Suretyship is an accessory contract by which a person binds himself to a creditor to fulfill the obligation of another upon the failure of the latter to do so." La. C.C. art. 3035.

"Suretyship may be qualified, conditioned or limited in any lawful manner." La. C.C. art. 3040.

A surety bond entered into by a subcontractor could place a time limitation upon the right of one of the signatories thereto to proceed against the other, shorter than the general prescriptive period, which would be enforceable by a plea of prescription or peremption. *Landis & Young v. Gossett & Winn*, 178 So. 760, 762 (La. App. 2d Cir. 1937).

"[I]t is clear that the two year prescriptive or peremptive period in the surety bond furnished ... in the present case is enforceable, and indeed, must be enforced." *Con-Plex, Div. of U.S. Indus., Inc. v. Vicon, Inc.*, 448 So. 2d 191, 193 (La. App. 1st Cir. 1984); *See also Kiva Constr. and Eng'g, Inc. v. Int'l Fid. Ins. Co.*, 749 F. Supp. 753, 756 (W.D. La. 1990); *Nat'l Tea Co. v. Plymouth Rubber Co., Inc.*, 663 So. 2d 801, 809 (La. App. 5th Cir. 1995).

"We conclude the specific and unambiguous prescriptive language contained in the [performance] bond, that any suit must be instituted within two years from the date of final payment, must take precedence over the general reference to the subcontract and incorporation of its provisions. We construe this language not as a waiver of the 10-year warranty period prescribed by Louisiana law, but rather, merely as a limitation on the enforceability of the bond, an accessory obligation to the underlying construction contract. An exception to the contractual conditions was specially stated in the bond." *J.B. Mouton & Sons, Inc. v. Alumawall, Inc.*, 583 So. 2d 157, 159 (La. App. 3d Cir. 1991).

## 7. Procedure

***Statutory or procedural rules that may affect handling or administration of lawsuits*** – Not applicable.

***Venue requirements and jurisdictional limitations***

**Public** – La. R.S. 38:2181(B) provides "a suit arising under any public contract regarding the construction, alteration, or repair of any public works or for the purchase of materials or supplies, may be instituted either in the parish in which the public entity is located or in any other parish where, by law, such action may be instituted."

**General Venue** – Louisiana's general rules of venue are set forth in La. C.C.P. art. 42.

An action on an insurance policy may be brought in the parish where the loss occurred or the insured is domiciled. La. C.C.P. art. 76.

An action on a contract may be brought in the parish where the contract was executed or the parish where any work or service was performed or was to be performed under the terms of the contract. La. C.C.P. art. 76.1.

***Court rules*** – Each Louisiana Judicial District has its own local rules regarding the procedure for that district.

***Particular agency regulations/rules*** – Not applicable.

***Arbitration requirements and application***

La. R.S. 9:4201 provides:

> [a] provision in any written contract to settle by arbitration a controversy thereafter arising out of the contract, or out of the refusal to perform the whole or any part thereof, or an agreement in writing between two or more persons to submit to arbitration any controversy existing between them at the time of the agreement to submit, shall be valid, irrevocable, and enforceable, save upon such grounds as exist at law or in equity for the revocation of any contract.

Louisiana has a strong public policy in favor of enforcement of arbitration clauses. *See Belleville Historic Dev., L.L.C. v. GCI Constr., Inc.*, 807 So. 2d 335, 338 (La. App. 4th Cir. 2002).

"The surety on a construction contract, is required to arbitrate a time-bar defense under its performance bond, pursuant to the bond's incorporation of the arbitration provision in the construction contract." *Jewish Fed'n of Greater New Orleans v. Fid. & Deposit Co. of Md.*, 273 F.3d 1094, 1094 (5th Cir. 2001).

Arbitration award in favor of town and against public contractor, which had defaulted by leaving project before completion, set only upper limits of the surety's obligation. *Town of Melville v. Safeco Ins. Co. of Am.*, 651 So. 2d 404 (La. App. 3d Cir. 1995).

## 8. Attorney's Fees

***Statutes and/or case law limiting or permitting recovery of attorney's fees***

"In Louisiana, attorney's fees are not allowable in the absence of statute or contract.... (However, we note, attorney's fees are recoverable if the performance bond so specifies. Couch on Insurance 2d, 58:114 (1966); 11 Appleman, Insurance Law and Practice, Section 6385 (1944))." *E. E. Rabalais & Son, Inc. v. United Bonding Ins. Co.*, 226 So. 2d 528, 533-34 (La. App. 3d Cir. 1969).

**Public** – The attorney's fees provisions of the Public Works Act, La. R.S. 38:2246 applies to claimants, not owners. "The only provision in the Public Works Act La R.S. 38:2241 *et seq.* for attorney's fees is that allowing attorney's fees to lien claimants under certain conditions." *Pittman Const. Co. v. Hous. Auth. of New Orleans*, 169 So. 2d 122, 138 (La. App. 1964).

**DOTD** – La. R.S. 48:255.2 provides "if the surety company has not timely completed the project and a court of competent jurisdiction has determined that the surety company has in bad faith refused to take over the project as provided in this Section, the surety company shall be responsible for the payment of any stipulated damages for any delay in the completion of the project as specified in the original contract and any reasonable attorney fees and court costs incurred by the public entity in collection of the payments required by this Section."

**Private** – Not applicable.

**Louisiana's Revised Statutes on Suretyship** – La. R.S. 9:3902 provides "[i]f the surety on a bond fails to pay his obligation and it becomes necessary for the creditor to sue thereon, the latter shall be entitled to 10 percent attorney's fees on the amount recovered, provided he has employed an attorney for the purpose, has made written amicable demand on the principal and surety and 30 days have elapsed from their receipt thereof without payment being made, and the full amount claimed in the demand is recovered."

Full recovery of the claim is a prerequisite to recovering attorney's fees under La. R.S. 9:3902. *See Val-U Inv. Corp. v. Trinity Universal Ins. Co.*, 170 So. 2d 723, 727-728 (La. App. 4th Cir. 1965).

"The contract and performance bond must be read together; thus ... surety was contractually obligated to pay attorney's fees to plaintiff." *Town of Melville v. Safeco Ins. Co. of Am.*, 651 So. 2d 404, 408 (La. App. 3d Cir. 1995).

Where bonded contract specifically provides for imposition of attorney's fees upon breach, and performance bond refers to and incorporates bonded contract, surety will be held liable for attorney's fees. *See Austin v. Parker*, 672 F.2d 508, 518 (5th Cir. 1982); *L & A Contracting Co., Inc. v. Ram Indus. Coatings, Inc.*, 762 So. 2d 1223, 1236-37 (La. App. 1st Cir. 2000).

***What fees are recoverable, if any***

One Louisiana case, *Austin v. Parker*, 672 F.2d 508, 520 (5th Cir. 1982), permitted a general contractor to recover attorney's fees and statutory penalties from the surety under Louisiana's insurance statute, La. R.S. 22:658.

**9. Special Provisions**

A surety's obligation will not be extinguished due to material changes to the bonded contract, extensions of time for performance or premature payments by the owner to the contractor. However, La. R.S. 9:4812(E) does provide the surety has the right to be indemnified by the owner, for any and all losses suffered by the surety for such actions, and will relieve the surety of any liability to the owner for overpayments or material modifications to the bonded contract.

A surety is granted a release from liability when an owner makes anticipatory payments, amends the contract, or grants an unauthorized extension of time to the contractor. *State v. Wilco Constr. Co., Inc.* 393 So. 2d 885, 890 (La. App. 4th Cir. 1981).

Louisiana law recognizes that a surety whose rights are impaired by the obligee is discharged to the extent the surety is prejudiced. *See* La. C.C. art. 3061; *See Town of Melville v. Safeco Ins. Co. of Am.*, 651 So. 2d 404, 408 (La. App. 3d Cir. 1995); *State v. Wilco Constr. Co.*, 393 So. 2d 885, 890 (La. App. 4th Cir. 1981).

**10. Remarks** – Not applicable.

## 11. Case Annotations

***Interpretation of AIA bond forms*** – Louisiana cases have not specifically addressed the interpretation of AIA forms of bonds A311 and A312.

***Cases in which surety steps into shoes of obligee***

"The surety who pays the principal obligation is subrogated by operation of law to the rights of the creditor." La. C.C. art. 3048.

A surety who advances money to its principal to complete a project becomes subrogated to the priority statutory position of the public owner with respect to retained contract funds and is entitled to set-off debts from one contract with another pursuant to the terms of the contract. *See U. S. Fidelity & Guaranty Co. v. Housing Authority of Town of Berwick*, 557 F.2d 482, 484 (5th Cir. 1977).

# MAINE

A. Robert Ruesch and John P. Giffune[1]

## 1. Requirement for Bond

***Statutory provisions for projects that are:***

**Public** – There are several Maine statutes that require performance bonds on public works projects.

Maine's Public Works Surety Bond Law of 1971, 14 M.R.S.A. § 871, requires performance bonds on any project for the construction, alteration, repair of any public building, or public work or other public improvement in excess of $100,000. The penal sum of the performance bond must be equal in value to the full contract amount being awarded. This statute applies to all contracts awarded by the state or any political subdivision, municipal corporation or public authority therein. Performance bonds must be conditioned upon the contractor's faithful performance of the contract in accordance with the plans and specifications. The performance bond is solely for the protection of the state or the awarding authority.

Maine's Department of Transportation is authorized by statute to develop its own standard contract specifications. 23 M.R.S.A. § 753. Under applicable case law, this statute is construed to allow Maine's

1 A. Robert Ruesch is a partner and John P. Giffune is an associate of:
Verrill Dana LLP
One Portland Square
Portland, Maine 04112-0586
(207) 774-4000

Department of Transportation full power in all matters related to the furnishing of bonds by successful bidders for the completion of their work and the fulfillment of contract obligations.

The construction, maintenance and repair of local highways, roads and bridges is governed by 23 M.R.S.A. § 3054. That statute provides that no contract shall be awarded unless its faithful performance is secured to the state by a bond in the penal sum of not less than 20 percent of the amount of the contract.

**Private** – No statutes, rules or regulations in Maine require performance bonds on private projects.

**Department of Transportation** – Maine's Department of Transportation has full power in all matters related to the furnishing of bonds by successful bidders for the completion of their work and the fulfillment of contract obligations. *Maine Sand & Gravel Co. v. Green & Wilson*, 133 Me. 313, 177 A. 185 (Me. 1935).

***Case law rules that might generally apply***

Notice by a subcontractor's materialman on a public construction project sent to, and received by, the general contractor by first-class mail, stating that the materialman had not received payment, and that the materialman's letter was to serve as notification to general contractor that there could be pending litigation, met the requirements of the Public Works Surety Bond Law that subcontractors not in privity of contract with the general contractor must give general contractor notice within 90 days of last day on which it furnished labor or materials, even though that statute provides that "notice shall be served by registered or certified mail." *Vacuum Systems, Inc. v. Washburn,* 651 A.2d 377 (Me. 1994).

Where adequate notice of lessor's claim against a subcontractor was provided to the general contractor, there was adequate compliance with the Public Works Surety Bond Law even in the absence of separate notice to surety. *Chadwick-BaRoss, Inc. v. T. Buck Const., Inc.,* 627 A.2d 532 (Me. 1993).

A statutory right to recover attorney's fees will be found only in the clearest kind of language, and a contractual right to attorney's fees is strictly limited to actions taken pursuant to that contract. *Chadwick-BaRoss, Inc. v. T. Buck Const., Inc.*, 627 A.2d 532 (Me. 1993).

## 2. Damages Covered

***Set forth in any statutes and/or case law***

Maine has a construction prompt payment statute set forth at 10 M.R.S.A. § 1111 *et seq*. The Prompt Payment Act, as it is commonly known, requires owners, contractors and subcontractors with downstream payment obligations to make timely payment of funds due in connection with a construction project. The statute applies to state, county and municipal projects, but not to contracts entered into by Maine's Department of Transportation. Late payments or a withholding of contract funds deemed not to be in good faith may subject the owner, contractor or subcontractor to liabilities for interest, penalties and legal fees incurred by the party seeking payment. This statute would apply to a surety stepping into a defaulting contractor's shoes on a construction project pursuant to the terms of the performance bond.

14 M.R.S.A. §§ 1602-B and 1602-C governs the award of pre- and post-judgment interest on civil claims generally. 14 M.R.S.A. §§ 1602-B (2) states that "[i]n all civil and small claims actions involving a contract or note that contains a provision relating to interest, prejudgment interest is allowed at the rate set forth in the contract or note." Under 14 M.R.S.A. §§ 1602-B(3), prejudgment interest in civil actions is allowed at the one-year United States Treasury bill rate plus 3 percent and is applicable where no interest rate is specified in the contract. Under 14 M.R.S.A. §§ 1602-C(1), post-judgment interest is allowed at the greater of the rate set forth in the parties' contract or at the one-year United States Treasury bill rate plus 6 percent.

***Obligations of surety to perform and/or pay***

Advance payment by owner to contractor did not discharge performance bond surety's obligations on the bond. *Maine Central R. Co. v. National Surety Co.*, 113 Me. 465, 94 A. 929 (Me. 1915).

***Whether failure to provide insurance transfers burden to surety*** – There are no Maine cases addressing this topic.

***Limitations on damages*** – There are no Maine cases addressing this topic.

***Whether obligee may set off bonded contract funds against other principal-obligee debts or obligations*** – There are no Maine cases addressing this topic.

***Incorporation of specific contract terms by reference***

Incorporation by reference of a subcontract, which contained an arbitration clause, into payment and performance bonds required the surety to submit to arbitration of a dispute arising out of the subcontract. *Cianbro Corp. v. Empressa Nacional De Ingenieria*, 697 F. Supp. 15 (D. Me. 1988).

## 3. Penal Sum Variations

***Limitations per statute*** – Except as noted above, Maine's Public Works Surety Bond Law of 1971 requires bonds to be provided in the amount of the contract.

***Effect of changes in work upon penal sum, if at all***

"The principle is elementary that any material alteration in the terms of a contract for the performance of which a surety is bound, if made without the surety's consent, releases him from liability." *Maine Cent. R. Co. v. National Surety Co.*, 94 A. 929, 113 Me. 465 (Me. 1915).

***Statutory or case law protections or dangers to penal sum*** – Maine has no case law addressing this issue.

## 4. Parties Covered

***Statutes and/or case law statements as to whether only obligees are covered***

Unpaid subcontractors and suppliers are not entitled to recovery under the performance bond. *Transamerica Premier Insurance Company v. Ober*, 849 F. Supp. 471 (D. Me. 1995).

***Coverage for:***

**Third-party beneficiaries** – There are no Maine cases on this topic.

**Assignees** – Contract progress payments received by a bank pursuant to an assignment by the bond principal/contractor were deemed to be held in trust for performing performance bond surety. *Aetna Casualty and Surety Co. v. Eastern Trust & Banking Co.,* 156 Me. 87, 161 A.2d 843 (Me. 1960).

**Dual obligees** – There are no Maine cases discussing dual obligee bonds.

## 5. Notice or Filing Required

***Statutory provisions***

Maine's Public Works Surety Bond Law of 1971 sets forth notice requirements and deadlines for filing suit for payment bond claimants only. No specific limitations period is provided in the statute as to performance bonds.

***Case law rules concerning condition precedent notice***

Notice by a subcontractor's materialman on a public construction project that was sent to, and received by, the general contractor by first-class mail, stating that materialman had received no payment, and that letter was to serve as notification to general contractor that there could be pending litigation, was sufficient to meet requirement of Public Works Surety Bond Law of 1971 that subcontractors not in privity of contract with the general contractor must give general contractor notice within 90 days of last day on which subcontractor furnished labor or materials, even though that statute provides that "notice shall be served by registered or certified mail." *Vacuum Systems, Inc. v. Washburn,* 651 A.2d 377 (Me. 1994).

Where adequate notice of lessor's claim against subcontractor was provided to general contractor, there was adequate compliance with public works surety bond law even in the absence of separate notice to surety. *Chadwick-BaRoss, Inc. v. T. Buck Const., Inc.,* 627 A.2d 532 (Me. 1993).

Where contract made no provision for notice, the surety on the contractor's performance bond was not discharged because the obligee/owner failed to provide notice of the contractor's default. *Maine Central R. Co. v. National Surety Co.*, 113 Me. 465, 94 A. 929 (Me. 1915).

### 6. Time for Suit

***Statutes of limitation particular to performance bonds and other applicable statutes of limitation***

Maine's general statute of limitations, 14 M.R.S.A. § 752, is applicable to contracts generally and provides:

> All civil actions shall be commenced within 6 years after the cause of action accrues and not afterwards, except actions on a judgment or decree of any court of record of the United States, or of any state or of a justice of the peace in this State, and except as otherwise specially provided.

As to foreign insurers (those organized under the laws of a state other than Maine), 24-A M.R.S.A. § 2433 provides:

> No conditions, stipulations or agreements in a contract of insurance shall deprive the courts of this State of jurisdiction of actions against foreign insurers, or limit the time for commencing actions against such insurers to a period of less than 2 years from the time when the cause of action accrues.

***Case law statements about enforceability of limitations contained in bonds*** – There are no Maine cases addressing this issue.

***Varying statutes of limitation by agreement in bond or contract***

With some exceptions not applicable to the law of performance bonds, Maine law permits contractual modification of the statute of limitations. *See,* 14 M.R.S.A. § 752-A; 24-A M.R.S.A. § 2433.

## 7. Procedure:

***Statutory or procedural rules that may affect handling or administration of lawsuits*** – Not applicable.

***Venue requirements and jurisdictional limitations***

Maine's Public Works Surety Bond Law of 1971, 14 M.R.S.A. § 871, requires bond claims be filed in the county where the contractor or surety has its principal place of business.

***Court rules*** – Not applicable.

***Particular agency regulations/rules*** – Not applicable.

***Arbitration requirements and application***

Maine has its own version of the Uniform Arbitration Act set forth at 14 M.R.S.A. § 5927 *et seq*. In pertinent part, that act states that:

> A written agreement to submit any existing controversy to arbitration or a provision in a written contract to submit to arbitration any controversy thereafter arising between the parties is valid, enforceable and irrevocable, save upon such grounds as exist at law or in equity for the revocation of any contract. This chapter also applies to arbitration agreements between employers and employees or between their respective representatives, unless otherwise provided in the agreement.

Incorporation by reference of a subcontract, which contained an arbitration clause, into payment and performance bonds requires the surety to submit to arbitration of a dispute arising out of the subcontract. *Cianbro Corp. v. Empressa Nacional De Ingenieria*, 697 F. Supp. 15 (D. Me. 1988).

## 8. Attorney's Fees

***Statutes and/or case law limiting or permitting recovery of attorney's fees***

Public Works Surety Bond Law of 1971 does not authorize recovery of legal fees. *Chadwick-BaRoss, Inc. v. T. Buck Const., Inc.*, 627 A.2d 532 (Me. 1993).

See, 10 M.R.S.A. § 1111 *et seq.*, *supra* regarding owner, contractor or subcontractor liability for legal fees.

***What fees are recoverable if any*** – See, 10 M.R.S.A. § 1111 *et seq.*, *supra.*

## 9. Special Provisions – Not applicable.

## 10. Remarks

Sureties are defined as "insurers" and thus fall within the coverage of Maine's Insurance Code. 24-A M.R.S.A. §§ 3, 4. "All contracts of surety insurance delivered or issued for delivery in this State and covering subjects resident, located or to be performed in this State are also subject to the applicable provisions of [the Maine Insurance Code]." 24-A M.R.S.A. § 3101.

The contractor's performance bond surety, however, is not the project obligee/owner's "own insurer" and, therefore, the obligee/owner cannot assert claims against the contractor's surety under the unfair claims settlement practices provision of the Maine Insurance Code. *Federal Insurance Company v. Maine Yankee Atomic Power Co.*, 183 F. Supp. 2d 76 (D. Me 2001).

Although sureties in Maine fall within the definition of the term "insurer" as defined by the Maine Insurance Code, at least one court has held that sureties are not subject to Maine's unfair insurance claims settlement practices statute, set forth at 24-A M.R.S.A. § 2436-A, at least in the context of a claim by a performance bond obligee against the performance bond surety. *Federal Insurance Company v. Maine Yankee Atomic Power Co.*, 183 F. Supp. 2d 76, 88 (D. Me. 2001).

## 11. Case Annotations

Condition of contractor's bond that contractor, as principal, shall faithfully perform contract and shall satisfy all claims and demands shall be liberally construed. *Newport Trust Co. v. Susi*, 153 Me. 51, 134 A.2d (Me. 1957).

***Interpretation of AIA bond forms*** – Maine has no cases or statutes on this issue.

***Cases in which surety steps into shoes of obligee***

Surety, which paid off obligee of performance bond for default of principal, became subrogated to obligee's rights against principal and third parties obligated to obligee. *Unity Telephone Co. v. Design Service Co., Inc.,* 201 A.2d 177 (Me. 1964).

# MARYLAND

Cynthia E. Rodgers-Waire and Nichole Velasquez[1]

## 1. Requirement for Bond

**Public** – Maryland "Little Miller Act," § 17-101, *et seq.*, Md. Code Ann., State Finance and Procurement Article.

The Maryland Little Miller Act requires contractors to provide payment security and performance security on all public construction contracts exceeding $100,000. The performance security must be "in an amount that the public body considers adequate for its protection" (generally the contract price) and the payment security must be in an amount that equals at least 50 percent of the contract price. A public body, other than the state or a unit of the state government, may require payment security or performance security for a construction contract that is greater than $25,000 but less than $100,000 if the amount of security does not exceed 50 percent of the contract amount.

The payment and performance security required under the Little Miller Act can be a bond provided by a surety company authorized to do business in the state, cash in an amount equivalent to the bond, or another form of security acceptable to the public obligee.

---

1 Cynthia E. Rodgers-Waire is a partner and Nichole Velasquez is an associate at:

Whiteford, Taylor & Preston L.L.P.
7 Saint Paul Street
Baltimore, Maryland 21202
(410) 347-8700

**Private** – None required

**Department of Transportation** – Md. Code Ann. § 8-646, Transportation Article, requires any non-governmental entity desiring to construct a commercial, industrial, or street entrance connecting with a state highway to obtain an entrance permit, which requires the applicant to provide performance surety, which may be in the form of a performance bond. The amount shall be the next highest even thousand dollar above 150 percent of the cost estimate for the construction. Anyone desiring to construct an entrance to a private residence must provide a performance bond in the amount of $1,000 for each entrance. COMAR 11.04.06.01

***Case law rules that might generally apply***

Traditional rules of contract interpretation apply to surety agreements ensuring performance and payment bonds. *Republic Ins. Co. v. Board of County Commissioners of St. Mary's County*, 68 Md. App. 428, 431, 511 A.2d 1136 (Md. App. 1986).

"The cardinal rule in the interpretation of bonds, as well as of other contracts, is to ascertain the intention of the parties and to give effect to that intention if it can be done consistently with legal principles." *Lange v. Board of Education*, 183 Md. 255, 260, 37 A.2d 317 (1944).

## 2. Damages Covered

***Set forth in any statutes and/or case law***

"The liability of a surety is coextensive with that of the principal, and it is clear that the liability of the surety is measured by the contract of the principal." *General Builders Supply Co., Inc. v. MacArthur*, 228 Md. 320, 326, 179 A.2d 868, 871-2 (Md. 1962).

A surety's liability for damages becomes fixed upon approval or acceptance of work by the obligee, rather than upon principal's default. *Republic Ins. Co. v. Prince George's County,* 92 Md. App. 528, 533, 608 A.2d 1301 (Md. App. 1992).

The Little Miller Act does not require a performance bond surety to assume liability for negligent acts of which contractor is guilty. State

Highway Administration v. Transamerica Ins. Co., 278 Md. 690, 707-708, 367 A.2d 509 (Md. 1976).

***Obligations of surety to perform and/or pay***

The specific obligations of the surety are governed by the language of its contract.

"While the contract of a surety for profit is not to be so strictly construed as one of a surety not for gain, it is clear that the liability of a surety is not to be extended, by implication, beyond the terms of its contract, but the nature of the duty of the obligor and the character of the obligee must be regarded as explanatory of their intent." *State Highway Admin. v. Transamerica Insur. Co.*, 278 Md. 690, 700-701, 367 A.2d 509 (1976).

"Nothing can be clearer, both upon principle and authority, than the doctrine, that the liability of a surety is not to be extended, by implication, beyond the terms of his contract. To the extent, and in the manner, and under the circumstances pointed out in his obligation, he is bound, and no farther." *Miller v. Stewart*, 9 Wheat. 680, 702-03 (1824).

***Whether failure to provide insurance transfers burden to surety*** – There are no cases addressing this issue.

***Limitations on damages***

The penal sum of the performance bond is the limit of a surety's liability under the performance bond. Maryland does not recognize the surety's failure to perform a contract as giving rise to a tort action for "bad faith" or breach of a duty of good faith or fair dealing. *Republic Ins. Co. v. Board of County Comm'rs of St. Mary's County*, 68 Md. App. 428, 431-32, 511 A.2d 1136 (Md. App. 1986); *Institute of Mission Helpers v. Reliance Insurance Company*, 812 F. Supp. 72 (D. Md. 1992). An obligee cannot recover consequential damages in excess of the stated limit of the bond based upon the surety's refusal to perform. *Bell BCI Co. v. HRGM Corp.*, 276 F. Supp. 2d 462, 463, n.1 (D. Md. 2004).

***Whether obligee may set off bonded contract funds against other principal-obligee debts or obligations*** – There are no cases addressing this issue.

***Incorporation of specific contract terms by reference***

"Where the contract incorporates as part of itself the specifications, and the contract is, by reference, incorporated as part of the bond, the contract, the specifications and the bond must all be construed together." *Lange v. Board of Education*, 183 Md., 255, 261, 37 A.2d 317 (Md. 1944).

## 3. Penal Sums Variation

***Limitations per statute and/or case law*** – Maryland does not have statutory limitations on performance bond penal sums. Generally, the penal sum of the bond is the contract price.

***Effect of changes in work upon penal sum, if at all*** – There are no cases addressing this issue.

***Statutory or case law protections or dangers to penal sum***

Maryland case law protects the penal sum liability limitation provided to the surety. Maryland courts have expressly rejected tort actions for "bad faith" or actions for breach of a duty of good faith or fair dealing. *Republic Ins. Co. v. Board of County Comm'rs of St. Mary's County*, 68 Md. App. 428, 431-32, 511 A.2d 1136 (Md. App. 1986); *Institute of Mission Helpers v. Reliance Insurance Company*, 812 F. Supp. 72 (D. Md. 1992).

## 4. Parties Covered

***Statutes and/or case law as to whether only obligees are covered***

"The common thread running through the cases cited is that liability under the bond extends, in any event, only to the parties intended to be benefited by the bond, ordinarily the State with respect to performance provisions, and persons furnishing labor and material used in the construction of the public work with respect to payment provisions (if not in a separate bond)." State Highway Admin. v. Transamerica Insur. Co. et. al., 278 Md. 690, 706, 367 A.2d 509, 519 (1976).

***Coverage for:***

**Third-Party Beneficiaries** – There are no cases addressing this issue.

**Assignees** – There are no cases addressing this issue.

**Dual obligees** – There are no cases addressing this issue.

## 5. Notice for Filing Required

***Statutory provisions*** – None applicable to performance bond claims.

***Case law concerning condition precedent notice*** – None pertaining to performance bond claims.

## 6. Time for Suit

***Statutes of limitation particular to performance bonds and other applicable statutes of limitation***

The 12-year statute of limitations applicable to specialties applies to actions on performance bonds, not the one year statute of limitations for payment bond claims under the Little Miller Act. *Anne Arundel County, Maryland v. Fidelity & Deposit Company of Maryland*, 336 Md. 282, 284, 648 A.2d 193 (1994).

Md. Code Ann., § 5-102(a), Courts and Judicial Proceedings Article, states:

Specialties

(a) *Twelve-year limitation.* An action on one of the following specialties shall be filed within 12 years after the cause of action accrues, or within 12 years from the date of the death of the last to die of the principal debtor or creditor, whichever is sooner:

* * *

(2) Bond except a public officer's bond;

Limitations begin to run on an obligee's performance bond claim on the date that final payment falls due. *Hagerstown Elderly Associates Ltd. Partnership v. Hagerstown Elderly Bldg. Associates Ltd. Partnership,* 368 Md. 351, 364, 793 A.2d 579 (Md. 2002).

***Case law statements about enforceability of limitations contained in bonds***

*Hagerstown Elderly Associates Ltd. Partnership v. Hagerstown Elderly Bldg. Associates Ltd. Partnership,* 368 Md. 351, 363, 793 A.2d 579 (Md. 2002) ("The Circuit Court was correct in substituting the 12-year statute of limitations contained in § 5-102(a)(2) for the two-year limitation contained in the performance bond, and none of the parties dispute that finding in the case before us.").

***Varying statutes of limitation by agreement in bond or contract***

Parties may not vary the limitations by agreement. Md. Code Ann., § 12-104(a), Insurance Article, prohibits the enforcement of any provision in a surety contract that shortens the applicable period of limitation required by the law of the State of Maryland.

**7. Procedure**

***Statutory or procedural rules that may affect handling or administration of lawsuits*** – Not applicable.

***Venue requirements and jurisdictional limitations*** – Not applicable.

***Court rules*** – Not applicable.

***Particular agency regulations/rules*** – Not applicable.

***Arbitration requirements and application***

A surety that issued a performance bond incorporating by reference a mandatory arbitration provision from the contract between the obligee and the bonded contractor could not enforce the arbitration agreement against the obligee in an action on the bond; the provision only incorporates the obligee's promise to arbitrate with the contractor. *Hartford Acc. & Indem. Co. v. Scarlett Harbor Associates Ltd. Partnership*, 346 Md. 122, 129, 695 A.2d 153 (Md. 1997).

**8. Attorney's Fees**

***Statutes and/or case law limiting or permitting recovery of attorney's fees***

When attorney's fees are provided for in the contract:

> "[a] contractual obligation to pay attorney's fees generally is valid and enforceable in Maryland." *Atlantic Contracting & Material Co. Inc., v. Ulico Casualty Co.*, 380 Md. 285, 316 844 A.2d 460, 477 (2004).

***What fees are recoverable, if any*** – There are no statutes or cases specifically addressing this issue.

**9. Special Provisions** – Not applicable.

**10. Remarks** – Not applicable.

**11. Case Annotations**

***Interpretation of AIA bond forms*** – Maryland has no cases or statutes on this issue.

***Cases in which surety steps into shoes of obligee***

Maryland courts have adopted the general rule that a performance bond surety who completes the contract upon the contractor's default is entitled to be subrogated to the rights which the obligee had to, or could assert against, such funds upon the contractor's default, to the extent necessary to reimburse himself for the outlay made to complete the contract. Finance Co. of America v. U.S. Fidelity & Guaranty Co., 277 Md. 177, 182-183, 353 A.2d 249 (Md. 1976).

# MASSACHUSETTS

Bradford R. Carver and Eric H. Loeffler[1]

## 1. Requirement for Bond

***Statutory provisions for projects that are:***

**Public Building** – M.G.L. c. 149, § 44E(2) requires contractors to furnish a performance bond equal to the contract price on public building projects. Terms of the performance bond are not prescribed by statute. M.G.L. c. 149, § 44F(3) provides that a general contractor may require certain subcontractors to furnish a performance bond in the full sum of the subcontract price.

**Public Works** – While M.G.L. c. 30, § 39M requires a payment bond for public works contracts, there is no requirement for a performance bond, although, in practice, virtually all public awarding authorities require performance bonds on public works projects.

**Private** – No statutes in Massachusetts require performance bonds on private projects.

**Department of Transportation** – Not applicable.

1 Bradford R. Carver is a partner and Eric H. Loeffler is an associate with:
Hinshaw & Culbertson LLP
One International Place, Third Floor
Boston, Massachusetts 02110
(617) 213-7000

***Case law rules that might generally apply***

"A surety's bond is a contract. It sets the limits of the surety's liability. The fact that this bond is required by statute does nothing to alter the settled principles of contract and suretyship law. That [the bond] is a statutory bond does not 'enlarge the risk' which the bonding company has undertaken." *Peerless Ins. Co. v. South Boston Storage & Warehouse, Inc.*, 397 Mass. 325, 327, 491 N.E.2d 253, 254 (1986), *citing Treasurer & Receiver Gen. v. Massachusetts Bonding & Ins. Co.*, 349 Mass. 256, 258, 207 N.E.2d 684 (1965).

## 2. Damages Covered

***Set forth in any statutes and/or case law***

A surety "cannot be holden beyond the fair scope of [its] engagement, as intended by the parties when undertaken." *Peerless*, 397 Mass. at 327, 491 N.E.2d at 254, *quoting President of Dedham Bank v. Chickering*, 4 Pick. 314, 340 (1827).

The rights and obligations of parties under a surety bond are to be determined by the terms of the bond, construed according to the usual rules of contract interpretation. *Miller v. Perry*, 333 Mass. 155, 158, 129 N.E.2d 143, 144-145 (1955); *In re Sinking of M/V Ukola*, 806 F.2d 1, 4 (1st Cir. 1986).

"The liability of a surety or guarantor is to be ascertained from the terms of the written instrument by which his obligation is expressed, construed according to the usual rules of interpretation in the light of the subject-matter, and the well-understood usages of the business, and the relations of the parties to the transactions. Where the words are unambiguous they alone can be examined to determine their meaning." *Gordon & Dilworth v. Abbott*, 258 Mass. 35, 38, 154 N.E. 523 (1926).

"The substantial correspondence of the obligations of principal and surety extends to the obligation to pay interest." *John W. Egan Co., Inc. v. Major Const. Management Corp.*, 46 Mass. App. Ct. 643, 647, 709 N.E.2d 66, 70 (1999) (construing statutory payment bond).

***Obligations of surety to perform and/or pay***

"The liability of [a] surety [is] to make good any default of the principal in regard to payments, within the amount stated as the penal sum of the bond." *Yanofsky v. Marinucci Bros & Co.*, 351 Mass. 698, 699, 218 N.E.2d 405, 406 (1966), *quoting George H. Sampson Co. v. Commonwealth*, 202 Mass. 326, 339, 88 N.E. 911, 916 (1909).

***Whether failure to provide insurance transfers burden to surety*** – Statutes do not transfer the burden to the surety.

***Limitations on damages*** – Not applicable.

***Whether obligee may set off bonded contract funds against other principal-obligee debts or obligations***

Pursuant to equitable subrogation, a surety who fulfills the duties of its principal is entitled to "step in the shoes" of and assert the rights of the principal against third persons. *National Shawmut Bk. of Boston v. New Amsterdam Gas Co.*, 411 F.2d 843, 844 (1st Cir. 1969) (applying Massachusetts law). A surety who pays the debt of another is entitled to all the rights of the person he paid to enforce his right to be reimbursed by a third party. *Pearlman v. Reliance Ins. Co.*, 371 U.S. 132, 137 (1962). When a surety "pays all the bills of the job to date and completes the job, it stands in the shoes of the contractor insofar as there are receivables due it; in the shoes of laborers and materialmen who have been paid by the surety - who may have had liens; and, not least, in the shoes of the government, for whom the job was completed." *National Shawmut*, 411 F.2d at 845. The right of the government that a surety succeeds to is the "right to apply to the cost of completion the earned but unpaid progress payments in its hands at the time of default." *Id.* at 848.

***Incorporation of specific contract by reference***

"[A] surety ... is generally obligated to arbitrate a dispute with a contractor or developer, if the performance bond incorporates by reference an underlying construction contract that contains an arbitration clause." *Travelers Cas. and Sur. Co. of Amer. v. Long Bay Mgmt. Co.*, 58 Mass. App. Ct. 786, 788, 792 N.E.2d 1013, 1015 (2003) (holding that performance bond's incorporation of contract by reference was not limited in scope to work to be performed under the contract, but included arbitration clause in the contract; the language of the bond stating that the contract was incorporated by reference meant that the construction contract was part of the bond itself); *see also Massachusetts Electrical Systems, Inc. v. R.W. Granger & Sons, Inc.*, 32 Mass. App. Ct. 982, 983, 594 N.E.2d 545, 546 (1992) (noting that surety may be bound by arbitration clause where a bond incorporates the underlying contract); *Kearsage Metallurgical Corp. v. Peerless Ins. Co.*, 383 Mass. 162, 167, 418 N.E.2d 580, 583 (1981) (bond contained language that made the underlying contract "a part of this bond, the same as though fully set forth herein"); *Commercial Union Ins. Co. v. Gilbane Building Co.,* 992 F.2d 386, 388 (1st Cir. 1993) (bond contained language that the underlying contract "is by reference made a part hereof"); *J&S Construction Co., Inc. v. Travelers Indemnity Co.*, 520 F.2d 809, 810 (1st Cir. 1975) (stating that "the contract was explicitly incorporated by reference in the surety bond); *Thomas O'Connor & Co. v. Insurance Co. of N. America*, 697 F. Supp. 563, 565 (D. Mass. 1988) (stating that the bond explicitly incorporated the underlying contract by reference); *Powers Regulator Co. v. United States Fid. & Guar. Co.*, 7 Mass. App. Ct. 913, 913-914, 388 N.E.2d 1205, 1206-07 (1979) (stating that the subcontract was incorporated by reference into the payment bond).

"[I]t is well established that a bond and the contract which it was written to guarantee should be read together when the bond makes appropriate reference to the contract." *In re Sinking of M/V Ukola*, 806 F.2d 1, 4 (1st Cir. 1986) (citations omitted). Indeed, "a surety's obligation should be construed by reading together all instruments, statutes, and regulations underlying the transaction." *Id.*

### 3. Penal Sum Variations

***Limitations per statute*** – Not applicable.

***Effect of changes in work upon penal sum, if at all*** – Not applicable.

***Statutory and/or case law protections or dangers to penal sum***

"'The liability of [a] surety [is] to make good any default of the principal in regard to payments, within the amount stated as the penal sum of the bond.'" *Yanofsky v. Marinucci Bros & Co.*, 351 Mass. 698, 699, 218 N.E.2d 405, 406 (1966), *quoting George H. Sampson Co. v. Commonwealth*, 202 Mass. 326, 339, 88 N.E. 911, 916 (1909).

The general rule in Massachusetts is that the penal amount limits recovery to that amount. *See Hartford Accident & Indem. Co. v. Casassa*, 301 Mass. 246, 255 256, 16 N.E.2d 860, 866 (1938); *Peerless Ins. Co. v. South Boston Storage & Warehouse, Inc.*, 397 Mass. 325, 491 N.E.2d 253 (1986) (holding that the penal sum is a limit not merely on each individual claim but on all claims in the aggregate).

"Where a surety company assumes the role of the principal and completes the contract, it is liable to pay sums in excess of the penal sum." *International Fidelity Ins. Co. v. Wilson*, 387 Mass. 841, 851, 443 N.E.2d 1308, 1314 (1983).

## 4. Parties Covered

***Statutes and/or case law as to whether only obligees are covered***

Where prime contractor executed payment bond to owner and only the owner was named as obligee, bond could not be construed to imply an obligation or offer by prime contractor to suppliers, and hence unpaid supplier to subcontractor was not entitled to recover on bond. *Waite Hardware Co. v. Ardini & Pfau, Inc.*, 339 Mass. 634, 638, 162 N.E.2d 13, 16 (1959) (construing payment bond).

A bond, given in connection with a construction contract, which is "valid as the basis of a common law obligation," may operate to benefit "all parties who, in reliance upon it, have furnished material or labor," if the bond contains certain "peculiar terms." *Morse Bros. Elec. Co. v. Martin Shore Realty Co.*, 344 Mass. 81, 84, 181 N.E.2d 549, 550 (1962), *quoting Johnson-Foster Co. v. D'Amore Const. Co.*, 314 Mass. 416, 419-420, 50 N.E.2d 89 (1943) (where bond expressly stated, not only that it created an obligation to the entity for which the work was being done, but that it was "also made for the use and benefit of all persons ... who may furnish any material or perform any labor for ... [the] contract ... and they and each of them are ... made obligees hereunder ... and ... may ...

sue hereon"). The principle of this case has been reaffirmed in cases where (a) the provisions of the bond or other contractual arrangement show an intention to benefit subcontractors and suppliers and to give them a direct right upon the bond or contract, and (b) there has been reliance by the subcontractors and suppliers. *See, e.g.*, *Robinson Clay Product Co. v. Beacon Const. Co. of Mass., Inc.*, 339 Mass. 406, 408-410, 159 N.E.2d 530 (1959).

***Coverage for:***

**Third party beneficiaries** – Sub-subcontractor on publicly funded construction project was not entitled to bring direct suit as a third party beneficiary on subcontractor's performance bond after subcontractor failed to pay for labor and materials furnished by sub-subcontractor. *Continental Bronze Co., Inc. v. Salvo & Armstrong Steel Co., Inc.*, 8 Mass. App. Ct. 799, 801-03, 397 N.E.2d 1143, 1144-45 (1979).

**Assignees** – There appears to be no case in Massachusetts discussing assignment of obligee's right to make a claim against a performance bond, although the general rule in Massachusetts is that rights arising under a contract may be assigned, absent a provision in the contract to the contrary. *Federal National Bank of Boston v. Commonwealth*, 282 Mass. 442, 450, 185 N.E. 9, 12 (1933) ("it is settled law that parties to a contract can agree that the contract in all its terms shall be non-assignable"); *American Employers' Insurance Co. v. City of Medford*, 38 Mass. App. Ct. 18, 22, 644 N.E.2d 241, 243 (1995) ("It is axiomatic that a contractual right can be assigned unless assignment is expressly forbidden by the terms of the contract").

**Dual obligees** – Where rider to performance bond naming construction lender as additional obligee along with owner provided that there was no liability on part of surety under bond to obligees or either of them unless obligees, or either of them, made payments to principal strictly in accordance with terms of contract as to payments and where construction lender did not step in to make payments to general contractor when owner fell in arrears, surety was not entitled under rider to reimbursement from lender for payments surety made to suppliers at general contractor's request. *U. S. Fidelity & Guaranty Co. v. N. J. B. Prime Investors*, 6 Mass. App. Ct. 455, 459, 377 N.E.2d 440, 443 (1978).

## 5. Notice or Filing Required

***Statutory provisions*** – Not applicable.

***Case law rules concerning condition precedent notice***

"The general rule is that a party suing on a bond must show strict compliance with its terms." *Simplex Time Recorder Co. v. Federal Ins. Co.*, 37 Mass. App. Ct. 947, 947, 641 N.E.2d 1358, 1359 (1994). "[W]hen the wording of a contract is unambiguous, the terms will be enforced." *Seaboard Sur. Co. v. Greenfield*, 370 F.3d 215, 219 n.5 (1st Cir. 2004) (construing performance bond).

Whether the provisions of a performance bond are conditions precedent is a question of law for the court to decide. *See Drake Fishing, Inc., v. Clarendon American Ins. Co.*, 136 F.3d 851, 853 (1st Cir.1998); *Shaw v. Commercial Ins. Co.*, 359 Mass. 601, 605-06, 270 N.E.2d 817 (1971); *see also Wood v. Roy Lapidus, Inc.*, 10 Mass. App. Ct. 761, 764, 413 N.E.2d 345 (1980) (noting that the court should "ascertain [] the intent of the parties as expressed in the instrument [and consider] the words used, the document taken as a whole, and surrounding facts") (internal citations omitted).

"While it is true that 'Massachusetts courts have held that lack of prompt notice to the compensated surety of a contractor's default (as required by a Performance Bond) does not discharge the surety if it is not harmed,' notice requirements 'exist [] precisely to provide the surety an opportunity to protect itself against loss by participating in the selection of the successor contractor to ensure that the lowest bidder is hired and damages mitigated." *Seaboard Sur. Co. v. Town of Greenfield*, 370 F.3d 215, 220 (1st Cir. 2004), *quoting Enterprise Capital, Inc. v. San-Gra Corp.*, 284 F. Supp. 2d 166, 177 (D. Mass. 2003) (citations omitted). "In the context of surety default, the notice provision similarly provides an opportunity for the surety to cure the breach and thus mitigate damages." *Id.* Even if surety must show injury, loss or prejudice, the surety meets this hurdle where it is deprived of its mitigation opportunities. *Enterprise Capital,* 284 F. Supp. 2d at 177.

Courts in Massachusetts have held that failure to comply with the default and termination provisions in the AIA A-312 bond results in a complete discharge of the surety. *See Seaboard Surety Co. v. Greenfield*, 266 F. Supp. 2d 189, 196 (D. Mass. 2003), *aff'd* 370 F.3d. 215, 219 (1st

Cir. 2004) ("... the surety default provisions of Paragraph 5 constitute an important contractual right of the surety... failure to provide this notice constitutes a material breach of the bond"); *Greenfield*, 266 F. Supp. 2d at 196-198 (obligee materially breached bond, and surety was discharged from "any and all liability under the bond" where obligee did not allow surety to exercise its completion options).

Surety was discharged of its obligations under performance bond where the owner materially breached the construction contract, which was incorporated by performance bond, by failing to comply with the construction contract's termination provision. *Enterprise Capital,* 284 F. Supp. 2d at 176.

Notices required under a performance bond must provide "clear, direct, and unequivocal" notice to the surety. *Enterprise Capital,* 284 F. Supp. 2d at 180-181.

### 6. Time for Suit

***Statutes of limitation particular to performance bonds and other applicable statutes of limitation***

M.G.L. c. 260, § 1 provides that actions upon contracts under seal "shall be commenced only within 20 years next after the cause of action accrues."

M.G.L. c. 260, § 2 states "Actions of contract, other than those to recover for personal injuries, founded upon contracts or liabilities, express or implied, except actions limited by section one or actions upon judgments or decrees of courts of record of the United States or of this or of any other state of the United States, shall, except as otherwise provided, be commenced only within six years next after the cause of action accrues."

The general rule is that contract action accrues, and six-year statute of limitations begins to run, at time contract is breached. *Berkshire Mut. Ins. Co. v. Burbank*, 422 Mass. 659, 661, 664 N.E.2d 1188, 1189 (1996).

***Case law statements about enforceability of limitations contained in bonds***

Endorsement to construction performance bond extending "effect" of bond and two year limitation provision of original bond were independent provisions; thus the endorsement did not extend or modify the limitations period. *Cooperatives of Charlesnewtown Housing, Inc. v. Drury Square*, 10 Mass. App. Ct. 901, 901, 409 N.E.2d 1335, 1336 (1980).

***Varying statutes of limitation by agreement in bond or contract***

Massachusetts law permits contractual modification of the statute of limitations. *General Elec. Co. v. Lexington Contracting Corp.*, 363 Mass. 122, 124, 292 N.E.2d 874, 876 (1973) (construing one year limitations period in payment bond).

## 7. Procedure

***Statutory or procedural rules that may affect handling or administration of lawsuits*** – Not applicable.

***Venue requirements and jurisdictional limitations***

"The general rule is that a party suing on a bond must show strict compliance with its terms, ... including, when applicable, a forum selection clause." *Simplex Time Recorder Co., Inc. v. Federal Ins. Co.*, 37 Mass. App. Ct. 947, 947, 641 N.E.2d 1358, 1359 (1994) (citations omitted).

M.G.L. c. 223, § 1 provides that "[a] transitory action shall, except as otherwise provided, if any one of the parties thereto lives in the commonwealth, be brought in the county where one of them lives or has his usual place of business ...."

M.G.L. c. 223, § 8 provides that "[t]ransitory actions, except those mentioned in the preceding section, to which a corporation, other than a county or the city of Boston, is a party, may be brought as follows: (1) If both parties are cities, towns or parishes, in the county where either party is situated. (2) If both parties are corporations, other than a city, town or parish, in any county in which either corporation has a usual place of business, or in which it held its last annual meeting, or usually holds its meetings. (3) If one party is a city, town or parish, and the other a corporation named in clause (2), in any county in which either party might sue or be sued. (4) If one party is a corporation named in clause (1) or (2), and the other an individual, in any county in which the corporation might sue or be sued, or in the county in which the individual lives or has a usual place of business."

***Court rules*** – Not applicable.

***Particular agency regulations/rules*** – Not applicable.

***Arbitration requirement and application***

In order for the court to compel arbitration, there must be a valid arbitration clause and the claims (or counterclaims) must fall within the scope of the clause. M.G.L. c. 251, the Massachusetts Arbitration Act, governs arbitration of commercial disputes and provides that a written agreement to arbitrate shall be valid, enforceable and irrevocable, save upon such grounds as exist at law or in equity for the revocation of any contract. M.G.L. c. 251, § 1. A party aggrieved by the refusal of the other party to proceed to arbitration to apply to the superior court for an order directing the parties to proceed to arbitration. M.G.L. c. 251, § 2.

Massachusetts has expressed "a strong public policy favoring arbitration as an expeditious alternative to litigation for settling commercial disputes." *Town of Danvers v. Wexler Constr. Co.*, 12 Mass. App. Ct. 160, 163, 422 N.E.2d 782 (1981). The Massachusetts Arbitration Act establishes that "any doubts concerning the scope of arbitrable issues should be resolved in favor of arbitration ..." *Carpenter v. Pomerantz*, 36 Mass. App. Ct. 627, 632, 634 N.E.2d 587 (1994). Counterclaims should be addressed through arbitration to the extent that they fall within the scope of the arbitration provision. *Town of Danvers*, 12 Mass. App. Ct. at 166. Where there is a valid arbitration agreement and that the issues raised in the court action are subject to arbitration, the court should stay the litigation of those issues and compel arbitration. *Id.* at 166, 422 N.E.2d 782.

## 8. Attorney's Fees

***Statutes and/or case law limiting or permitting recovery of attorney's fees***

Attorney's fees in action against surety to recover for surety's breach of obligation on performance bond were not recoverable. *Town of East*

*Longmeadow v. Maryland Cas. Co.*, 348 Mass. 722, 729, 206 N.E.2d 54, 59 (1965).

Massachusetts generally follows the traditional American Rule, which provides that a prevailing party is not entitled to attorney's fees in the absence of a specific statute, court rule or contractual stipulation which provides for such recovery. *Preferred Mut. Ins. Co. v. Gamache*, 426 Mass. 93, 95, 686 N.E.2d 989 (1997); *Curtis v. Surrette*, 49 Mass. App. Ct. 99, 107, 726 N.E.2d 967 (2000).

***What fees are recoverable, if any***

The decision to award attorney's fees rests within the sound discretion of the trial judge. *Drapek v. Drapek*, 399 Mass. 240, 248, 503 N.E.2d 946 (1987). It is for the trial judge to review the evidence and determine whether to award attorney's fees as well as the amount of that award. *Brash v. Brash*, 407 Mass. 101, 106, 551 N.E.2d 523, 526 (1990).

"As long as the amount awarded is not incommensurate with an objective evaluation of the services performed ... '[t]he award of such costs generally rests in sound judicial discretion .... [T]he award ... may be presumed to be right and ordinarily ought not to be disturbed.'" *Ross v. Ross*, 385 Mass. 30, 38-39, 430 N.E.2d 815 (1982), *quoting Old Colony Trust Co. v. Third Universalist Soc'y*, 285 Mass. 146, 151, 188 N.E. 711 (1934).

**9. Special Provisions** – Not applicable.

**10. Remarks** – Not applicable.

**11. Case Annotations**

***Interpretation of AIA bond forms***

Courts in Massachusetts have held that failure to comply with the default and termination provisions in the AIA A-312 bond results in a complete discharge of the surety. *See Seaboard Surety Co. v. Greenfield*, 266 F. Supp. 2d 189, 196 (D. Mass. 2003), *aff'd* 370 F.3d. 215, 219 (1st Cir. 2004) ("... the surety default provisions of Paragraph 5 constitute an important contractual right of the surety ... failure to provide this notice constitutes a material breach of the bond").

Obligee's refusal to allow surety to complete the project renders the performance bond null and void and discharges the surety from any and all liability under the bond. *Greenfield*, 266 F. Supp. 2d at 196.

***Cases in which surety steps into shoes of obligee***

When a surety "pays all the bills of the job to date and completes the job, it stands in the shoes of the contractor insofar as there are receivables due it; in the shoes of laborers and materialmen who have been paid by the surety - who may have had liens; and, not least, in the shoes of the government, for whom the job was completed." *National Shawmut Bk. of Boston v. New Amsterdam Gas Co.*, 411 F.2d 843, 845 (1st Cir. 1969).

**Material alteration of bonded obligation** – To avoid liability under performance bond because of modification of contract without its knowledge or consent, surety has burden of showing that modification materially increased its risk or that some of the liability for which it is answerable resulted from modification. *Town of Hingham v. B. J. Pentabone, Inc.*, 354 Mass. 537, 238 N.E.2d 534 (1968).

# MICHIGAN

Phillip G. Alber and Omar J. Harb[1]

## 1. Requirement for Bond

***Statutory provisions for projects that are:***

**Public** – All public projects in Michigan were traditionally governed by a single bond statute, MCL 570.101 *et seq*. However, in 1963, the Michigan Legislature enacted a new public works bond statute, MCL 129.201 *et seq*. However the new statute specifically provided that the older statute would continue to apply to "construction and maintenance contracts of the state highway commissioner." MCL 129.211. Pursuant to MCL 247.802, "any law referring to the State Highway Commissioner or office of State Highway Commissioner shall be considered to refer to the department [of transportation]". Accordingly, Michigan Department of Transportation ("MDOT") projects continue to be governed by MCL 570.101 *et seq*.

MCL 129.201 requires a contractor on a public construction project to furnish a performance bond if the contract price exceeds $50,000. A public project includes "any public building or public work or improvement of the state or a county, city, village, township, school

---

[1] Phillip G. Alber and Omar J. Harb are shareholders with:
Alber Crafton, PSC
2301 West Big Beaver Road, Suite 300
Troy, Michigan 48084
(248) 822-6190

district, public educational institution, or other political subdivision, public authority, or public agency." *Id.*

Note that case law initially excluded constitutionally created state universities from the bond requirement, the Michigan Supreme Court reversed earlier decisions and held that the public works bond statute is applicable to the University of Michigan and other such universities. *W.T. Andrew Co. v. Mid-State Surety Corp.*, 450 Mich. 655; 545 N.W.2d 351 (1996).

A public utility (phone company) laying telephone cables under sidewalks, and agreeing to repair and replace the sidewalks, does not fall under MCL 129.201. "We believe that the statute was intended to cover only situations where the governmental unit hired a private contractor to perform construction work on governmental property. Instances such as the present, where a public utility seeks to enforce an easement and agrees to repair damage done to the governmental property, are distinguishable." *Modern Transit Mix, Inc. v Michigan Bell Telephone Co.*, 130 Mich. App. 300; 343 N.W.2d 14 (1983).

**Private** – No statutes in Michigan require performance bonds on private projects.

**Department of Transportation** – As noted above, MCL 570.101 *et seq*. now applies only to MDOT projects. However, that statute does not reference any requirement for a performance bond, only payment bonds. Accordingly, it is unclear under Michigan law whether highway (MDOT) projects carry with them any performance bond requirement. In any event, MDOT routinely requires performance bonds from the principal contractor, and a requirement for a performance bond for at least 100 percent of the total contract price is contained in MDOT's Standard Specifications for Construction, at Section 102.16.

***Case law rules that might generally apply***

The public works bond statute was intended to fill the void left by the mechanics' lien (construction lien) law in Michigan, which does not apply to public projects. The statute thus only applies to public projects. Even though a public agency, the Michigan Department of Social Services, was to be the ultimate lessee of a building being constructed, the operative issue was whether the land on which the building was being constructed was publicly owned. *The Milbrand Co. v. State of Michigan, Dept. of Social Services*, 117 Mich. App. 437; 324 N.W.2d 41 (1982).

The Michigan public works bond statute should be liberally construed to effectuate the legislative intent. *Trustees v. Warranty Builders, Inc.*, 921 F. Supp. 471 (E.D. Mich. 1996).

## 2. Damages Covered

### *Set forth in any statutes and/or case law*

MCL 129.202 provides that performance bonds are "conditioned upon the faithful performance of the contract in accordance with the plans, specifications and terms thereof."

### *Obligations of surety to perform and/or pay*

A performance bond surety is responsible for latent defects appearing within the contract's warranty period. *Hunters Pointe Partners Ltd Partnership v. Hoffman Const. Co.*, 194 Mich. App. 294; 486 N.W.2d 136 (1992).

### *Whether failure to provide insurance transfers burden to surety*

The Michigan Supreme Court held that a surety's performance bond covered all obligations of the principal, including the contractor's obligation to assume liability resulting from property damage to third parties. While presumably the principal had not obtained insurance to cover the damage, the opinion was silent on that issue, as well as with respect to whether insurance coverage was required under the contract. *Hardware Dealers Mutual Ins. Co. v. R. H. Hidey, Inc.*, 349 Mich. 490; 84 N.W.2d 795 (1957).

### *Limitations on damages*

The liability of a surety is coextensive with that of the principal. The surety may plead any defense available to its principal. If no action could be maintained by the obligee against the principal, none can be maintained against the surety. *Ackron Contracting Co. v. Oakland County*, 108 Mich. App. 767; 310 N.W.2d 874 (1981).

***Whether obligee may set off bonded contract funds against other principal-obligee debts or obligations*** – There are no Michigan cases on this issue.

***Incorporation of specific contract terms by reference***

The general rule in Michigan is that "where one writing references another instrument for additional contract terms, the two writings should be read together." *Forge v. Smith*, 458 Mich. 198; 580 N.W.2d 876 (1998).

A court can look to the underlying contract as an aid in interpreting the language of a bond. *Utter v. Leach*, 214 Mich. 31; 181 N.W. 999 (1921).

### 3. Penal Sum Variations

***Limitations per statute***

Pursuant to MCL 129.201, performance bonds are only required for non-MDOT public projects in excess of $50,000. The performance bond amount can be fixed by the governmental unit, but must be at least 25 percent of the contract amount. MCL 129.202.

***Effect of changes in work upon penal sum, if at all***

A surety can be relieved of its obligations based on a change in the underlying contract of its principal only if there is a material departure from the contract resulting in some harm to the surety. *Grinnell Realty Co. v. General Casualty & Surety Co.*, 253 Mich. 16; 234 N.W. 125 (1931).

***Statutory or case law protections or dangers to penal sum*** – There are no Michigan cases or statutes on this issue.

## 4. Parties Covered

***Statutes and/or case law as to whether only obligees are covered***

The public works bond statute provides that "the [performance] bond shall be solely for the protection of the governmental unit awarding the contract." MCL 129.202.

***Coverage for:***

**Third-party beneficiaries** – The Michigan Court of Appeals has held that a co-prime contractor was a third-party beneficiary of the performance bond issued on behalf of another co-prime contractor. *Chris Nelson and Son, Inc. v. Atlas Concrete Pipe, Inc.*, 84 Mich. App. 29; 269 N.W.2d 295 (1978). Part of the principal's contract was to make timely deliveries to the other prime contractor. When timely delivery was not made, the other prime contractor was deemed to have a cause of action on the performance bond for damages.

**Assignees** – Where there is no express prohibition against assignment in the performance bond, assignment can be made without the consent of the surety. *Hunters Pointe Partners Ltd. Partnership v. USF&G*, 177 Mich. App 745; 442 N.W.2d 778 (1989); and *Chris Nelson and Son, Inc. v. Atlas Concrete Pipe, Inc.*, 84 Mich. App. 29; 269 N.W.2d 295 (1978).

**Dual obligees** – There are no Michigan cases addressing this issue.

## 5. Notice or Filing Required

***Statutory provisions*** – Michigan statutes do not contain any notice requirements for a claim or suit under a performance bond.

***Case law rules concerning condition precedent notice*** – There are no published Michigan cases on this issue.

## 6. Time for Suit

***Statutes of limitation particular to performance bonds and other applicable statutes of limitation***

There is no specific statute of limitations contained in the public works bond statute relating to actions on performance bonds.

The general statute of limitations on a contract action is six years pursuant to MCL 600.5807(8).

***Case law statements about enforceability of limitations contained in bonds***

There are no published Michigan decisions relating to the enforceability of a limitations period contained in a performance bond. The Michigan Supreme Court has held that a one-year limitations period in a private project payment bond was enforceable, deeming it to be "reasonable." *Camelot Excavating Co., Inc. v. St. Paul Fire & Marine Ins. Co.*, 410 Mich. 118; 301 N.W.2d 275 (1981). (See note in the following section relating to the "reasonableness" requirement).

***Varying statutes of limitation by agreement in bond or contract***

Michigan courts allow parties to contractually shorten the limitations period. *Rory v. Cont'l Ins. Co.*, 473 Mich. 457 (2005) (relating to a provision in an insurance policy. Note that this recent decision expressly overruled *Camelot, supra,* to the extent of its requirement that the shortened period be "reasonable").

## 7. Procedure

***Statutory or procedural rules that may affect handling or administration of lawsuits*** – There are no rules relating to this issue in Michigan.

***Venue requirements and jurisdictional limitations*** – The Michigan public works bond statute does not address venue or jurisdictional issues for performance bond suits.

***Court rules*** – None relating to performance bond issues.

***Particular agency regulations/rules***– None relating to performance bond issues.

***Arbitration requirements and application***

The statute in Michigan generally covering arbitrations is MCL 600.5001 *et seq*. In addition, arbitration proceedings are governed by Michigan Court Rules (MCR) 3.602.

Just as other judgments against a principal, an arbitration award against a principal is prima facie evidence against a surety, shifting the burden of proceeding to the surety to rebut the presumption. *P.R. Post Corp. v. Maryland Casualty Co.*, 403 Mich. 543; 271 N.W.2d 521 (1978).

## 8. Attorney's Fees

***Statutes and/or case law limiting or permitting recovery of attorney's fees*** – There are no statutes or cases in Michigan permitting the recovery of attorney's fees with respect to a performance bond action.

***What fees are recoverable, if any*** – Not applicable.

## 9. Special Provisions – Not applicable.

## 10. Remarks

**Effect of judgment against principal** – A judgment against a principal is admissible as prima facie evidence against the surety, even if the surety was not a party to the prior action and had no notice. The burden of proceeding is then shifted to the surety, which can rebut the presumption. *P.R. Post Corp. v. Maryland Casualty Co.*, 403 Mich. 543; 271 N.W.2d 521 (1978).

## 11. Case Annotations:

**Discharge of surety based on overpayment to principal** – The traditional rule in Michigan was that an overpayment by the obligee to the principal results in a discharge of the Surety. See *Backus vs. Archer,* 109 Mich. 666; 67 N.W. 913 (1896) and *Sandusky Grain Co. vs. Borden's Condensed Milk Co.*, 214 Mich. 306; 183 N.W. 218 (1921).

However, the Sixth Circuit Court of Appeals, applying Michigan law, held that a surety should only be discharged to the extent it was prejudiced by the overpayments. *Ramada Development Co. v. USF&G,* 626 F.2d 517 (6th Cir. 1980). In Ramada, the contractor/obligee had made advance payments to the subcontractor/principal, but the principal had used those advance payments to pay its employees and to obtain supplies for the project. Because those advance payments were put into the project, the court held they benefited the surety, and there was no prejudice (and therefore no discharge).

**Discharge of surety based on release of principal** – The Michigan Court of Appeals performed an extensive analysis under the Restatement of Suretyship and Guaranty, 3d, on the issue of whether the release of the principal serves to discharge the surety. *Will H. Hall & Son, Inc. v Capitol Indemnity Corp.* 260 Mich. App. 222; 677 N.W.2d 51 (2003); lv app den, 470 Mich. 887; 682 N.W.2d 97 (2004). The court found that the surety was discharged by the release of the principal because the language and circumstances of the release did not evidence the obligee's intent to retain its claim against the surety, pursuant to Restatement of Suretyship, 3d, § 39.

**Change in obligations or duties of surety** – "A prejudicial change in obligations or duties is necessary to discharge a paid surety from liability." *Hunters Pointe Partners Ltd. Partnership v. USF&G,* 177 Mich. App 745; 442 N.W.2d 778 (1989); and *Chris Nelson and Son, Inc. v. Atlas Concrete Pipe, Inc.*, 84 Mich. App. 29; 269 N.W.2d 295 (1978). In each of these cases, the obligee assigned rights under the performance bond without the consent of the surety, and the court found that such assignment did not discharge the surety's obligations.

**Assignment rights of surety** – A surety's payment under a performance bond triggered its assignment rights under the bond application. The court held that the assignment was effective as of the date of the bond, pursuant to the language of the bond application. *R.C. Mahon Co. v. R.S. Knapp Co.*, 268 Mich. 67; 255 N.W. 453 (1934).

In a case in which the assignment in the indemnity agreement provided that it was "effective as of the date of any such bond, but only in the event of a default," the Michigan Court of Appeals held that the surety's priority rights vis-à-vis the garnishments of judgment creditors of the principal date back to the date of default of the principal. *Earl Dubey & Sons, Inc. v. Macomb Contracting Corp.*, 97 Mich. App. 553; 296 N.W.2d 582 (1980).

A performing surety is subrogated to all rights and remedies of the principal/contractor under a subcontract, entitling the surety to maintain an action against the principal's subcontractor. *Sentry Ins. v. Lardner Elevator Co.*, 153 Mich. App. 317; 395 N.W.2d 31 (1986).

The Michigan Court of Appeals held that a surety (that had completed a project under a performance bond) had priority to contract balances over the principal's secured lender. The bonds were issued prior to the perfection of the lender's security interests. While default of the principal occurred after the lender's rights were perfected, the court apparently (though not explicitly) held that the surety's rights related back to the dates of the bonds. *Old Kent Bank-Southeast v. City of Detroit*, 178 Mich. App. 416; 444 N.W.2d 162 (1989).

***Interpretation of AIA bond forms*** – There have been no published Michigan cases specifically addressing performance bond issues under AIA forms A311 or A312.

***Cases in which surety steps into shoes of obligee***

A surety that completes the work becomes the subrogee of the owner, and is entitled to the rights of the owner in retained funds. *Earl Dubey & Sons, Inc. v. Macomb Contracting Corp.*, 97 Mich. App. 553; 296 N.W.2d 582 (1980).

"Equitable subrogation allowed the surety, who had completed the contractor's performance under the contract, to step into the shoes of the government and assert any rights that the government had to withhold or retain funds upon default of the general contractor." *In re RAH Dev. Co.*, 184 B.R. 525, 529 (Bankr. D. Mich. 1995).

# MINNESOTA

Patrick J. O'Connor and Sara K. Van Norman[1]

## 1. Requirement for Bond

***Statutory provisions for projects that are:***

**Public** – Minn. Stat. § 574.26-574.32 is Minnesota's Public Contractors' Performance and Payment Bond Act (the "Act" ). Minn. Stat. § 574.26 subd. 2 requires contractors to secure bonds for all public contracts above $75,000.

**Private** – Not required.

**Department of Transportation** – Minn. Stat. § 574.26 subd. 1a(b) states that "at the discretion of the commissioner of transportation, [the Act does] not apply to any projects of the Department of Transportation (1) costing less than $75,000, or (2) involving the permanent or semipermanent installation of heavy machinery, fixtures, or other capital equipment to be used primarily for maintenance or repair."

---

1 Patrick J. O'Connor is a partner and Sara K. Van Norman is an associate of:
Faegre & Benson LLP
2200 Wells Fargo Center
90 South Seventh Street
Minneapolis, Minnesota 55402-3901
(612) 766-7413

**Other** – Under Minn. Stat. § 574.263 subd. 2, the commissioner of the Department of Natural Resources has the discretion as to whether to require a performance bond on a natural resource development project, and if so, it shall be not less than five percent of the contract price.

***Case law rules that might generally apply***

It is well-established in Minnesota, as elsewhere, that a surety bond is to be liberally construed in favor of the obligee. *See First National Bank v. Iowa Bonding and Cas. Co.*, 149 Minn. 279, 282, 183 N.W. 832, 833 (1921).

"The bond must be construed in accordance with the general rules for the construction of written instruments, guided in their application by the further rule that sureties are not liable beyond the strict letter of their contract." *Union Sewer-Pipe Co. v. Olson*, 82 Minn. 187, 189, 84 N.W. 756, 757 (1901).

## 2. Damages Covered

***Set forth in any statutes and/or case law***

Under Minn. Stat. § 337.10 subd. 3, prompt payment of subcontractors is required on all construction projects:

> The contract shall be deemed to require the party responsible for payment to pay interest of 1-1/2 percent per month to the party requesting payment on any undisputed amount not paid on time ... A party requesting payment who prevails in a civil action to collect interest penalties from a party responsible for payment must be awarded its costs and disbursements, including attorney fees incurred in bringing the action.

***Whether failure to provide insurance transfers burden to surety*** – No, not under Minnesota statutes or case law.

***Limitations on damages***

Under the rule of *Barr/Nelson, Inc. v. Tonto's, Inc.*, 336 N.W.2d 46, 52 (Minn. 1983), no punitive damages are allowed even where a performance bond surety maliciously or willfully breaches the bond terms, unless such breach is accompanied by an independent tort.

The extent of a surety's liability is usually the penal sum, plus interest. *See Nelson & Albin Creamery & Cheese Mfg. Co. v. M.K. Armstrong*, 93 Minn. 449, 102 N.W. 731 (1904) (reducing judgment where it went $120 over bond's penal sum and interest on penal sum); *but see Iowa Concrete Breaking Corp. v. Jewat Trucking, Inc.*, 444 N.W.2d 872 (Minn. Ct. App. 1989) (surety was obligated to pay attorney's fees even above penal sum).

"The designation by statute of a specific sum as a penalty has the effect of constituting a bond given in compliance therewith, a covenant for liquidated damages, or a penalty imposed by the sovereign power * * * unless a different intent appears." *City of St. Cloud v. Marie Willenbring*, 195 Minn. 70, 76, 261 N.W. 585, 588 (1935).

*See also U.S. v. U.S. Fid. & Guar. Co.*, 236 U.S. 512 (1914) (holding surety can be liable for interest above penal sum).

***Whether obligee may set off bonded contract funds against other principal-obligee debts or obligations***

To the contrary, it is established that a "surety has an equitable right of subrogation to contractor funds retained by a project owner when the surety pays the debts of the contractor to subcontractors under a payment bond." *Mon-Ray, Inc. v. Granite Re, Inc.*, 677 N.W.2d 434, 441 (Minn. Ct. App. 2004).

***Incorporation of specific contract terms by reference***

Performance bond language must expressly demonstrate an intent to incorporate the terms of the underlying contract in order for third party subcontractors and suppliers to benefit from the bond. *See Cretex Cos. v. Constr. Leaders*, 342 N.W.2d 135, 139-41 (Minn. 1984).

## 3. Penal Sum Variations

***Limitations per statute***

Under Minn. Stat. § 574.26 subd. 3, "[t]he penalty of each bond must not be less than the contract price, and if after the giving of the bond the contract price is increased, for any reason, the public body may require additional bonds, the penalties of which shall be not less than the amount of the increase, and if the additional bonds are not furnished within 10 days after demand, the work on the contract shall cease until the additional bonds are furnished."

There are also particular exceptions to accommodate the discretion (discussed above) that is statutorily granted to the commissioners of the Department of Transportation and the Department of Natural Resources. No other financial limits are imposed by statute.

***Statutory or case law protections or dangers to penal sum***

Under *Iowa Concrete Breaking Corp. v. Jewat Trucking, Inc.*, 444 N.W.2d 872 (Minn. Ct. App. 1989), where a surety is also obligated to pay attorney's fees, it can be liable above the penal sum.

*See Barr/Nelson, Inc. v. Tonto's, Inc.*, 336 N.W.2d 46, 52 (Minn. 1983) (no punitive damages allowed even where a performance bond surety intentionally breaches without independent tort).

## 4. Parties Covered

***Statutes and/or case law as to whether only obligees are covered***

The intended beneficiaries of bonds are "the public corporation, laborers, and materialmen." *Den Mar Const. Co. v. American Ins. Co.*, 290 N.W.2d 737, 740-41 (Minn. 1979).

***Coverage for:***

**Third-party beneficiaries** – In the private context: "While we acknowledge that third-party recovery is warranted in cases where the surety bond explicitly or by reasonable implication expresses an intent to benefit third-party subcontractors and materialmen, we do not believe an 'intent to benefit' third parties should be imputed to a surety on the basis of a private construction contract to which that surety was not a party, when the language of the surety's bond, though incorporating the construction contract by reference, evinces no more than an incidental intent to benefit those third parties." *Cretex Cos. v. Constr. Leaders*, 342 N.W.2d 135, 139-41 (Minn. 1984).

In the public context: A performance bond not incorporating language requiring payment of subcontractors and suppliers will not satisfy the statutory payment bond requirement. *See Green Elec. Sys., Inc. v. Metropolitan Airports Comm'n.*, 486 N.W.2d 819, 822-23 (Minn. Ct. App. 1992), *citing Crow & Crow, Inc. v. St. Paul Mercury Indem. Co.*, 247 Minn. 426, 429-31, 77 N.W.2d 429, 431-32 (1956).

Where a third party takes over the performance of the contract, the surety is not liable for the third party's work. *See Northern Minnesota Drainage Co. v. Mageau*, 131 Minn. 243, 154 N.W. 1092 (Minn. 1915).

**Assignees** – "Where an assignor principal seeks to prove a novation in order to be discharged from a binding contract to indemnify its surety, a clearly defined expression of consent by the surety to release the assignor principal must be shown." *Tony and Leo, Inc. v. U.S. Fid. & Guar. Co., et al.*, 281 N.W.2d 862, 865 (Minn. 1979). In the case, the court held there was no sufficiently clear evidence of novation. Hence, the surety could not be indemnified by solvent assignee, who was successor of now-insolvent original principal, where the surety did not clearly release the original principal from its obligations under the indemnity agreement, and was confused even as to the identity and corporate status of assignee.

*See Farmers State Bank of Madelia v. Burns*, 212 Minn. 455, 462, 4 N.W.2d 330, 334 (1942) (where contractor assigned rights to payment under contract to bank, surety did not have superseding right to pay subcontractors and suppliers out of contract funds); *but see National Surety Co. v. Berggren*, 126 Minn. 188, 148 N.W. 55 (1914):

"[T]he equity of the surety who had been compelled to pay and had paid claims against the principal was superior to that of one who loaned money to the contractor to be by him used as he saw fit, either in the performance of his contract or in any other way."

*See Barrett Bros. Co. v. St. Louis County*, 165 Minn. 158, 161-62, 206 N.W. 49, 50 (1925), quoted below.

**Dual obligees** – Not applicable.

### 5. Notice or Filing Required

***Statutory provisions***

The act does not require notice to the surety before bringing suit on the bond. However, Minn. Stat. § 574.31, subd. 1 states "[n]othing in this subdivision may be construed to otherwise affect the common law or equitable rights of performance bond sureties, principals, or public bodies that are obligees." Because reasonable notice to the surety is a common law defense, it is still preserved.

Treating a payment bond: "The settlement agreement ultimately entered into between [the surety] and the city purported to backdate the official completion and acceptance of the new construction.... [The surety] argues that this date should control for the purposes of Minn. Stat. 574.31 a position which the trial court correctly rejected. Adoption of [the surety's] argument in theory would allow the parties to a construction contract to backdate acceptance far enough to actually eliminate the 90-day notice period and thereby bar any claims against the performance bond. It is hornbook law that no one by contract may barter away the rights of persons not privy to the contract." *A. J. Chromy Const. Co. v. Commercial Mechanical Services, Inc.*, 260 N.W.2d 579, 581-82 (Minn. 1977).

***Case law rules concerning condition precedent notice***

Condition precedent notice is only required by statute on payment bonds. *See* Minn. Stat. § 574.31, subd. 2. Notice to the performance bond surety is controlled by common law and the bond language itself.

"For a claim against a bond, it is reasonable that the claimant not be held to the notice requirement unless the bond discloses the address at which the surety can be served. If the bond contains no address for service on the surety, it is a reasonable conclusion that the legislature intended that the surety is not entitled to the benefit of the statutory notice requirement." *Edward Kraemer & Sons, Inc. v. Ashbach Const. Co.*, 608 N.W.2d 559 (Minn. Ct. App. 2000).

However, even without notice, a surety may still be liable for a judgment against its principal in certain circumstances: "... [W]here a surety has undertaken to pay 'any judgment rendered' in an action, the surety has neither a right to notice of such an action or a right to reopen a judgment entered against its principal, even though it was obtained by consent or default." *R & L Lumber Co. v. Summit Fidelity & Sur. Co.*, 284 Minn. 489, 494, 170 N.W.2d 594, 598 (Minn. 1969).

## 6. Time for Suit

***Statutes of limitation particular to performance bonds and other applicable statutes of limitation***

Minn. Stat. § 574.31 states that no action by a public body on a performance bond "may be maintained later than permitted under the statute of limitations applicable to the claim."

Minn. Stat. § 541.05 limits suits for breach of contract to six years.

Minnesota's statute of limitation regarding defective construction work (Minn. Stat. § 541.051) requires plaintiffs to sue within two years of discovering the injury due, which applies to protect sureties as well as other parties in the construction business. *See Travelers Indem. Co. v. Hennepin County, Minnesota*, 918 F.2d 66, 68 (8th Cir. 1990) (applying Minnesota law).

***Case law statements about enforceability of limitations contained in bonds***

Short limitations periods have been upheld in actions on performance bonds on private projects. *See Fitger Brewing Co. v. American Bonding Co. of Baltimore*, 127 Minn. 330, 149 N.W. 539 (1914) (noting that six month period statute of limitations for actions on performance bond was acceptable).

*See Nelson Roofing & Contracting, Inc. v. C. W. Moore Co.*, 310 Minn. 140, 245 N.W.2d 866 (Minn. 1976) (upholding longer statute of limitations on payment bond and construing statutory one-year limit as only a minimum).

At least in the insurance context, the statue of limitations may be shortened, where there is only a general statute of limitations required by statute, and the contractual time period is not unreasonably short. *See O'Reilly v. Allstate Ins. Co.*, 474 N.W.2d 221, 222 (Minn. Ct. App. 1991).

## 7. Procedure

***Statutory or procedural rules that may affect handling or administration of lawsuits*** – Not applicable.

***Venue requirements and jurisdictional limitations***

Minn. Stat. § 543.19 is Minnesota's long-arm statute. Furthermore, "the long-arm statute is intended to permit Minnesota courts to exercise jurisdiction over such defendants to the full extent that federal constitutional requirements of due process will allow." *State Farm Mutual Auto Ins. Co. v. Tenn. Mutual Farmers Ins. Co.*, 645 N.W.2d 169 (Minn. Ct. App. 2002), *citing Valspar Corp. v. Lukken Color Corp*, 495 N.W.2d 408, 410 (Minn. 1992).

***Court rules*** – Not applicable.

***Particular agency regulations/rules*** – Not applicable.

***Arbitration requirements and application***

The Minnesota Uniform Arbitration Act is found at Minn. Stat. §§ 572.08 to 572.30. Minn. Stat. § 572.08 states that "[a] written agreement to submit any existing controversy to arbitration or a provision in a written contract to submit to arbitration any controversy thereafter arising between the parties is valid, enforceable, and irrevocable, save upon such grounds as exist at law or in equity for the revocation of any contract."

In any case, whether arbitration is required is "solely a matter of contract." *Twin City Monorail, Inc. v. Robbins & Meyers, Inc.*, 728 F.2d 1069, 1072 (8th Cir. 1984).

## 8. Attorney's Fees

***Statutes and/or case law limiting or permitting recovery of attorney's fees***

Under Minn. Stat. § 574.26 subd. 2, the public contract will not be valid unless a performance bond is "conditioned on saving the public body harmless from all costs and charges that may accrue on account of completing the specified work ...." Furthermore, as to both performance and payment bonds on public contracts, "[r]easonable attorney's fees, costs, and disbursements may be awarded in an action to enforce claims under the [A]ct if the action is successfully maintained or successfully appealed."

Under Minn. Stat. § 549.211 subd. 5, following Federal Rule of Civil Procedure 11, reasonable attorney's fees may be awarded as a sanction where a party or attorney acts in bad faith as to some element of the litigation itself. However, in general, no attorney's fees are ever recoverable unless authorized by contract or statute. *See Barr/Nelson*, 336 N.W.2d at 53 (citations omitted).

In *Iowa Concrete Breaking Corp. v. Jewat Trucking, Inc.*, 444 N.W.2d 865, 872 (Minn. Ct. App. 1989), dealing with a performance bond given to a contractor by a subcontractor on a state highway project, the court held that "where a bond covers both a sum and attorney fees, the surety is liable for attorney fees in addition to the penalty sum of the bond."

"We are similarly unpersuaded by [the city's and the contractor's surety's] contention that [subcontractor] Alexander's attorney's fees were unreasonably high because the company chose to be represented by two firms. That 'choice' was forced upon Alexander by appellants' contention that attorney Young committed malpractice by failing to file a timely notice of claim. This court notes that, on the contrary, he was remarkably diligent in trying to ascertain the date of acceptance of the project. Appellants' actions forced Alexander to seek double representation, so it is reasonable to require appellants to pay the full $10,708.63 in attorney's fees incurred by Alexander." *Alexander Const. Co., Inc. v. C & H Contracting, Inc.*, 354 N.W.2d 535, 539 (Minn. Ct. App. 1984).

## 9. Special Provisions – Not applicable.

10. **Remarks** – Not applicable.

## 11. Case Annotations

***Interpretation of AIA bond forms*** – *See Barr/Nelson*, 336 N.W.2d at 53 (noting only that bond at issue was an AIA standard performance bond).

***Cases in which surety steps into shoes of obligee***

Limits of subrogation: Under *Anderson v. U.S.,* 561 F.2d 162, 167 (8th Cir. 1977), a surety's "right of subrogation out of funds taken in completion of the projects in no event existed beyond the extent necessary to reimburse itself for expenditures made in fulfilling its obligations under the bonds."

Subrogation right of surety vs. right of assignee: "[T]he surety's equity of subrogation attaches to the contract and the prospective earnings of the contractor thereunder at the very moment he becomes surety. The right of subrogation and its automatic equitable assignment 'relate to the date of the suretyship, as against the principal and those claiming under him.'... That 'equitable assignment' to the surety of the 'principal's rights and remedies' when completed by the surety's performance of his principal's obligation "relates back * * * to that earlier time" when the surety first obligated himself as such ...." In this case the contracts and bonds took effect at the same time. In consequence and from that moment, the rights of the contracting parties, the builder and the county, were qualified insofar as they became subject to the surety's equity of subrogation. It follows that there was no part of the prospective earnings, whether reserved or unreserved, which the contractor could assign to a mere stranger, such as plaintiff, having no independent equity, and thereby given to the assignee a right superior to that of the surety. That is the precise holding, as we understand the decision, in *Henningsen v. U.S.F. & G. Co.*, 208 U.S. 404, 28 Sup. Ct. 389, 52 L. ed. 547, where the surety of a government building contractor was held entitled to *all* of the earnings of a contractor as against the latter's assignment to a creditor. True, the effect of the "reserved percentage" provision, if any, of the controlling contract was not considered. But is it not clear that any other holding, based upon such a provision, subjects the surety's highly valuable and obviously moral right of subrogation to easy destruction by the mere omission of any provision for a reserved percentage? Where nothing is agreed to be reserved, the surety as a subrogee has no recourse, if it is to be held that his right can attach only to earnings which are reserved or subject to reservation by the contract." *Barrett Bros. Co. v. St. Louis County*, 165 Minn. 158, 161-62, 206 N.W. 49, 50 (1925) (citations omitted).

A surety could not recover forfeited contract funds under a claim for equitable subrogation merely because it had paid a defaulting contractor's subcontractors under its payment bond obligation. *See Mon-Ray, Inc. v. Granite Re, Inc.*, 677 N.W.2d 434 (Minn. Ct. App. 2004). Even by completing a contract where the principals defaulted, the surety could not step into the contractor's shoes and recover these monies, as the funds were already forfeited for failure to comply with the contract provision regarding submission of final documents. *Id.*

# MISSISSIPPI

Ron A. Yarbrough[1]

## 1. Requirement for Bond

***Statutory provisions for projects that are:***

**Public** – As explained hereafter, separate statutory provisions exist for contracts with the State of Mississippi, including any county, city or political subdivision or other public authority, and for contracts with the Mississippi Transportation Commission.

Miss. Code Ann. § 31-5-51 requires a separate performance bond and payment bond covering all contracts of $25,000 or more, whenever a party enters into a contract with the State of Mississippi or any county, city, political subdivision or other public authority for construction, alteration or repair of a public building or public work. Both bonds are required to be in the full amount of the contract.

Miss. Code Ann. § 65-1-85 requires a single bond for all construction contracts entered into with the Mississippi Transportation Commission in excess of $1,500. The bond is to be equal to the contract price.

---

1 Ron A. Yarbrough is a partner at:
Brunini, Grantham, Grower & Hewes, PLLC
P.O. Drawer 119
Jackson, Mississippi 39205
(601) 948-3101

**Private** – There is no requirement for a bond covering private work. If a performance bond is provided for a private work contract the statutory provision controls.

Miss. Code Ann. § 85-7-185 provides that where a performance bond is given covering a private construction contract, the bond includes a payment obligation that has been held to protect the contractor's first tier subcontractors and material suppliers. The statute has no requirement regarding the amount of the bond.

**Department of Transportation** – Not applicable.

***Case law rules that might generally apply***

In construing a contract surety bond, its terms are to be given their ordinary and usual meaning. *Alexander v. Fid. & Cas. Co.,* 100 So. 2d 347 (Miss. 1958).

A project architect (or engineer) is an agent of the owner, making the owner liable for damages forseeably suffered by third parties as a consequence of the architect's (or engineer's) negligence. *Mayor and City Council of Columbus, MISS. v. Clark-Dietz and Assoc.,* 550 F. Supp. 610 (N.D. Miss. 1982).

A surety is entitled to recover against an architect for improper release of retainage to the bond principal. *State for the Use of National Surety Corp. v. Malvaney*, 72 So. 2d 424 (Miss. 1954).

A surety is entitled to rely upon the obligee paying the principal in accordance with the requirements of the contract. *Natl. Union Indem. Co. v. G.E. Bass & Co.,* 369 F.2d (5th Cir. 1966).

## 2. Damages Covered

***Set forth in any statutes and/or case law***

For public work, excluding contracts with the Mississippi Transportation Commission, owners typically use a variety of performance bond forms, ranging from the AIA-312 standard form to modified AIA forms or federally-mandated performance bonds, such as those required by the United States Department of Housing and Urban Development. The damages for which a surety is liable are generally understood to be measured by the terms of the bond, e.g., liquidated damages, additional design and legal fees resulting from a default, if so provided by the bond.

Contracts with the Mississippi Transportation Commission involve a single bond covering both performance and payment obligations and are designated as a Section 903 bond. These MTC bonds cover a wide variety of damages not always generally considered to be covered by a bond. These damages include, among other things, double the amount that the obligee pays the principal due to the principal's fraud.

Even if the principal is liable for punitive damages, the surety is not similarly liable unless its own conduct justifies the imposition of punitive damages. *U.S.F.&G. v. State f/u/b Stringfellow,* 182 So. 2d 919 (Miss. 1966).

Where by the terms of the contract, a co-prime was entitled to recover on the performance bond of another co-prime, the surety was liable for such items as home office overhead and loss of labor productivity. *Aetna Cas. & Surety Co. v. Doleac Electric Co., Inc.*, 471 So. 2d 325 (Miss. 1985).

A surety is liable to an unpaid material supplier for interest at the "legal rate" in the absence of an agreement respecting interest. Otherwise, the surety is liable for interest at the rate agreed upon between the principal and the material supplier. *Faulkner Concrete Prods. Co. v. U.S.F.&G.,* 218 So. 2d 1 (Miss. 1969).

### *Obligations of surety to perform and/or pay*

The liability of a surety is measured by the express terms of its undertaking. *Metropolitan Cas. Ins. Co. New York v. Koelling*, 57 So. 2d 562 (Miss. 1952).

A surety who issues a separate performance bond and a payment bond is not liable to the performance bond obligee on the payment bond even if the damages exceed the penal sum of the performance bond. *McQueen Contracting, Inc. v. Fid. and Dep. Co. of Maryland*, 863 F.2d 1216 (5th Cir. 1989).

### *Whether failure to provide insurance transfers burden to surety*

Generally there are no cases addressing this. However, in *Continental Ins. Co. v. Harrison Co.*, 153 F.2d 671 (5th Cir. 1946), the court refused to impose liability in favor of the owner (or the owner's insurer) and against the surety for damages to barges caused by negligence of the principal's employees.

***Limitations on damages***

A surety's liability is limited by the express terms and extent of its undertaking and, while its liability may not be extended beyond the terms of the bond, if it is susceptible of two constructions, one of which will uphold and the other defeat the claim, the construction favorable to the claimant will be adopted. *Metropolitan Cas. Ins. Co. New York v. Koelling*, 57 So. 2d 562 (Miss. 1952).

If the bond principal is not liable, the surety is not liable. *Mohundro v. Alcorn County,* 675 So. 2d 848 (Miss. 1996).

***Whether obligee may set off bonded contract funds against other principal-obligee debts or obligations*** – Not applicable.

***Incorporation of specific contract terms by reference*** – Not applicable.

### 3. Penal Sum Variations

***Limitations per statute***

Miss. Code Ann. § 31-5-51 requires a performance bond in the amount of the contract for all public work exceeding $25,000. There is no penal sum requirement for a bond covering a private contract.

***Effect of changes in work upon penal sum, if at all***

There are no statutes or cases dealing with this issue but many bond forms acknowledge that changes which increase the contract sum will be covered by the bond. The underlying, bonded contract frequently provides the same.

***Statutory or case law protections or dangers to penal sum***

The general rule that a surety's liability is limited to the terms of its undertaking, *Metropolitan Cas. Ins. Co. v. Koelling,* 58 So. 2d 562 (Miss. 1952), would seem to have application to this issue.

## 4. Parties Covered

***Statutes and/or case law as to whether only obligees are covered***

Because both a performance bond and a payment bond are required for contracts covering public work, and in view of *McQueen Contracting, Inc. v. Fid. & Dep. Co. of Md.,* 836 F.2d 1216 (5th Cir. 1989), only the performance obligee can recover on the performance bond and only statutorily qualified subcontractors and material suppliers can recover on the payment bond. For single limit performance bonds issued for contracts with the Mississippi Transportation Commission, not only is the commission entitled to recover but subcontractors and material suppliers may also recover on the same bond.

The statutory framework for bonds required by the Mississippi Transportation Commission does not, however, specify which unpaid subcontractors and material suppliers are entitled to recover. Based upon a case decided prior to the present statute, it should be safe to assume that the same subcontractors and material suppliers allowed recovery on a general public works payment bond, prescribed by Miss. Code Ann. § 31-5-51, are entitled to recover on a performance bond issued in connection with a project for the Mississippi Transportation Commission. *Dixie Contractors, Inc. v. Ballard,* 249 So. 2d 653 (Miss. 1971).

For bonds covering private contracts, the scope of protection can be quite different from that allowed for bonds covering public work or contracts with the Mississippi Transportation Commission. "Private contracts" include subcontracts on public work and are governed by the private work bond statutes at Miss. Code Ann. 85-7-185, *et seq. Davis Co. v. D'Lo Guar. Bank,* 138 So. 802 (Miss. 1932).

Miss. Code Ann. § 85-7-185 provides that, where only a performance bond is given, a payment bond feature is read into the performance bond, and unpaid subcontractors and material suppliers have a right of recovery on the bond, but only after the performance bond obligee has been fully satisfied. If the bond obligee is fully satisfied and the remaining amount of the penal sum is insufficient to satisfy all claims of unpaid subcontractors and suppliers, they share pro rata. Moreover, unless the terms of the bond provide otherwise, coverage for unpaid subs and suppliers extends only to those in privity with the principal who provided the bond. *Alabama Marble Company v. USF&G*, 111 So. 573 (Miss. 1927). If the terms of the bond allow broader coverage than provided by the statute or if a separate payment bond is given in addition to the performance bond, the rights of unpaid subcontractors and material suppliers will be governed by the terms of the bond as issued. *Linde Air Products Co. v. American Surety Co.*, 152 So. 292 (Miss. 1934).

***Coverage for:***

**Third-party beneficiaries** – Not applicable.

**Assignees** – Not applicable.

**Dual obligee** – Not applicable.

## 5. Notice or Filing Required

There are no statutes in Mississippi requiring that any contract bond be filed.

***Case law rules concerning condition precedent notice***

In *Western Cas. and Sur. Co. v. Honeywell, Inc.,* 380 So. 2d 1385 (Miss. 1980), the court held that the bond language requiring a second-tier claimant to give notice within 90 days after last providing labor or material was enforceable as a necessary condition precedent to recovery on the bond.

## 6. Time for Suit

***Statutes of limitation particular to performance bonds and other applicable statutes of limitation***

Curiously, Miss. Code Ann. § 65-1-85, the statutory framework for bonds covering contracts with the Mississippi Transportation Commission, is devoid of any reference to a period of limitations for bringing suit on the bond. In *Dixie Contractors, Inc. v. Ballard*, 249 So. 2d 653 (Miss. 1971), a case decided prior to adoption of the current statute governing bonds on general public work in Mississippi, the court held that the same procedural requirements applicable to the general public works bond should be applied to claims arising under bonds issued for contracts with the Mississippi Transportation Commission. Accordingly, the limitations period in Miss. Code Ann. § 31-5-53 appears to apply to bonds for contracts with the Mississippi Transportation Commission. That statute provides as follows:

> 31-5-53. (a) When suit is instituted on a performance bond given in accordance with this chapter, it shall be commenced within one year after the obligee shall have made final payment on the contract; provided, however, if the contract is abandoned by the general contractor as bond principal or is terminated by the bond obligee, suit shall be commenced within one year after the earlier of the abandonment by the bond principal or termination by the bond obligee.
>
> (b) When suit is instituted on a payment bond given in accordance with this chapter, it shall be commenced within one year after the day on which the last of the labor was performed or material was supplied by the person bringing the action and not later.

The statutes of limitations for a suit on a private works bond are substantially different from that for public work contracts. Those statutes provide:

> 85-7-187. If only a performance bond has been provided in accordance with this chapter and if no suit shall be brought by the obligee within six months from the date of the earlier of final completion or actual use or occupancy of the project for its intended purpose, then any person supplying labor or materials to the bond principal on the project shall have a right of action on said bond for his use and benefit against said

bond principal and the sureties thereon and to prosecute same to final judgment and execution, subject to the rights and demands of the bond obligee.

85-7-189 (1) Suit on a performance claim by an obligee on a bond given in accordance with this chapter shall be commenced as follows:

(a) If the obligee is the owner of the project being constructed, such obligee shall bring suit within one year after the earlier of final completion or actual use or occupancy of the project for its intended purpose; or

(b) If the obligee is other than an owner of the project being constructed, such obligee shall bring suit within one year after such obligee receives final payment with respect to the project.

(2) When suit is instituted on a claim for payment on a payment bond given in accordance with this chapter, it shall be commenced within one year after the day on which the last of the labor was performed or material was supplied by the person bringing the action and not later.

85-7-191. If only a performance bond is given in accordance with this chapter and if suit is instituted on said performance bond only one action shall be brought for performance and payment claims and any person entitled to sue may upon application intervene and be made a party to said suit and such intervention must occur within the time limited for such person to bring an original action; provided, however, if a separate payment bond is given then only one separate action for payment claims shall likewise be brought on the payment bond and intervention shall be allowed in accordance with this statute.

***Case law statements about enforceability of limitations contained in bonds***

Because the referenced limitations period for bonds covering public works contracts and private works contracts represent recent amendments to the statutes, there are no cases construing these limitations periods. However, the recently amended statute of limitations for suits on private works bonds appears to effectively moot the holding in *Cooper Indus., Inc. v. Tarmac Roofing Systems*, 276 F.3d 704 (5th Cir. 2002), holding, *inter alia*, that the predecessor statute's limitations period did not apply to a performance bond obligee unless the obligee had provided labor or materials for the project.

### *Varying statute of limitations by agreement in bond or contract*

Miss. Code Ann. § 15-1-5 prohibits any change in any of the limitations periods "prescribed in this chapter" and makes any such stipulation "absolutely null and void." Significantly, neither the statute of limitation for suits on public work bonds or for suits on private work bonds appear in that "chapter," so that statutory prohibition is inapplicable. As a practical matter, however, with respect to suits on a public works bond, the issue almost never arises, and there are no cases construing the issue. This is primarily – probably solely – because most of the standard form bonds which contain a limitations period also contain a disclaimer that the limitations contained in the bond will not be enforced if it is in derogation of a statute containing a limitations period.

The issue is more unsettled with respect to a private works bond. While the holding in *Cooper Indus., Inc. v. Tarmac Roofing Systems, Inc.,* 276 F.3d 704 (5th Cir. 2002), appears to mean that the limitations period for a private works bond cannot be changed from what the statute requires, the Mississippi Supreme Court in *Linde Air Products v. American Surety Co.*, 152 So. 292 (Miss. 1934), instructs that private parties may insert in a bond whatever terms they agree to.

## 7. Procedure

### *Statutory or procedural rules that may affect handling or administration of lawsuits*

Mississippi has adopted Rules of Civil Procedure, patterned generally after the Federal Rules of Civil Procedure. Other than how these rules are applicable to suits in state and federal court, there are no particular statutory or other procedural rules relevant to actions on a performance bond.

### *Venue requirements and jurisdictional limitations*

Miss. Code Ann. § 31-5-53(c) provides as follows:

> Any suit brought on a performance or payment bond given in accordance with this chapter shall be brought in the county in which the contract or some part thereof was performed or in the county in which

> service of process may be obtained upon either the principal or the surety on such bond.

This venue provision applies to a suit on a bond covering general public work as well as a bond covering a contract with the Mississippi Transportation Commission.

For suits on bonds covering private work, Miss. Code Ann. § 85-7-189(3) has language almost identical to its public works counterpart:

> Any suit on a bond given in accordance with this chapter shall be brought in the county in which the contract or some part thereof was performed or in the county in which service of process may be obtained upon either the principal or the surety on such bond.

Miss. Code Ann. § 9-9-21 vests county courts with jurisdiction of disputes not exceeding $75,000. For disputes in excess of that amount, jurisdiction is proper in circuit court in Mississippi. Miss Code Ann. § 9-7-81. Federal court jurisdiction is typically determined by 28 U.S.C. § 1332 if there is complete diversity of citizenship between the parties and the amount in controversy exceeds the sum of $75,000, exclusive of interest and costs. 28 U.S.C. § 1352 vests federal district courts with original jurisdiction, concurrent with state courts, for suits involving bonds executed under any law of the United States (except "matters within the jurisdiction of the Court of International Trade under Section 1582 of this Title"). This concurrent jurisdiction of the federal courts means suits that otherwise would not satisfy the requirements of 28 U.S.C. § 1332 may also be filed in federal district court, including suits on such bonds as those required by the United States Department of Housing and Urban Development for use on contracts with certain local agencies.

***Court rules***

In addition to the Mississippi Rules of Civil Procedure, there are Uniform Rules of Circuit Court and County Court practice and Uniform Chancery Court Rules which may be applicable.

***Particular agency regulations/rules*** – Not applicable.

### *Arbitration requirements and application*

Under Mississippi law, where there is an agreement to arbitrate a construction dispute, that provision is binding and enforceable. Miss. Code Ann. § 11-15-101, *et. seq.* If suit is commenced involving a contract with a binding arbitration provision, the defendant is entitled to a stay of the court action pending arbitration by the parties.

Miss. Code Ann. § 31-5-51(2), applicable to bonds covering public work contracts, provides as follows:

> Notwithstanding anything to the contrary contained herein, if the amount claimed in such action is subject to contractual provisions or conditions, between the parties involved in such action, the action shall be abated pending the performance of such provisions and the fulfillment of such conditions.

Although there are no reported cases construing this provision, arguably it would entitle a surety to a stay of litigation, pending the outcome of arbitration between the obligee and principal, where there is an enforceable arbitration provision in the underlying contract and the principal is sued with the surety.

## 8. Attorney's Fees

### *Statutes and/or case law limiting or permitting recovery of attorney's fees*

The general rule in Mississippi is that attorney's fees may not be awarded except as provided by contract or statute or where a party's conduct is so outrageous as to justify the imposition of punitive damages. In the context of suits on contract surety bonds, there are specific statutes applicable to such suits involving bonds covering general public work contracts and private work contracts. Note that the Section 903 bond required for contracts with the Mississippi Transportation Commission includes a right of recovery for attorney's fees to enforce the terms and conditions of that bond, either by the performance obligee or by unpaid subcontractors and material suppliers.

Miss. Code Ann. § 31-5-57 provides as follows:

> Whenever any person supplying labor or material in the prosecution of the work brings an action on such payment bond and the trial judge finds that the defense raised to such action by the contractor or surety was not reasonable, or not in good faith, or merely for the purpose of delaying payment, then the trial judge may, in his discretion, award the claimant a reasonable amount to be determined by the trial judge as claimant's attorney's fees in bringing such successful action. Likewise, if the trial judge finds that such action was brought by claimant without just cause or in bad faith, the trial judge may, in his discretion, award the contractor or surety a reasonable amount to be determined by the trial judge as attorney's fees for defending such action; provided, however, this section shall not affect the right of any person to recover attorney's fees where provided by contract or bond.

For suits on private work bonds, Miss Code Ann. § 85-7-193 allows recovery of "reasonable attorney's fees in an amount to be set by the judge, pro rata of the amount of the recovery."

**9. Special Provisions** – Not applicable.

**10. Remarks**

Mississippi follows the minority rule regarding the surety's priority to earned but unpaid contract funds in the possession of the obligee. An assignee holding a perfected security agreement is entitled to earned but unpaid "progress payments" and the surety is entitled to earned but unpaid retainage. *Reliance Ins. Co. v. First Miss. National Bank,* 263 So. 2d 555 (Miss. 1972).

**11. Case Annotations**

Whether a surety is bound by a judgment against its principal appears to be unsettled. In *U.S.F.&G. v. State of Miss. f/u/b Stringfellow,* 182 So. 2d 919 (Miss. 1966), the court held that a surety on a sheriff's bond was entitled to defend a suit against it even though the plaintiff had already recovered a judgment against the sheriff in a separate action. Without overruling that case or even mentioning it, the court in *First Mobile Home Corp. v. Little,* 298 So. 2d 676 (Miss. 1974), held that a default judgment against the principal on a blue sky bond is conclusive against the surety unless the judgment was obtained through the principal's consent or collusion with the principal.

***Interpretation of AIA bond forms*** – Mississippi has no cases or statutes on this issue.

***Cases in which surety steps into shoes of obligee***

A surety who satisfies a county's claims against a failed bank, as required by its depository bond, is subrogated to the county's position. *Coahoma County, Miss. v. Mississippi Fire Ins. Co.*, 68 F.2d 489 (5th Cir. 1934).

# MISSOURI

Lawrence Lerner[1]

## 1. Requirement for Bond

The State of Missouri does not have a statute that requires performance bonds to be furnished on all public or private work, however, cities, counties and state agencies require such bonds as part of the procurement process.

***Statutory provisions for projects that are:***

**Public** – R.S.Mo. 229.060 requires contractors to obtain bonds for all *public roads and waterways* "conditioned that the contractor will faithfully discharge his duties under the contract within the time and in the manner therein provided and that he will furnish and promptly pay all labor employed and materials used and equipment rented in the performance of the contract and the state, county or political subdivision, or any laborer, materialman or other person injured by breach of such contract may sue on such bond."

**Private** – No statutes in Missouri require performance bonds on private projects.

---

1 Lawrence Lerner is a shareholder of:
Levy & Craig, a Professional Corporation
1301 Oak Street
Kansas City, Missouri 64106
(816) 474-8181

**Department of Transportation** – R.S.Mo. 227.100 requires contractors to obtain performance bonds on *state highway system* contracts as follows:

> The successful bidders ... shall give good and sufficient bond, in a sum equal to the contract price, to the state of Missouri, with sureties approved by the commission and to ensure the proper and prompt completion of said work in accordance with the provisions of said contracts, and plans and specifications; provided, that if, in the opinion of the majority of the members of the commission, the lowest bid or bids for the construction of any of the roads, or parts of roads, herein authorized to be constructed, shall be excessive, then, and in that event, said commission shall have the right, and it is hereby empowered and authorized to reject any or all bids, and to construct, under its own direction and supervision, all of such roads and bridges, or any part thereof.

***Case law rules that might generally apply***

"The bond covenanted that the bridge should stand and remain for four years; and if it did not do so, a breach took place, and a right of action accrued to the obligee." *Buchanan County v. Kirtley,* 42 Mo. 534 (1868).

"Where, in an action on a bond given by a contractor to secure the performance of his contract for the erection of a bridge for a county, it appeared that the county court appointed a third person to examine and receive the bridge from the contractor, that the third person reported to the court that the contractor had complied with his contract, and that the court then paid the contractor the contract price, evidence giving the conversation of the contractor with the judges was admissible on the issue whether the county had waived defects in the bridge." *Johnson County v. Lowe,* 72 Mo. 637 (1880).

## 2. Damages Covered

***Set forth in any statutes and/or case law***

R.S.Mo. 229.060 – Provides that the contractor will furnish and promptly pay for all labor employed and materials used and equipment rented in the performance of the contract.

R.S.Mo. 375.420 – Provides that "if it appears from the evidence that such company has refused to pay such loss without reasonable cause or excuse, the court or jury may, in addition to the amount thereof and interest, allow the plaintiff damages not to exceed 20 percent of the first $1,500 of the loss, and 10 percent of the amount of the loss in excess of $1,500 and a reasonable attorney's fee; ..."

R.S.Mo. 408.020 – The surety may be liable for prejudgment interest from the date of demand beyond the penal sum if the principal is found liable and/or surety litigates the issue of liability. R.S.Mo. 408.020 provides that "creditors shall be allowed to receive interest at the rate of nine percent per annum, when no other rate is agreed upon, for all moneys after they become due and payable on written contracts, and on accounts after they become due and demand of payment is made...." *See also Howard Construction Company v. Teddy Woods Construction Co.*, 817 S.W.2d 556, 564 (Mo. App. W.D. 1991)

***Obligations of surety to perform and/or pay***

"In the case of a performance bond, the surety has the option of completing performance or of assuming the liability for the obligee's costs in completing the contract, which are in excess of the contract price." *Miller-Stauch Construction v. Williams-Bungart Electric, Inc.*, 959 S.W.2d 490, 494 (W.D. Mo. 1998).

***Whether failure to provide insurance transfers burden to surety*** – Statutes do not transfer the burden to surety.

***Limitations on damages***

"... as a general rule, a surety's liability for contract damages is coextensive with that of the principal." *Sheffield Assembly of God Church, Inc. v. American Ins. Co.,* 870 S.W.2d 926, 932 (Mo. App.

1994). In the absence of an agreement to the contrary, the rights and liabilities of a surety are measured by those of the principal. *City of Kansas City ex rel. Jennings v. Integon Indem. Corp.*, 857 S.W.2d 233, 236 (Mo. App. 1993). *City of Independence for use of Briggs v. Kerr Construction Paving Company, Inc.*, 957 S.W.2d 315, 319 (Mo. App. W.D. 1997).

"There is no Missouri statute authorizing interest in this type of case. [citation omitted] Nor do any of the contracts provide for such an award. Absent statutory or contractual authorization, prejudgment interest is not generally allowed on an unliquidated claim, such as the claim at bar. Recovery of prejudgment interest may be allowed only for liquidated claims under these circumstances for an amount 'readily ascertainable by computation or by determination according to a recognized standard.' [citation omitted] this court affirmed the district court's refusal to award prejudgment interest, finding that as in this case, the claim asserted was unliquidated." *Continental Bank & Trust Co. v. American Bonding Co.*, 630 F.2d 606, 612 (C.A. Mo. 1980); also see *General Ins. Co. of Amer. v. Hercules Construction Co.*, 385 F.2d 13, 25 (8th Cir. 1967) and *Ehrle v. Bank Bldg. & Equip. Corp. of America,* 530 S.W.2d 482, 496 (Mo. App. 1975).

"As with contract damages, the liability of a surety for interest is coextensive with that of its principal. *City of St. Louis ex rel. Esmar v. Tru-Bounce,* 562 S.W.2d at 162. The liability of the principal, for contract damages, was fixed in the interlocutory default judgment. Accordingly, the trial court revised the jury's award of contract damages because Integon's liability for contract damages could not exceed the liability of its principal. The trial court also limited the amount of prejudgment interest as entered against Woods Construction in the interlocutory default judgment. By so doing, the trial court denied interest for the period between the interlocutory default judgment and judgment against Integon. Pursuant to § 408.020, R.S.Mo. 1986, Howard Construction is entitled to interest under the circumstances herein at the rate of 9 percent from the date of the interlocutory default judgment against Woods Construction. To allow otherwise would be to grant Integon a windfall by relieving it of interest for the period. A surety is not entitled to a windfall by being relieved of interest on the amount due under its bonds. *State ex rel. Neese v. IGF Insurance Co.,* 706 S.W.2d 856, 860 (Mo. banc 1986). The trial court erred by limiting interest to the date of the interlocutory default judgment rather than allowing interest to the date of judgment against Integon." *Howard Construction Co. v. Teddy Wood Construction Co.,* 817 S.W.2d 556, 564 (Mo. App. 1991).

Generally, a surety is not liable for its principal's tortious acts. *J. Louis Crum Corp. v. Alfred Lindgren, Inc.,* 564 S.W.2d 544, 549-50 (Mo. App. W.D. 1978).

***Whether obligee may set off bonded contract funds against other principal-obligee debts or obligations***

"However, while it is true that the rights and liabilities of a surety are measured by those of the principal, it is also true that a performance bond surety confers a benefit upon the obligee and thus becomes subrogated not only to the rights of the principal but also to the rights of the obligee, and has a right to retained funds free from set-off by the obligee." *Miller-Stauch Construction v. Williams-Bungart Electric, Inc.*, 959 S.W.2d 490, 495 (W.D. Mo. 1998).

"The Court holds that ESI, as general contractor, had a contractual right of setoff; that the right is absolute and not qualified by any other provision in the subcontract; and that the setoff right is superior to NAS's [surety] right of subrogation. The exact amount that ESI was entitled to setoff is a factual issue for the jury." The subcontract contained the following language "... Notwithstanding anything herein to the contrary Contractor has the absolute right to withhold and set off from funds otherwise due Subcontractor on this Project any amounts due Contractor from Subcontractor on any other project and if Contractor exercises such right of set off, then Subcontractor hereby waives any lien claims and bond rights on this Project as to such amounts so set off." *Environmental Specialists, Inc. v. North American Specialty Insurance Co.,* 2005 WL 1345256, 3 (W.D. Mo. 2005).

***Incorporation of specific contract terms by reference***

"A separate document may be incorporated in the contract by reference; however, 'when the reference is made only for specific purposes, the separate document becomes a part of the contract only for such purposes.'" *Lusk v. Lyon Metal Products, Inc.*, 247 S.W.2d 617, 618 (1952) (citing *Spitcufsky v. State Highway Commission of Missouri*, 159 S.W.2d 647).

"Reference in subcontract to main contract or other extraneous writing for a particular purpose makes it part of subcontract only for purpose specified." *Guerini Stone Company v. P.J. Carlin Construction Company*, 240 U.S. 264 (1916).

"Liability of a surety is limited to the terms and conditions stated in the bond." "A court cannot make a contract for the parties that they did not make for themselves, or impose upon the parties obligations they have not assumed." *Frank Powell Lumber Co. v. Federal Insurance Co.*, 817 S.W.2d 648, 651 (Mo. App. S.D. 1991).

"The obligation of the bond may not in the guise of construction be enlarged beyond the plain terms and stipulations, and with respect to contracts generally." *Executive Hills Home Builders v. Whitley*, 770 S.W.2d 507, 508 (Mo. App. 1989).

"Two parties to a three-party contract cannot waive the rights of the third party under the contract." *Welch v. North Hills Bank*, 442 S.W.2d 98, 103 (1969).

### 3. Penal Sum Variations

***Limitations per statute*** – Missouri does not have statutory limitations on performance bond penal sums.

***Effect of changes in work upon penal sum, if at all***

"Therefore, if the original parties to the contract make changes or alterations which go to vary and alter its terms through substituting other matters for those called for in the contract, so as to destroy its identity in the matter of performance, without the consent of the surety, he is thereby relieved and discharged from the secondary obligation undertaken on the ground that the identity of the contract on which he assumed to respond has been destroyed through the act of the original parties without consulting him." ... "In other words, as the thought is expressed by the Kansas City Court of Appeals, where the different matter does not consist of a change of that provided for or contemplated by the contract, but is something additional not included in the contract, then it is an independent transaction, and does not affect the contract, and consequently does not release the surety." *Neuwirth v. Moydell*, 188 Mo. App. 467, 174 S.W. 206, 207-08 (1915).

***Statutory or case law protections or dangers to penal sum*** – There are no cases that require a variation in the penal sum.

## 4. Parties Covered

***Statutes and/or case law as to whether only obligees are covered***

"Moreover, a plain reading of the performance bond gives no right of action to anyone other than West Side [obligee]. It expressly speaks in terms of a right of action of West Side and Travelers Ins. Co. (lender) and says that the aggregate liability of USF&G to obligees or their assigns is limited to the penal sum of the bond, $1,340,503. Nowhere does it purport to give anyone else a right of action. Therefore, if plaintiffs are entitled to a recovery it must be found under the policy terms of the payment bond, not the performance bond." *Coates v. U. S. Fidelity & Guar. Co.,* 525 S.W.2d 654, 655 (Mo. App. 1975).

"Finally Waggoner argues that to avoid obligations to materialmen and laborers the surety must expressly exclude liability to them in the bond, referring to dictum from *LaSalle, supra at 91*, wherein the court, discussing a hypothetical situation stated: If the surety wishes to exclude this type of liability it may consider such a bond as is shown in *Bourrett v. W. M. Bride Construction Company*, 248 Iowa 1080, 84 N.W.2d 4, where all rights of action by any one except the named obligee in the bond were expressly excluded. The cited language suggests sureties may wish to consider use of such terms, but neither *LaSalle* nor the later *Ill-Mo* impose the requirement of express exclusion provisions in the bond to avoid such liability by the surety." *Wilbur Waggoner Equip. Rental and Excavating Co., Inc. v. Bumiller,* 542 S.W.2d 32, 36 (Mo. App. E.D. 1976).

***Coverage for:***

**Third-party beneficiaries** – "Waggoner contends this quoted portion of the contract constitutes an implied promise to pay all laborers and materialmen, providing it (Waggoner) a direct right of action on the bond under the holding in *LaSalle Iron Works, Inc. v. Largen*, 410 S.W.2d 87, 92 (Mo. banc 1966). We do not agree. The bond was executed to Bumiller as sole obligee, conditioned on Hart's performance of the contract. Before a third party, furnishing labor or material but not named in the bond or contract nor privy to the consideration, may sue thereon, it must be found the bond was entered into for his benefit. The intention to benefit the 'third-party' laborer or materialman may be found if, as found in *LaSalle*, *supra* at 89, the bond is conditioned 'that the contractor shall pay all claims for labor and materials, or that he shall pay laborers and materialmen.'" *Wilbur Waggoner Equip. Rental and Excavating Co., Inc. v. Bumiller,* 542 S.W.2d 32, 35 (Mo. App. E.D. 1976); also see *Marks and Masters Const., Inc. v. Western Cas. & Sur. Co.,* 684 S.W.2d 863, 866 (Mo. App. W.D. 1984) and *City of University City ex rel. and to Use of Mackey v. Frank Miceli*, 347 S.W.2d 131, 134 (Mo. 1961).

**Assignees** – There are no Missouri cases discussing assignment of an obligee's right to make a claim against a performance bond.

**Dual obligees** – "Where two or more obligees are named in the bond, each has a separate right to recover thereon in the event of a breach." *Continental Bank & Trust Co. v. American Bonding Co.,* 605 F.2d 1049, 1056 (C. A. Mo. 1979) (citing *Curtis v. Tozer*, 374 S.W.2d 557, 588 (Mo. App. 1964)).

## 5. Notice or Filing Required

***Statutory provisions*** – Missouri statutes do not provide for any unusual notice requirements for suit under a performance bond.

***Case law rules concerning condition precedent notice***

"In the absence of a provision in the bond agreements requiring notice to the surety upon the principal's default, the surety is not discharged by the obligee's failure to communicate such notice. Restatement of Security § 136 (1941). Nevertheless, the obligee may not delay before notifying the surety and then insist that the measure of the surety's liability includes escalated costs arising in the interim between default and demand." *Continental Bank & Trust Co. v. American Bonding Co.,* 605 F.2d 1049, 1059 (Mo. App. 1979).

## 6. Time for Suit

***Statutes of limitation particular to performance bonds and other applicable statutes of limitation***

R.S.Mo. 516.120, states "Within 5 years: All actions upon contracts, obligations or liabilities, express or implied, except those mentioned in section 516.110, and except upon judgments or decrees of a court of record, and except where a different time is herein limited;"

R.S.Mo. 516.110, states "Within 10 years: An action upon any writing, whether sealed or unsealed, for the payment of money or property;"

***Case law statements about enforceability of limitations contained in bonds***

It has been held by the Missouri Supreme Court that an "action upon any writing, whether sealed or unsealed, for the payment of money or property, may be brought within 10 years after the cause of action shall accrue." An action upon an administrator's bond may be brought within 10 years from the date of the accruing of the cause of action. *State ex. rel. Enter. Miller Co. v. Brown*, 106 S.W. 630, 631 (Mo. 1907); also *see Missouri K.&T.Ry. Co. v. American Surety Co. of N.Y.*, 236 S.W. 657 (Mo. banc 1921).

***Varying statute of limitations by agreement in bond or contract***

Missouri does not permit this in any contract.

R.S.Mo. 431.030 "All parts of any contract or agreement hereafter made or entered into which either directly or indirectly limit or tend to limit the time in which any suit or action may be instituted, shall be null and void."

## 7. Procedure

***Statutory or procedural rules that may affect handling or administration of lawsuits*** – Not applicable.

***Venue requirements and jurisdictional limitations***

"To subject a non-resident defendant to the long arm jurisdiction of this state, the plaintiff must plead and prove two elements: first, that the suit arose from any of the activities enumerated in the long arm statute, § 506.500, R.S.Mo. 1994; and second, that defendant has sufficient minimum contacts with Missouri to satisfy due process requirements." *Chromalloy,* 955 S.W.2d at 4. *See also State ex rel. William Ranni Associates, Inc. v. Hartenbach,* 742 S.W.2d 134, 137 (Mo. banc 1987) *Capitol Indem. Corp. v. Citizens Nat. Bank of Fort Scott, N.A.*, 8 S.W.3d 893, 899 (Mo. App. W.D. 2000).

***Court rules*** – Not applicable.

***Particular agency regulations/rules*** – Not applicable.

**Arbitration requirements and application**

In general R.S.Mo. 435.350 through 435.470, the Missouri Uniform Arbitration Act apply.

"A written agreement to submit a present or future controversy to arbitration is 'valid, enforceable and irrevocable, save upon such grounds as exist at law or in equity for the revocation of any contract' – both under the Federal and Missouri Acts. On these principles, "a party cannot be required to submit to arbitration any dispute which he has not agreed to submit." *Village of Cairo, Mo. v. Bodine Contracting Co.*, 685 S.W.2d 253, 258 (Mo. App. W.D. 1985).

"Arbitration is a matter of contract, and a party cannot be required to arbitrate a dispute that it has not agreed to arbitrate. *AgGrow Oils, L.L.C. v. Nat'l Union Fire Ins. Co. of Pittsburgh, Pa.,* 242 F.3d 777, 780 (8th Cir. 2001). As such, a guarantor who is not a signatory to a contract containing an arbitration clause is generally not bound by the arbitration clause. *Grundstad v. Ritt,* 106 F.3d 201, 204 (7th Cir. 1997). However, in a majority of state courts, including Missouri, due to the strong federal policy in favor of arbitration, arbitration agreements are enforced against guarantors or sureties where the arbitration agreement is incorporated by reference into the guaranty or performance bond." *Dunn Indus. Group, Inc. v. City of Sugar Creek* 112 S.W.3d 421, 435 (Mo. banc 2003).

"We hold that an arbitration award entered against the principal is equally binding against the surety, even if the surety is not a named party in the arbitration proceedings, when the surety has judicially admitted that it is bound by the arbitration proceeding." *Sheffield Assembly of God Church, Inc. v. American Ins. Co.,* 870 S.W.2d 926, 931 (Mo. App. W.D. 1994).

## 8. Attorney's Fees

***Statutes and/or case law limiting or permitting recovery of attorney's fees***

R.S.Mo. 375.420 provides that "reasonable attorney's fees" are recoverable.

"Vexatious means without reasonable cause or excuse, and 'there must be evidence from which it may be found that the refusal to pay the loss was willful and without reasonable cause as that fact would appear to a reasonable and prudent man prior to trial.'" *Lindsey Masonry Company, Inc. v. Jenkins & Associates, Inc.*, 897 S.W.2d 6, 17 (Mo. App. W.D. 1995) (citing *Housing Authority of Clinton v. Baumann*, 512 S.W.2d 436, 440 (Mo. App. 1974)).

"It is error to submit to jury the question of attorney fees as award for insurer's vexatious refusal to pay where there is no evidence in record showing reasonable value of attorney's services." *Tate v. Golden Rule Ins. Co.,* 859 S.W.2d 831 (Mo. App. W.D. 1993).

"Litigation expenses other than attorney fees are not recoverable under the statute." *Legg v. Certain Underwriters at Lloyd's of London,* 18 S.W.3d 379 (Mo. App. W.D. 1999).

***What fees are recoverable, if any***

"In determining the reasonable value and amount of attorney fees recoverable, there are many factors appropriate for consideration. The rates customarily charged by the attorneys involved and by other attorneys in the community for similar services are relevant factors. *Id.* Time taken is a consideration as is the nature and character of the services rendered, the nature and importance of the matter in which services are rendered, the degree of responsibility imposed upon the attorney, the value of the property or money involved, the degree of professional ability called for and used, and the result. *Ozark Production Credit Association v. Walden,* 695 S.W.2d 919, 921 (Mo. App. 1985). The trial court is an expert on the value of legal services, *Id.* at 922, however, a jury is not." "The question of attorney fees for vexatious refusal to pay was properly submitted to the jury in the case at bar, but there was no expert testimony upon which the jury could base a finding as to the reasonable value of the attorney fees requested. However, the evidence did show that $39,924.88 in attorney fees had been paid." *Howard Construction Co. v. Teddy Woods Construction Co.,* 817 S.W.2d 556, 563-64 (Mo. App. 1991).

**9. Special Provisions** – Not applicable.

**10. Remarks** – Not applicable.

**11. Case Annotations**

***Interpretation of AIA bond forms*** – Missouri cases have not specifically addressed AIA forms of bonds A311 and A312.

***Cases in which surety steps into shoes of obligee***

"A surety who makes good under his contract of suretyship upon default of the principal contractor, acquires an equitable lien against the unpaid balance in the hands of the person in whose favor the bond runs, and that such equitable lien upon payment by the surety relates back to the date of the contract and is superior to a claim of the United States for unpaid taxes for periods subsequent to the date of the contract of suretyship, although prior to the date of payment by the surety." *Home Indemnity Company v. United States of America,* 313 F. Supp. 212, 215-216 (W.D. Mo. 1970) (citing *Glenn v. American Surety Co.*, 160 F.2d 977, 982 (C.A. 6 1947)).

"The general rule is that a surety which executes a performance bond on a construction contract, and is thereafter required to pay unpaid labor and materials claims, or to complete the contract upon default by the contractor, has an equitable right of subrogation and an equitable lien upon funds retained by the owner or obligee; this right of subrogation or equitable lien is superior to the right of one who takes by assignment from the contractor after the execution of the bond, and relates back to the date of the surety's bond." *First State Bank v. Reorganized School Dist. R-3,* 495 S.W.2d 471, 480 (Mo. App. 1973).

# MONTANA

Mark D. Etchart and Daniel J. Auerbach[1]

## 1. Requirement for Bond

The State of Montana statute which generally requires performance bonds to be furnished on public construction projects is M.C.A. § 18-2-201(1) which states, "whenever any board, council, commission, trustees, or body acting for the state or any county, municipality, or public body contracts with a person or corporation to do work for the state, county, or municipality or other public body, city, town, or district, the board, council, commission, trustees, or body shall require the person or corporation with whom the contract is made to make, execute, and deliver to the board, council, commission, trustees, or body a good and sufficient bond with a surety company, licensed in this state, as surety, conditioned that the person or corporation shall:

(i) faithfully perform all of the provisions of the contract;

(ii) pay all laborers, mechanics, subcontractors, and materials suppliers; and

(iii) pay all persons who supply the person, corporation, or subcontractors with provisions, provender, material, or supplies for performing the work."

---

1 Mark D. Etchart is a shareholder and Daniel J. Auerbach is an associate of:
Browning, Kaleczyc, Berry & Hoven, P.C.
139 North Last Chance Gulch
Helena, Montana 59601
(406) 443-6820

There are three exceptions to the bonding requirements of M.C.A. § 18-2-201(1):

(1) Pursuant to M.C.A. § 18-2-201(4), the state or other governmental entity may waive the performance bond requirements of M.C.A. § 18-2-201(1) for the construction, alteration, repair, maintenance, and remodeling of a building, facility, or structure which: is constructed or purchased wholly or in part with state money; or is at a state institution; or is owned or will be owned by a state agency; or which is constructed for the use or benefit of the state with federal or private money; AND costs less than $50,000.

(2) Pursuant to M.C.A. § 18-2-201(5), a school district may waive the performance bond requirements of M.C.A. § 18-2-201(1) for the construction, alteration, repair, maintenance, and remodeling of a building, facility, or structure which: is constructed or purchased wholly or in part with state money; or is at a state institution; or is owned or will be owned by a state agency; or which is constructed for the use or benefit of the state with federal or private money; AND costs less than $7,500.

(3) Pursuant to M.C.A. § 85-1-219(4)(b) the performance bond requirements of M.C.A. § 18-2-201(1) do not apply to contracts on state-owned works for the conservation and distribution of water, including reservoirs, dams, diversion canals, distribution canals, waste canals, drainage canals, dikes, lateral ditches and pumping units, mains, pipelines, and waterworks systems for which the proposed construction costs are $50,000 or less.

M.C.A. § 18-2-203 requires performance bonds subject to M.C.A. § 18-2-201(1) to be in an amount equal to the full contract price and must be to the state of Montana except for cities and towns, wherein the municipality may by ordinance fix and determine the amount of the security and the name of the secured party, provided that the amount may not be for less than 25 percent of the contract price, and the bond may designate the city or town as the obligee.

M.C.A. § 18-4-312 requires "For state contracts for the procurement of services or of supplies, the department may in its discretion require: (a) bid [bond]; (b) contract performance [bond] to guarantee the faithful performance of the contract and the payment of all laborers, suppliers, mechanics, and subcontractors; or (c) both bid and contract performance [bonds]."

***Statutory provisions for projects that are:***

**Public** – There are several Montana statutes that require public performance bonds.

M.C.A. § 7-8-2606 requires purchasers of *county timber or other forest crops* to furnish a performance bond to the county in an amount equal to at least 20 percent of the estimated value of the timber sold.

M.C.A. § 7-12-2138 requires all contractors and contracting owners that contract with the board of county commissioners for *any work* in a rural improvement district to provide a performance bond.

M.C.A. § 7-12-4151 requires all contractors and contracting owners that contract with a city council for *street work* in a special improvement district to provide a performance bond.

M.C.A. § 7-14-2405 requires contractors that contract with the board of county commissioners for the *construction, maintenance, and improvement of county roads and bridges* to provide a performance bond.

M.C.A. § 7-14-2717 requires contractors that contract with a local improvement district committee of supervisors for the *laying out, opening, construction and improvement of county roads* to provide a performance bond.

**Private** – No statutes in Montana require performance bonds on private projects.

**Department of Transportation** – *See* M.C.A. §§ 18-2-201(1) and 18-4-312 *supra*.

***Case law rules that might generally apply***

M.C.A. § 28-11-403 states "In interpreting the terms of a contract of suretyship, the same rules are to be observed as in the case of other contracts."

"Historically, courts have liberally construed bonding statutes to effectuate the overall purpose of compensating those who contribute materials and supplies to a public project." *Luciano v. Northwest Pipe & Casing Co.*, 264 Mont. 148, 152, 870 P.2d 99, 101 (1994).

"Ambiguities in a bond should be construed in favor of the assured and against the entity that drafted the bond." *Transamerica Premier Ins. Co. v. Miller*, 41 F.3d 438, 441 (9th Cir. 1994).

## 2. Damages Covered

***Set forth in any statutes and/or case law***

M.C.A. § 18-2-207 states "In a suit or action brought against the surety ... on the [bond] by a person or corporation to recover for any of the items specified in this part, the prevailing party is entitled to recover, in addition to all other costs, attorney fees in a sum that the court finds reasonable. However, attorney fees may not be allowed in a suit or action brought or instituted before the expiration of 30 days following the date of filing of the notice required in 18-2-206." *See* M.C.A. § 18-2-206, *infra*.

"[I]n an action against a surety company upon a bond issued by that company, interest may be awarded even if that interest, in addition to the amount of damages awarded, exceeds the amount of liability stated in the bond." *Lapke v. Hunt*, 151 Mont. 450, 460, 443 P.2d 493, 498 (1968).

***Obligations of surety to perform and/or pay***

Prejudgment interest may be awarded in an action to collect on a surety bond where "the amount of damages 'is certain or capable of being made certain by calculation.'" *Transamerica Premier Ins. Co. v. Miller*, 41 F.3d 438, 445 (9th Cir. 1994).

"The universal rule is that in construing the bond of a surety company, acting for compensation, the contract is construed most strongly against the surety, and in favor of the indemnity which the obligee has reasonable grounds to expect. Such contracts are generally regarded as contracts of insurance, and are construed most strictly against the surety." However, "the liability of a surety cannot be extended beyond that which the law has required it to assume and to discharge." *Kohles v. St. Paul Fire & Marine Ins. Co.*, 144 Mont. 395, 397-400, 396 P.2d 724, 725-26 (1964).

A surety may be required to pay penalties associated with the late payment of wages after the contractor fails to pay obligations under a performance bond. The court will look to the terms of the written agreements to determine whether the bond contains a restriction limiting the surety's liability. *Ring v. Hoselton*, 197 Mont. 414, 428, 643 P.2d 1165, 1173 (1982).

"As a general rule, a performance bond on a public works contract is for the benefit and protection of the municipality. The municipality is not liable to a person who has furnished materials to a contractor for a public works project unless provided by statute." Montana law "allows a materialman who has supplied a subcontractor a direct action against the original or general contractor and surety; but it does not establish a claim or right of action against the City." *C.E. Mitchell & Sons v. Davis*, 162 Mont. 221, 224, 511 P.2d 316, 317, (1973) (citations omitted).

Absent an agreement, "payment means the discharge of a debt or obligation in money and the mere delivery and acceptance of a note for the amount of the account, whether it be the note of the debtor or of another does not operate to discharge the debt. However, by agreement anything of value may be given by the debtor and accepted by the creditor in satisfaction of a debt; and, if such was the agreement, the delivery and acceptance constitute payment and discharge of indebtedness." When a principal pays an obligation with a promissory note and then is subsequently adjudicated bankrupt, the surety is not relieved of its obligation by the delivery of the note by the insolvent principal. *Falls Implement Co. v. Gen. Ins. Co. of Am.*, 152 Mont. 250, 252-53, 448 P.2d 675, 676-77 (1968) (citations omitted).

***Whether failure to provide insurance transfers burden to surety*** – There are no cases addressing this.

***Limitations on damages***

M.C.A. § 28-11-411 states "A surety cannot be held beyond the express terms of his contract, and if such contract prescribes a penalty for its breach, he cannot in any case be liable for more than the penalty."

M.C.A. § 28-11-412 states "A surety is exonerated: (1) in like manner with a guarantor; (2) to the extent to which he is prejudiced by any act of the creditor which would naturally prove injurious to the remedies of the surety or inconsistent with his rights or which lessens his security; or (3) to the extent to which he is prejudiced by an omission of the creditor, when required by the surety, to do anything which it is the creditor's duty to do."

M.C.A. § 28-11-413 states "Performance of the principal obligation or an offer of such performance, duly made as provided in this code, exonerates a surety."

M.C.A. § 18-2-208 states that when a contractor loans or advances money to a contractor, subcontractor or other person, that person cannot seek to recover against the lending contractor's bond.

Statutes such as M.C.A. § 18-2-208 which limit recovery on a contractor's bond, however, are applied narrowly and only prevent recovery if the contractor has loaned or advanced money to that specific subcontractor or other person seeking to recover against the contractor's bond. *Luciano v. Northwest Pipe & Casing Co.*, 264 Mont. 148, 152, 870 P.2d 99, 102 (1994).

While a surety's contract liability is limited to the express terms of its contract, the surety may be "held liable in tort for its independent violation of statutory or common law duties in the handling of a claim under the bond. Under common law, an insurer who breaches the duty of good faith and fair dealing may be held liable in tort beyond the limits of the policy." *K-W Indus. v. Nat'l. Surety Corp.*, 231 Mont. 461, 467, 754 P.2d 502, 506 (1988).

***Whether obligee may set off bonded contract funds against other principal-obligee debts or obligations*** – Montana has no case law or statutes discussing the right of an obligee to set off bonded contract funds.

***Incorporation of specific contract terms by reference*** – *See Treasure St. Indus. Inc., v. Welch*, 173 Mont. 403, 407-08, 567 P.2d 947, 949-50 (1977), *infra* Section 4.

## 3. Penal Sum Variations

***Limitations per statute*** – Montana does not have statutory limitations on performance bond penal sums.

***Effect of changes in work upon penal sum, if at all*** – Montana has no case law interpreting such changes in work.

***Statutory or case law protections or dangers to penal sum*** – Montana has no cases that require a variation in the penal sum.

## 4. Parties Covered

### *Statutes and/or case law as to whether only obligees are covered*

M.C.A. § 18-2-204 states that all laborers, mechanics, subcontractors, and material suppliers; and all persons who supply the person, corporation, or subcontractors with provisions, provender, material, or supplies for performing the work have a right of action in their own name on any performance bond provided pursuant to M.C.A. § 18-2-201 for work done by the laborers or mechanics and for provender, materials, supplies, provisions, or goods supplied and furnished in the work. "The persons do not have any right of action on the [bond] unless within 90 days after the completion of the contract with an acceptance of the work by the affirmative action of the board, council, commission, trustees, officer, or body acting for the state, county, or municipality or other public body, city, town, or district, the laborer, mechanic or subcontractor, or materialman or person claiming to have supplied provender, materials, provisions, or goods for the prosecution of the work of the making of the improvement presents to and files with the board, council, commission, trustees, or body acting for the state, county, or municipality or other public body, city, town, or district a notice in writing [stating their name, the amount of the claim, the names of the principal and surety, and a description of the work]." The notice must be signed by the person or corporation making the claim.

M.C.A. § 18-2-205 states "A corporation or person performing services or furnishing provender, provisions, supplies, or material to a subcontractor has the same right under the [bond] as if the work, services, provender, provisions, supplies, or material was furnished to the original contractor."

"[A]lthough the surety bond and the underlying contract must be read together to ascertain the parties' intentions, the surety's obligations are not coextensive with obligations of the underlying contract. ... [T]he mere fact the underlying subcontract ... contained a promise to pay all materialmen in no way creates an obligation on the part of Aetna, the surety, unless the bond itself contains a similar promise to pay the materialmen." *Treasure St. Indus. Inc., v. Welch*, 173 Mont. 403, 407-08, 567 P.2d 947, 949-50 (1977).

***Coverage for:***

**Third-party beneficiaries** – "[A] third person who is a stranger to a contract or a bond thereunder, cannot recover from the surety even when the contract and bond, as here, contain some reference to him or to the class to which he belongs, unless there is a specific promise to pay such third person or such class, contained in the contract and bond. The mere statement of a duty to be discharged by the contractor, which may incidentally benefit a third party or class to which the latter belongs, without more, does not make the surety liable for such third person for the contractor's failure to discharge that duty." *Nat'l. Surety Co. of New York v. Ulmen*, 68 F.2d 330, 336 (9th Cir. 1933).

**Assignees** – "The general rule under subrogation is that a claim for money loaned or advanced to a building or construction contractor is not within the coverage of the ordinary form of contractor's bond conditioned upon the performance of the contract and the payment of claims for labor and material, even though the borrowed money has been wholly applied to the payment of the cost of labor and material actually going into the construction project." However, where a party lends money to the principal such that the principal can make payments to laborers and materialmen and the lender is induced by the surety not to obtain assignments of interest on the bond, the principle of equitable subrogation grants the lender an interest in the surety bond. "To decide otherwise would allow the surety to be unjustly enriched at the expense of the plaintiffs." *Bower v. Tebbs*, 132 Mont. 146, 155-58, 314 P.2d 731, 736-38 (1957).

**Dual obligees** – There are no cases addressing this.

## 5. Notice or Filing Required

***Statutory provisions***

*See* M.C.A. § 18-2-204, *supra*.

M.C.A. § 18-2-206 states:

(1) A person, firm, or corporation furnishing provender, provisions, materials, or supplies to be used in the construction, performance, carrying on, prosecution, or doing of any work for the state or any county, city, town, district, municipality, or other public body shall, not later than 30 days after the date of the first delivery to a subcontractor or agent of a person, firm, or corporation having a subcontract for the construction, performance, carrying on, prosecution, or doing of the work, give a notice of a right of action on the [bond].
(2) (a) The notice must be delivered personally or sent by certified mail to the contractor.
(b) The notice must be in writing and state:
(i) that it is a notice of a right of action on the [bond];
(ii) that the person, firm, or corporation giving the notice has commenced to deliver provender, provisions, materials, or supplies;
(iii) the name of the subcontractor or agent who placed the order or to whom the provender, provisions, materials, or supplies were delivered; and
(iv) that the contractor and the contractor's [bond] will be held for the unpaid price if the supplier is not paid.
(3) To have a right of action against the contractor and the [bond]..., a person, firm, or corporation shall give the written notice required by this section in substantially the form described in subsection (2). Any other type of actual or constructive notice is not sufficient.
(4) A suit or action may not be maintained in any court against the contractor or the [bond] to recover for the provender, provisions, materials, or supplies or any part thereof unless the provisions of this part have been complied with.

***Case law rules concerning condition precedent notice*** – Generally there are no cases addressing this.

### 6. Time for Suit

***Statutes of limitation particular to performance bonds and other applicable statutes of limitation***

M.C.A. § 27-2-202 states "The period prescribed for the commencement of an action upon any contract, obligation, or liability founded upon an instrument in writing is within 8 years."

***Case law statements about enforceability of limitations contained in bonds*** – A surety may "limit the period during which their liability should attach." *State v. Rosman*, 84 Mont. 207, 274 P. 850, 852 (1929).

***Varying statutes of limitation by agreement in bond or contract***

M.C.A. § 28-2-708 states "Every stipulation or condition in a contract by which any party thereto is restricted from enforcing his rights under the contract by the usual proceedings in the ordinary tribunals or which limits the time within which he may thus enforce his rights is void." This provision does not affect the validity of an agreement to arbitrate.

### 7. Procedure

***Statutory or procedural rules that may affect handling or administration of lawsuits***

"Plaintiff had a right to sue only [the surety] without joining [the principal] because a contract of suretyship is a direct liability of the surety to the assured and when the principal ... fails to perform, the surety becomes directly responsible at once, as it is unnecessary for the assured to establish that the principal failed to carry out his contract before the obligation of the surety becomes absolute." *Morgen & Oswood Constr. Co., v. U.S. Fidelity & Guaranty Co.*, 167 Mont. 64, 68, 535 P.2d 170, 172 (1975).

M.C.A. § 25-4-202 states "The insertion in a pleading of a copy of a written instrument is equivalent to setting forth the instrument according to its legal effect."

### *Venue requirements and jurisdictional limitations*

M.C.A. § 25-2-121 provides that the proper venue for an action upon a contract is either the county in which any defendant resides or the county in which the contract was to be performed. For a labor or construction contract, the proper venue for an action is the county where the labor or services are to be performed or the county where the object is to be constructed or repaired.

M.C.A. § 18-1-401 states "The district courts of the state of Montana shall have exclusive original jurisdiction to hear, determine, and render judgment on any claim or dispute arising out of any express contract entered into with the state of Montana or any agency, board, or officer thereof."

### *Court rules*

Generally, the Montana District Courts observe the Montana Uniform District Court Rules, however, most district courts also have local district court rules.

***Particular agency regulations/rules*** – Generally, there are no significant rules.

### *Arbitration requirements and application*

M.C.A. § 27-5-114 states:

> (1) A written agreement to submit an existing controversy to arbitration is valid and enforceable except upon grounds that exist at law or in equity for the revocation of a contract.
> (2) A written agreement to submit to arbitration any controversy arising between the parties after the agreement is made is valid and enforceable except upon grounds that exist at law or in equity for the revocation of a contract. ...[T]his subsection does not apply to: ... (c) any agreement concerning or relating to insurance policies or annuity contracts except for those contracts between insurance companies....

"Judicial review of arbitration awards is limited by statute. When a matter has been submitted to binding arbitration, courts are not permitted to review the merits of the controversy, but may only confirm, vacate, modify, or correct an arbitration award pursuant to §§ 27-5-311, -312 and -313, MCA." *Terra West Townhomes v. Stu Henkel Realty*, 298 Mont. 344, 350, 996 P.2d 866, 870 (2000).

## 8. Attorney's Fees

***Statutes and/or case law limiting or permitting recovery of attorney's fees***

*See* M.C.A. § 18-2-207, *supra*.

In spite of an explicit limitation on aggregate liability of the surety, a claimant may recover an amount greater than the penal sum of the bond. "Costs of suit are recognized to be collectable beyond the face value of the bond and hence with precise statutory authority attorney fees in this instance will be a part of the cost of suit." *Twite v. Western Surety Co.*, 176 Mont. 286, 291-92, 577 P.2d 1219, 1222 (1978).

***What fees are recoverable, if any***

M.C.A. § 28-2-2105 states "In a civil action on a contract to enforce an obligation imposed by this part, the prevailing party is entitled to reasonable attorney fees and costs, both for trial and appeal. If the parties to a construction contract or subcontract use arbitration, the arbitrator may award fees and costs as the arbitrator may determine."

**9. Special Provisions** – There are no special provisions.

## 10. Remarks

"A surety who has undertaken to pay the creditors of the principal, though not beyond a stated limit, may not share in the assets of the principal by reason of such payment until the debts thus partially protected have been satisfied in full. Here the bond was intended to protect materialmen and laborers who worked on the job from [the principal's] insolvency. They could have recovered had [the principal] not become insolvent irrespective of what their rights against the surety might have been. Consequently, the surety cannot claim under subrogation or indemnity for money paid some creditors for whose benefit the bond was intended and be allowed to reduce the insolvent [principal's] interest in the retained fund as against unpaid creditors." *Gen. Ins. Co. of Am. v. State Highway Commn.*, 147 Mont. 450, 457, 414 P.2d 526, 529-30 (1966) (quotations omitted).

## 11. Case Annotations

***Interpretation of AIA bond forms*** – Montana statutes and cases have not specifically addressed AIA forms of bonds A311 and A312.

***Cases in which surety steps into shoes of obligee*** – Generally, there are no cases on this.

# NEBRASKA

Victor E. Covalt III[1]

## 1. Requirement for Bond

***Statutory provisions for projects that are:***

**Public** – A performance bond is required on any building project by the state of Nebraska or any department or agency thereof if the total cost of the project exceeds $40,000. Neb. Rev. Stat. § 72-803 (Reissue 2003). A bond can also be required for smaller projects if required by the specifications for bids. Id. *Accord,* Neb. Rev. Stat. § 83-134 (Reissue 1999) (Department of Health and Human Services); Neb. Rev. Stat. § 83-916 (Reissue 1999) (Department of Correctional Services).

Counties and drainage districts are also required to obtain performance bids for certain contracts for materials and supplies when the contract is for less than $50,000. Neb. Rev. Stat. §§ 23-315, -342 (Reissue 1997); *Id.* §§ 31-118, -355, -912 (Reissue 2004); *Id.* §§ 39-820, -825.

Where a bond is taken which is not required by statute, it will be enforced as a common-law contract. *Nye-Schneider-Fowler Co. v. Bridges, Hoye & Co.,* 98 Neb. 27, 151 N.W. 942 (1915).

---

[1] Victor E. Covalt III is a member of:
Ballew Schneider Covalt Gaines & Engdahl, PC, LLO
440 So. 13th Street, Suite C
P.O. Box 81229
Lincoln, Nebraska 68501
(402) 436-3030

**Private** – There are no statutory provisions requiring or governing performance bonds for private projects. However, they are commonly used and are enforced under the standards for contract interpretation and enforcement. *See, e.g., Farmers Union Co-operative Association v. Mid-States Constr. Co.*, 212 Neb. 147, 322 N.W.2d 373 (1982).

**Department of Roads** – The Department of Roads has complete authority over bidding, contract letting and qualifications of bidders for state and local road construction. Neb. Rev. Stat. §§ 39-1348 to -1354 (Reissue 2004). There is no statutory requirement for performance bonds on highway projects. *See id.*

**Other** – Payment Bonds are required for public construction contracts in excess of
$5,000 for local projects and in excess of $15,000 for state projects. Neb. Rev. Stat. §§ 52-118, -118.01 (Reissue 2004).

## 2. Damages Covered

***Set forth in any statutes and/or case law***

The liability of the surety for the debt to the holder of an obligation is no greater and no less than that of the principal. *Sawyer v. State Surety Company*, 251 Neb. 440, 558 N.W.2d 43 (1997).

***Obligations of surety to perform and/or pay***

A performance bond guarantees that the contractor will perform the contract, and usually provides that if the contractor defaults and fails to complete the contract, the surety can itself complete the contract or pay damages up to the limit of the bond. *Cagle, Inc. v. Sammons*, 198 Neb. 595, 599, 254 N.W.2d 398, 402 (1977).

Surety is not liable for repairs made by the owner under a new contract let without demand on the general contractor who posted the bond and without notice to the surety. *Twin Cities Plaza v. Central Surety and Insurance Corp.*, 409 F.2d 1195 (8th Cir. 1969) (Nebraska law).

***Whether failure to provide insurance transfers burden to surety*** – Nebraska has no statute nor case law addressing this issue.

***Limitations on damages***

Nebraska does not allow recovery of punitive damages. *Scurlocke v. Hansen* , 268 Neb. 548, 684 N.W.2d 565 (2004); *Abel v. Conover,* 170 Neb. 926, 104 N.W.2d 684 (1960).

Damages against the surety are limited to those contemplated by the parties at the time the bond was issued. *O'Shea v. North American Hotel Co.,* 109 Neb. 317, 191 N.W. 321 (1922)

Damages which are not proximately caused by the acts covered by the bond are not recoverable. *Adams Bank & Trust v. Empire Fire and Marine Insurance Co.*, 244 Neb. 262, 506 N.W.2d 52 (1993).

***Whether obligee may set off bonded contract funds against other principal-obligee debts or obligations***

Surety who pays claims for labor or material on public building, after contractor's default, has interest in balance due contractor superior to one who advanced money and took assignment from latter. *First Nat. Bank of Auburn v. Pesha,* 99 Neb. 785, 157 N.W. 924 (1916).

Surety is discharged pro tanto for the wrongful loss or release of security. *Adams Bank & Trust v. Empire Fire and Marine Ins. Co.,* 244 Neb. 262, 506 N.W.2d 52 (1993).

Unauthorized payment by the owner to the contractor may reduce liability of surety pro tanto to the extent of the unauthorized payment. *Cf. School District No. 65R of Lincoln County v. Universal Surety Company,* 178 Neb. 746, 135 N.W.2d 232 (1965) (dicta).

***Incorporation of specific contract terms by reference***

The terms of the general contract when incorporated within the bond by reference control the obligations between surety and owner. *School District No. 65R of Lincoln County v. Universal Surety Company,* 178 Neb. 746, 135 N.W.2d 232 (1965).

Where a bond and another contract or instrument relate to and form one and the same transaction, or the bond refers to such other instrument or is conditioned for the performance of specific agreements set forth therein, such instrument with all its stipulations, limitations, or restrictions becomes a part of the bond, and the two should be read together and construed as a whole. Thus a bond given by a contractor should be construed in connection with the contract or undertaking it is intended to secure. *Luikart v. Massachusetts Bonding & Ins. Co.*, 129 Neb. 771, 263 N.W. 124, 131 (1935).

### 3. Penal Sum Variations

***Limitations per statute***

A penal sum limits the liability of the surety. *Hsuth v. Sambo,* 100 Neb. 160, 158 N.W. 1036 (1916); *Morrison v. Boggs*, 44 Neb. 248, 62 N.W. 473 (1895); *Mullen v. Morris*, 43 Neb. 596, 62 N.W. 74, 79 (Neb. 1895).

Where the damages sustained exceed the penalty, interest may be recovered from the time the condition of the bond was broken, or the damages became due. *Mullen v. Morris*, 43 Neb. 596, 62 N.W. 74, 79 (Neb. 1895).

***Effect of changes in work upon penal sum, if at all***

A material and substantial change in the character or nature of the obligation is required before a surety is released from its obligations under the bond obligation. *State v. Smith*, 135 Neb. 423, 281 N.W. 851 (1938).

***Statutory or case law protections or dangers to penal sum***

"There are numerous cases in which the law does not enforce contracts according to their literal interpretation. This is true generally of bonds, other than penal ones, which usually provide for a fixed liability upon condition, but upon condition broken the law enforces, not the contract according to its literal interpretation, but for the amount of the actual damages." *Northwestern Terra Cotta Co. v. Caldwell,* 234 F. 491, 496 (8th Cir. 1916) (denying enforcement of $50 per day late charge as a penalty).

## 4. Parties Covered

***Statutes and/or case law as to whether only obligees are covered***

A surety in general is bound only on the contract he makes and if he excludes any purpose to benefit those outside the contract, there will be no third party beneficiaries assuming the exclusion is valid. *Nebraska Beef Ltd. v. Universal Surety Company*, 9 Neb. App. 40, 607 N.W.2d 227 (2000), *quoting with approval,* Restatement of Security § 165, comment c at 459 (1941).

But a bond issued to the City of Omaha that required the principal and surety to pay for labor materials and equipment furnished for a refuse company did not make the surety liable for the deficiency remaining on time purchase of garbage trucks, after the seller repossessed and sold them. The court held the bond was for the protection of the city if it had to take over the garbage collection service on default and refused to allow the creditor to recover thereon. *Cornett v. White Motor Corporation,* 190 Neb. 496, 209 N.W.2d 341 (1973).

***Coverage for:***

**Third-party beneficiaries** – It must appear by express stipulation or by reasonable intendment that the rights and interests of unnamed parties were contemplated and provision was made for them. *Nebraska Beef Ltd. v. Universal Surety Company*, 9 Neb. App. 40, 607 N.W.2d 227 (2000).

A materialman may sue on a performance bond for unpaid materials if the bond is conditioned upon the faithful performance of the contract by the contractor and the contract requires the contractor to pay all labor and materialmen as a part of his duties due to the owner. *Dealers Electric Supply v. United States Fidelity and Guaranty Co.,* 199 Neb, 269, 258 N.W.2d 131 (1977).

One furnishing labor or supplies to highway contractor may sue in own name on surety bond as contract made with third person for his benefit. *West v. Detroit Fidelity & Surety Co.*, 118 Neb. 544, 225 N.W. 673 (1929).

A subcontractor has no cause of action against department or agency in absence of express or implied contract and must look to contractor or his bond for payment. *Boyd v. Benkelman Public Housing Authority*, 188 Neb. 69, 195 N.W.2d 230 (1972).

**Assignees** – An assignment of a claim assigns the claim on the bond securing the claim. *Luikart v. Massachusetts Bonding & Ins. Co.* 129 Neb. 771, 263 N.W. 124 (1935).

Since the plaintiff was the assignee of the construction company and the surety, all her rights were subject to the defenses the [subcontractor who provided the performance bond] had against the construction company and the surety. *Barnes v. Hampton*, 198 Neb. 151, 153, 252 N.W.2d 138, 139 (Neb. 1977).

**Dual obligees** – One obligee can bring an action on behalf of all named obligees. *O'Shea v. North American Hotel Co.,* 109 Neb. 317, 191 N.W. 321 (1922).

## 5. Notice or Filing Required

***Statutory provisions*** – Nebraska does not have any statutory provisions governing notices on performance bonds.

***Case law rules concerning condition precedent notice***

When the giving of notice of loss within a prescribed time was made a condition to liability, plaintiffs' failure to do so prevents recovery. *Dockendorf v. Orner,* 206 Neb. 456, 293 N.W.2d 395 (1980).

The terms of the contract and the bond govern whether notice to the surety of default by the principal or of final payment is required. *School District No. 65R of Lincoln County v. Universal Surety Company,* 178 Neb. 746, 135 N.W.2d 232 (1965).

Surety of general contractor is not liable for repairs made under a new contract by owner with a different company where the general contractor was not provided notice or a demand for performance of the repair work before the new contract was let. *Twin Cities Plaza v. Central Surety and Insurance Corp.*, 409 F.2d 1195 (8th Cir. 1969) (Nebraska law).

## 6. Time for Suit

***Statutes of limitation particular to performance bonds and other applicable statutes of limitation***

Actions on official bonds or bonds required by statute must be brought within 10 years. Neb. Rev. Stat. § 25-209 (Reissue 1995); *Stock v. Meissner,* 217 Neb. 56, 348 N.W.2d 426 (1984) (grain dealer's bond).

Actions on written contracts must be brought within five years of the date the cause of action accrues. Neb. Rev. Stat. § 25-205(1) (Cum. Supp. 2004).

Actions on oral contracts and torts must be commenced within four years. Neb. Rev. Stat. §§ 25-206, -207, -211 (Reissue 1995).

Contract claims against the state or any agency thereof must be presented to the state risk manager within two years of the date of occurrence under the State Contract Claims Act, Neb. Rev. Stat. §§ 81-8,302 to -81-8,806 (Reissue 2003).

***Case law statements about enforceability of limitations contained in bonds***

A three year guarantee in the contract prevented the surety from being liable on a construction bond for a failure of the work occurring 11 years later. "General or indefinite words in the instrument as to the time during which the surety shall remain liable will be limited by a recital specifying the time during which the prescribed duty is to be performed by the principal." Farmers Union Co-operative Association v. Mid-States Constr. Co., 212 Neb. 147, 322 N.W.2d 373 (1982).

***Varying statutes of limitation by agreement in bond or contract***

The general rule in Nebraska is that a contract cannot limit the period in which to bring a claim thereon. *Dunlop Tire & Rubber Corp. v. Ryan,* 171 Neb. 820, 108 N.W.2d 84 (1961).

A party may be estopped from asserting a statute of limitation defense by subsequent conduct. *See Manker v. Manker*, 263 Neb. 944, 644 N.W.2d 522 (2002).

## 7. Procedure

***Statutory or procedural rules that may affect handling or administration of lawsuits***

Nebraska District Courts are courts of general jurisdiction. County courts have law jurisdiction for claims up to $51,000. *See* Neb. Rev. Stat. § 24-517 (Cum. Supp. 2004). Bond actions are generally treated as civil actions. Court jurisdiction is covered by Chapter 24 of the Nebraska Revised Statutes. Civil procedure is governed by Chapter 25 of the Nebraska Revised Statutes.

***Venue requirements and jurisdictional limitations***

Venue lies in the county where the action arose, where the transaction or any part thereof occurred, or where the defendant or any one of the defendants may be served. Neb. Rev. Stat. 25-403.01 (Reissue 1995).

***Court rules***

Nebraska Court rules may be found at http://court.nol.org/courts.htm.

Nebraska has adopted notice pleading under the Nebraska Rules of Pleading in Civil Actions as reproduced Nebraska Court Rules and Procedures at 718-724 (Thompson West 2005). These track the Federal Rules of Civil Procedure, Rules 1 through 15 with minor variation. Discover is governed by the Nebraska Discovery Rules for All Cases which generally coincide with the Federal Rules of Civil Procedure Rule 26 through 37 with the notable addition of Rule 34A which allows document requests to be sent to non-parties.

***Particular agency regulations/rules*** – The Nebraska Administrative Code may be found at http://www.sos.state.ne.us/business/regsearch/.

***Arbitration requirements and application***

Arbitration agreements are enforceable in Nebraska and arbitration awards may be registered as judgments. Neb. Rev. Stat. §§ 25-2601 to - 2622 (Reissue 1995 and Cum. Supp. 2004).

## 8. Attorney's Fees

***Statutes and/or case law limiting or permitting recovery of attorney's fees***

Generally, costs and expenses of litigation, including attorney fees, may not be recovered unless provided for by statute or as a uniform course of procedure. *Southwest Trinity Constructors, Inc. v. St. Paul Fire & Marine Ins. Co.* 243 Neb. 55, 59, 497 N.W.2d 366, 368 (1993).

Neb. Rev. Stat. § 44-359 (Reissue 2004) provides for recovery of attorney's fees to a successful party who sues on an insurance contract. This has been held to apply to suits on surety bonds. *Adams Bank & Trust v. Empire Fire and Marine Insurance Co.*, 244 Neb. 262, 506 N.W.2d 52 (1993).

In action on performance bond where surety admits execution of bond but does not admit defective performance by contractor, the plaintiff may recover attorney's fee. *Omaha Home for Boys v. Stitt Constr. Co., Inc.*, 195 Neb. 422, 238 N.W.2d 470 (1976).

There is no statutory provision providing for attorney fees in an indemnity agreement. *Havelock Bank of Lincoln v. Western Sur. Co.*, 217 Neb. 560, 567, 352 N.W.2d 855, 859 (1984).

***What fees are recoverable, if any***

The amount of attorney's fees to be awarded is committed to the discretion of the trial court. *Adams Bank & Trust v. Empire Fire and Marine Insurance Co.*, 244 Neb. 262, 506 N.W.2d 52 (1993).

## 9. Special Provisions

Any claims against the state of Nebraska must be brought within two years of the date when the claim arose. Neb. Rev. Stat. § 25-218 (Reissue 1995).

Contract claims against the state or any agency thereof must be presented under the State Contract Claims Act, Neb. Rev. Stat. §§ 81-8,302 to -81-8,806 (Reissue 2003).

Other claims against the state are subject to the State Tort Claims Act, Neb. Rev. Stat. §§ 81-8,209 *et. seq.* (Reissue 2003).

Claims against political subdivisions may be subject to the requirements of the Political Subdivision Tort Claim Act, Neb. Rev. Stat. §§ 13-901, et. Seq. (Reissue 1997 and Cum. Supp. 2004).

Claims against counties for labor or materials must be presented within 90 days of when furnished or preformed. Neb. Rev. Stat. § 23-135 (Reissue 1997).

**10. Remarks** – None.

**11. Case Annotations**

***Interpretation of AIA bond forms*** – None.

***Cases in which surety steps into shoes of obligee***

"The doctrine of subrogation includes every instance in which one person pays a debt for which another is primarily liable, and which in equity and good conscience should have been discharged by the latter, so long as the payment was made under compulsion or for the protection of some interest of the one making the payment and in discharge of an existing liability." *Sheridan v. Dudden Implement, Inc.*, 174 Neb. 578, 119 N.W.2d 64 (1962). The doctrine applies where a party is compelled to pay the debt of a third person to protect his own rights or interest, or to save his own property. *Luikart v. Buck*, 131 Neb. 866, 270 N.W. 495 (1936). *Cagle, Inc. v. Sammons*, 198 Neb. 595, 602, 254 N.W.2d 398, 403 (1977).

Upon payment of the obligation of the principal, a surety is subrogated to the rights of the creditor against the principal. *Barnes v. Hampton*, 198 Neb. 151, 152, 252 N.W.2d 138, 139 (1977).

The rights of a bank as assignee of the rights under a construction claim are junior to those of a surety who has preformed in accordance with its bond because the bond "became an essential part of the contract." The claims held by the bank are based upon work done under the contract. The rights of the bank necessarily rest upon the provisions of the contract, including the bond. The surety had a prior claim on the funds because, *by the terms of its bond,* it had assumed obligation to make certain payments, that obligation related back to the date of its entering into the obligation under its bond, and the surety company had a prior obligation, and therefore, a right prior to the assignee. *Dakota*

*County v. Central Bridge & Const. Co.*, 136 Neb. 118, 285 N.W. 309, 313 (1939); *First Nat. Bank v. Pesha*, 99 Neb. 785, 157 N.W. 924 (1916).

A surety on a fidelity bond who partially restores a loss created by the fraud of the principal obligor cannot thus acquire by subrogation a greater right than that formerly possessed by the party for whose benefit the bond was given. *Federal Land Bank of Omaha v. Worley*, 135 Neb. 493, 282 N.W. 476, (1938).

In *Nebraska Beef v. Universal Surety Co.,* 9 Neb. App. 40, 607 N.W.2d 227 (2000) the court of appeals also held that Nebraska Beef should have been given leave to amend its petition to allege a subrogation theory of recovery, i.e., that it had paid subcontractors to complete the obligations of ABC Electric who should have been paid by Universal pursuant to its performance bond, and that it was entitled to recover these payments from Universal. *But see J.B. Contracting Services, Inc. v. Universal Sur. Co*. 261 Neb. 586, 595, 624 N.W.2d 13, 20-21 (2001).

# NEVADA

Kurt C. Faux[1]

## 1. Requirement for Bond

The State of Nevada has two primary statutes requiring a performance bond on certain public works. Quasi-performance bond related obligations may also be found in certain statutory requirements regarding private contracts.

***Statutory provisions for projects that are:***

**Public** – *NRS 339.025, Contractor's Bonds on Public Works*. Effective October 1, 2005, a performance bond to be fixed by the contracting body in an amount not less than 50 percent of the contract amount must be furnished for any contract exceeding $100,000 involving "the new construction, repair or reconstruction of any public building or other public work or public improvement" excluding work for the Nevada Department of Transportation. NRS 339.025.

The performance bond is conditioned upon the "faithful performance of the contract in accordance with the plans, specifications and conditions of the contract." NRS 339.025(1)(a). The bond must be solely for the protection of the contracting body which awarded the contract.

---

[1] Kurt C. Faux is a member of:
Faux & Associates
2785 E. Desert Inn Road, Suite 270
Las Vegas, Nevada 89121
(702) 458-5790

*Id.* The "contracting body" means "the State, county, city, town, school district, or any public agency of the State or its political subdivisions which has authority to contract for the construction, alteration or repair of any public building or other public work or public improvement." NRS 339.015(2).

If the contract is with the State Public Works Board, then each subcontractor who will perform work on the contract that exceeds $50,000 or 1 percent of the proposed project, whichever amount is greater, shall furnish a bond to the board in an amount to be fixed by the board. NRS 339.025(2).

**Private – *Pool Contractors*** – Certain consumer protections have been enacted to protect residential homeowners against incomplete pool construction. These are discussed below.

***NRS 597.719(3)(b)(2), Consumer Protection*** – Contracts for the construction of a residential pool or spa must contain a provision in close proximity to the signatures of the owner and the contractor a notice stating that the owner "has the right to request a bond for payment and performance if such a bond is not otherwise required pursuant to NRS 624.270." Failure to include this provision renders the contract void and unenforceable against the owner. *Id.*

Financing of the principal by the surety may also render a contract with a residential pool or spa owner unenforceable. A contract is unenforceable if the contractor receives from a third party, either directly or indirectly, remuneration or any other thing of value for a loan to finance the work and it is not disclosed in the contract. NRS 597.7194(5). A "third party" means a bonding company, finance company, or any other corporation or business financing the work concerning a residential pool or spa. NRS 597.7194(6). This law became effective July 1, 2005.

***NRS 624.270(8), Pool Contractors*** – A residential pool and spa contractor may be required to furnish a performance bond from an "A" rated surety by the Nevada State Contractors Board ("NSCB"). NRS 624.270(8). The performance bond must be in an amount equal to not less than 50 percent of the amount of the contract, conditioned upon the faithful performance of the contract in accordance with the plans, specifications and conditions set forth in the contract. The NSCB is authorized to demand a performance bond if the contractor (i) is determined to have violated one or more provisions of NRS 624.301 to

624.305[2]; (ii) enters into a contract after July 1,2001, that is found to be void and unenforceable pursuant to NRS 597.719(5)[3] or pursuant to any regulation adopted by NSCB; and (iii) has five valid complaints filed against him with the NSCB within any 15-day period. As of October 2005, the NSCB is in the process of adopting a mandatory bond form which requires coverage for an owner who is damaged either by the contractor's failure to perform the contract or injured by the contractor's unlawful act or omission. NRS 624.276(13).[4]

***NRS 624.273, Contractors*** – Each licensed contractor is required to have a contractor's license bond unless waived by the Nevada State Contractors Board. NRS 624.270(1). One beneficiary of this bond is an owner of the property to be improved who entered into a construction contract with the contractor and is damaged by the failure of the contractor to perform the contract or to remove liens filed against the property. NRS 624.273(1)(a). Arguably, this provision has a performance aspect as the surety may be entitled to perform the contract. In practice, however, a surety faced with liability under this provision typically pays a lump sum in exchange for a release.

**Department of Transportation** – ***NRS 408.357, Nevada Department of Transportation*** – Every contract must provide for the filing and furnishing of a performance bond or bonds equal to the full or total amount of the contract awarded. The performance bond must (i) guaranty the faithful performance of the contract in accordance with the plans, specifications and terms of the contract; and (ii) be maintained for one year after the date of completion of the contract. The performance bond requirement may be excused for a contract awarded to a railroad company for the construction, reconstruction, improvement or maintenance of a highway

---

2 These sections specify the grounds for disciplinary action against a contractor.

3 NRS 597.719(5) concerns the violation of consumer protection laws applicable to residential pool and spa contractors. These provisions are in the process of being transferred to NRS 624 governing contractors.

4 NRS 624.276 requires an additional bond of residential pool and spa contractors solely for the protection of consumers in an amount not less than $10,000 or more than $400,000. Hence, a pool and spa subcontractor possibly could be required to obtain four bonds. NRS 624.270; NRS 624.270(8); NRS 624.276; NRS 597.719(3)(b)(2).

located on property owned or under the control of a railroad company. NRS 408.354.

### *Case law rules might generally apply*

A public contractor's payment bond given as required by statute is deemed to be a "statutory bond," and the statutory provisions must be read into the bond and are operative by force of statute without recitation in the bond. *Capriotti, Lemon and Associates, Inc. v. Johnson Service Co.*, 84 Nev. 318, 321, 440 P.2d 386 (1968).

The general rules of contractual construction are applied to interpret the surety bond. *Royal Indemnity Co. v. Special Service Supply Co.*, 82 Nev. 148, 151, 413 P.2d 500, 502 (1966).

There is no special element of reliance or fiduciary duty to support a tort action for breach of the implied covenant of good faith and fair dealing between a commercial principal and the surety. The principal has no standing to make a claim against the bonds themselves. *Great American Ins. V. General Builders*, 113 Nev. 346, 934 P.2d 257 (1997).

If the terms of a building contractor's surety bond are susceptible of two interpretations, that most favorable to the beneficiary should be adopted, if consistent with the purpose to be accomplished. *Gill v. Paysee*, 48 Nev. 12, 226 P. 302 (1924).

## 2. Damages Covered

### *Set forth in any statutes and/or case law*

Public works, other than Nevada Department of Transportation projects, require a performance bond in an amount to be fixed by the contracting body, but not less than 50 percent of the contract amount, conditioned upon the faithful performance of the contract in accordance with the plans, specifications and conditions of the contract. The bond must be solely for the protection of the contracting body which awarded the contract. NRS 339.025(1)(a).

If a general contractor has been awarded a contract, except one subject to the provisions of chapter 408 of NRS (the Nevada Department of Transportation), by the State Public Works Board for any project for new construction, repair or reconstruction of any public building or other public work or public improvement, each of his subcontractors who will perform work on the contract that exceeds $50,000 or 1 percent of the proposed project, whichever amount is greater, shall furnish a bond to the board in an amount to be fixed by the board.

Nevada Department of Transportation jobs require that the performance bond guaranty the faithful performance of the construction contract in accordance with plans, specifications, terms of the contract, and be maintained for one year after the date of completion. NRS 408.357(1).

Contractor's license bonds, which contain a quasi-performance provision, may be in the amount as determined by the contractor's board between $1,000 and $500,000. NRS 624.270(4).

***Obligations of surety to perform and/or pay***

Performance is due when the surety breached the contract to pay a definite sum of money, or to render a performance the value of which in money was stated in contract, or was ascertainable by mathematical calculations from a standard fixed in the contract or from established market prices of the subject matter. Surety on a performance bond is subject to paying interest from the time performance is due. *Paradise Homes, Inc. v. Central Surety and Insurance Corporation*, 84 Nev. 109, 437 P.2d 78, 84 (1968).

Contractor's license bond could not be construed to cover faulty workmanship. *E.A. Boswell v. Insurance Company of North America,* 85 Nev. 359, 455 P.2d 174 (1969). Compare to NRS 624.273(1).

***Whether failure to provide insurance transfers burden to surety*** – Generally there are no cases addressing this.

***Limitations on damages***

A bond obligation to pay "all damages" does not include punitive damages. *New Hampshire Insurance Co. v. Gruhn*, 99 Nev. 771, 670 P.2d 941 (1983).

The bond may not be expanded to embrace occurrences not within the statute unless the bond discloses an intention to cover such occurrences. *Day & Night Manufacturing Co. v. Fidelity & Deposit Casualty Co. of New York*, 85 Nev. 227, 452 P.2d 906, 908 (1969). (license bond).

Effective July 1,2005, delay damages may not be assessed against a surety if the contract is terminated or the work is stopped for a reasonable basis in law or pursuant to NRS 624. NRS 624.610(9); NRS 624.626(9).

Effective July 1, 2005, contracts requiring a contractor or subcontractor to waive a right for damages or extension of time may be void as against public policy. NRS 624.622(2); NRS 624.628(3).

***Whether obligee may set off bonded contract funds against other principal-obligee debts or obligations***

After making all the deductions to which the defendant may be entitled, prejudgment interest shall be allowed on the amount of the debt. *Paradise Homes, Inc. v. Central Surety and Insurance Corporation*, 84 Nev. 109, 437 P.2d 78, 80, 83, 84 (1968).

***Incorporation of specific contract terms by reference***

The surety issued a contract bond to the owner in connection with a construction contract. The bond stated that the contract was "by specific reference ... made a part hereof." An unpaid subcontractor's suit against the surety was dismissed based on the trial court's finding that the bond was limited to indemnification of the owner and conferred no rights upon job creditors. The Nevada Supreme Court reversed relying, in part, upon the contract incorporation provision of the bond wherein the contractor promised the owner that the contractor would pay all valid bills of the subcontractor. The surety had, by the terms of the bond, expressly undertaken the obligations of the general contractor in all respects. If the contractor fails to perform, the surety has promised performance. It has thus promised that it will pay the subcontractors. As this was an indemnity bond, the court held that the bond falls in the middle of two classes: those which expressly give creditors a direct right of action against the surety and those which expressly limit the rights under the bond to those of indemnification. The court noted that the condition of the performance bond in this case was not limited (as is frequently the case) to performance of the construction work agreed to be performed. The court noted that the bond was poorly drawn. *Acoustics Inc. v. American Surety Company of New York*, 74 Nev. 6, 320 P.2d 626, 627-628 (1958).

Immaterial variances in names of the parties in contract documents is of no effect. Parties may adopt a written contract through performance of its conditions even though it is not signed. *U.S. Fidelity & Guaranty Co. v. Reno Electrical Works*, 43 Nev. 191, 183 P. 386 (1919).

Where reference in a contract to "plans and specifications" indicates an intention to incorporate them generally, such reference becomes a part of the contract for all purposes. *Lincoln Welding Works, Inc. v. Ramirez*, 98 Nev. 342, 647 P.2d 381 (1982).

### 3. Penal Sum Variations

#### *Limitations per statute*

Contractor's license bonds, which contain a quasi-performance provision, may be in the amount as determined by the contractor's board between $1,000 and $500,000. NRS 624.270(4).

If a pool performance bond is required, it must be in an amount equal to not less than 50 percent of the amount of the contract. NRS 624.270(8)(a).

#### *Effect of changes in work upon penal sum, if at all*

Where general contractor and subcontractor renegotiated and materially changed the contract to increase its price by approximately 32 percent, the surety on the subcontractor's performance bond was not liable for the subcontractor's failure to perform the additional work but was liable for the failure to perform the original contract. *Zuni Construction Co. v. Great American Ins. Co.*, 86 Nev. 364, 468 P.2d 980 (1970).

If the principal is discharged by novation, then the surety on the principal's performance bond is discharged. *Zuni Construction Co. v. Great American Ins. Co.*, 86 Nev. 364, 468 P.2d 980, 982 (1970).

A performance bond surety cannot be discharged when there is an alteration or modification unless it shows it was prejudiced or injured by the variance. *Zuni Construction Co. v. Great American Ins. Co.*, 86 Nev. 364, 468 P.2d 980, 982 (1970).

The novation of a contract, the performance of which is guaranteed by sureties who do not consent to the novation absolves them of their liability, which disappears with the debt to which it was collateral. *Williams v. Crusader Discount Corp.*, 75 Nev. 67, 334 P.2d 843 (1959).

Prejudice or injury must be shown to avoid bond liability based on assignment. *Midland Ins. Co. v. Yanke Plumbing and Heating, Inc.*, 99 Nev. 66, 657 P.2d 1152 (1983) (license bond).

***Statutory or case law protections or dangers to penal sum***

A bond obligation to pay "all damages" does not include punitive damages. *New Hampshire Insurance Co. v. Gruhn*, 99 Nev. 771, 670 P.2d 941 (1983).

The bond may not be expanded to embrace occurrences not within the statute unless the bond discloses an intention to cover such occurrences. *Day & Night Manufacturing Co. v. Fidelity & Deposit Casualty Co. of New York*, 85 Nev. 227, 452 P.2d 906, 908 (1969) (license bond).

Provided that the minimum statutory requirements are satisfied, the express language of the bond controls and liability may not be imposed beyond the express contractual terms. *Carson Opera House Association v. Miller*, 16 Nev. 327, 334 (1881); *Adelson v. Wilson & Co.*, 81 Nev. 15, 21, 398 P.2d 106, 109 (1965).

The court must apply the law as it finds it. *Union Indemnity Co. v. A.D. Drumm, Jr.*, 57 Nev. 242, 62 P.2d 698, 700 (1936).

The contract of a compensated surety should be interpreted liberally in the interest of the promisee and beneficiaries, rather than strictly in favor of the surety. *Acoustics Inc. v. American Surety Company of New York*, 74 Nev. 6, 320 P.2d 626 (1958).

## 4. Parties Covered

***Statutes and/or case law as to whether only obligees are covered*** – Not applicable.

***Coverage for:***

**Third-party beneficiaries** – The court held that an unpaid subcontractor was the third party beneficiary of an indemnity bond promising the contractor's performance to the owner, *Acoustics Inc. v.*

*American Surety Company of New York*, 74 Nev. 6, 320 P.2d 626, 627 (1958).

**Assignees** – Surety brought suit to restrain the Department of Highways from distributing to the principal the balance due on the contract and to compel its application to the payment of debts incurred by the principal in performing the contract. Three parties sought the balance due: oil companies assigned the construction funds four months prior to the principal's bankruptcy, the bankruptcy trustee, and the surety. The state controller filed a separate action to compel the principal's creditors to interplead and establish their claims to the balance due. These actions were consolidated. Before judgment was entered, an involuntary petition for bankruptcy was filed as to the principal, and the trustee intervened in the consolidated action. The trial court upheld the assignments to the oil companies and the job creditors' (not general creditors) claims for an equitable lien. The trustee appealed. The appellate court held that job creditors possessed no equitable lien rights given the terms of the then statute that the retained percentage shall be paid to the principal without regard to creditors' claims filed with the state highway department. *Union Indemnity Co. v. A.D. Drumm, Jr.*, 57 Nev. 242, 62 P.2d 698 (1936), rehearing, *Union Indemnity Co. v. A.D. Drumm, Jr.*, 57 Nev. 242, 70 P.2d 727 (1937) (equitable lien and not a subrogation case; trial court judgment reversed).

**Dual obligees** – Generally there are no cases addressing this.

## 5. Notice or Filing Required

***Statutory provisions***

Every contract with the Nevada Department of Transportation must provide for the filing and furnishing of bonds. NRS 408.357.

Public work bonds, other than those with the Nevada Department of Transportation, "must be filed in the office of the contracting body which awarded the contract for which the bonds were given." NRS 339.025(4).

***Case law rules concerning condition precedent notice*** – This has not been specifically addressed as to performance bond.

## 6. Time for Suit

***Statutes of limitation particular to performance bonds and other applicable statutes of limitation***

An action upon a contract, obligation or liability founded upon an instrument in writing, judgment or court decree must be brought within 6 years. NRS 11.190(1)(a) and (b).

In a Miller Act setting, the court has held that Nevada's six year limitation for contract actions apply. *Trustees of Bricklayers Local No. 3 v. REECO*, 747 F. Supp. 606, 613 (D. Nev. 1990); NRS 11.190(1)(b).

NRS 11.190(3)(a) provides that an action must be commenced within three years "upon a liability created by statute...." Case law concerning state agencies' claims for past-due payments applies this three year statutory limitation period. *State Tax Commission v. Cord*, 404 P.2d 422, 426 n.1 (Nev. 1965) ("We are satisfied that NRS 11.190(3) applies to tax liabilities."); *State of Nevada v. The Yellow Jacket Silver Mining Co.*, 14 Nev. 220 (1879). But see, *The State of Nevada v. American Bankers Ins. Co.*, 105 Nev. 692, 782 P.2d 1316 (1989) (six year limitation applied to bail bond based on written contract).

An action by a contractor against the Department of Transportation upon a contract for the construction, reconstruction, improvement or maintenance of a highway must be commenced within 3 years after the date of the:

1. Completion of the contract; or
2. Determination of the engineer or decision of the Board of Directors of the Department of Transportation on an appeal of a claim arising from the contract as provided in the standard specifications for construction of roads and bridges adopted by the Department, whichever occurs later. NRS 11.208.

***Case law statements about enforceability of limitations contained in bonds***

In enforcing a bail bond with a one year limitation period, the court determined that the language of the bond is strictly construed in accordance with the terms contained therein. A contract should not be revised under the guise of construing it. Neither a court of law nor a court of equity can interpolate in a contract what the contract does not contain. *All Star Bonding v. The State of Nevada*, 119 Nev. 47, 62 P.3d 1124, 1125 (2003) (bail bond).

***Varying statutes of limitation by agreement in bond or contract***

A contractual stipulation limiting the time for bringing an action upon the contract is enforceable as long as it is reasonable. *Davis v. State Farm Fire & Cas. Co.*, 545 F. Supp. 370 (D. Nev. 1982).

Insurance contract clause requiring that suits be brought within 12 months after the "inception of the loss" allowed the period of limitations to run from the date of the casualty, but the period was tolled from the time the insured gave notice of loss until the insurer formally denied liability. *Clark v. Truck Ins. Exchange,* 95 Nev. 544, 598 P.2d 628 (1979).

## 7. Procedure

***Statutory or procedural rules that may affect handling or administration of lawsuits***

A foreign surety must be served with a lawsuit through the Nevada Insurance Commissioner. A claimant is precluded from accomplishing service of process on a foreign insurer in any other manner. NRS 680A.250(3); *Transamerica Ins. Co. v. C. B. Concrete*, 99 Nev. 677, 669 P.2d 246 (1983).

A foreign surety served through the insurance commissioner has 10 additional days (thirty days) to answer a complaint. NRS 680A.260 (3).

Effective May 18, 2005, all civil actions commenced in state district court that have a probable jury award value not in excess of $50,000 per plaintiff (exclusive of attorney's fees, interest and court costs) are subject to nonbinding arbitration pursuant to Nevada Arbitration Rule 3(A) (unless the parties stipulate to mediation or the short trial program). Actions involving declaratory relief and title to real property are also excluded if timely requested.

An unlicensed contractor is precluded from prosecuting an action for collection. NRS 624.320.

***Venue requirements and jurisdictional limitations***

A court of this state may exercise jurisdiction over a party to a civil action on any basis not inconsistent with the constitution of this state or the Constitution of the United States. NRS 14.065(1).

When a person has contracted to perform an obligation at a particular place, and resides in another county, the action must be commenced, and, subject to the power of the court to change the place of trial as provided in this chapter, must be tried in the county in which such obligation is to be performed or in which he resides; and the county in which the obligation is incurred shall be deemed to be the county in which it is to be performed, unless there is a special contract to the contrary. NRS 13.010(1).

***Court rules*** – Not applicable.

***Particular agency regulations/rules*** – Agency rules regarding the pool performance bond are currently under discussion. NAC 624.

***Arbitration requirements and applications***

Effective October 1, 2005, any public body charged with the drafting of specifications for a public work shall include in the specifications a clause requiring arbitration of a dispute arising between the public body and the contractor engaged on a public work if the dispute cannot otherwise be settled. NRS 338.150(1).

Effective May 18, 2005, all civil actions commenced in state district court that have a probable jury award value not in excess of $50,000 per plaintiff (exclusive of attorney's fees, interest and court costs) are subject to nonbinding arbitration pursuant to Nevada Arbitration Rule 3(A) (unless the parties stipulate to mediation or the short trial program). Actions involving declaratory relief and title to real property are also excluded if timely requested.

## 8. Attorney's Fees

***Statutes and/or case law limiting or permitting recovery of attorney's fees***

Fact that costs and interest when added to the principal sum of recoverable damages exceeded the penal sum of the bond would not preclude recovery of costs and interest from the surety, particularly when conceded by the surety. Attorney's fees could not exceed the penal sum. *Basic Refractories, Inc. v. Bright*, 72 Nev. 183, 298 P.2d 810, 817-818 (1956).

If a secured entity becomes obligated to pay attorney fees in third-party litigation, the surety is not liable for these fees if they exceed the bond amount. When the secured entity incurs attorney fees in direct litigation with the surety over the bond, attorney fees may be awarded under NRS 17.115 (offer of judgment); NRCP 68 (offer of judgment); and NRS 18.010 (bad faith litigation or recovery under $20,000). *Trustees of the Plumbers and Pipefitters Union Local 525 v. Developers Surety & Indemnity Co.*, 120 Nev. 56, 84 P.3d 59 (2004).

***What fees are recoverable if any***

Nevada Supreme Court Rule 155 generally dictates that the standard for recovery of attorney's fees is reasonableness. Factors determining reasonableness include the time and labor required, the novelty of the issue, the fee customarily charged in the area, and related factors. The court has enforced a good faith standard for the recovery of attorney's fees. *Transamerica Premier Ins. Co. v. Nelson*, 110 Nev. 951, 878 P.2d 314, 317 (1994).

**9. Special Provisions** – Not applicable.

**10. Remarks** – Not applicable.

## 11. Case Annotations

***Interpretation of AIA bond forms*** – Nevada cases have not specifically addressed AIA forms of bonds A311 and A312.

***Cases in which surety steps into shoes of obligee***

The subrogation rights of a surety compelled to complete performance of a construction contract are not limited to the rights of the contractor. The surety is subrogated to the right of the state to apply the retent against the cost of completing performance. Therefore, the surety's right to retent is free from any claim thereto which might be asserted by the materialman. If the surety, instead of performing the contract, elects to pay damages, the surety is given credit for the current estimates as well as the retained percentages. Equity will not place the surety in a worse position. *Globe Indemnity Co. v. Peterson-McCaslin Lumber Company*, 72 Nev. 282, 303 P.2d 414 (1956), quoting in part, *Lacy v. Maryland Casualty Co.*, 32 F.2d 48, 51 (4th Cir. 1929).

Under the terms of the agreement between the contractor and the surety, all rights to the retained contract price passed to the surety upon completion of the contract and failure of the contractor to satisfy liens. *Continental Casualty Co. v. H.D. Farrow*, 79 Nev. 428, 386 P.2d 90 (1963).

Surety company that wrote the performance bond and took over the completion of the contract obtained the final payment of the contract funds. *Fitch v. La Tourette*, 75 Nev. 484, 346 P.2d 704, 707 (1959).

Surety's liability coincides with that of the principal. *Trustees of Bricklayers Local No. 3 v. REECO*, 747 F. Supp. 606, 614 (D. Nev. 1990).

In an action by an owner against the contractor and performance bond surety, the court held that the liquidated damages clause was valid as to delay damages and did not preclude actual damages for defective workmanship. *Spinella v. B-Neva, Inc.*, 94 Nev. 373, 580 P.2d 945, 947 (1978).

A surety who completes a contract or satisfies the claims of laborers and materialmen has established a subrogation right to all funds, progress payments, or retained percentages, which are in the hands of the contractee. *Bennett v. Fidelity & Deposit Company of Maryland*, 98 Nev. 449, 652 P.2d 1178, 1180 (1982), quoting *Reliance Ins. Co. v. Alaska State Housing Authority*, 323 F. Supp. 1370, 1373 (D.C. Alaska 1971).

Default judgment against the principal does not bind the surety. *Gearhart v. Pierce Enterprises*, 105 Nev. 517, 779 P.2d 93 (1989).

Surety not obligated to pay punitive damages assessed against the principal. *The New Hampshire Ins. Co. v. Gruhn*, 99 Nev. 771, 670 P.2d 941 (1983).

The bond may not be expanded to embrace occurrences not within the statute unless the bond discloses an intention to cover such occurrences. *Day & Night Manufacturing Co. v. Fidelity & Deposit Casualty Co. of New York*, 85 Nev. 227, 452 P.2d 906, 908 (1969). (license bond). *Pierce Enterprises,* 105 Nev. 517, 779 P.2d 93 (1989).

# NEW HAMPSHIRE

James E. Owers and Kevin M. O'Shea[1]

## 1. Requirement for Bond

***Statutory provisions for projects that are:***

**Public** – RSA 447:16 requires officers, public boards or agents or other persons who contract on behalf of the state or any political subdivisions for the construction, repair or rebuilding of public buildings, public highways, bridges or other public works to obtain a bond if the contract involves an expenditure of more than $25,000.

**Private** – There are no requirements to bond private construction projects, but local planning boards may require a performance bond as part of subdivision regulation or site plan review. RSA 674:36, III allows a planning board to require a bond for the performance of completing streets, water and sewer lines and other improvements on a private subdivision project.

**Department of Transportation** – Covered by RSA 447:16 above.

***Case law rules that might generally apply*** – Not applicable.

---

1 James E. Owers is a partner and Kevin M. O'Shea is an associate of:
Sulloway & Hollis, P.L.L.C.
9 Capitol Street
Concord, New Hampshire 03820
(603) 224 2341

## 2. Damages Covered

***Set forth in any statutes and/or case law***

RSA 447:16 requires the bond on a public project to be in an amount equal to at least 100 percent of the contract price or of the estimated cost of the work if no aggregate price is agreed upon. If a suit is successful the prevailing party is in addition entitled to prejudgment and post judgment interest. RSA 336:1, II provides that the annual simple rate of interest on judgments, including prejudgment interest, shall be a rate equal to the interest on 26-week United States Treasury bills plus 2 percentage points.

***Obligations of surety to perform and/or pay*** – No statute or case on point.

***Whether failure to provide insurance transfers burden to surety*** – No statute or case on point.

***Limitations on damages***

New Hampshire does not allow punitive damages. RSA 507:16. However, New Hampshire does recognize enhanced compensatory damages when the defendant's conduct is "wanton, malicious or oppressive." *Figlioli v. R.J. Moreau Companies, Inc.*, 866 A.2d 962, 967 (N.H. 2005) (citations omitted).

***Whether obligee may set off bonded contract funds against other principal-obligee debts or obligations*** – No statute or case on point.

***Incorporation of specific contract terms by reference*** – No statute or case on point.

### 3. Penal Sum Variations

***Limitations per statute***

There are no statutes that limit or enhance bond penal sums under RSA 447:16 or 674:36, 44 except that the penal sum of the bond must equal 100 percent of the contract price under RSA 447:16.

***Effect of changes in work upon penal sum, if at all*** – No statute or case on point.

***Statutory or case law protections or changes to penal sum*** – No statute or case on point.

### 4. Parties Covered

**Statutes and/or case law as to whether only obligees are covered**

RSA 447:16 requires payment of contractors and subcontractors for all labor performed or furnished, for all equipment hired, and for all material used and for fuels, lubricants, power, tools, hardware and supplies purchased and used in carrying out a contract.

Materialman of a subcontractor can recover under the bond. RSA 447:17. *Lyle Signs Inc. v. Evroks Corp.*, 562 A.2d 785, 786 (N.H. 1989) (citing *Naylor Pipe v. Walter Murray Company*, 421 A.2d 1012, 1013 (N.H. 1980)). However, "RSA 447:16 does not protect a materialman's materialman. The clear statutory language provides for protection for the payment by the contractors and subcontractors for all labor performed or furnished and for all materials used. Clearly this anticipates protecting only those parties who are in privity of contract with either a contractor or a subcontractor." *Lyle Signs Inc. v. Evroks Corp.*, 562 A.2d 785, 786 (N.H. 1989). Those not in privity of contract cannot recover on a bond.

***Coverage for:***

**Third-party beneficiaries, assignees, and dual obligees** – New Hampshire statutes and case law do not define the rights of third parties, assignees, and dual obligees specifically under surety bonds, but the courts will look generally to the Restatement of Contracts and Restatement of Surety.

### 5. Notice or Filing Required

***Statutory provisions***

RSA 447:17 requires that to obtain benefit of the bond, any person, firm or corporation having any claim for the labor preformed, materials, machinery, tools or equipment furnished shall, within *90 days* after the completion and acceptance of the project by the contracting party, file a notice in:

(i) The office of the secretary of state if the state is a contracting party, or

(ii) With the department of public works and highways, if the state is a party to the contract, or

(iii) In the office of the clerk of the superior court for the county within which the contract shall be principally performed, if any political subdivision of the state is a contracting party.

***Case law rules concerning condition precedent notice***

Strict compliance with the statutory notice is required: "Failure to comply with the statutory requirement that a statement of claim shall be filed with a designated party is usually fatal." *Crushing Services Inc. v. Abatement International/Advantex Associates, Inc.*, 827 A.2d. 1019, 1023 (N.H. 2003) (citing *American Fidelity Co. v. Cray*, 194 A.2d 763 (N.H. 1963).

### 6. Time for Suit

***Statutes of limitation particular to performance bonds and other applicable statutes of limitation***

RSA 447:18 requires that claimant shall, within *one year* after filing notice of a claim (as outlined in RSA 447:17), file a petition in the superior court for the county within which the contract shall be principally performed to enforce his claim or to intervene in a petition already filed.

RSA 508:4-b, I, provides an *eight year* statute of repose for construction contracts generally:

> except as otherwise provided in this section, all actions to recover damages for injury to property, injury to the person, wrongful death or economic loss arising out of any deficiency in the creation of an improvement to real property, including without limitation the design, labor, materials, engineering, planning, surveying, construction, observation, supervision or inspection of that improvement, shall be brought within 8 years from the date of substantial completion of the improvement, and not thereafter.

The statute has been upheld in *Winnisquam Reg'l Sch. Dist. v. Levine*, 2005 WL 1981060; 2005 N.H. LEXIS 134. (N.H. 2005).

***Case law statements about enforceability of limitations contained in bonds***

New Hampshire would probably examine a surety contract that is not mandated by statute as an ordinary contract. Under RSA 508:A, "a contract claim must be brought within three years of the contract's breach." *A & B Lumber Co., LLC v. Vrusho*, 871 A.2d 64, 65 (N.H. 2005). "A breach of contract occurs when there is a failure without legal excuse, to perform any promise which forms the whole or part of a contract. While a party may be able to invoke the discovery rule if the injury is not discovered until a later time, the action arises once there has been a breach." *Bronstein v. GZA GeoEnvironmental, Inc.*, 665 A.2d 369, 371 (N.H. 1995) (citations and quotations omitted).

***Varying statutes of limitation by agreement in bond or contract***

Depending on the language and period allowed, a shorter period for filing suit may be enforced. "Contractual time limits provided as part of a plan are enforceable, despite different state law limitations periods, as long as the agreed-upon period is reasonable." *Berlin L. Ayotte v. Matthew Thornton Health Plan, Inc. and Anthem Health Plans of New Hampshire, Inc.,* U.S. District Ct. N.H., unpublished Op. No. 2004 D.N.H. 098(6/28/04). *See also, Newell v. Clark,* 61 A. 555 (N.H. 1905); *Tasker v. Kenton Ins. Co.,* 58 N.H. 469 (1878).

## 7. Procedure

***Statutory or procedural rules that may affect handling or administration of lawsuits*** – Not applicable.

***Venue requirements and jurisdictional limitations***

While RSA 447:17 and 18 outline specific venues for public performance bond suits, RSA 507:9 sets venue in transitory actions for other common law actions, "in which any one of the parties is an inhabitant of the state, shall be brought in the county or judicial district thereof where some one of them resides. If no one of the parties is an inhabitant of the state, the action may be brought in any county or judicial district."

In New Hampshire, the superior court is the court of general jurisdiction. *See* N.H. Const. Pt. 2, Art. 72-a; *see also* RSA 491:7.

***Court rules*** – Not applicable.

***Particular agency regulations/rules*** – Not applicable.

***Arbitration requirements and application***

RSA 542:1 provides that a "provision in any written contract to settle by arbitration a controversy thereafter arising out of such contract, or an agreement in writing to submit to arbitration any controversy existing at the time of the agreement to submit, shall be valid, irrevocable, and enforceable, save upon such grounds as exist at law or in equity for the revocation of any contract."

## 8. Attorney's Fees

***Statutes and/or case law limiting or permitting recovery of attorney's fees***

Under New Hampshire law, "in the absence of a statute or contract providing for the allowance of attorney's fees, the prevailing party is not entitled to recover such costs." *H. Loney Construction Co. v. Manchester Housing and Redevelopment Authority v. Aetna Casualty and Surety*

*Corporation*, 1995 U.S. Dist. LEXIS 12486 at *11-12 (D.N.H.) (August 18, 1995) (citing *Smith v. Town of Wolfeboro*, 573 A.2d 451 (N.H. 1990); *Maguire v. Merrimack Mut. Ins. Co.*, 573 A.2d 1252 (N.H. 1992)). The American rule applies unless fees are contractually shifted to the prevailing party.

RSA 507:15 provides for an award of fees for a "frivolous" action:

> If, upon the hearing of any contract or tort action, it clearly appears to the court that the action or any defense is frivolous or intended to harass or intimidate the prevailing party, then the court, upon motion of the prevailing party or on its own motion, may order summary judgment against the party who brought such action or raised such defense, and award the amount of costs and attorney's fees incurred by the prevailing party plus $1,000 to be paid to the prevailing party, provided such costs and fees are reasonable. The trial judge shall also report such conduct to the supreme court committee on professional conduct.

Under Superior Court Rule 59 the "Court may assess reasonable costs, including reasonable counsel fees, against any party whose frivolous or unreasonable conduct makes necessary the filing of or hearing on any motion."

"[W]hen overriding considerations so indicate, the award of fees lies within the power of the court, and is an appropriate tool in the court's arsenal to do justice and vindicate rights. Bad faith conduct held to justify the award of counsel fees has been found where one party has acted 'in bad faith, vexatiously, wantonly, or for oppressive reasons' where the litigant's conduct can be characterized as unreasonably obdurate or obstinate, and where it should have been unnecessary for the successful party to have brought the action." *Harkeem v. Adams*, 377 A.2d 617, 619 (N.H. 1977) (citations omitted).

***What fees are recoverable, if any***

Superior Court Rule 87 allows for the recovery of filing fees, deposition expenses, and other costs associated with the trial of a case.

**9. Special Provisions** – None.

**10. Remarks** – None.

## 11. Case Annotations

Included above where relevant.

***Interpretation of AIA bond forms*** – Not applicable.

***Cases in which surety steps into shoes of obligee*** – Not applicable.

# NEW JERSEY

Kevin J. Russell[1]

## 1. Requirement for Bond

***Statutory provisions for projects that are:***

**Public** – The New Jersey Public Works Contractors Bond Law ("New Jersey Bond Act") N.J.S.A. 2A:44-143 *et seq.*, requires a successful bidder on a public project to supply a single bond that is generally equal to the amount of the contract. The statute defines "public projects" broadly to encompass construction, erection, alteration and repairs contracted for, by or on behalf of the State, or "any contracting unit," or any school district. Consequently, although projects performed by different public contracting units are governed by different statutory sections, the bonding requirements are contained exclusively in N.J.S.A. 2A:44-143 through N.J.S.A. 2A:44-147.

**Private** – New Jersey does not require performance bonds on private construction projects. Although not mandated by statute, private projects that are bonded, frequently but not exclusively, use the AIA 311 and AIA 312 bond form.

---

[1] Kevin J. Russell is with:
Lindabury, McCormick & Estabrook, P.A.
53 Cardinal Drive, P. O. Box 2369
Westfield, New Jersey 07091
(908) 233-6800

**Department of Transportation** – Not applicable.

***Case law rules that might generally apply***

Unlike the Miller Act that mandates a separate performance bond and payment bond, the New Jersey Bond Act requires that the contractor provide only a single bond covering both performance and payment obligations.

The form of the bond for public construction projects is specified by statute and can be found at N.J.S.A. 2A:44-147. If a public entity accepts a bond form that does not comply with the statutory requirements, the courts will "read out" the conditions of the bond that are not included in the statutory bond form. See, *Gloucester City Bd. of Educ. v. American Arbitration Association*, 333 N. J. Super. 511, 755 A.2d 1256 (App. Div. 2000). What this means is that regardless of the type of bond provided on a public project, the court will read the bond as if it complies with the statutory bond form and conditions on the surety's liability that are not mandated by the statute are read out of the bond.

Significantly, the statutory bond form does not contain language requiring a formal declaration of default and a demand against the surety for the surety to have liability under its bond. Thus, the court in *Gloucester City Bd. Educ. v. American Arbitration Association*, 333 N.J. Super. 511, 755 A.2d 1256, found that a surety on a statutory performance bond faces exposure without the condition precedent that the obligee issue a formal declaration of default and makes a demand on the surety. As a result, under a statutory performance bond a surety faces potential liability even if the principal is not formally defaulted and terminated.

## 2. Damages Covered

The New Jersey courts have articulated what could best be described as fundamental principles of surety law. A surety is chargeable only according to the strict terms of its undertaking and its obligations should not be extended by implication or construction beyond the confines of its contract. Moreover, the surety's liability is capped at the penal sum of the bond. *Monmouth Lumber Company v. Indemnity Insurance Co. of North America,* 21 N.J. 439, 122 A.2d 604 (1956).

***Set forth in any statutes and/or case law***

N.J.S.A. 2A:44-143 articulates the general scope of the surety's liability under a statutory performance bond. The statute provides in part that:

> A surety's obligation shall not extend to any claim for damages based upon alleged negligence that resulted in personal injury, wrongful death, or damage to real or personal property, and no bond shall in any way be construed as a liability insurance policy. Nothing herein shall relieve the surety's obligation to guarantee the contractor's performance of all conditions of the contract including the maintenance of liability insurance if and as required by the contract. Only the obligee named on the bond and any subcontractor performing labor or any subcontractor or materialman providing materials for the construction, erection, alteration or repair of the public building, work or improvement for which the bond is required pursuant to this section, shall have any claim against the surety under the bond. N.J.S.A. 2A:44-143(b).

**Performance bond does not cover negligence claims** – Under the plain language of N.J.S.A. 2A:44-143(b), a statutory performance bond shall not cover claims for negligence, nor shall the bond be construed as an insurance policy. See, *Wyckoff Twp. v. Sarna*, 136 N.J. Super. 512, 347 A.2d 16 (A.D. 1975) where the court found that neither the provisions of the municipal planning act nor the terms of the performance bond issued for the installation of the storm sewer insured the township against liability for its own negligence in connection with the installation of the storm sewer, and the surety was not obligated to indemnify the township with respect to a judgment obtained by grantors of the easement for the storm sewer.

**Surety's liability is co-extensive with its principal** – Significantly, N.J.S.A. 2A:44-143(b) also states that the surety's obligation is to "guarantee the contractor's performance of all conditions of the contract." Consequently, under a performance bond, the surety's liability is co-extensive with that of its principal.

***Obligations of surety to perform and/or pay***

The statutory bond form does not delineate specific performance options for the surety to respond to legitimate claims against the bond. However, following a contractor's default on a contract to construct a school building for township board of education, surety was at liberty to choose a contractor to complete the work. *Central Sur. & Ins. Corp. v. Martin Infante Co.,* 272 F.2d 231 (3rd 1959).

***Whether failure to provide insurance transfers burden to surety***

Although the statute excludes negligence claims under a performance bond, the statute specifically states that if the contractor fails to provide the contractually required insurance, it is covered under the bond. See *also Hartford Fire Ins. Co. v. Riefolo Const. Co., Inc.*, 81 N.J. 514, 410 A.2d 658 (1980), where the New Jersey Supreme Court found that a school board's insurer as subrogree had standing to recover against the performance bond if the general contractor failed to maintain the required liability insurance.

***Limitations on damages***

"It has long seen settled law that a surety is chargeable only according to the strict terms of its undertaking and its obligations cannot and should not be extended either by implication or by construction beyond the confines of its contract." *Eagle Fire Protection Corp. v. First Indemnity of America Insurance Company*, 145 N.J. 345, 356, 678 A.2d 699 (1996).

There are no cases in which a court has held the surety liable for punitive damages.

***Whether obligee may set off bonded contract funds against other principal-obligee debts or obligations***

There are no cases involving an obligee setting off funds against other principal-obligee debts or obligations.

***Incorporation of specific contract terms by reference*** – Not applicable.

## 3. Penal Sum Variations

***Limitations per statute***

**Public Projects** – N.J.S.A. 2A:44-143(a)(2) and (3) permit the head of the public contracting unit or agency to establish the penal sum for the specific bonded contract at any percentage not exceeding 100 percent of the contract price based on the assessment of the risk presented to the contracting entity by the type of contract and other relevant factors. However, despite the ability for a public owner to accept a bond with a penal sum less than the contract amount, public owners almost uniformly require that the penal sum for the statutory performance bond be equal to the amount of the contract.

**Private Projects** – Since private parties are free to determine if they want a performance bond for a construction project, they are likewise free to agree upon a state penal sum.

***Effect of changes in work upon penal sum, if at all*** – There are no cases interpreting a change in the work and its affect upon the penal sum.

***Statutory or case law protections or dangers to penal sum*** – Not applicable.

## 4. Parties Covered

***Statutes and/or case law as to whether only obligees are covered***

Under the plain language of the statute, "only the obligee named on the bond ... shall have any claim against the surety under the bond." N.J.S.A. 2A:44-143(b).

***Coverage for:***

**Third-party beneficiaries, assignees** – There are no cases involving either assignees or third party beneficiaries.

**Dual obligees** – Although there are no cases involving a dual obligee, presumably, if both are listed as the obligee, both may be permitted to pursue a claim against the bond. Lastly, in *Hartford Fire*, 81 N.J. 514, 410 A.2d 658, discussed above, the New Jersey Supreme Court concluded that the insurer as subrogree of a school board could assert a claim against a performance bond surety.

## 5. Notice or Filing Required

***Statutory provisions***

The statutory bond form does not contain any notice or filing requirements for an obligee that are conditions precedent to asserting a claim or filing suit against a performance bond. Payment bond claimants under a statutory bond are required to file a notice as a condition precedent to filing suit. *See e.g.*, N.J.S.A. 2A:44-145.

Private bonds will be construed according to the terms and conditions. To the extent a private bond contains conditions precedent or pre-filing requirements, those should be enforced.

***Case law rules concerning condition precedent notice*** – Not applicable.

## 6. Time for Suit

***Statutes of limitation particular to performance bonds and other applicable statutes of limitation***

Although the statute proscribes a one-year limitations period for payment bond claims, N.J.S.A. 2A:44-145 and 146, the New Jersey Bond Act does not contain a specific limitations period for claims against performance bond claims.

***Case law statements about enforceability of limitations contained in bonds***

**Public Bonds** – Under N.J.S.A. 2A:14-1.2, a public owner has 10 years to file a suit against a contractor on a public project. Consequently, in *Gloucester City Bd. of Educ. v. American Arbitration Association*, 333 N. J. Super. 511, 755 A.2d 1256, the court found that the 10-year limitations period for a public owner to assert a claim against a contractor is also applicable to claims against the contractor's performance bond. The court reasoned that because the statute places an unqualified obligation on the surety to guarantee its principal's performance, the limitations period applicable to claims against the principal should also apply to claims against the surety.

***Varying statutes of limitation by agreement in bond or contract***

**Private Bonds** – Under N.J.S.A. 2A: 14-1, the statute of limitations for contract actions in New Jersey is six years. However, parties are permitted to shorten the period by agreement. The shorter limitations period, however, must be "reasonable." *See Eagle Fire Protection Corp. v. First Indemnity of America Insurance Company*, 145 N.J. 345, 678 A.2d 699 (1996).

## 7. Procedures

***Statutory or procedural rules that may affect handling or administration of lawsuits***

There are no unique procedural rules applicable to lawsuits against performance bonds.

If a surety is sued on a performance bond, provided it meets the diversity requirement and is not subject to the Eleventh Amendment bar for suits against the state, under 28 U.S.C. 1441 *et seq.*, a surety can remove an action to federal court. Under *28 U.S.C.* 1446(b), it must be filed within 30 days after service of the summons.

***Venue requirements under jurisdictional limitations***

Venue for "actions brought by or against municipal corporations, public agencies or officials," shall be laid in the county in which the cause of action arose. New Jersey Court Rule 4:3-2(a)(2). This extends to the state and its agencies and officials. *Id.* at Comment 1.

***Court rules***

New Jersey Court Rule 4:6-1(a), requires that an answer be filed within 35 days after service of the summons and complaint. The time for service of a responsive pleading may be enlarged for a period not exceeding 60 days by the written consent of the parties, which shall be filed with the responsive pleading. Any additional extension is only permitted on notice by court order upon a showing of good cause. Rule 4:6-1(1)(c).

***Particular agency regulations/rules*** – Not applicable.

***Arbitration requirements and application***

Parties can only be compelled to arbitrate if they have agreed to this alternative form of dispute resolution. The courts determine whether a particular contract contains an arbitration clause. *Commerce Bank, N.A. v. DiMaria Constr., Inc.*, 300 N.J. Super. 9, 692 A.2d 54, (App. Div.), *certif. denied*, 151 N.J. 73, 697 A.2d 546 (1997).

Consequently, if a performance bond contains an arbitration clause, a surety can be compelled to submit disputes to arbitration because through the bond it agreed to arbitrate.

Many performance bonds, including the statutory bond form do not contain arbitration clause. Rather, many performance bonds, including the statutory form incorporate the terms of the underlying contract. The statutory bond in part states "which said contract is made a part of this bond the same as though set forth herein." N.J.S.A. 2A:44-147. The question this presents is whether a surety in New Jersey can be compelled to arbitrate with an obligee based on an arbitration agreement contained in a construction contract that is incorporated into the bond? In *Gloucester City Bd. of Educ. v. American Arbitration Association*, 333 N. J. Super. 511, 755 A.2d 1256, the New Jersey Appellate Division adopted the minority view and found that if a performance bond incorporates by reference a contract containing an arbitration clause, disputes regarding the principal's performance will be resolved through arbitration. Although the disputes regarding the principal's performance is subject to arbitration, any defenses the surety has to a claim against a performance bond are not subject to arbitration and may be decided by the court. New Jersey adopted the New York Court of Appeals reasoning in *Fidelity & Deposit Co. v. Parsons & Whittemore Contractors Corp.*, 48 N.Y.2d 127, 421 N.Y.S.2d 869, 397 N.E.2d 380 (1979).

This creates a two step process. In the first, issues regarding the principal's performance are settled through arbitration as required by the underlying construction contract. Then, if a claim is preserved against the surety, the surety has the right to litigate its personal defenses. In the second proceeding, the surety is not permitted to re-litigate issues of its principal's performance that were settled in the arbitration.

Although *Gloucester* presented the issue in the context of a public project, the same analysis should apply in the context of a private contract.

## 8. Attorney's Fees

***Statutes and/or case law limiting or permitting recovery of attorney's fees***

The New Jersey Bond Act form does not permit the recovery of attorney's fees. Moreover, New Jersey follows the American Rule that requires each side to bear the cost of litigation.

***What fees are recoverable, if any***

**New Jersey Court Rules** – The New Jersey Court Rules do, however, allow a very limited exception permitting the recovery of attorney's fees. Rule 4:42-9 permits the allowance of attorney's fees "in an action upon a liability or indemnity policy of insurance in favor of a successful claimant." Rule 4:42-9(a)(6). This does not apply to performance bonds.

**Applicable case law prohibiting recovery of attorney's fees in context of performance bond** – The New Jersey Supreme Court specifically addressed the applicability of this rule in the context of a surety bond. The Court found that a surety bond is materially different from an indemnity policy and does not fall within the exception. See *Eagle Fire Protection Corp. v. First Indemnity of America Ins. Co.*, 145 N.J. 345, 364-65, 678 A.2d 699 (1996). Therefore, a surety on a performance bond in New Jersey should not be exposed to the potential for any attorney's fees.

Although attorney's fees are not recoverable through a performance bond, in *The Matter of the Estate of Lash*, N.J. 20, 776 A.2d 765 (2001), the New Jersey Supreme Court found that the surety on an administrator's bond was responsible for attorney's fees incurred by the estate in proceeding to recover against the bond for the administrator's malfeasance. In reaching its conclusion, the majority distinguished the context of the administrator's bond from performance bonds. As a result, although on an administrator bond the surety faces exposure for attorney's fees, that should not extend to a performance bond surety.

**9. Special Provisions** – Not applicable.

**10. Remarks**

New Jersey does not have a well-developed body of case law regarding performance bonds. The *Gloucester City Bd. of Educ. v. American Arbitration Association*, 336 N.J. Super. 511, 755 A.2d 1256 decision is significant because of its holding that a declaration of default was not required as a precondition of a surety's liability.

**11. Case Annotations**

The significant New Jersey cases involving performance bonds have been noted above.

***Interpretation of AIA bond forms*** – Not applicable.

***Cases in which surety steps into shoes of obligee*** – Not applicable.

# NEW MEXICO

Ann M. Conway[1]

## 1. Requirement for Bond

The State of New Mexico has a "Little Miller Act." Some provisions of the act are consistent with the federal Miller Act, but there are important differences between the federal and state acts. Section 13-4-18 provides that when a construction contract is awarded in excess of $25,000 a performance and payment bond shall be delivered to the state agency or local public body in charge of the construction project.

***Statutory provisions for projects that are:***

**Public** – Section 13-4-18 requires contractors to obtain bonds for all public works construction contracts in excess of $25,000. Section 13-4-18(A) provides:

> When a construction contract is awarded in excess of $25,000 the following bonds or security shall be delivered to the State agency or local public body and shall be combining on the parties upon the execution of the contract. If a contractor fails to deliver the required performance and payment bonds, the contractor's bid shall be rejected, its bid security shall be enforced to the extent of actual damages ...

---

[1] Ann M. Conway is Counsel with the law firm of:
Miller Stratvert P.A.
Post Office Box 25687
Albuquerque, New Mexico 87125-0687
(505) 842-1950

> (1) a performance bond satisfactory to the state agency or local public body, executed by a surety company authorized to do business in this State and such surety to be approved in Federal Circular 570 as published by the United States Treasury Department or the State Board of Finance or the local governing authority, in an amount equal to 100 percent of the price specified in the contract; ...

**Private** – No statutes in New Mexico require performance bonds on private projects.

**Department of Transportation** – Section 13-4-18, *supra*, governs New Mexico DOT projects.

***Case law rules that might generally apply***

"Although the general rule is that the liability of a surety cannot be extended beyond the fair import of the undertaking in the bond, this rule has certain exceptions: (1) where bonds are given pursuant to a statute for a public or quasi public purpose; or (2) when by special provision of statute, the conditions and obligations prescribed in the statute requiring the bond must be read into the bond, whether contained therein or not and in such cases, the liability of the surety will be determined by the conditions and obligations prescribed by the statute, in the first instance, on principles of public policy, and the second, by force of statutory provision." *Employment Sec. Comm'n v. C.R. Davis Contracting Co.*, 81 N.M. 23, 462 P.2d 608 (1969).

## 2. Damages Covered

***Set forth in any statutes and/or case law***

Section 13-4-18(A)(1) provides that the performance bond must be executed in an amount equal to 100 percent of the price specified in the contract.

Section 48-2-17 provides that unpaid premiums or charges for the furnishing of workers' compensation insurance is defined to be material furnished to the contractor for use in the performance of the contract. In *State ex rel. Mountain States Mutual Casualty Co. v. KNC*, the New Mexico Supreme Court construed Section 48-2-17 to provide coverage to a workers' compensation carrier who insured subcontractors on two projects, where the performance bonds that were the subject of the lawsuit had been executed by the general contractor and not by either of the insured subcontractors. The subcontractors were required by the terms of the subcontracts to secure workers' compensation insurance but were not required to execute separate and distinct bonds. When the subcontractors defaulted on their insurance premiums, the insurer sued the general contractor and its surety to foreclose a claim of lien on the bonds executed by the general contractor. The court also ruled that the remedy provided under Section 48-2-17 is to be treated as a lien right governed by the requirements of the New Mexico Mechanics' and Materialmen's Lien Act, N.M. Stat. Ann., §§ 48-2-1 to 48-2-17.

***Obligations of surety to perform and/or pay***

"If the contractor fails to complete the job, the government can apply the retained funds and any remaining money to costs completing the job. The surety is liable under the performance bond for any damage incurred by the government in completing the job. On the other hand, the surety may undertake to complete the job itself. In so doing, it performs a benefit for the government, and has a right to the retained funds and remaining progress money to defray its costs." *Employment Security Commission v. Big 4 Paving, Inc.*, 81 N.M. 26, 462 P.2d 611 (1969)

***Whether failure to provide insurance transfers burden to surety*** – New Mexico statutes do not transfer the burden to the surety.

***Limitations on damages***

Generally, the damages covered are limited to amounts necessary to complete performance up to the penal limit of the performance bond. The surety completion options are not addressed by statute or case law and, therefore, should be governed by the terms of the applicable bond form.

***Whether obligee may set off bonded contract funds against other principal-obligee debts or obligations***

"The surety who undertakes to complete the project is entitled to the funds in the hands of the government not as a creditor and subject to setoff, but as a subrogee having the same rights to the funds as the government." *Employment Security Commission v. Big 4 Paving, Inc.*, 81 N.M. 26, 462 P.2d 611 (1969).

***Incorporation of specific contract terms by reference***

"In determining the surety's liability to third persons on a bond given for their benefit and to secure the faithful performance of a building contract, the contract and the bond are to be read together.... The obligation of the bond is to be read in the light of the contract it is given to secure, and ordinarily the extent of engagement entered into by the surety is to be measured by the terms of the principal's agreement." *Southwestern Sash & Door v. American Employers' Ins. Co.*, 37 N.M. 212, 20 P.2d 928 (1933).

### 3. Penal Sum Variations

**Limitations per statute** – New Mexico does not have statutory limitations on performance bond penal sums.

**Effect of changes in work upon penal sum, if at all** – New Mexico law does not address this issue. The penal sum of the bond should control.

***Statutory or case law protections or dangers to penal sum***

There are no New Mexico cases requiring a variation in the penal sum.

There are no New Mexico appellate cases addressing whether an obligee may sue a surety for bad faith or unfair insurance practices in New Mexico, which would allow damages in excess of the penal sum of the bond. There is a recent federal district court decision which holds that the New Mexico Unfair Insurance Practices Act does not apply to sureties. *Carnes/Melvin Blake Road Partnership v. The St. Paul Travelers Companies, Inc., et al.*, No. CIV 04792 (2005).

## 4. Parties Covered

### *Statutes and/or case law as to whether only obliges are covered*

"In determining the surety's liability to third persons on a bond given for their benefit and to secure the faithful performance of a building contract, the contract and the bond are to be read together.... The obligation of the bond is to be read in the light of the contract it is given to secure, and ordinarily the extent of engagement entered into by the surety is to be measured by the terms of the principal's agreement." *Southwestern Sash & Door v. American Employers' Ins. Co.*, 37 N.M. 212, 20 P.2d 928 (1933).

***Coverage for:***

**Third-party beneficiaries** – *See Southwestern Sash & Door*, discussed, *supra*.

**Assignees** – No data.

**Dual obligees** – No data.

## 5. Notice or Filing Required

**Statutory provisions** – New Mexico statutes do not provide for any unusual notice requirements for suit under a performance bond.

**Case law rules concerning condition precedent notice** – There are no case law rules concerning condition precedent notice for suit under a performance bond.

## 6. Time for Suit

**Statutes of limitation particular to performance bond or other applicable statutes of limitation** – NMSA § 37-1-3 provides for a six-year statute of limitation for causes of action founded upon a bond.

***Case law statements about enforceability of limitations contained in bonds***

"We recognized in *Jim* [*Jim v. CIT Financial Services Corp.*, 87 N.M. 362, 533 P.2d 751 (1975)] that parties may include a time to sue provision in a contract. In other words, parties can put their own statute of limitations period in a contract, and our courts will honor it. *See Electric Gin Co. v. Firemen's Fund Ins. Co.*, 39 N.M. 73, 39 P.2d 1024 (1935) (fire insurance policy contained a provision that a suit must be commenced within 12 months after loss, which this court upheld); *Turner v. New Brunswick Fire Ins. Co.*, 45 N.M. 126, 112 P.2d 511 (1941) (insurance policy provision stipulating a one-year limitation period is not void when it shortens a general six-year contract statute of limitations period); *Wiseman v. Arrow Freightways, Inc.*, 89 N.M. 392, 552 P.2d 1240 (Ct. App.), *cert. denied*, 90 N.M. 9, 558 P.2d 621 (1976) (trial court erred in failing to give effect to a time to sue provision found in an insurance policy). However, in *Sandoval v. Valdez*, 91 N.M. 705, 580 P.2d 131 (Ct. App. 1978), our court of appeals held that a one-year limitation period in an insurance contract was not controlling when it conflicted with New Mexico public policy set forth in our uninsured motorist statute." *Nez v. Forney*, 109 N.M. 161, 783 P.2d 471 (N.M. 1989).

***Varying statute of limitations by agreement in bond or contract*** – See above.

## 7. Procedure

***Statutory or procedural rules that my affect handling or administration of lawsuits***

Unless the contract provides for mandatory arbitration of disputes, New Mexico's Public Works Mediation Act requires the parties to a dispute to mediate before commencing litigation. N.M. Stat. Ann., §§ 13-4C-1 to 13-4C-11.

**Venue requirements and jurisdictional limitations** – New Mexico has no unusual venue requirements or jurisdictional limitations.

***Court rules*** – Not applicable.

***Particular agency regulations/rules*** – Not applicable.

**Arbitration requirements and application** – New Mexico has adopted the New Mexico Uniform Arbitration Act, which governs arbitration agreements. N.M. Stat. Ann., §§ 44-7A-1 to 44-7A-32.

## 8. Attorney's Fees

***Statutes and/or case law limiting or permitting recovery of attorney's fees.***

There are no statutory provisions or case law allowing attorney's fees in connection with the suit upon the bond. However, if the bonded contract allows for attorney's fees, it is arguable they would be covered under the bond.

The New Mexico appellate courts have not addressed the issue of whether a surety would be subject to a claim for common law bad faith or under the Unfair Insurance Practices Act. If the courts were to do so, then arguably attorney's fees could be recoverable as part of such a claim. However, there is a recent federal district court decision which holds that the New Mexico Unfair Insurance Practices Act does not apply to sureties. *Carnes/Melvin Blake Road Partnership v. The St. Paul Travelers Companies, Inc., et al.*, No. CIV 04792 (2005).

## 9. Special Provisions – Not applicable.

## 10. Remarks – Not applicable.

## 11. Case Annotations

**Interpretation of AIA bond forms** – New Mexico cases have not specifically addressed AIA forms of bonds.

***Cases in which surety steps into shoes of obligee***

"A surety that issues performance and payment bonds, and then satisfies the claims against the contractor by paying laborers and materialmen, has superior rights as against the contractor's secured creditors to final progress payments and retainage funds held by the project owner." *New Mexico State Highway & Transportation Dept. v. Gulf Insurance Co.*, 2000-NMCA-007, 128 N.M. 634, 996 P.2d 424.

# NEW YORK

Theodore M. Baum[1]

## 1. Requirement for Bond

***Statutory provisions for projects that are:***

**Public** – There are several New York statutes that require public performance bonds.

N.Y. State Fin. Law §§ 127(2) and 136 both include a general requirement for performance bonds on public projects in excess of $5,000; however, the statutes offer little in the way of details. The only specific requirement is that the bond be "sufficient," be in an amount specified in the contract, and be approved by the State Comptroller.

N.Y. Public Buildings Law § 20 excludes the performance bond requirement from contracts for "special orders," which are defined as minor work of less than $50,000 as determined by the commissioner of general services.

N.Y. Education Law § 376(8) permits the State University Construction Fund, the entity in charge of constructing buildings within the State University system, to dispense with the requirements for all bonding on projects less than $50,000 in value.

---

1 Theodore M. Baum is a member of:
Ernstrom & Dreste, LLP
180 Canal View Boulevard, Suite 600
Rochester, New York 14623
(585) 473-3100

Most statutes governing performance bonds in New York do not specifically dictate the amount of the bond, but performance bonds are typically issued in an amount equal to the initial contract price.

**Private** – No statutes in New York require performance bonds on private projects.

**Department of Transportation** – The New York Highway Law generally governs projects built under the auspices of the New York State Department of Transportation. However, many municipalities, public entities and authorities, such the New York State Thruway Authority, adopt the NYSDOT standard specifications for use on their projects, thus incorporating the Highway Law.

N.Y. Highway Law § 38(6) requires a performance bond in the form prescribed by the commissioner of transportation, but also requires that the commissioner may dispense with the requirement of a bond upon a written request submitted by the contractor. As noted above, although most statutes governing performance bonds in New York do not specifically dictate the amount of the bond, Highway Law § 193, relating to town highways, requires that a performance bond be not less than one-half of the contract amount.

***Case law rules that might generally apply*** – See cases cited in sections below.

## 2. Damages Covered

***Set forth in any statutes and/or case law***

N.Y. General Obligations Law § 7-301 expressly limits the surety's liability to the penal sum of bond *if* the surety elects payment. However, interest may be recovered on a bond claim in New York (*see* Penal Sum Variations below).

N.Y. Highway Law § 38(6). The State Highway Law, relating to state road projects such as those constructed by the NYSDOT, requires that a performance bond protect the owner from any "direct or indirect damage."

### *Obligations of surety to perform and/or pay*

N.Y. General Obligations Law § 7-301 provides in part that "[W]hen any undertaking executed within or without the state specifies that it is to be void upon payment of an amount or performance of an act, the undertaking shall be deemed to contain a covenant either to pay the amount or to perform the act specified." This provides statutory authority to the surety the option of tendering the appropriate sum in lieu of performance.

Where the performance bond obligates the surety to complete the project upon default, the failure to do so makes the surety liable not only for the costs to complete, but also for the damages caused to the obligee by virtue of the surety's refusal to perform, to the limit of the penal sum. *Hunt v. Bankers & Shippers Ins. Co. of New York,* 73 A.D.2d 797, 423 N.Y.S.2d 718 (4th Dep't 1979).

### *Whether failure to provide insurance transfers burden to surety*

Statutes do not transfer the burden to surety. While some cases hold that a contractor which fails to provide insurance as required by the contract will be liable for the damages to so provide, no cases have extended that theory of liability to a surety.

### *Limitations on damages*

As a general rule, a surety is chargeable only according to the strict terms of its undertaking and its obligations cannot be extended either by implication or construction beyond the confines of its contract. *Davis Acoustical Corp. v. Hanover Ins. Co*., 22 A.D.2d 843, 254 N.Y.S.2d 14 (3rd Dep't 1964); *See also MacKennan v. American Casualty Co. of Reading, Pennsylvania*, 169 A.D. 2d 709, 564 N.Y.S.2d 462 (2nd Dep't 1991); *Venus Mechanical, Inc. v. Insurance Company of North America*, 245 A.D.2d 559, 667 N.Y.S.2d 60 (2nd Dep't 1997); *Hall & Co., Inc. v. Continental Casualty Co.*, 34 A.D.2d 1028, 310 N.Y.S.2d 950 (3rd Dep't 1970).

The correct measure of a surety's liability on a performance bond is "the difference between the contract price and what it would cost the plaintiff to complete the contract." *Juell v. New Amsterdam Casualty Co.,* 223 A.D. 612, 229 N.Y.S. 190 (1st Dep't 1928).

Where a performance bond is unambiguous, the surety's obligation is construed *strictissimi juris* in the surety's favor, and its liability cannot be extended beyond the plain terms of the bond. *Mendel-Mesick-Cohen Architects v. Peerless Ins. Co.*, 74 A.D.2d 712, 426 N.Y.S.2d 124 (1st Dep't 1980).

A performance bond is not an instrument of forfeiture without regard to the principal's performance, but requires the obligee to establish the default of the principal before collecting on the bond. *General Authority for Supply Commodities v. Ins. Co. of N. America,* 951 F. Supp. 1097 (S.D. N.Y. 1997).

A contract of surety shall not be construed to have retroactive operation unless express words or necessary implication dictate such effect. *Crisafulli Bros., Inc. v. Clanton,* 128 A.D.2d 963, 512 N.Y.S.2d 927 (3rd Dep't 1987).

***Whether obligee may set off bonded contract funds against other principal-obligee debts or obligations***

There are no New York statutes which specifically address this issue. However, as a result of N.Y. Lien Law Article 3-A, § 70 *et seq.*, New York's construction trust fund statute, New York's highest court held that the various state agencies are not permitted to off-set obligations owed by the principal on unrelated projects, only for project specific obligations. *RLI Insurance Co. v. N.Y.S. Dep't of Labor,* 97 N.Y.2d 256, 740 N.Y.S.2d 272 (N.Y. 2002).

A completing surety's rights to contract funds are superior to the principal's rights in the same funds, and therefore to creditors of the principal claiming an interest in such funds. *U.S. Fidelity & Guaranty Co. v. Triborough Bridge Authority*, 297 N.Y. 31, 74 N.E.2d 226 (N.Y. 1947).

***Incorporation of specific contract terms by reference***

In general, "the surety bond attaches to the principal contract and must be construed with it," *Carrols Equities Corp. v. Villnave,* 57 A.D.2d 1044, 1045, 395 N.Y.S.2d 800 (4th Dep't 1977), *app. denied,* 42 N.Y.2d 810, 399 N.Y.S.2d 1026, 369 N.E.2d 775 (1977).

General rules of New York contract construction provide that a general incorporation of reference provision means that the referenced contract is only incorporated with respect to "the scope, quality, character and manner of the work to be performed." *Bussanich v. 310 East 55th Street Tenants,* 282 A.D.2d 243, 244, 723 N.Y.S.2d 444, 445 (1st Dep't 2001), citing *S. Leo Harmonay Inc. v. Binks Mfg. Co.,* 597 F. Supp. 1014, 1023-24, *aff'd,* 762 F.2d 990 (citing *Guerini Stone Co. v. P.J. Carlin Constr. Co.,* 240 U.S. 264, 277; *U.S. Steel Corp. v. Turner Constr. Co.,* 560 F. Supp. 871).

### 3. Penal Sum Variations

#### *Limitations per statute*

Pursuant to N.Y. General Obligations Law § 7-301, the total amount for which the surety may be liable "shall not exceed" the penal sum, "except that" interest shall be awarded from the time of the surety's default. One court has interpreted the accrual of the surety's time of default as the date upon which the surety actually received notice of the principal's default. *Town of Clarkstown v. North River Ins. Co.,* 803 F. Supp. 827 (S.D. N.Y. 1992). In light of New York's statutory interest rate of 9 percent for breach of contract actions, this can be a significant factor in determining liability.

#### *Effect of changes in work upon penal sum, if at all*

As a general rule, any material or substantial alteration of the terms of a contract, for whose performance a surety is bound, when made without the surety's consent, releases the surety from his or her obligations. *Midland Steel Warehouse Corp., v. Godinger Silver Art Ltd.,* 276 A.D.2d 341, 714 N.Y.S.2d 466 (1st Dep't 2000).

#### *Statutory or case law protections or dangers to penal sum*

Although a surety's liability is generally defined by its bond and by the obligations of its principal, a surety may take on greater collateral responsibility than its principal assumed. *See, e.g., Jones v. Gelles,* 167 A.D.2d 636, 562 N.Y.S.2d 992 (3rd Dep't 1990); *American Trading Co. v. Fish,* 42 N.Y.2d 20, 364 N.E.2d 1309, 396 N.Y.S.2d 617 (N.Y. 1977).

## 4. Parties Covered

### *Statutes and/or case law as to whether only obligees are covered*

There are no statutes which define who may be an obligee under a performance bond, and so ordinary rules of contract construction apply. Generally, the case law demonstrates that only the named obligee is a proper claimant, barring a dual obligee rider or other writing establishing the right of another party.

### *Coverage for:*

**Third-party beneficiaries** – "[W]hether a contractor's bond, be it a performance bond or a payment bond, or both, is intended to grant a third party the right to sue upon it depends upon whether it manifests a clear intent to grant that right to the third party." *Novak & Co., Inc. v. The Travelers Indemnity Co.,* 56 A.D.2d 418, 392 N.Y.S.2d 901 (2nd Dep't 1977) (holding that a co-prime contractor on multiple prime project was not a third-party beneficiary eligible to make a claim on another prime contractor's bond). *To same effect: Anron Heating & Air Conditioning, Inc. v. City of New York, et al.*, Supreme Court, N.Y. County 605981/97, unreported decision dated November, 1998).

"Because there is no evidence of intent to benefit third parties, the appellant, as an unpaid subcontractor, has no right to recover from the [performance] bond proceeds as an intended third-party beneficiary." *Town of Southeast v. Seaboard Surety Company,* 208 A.D.2d 520, 616 N.Y.S.2d 812 (2nd Dep't 1994).

**Assignees** – In an unreported case interpreting language similar to AIA A312:

> "The performance bond contains no provision prohibiting its assignment. The right of action upon the performance bond, however, by its terms, is enforceable only by [the obligee] or its 'heirs, executors, administrators, or successors'. The performance bond, thus, while assignable, may not be enforced by the assignee, as the right of enforcement is clearly restricted." *In re DAK Electric Contracting Corp. (New York City School Construction Authority)*, Supreme Court, Queens County (Lonschein, J.), January 12, 1995 NYLJ, p. 32, col. 6.

**Dual obligees** – A dual obligee is entitled to the same rights as its co-dual obligee, but the surety's total liability remains limited by the penal sum of the bond. *Fidelity New York, FSB v. Aetna Ins. Co.,* 234 A.D.2d 261, 651 N.Y.S.2d 58 (2nd Dep't 1996) (fact that there were dual obligees did not permit double recovery on bond).

## 5. Notice or Filing Required

### *Statutory provisions*

New York statutes do not provide for any unusual notice requirements for suit under a performance bond.

### *Case law rules concerning condition precedent notice*

Case law in New York State and federal courts applying New York law is well-developed with respect to the requirement of condition precedent notice. Generally, the case law requires strict compliance with notice provisions contained in all contracts, including performance bonds. Again, no statutory notice requirements apply. However, some recent case law holds that where a performance bond such as the AIA A311 does not expressly provide for notice to the surety, no such notice is required prior to the owner taking steps to cure a default. *Walter Concrete Construction Corp. v. Lederle Laboratories,* 99 N.Y.2d 603, 788 N.E.2d 609, 758 N.Y.S.2d 260 (2003). However, the decision in this case does not necessarily square with the concept of a notice and opportunity to cure or other decisions. *See, e.g., Town of Clarkstown v. North River Ins. Co.,* 803 F. Supp. 827 (S.D. N.Y. 1992), holding that "Notice provisions are ordinarily incorporated into insurance instruments, but even where they are not, the law will imply an obligation that the obligee notify the insurer of an occurrence or claim within a reasonable time." (analyzing accrual of performance bond surety's obligation).

Court summarily dismissed surety's defense of the owner's default in complying with provisions concerning "notice, default and/or termination" by neglecting to identify any specific procedure required by the performance bond as required by New York strict pleading requirements for a condition precedent. *1199 Housing Corp. v.*

*International Fidelity Company*, 14 A.D.3d 383, 788 N.Y.S.2d 88 (1st Dep't 2005).

### 6. Time for Suit

***Statutes of limitation particular to performance bonds and other applicable statutes of limitation***

N.Y. Civ. Prac. L&R § 213(2). For statute of limitations purposes, among other purposes, New York courts analyze surety bonds as contracts, and absent any contrary agreement, a cause of action for breach of contract carries a six year statute of limitations.

N.Y. Civ. Prac. L&R § 201. Under New York law, parties may, prior to any dispute arising, prescribe by written agreement a shorter period of limitations than that allowed by law. Therefore, New York courts will uphold a shortened statute of limitations contained in a performance bond, so long as the shortened period is reasonable (as little as six months has been deemed reasonable). The typical limitations of actions period in a performance bond is two years, but accrual of that period may vary. If the performance bond contains no provision for limitations of actions, then the six-year statute of limitations for breach of contract claims pursuant to § 213(2) will apply.

***Case law statements about enforceability of limitations contained in bonds***

A provision in a performance bond to shorten the limitations of actions period provided by statute is permitted by New York public policy. *Yeshiva University v. Fidelity and Deposit Co. of Maryland,* 116 A.D.2d 49, 500 N.Y.S.2d 241 (1st Dep't 1986).

### 7. Procedure

***Statutory or procedural rules that may affect handling or administration of lawsuits***

There are no special court rules which affect venue or procedure for surety disputes in New York state courts, with the exception that some counties, including the counties of New York (New York City), Erie

(City of Buffalo) and Monroe (City of Rochester), have established commercial divisions, to which most surety performance bond disputes will be assigned. The Commercial Divisions have some court rules which apply to the cases handled by those courts, usually with regard to discovery.

***Venue requirements and jurisdictional limitations***

As for claims against surety bonds, none other than ordinary rules of procedure for contract actions. *See* below concerning affirmative claims asserted by sureties.

***Court rules***

No special rules apply to claims against sureties.

Sureties pursuing affirmative claims against public entities should also be aware that in addition to the sometimes Byzantine contractual notice provisions applicable to claims against the owner in which are typical New York public contracts, special notice, statutory notice provisions and venue provisions may apply to breach of contract claims asserted against the State of New York (N.Y. Court of Claims Act), Public Authorities (N.Y. Authorities Law § 1744); School Districts (N.Y. Education Law § 3813), Towns (N.Y. Town Law), Villages (N.Y. Village Law).

***Particular agency regulations/rules*** – Not applicable (except as noted above).

***Arbitration requirements and application***

While a surety will be bound by a substantive determination arising from an arbitration result between principal and obligee, the surety is not obligated to directly arbitrate the obligee's claim, notwithstanding general incorporation by reference provisions, and the surety remains free to litigate its surety specific defenses in court. *Fid. & Deposit Co. of Maryland v. Parsons & Whittemore Contractors Corp.,* 48 N.Y.2d 127, 397 N.E.2d 380, 421 N.Y.S.2d 869 (N.Y. 1979).

Where surety in takeover agreement agreed "to procure the performance of all work remaining to be completed *in accordance with all the terms and conditions of the original contract*" (emphasis added by court), disputes over the adequacy of the surety's performance were subject to arbitration. *In re Arbitration between International Fid. Ins. Co. v. Saratoga Springs Public Library,* 236 A.D.2d 719, 653 N.Y.S.2d 729 (3rd Dep't 1997); however, a general incorporation by reference provision may *not* be sufficient to incorporate dispute resolution procedures, because a party's agreement to arbitrate must be "clear, explicit and unequivocal." *General Railway Signal Corp. v. L.K. Comstock & Co., Inc.,* 254 A.D.2d 759, 678 N.Y.S.2d 208 (4th Dep't 1998).

Performance surety entitled to invoke arbitration clause in underlying agreement against obligee by virtue of incorporation by reference provisions. *See, Choctaw Generation Ltd. Partnership v. American Home Assurance Co.,* 271 F.3d 403 (2d Cir. 2001).

Where a claimant takes a judgment by default against the principal in litigation, however, such default is not binding on the surety in subsequent litigation on the bond. See *S.D.I Corporation v. Fireman's Fund Insurance Companies,* 208 A.D.2d 706, 617 N.Y.S.2d 790 (2nd Dep't 1994) and *Shapiro v. Marstone Distributors, Inc.,* 38 A.D.2d 604, 328 N.Y.S.2d 592 (2nd Dep't 1971).

## 8. Attorney's Fees

***Statutes and/or case law limiting or permitting recovery of attorney's fees***

Generally, New York State case law provides that attorney's fees are not recoverable unless provided by statute, court rule or by contract. Although New York's "Little Miller" Act for payment bonds, N.Y. State Finance Law § 137 provides that a court may award attorney's fees in connection with a payment bond claim where the claim is "without substance in law or in fact," no similar provision exists for performance bond claims. Where a bond does not contain a provision for attorney's fees, such fees are generally not recoverable.

***What fees are recoverable, if any***

Where a bond expressly provides for the recovery of attorney's fees incurred by the obligee, such as the AIA A312, it has been held that this language was intended to reimburse the obligee for the legal fees required to re-procure the work, *not* the fees incurred by the obligee to litigate the surety's liability under the performance bond. *USF&G v. Braspetro Oil Services Co.,* 369 F.3d 34 (2d Cir. 2004).

## 9. Special Provisions

Where performance bonds are required, N.Y. General Municipal Law § 106-b, relating to construction by municipalities, limits the owner to 5 percent retention. However, where the requirement of a bond is excused, retainage of up to 10 percent may be withheld by the owner. Similarly, the Highway Law permits up to 20 percent to be retained where the performance bond requirement has been dispensed with.

## 10. Remarks

Under New York case law, sureties can lose the protection of bond penal sum and other limitations on liability if the surety undertakes completion without any kind of agreement limiting penal sum, or because the terms of a completion contract supplant the terms of the bond itself.

## 11. Case Annotations

### *Interpretation of AIA bond forms*

Under A311 Performance Bond, unlike A312, the surety's liability is not tied to a notice of default, and the surety is liable to the obligees for the cost to complete, even if the surety could have reduced such costs if given notice and an opportunity to mitigate such costs. *Walter Concrete Construction Corp. v. Lederle Laboratories,* 99 N.Y.2d 603, 788 N.E.2d 609, 758 N.Y.S.2d 260 (2003).

Under A312 Performance Bond, unlike A311, the obligee's declaration of default was required as a condition precedent to the surety's liability, and the obligee's failure to declare such a default was fatal to its performance bond claim. *120 Greenwich Development Associates, LLC v. Reliance Insurance Co.*, 2004 WL 1277998 (S.D. N.Y. June 8, 2004) (not reported in F. Supp.); to same effect: *USF&G v. Braspetro Oil Services Co.*, 369 F.3d 34 (2d Cir. 2004).

Under A311 Performance Bond, principal's default and obligee's unequivocal declaration of default were conditions precedent to surety's liability on performance bond claim, and numerous letters sent by the obligee to the surety were insufficient to constitute such declaration of default. *Elm Haven Construction Limited Partnership v. Neri Construction LLC,* 376 F.3d 96 (2d Cir. 2004) (applying Connecticut law).

Under A312 Performance Bond, surety was not liable to obligee for attorney's fees incurred by obligee in litigating against surety for claim on performance bond, only for such fees as were incurred in "remedying" the default. *USF&G v. Braspetro Oil Services Co.,* 369 F.3d 34 (2d Cir. 2004).

Obligee's failure to provide condition precedent notice of default to surety and principal precluded claim on performance bond. *153 Hudson Development, LLC v. DiNunno,* 8 A.D.3d 77, 778 N.Y.S.2d 482 (1st Dep't 2004).

***Cases in which surety steps into shoes of obligee***

"Plaintiff [surety] succeeded under principles of subrogation to all rights which defendant Authority might have against the contractor, including that of withholding money due the contractor and of applying it to the payment of unsatisfied claims for labor and materials furnished." *U.S. Fidelity & Guaranty Co. v. Triborough Bridge Authority*, 297 N.Y. 31, 74 N.E.2d 226 (N.Y. 1947); *see also Titan Indemnity Co. v. Triborough Bridge & Tunnel Authority, Inc.,* 135 F.3d 831 (2d Cir. 1998) (applying New York law).

A surety's right of subrogation, which attaches at the time the bond is issued, entitles the surety to a priority recovery in all additional collateral held by creditor. *Chemical Bank v. Meltzer,* 93 N.Y.2d 296, 712 N.E.2d 656, 690 N.Y.S.2d 489 (1999).

A completing surety steps into the shoes of the state as obligee where the contractor principal forfeits its rights in the contract upon default. *Firemen's Ins. Co. v. State of New York,* 91 Misc. 2d 183 (Ct. Claims 1977), *aff'd,* 65 A.D.2d 241 (3rd Dep't 1979). *See also, Scarsdale Nat. Bank & Trust Co. v. United States Fidelity & Guaranty Co.,* 264 N.Y. 159 (N.Y. 1934).

A completing surety is subrogated not only to the rights of the obligee, but may also be subrogated to any claims which the defaulting principal might have against its subcontractors whose wrongful conduct allegedly was a cause of the default. *Menorah Nursing Home, Inc., v. Zukov*, 153 A.D.2d 13, 548 N.Y.S.2d 702 (2nd Dep't 1989).

# NORTH CAROLINA

William H. Sturges and Daniel R. Hansen[1]

## 1. Requirement for Bond

***Statutory provisions for projects that are:***

**Public** – The Model Payment and Performance Bond Act is codified at N.C. Gen. Stat. § 44A-25 *et. seq*. (the "Little Miller Act"). In addition, there are numerous provisions concerning public contracts at N.C. General Statutes § 143-128 *et. seq*.

N.C. Gen. Stat. § 44A-26 requires that in a contract with any department, agency, or political subdivision of the State of North Carolina for the performance of any one project where the total cumulative amount of construction contracts is in excess of $300,000 a contractor who has a contract over $50,000 must provide a performance bond in the amount of his contract.

N.C. Gen. Stat. § 44A-33 states that a performance bond form shall comply with the Little Miller Act, by including the date the bond is executed, the names of the principal, surety, and contracting body, an appropriate place for execution by the surety and principal, the amount of

---

1 William H. Sturges and Daniel R. Hansen are partners in the law firm of:
Shumaker, Loop & Kendrick, LLP
128 South Tryon Street, Suite 1800
Charlotte, North Carolina 28202
(704) 375-0057
They were assisted in this paper by Patricia Wilson Magee of the firm.

the bond, and the contract number, and by specifically reciting certain conditions and provisions as follows:

> KNOW ALL MEN BY THESE PRESENTS, That we, the PRINCIPAL AND SURETY above named, are held and firmly bound unto the above named Contracting Body, hereinafter called the Contracting Body, in the penal sum of the amount stated above for the payment of which sum well and truly to be made, we bind ourselves, our heirs, executors, administrators, and successors, jointly and severally, firmly by these presents.
>
> THE CONDITION OF THIS OBLIGATION IS SUCH, that whereas the Principal entered into a certain contract with the Contracting Body, numbered as shown above and hereto attached;
>
> NOW THEREFORE, if the Principal shall well and truly perform and fulfill all the undertakings, covenants, terms, conditions, and agreements of said contract during the original term of said contract and any extensions thereof that may be granted by the Contracting Body, with or without notice to the Surety, and during the life of any guaranty required under the contract, and shall also well and truly perform and fulfill all the undertakings, covenants, terms, conditions, and agreements of any and all duly authorized modifications of said contract that may hereafter be made, notice of which modifications to the Surety being hereby waived, then, this obligation to be void; otherwise to remain in full force and virtue.
>
> IN WITNESS WHEREOF, the above-bounden parties have executed this instrument under their several seals on the date indicated above, the name and corporate seal of each corporate party being hereto affixed and these presents duly signed by its undersigned representative, pursuant to authority of its governing body.

N.C. Gen. Stat. § 143-129 sets forth the procedure for letting of public contracts. Under subsection (c), the statute provides:

> All contracts to which this section applies shall be executed in writing. The board or governing body shall require the person to whom the award of a contract for construction or repair work is made to furnish a bond as required by Article 3 of Chapter 44A; or require a deposit of money, certified check or government securities for the full amount of said contract to secure the faithful performance of the terms of said contract and the payment of all sums due for labor and materials in a manner consistent with Article 3 of Chapter 44A; and the contract shall not be altered except by written agreement of the contractor and

> the board or governing body. The surety bond or deposit required herein shall be deposited with the board or governing body for which the work is to be performed. When a deposit, other than a surety bond, is made with the board or governing body, the board or governing body assumes all the liabilities, obligations and duties of a surety as provided in Article 3 of Chapter 44A to the extent of said deposit.
>
> The owning agency or the Department of Administration, in contracts involving a State agency, and the owning agency or the governing board, in contracts involving a political subdivision of the State, may reject the bonds of any surety company against which there is pending any unsettled claim or complaint made by a State agency or the owning agency or governing board of any political subdivision of the State arising out of any contract under which State funds, in contracts with the State, or funds of political subdivisions of the State, in contracts with such political subdivision, were expended, provided such claim or complaint has been pending more than 180 days.

N.C. Gen. Stat. § 58-31-66 provides that neither the state nor any county, city, or other political subdivision of the state, or any officer, employee, or other person acting on behalf of any such entity shall, with respect to any public building or construction contract, require any contractor, bidder, or proposal to procure a bid bond, payment bond, or performance bond from a particular surety, agent, producer, or broker.

N.C. Gen. Stat. § 143B-472.92 provides that the North Carolina Small Business Contractor Authority may execute and perform performance bonds for the benefit of an applicant in connection with a contract, of which the majority of the funding is provided by a government agency or a combination of government agencies. (Note: this provision expires June 30, 2006).

**Private** – No statutes in North Carolina require performance bonds on private projects. Further, a performance bond on a non-public project would not be controlled by the Model Payment and Performance Bond Act. *See* N.C. Gen. Stat. § 44A-25(3) (defining "construction contract" under the statute as only those contracts for public buildings, public works, or public improvements, including highways).

**Department of Transportation** – Not applicable.

***Case law rules that might generally apply***

The provisions of the Model Payment and Performance Bond Act are presumed conclusively to have been written into every performance bond for a public project for the general or prime contractor, whether or not the bond was drawn in accordance with the statutes. N.C. Gen Stat. § 44A-30(b). *Mason C. Day Excavating, Inc. v. Crowder Constr. Co.*, 676 F. Supp. 670, 674 (W.D. N.C. 1987); *see also Pyco Supply Co. v. American Centennial Ins. Co.*, 321 N.C. 435, 364 S.E.2d 380 (1988).

The performance bond must be construed together with the contract, for the performance of which the bond was given:

> The liability of the surety does not rest solely upon the terms of its bond. It grows out of and is dependent upon the terms of the contract executed by its principal. If there has been no default by the principal, there can be no enforceable debt against the surety. The obligation of the bond is to be read in the light of the contract it is given to secure.

*Builders Corp. v. Casualty Co.,* 236 N.C. 513, 515, 73 S.E.2d 155, 156 (1952) (citations omitted); *see also Foundry Co. v. Construction Co.*, 198 N.C. 177, 151 S.E. 93 (1930) (applying rule to bond on private construction project).

## 2. Damages Covered

***Set forth in any statutes and/or case law***

**Prompt Payment** – Should the performance-bond surety take over a project for the general contractor, the surety should be aware of certain prompt payment statutes that might subject the surety to liability. When a subcontractor has performed its contractual obligations, the subcontractor is entitled to be paid within seven days of receipt by the general contractor (or surety if the surety has taken over the job) of any periodic or final payments from the project owner. N.C. Gen. Stat. § 22C-3. Should the general contractor (or surety if the surety has taken over the job) fail to promptly make payment within seven days, the subcontractor is entitled to recover interest "at the rate of one percent (1 percent) per month or a fraction thereof on such unpaid balance as may be due." N.C. Gen. Stat. § 22C-5. If the bonded project is a public project "let by a board or governing body of the State government or any political subdivision thereof," then the same interest charge applies for payments to subcontractors that are more than seven days late. *See* N.C. Gen. Stat. § 143-134.1 (tracking language of section 22C-5 and applying the same rule to state public projects).

**Pay-When-Paid Clauses** – On all contracts for construction, pay-when-paid clauses are generally unenforceable in North Carolina by statute. N.C. Gen. Stat. § 22C-2. Thus, a clause in a contractor-subcontractor contract stating that the contractor need not pay his subcontractor for satisfactory work until the contractor gets paid by the owner, is not enforceable. There are exceptions, however, to the pay-when-paid prohibition. A contractor may still refuse to pay the subcontractor for:

> "unsatisfactory job progress; defective construction not remedied; disputed work; third party claims filed or reasonable evidence that claim will be filed; failure of subcontractor to make timely payments for labor, equipment, and materials; damage to contractor or another subcontractor; reasonable evidence that subcontract cannot be completed for the unpaid balance of the subcontract sum; or a reasonable amount for retainage not to exceed the initial percentage retained by the owner." N.C. Gen. Stat. § 22C-4.

**Attorney's Fees** – On bonded public projects governed by North Carolina's "Little Miller Act[2]," attorney's fees may be awarded in the judge's discretion to the "prevailing party" upon a finding by the judge that the losing party unreasonably refused to fully resolve the matter. N.C. Gen. Stat. § 44A-35. The attorney's fees statute explains that the "prevailing party" is the one "who obtains a judgment of at least 50 percent of the monetary amount sought in a claim or is a party defendant or third party defendant against whom a claim is asserted which results in a judgment of less than 50 percent of the amount sought in the claim defended." If a Rule 68 Offer of Judgment was served in the case, the plaintiff must obtain a verdict (or the defendant receive a verdict less than) the amount stated in the Offer of Judgment to "prevail" for purposes of section 44A-35.[3] *Id.* Note, however, that the above attorney's fees statute will normally not apply to bonds given by subcontractors on

---

2 N.C. Gen. Stat. §§ 44A-25 *et seq.*

3 *See also* "Limitations on Damages" *infra.*

public jobs. The Little Miller Act generally applies only to bonds given by prime contractors for the benefit of the public owner/obligee. If the prime contractor requires a performance bond from its subcontractor for the benefit of the prime contractor (i.e., the prime contractor would be the bond obligee), then the Little Miller Act would not cover the prime contractor/subcontractor bond. The reason is that the subcontractor's bond retains its status as a private, as opposed to a "public" or Little Miller Act, bond, unless the subcontractor's bond expressly incorporates the Little Miller Act. *See* 3 Philip L. Bruner & Patrick J. O'Connor, Jr., *Bruner & O'Connor on Construction Law* § 8:156 (2003) (explaining the difference between private or "common law" bonds and statutory bonds). Thus, a claimant seeking attorney's fees under a private, subcontractor's bond or other private bond would have only common law remedies. *See Stillwell Enterprises, Inc. v. Interstate Equip. Co.*, 300 N.C. 286, 266 S.E.2d 812 (1980) (explaining that bond claimants on private bonds can recover attorney's fees only if: (1) there is statutory authority for such recovery [and in construction cases, there usually is not]; and (2) the parties have contractually agreed to pay attorney's fees).

**Interest** – The accrual of pre-judgment interest in North Carolina is governed by statute. *Farmah v. Farmah*, 348 N.C. 586, 500 S.E.2d 662 (1998). For all bonds and contracts, interest begins to accrue "from the time they [the bonds and contracts] become due ...." N.C. Gen. Stat. § 24-3. By statute, a party becomes obligated to pay interest on a contract from the date of the party's breach. N.C. Gen. Stat. § 24-5. But the statute specifically excludes "penal bonds" from the general rule that interest begins to run on the date of contract breach. The statute states that:

> "In an action for breach of contract, except an action on a penal bond, the amount awarded on the contract bears interest from the date of breach." Thus, a surety can become liable for pre-judgment interest only when the surety becomes obligated to pay the claim.

No reported North Carolina case expressly states when pre-judgment interest begins to accrue against the surety on a performance bond claim. But based on the interest statutes cited above and various other authorities, it appears that at the earliest, interest begins to run when the surety first receives notice of a liquidated claim. However, an unliquidated claim does not begin to accrue interest until after the claim has been judicially ascertained, *i.e.*, made "liquidated." *Tilghman v. Proctor*, 125 U.S. 136, 8 S. Ct. 894, 31 L. Ed. 664 (1888). The U.S. Supreme Court and other federal courts have held that pre-judgment interest does not accrue against the surety until it has received notice of the principal's breach. *United States v. U.S. Fid. & Guar. Co.*, 236 U.S. 512 (1915); *New Amsterdam Cas. Co. v. United States Shipping Bd. Emer. Fleet Corp.*, 16 F.2d 847, 853 (4th Cir. 1927); *see also* 12 AM. JUR. 2D *Bonds* § 48; 74 AM. JUR. 2D *Suretyship* § 137; 25 *Williston on Contracts* § 66:114 (4th ed.) (all explaining the general rule that the surety cannot be liable for interest before notice of the claim to the surety, regardless of when the principal became liable for the claimant's claim). These authorities are consistent with North Carolina law, which holds in non-surety contexts that interest on an account does not begin to run until there is a proper demand to pay. *Hunt v. Hunt*, 261 N.C. 437, 135 S.E.2d 195 (1964) (explaining that if there is no proper demand to pay, then interest does not begin to run until suit is filed for recovery of damages).

The pre-judgment amount awarded against the surety, however, may not exceed the penal sum of the bond. *Lee v. Martin*, 188 N.C. 119, 123 S.E. 631 (1924) (explaining that the surety's liability for the combined amount of principal and interest cannot exceed the penal sum of the bond). The *Lee* court made clear, however, that once judgment has been entered against the surety, the unpaid judgment accrues interest at the legal rate, and the surety may not use the penal sum of the bond as a defense to paying post-judgment interest. *Id.*

Post-judgment interest is collectible against sureties, regardless of the penal sum of the bond. Should the surety be found liable under its bond, the claimant may recover post-judgment interest at the legal rate of eight percent[4] "from the date of entry of judgment ... until the judgment is satisfied."

***Obligations of surety to perform and/or pay***

The obligation of the surety under a performance bond is determined by the bond and the contract that the bond secures. *Realty Co. v. Batson*, 256 N.C. 298, 123 S.E.2d 744 (1962); *see also Builders Corp. v.*

---

[4] N.C. Gen. Stat. § 24-1.

*Casualty Co.* 236 N.C. 513, 515, 73 S.E.2d 155, 156 (1952); *Blue Cross & Blue Shield v. Odell Assoc., Inc.*, 61 N.C. App. 350, 364, 301 S.E.2d 459, 467 ("The liability of a surety is measured in terms of the principal's agreement."), *disc. rev. denied*, 309 N.C. 319, 306 S.E.2d 791 (1983). It stands to reason, then, that sureties and principals are co-obligors to the obligee (usually the project owner), and a written acknowledgment or payment by one co-obligor is binding on the other. *Pickett v. Rigsbee*, 252 N.C. 200, 113 S.E.2d 323 (1960).

**Actual Damages** – If the surety breaches its performance bond obligations, the surety is liable for actual damages. Actual damages are the reasonable cost of labor and materials necessary to bring the project into conformity with the contract specifications. *Robbins v. Trading Post, Inc.*, 251 N.C. 663, 111 S.E.2d 884 (1960). An alternative measure of actual damages is the difference in value between the project as contracted and the project as built by the general contractor/principal. *Patrick v. Mitchell*, 44 N.C. App. 357, 260 S.E.2d 809 (1979). The difference-in-value measure of actual damages is usually limited, however, to cases where construction defects could not be remedied without substantially deconstructing or destroying the project. *Id.*

**Consequential Damages** – Consequential and special damages are often used interchangeably by North Carolina courts. Normally, consequential damages are not recoverable unless the party claiming them can show that the breaching party knew that consequential damages might result and the breaching party agreed to undertake responsibility for them. Generally, to recover consequential damages, the claiming party must prove two elements: (1) the party must show it suffered special damages that were within the parties' contemplation at contract formation; and (2) the party must show the amount of its special damages to a reasonably certain degree. *Nello L. Teer Co. v. Dickerson, Inc.*, 257 N.C. 522, 126 S.E.2d 500 (1962). In order to show that the parties specifically contemplated special damages, the claiming party must show: (a) that the parties were aware of special circumstances or conditions that would give rise to special damages; and (b) the special damages were reasonably foreseeable. *Troitino v. Goodman*, 255 N.C. 406, 35 S.E.2d 277 (1945). The language of the bond will provide some evidence of what the parties contemplated. A broadly worded performance bond may subject the surety to liability for certain kinds of consequential damages. *See Donlan v. American Bonding & Trust Co.*, 139 N.C. 212, 51 S.E. 924 (1905) (holding surety liable for lost rents); *Knutton v. Cofield*, 273 N.C. 355, 362-63,160 S.E.2d 29, 34 (1968) (explaining when a party may be liable for liquidated damages); *United States v. Phoenix Indem. Co.*, 231 F.2d 573, 575 (4th Cir. 1956) (applying North Carolina law and holding surety liable for a variety of employment related taxes).

**Liquidated Damages** – A contract that provides for liquidated damages is generally enforceable in North Carolina, provided the liquidated damages do not constitute a penalty. *Bradshaw v. Millikin*, 173 N.C. 432, 92 S.E. 161 (1917). The particular case facts determine whether a liquidated damages clause is a penalty. *Ledbetter Bros., Inc. v. North Carolina Dept. of Trans.*, 68 N.C. App. 97, 314 S.E.2d 761 (1984). If the contract amount of liquidated damages is "reasonably proportionate" to the actual damages the party suffered, and the damages that the party might suffer are difficult to estimate at the time of contracting, then the clause is not a penalty. *Id.* (quoting *Knutton v. Cofield*, 273 N.C. 355, 361, 160 S.E.2d 29, 34 (1968)). A penalty will be found only where the stipulated amount of liquidated damages is so disproportionate as to "shock the judicial conscience." *Ledbetter Bros.*, 68 N.C. App. at 107, 314 S.E.2d at 768.

***Whether failure to provide insurance transfers burden to surety***

If the surety's principal is negligent and there is no liability insurance coverage, the surety may be liable to the obligee/project owner for the principal's negligence. *Haywood County Consol. School Dist. v. U.S.F. & G.*, 43 N.C. App. 71, 73, 257 S.E.2d 670 (1979). The *Haywood County* court explained that the "Contractor's liability is the measure of defendant's [surety's] liability. As Contractor is liable for damages resulting from his negligent performance of the work, so is defendant [surety]." *Id.* (citation omitted).

***Limitations on damages***

*Generally* – In most cases, the surety's liability is limited to the penal sum of the bond. *State v. U.S. Guarantee Co.*, 207 N.C. 725, 178 S.E. 550 (1935). The surety is liable only if its principal is in default and is also liable. *RGK, Inc. v. U.S.F.&G*, 292 N.C. 668, 235 S.E.2d 234 (1977). In accordance with the general rule that sureties are liable for only actual damages (unless the conditions for consequential liability can be proven), a surety's liability "'will be construed to cover all losses, damages, and liabilities which reasonably appear to have been within contemplation of the parties, but it cannot be extended to cover any losses which are neither expressly within its terms nor of such character that it can reasonably be inferred that they were intended to be within the contract.'" *Triplett v. James*, 45 N.C. App. 96, 262 S.E.2d 374, 375 (quoting *Dixie Container Corp. v. Dale*, 273 N.C. 624, 627, 160 S.E.2d 708 (1968)), *cert. denied*, 300 N.C. 202, 269 S.E.2d 621 (1980).

**Attorney's fees in bond** – As stated earlier, in public projects governed by the "Little Miller Act," the court may award attorney's fees to the prevailing party. Recall, however, as stated earlier in Section 2, that attorney's fees are collectible only if there is statutory authority and a contractual agreement to pay such fees. In public bond cases involving a performance bond given by the prime contractor to the public owner/obligee, the Little Miller Act provides the statutory and contractual authority for attorney's fees.[5] However, private bonds must have some other statutory authority (besides the Little Miller Act) that allows attorney's fees. A contractual agreement to pay attorney's fees that is expressly included in a performance bond is not sufficient. There are no other statutes besides the Little Miller Act that address attorney's fees in bonds. The general statute allowing for attorney's fees in contracts that are "evidence of indebtedness" has been narrowly construed to allow attorney's fees only for certain debt instruments, and not all contracts generally. *See* N.C. Gen. Stat. § 6-21.2 and *Lee Cycle Center, Inc. v. Wilson Cycle Center, Inc.*, 143 N.C. App. 1, 545 S.E.2d 745, *aff'd per curiam*, 556 S.E.2d 293 (2001).

**Bad faith/treble damages** – North Carolina law does not allow recoveries against sureties for bad faith or for treble damages under North Carolina's Unfair and Deceptive Trade Practices Act, N.C. Gen. Stat. §§ 75-1.1 *et seq.* Furthermore, the case law specifically holds that a surety cannot be liable for treble damages assessed against the principal.

---

5 Remember, under N.C. Gen. Stat. § 44A-30(b), the terms of the Little Miller Act are deemed written into the performance bond.

*Tomlinson v. Camel City Motors, Inc.*, 330 N.C. 76, 408 S.E.2d 853 (1991) (explaining that to hold otherwise would contradict the deterrent effect intended by the legislature in creating the unfair trade act). Also, there are no authorities that allow a bad faith or treble damage recovery against a surety for the surety's own alleged misconduct. The authorities that address tort recovery against sureties tend to suggest that bad faith and unfair trade recoveries would not be allowed against sureties. *See, e.g., Angelo v. Property Devel. Corp.*, 63 N.C. App. 569, 306 S.E.2d 162 (1983) (explaining the differences between suretyship and insurance and holding that North Carolina insurance statutes do not control sureties); *Cincinnati Ins. Co. v. Centech Bldg. Corp.*, 286 F. Supp. 2d 669 (M.D. N.C. 2003) (relying on *Angelo* and holding that the obligee's claims against the surety for bad faith and unfair trade practices would not be allowed under North Carolina law); *Wilson v. Wilson*, 121 N.C. App. 662, 468 S.E.2d 495 (1996) (holding in the liability insurance context that the injured party may not bring a tort claim directly against the tort-feasor's insurance carrier because such a claim would put the insurer in an irreconcilable conflict with its insured).

**Punitive Damages** – Punitive damages are generally not recoverable against sureties. The same reasoning that prevents bad faith claims against sureties also militates against recovering punitive damages from sureties. Moreover, the surety's liability is contractual, and North Carolina does not permit recovery of punitive damages for breach of contract. *Shore v. Farmer*, 351 N.C. 166, 170, 522 S.E.2d 73, 76 (1999).

**Delay Damages** – Delay damages are usually recoverable if the damages are costs resulting directly from delays caused by the defendant and there is no clause in the defendant's contract relieving it of damages for delay. *See generally Biemann & Rowell Co. v. Donohoe Cos., Inc.*, 147 N.C. App. 239, 556 S.E.2d 1 (2001) (discussing delay damages generally and their enforceability); *Metric Constructors v. Hawker, Siddeley, Power Eng'g.*, 121 N.C. App. 530, 468 S.E.2d 435 (1996). Contracts that contain a "no damages for delay" clause that exempts the owner from paying for owner-caused delays are generally enforceable in North Carolina. *APAC-Carolina, Inc. v. Greensboro-High Point Airport Auth.*, 110 N.C. App. 664, 431 S.E.2d 508, *disc. rev. denied*, 335 N.C. 171, 438 S.E.2d 197 (1993). But there is a statutory exemption to the rule that "no damages for delay" clauses are generally enforceable. On state public projects, such clauses are prohibited by statute for delays caused *solely* by the owner or its agent. *See* N.C. Gen. Stat. § 143-134.3.

***Whether obligee may set off bonded contract funds against other principal-obligee debts or obligations***

The answer to this question requires an analysis of subrogation law and set-off law.

There is little recent North Carolina case law discussing subrogation as it relates to suretyship. However, older cases concerning promissory notes and deeds of trust have established that the doctrine of "[s]ubrogation is of equitable origin, not dependent on contract, and is always invoked to prevent injustice." *Moring v. Privott*, 146 N.C. 558, 564, 60 S.E. 509, 511 (1908). The doctrine of subrogation was summarized in *Liverman v. Cahoon*, 156 N.C. 187, 193-94, 72 S.E. 327, 330 (1911) as follows:

> It is a doctrine primarily of equity jurisprudence ... [I]t is a substitution of one person in the place of another, whether as a creditor or as the possessor of any other rightful claim. The substitute is put in all respects in the place of the party to whose rights he is subrogated.... It is broad enough to include every instance in which one party pays a debt for which another is primarily answerable, and which, in equity and good conscience, should have been discharged by the latter.

The scope of subrogation is broad. As stated in *Exxon Chemical Americas, Div. of Exxon Chemical Co. v. Kennedy*, 59 N.C. App. 90, 93, 295 S.E.2d 770, 771-72 (1982) (quoting *Peebles v. Gay,* 115 N.C. 38, 40, 20 S.E. 173, 174 (1894)); "[u]pon general principles of equity a surety, paying the debt of his principal, is entitled to be substituted to all the rights of the creditor." *See also Brown v. Harding,* 170 N.C. 253, 268, 86 S.E. 1010, 1017 (1915) ("a party secondarily liable, but who has paid the debt, [is entitled] to reap the benefit of any securities or remedies which the creditors may hold as against the principal debtor and by the use of which the party paying may thus be made whole."), *reh'g denied*, 171 N.C. 686, 89 S.E. 222 (1916).

The Fourth Circuit Court of Appeals has discussed subrogation rights of a performance bond surety in connection with contracts between a contractor and the State Highway Commission of North Carolina. In

*Hartford Accident & Indem. Co. v. Coggin*, 78 F.2d 471, 477-78 (4th Cir. 1935), the court stated:

> The obligee, upon default, is of course entitled to apply all unpaid moneys towards the performance of the contract, and it necessarily follows that when the surety performs the contract, he is subrogated to the rights of the obligee, and is entitled to the moneys unpaid so far as necessary to reimburse him for his loss.

*See also Lacy v. Maryland Cas. Co.*, 32 F.2d 48 (4th Cir. 1929).

North Carolina subrogation case law suggests that it will not permit the obligee to set-off other obligations of the principal against the subrogated party.

There is recent North Carolina case law discussing the right of set-off, but not in the surety context. The North Carolina Supreme Court has stated the right of set-off "may be invoked only where there is mutuality of parties and of demands." *In Re: Battery King Mfg. Co.*, 240 N.C. 586, 589, 83 S.E.2d 490, 492 (1954). Further, as stated in *In Re Bank of Sampson*, 205 N.C. 333, 335, 171 S.E. 436, 437 (1933), mutuality is essential to set-off and:

> "Such right of set-off only exists between the same parties and in the same right." *Adams v. Bank*, 113 N.C. 332, 18 S.E. 513. "Where the debts are not due to and from the same persons in the same capacity the right of set-off does not exist." 7 C.J., 745.

In regard to mutuality of the parties, the debts must be due to and from the same persons in the same capacity. Thus, the debt of a partnership could not be set off against the bank accounts of individual partners. *In Re Bank of Sampson*, 205 N.C. 333, 171 S.E. 436. The North Carolina courts have also denied set-off claims between the same parties where the claims grew out of separate transactions. In *Townsend v. Bentley*, 57 N.C. App. 581, 292 S.E.2d 19 (1982), plaintiffs sued defendants on a promissory note and defendants attempted to set off the amount due by their claim against plaintiffs for work unperformed on a home sold by the plaintiffs to the defendants. The court stated:

> We do not believe the defendants are entitled to set off their claim against the plaintiffs in this action. The claims of the parties against

each other grew out of separate transactions. *Id.* at 583, 292 S.E.2d at 20.

Although there is no North Carolina case law directly on point, it is likely that an obligee may not set off bonded contract funds against other principal-obligee obligations in light of case authority on subrogation and set-off law.

***Incorporation of specific contract terms by reference***

N.C. Gen. Stat. § 44A-33 sets forth the required conditions and provisions to be included in all bonds for a public project and specifically states, "THE CONDITION OF THIS OBLIGATION IS SUCH, that whereas the Principal entered into a certain contract with the Contracting Body, numbered as shown above and *hereto attached* ...." (emphasis added). As such provision is required under N.C. Gen. Stat. § 44A-33, performance bonds for public projects generally refer to the entire contract, but may not specifically mention or incorporate by reference the specific terms of the contract. It is unclear whether the "hereto attached" language is sufficient to incorporate the underlying contract by reference. However, in *Burgess v. Jim Walter Homes*, 161 N.C. App. 488, 491, 588 S.E.2d 575, 578 (2003) (citations and quotations omitted), the court considered such language in reference to an arbitration agreement that was mentioned, but not attached, to a contract. The *Burgess* court held that a contract stating "attached hereto and incorporated by reference" is insufficient to incorporate the document by reference unless the document is actually attached to the contract. *Id.* at 491-92, 588 S.E.2d at 578. Although *Burgess* did not involve a performance bond, its holding may be applicable to disputes regarding whether specific terms of the underlying contract are incorporated by reference where the performance bond attempts to incorporate such terms by reference to an "attached" document.

Where the terms of the bond incorporate the construction contract, the contract provisions are to be considered "in any question of construction of any ambiguous language in the condition of the bond itself." *RGK, Inc. v. United States Fidelity & Guaranty Co.*, 292 N.C. 668, 679, 235 S.E.2d 234, 241 (1977) (noting the contract between the prime contractor and project owner, principal and obligee, respectively, must be consulted to determine whether the work done and materials furnished by the subcontractor were done and furnished for use in the performance of that contract and are, therefore, within the coverage of the bond).

### 3. Penal Sum Variations

***Limitations per statute*** – There are no statutory limitations on performance bond penal sums.

***Effect of changes in work upon penal sum, if at all*** – There is no case law interpreting the effect upon the penal sum of changes in the work.

***Statutory or case law protections or dangers to penal sum***

Although there is a statute limiting payment bond liability to the penal sum (N.C. Gen. Stat. § 44A-29), there is no corresponding statute for performance bonds. There are no cases specifically setting forth protections or dangers to the penal sum in performance bonds. Courts may, however, apply general surety law to limit the amount of recovery to the bond penal sum. In *Lee v. Martin*, 188 N.C. 119, 122, 123 S.E. 631, 633 (1924), a case involving an official bond, the supreme court noted the general rule in most jurisdictions:

> [A]lthough the penalty of the bond fixes the limit of liability of the surety at the time liability arises thereunder, yet, if the principal or surety fail to discharge that liability when it matures, interest may be allowed on the amount from the time the liability accrues, even if the amount of recovery exceed the penalty named in the bond. As against the sureties, however, interest is allowed only from the date of notice to them of the breach, or from the date of a demand on them to make good such breach. (Internal citation omitted).

The court did not adopt the general rule, and in regard to the penal sum on bond claims in North Carolina, the court held:

> [T]he surety's liability may not exceed the penalty of the bond until judgment has been rendered against the surety. Interest may then be collected on said judgment without regard to the limit of liability named in the bond, because the nature of the demand is altered by the

judgment, and under the statute such judgment would bear interest at the rate of 6 percent [former legal rate] per annum until paid. *Id.* at 123, 123 S.E.2d at 633; *see also State v. U.S. Guarantee Co.*, 207 N.C. 725, 178 S.E. 550 (1935) (involving depository bond).

This holding was followed in *Robinson Mfg. Co. v. Blaylock*, 192 N.C. 407, 416, 135 S.E. 136, 140 (1926), a case involving a "bond given for their benefit and to secure the faithful performance of a building contract." In *Robinson*, the court held, "The surety is also allowed, by paying into court in such suit the full amount of the penalty of the bond, to be relieved from any other or further liability thereon." *Id.* at 410, 135 S.E. at 137-38 (citing *Electric Co. v. Deposit Co.*, 191 N.C. 653, 132 S.E. 808 (1926) (noting application of rule to surety on a performance bond)).

## 4. Parties Covered

***Statutes and/or case law as to whether only obligees are covered***

In public projects governed by North Carolina's "Little Miller Act," the performance bond is a contract solely between the governing body (who is the project owner and obligee) and the general or prime contractor. N.C. Gen. Stat. § 44A-26(a)(1) (stating that a performance bond under the act "shall be solely for the protection of the contract body [public owner] which awarded the contract").

***Coverage for:***

**Third-party beneficiaries** – North Carolina courts have interpreted the Little Miller Act to mean that subcontractors and suppliers are not third-party beneficiaries of the performance bond. *Bolton Corp. v. State*, 95 N.C. App. 596, 383 S.E.2d 671 (1989), *disc. rev. denied*, 326 N.C. 47, 389 S.E.2d 85 (1990). The rule is the same for co-prime contractors on multi-prime public projects: the co-primes are not third-party beneficiaries under one another's performance bonds. *Id.*; *see also Bolton Corp. v. The United Pacific Ins. Co.*, No. 89-1773, 1990 WL 76518 (4th Cir., May 25, 1990) and *Hartford Fire Ins. Co. v. Hayes & Lunsford Elec. Contractors*, No. 94-2559, 1995 WL 419982 (4th Cir., July 14, 1995) (both federal courts came to the same conclusion as the

North Carolina Court of Appeals in *Bolton Corp. v. State* and barred recovery to a co-prime contractor).

**Assignees** – No North Carolina cases directly address the right of an obligee's assignee to enforce the obligee's rights against the performance bond surety. Generally, however, North Carolina law allows parties to assign their rights, and the assignee is entitled to enforce such rights against the obligor. *See, e.g.*, *Kraft Foodservice v. Hardee*, 340 N.C. 344, 348, 457 S.E.2d 596, 598 (1995); *Gillespie v. De Witt*, 53 N.C. App. 252, 262, 280 S.E.2d 736, 743, *cert. denied*, 304 N.C. 390, 285 S.E.2d 832 (1981). The cited cases, however, do not concern performance bonds. But, as noted earlier in Section 4, performance bonds are generally considered to be contracts solely for the benefit of the obligee. Indeed, on public projects covered by the Little Miller Act, this "exclusivity of benefit" is statutory. Other jurisdictions that have addressed the issue have held that the obligee's assignee could *not* enforce claims against the surety, because the bond stated it was solely for the obligee's benefit. Had the surety intended to benefit assignees as well, the bond would have stated that it was issued for the obligee and "its successors and assigns." *See Citibank v. Grupo Cupex, Inc.*, 2004 WL 1921825 (1st Cir., 2004).

**Dual obligees** – No North Carolina cases specifically state that each dual obligee has a right to recover on a performance bond if there is a breach. The cases imply, however, that dual obligees have such rights. In *Fitts ex rel. Slade v. Green*, 14 N.C. 291 (1831), the court found that only one party could prove that he was an obligee under the bond and, therefore, only that party could recover. If the bond had been more specific about the identity of other obligees, each of them would likely have had a right under the bond. Similarly, in *T.A. Loving Co. v. Latham*, 20 N.C. App. 318, 201 S.E.2d 516 (1974), the general contractor sued all three co-obligees under a performance bond, which the court referred to as a "dual-obligee bond." The co-obligees were the joint owners of the construction project and their lender. All of the co-obligees also filed counterclaims against the general contractor and its surety. Although the court did not specifically address whether co-obligees enjoyed the same rights under the bond, the case could not have proceeded unless such was the case.

## 5. Notice or Filing Required

***Statutory provisions*** – There are no statutory provisions concerning notice.

***Case law rules concerning condition precedent notice***

Generally, the law regarding conditions precedent in North Carolina is well-settled:

> The provisions of a contract will not be construed as conditions precedent in the absence of language plainly requiring such construction. The weight of authority is to the effect that the use of such words as 'when,' 'after,' 'as soon as,' and the like, gives clear indication that a promise is not to be performed except upon the happening of a stated event.

*In re Foreclosure of Goforth Properties, Inc.*, 334 N.C. 369, 375-76, 432 S.E.2d 855, 859 (1993) (internal citations and quotations omitted).

A basic condition precedent to performance bond claims is a default by the principal. *Builders Corp. v. Casualty Co.*, 236 N.C. 513, 515, 73 S.E.2d 155, 156 (1952). In the case of *RGK, Inc. v. U.S. Fidelity & Guaranty Co.,* 292 N.C. 668, 235 S.E.2d 234 (1977), the supreme court elaborated and narrowed the condition precedent requirement as set forth in the *Builders Corp.* case. In *Builders Corp*., the plaintiff, in the complaint, had not alleged a default and a right to recover from the defendant surety. The court held this supported the trial court's dismissal of the complaint against the surety. The *RGK* court, however, refused to dismiss a complaint with a similar pleading deficiency where "there was default by the principal of the bond ... upon the contract which the bond was given to secure. This is clearly alleged in the complaint and the bond sued upon, and the contract secured thereby, are sufficiently alleged, as to their legal effect, in the complaint." 292 N.C. at 686, 235 S.E.2d at 245.

In regards to the notice requirement after default, the Federal Court for the Middle District of North Carolina has applied state law to resolve the issue of whether a surety must be provided notice and an opportunity to perform on the bond prior to the obligee making a claim on the bond. *MCI Constructors, Inc. v. Hazen & Sawyer*, 310 F. Supp. 2d 754, 762n.7

(M.D. N.C., 2004), *aff'd in part, rev'd in part on other grounds*, 125 Fed. Appx. 471 (4th Cir. 2005). In *MCI*, the court stated:

> While acknowledging that the duty of a surety in a performance bond is to insure performance, not merely payment, it is equally true that the beneficiary of a performance bond is the obligee of the bond, ... and not ... the surety. N.C. Gen. Stat. § 44A-26 (2003) ("[The performance bond] shall be solely for the protection of the contracting body that is constructing the project.").... Therefore, [the surety's] assertion that it was deprived of the opportunity to perform by completing the project on its own is not supported by the plain language of the statutory bond requirement. In addition, the contract clearly states that the [obligee] has the right to complete the work itself.

In a case involving the notice requirement in an insurance policy, the North Carolina Supreme Court has held:

> [Where a] policy makes the giving of notice a condition precedent, the party seeking to enforce the contract has, under general common law contract principles, the burden of pleading and proving strict compliance. Since notice was given eight months after the accident and plaintiff presented no evidence to justify or explain the delay, notice was not given "as soon as practicable" as a matter of law....

*Great American Ins. Co. v. C. G. Tate Constr. Co.*, 303 N.C. 387, 391, 279 S.E.2d 769, 772 (1981).

## 6. Time for Suit

***Statutes of limitation particular to performance bonds and other applicable statutes of limitation***

The Model Payment and Performance Bond Act, or "Little Miller Act", (N.C.G.S. § 44A-25 *et seq.*) does not set forth a time limitation for performance bond claims. Therefore, the time limitation for legal action is governed by the statute of limitations for contract actions, which is three years. *See* N.C.G.S. § 1-52. Although most performance bonds are under seal, and there is a 10-year statute of limitations for documents under seal, North Carolina will likely still apply the three year statute of limitations. *Blue Cross & Blue Shield v. Odell Associates, Inc.*, 61 N.C. App. 350, 362, 301 S.E.2d 459, 465 ("routine use of a corporate seal is merely to demonstrate authority to execute a document, the mere presence of a corporate seal, without more, does not convert the document into a specialty"), *disc. rev. denied*, 309 N.C. 319, 306 S.E.2d 791 (1983); *see also Chappell v. National Surety Co.*, 191 N.C. 703, 708, 133 S.E. 21, 23 (1926) (discussing applicability of three year statute of limitations and inapplicability of 10-year statute of limitations in action to enforce the bond against a surety).

***Case law statements about enforceability of limitations contained in bonds***

Time limitations contained in the performance bond are enforceable. *See Town of Pineville v. Atkinson/Dyer/Watson Architects, P.A.*, 114 N.C. App. 497, 442 S.E.2d 73 (1994).

In *Fayetteville Investors v. Commercial Builders*, 936 F.2d 1462 (4th Cir. 1991), the court enforced the time limitation set forth in the AIA Performance Bond that required an action on the bond to be filed "within two years after Contractor Default *or* within two years after the Contractor ceased working...." *Id.* at 1464. The court held the plaintiff timely brought a claim against the contractor where a subcontractor of the contractor performed work on the project within two years of suit being filed. *Id.*

***Varying statutes of limitation by agreement in bond or contract***

Since there is no claim limitation period in the Model Payment and Performance Bond Act, the parties can agree upon a shorter statute of limitations for bringing claims. See *Town of Pineville v. Atkinson/Dyer/Watson Architects, P.A.*, 114 N.C. App. 497, 442 S.E.2d 73 (1994).

## 7. Procedure

***Statutory or procedural rules that may affect handling or administration of lawsuits***

North Carolina has no statutory or procedural rules specifically governing lawsuits involving performance bonds; however, the general rules contained within the North Carolina Rules of Civil Procedure are applicable.

N.C. Gen. Stat. § 1A-1, Rule 12(a) allows a defendant 30 days to file an answer after service of the summons and complaint.

Under N.C. Gen. Stat. § 1A-1, Rule 38(b), a party is entitled to demand trial by jury but must do so in writing within 10 days after the service of the last pleading.

***Venue requirements and jurisdictional limitations***

North Carolina has no specific statutes regarding venue and jurisdictional limitations for performance bond lawsuits. The general rules governing venue and jurisdiction are applicable.

Where there is no specific statute addressing venue for a cause of action, N.C. Gen. Stat. § 1-82 provides the general rule regarding the proper venue:

> In all other cases the action must be tried in the county in which the plaintiffs or the defendants, or any of them, reside at its commencement, or if none of the defendants reside in the State, then in the county in which the plaintiffs, or any of them, reside; and if none of the parties reside in the State, then the action may be tried in any county which the plaintiff designates in his summons and complaint, subject to the power of the court to change the place of trial, in the cases provided by statute; provided that any person who has resided on or been stationed in a United States army, navy, marine corps, coast guard or air force installation or reservation within this State for a period of one year or more next preceding the institution of an action shall be deemed a resident of the county within which such installation or reservation, or part thereof, is situated and of any county adjacent to such county where such person stationed at such installation or reservation lives in such adjacent county, for the purposes of this section....

When determining the proper venue to sue or be sued by a domestic corporation, limited partnership, limited liability company, or registered limited liability partnership, N.C. Gen. Stat. § 1-79(a) sets forth the considerations for determining the "residence" of said entity as follows:

> (1) Where the registered or principal office of the corporation, limited partnership, limited liability company, or registered limited liability partnership is located, or
> (2) Where the corporation, limited partnership, limited liability company, or registered limited liability partnership maintains a place of business, or
> (3) If no registered or principal office is in existence, and no place of business is currently maintained or can reasonably be found, the term "residence" shall include any place where the corporation, limited partnership, limited liability company, or registered limited liability partnership is regularly engaged in carrying on business.

N.C. Gen. Stat. § 1-80 provides the proper venue for actions against foreign corporations:

> An action against a corporation created by or under the law of any other state or government may be brought in the appropriate trial court division of any county in which the cause of action arose, or in which the corporation usually did business, or has property, or in which the plaintiffs, or either of them, reside, in the following cases:
> (1) By a resident of this State, for any cause of action.
> (2) By a nonresident of this State in any county where he or they are regularly engaged in carrying on business.
> (3) By a plaintiff, not a resident of this State, when the cause of action arose or the subject of the action is situated in this State.

In actions asserted by a foreign corporation, the other venue statutes, including the general rule set forth in N.C. Gen. Stat. § 1-82, apply. *See* N.C. Gen. Stat. §§ 1-76 *et. seq.*

N.C. Gen. Stat. § 1-75.4, North Carolina's "Long-Arm Statute" provides the general rules for determining whether a court in this state has jurisdiction:

> A court of this State having jurisdiction of the subject matter has jurisdiction over a person served in an action pursuant to Rule 4(j),

Rule 4(j1), or Rule 4(j3) of the Rules of Civil Procedure under any of the following circumstances:

(1) Local Presence or Status. – In any action, whether the claim arises within or without this State, in which a claim is asserted against a party who when service of process is made upon such party:
   a. Is a natural person present within this State; or
   b. Is a natural person domiciled within this State; or
   c. Is a domestic corporation; or
   d. Is engaged in substantial activity within this State, whether such activity is wholly interstate, intrastate, or otherwise.

(2) Special Jurisdiction Statutes. – In any action which may be brought under statutes of this State that specifically confer grounds for personal jurisdiction.

(3) Local Act or Omission. – In any action claiming injury to person or property or for wrongful death within or without this State arising out of an act or omission within this State by the defendant.

(4) Local Injury; Foreign Act. – In any action for wrongful death occurring within this State or in any action claiming injury to person or property within this State arising out of an act or omission outside this State by the defendant, provided in addition that at or about the time of the injury either:
   a. Solicitation or services activities were carried on within this State by or on behalf of the defendant;
   b. Products, materials or thing processed, serviced or manufactured by the defendant were used or consumed, within this State in the ordinary course of trade; or
   c. Unsolicited bulk commercial electronic mail was sent into or within this State by the defendant using a computer, computer network, or the computer services of an electronic mail service provider in contravention of the authority granted by or in violation of the policies set by the electronic mail service provider. Transmission of commercial electronic mail from an organization to its members shall not be deemed to be unsolicited bulk commercial electronic mail.

(5) Local Services, Goods or Contracts. – In any action which:
   a. Arises out of a promise, made anywhere to the plaintiff or to some third party for the plaintiff's benefit, by the defendant to perform services within this State or to pay for services to be performed in this State by the plaintiff; or
   b. Arises out of services actually performed for the plaintiff by the defendant within this State, or services actually performed for the defendant by the plaintiff within this State if such

performance within this State was authorized or ratified by the defendant; or

c. Arises out of a promise, made anywhere to the plaintiff or to some third party for the plaintiff's benefit, by the defendant to deliver or receive within this State, or to ship from this State goods, documents of title, or other things of value; or

d. Relates to goods, documents of title, or other things of value shipped from this State by the plaintiff to the defendant on his order or direction; or

e. Relates to goods, documents of title, or other things of value actually received by the plaintiff in this State from the defendant through a carrier without regard to where delivery to the carrier occurred.

***Court rules*** – Some North Carolina Judicial Districts have their own local procedure rules.

***Particular agency regulations/rules***

Although not containing any provisions specifically applicable to performance bonds, the North Carolina Administrative Procedure Act, N.C. Gen. Stat. § 150B-1 *et. seq.*, ("NCAPA") establishes a uniform system of administrative rule making and adjudicatory procedures for state agencies.

***Arbitration requirements and application***

North Carolina has enacted the Uniform Arbitration Act, N.C. Gen. Stat. § 1-569.1 *et. seq.*, which requires that arbitration agreements be in writing. The act does not require the agreement to arbitrate be signed by the parties. Written arbitration agreements can bind the state, its agencies, and its political divisions.

N.C. Gen. Stat. § 1-569.6 provides the requirements and procedure for determining the validity of an arbitration agreement:

(a) An agreement contained in a record to submit to arbitration any existing or subsequent controversy arising between the parties to the agreement is valid, enforceable, and irrevocable except upon a ground that exists at law or in equity for revoking a contract.

(b) The court shall decide whether an agreement to arbitrate exists or a controversy is subject to an agreement to arbitrate.
(c) An arbitrator shall decide whether a condition precedent to arbitrability has been fulfilled and whether a contract containing a valid agreement to arbitrate is enforceable.
(d) If a party to a judicial proceeding challenges the existence of, or claims that a controversy is not subject to, an agreement to arbitrate, the arbitration proceeding may continue pending final resolution of the issue by the court, unless the court otherwise orders.

A surety is generally bound by an arbitration award between the obligee and the principal if the surety contract considered or incorporated by reference: (1) the agreement to arbitrate; and (2) the obligation ordered by the arbitration award. *George v. Hartford Acc. and Indem. Co.,* 102 N.C. App. 761, 404 S.E.2d 1, *aff'd as modified*, 330 N.C. 755, 412 S.E.2d 43 (1991).

In the context of public construction contracts, the North Carolina Court of Appeals has upheld the arbitration requirement provided for in the standard AIA construction contract. *Carteret County v. United Contractors*, 120 N.C. App. 336, 342, 462 S.E.2d 816, 820 (1995) ("It is reasonable to expect that a building contractor and a body politic frequently involved in capital construction know the contents of a standard AIA construction contract.... The arbitration provision is valid and enforceable by the defendant [contractor].").

The arbitration award must also be consistent with the contract between the principal and the contractor. *J. M. Owen Bldg. Contractors, Inc. v. College Walk, Ltd.*, 101 N.C. App. 483, 488, 400 S.E.2d 468, 471 (1991). Although *College Walk* involved a payment bond, it is instructive as to arbitration agreements involving sureties. "An [arbitration] award is conclusive on matters of law and fact if decided in accordance with the legal construction of the contract in which the arbitrators derive their authority." *Id.* Under *College Walk*, the surety is not obligated beyond what was contemplated under the contract between the principal and the contractor.

For arbitrator's authority to award attorney's fees, see Section 8, *infra*.

## 8. Attorney's Fees

***Statutes and/or case law limiting or permitting recovery of attorney's fees***

In North Carolina, attorney's fees are not recoverable unless there is a specific statute allowing their recovery. *Lee Cycle Center, Inc. v. Wilson Cycle Center, Inc.*, 143 N.C. App. 1, 11-12, 545 S.E.2d 745, 752, *aff'd*, 354 N.C. 565, 556 S.E.2d 293 (2001). As stated above in Section 2, attorney's fees can be recovered against the surety if: (1) there is statutory authority for them and the bond specifically allows them; or (2) the claimant in a Little Miller Act action is the prevailing party and the judge awards such fees in his discretion. The performance bond surety may recover attorney's fees from its principal for the attorney's fees incurred in defending claims under the bond. *Maryland Cas. Co. v. Teer*, 214 N.C. 29, 197 S.E. 558 (1938).

If the parties are involved in arbitration, then attorney's fees may be awarded by the arbitrator only if the parties' arbitration agreement expressly gives the arbitrator such authority. North Carolina's Revised Uniform Arbitration Act ("Revised Act") provides, "An arbitrator may award reasonable attorney's fees if: (1) The arbitration agreement provides for an award of attorney's fees; and (2) an award of attorney's fees is authorized by law in a civil action involving the same claim." N.C. Gen. Stat. § 1-569.21. The Revised Act, however, applies only to arbitration agreements entered into on or after January 1, 2004. For arbitration agreements predating January 1, 2004, the common law applied this same standard for an arbitrator to award attorney's fees, notwithstanding the fact the Revised Act had not yet been adopted. *See J.M. Owen Bldg. Contractors v. College Walk*, 101 N.C. App. 483, 400 S.E.2d 468 (1991).

## 9. Special Provisions – Not applicable.

## 10. Remarks

North Carolina courts have addressed overpayment by the obligee as a defense to performance bond claims. In *Crouse v. Stanley*, 199 N.C. 186, 154 S.E. 40 (1930), the court stated that a contractor's [obligee] failure to preserve and hold the retained percentage does not release a surety from any and all obligations on a performance bond, but equitable principles dictate that the surety is discharged and relieved to the extent of the loss actually suffered by the surety, which can be equal to the amount that should have been retained by the contractor [obligee]. *See also Fidelity & Deposit Co. v. Board of Education*, 202 N.C. 354, 162 S.E. 763 (1932). In other words, "[T]he surety is held entitled to a credit to the extent the owner makes premature payments, that is, payments in excess of the amount the contractor is entitled to receive as progress payments on account of completed work." *Salem Realty Co. v. Batson*, 256 N.C. 298, 307, 123 S.E.2d 744, 751 (1962); *see also Commercial Cas. Ins. Co. v. Durham County*, 190 N.C. 58, 128 S.E. 469 (1925).

## 11. Case Annotations

### *Interpretation of AIA bond forms*

In addressing whether the surety was obligated to pay for damages caused by the contractor's improper performance under the construction contract, the North Carolina Court of Appeals interpreted the provisions contained within the AIA form performance bond in the case of *Haywood Cty. Consol. School Sys. v. U.S. Fidelity and Guar. Co.*, 43 N.C. App. 71, 257 S.E.2d 670 (1979). The court rejected the surety's argument that the subsection requiring the contractor to carry liability insurance against "claims for damages because of injury to or destruction of tangible property" relieved the contractor, and thus the surety, for liability caused by the contractor's improper performance. *Id.* at 73, 257 S.E.2d at 671. Instead, the provisions of the performance bond explicitly provided, "The Contractor shall indemnify ... the Owner ... against all ... damages, losses and expenses ... arising out of or resulting from the performance of the Work ...." *Id.* The court held, "As Contractor is liable for damages resulting from his negligent performance of the work, so is defendant [surety]." *Id.*

### *Cases in which surety steps into shoes of obligee*

Once the surety has performed its contractual obligations under the bond, it is entitled to receive all remaining contract proceeds from the owner. *Robinson Mfg. v. Blaylock*, 192 N.C. 407, 135 S.E. 136 (1926); *Hartford Acc. & Indem. Co. v. Coggin*, 78 F.2d 471, 477-78 (4th Cir.

1935) (holding that under North Carolina law the surety was "entitled to ... the moneys earned by the contractor [bond principal] but not paid to him before he abandoned the work" and that "when the surety performs the contract, [it] is subrogated to the rights of the obligee, and is entitled to the moneys unpaid so far as necessary to reimburse [the surety] for [its] loss."); *Lacy v. Maryland Cas. Co.*, 32 F.2d 48 (4th Cir. 1929); *United States Fidelity & Guaranty Co. v. Miller*, 143 F. Supp. 941, 944 (W.D. N.C. 1956). The surety's rights in the contract proceeds held by the owner include retainage. *Commercial Cas. Ins. Co. v. Durham County*, 190 N.C. 58, 128 S.E. 469 (1925). The surety's rights are even superior to government tax liens. *See Miller*, 143 F. Supp. 941, *supra*.

If the owner has made any overpayments to the contractor, the surety is "entitled to a credit" for all "payments in excess of the amount the contractor is entitled to receive as progress payments on account of completed work." *Salem Realty* Co. *v. Batson*, 256 N.C. 298, 307, 123 S.E.2d 744, 751 (1962).

In *Lacy v. Maryland Gas Co.*, 32 F.2d 48 (4th Cir. 1929), a party claimed the surety was not entitled to subrogation rights because the owner did not give notice of default of the contractor/principal's contract. The Fourth Circuit, in a case involving North Carolina road work, said that it is clear that the right of subrogation arose because the contractor became insolvent, the contractor abandoned the job, and the surety took over the work. *Id.* at 53.

For more on the surety's subrogation rights and the obligee's potential set-off rights, *see* Section 2, *supra.*

# NORTH DAKOTA

Douglas W. Gigler[1]

## 1. Requirement for Bond

***Statutory provisions for projects that are:***

**Public** – N.D.C.C. § 48-02-06.2 requires a contractor to furnish a performance bond on all contracts for the construction of a public improvement in excess of $100,000. The bond must be for an amount at least equal to the contract price. The bond runs to the governing body, but any person having a lawful claim against the contractor or any subcontractor may sue on the bond.

**Private** – North Dakota does not require contractors to provide performance bonds on private projects.

**Department of Transportation** – N.D.C.C. § 24-02-23 requires a contractor to furnish a suitable performance bond on all Department of Transportation construction projects in excess of $20,000. The bond must be for an amount at least equal to the contract price. Any person

---

1 Douglas W. Gigler is a shareholder of:
Nilles, Ilvedson, Stroup, Plambeck & Selbo, Ltd.
1800 Radisson Tower
201 North Fifth Street
P.O. Box 2626
Fargo, North Dakota 58108-2626
(701) 237-5544

who furnished labor, materials or supplies on a department project, but who has not been paid in full by the time of final acceptance, has the right to file a claim against the contractor and surety furnishing the bond. N.D.C.C. § 24-02-25.1.

***Case law rules that might generally apply***

A general contractor is required to furnish a bond as security for all bills and claims of subcontractors under this section. *Kuchenski v. Kramer Sheet Metal, Inc.*, 377 N.W.2d 133 (N.D. 1985).

A remote materialman, that is, one furnishing materials to a supplier or materialman, rather than to a contractor or subcontractor, cannot recover on a public contractor's bond. *Kinney Electrical Mfg. Co. v. Modern Electric Co.*, 149 N.W.2d 69 (N.D. 1967).

## 2. Damages Covered

***Set forth in any statutes and/or case law***

N.D.C.C. § 48-02-06.2 requires contractors and subcontractors to pay all bills and claims for labor, materials and supplies used in the performance of the contract. The requirement that all bills and claims be paid includes interest on those not paid within 90 days.

N.D.C.C. § 24-02-25.1 provides that any claim against the contractor's performance bond bears interest on each transaction for labor, materials or supplies, commencing 30 days after the last transaction.

**Obligations of surety to perform and/or pay** – Generally there are no cases addressing this.

***Whether failure to provide insurance transfers burden to surety*** – Statutes do not transfer the burden to surety and generally there are no cases addressing this.

***Limitations on Damages***

N.D.C.C. § 22-03-01 provides that, "[a] surety cannot be held beyond the express terms of the surety's contract and if such contract prescribes a penalty for its breach, the surety cannot be liable in any case for more than the penalty."

***Whether obligee may set off bonded contract funds against other principal-obligee debts or obligations*** – There are no North Dakota cases addressing this subject.

***Incorporation of specific contract terms by reference*** – There are no North Dakota cases addressing this subject.

### 3. Penal Sum Variations

**Limitations per statute and/or case law** – North Dakota does not have statutory limitations on performance bond penal sums, nor is there case law addressing this.

***Effect of changes in work upon penal sum, if at all*** – North Dakota has no case law interpreting such changes in the work.

***Statutory or case law protections or damages to penal sum*** – There are no North Dakota cases on this subject.

### 4. Parties Covered

***Statutes and/or case law as to whether only obligees are covered*** – There are no North Dakota cases on this subject.

***Coverage for:***

**Third-party beneficiaries** – There are no North Dakota cases on this subject.

**Assignees** – There are no North Dakota cases on this subject.

**Dual obligees** – There are no North Dakota cases on this subject.

## 5. Notice or Filing Required

***Statutory provisions***

N.D.C.C. § 48-02-15 states in relevant part, "[a]ny person having a direct contractual relationship with a subcontractor, but no contractual relationship with the contractor furnishing the bond, does not have a claim for relief upon the bond unless that person has given written notice to the contractor within 90 days from the date on which the person completed the contribution[.]" The notice must state with substantial accuracy the amount claimed and the name of the person for whom the contribution of labor or materials was performed. Each notice must be served by registered mail, postage prepaid, in an envelope addressed to the prime contractor at any place the prime contractor maintains an office, conducts business or has a residence. Id.

With regard to Department of Transportation projects, the person making a claim must give written notice to the contractor or surety furnishing the performance bond. N.D.C.C. § 24-02-25.2. The notice must provide a clear and concise statement of the labor, materials and supplies furnished, to whom it was furnished and the monetary value of the same. The notice must be served by registered mail, postage prepaid, addressed to the contractor at any place the contractor maintains an office or has a residence. The notice must be posted within 180 days from the date on which the person completed the contribution giving rise to the claim. Id.

***Case law rules concerning condition precedent notice***

Recovery from a bond furnished under N.D.C.C. § 48-02-06.2 is expressly conditioned by the notice requirement contained in § 48-02-15. *Kuchenski v. Kramer Sheet Metal, Inc.*, 377 N.W.2d 133 (N.D. 1985).

## 6. Time for Suit

***Statutes of limitation particular to performance bonds and other applicable statutes of limitation***

N.D.C.C. § 48-02-17, provides in relevant part, "[a]ll claims for any labor, material, or supplies furnished for improvements, upon which suit is not commenced within one year after completion and acceptance of the project, shall be barred as liens or claims against the contractor and the contractor's surety."

Department of Transportation projects also have a one-year statute of limitations. "Any person who has furnished labor, materials, or supplies and made a claim under section 24-02-25.1 has the right to commence an action to recover the amount of the person's claim against the contractor or surety within one year of the date of the final acceptance of the project by the department." N.D.C.C. § 24-02-25.2.

***Case law statements about enforceability of limitations contained in bonds*** – Generally there are no North Dakota cases addressing this subject.

***Varying statutes of limitation by agreement in bond or contract*** – There is no North Dakota law addressing this subject.

## 7. Procedure

***Statutory or procedural rules that may affect handling or administration of lawsuits*** – Not applicable.

***Venue requirements and jurisdictional limitations***

As to venue, an action must be tried in the county in which the defendant or one of the defendants resides at the time of the commencement of the action. If none of the defendants reside in the state, the action must be tried in the county designated by the plaintiff in the summons. N.D.C.C. § 28-04-05.

As to jurisdictional limitations, Rule 4(b)(2) of the North Dakota Rules of Civil Procedure provides as follows,

> *Rule 4. Persons subject to jurisdiction–Process–Service–*
>
> * * *
>
> (b) Jurisdiction Over Person.
>
> * * *
>
> (2) *Personal Jurisdiction Based Upon Contacts.* A court of this state may exercise personal jurisdiction over a person who acts directly or by an agent as to any claim for relief arising from the person's having such contact with this state that the

exercise of personal jurisdiction over the person does not offend against traditional notions of justice or fair play or the due process of law, under one or more of the following circumstances:

(A) transacting any business in this state;
(B) contracting to supply or supplying services, goods, or other things in this state;
(C) committing a tort within or without this state causing injury to another person or property within this state;
(D) committing a tort within this state, causing injury to another person or property within or without this state;
(E) owning, having any interest in, using, or possessing property in this state;
(F) to insure another person, property, or other risk within this state;
(G) as a director, manager, trustee, or officer of a corporation organized under the laws of, or having its principal place of business within, this state;
(H) any other legal status or capacity within this state; or
(I) engaging in any other activity, including cohabitation or sexual intercourse, within this state.

"The determination that must be made in resolving the question of personal jurisdiction is two fold. First, it must be determined if the requirements of the applicable subparagraphs contained in Rule 4(b)(2), N.D. R.Civ.P., have been satisfied. Secondly, it is necessary to determine whether or not the nonresident party has had such contact with the forum State that the exercise of personal jurisdiction over the nonresident does not offend against the traditional notions of justice and fair play under the concept of due process of law." *Hust v. Northern Logs, Inc.*, 297 N.W.2d 429 (N.D. 1980).

**Court rules** – Each North Dakota Judicial District has its own local rules regarding the procedure for that district.

***Particular agency regulations/rules*** – Not applicable.

***Arbitration requirements and application***

All controversies arising out of any contract for the construction or repair of highways must be submitted to arbitration. Any person who voluntarily enters into a contract for the construction or repair of highways must be considered as having agreed to arbitration of all controversies arising out of the contract. N.D.C.C. § 24-02-26.

The validity of arbitration agreements is recognized by N.D.C.C. § 32-29.2-01, which provides:

> A written agreement to submit any existing controversy to arbitration or a provision in a written contract to submit to arbitration any controversy thereafter arising between the parties is valid, enforceable, and irrevocable, except on such grounds as exist at law or in equity for the revocation of any contract.

## 8. Attorney's Fees

***Statutes and/or case law limiting or permitting recovery of attorney's fees***

The general threshold rule is that, "[A]bsent specific contractual or statutory authority, the 'American Rule' requires parties to bear their own attorney's fees." *State Farm Mut. Auto. Ins. Co. v. Estate of* Gabel, 539 N.W.2d 290, 294 (N.D. 1995).

Section 28-26-01 N.D.C.C. provides as follows,

> *Attorney's fees by agreement–Exception–Awarding of costs and attorney's fees to prevailing party.*
>
> 1. Except as provided in subsection 2, the amount of fees of attorneys in civil actions must be left to the agreement, express or implied, of the parties.
> 2. In civil actions the court shall, upon a finding that a claim for relief was frivolous, award reasonable actual and statutory costs, including reasonable attorney's fees to the prevailing party. Such costs must be awarded regardless of the good faith of the attorney or party making the claim for relief if there is such a complete absence of actual facts or law that a reasonable person could not have thought a court would render judgment in their favor, providing the prevailing party has in responsive pleading alleged the frivolous nature of the claim. This subsection does not require the award of costs or fees against an attorney or party advancing a claim unwarranted under existing law, if it is supported by a good

faith argument for an extension, modification, or reversal of the existing law.

***What fees are recoverable, if any*** – Not applicable.

**9. Special Provisions** – Not applicable.

**10. Remarks** – Not applicable.

**11. Case Annotations**

**Interpretation of AIA bond forms** – North Dakota cases have not specifically addressed AIA forms of bonds A311 and A312.

***Cases in which surety steps into shoes of obligee*** – There is no North Dakota case law addressing this issue.

# OHIO

David Olson and Dan Hendy[1]

## 1. Requirement for Bond

The State of Ohio does not have a statute that requires performance bonds to be furnished on private work. Every public construction contract, however, which requires a competitive bid, also requires the use of a bid guaranty and surety bond in accordance with O.R.C. § 153.54 *et seq.* The Department of Transportation also requires the use of bid guaranties and surety bonds through a separate statute, O.R.C. § 5526.16.

The following Revised Code sections mandate compliance with O.R.C. § 153.54 *et seq.* as part of the competitive bidding processes for the specified entity:

Board of education school districts, O.R.C. §§ 3313.46, 3318.10.
Board of hospital trustees, O.R.C. § 749.29.
Board of library trustees, O.R.C. § 3375.41.
Board of park trustees, O.R.C. § 755.31.
Bridge commission, O.R.C. § 5593.08.
Community college district board of trustees, O.R.C. § 3354.16.
Community urban redevelopment corporation, O.R.C. § 1728.08.
Conservancy district, O.R.C. § 6101.16.

---

[1] David Olson and Dan Hendy are with:
Frost Brown Todd LLC
2200 PNC Center
201 East Fifth Street
Cincinnati, Ohio 45202
(513) 651-6905

Construction manager to provide financial assurance; waiver, O.R.C. § 933.3.
County commissioners, contracts for grading, draining, paving streets, O.R.C. § 5559.13.
Single county ditches; improvements, O.R.C. §§ 6131.14, 6131.44.
Department of natural resources, O.R.C. § 1501.01.1.
Department of public service, O.R.C. § 735.06.
Director of development, O.R.C. § 122.42.
Minority business development loan program, O.R.C. § 122.75.
Powers and duties re minority development financing, O.R.C. § 122.74.
Fire and ambulance district, O.R.C. § 505.37.6.
Hospital building, O.R.C. § 749.12.
Municipal corporation; water works, O.R.C. § 743.11.
Ohio air quality development authority, O.R.C. § 3706.04.
Ohio building authority; emergencies, O.R.C. § 152.18.
Ohio turnpike commission, O.R.C. § 5537.04.
Contracts exceeding $35,000, O.R.C. § 5537.07.
Ohio water development authority, O.R.C. §§ 6121.04, 6123.04.
Port authority, O.R.C. § 4582.12.
Regional airport authority, O.R.C. § 308.13.
Regional transit authority, O.R.C. § 306.43.
Regional water and sewer district, O.R.C. § 6119.10.
Sanitary district board, O.R.C. § 6115.20.
Soil and water conservation district, O.R.C. § 1515.08.
State buildings, O.R.C. § 153.08.
Technical colleges, O.R.C. § 3357.16.
Township, contracts for private sewage collection tiles improvements, O.R.C. § 521.05.
Township lighting, O.R.C. § 515.07.
Township memorial buildings, monuments, O.R.C. § 511.12.
Township roads, O.R.C. § 5575.02.
University branch district, O.R.C. § 3355.12.
Village legislative authority, O.R.C. § 731.15.
Water improvements, O.R.C. § 1523.03.

***Statutory provisions for projects that are:***

**Public** – O.R.C. § 153.54 provides as follows:

Each person bidding for a contract with the state or any political subdivision, district, institution, or other agency thereof, excluding therefrom the department of transportation, for any public improvement shall file with the bid, a bid guaranty.

The bond shall "indemnify the state, political subdivision, district, institution, or agency against all damage suffered by failure to perform the contract according to its provisions and in accordance with the plans, details, specifications, and bills of material therefore and to pay all lawful claims of subcontractors, materialmen, and laborers for labor performed or material furnished in carrying forward, performing, or completing the contract."

The bond must be an amount equal to the contract price. O.R.C. § 153.54.

O.R.C. § 153.54(F) provides as follows:

> All bid guaranties filed pursuant to [§ 153.54] shall be payable to the state, political subdivision, district, institution, or agency, be for the benefit of the state, political subdivision, district, institution, or agency or any person having a right of action thereon, and be deposited with, and held by, the board, officer, or agent contracting on behalf of the state, political subdivision, district, institution, or agency. All bonds filed pursuant to [§ 153.54] shall be issued by a surety company authorized to do business in this state as surety approved by the board, officer, or agent awarding the contract on behalf of the state, political subdivision, district, institution, or agency.

The statute sets forth the form for the bond. O.R.C. § 153.54(C)(1) provides that the bond shall be in substantially the same form as the following portion of O.R.C. § 153.57:

> KNOW ALL PERSONS BY THESE PRESENTS, that we, the undersigned ......... as principal and ......... as sureties, are hereby held and firmly bound unto........ in the penal sum of ......... dollars, for the payment of which well and truly to be made, we hereby jointly and severally bind ourselves, our heirs, executors, administrators, successors, and assigns.
>
> Signed this ........ day of ........., ...
>
> THE CONDITION OF THE ABOVE OBLIGATION IS SUCH, that whereas the above named principal did on the ...... day of .........., ....., enter into a contract with .........., which said contract is made a part of this bond the same as though set forth herein;

> Now, if the said ......... shall well and faithfully do and perform the things agreed by ......... to be done and performed according to the terms of said contract; and shall pay all lawful claims of subcontractors, materialmen, and laborers, for labor performed and materials furnished in the carrying forward, performing, or completing of said contract; we agreeing and assenting that this undertaking shall be for the benefit of any materialman or laborer having a just claim, as well as for the obligee herein; then this obligation shall be void; otherwise the same shall remain in full force and effect; it being expressly understood and agreed that the liability of the surety for any and all claims hereunder shall in no event exceed the penal amount of this obligation as herein stated.
>
> The said surety hereby stipulates and agrees that no modifications, omissions, or additions, in or to the terms of the said contract or in or to the plans or specifications therefore shall in any wise affect the obligations of said surety on its bond.

**Private** – As noted above, no statutes in Ohio require performance bonds on private projects.

**Department of Transportation** – Under O.R.C. § 5525.16, the director of transportation, before entering into a contract, shall:

> require a contract performance bond and a payment bond with sufficient sureties, as follows:
>
> (1) A contract performance bond in an amount equal to 100 percent of the estimated cost of the work, conditioned, among other things, that the contractor will perform the work upon the terms proposed, within the time prescribed, and in accordance with the plans and specifications, will indemnify the state against any damage that may result from any failure of the contractor to so perform, and, further, in case of a grade separation will indemnify any railroad company involved against any damage that may result by reason of the negligence of the contractor in making the improvement.
>
> (2) A payment bond in an amount equal to 100 percent of the estimated cost of the work, conditioned for the payment by the contractor and all subcontractors for labor or work performed or materials furnished in connection with the work, improvement, or project involved.

***Case law rules that might generally apply***

Under the former statute that required bonds for public projects, the Ohio Supreme Court held that a bond which did not fully conform to the statutory mandate would be interpreted to include all such provisions. *Southern Surety Co. v. Chambers* (1926) 115 Ohio St. 434. In addition, compliance with the notice requirements of the statute is mandatory. "A notice of claim and an action under the payment portion of the bond asserted by a subcontractor, materialman, or laborer, alleging that money is due for labor or work performed or material furnished in a public improvement contract must be timely presented within the limitations periods set forth in R.C. 153.56." *Thomas Steel, Inc. v. Wilson Bennett, Inc.*, 127 Ohio App. 3d 96, 102 (1998).

## 2. Damages Covered

***Set forth in any statutes and/or case law***

The liability of the surety parallels that of the principal. "Suretyship is the contractual relation whereby one person, the surety, agrees to answer for the debt, default, or miscarriage of another, the principal, with the surety generally being primarily and jointly liable with the principal debtor. Because the surety's obligation is derived from that of the principal, the liability of the surety is ordinarily measured by the liability of the principal. As a general rule, a surety on a bond is not liable unless the principal is and, therefore, may plead any defense available to the principal with the exception of defenses which are purely personal to a principal, such as infancy, incapacity, or bankruptcy." *Hopkins v. INA Underwriters Ins. Co.*, 44 Ohio App. 3d 186, 188, 542 N.E.2d 679-89 (1988) (citations omitted).

"It has long been the law in Ohio that a 'surety is entitled to stand upon the letter of his undertaking, including his designations of the persons who may become his creditors.' 'A bond is a contract and, in the absence of some controlling statute, is to be construed according to the fair import of the language used.' A surety, then, will generally not be liable beyond the terms of the contract." *Dean v. Seco Electric Co.*, 35 Ohio St. 3d 203, 205 (1988) (internal citations omitted).

***Obligations of surety to perform and/or pay***

As shown in the statutory bond form, the extent of the liability of the surety is limited to the penal sum. Unless otherwise contracted, the liability of the surety for any and all claims under the bond shall in no event exceed the penal amount of the obligation stated in the bond. *See* O.R.C. § 153.57.

***Whether failure to provide insurance transfers burden to surety*** – Statutes do not transfer the burden to the surety.

***Limitations on damages***

Interpreting the former statute, Ohio courts have held that the statutory remedy of materialmen or laborers on bond of public improvement contractor is exclusive. *General Elec. Supply Corp. v. Wiley Elec. Co.*, 47 Ohio App. 196, 191 N.E. 706 (1933).

Ohio courts have recognized the liability of a compensated surety for punitive damages. *Suver v. Personal Service Insurance Company* (1984) 11 Ohio St. 3d 6. That case arose from a financial responsibility bond issued for an automobile and requires that there be a showing of the breach of the duty of good faith upon proof of actual malice, fraud or oppression. That holding has been applied to contract suretyship and allows the award of punitive damages only upon a showing that the act of the principal was authorized, participated in, or ratified by the surety. *Dean v. Seco Electric Co.*, 35 Ohio St. 3d 203, 206 (1988).

***Whether obligee may set off bonded contract funds against other principal-obligee's debts or obligations***

Where a surety fulfills the terms of its bond and completes a construction project by paying debts of a contractor, the surety acquires an equitable right to be paid funds retained by the owner until the condition is satisfied that all "bills for materials, supplies and equipment" have been paid or otherwise satisfied. *In re Design Int'l Ohio Corp.*, No. 1-92-00642, 1994 WL 912422 (Bankr. S.D. Ohio, Sept. 14, 1994).

***Incorporation of specific contract terms by reference*** – Not applicable.

## 3. Penal Sum Variations

***Limitations per statute and/or case law***

"A cause of action can not exist against a surety, as such, unless a cause of action exists against his principal. This rule results as a corollary, from the very definition of the contract of suretyship, that the obligation of the surety being accessory to the obligation of the principal debtor or obligor, it is of its essence that there should be a valid obligation of such a principal, and that the nullity of the principal obligation necessarily induces the nullity of the accessory. And as a general rule the obligation of the surety, as such, cannot exceed that of the principal, it being said that it would be most unjust and incongruous to hold the surety liable, where the principal is not bound." *East Cleveland v. Fidelity & Deposit Co.*, 5 F. Supp. 212, 214 (D. Ohio 1933).

***Effect of changes in work upon penal sum, if at all***

O.R.C. § 153.11 addresses the issue of changes in the work and the impact on the penal sum of the bond.

> Whenever the change referred to in section 153.10 of the Revised Code is approved by the owner as defined in section 153.01 of the Revised Code, accepted in writing by the contractor, and filed, the same shall be considered as being a part of the original contract, and the bond theretofore executed shall be held to include and cover the same.

"Generally speaking, a suretyship contract for the performance of public work, which under the law is operative for the benefit and protection of laborers, mechanics, and materialmen, will be effective for their protection regardless of changes and alterations subsequently made between the principal contractor and the other contracting party, even though the same are made without the knowledge and consent of the surety on the contractor's bond. This is so because the laborers, mechanics, and materialmen have no control of the actions of the contracting parties." *Bailey Lumber Co. v. Ohio Dep't of Natural Resources*, 79 Ohio App. 3d 434, 438 (1992).

***Statutory or case law protections or dangers to penal sum***

Under a bond issued pursuant to O.R.C. § 153.54 *et seq*. a surety should never be liable for more than what it contracted for. *See* O.R.C. § 153.57.

## 4. Parties Covered

***Statute and/or case law as to whether obligees covered***

O.R.C. § 153.54 provides that the bond shall "indemnify the state, political subdivision, district, institution, or agency against all damage suffered by failure to perform the contract according to its provisions and in accordance with the plans, details, specifications, and bills of material therefore and to pay all lawful claims of subcontractors, materialmen, and laborers for labor performed or material furnished in carrying forward, performing, or completing the contract."

***Coverage for:***

**Third-party beneficiaries** – The statutory bond is available to pay claims for the designated entities. At the same time, the claimants are charged with the obligation to comply with the requirements to perfect their claims. "When parties execute a bond pursuant to [R. C. § 153.54 - 153.57] they are chargeable with notice of the provisions of the statute, and materialmen and subcontractors may avail themselves of the security of the bond although they are not expressly named therein." *L.M. Builders Co. v. Jefferson*, 61 Ohio St. 2d 91, 97 (1980).

The coverage under the bond is not without limits. "As used in [R.C. § 153.54 *et seq*.], the word 'subcontractor' will be given its ordinary meaning so that it may include one who, under a contract with the general contractor, merely furnishes material for use in performance of the general contract, but so that it will exclude a subcontractor of a subcontractor of the general contractor." *Cadillac Plastic Group v. Advanced Glazing Tech.*, 97 Ohio App. 3d 37, 40 (1994).

**Assignees** – There are no Ohio cases discussing assignment of obligee's right to make claim against a performance bond.

**Dual obligees** – "The rule generally applied by federal courts is that where two or more parties are joint obligees, they are indispensable parties in an action for enforcement of that obligation. ... The rationale behind this position is that the duty or promise was made to the obligees jointly, not separately; mandatory joinder of joint obligees is therefore justified to avoid inconsistent judgments, prevent multiple lawsuits, and to obtain final and complete relief between all interested parties." *Dublin Transp., Inc. v. Goebel*, 133 Ohio App. 3d 272, 278 (1999) (internal citations omitted).

## 5. Notice or Filing Required

***Statutory provision***

Ohio allows for the use of a unified bond form to cover both the bid bond requirement and also the performance/payment bond requirement. Under this process, the principal tenders one instrument containing both obligations. Since the surety may not have collected a premium for the performance bond, O.R.C. § 9.32 requires that the public owner notify the surety for the successful bidder of the impending award. The statute provides the following:

> Whenever the state, or any political subdivision, district, institution, or other agency thereof awards a contract for the construction, demolition, alteration, repair, or reconstruction of a public improvement, the contracting authority shall simultaneously notify the surety on the contractor's bond of the award and the agent of the surety who executed the bond on behalf of the surety. The notice shall be given in writing and mailed to the surety and the agent whose names and addresses appear on the bond.

The statute allowing for the pursuit of bond claims also provides that the claimant must provide notice to the surety. O.R.C. § 153.56 provides as follows:

> Any person to whom any money is due for labor or work performed or material furnished in a public improvement as provided in section 153.54 of the Revised Code, at any time after performing the labor or work or furnishing the materials, but not later than 90 days after the acceptance of the public improvement by the duly authorized

> board or officer, shall furnish the sureties on the bond, a statement of the amount due the person.
>
> A suit shall not be brought against sureties on the bond until after 60 days after the furnishing of the statement described in this section.

*See also, Thomas Steel, Inc. v. Wilson Bennett, Inc.*, 127 Ohio App. 3d 96, 102 (1998).

If the claimant does not have a direct contract with the principal it must also provide notice to the surety under certain circumstances. To exercise rights under O.R.C. § 153.56,

> a subcontractor or materials supplier supplying labor or materials that cost more than $30,000 who is not in direct privity of contract with the principal contractor for the public improvement, shall serve a notice of furnishing upon the principal contractor in the form provided in section 1311.261 [1311.26.1] of the Revised Code. O.R.C. § 153.56(C).

This notice requirement parallels the requirement to provide notice to the owner to assert a lien claim under O.R.C. § 1311.261.

***Case law rules concerning condition precedent notice***

As noted above, a claimant must provide notice within 90 days of "acceptance" by the public owner, but that term is not defined in the statute. Case law has provided a gloss for the concept. Some action by the public entity is required, but a formal resolution of acceptance of work performed under a public contract is not necessary to constitute an acceptance within the meaning of O.R.C. § 153.56. For example, the board of education accepted work within the purview of O.R.C. § 153.56, when its treasurer on May 1, 1953, after the board had been notified by the "architect and chief engineer that they certified final payment under the contract, certified such payment was correct, which action was approved by the president of the board and payment made on that date, and a statement furnished by the contractor to the bonding company more than 90 days after such acceptance and a suit filed more than one year after May 1, 1953, did not comply with the limitations provided for in RC § 153.56." *Johnson Service Co. v. American Casualty Co.*, 6 Ohio Op. 2d 290, 148 N.E.2d 112 (CP 1957).

**6. Time for Suit**

***Statutes of limitation particular to performance bonds and other applicable statutes of limitation***

A suit on a performance bond issued pursuant to O.R.C. § 153.54 *et seq.* must be brought no later than one year from the date of acceptance of the public improvement. O.R.C. § 153.56; *Thomas Steel, Inc. v. Wilson Bennett, Inc.*, 127 Ohio App. 3d 96, 102 (Ohio Ct. App. 1998).

***Case law statements about enforceability of limitations contained in bonds***

Statute of limitations contained in O.R.C. § 153.56 cannot be extended via a local government ordinance. *Thomas Steel, Inc. v. Wilson Bennett, Inc.*, 127 Ohio App. 3d 96, 105 (Ohio Ct. App. 1998) ("In selecting which statute of limitations to apply in the Revised Code, "a special statutory provision which relates to the specific subject matter involved in the legislation is controlling over a general statutory provision which might otherwise be applicable. ...A bond claim statute which applies to a contract with 'any political subdivision' of the state for 'any public improvement' is squarely on point.")

***Varying statements of limitation by agreement in bond or contract***

While no Ohio case discusses this issue, based on the language of O.R.C. § 153.56, it would seem that parties could not vary the one-year statute of limitations by agreement.

## 7. Procedure

***Statutory or procedural rules that may affect handling or administration of lawsuits***

There are some general statutes governing actions on bonds. O.R.C. § 2307.06 allows for multiple actions on a bond by several claimants who otherwise have valid claims:

> When a person forfeits his bond, or renders his sureties liable thereon, a person injured thereby, or who is entitled to the benefit of the security, may bring an action thereon, in his own name, against the person and

> his sureties, to recover the amount to which he is entitled by reason of the delinquency, which action may be prosecuted on a certified copy of the bond. A judgment for one delinquency does not preclude the same for another person from bringing an action on the instrument for another delinquency.

O.R.C. § 2307.07 also addresses actions on bond claims:

> On tender of the proper fee, the custodian of the bond referred to in section 2307.06 of the Revised Code shall deliver a copy thereof to a person claiming to be injured. The requirements of such section are not imperative, if other provision is made by law.

***Venue requirements and jurisdictional limitations***

Typically, the action on a surety bond must be brought in the county where the project was being performed. O.R.C. § 153.05 provides as follows:

> The bond required by section 153.08 of the Revised Code may be enforced against the person executing such bond, by any claimant for labor or material, and suit may be brought on such bond in the name of the state on relation of the claimant within one year from the date of delivering or furnishing such labor or material, in the court of common pleas of the county wherein such labor or material was furnished or delivered. Such bond shall not be released by the execution of any additional security, notes, retentions from estimates, or other instrument on account of such claim, or for any reason, except the full payment of such claim for labor or material.

***Court rules*** – Not applicable.

***Particular agency regulations/rules*** – Not applicable.

***Arbitration requirements and application***

In *Council of Smaller Enterprises v. Gates, McDonald & Company*, 80 Ohio St. 3d 661, 665 (1998), the Supreme Court of Ohio stated that, "arbitration is a matter of contract and a party cannot be required to submit to arbitration any dispute which he has not agreed to so submit ... This axiom recognizes the fact that arbitrators derive their authority to resolve disputes only because the parties have agreed to submit such grievances to arbitration." (internal citations omitted).

In *Teramar Corp. v. Rodier Corp.*, 40 Ohio App. 3d 39 (1987), the trial court ordered a surety to submit to arbitration pursuant to an arbitration clause contained not in the guaranty signed by the surety, but in the underlying franchise agreement to which the surety was not a party. The court of appeals reversed, holding that, "arbitration is a matter of contract and, in spite of the strong policy in its favor, a party cannot be compelled to arbitrate a dispute which he has not agreed to submit to arbitration." *Id.* at paragraph one of the syllabus.

## 8. Attorney's Fees

***Statutes and/or case law limiting or permitting recovery of attorney's fees***

"In the absence of an express provision to the contrary, a surety's liability upon a labor and material payment bond is limited to payment for labor and material only and does not extend to liability for the statutory penalty, attorney fees, and costs for violation of the prevailing wage statute." *Dean v. Seco Electric Co.*, 35 Ohio St. 3d 203, paragraph 1 of syllabus (1988).

The general American Rule concerning the award of attorney fees does not permit the prevailing party to recover such fees as part of the cost of litigation, in the absence of statutory authorization or contract. "Bad faith vexatious, wanton, obdurate or oppressive conduct is an exception to the 'American Rule' that attorney fees are not recoverable in the absence of statutory authorization is not properly presented in the instant cause." *Sorin v. Bd. of Edn.*, 46 Ohio St. 2d 177, 183 (1976).

***What fees are recoverable if any*** – Not applicable.

## 9. Special Provisions – Not applicable.

## 10. Remarks – Not applicable.

## 11. Case Annotations

***Interpretation of AIA bond forms*** – Ohio has no cases or statutes on this issue.

***Cases in which surety steps into shoes of obligee***

"Since the state of Ohio has a statutory requirement of a payment bond and, in addition, has a legal obligation to pay the laborers and materialmen out of the retainages if they are not otherwise paid, the surety on the road construction contractor's bond can be held to have subrogated to the rights of the state in retained funds as well as rights of laborers and materialmen in the funds." *Western Casualty & Surety Co. v. Brooks*, 37 Ohio Op. 2d 317 (1966).

# OKLAHOMA

Evan B. Gatewood[1]

## 1. Requirement for Bond

***Statutory provisions for projects that are:***

**Public** – Pursuant to Title 61 O.S. § 113, a performance bond is required for all public works construction contracts in amounts in excess of $25,000. The performance bond must be in an amount equal to the contract price and must "ensure the proper and prompt completion of the work in accordance with the provisions of the contract and bidding documents." The term "Public Construction Contract" means any contract awarded by any public agency for the purpose of making any public improvements or constructing any public building or making repairs to or performing maintenance on the same. 61 O.S. § 102. A public agency is any county, city, town, school district or other political subdivision of the state, any public trust, any public entity specifically created by the statutes of the State of Oklahoma, and any department, agency, board, bureau, commission, committee or authority of any of the foregoing public entities. 61 O.S. § 102.

---

1 Evan B. Gatewood is a member of:
Hayes Magrini & Gatewood
1220 N. Walker
P.O. Box 60140
Oklahoma City, Oklahoma 73146-0140
(405) 235-9922

**Private** – There are no statutes in Oklahoma which require performance bonds on private projects.

**Department of Transportation** – Not applicable.

***Case law rules that might generally apply*** – Not applicable.

## 2. Damages Covered

***Set forth in any statutes and/or case law***

61 O.S. § 113B.2. – Provides that the performance bond will ensure the proper and prompt completion of the construction work in accordance with the provisions of the contract and bidding documents. The performance bond protects the owner of the property by assuring completion of the project in the event of default by the general contractor. *Boren v. Thompson & Associates*, 999 P.2d 438 (Okla. 2000).

***Obligations of surety to perform and/or pay*** – Not applicable.

***Whether failure to provide insurance transfers burden to surety*** – Statutes do not transfer the burden to provide insurance to surety.

***Limitations on damages***

A surety is liable to the same extent as its principal. *U.S. Fidelity & Guaranty Co. v. Kern*, 62 P.2d 1173 (Okla. 1936). The surety's liability is limited to the penal sum of the bond. *Western Surety Co. v. Childers*, 372 P.2d 214 (Okla. 1962). However, Oklahoma courts have allowed an award of interest in addition to the penal sum. *Southern Surety Co. v. Enfield*, 229 P. 446 (Okla. 1924).

A surety may not be held liable beyond the express terms of its contract. *Barbero v. Equitable General Ins. Co.*, 607 P.2d 670 (Okla. 1980). Bonds required by statute are to be strictly construed and are not to be extended by implication beyond the clearly expressed intent of the statute. *Culver v. Mid-Continent Cas. Co.*, 526 P.2d 496 (Okla. 1974). A surety on a statutory bond is liable in accordance with the terms of the statute. When a statute requires a bond to be given and surety undertakes to furnish it, obligation imposed by statute is read into the terms of the bond. *Lum v. Lee Way Motor Freight, Inc.*, 757 P.2d 810 (Okla. 1987). If the terms of the bond are broader than those imposed by statute, additional liability may be enforced in accordance with the terms of the bond. *Lum v. Lee Way Motor Freight, Inc.*, 757 P.2d 810 (Okla. 1987). However, the liability of a surety is not to be extended by implication. *Culver v. Mid-Continent Cas. Co.*, 526 P.2d 496 (Okla. 1974). Oklahoma courts have found that claims for impaired bonding capacity or consequential loss of contracting capacity cannot be implied from the terms of a performance bond. *Professional Construction Consultants, Inc. v. The State of Oklahoma*, 646 P.2d 1262 (Okla. 1982).

The obligation of a surety on a performance bond, upon default of principal or contractor, is to perform or furnish work agreed upon or to pay owner costs of performing or finishing the work. *American Casualty Co. v. Town of Shattuck*, 228 F. Supp. 834 (D.C. Okla. 1964).

## 3. Penal Sum Variations

***Limitations per statute*** – Title 61 O.S. § 113 requires the performance bond on public works construction projects to be in a sum equal to the contract price.

***Effect of changes in work upon penal sum, if at all*** – There is no Oklahoma case law or statute which would indicate that change orders issued during construction would affect the penal sum of the bond.

***Statutory or case law protections or dangers to penal sum*** – Not applicable.

## 4. Parties Covered

***Statutes and/or case law as to whether only obligees are covered***

Title 61 O.S. § 113B.2 provides that the performance bond will be issued "for the benefit of the state, on behalf of the awarding public agency." Thus, the State of Oklahoma or the public agency awarding the public works project is the only proper obligee under the statutory performance bond.

***Coverage for:***

**Third-party beneficiaries** – Whether a materialmen, supplier or subcontractor can recover as a third-party beneficiary under the prime contract and its corresponding performance bond depends on the intention of the parties. However, Oklahoma courts have found that where the prime contract requires a payment bond, materialmen, suppliers and subcontractors could not recover on the performance bond as third-party beneficiaries. *See*, *G.A. Mosites Company of Ft. Worth v. Aetna Casualty and Surety Company*, 545 P.2d 746 (Okla. 1976).

**Assignees** – Unless the bond contains a clear provision relieving surety of liability in the event of an assignment, the surety remains liable for the performance of the contract notwithstanding any assignment. *Leader Printing Co. v. Lowry*, 59 P. 242 (Okla. 1899) and *American Surety Co. of New York v. U.S.*, 112 F.2d 903 (C.A. 10th Cir. 1940).

**Dual obligees** – Not applicable.

## 5. Notice or Filing Required

***Statutory provisions*** – Oklahoma statutes do not provide for any unusual notice requirements or suit under a performance bond.

***Case law rules concerning condition precedent notice***

"As a general rule, a surety is bound to perform the obligation of its principal, and cannot complain when the creditor does not notify him of the default of his principal ... mere inaction of the creditor will not discharge the surety, and the fact that the principal is delinquent in payments of sums due, does not affect the liability of the surety. But this rule does not apply where there is a question of moral turpitude involved, or where the principal is guilty of conduct indicating dishonesty, or bad faith, or other unfitness for trust, after the knowledge of such conduct has come to the obligee's attention. (Cite omitted). 'If, however, the obligation of the surety is a continuing one, and the extent of the liability of the principal rests entirely within the knowledge of the obligee, notice of the principal's default must be given to the surety within a reasonable time or they will be discharged.'" *J.R. Walker Co. v. Jennings*, 269 P. 265 (Okla. 1928).

If the bond does require the obligee to give notice of default, a failure to notify surety of principal's defaults may relieve the surety of liability on the bond. However, the performance bond surety must establish prejudice. An obligee's failure to provide the required notice to surety of principal's default is not fatal to recovery on the bond. Unless it is clearly set forth as a condition precedent to liability, such failure to give notice will simply be considered a breach and the surety will be entitled to recoup any loss it can establish because of the obligee's failure to give notice. *Southern Surety Co. v. MacMillan Co.*, 58 F.2d 541 (10th Cir. 1932).

## 6. Time for Suit

***Statutes of limitation particular to performance bonds and other applicable statutes of limitation***

The limitations period for both statutory and private performance bonds is five years. Title 12 O.S. §95 provides:

> "An action upon the official bond or undertaking of an executor, administrator, guardian, sheriff or any other officer, or upon the bond or undertaking given an attachment, injunction, arrest, or in any case whatever required by the statute, can only be brought within five years after the cause of action shall have accrued..."

In addition, 12 O.S. §99A.1 provides:

> Within five years: an action upon any contract, agreement, or promise in writing;

***Case law statements about enforceability of limitations contained in bonds*** – Not applicable.

***Varying statutes of limitation by agreement in bond or contract*** – Oklahoma law does not allow parties to reduce the limitations period by agreement. Title 15 O.S. § 216 provides:

"Every stipulation or condition in a contract, by which any party thereto is restricted from enforcing his rights under the contract by the usual legal proceedings in the ordinary tribunals, or which limits the time within which he may thus enforce his rights, is void." *See*, *Sherwood Forest No. 2 Corp. v. City of Norman*, 632 P.2d 368 (Okla. 1980) (where the court found that the five year limitations period for actions on contracts in writing applied as opposed to the two year limitations period set forth in a subdivision improvement bond).

## 7. Procedure

***Statutory or procedural rules that may affect handling or administration of lawsuits*** – Not applicable.

***Venue requirements and jurisdictional limitations*** – Not applicable.

***Court rules*** – Not applicable.

***Particular agency regulations/rules*** – Not applicable.

***Arbitration requirements and application*** – Not applicable.

## 8. Attorney's Fees

***Statutes and/or case law limiting or permitting recovery of attorney's fees***

Although there are no Oklahoma cases dealing with a performance bond, the Oklahoma Court of Appeals has allowed a payment bond claimant to recover its attorney's fees under §936 on a private payment bond. *Builders Overhead Cranes v. Nashco Building Co., Inc.*, 85 P.3d 851 (Okla. Civ. App. 2003). Title 12 O.S. §936 provides:

> In any civil action to recover for labor or services rendered, ... or a contract relating to the purchase or sale of goods ... the prevailing party shall be allowed a reasonable attorney's fee to be set by the court.

Oklahoma courts have typically interpreted the provisions of §936 conservatively. Thus, since a performance bond claim is not an "action to recover for labor and services rendered," a performance bond claimant should not be entitled to attorney fees.

**9. Special Provisions** – Not applicable.

**10. Remarks** – Not applicable.

**11. Case Annotations**

***Interpretation of AIA bond forms*** – Oklahoma cases have not specifically addressed AIA forms of bonds A311 and A312.

***Cases in which surety steps into shoes of obligee*** – Not applicable.

# OREGON

Loren D. Podwill and Randy L. Arthur[1]

## 1. Requirement for Bond

*Statutory provisions for projects that are:*

**Public –**

### a. Public Improvement Contracts

ORS 279A.005 provides that Oregon Revised Statutes ("ORS") Chapters ("Chs.") 279A ("Public Contracting-General Provisions"), 279B ("Public Contracting-Public Procurements"), and 279C ("Public Contracting-Public Improvements") "may be cited as the Public Contracting Code." ORS Chapter 279A became "operative" March 1, 2005, and generally "applies only to public contracts first advertised, but if not advertised then entered into, on or after March 1, 2005." *See* Note following ORS 279A.005.

---

1 Loren D. Podwill and Randy L. Arthur are shareholders of:
Bullivant Houser Bailey PC
300 Pioneer Tower
888 S.W. 5th Ave.
Portland, Oregon 97204
(503) 228-6351

### *Definitions*

ORS 279A.010, *as amended*, 2005 Oregon Laws Chs. 22; 103, §§ 1a, 40; 153; 360, § 13, provides definitions for the Public Contracting Code "unless the context or a specifically applicable definition requires otherwise."

ORS 279A.010(b) – A "contracting agency" is "a public body authorized by law to conduct a procurement."

ORS 279A.010(aa) – A "public improvement" is "a project for construction, reconstruction or major renovation on real property by or for a contracting agency."

ORS 279A.010(aa)(A) – "Public improvement" does not include:

> "(A) Projects for which no funds of a contracting agency are directly or indirectly used, except for participation that is incidental or related primarily to project design or inspection."

ORS 279A.010(aa)(B) – "Public improvement" does not include:

> "(B) Emergency work, minor alteration, ordinary repair or maintenance necessary to preserve a public improvement."

ORS 279A.010(bb) – A "public improvement contract" means "a public contract for a public improvement. 'Public improvement contract' does not include a public contract for emergency work, minor alterations, or ordinary repair or maintenance necessary to preserve a public improvement."

### *Performance Bonds*

Public contracting under Chapter 279C is subject to ORS Chapter 279A. ORS 279C.010. ORS Chapter 279C became "operative" March 1, 2005, "and applies only to public contracts first advertised, but if not advertised then entered into, on or after March 1, 2005." *See* Note following ORS 279C.005.

ORS 279C.375, *as amended*, 2005 Oregon Laws Ch. 103, § 17; Ch. 376, § 1, pertains to "[a]ward of contract" and "bonds" for public improvements.

ORS 279C.375(4) – The successful bidder of a public improvement contract must "(a) "Promptly execute a formal contract; and (b) Execute and deliver to the contracting agency a performance bond and a payment bond when required under ORS 279C.380."

ORS 279C.380, *as amended*, 2005 Oregon Laws Ch. 103, § 20 - Applies to performance bonds, payment bonds, and waiver of such bonds for public improvement contracts, including design-build contracts.

ORS 279C.380(1)(a) – "Except as provided in ORS 279C.390" ["Exemption of Contracts from Bid Security and Bonds"], a successful bidder for a public improvement contract must "promptly execute and deliver to the contracting agency" a performance bond that is in an amount equal to the full contract price and "conditioned on the faithful performance of the contract in accordance with the plans, specifications and conditions of the contract." The contracting agency may waive the performance bond requirement. The contracting agency may permit the successful bidder to submit a cashier's or certified check in lieu of all or part of the required performance bond. (Note: The successful bidder must also submit a payment bond. *See* ORS 279C.380(1)(b).).

ORS 279C.380(1)(a) – For design-build public improvement contracts, the performance bond must cover both the performance of the contract and "the preparation and completion of the design and related services covered under the contract." The surety is not liable after the final completion of the contract, or longer if provided for by the contract, "for damages of any nature economic or otherwise including corrective work, attributable to the design aspect of a design-build project, or for the costs of design revisions needed to implement corrective work."

ORS 279C.380(3) – A performance bond "must be executed solely by a surety company or companies holding a certificate of authority to transact surety business in this state. An individual or group of individuals cannot act as a surety."

ORS 279C.380(4) – In cases of emergency, the contracting agency may waive the requirement for a performance bond (and a payment bond).

ORS 279C.380(5) – ORS 279C.380 applies only to public improvement contracts of more than $100,000 or to public improvement contracts of more than $50,000 for highways, bridges, and other transportation projections. Provision added by 2005 Oregon Laws Ch. 103, § 20(5).

ORS 279C.385(2), *as amended*, 2005 Oregon Laws Ch. 103, § 21 – A successful bidder failing to "promptly and properly" execute the awarded contract and failing to deliver the appropriate performance bond (and payment bond and insurance) forfeits its bid security, which is taken as liquidated damages, not as a penalty.

ORS 279C.470(1)(a), (c) – A court may determine that a public improvement contract is void because of the contracting agency's failure to comply with statutory or regulatory procurement requirements. But, if the contractor has not intentionally violated any applicable laws, then the contractor is entitled to reimbursement unless the court determines that "substantial injustice" would result. If the work is substantially complete, the contracting agency must ratify the contract. A ratified contract is deemed "valid, binding and legally enforceable," and the contractor's payment and performance bonds remain in "full force and effect."

ORS 279C.580(3), (4), (5), *as amended*, 2005 Oregon Laws Ch. 103, §§ 3 4(3), (4), (5) – Contractors and first-tier subcontractors and lower-tier subcontractors must include in their contracts a payment penalty clause and an interest penalty clause for specified late payments. In the event of a good-faith dispute over amounts due, the contractor or subcontractor can retain up to 150 percent from the amount due a subcontractor without having to pay a late payment interest penalty, "giving such recognition as the parties consider appropriate to the ability of a subcontractor to furnish a performance bond and a payment bond."

**Public –**

**b. Contracts for Construction Other than Public Improvements**

ORS 279C.320(3) – When construction services are not "a public improvement" because the funds of a public agency have not been "directly or indirectly used, except for participation that is incidental or related primarily to project design or inspection," the benefiting public body "may" condition acceptance of the services on receipt of a performance bond, a payment bond, and appropriate insurance.

ORS 701.035, *as amended*, 2005 Oregon Laws Ch. 249, § 1; 2005 Oregon Laws Ch. 432, § 8 (concerns licensing of independent contractors).

ORS 701.055(1) – "A person may not undertake, offer to undertake or submit a bid to do work as a contractor unless that person has a current, valid license issued by the Construction Contractors Board.

ORS 701.055(3) – "... A county, city or state agency that requires the issuance of a permit as a condition precedent to construction, alteration, improvement, demolition, movement or repair of any building or structure or the appurtenances to the structure shall, as a condition for issuing the permit, require that the applicant for a permit file a written statement ... affirm[ing] that the applicant is licensed ... or, if the applicant is exempt from licensing ... list[ing] the basis for the exemption."

**Private** – No statutes in Oregon specifically require performance bonds on private projects. Nevertheless, licensed contractors in Oregon must post a statutory bond in connection with an application for a contractor's license.

ORS 701.035, *as amended*, 2005 Oregon Laws Ch. 249, § 1; 2005 Oregon Laws Ch. 432, § 8 (concerns licensing of independent contractors).

ORS 701.055(1) – "A person may not undertake, offer to undertake or submit a bid to do work as a contractor unless that person has a current, valid license issued by the Construction Contractors Board."

ORS 701.055(3) – "A city, county or the State of Oregon may not issue a building permit to any person required to be licensed ... that does not have a current, valid license... ."

ORS 701.085(1) – A person who applies for or seeks renewal of a contractor's license must file a surety bond with the state Construction Contractors Board. The bond must be issued by one or more corporate sureties authorized to do business in the State of Oregon.

The amount of the surety bond depends upon the type of contractor:

General contractor or licensed developer – $15,000, ORS 701.085(2);
Specialty contractor – $10,000, ORS 701.085(3);
Inspector – $10,000, ORS 701.085(4);
Limited contractor – work not exceeding $40,000 in gross annual volume and contracts not exceeding $5,000, ORS 701.085(5).

The bond required under ORS 701.085 "is for the exclusive purpose of payment of final orders and arbitration award of the board...." ORS 701.085(9).

ORS 701.139 – The Construction Contractors Board "may resolve a dispute against a licensed contractor only if a claim is made against the contractor's surety bond required by ORS 701.085 [*supra*]."

Claims allowed against a licensed contractor's surety bond are limited to the following:

ORS 701.140(1) – A claim against a contractor by the owner of a structure or other real property for negligent work, improper work, or breach of contract.

ORS 701.140(2) – A claim against a contractor by the owner of a structure or other real property to "discharge, or to recoup funds expended in discharging, a lien."

ORS 701.140(3) – A claim against a licensed subcontractor by a licensed contractor for negligent work, improper work, or breach of contract.

ORS 701.140(4) – A claim by a person furnishing labor to a contractor.

ORS 701.140(5) – A claim, as limited by rule of the board, by "a person furnishing material or renting or supplying equipment to a contractor. The minimum limit set by the board shall not exceed $150."

ORS 701.140(6) – A claim by a subcontractor against a contractor for "unpaid labor or materials arising out of a contract."

ORS 701.430(1) – Before beginning construction, a contractor or subcontractor "may" execute and deliver to the owner, contractor, or subcontractor "a good and sufficient bond in a sum equal to the contract price for the faithful performance of the contract." The bond term must include that time period during which "claims of lien or notices of other encumbrances based on the construction performed under the contract may be filed under applicable law." If such a bond is not obtained, the owner, contractor, or subcontractor may withhold retainage. ORS 701.430(3).

**Department of Transportation** – The Department of Transportation is a "contracting agency" within the meaning of the Public Contracting Code. *State ex rel. Town Concrete Pipe, Inc. v. Andersen*, 264 Or. 565, 570, 505 P.2d 1162, 1164 (1973). Except as otherwise provided in the Public Contracting Code, the Director of Transportation has all of the rights, powers and authority to, *inter alia*, "procure or supervise the procurement of all goods, services, public improvements and personal services relating to the operation, maintenance or construction of highways, bridges and other transportation facilities that are subject to the authority of the Department of Transportation." ORS 279A.050 (3)(b).

ORS 279C.390(1) – The Director of Transportation may exempt certain contracts or classes of the public improvement contracts described in ORS 279A.050(3)(b), *supra*, from the requirement for a performance bond (as well as the requirements for bid security and payment bonds).

ORS 279C.390(2) – The contracting agency "may" still require "a good and sufficient performance bond" (as well as bid security and "a good and sufficient payment bond, or any combination of such bonds"), even though the subject contract is in a class exempted from such requirements by the Director of Transportation.

ORS 279C.390(3)(a) – The Director of Transportation "may" exempt contracts or classes of contracts financed from the proceeds of Highway User Tax Bonds (ORS 367.620(3)(a)) from the requirement for "a good and sufficient bond" to ensure the contract's performance (and exempt such contracts from the bid security requirement).

ORS 279C.390(3)(b) – In the alternative to exemption under ORS 279C.390(3)(a), the Director of Transportation may reduce the amount of the performance bond for contracts or classes of contracts financed from Highway User Tax Bonds to less than 100 percent of the contract price.

ORS 279C.390(4) – The Department of Transportation is solely responsible for any recoverable damages exceeding the amount of the performance bond required under ORS 279C.390(3).

ORS 802.179(13)(a),(b) – The Department of Transportation must disclose personal information from a motor vehicle record to a person who is in the business of "disseminating" such information. The disseminator must enter into a contract with the department, ORS 802.179(13)(b), and file a performance bond in the amount of $25,000. The bond must be in favor of the State of Oregon on a form subject to approval by the state attorney general. ORS 802.179(13)(a).

**Other** – ORS 273.815(1), (b), (c), (e) – The Department of State Lands may lease common school grazing lands and may loan monies belonging to the Common School Fund to lessees of such lands. The department may require performance bonds to secure performance of any such lease or loan.

ORS 376.340(1) – A forest road contractor must execute and file a performance bond with the county clerk. The county court fixes the amount of the bond.

ORS 279B.055(11) – For public procurements pursuant to competitive sealed bidding, the successful bidder must promptly execute a contract. The duty to execute the contract includes "the posting of performance security" where required.

ORS 279B.060(3)(c) – For public procurements pursuant to competitive sealed proposals, the successful bidder must promptly execute a contract. Execution of the contract includes "the posting of performance security" where required.

ORS 297.435(2)(c) – A municipal corporation is exempt from audit if, in part, "the principal responsible official" of the corporation is covered during the entire year by "a fidelity or faithful performance bond in an amount at least equal to the total amount of money received by the municipal corporation during the year. For municipal corporations with total receipts and expenditures of more than $150,000, but not exceeding $500,000, the fidelity or "faithful performance bond" must be in an amount "at least equal to 10 percent of the total receipts for the year, but not less than $10,000." ORS 297.435(3)(c).

***Case law rules that might generally apply***

"The general rule when claims are made against performance bonds on public-works projects has been to construe the relevant statutes so as to protect laborers and suppliers against mismanagement or dishonesty by public-works contractors insofar as it is possible for a performance bond to do so." *State ex rel. Thuney Logging, Inc. v. Fireman's Fund Ins. Co.*, 254 Or. 145, 147, 458 P.2d 413, 414 (1969).

"... [S]ince performance of a contract involving esthetic judgment cannot be measured objectively, it would not be reasonable to require an architect to post a performance bond." *Mongiovi v. Doerner*, 24 Or. App. 639, 645, 546 P.2d 1110, 1113 (1976).

"We must first seek to ascertain the intention of the parties as expressed in the instrument itself, bearing in mind that [the surety] was a compensated surety and that if the bond is susceptible of two constructions, the one which favors the insured must be adopted." *U.S. Fidelity & Guaranty Co. v. Thomlinson-Arkwright Co.*, 172 Or. 307, 317, 141 P.2d 817, 821 (1943).

Oregon case law recognizes that the liabilities of sureties under bonds required by statute are different from the liabilities of insurance companies under private contracts of insurance. *Harrell v. Travelers Indem. Co.,* 279 Or. 199, 218 n22, 567 P.2d 1013, 1022 n22 (1977).

Although a performance bond is not an insurance policy, Oregon courts may apply similar rules of construction to performance bond language as are used when interpreting the wording of insurance policies.

Oregon follows the general rule that, except as otherwise dictated by statute or public policy, insurance contracts are regarded in the same light as ordinary business contracts between individuals and are subject to the same general principles of construction. *See e.g. Hoffman Const. Co. v. Fred S. James & Co. of Oregon,* 313 Or. 464, 469-72, 836 P.2d 703, 706-07 (1992).

For purposes of statutory construction in connection with public improvement contracts, to discern the legislature's intent, "the first level of analysis requires an examination of the text and context of the statutory provision." *State ex rel. Dept. of Administrative Services v. United Pacific Ins. Co.,* 172 Or. App. 435, 440-41, 18 P.3d 491, 493-94, *rev. denied sub nom. State ex rel. Oregon Waste Systems v. United Pacific Ins. Co. and Dept. of Transp.,* 332 Or. 431, 30 P.3d 1184 (2001) (citing *Portland General Elec. Co. v. Bureau of Labor and Industries,* 317 Or. 606, 610, 859 P.2d 1143, 1146 (1993)).

## 2. Damages Covered

### *Set forth in any statutes and/or case law*

"The general rule is: '... (A) surety is liable only for the payment of actual damages caused by the principal and may not be held for exemplary or punitive damages, in the absence of any statutory provision imposing such liability.'" *Butler v. United Pacific Ins. Co.*, 265 Or. 473, 474-75, 509 P.2d 1184, 1185 (Or. 1973) (quoting 11 Appleman, Insurance Law and Practice s 6361, p. 86 (1944)) (other citations omitted).

"We adhere to the doctrine ... to the effect that the surety is liable in the aggregate only to the extent of the penalty named in the bond. 'This of course does not include attorney fees, interest, or costs.'" *U.S. Fidelity & Guaranty Co. v. Zidell-Steinberg Co.*, 151 Or. 538, 555, 50 P.2d 584, 591, *modified*, 151 Or. 538, 51 P.2d 687 (1935) (citations omitted).

In *Stirling v. Dari-Delite, Inc.*, 262 Or. 359, 372, 498 P.2d 753, 756 (1972), the court held the surety liable on a cost bond for statutory delay damages in the amount of 10 percent of the original judgment because of the surety's "frivolous" appeal.

ORS 19.445 [formerly ORS 19.160], 2003 Oregon Laws Ch. 576, § 284 – "Whenever a judgment is affirmed on appeal, and it is for recovery of money, or personal property or the value thereof, the judgment shall be given for 10 percent of the amount thereof, for damages for the delay, unless it appears evident to the appellate court that there was probable cause for taking the appeal."

ORS 19.450(5) [formerly ORS 19.190(2)], 2003 Oregon Laws Ch. 576, § 89 – "If the appellate judgment terminating an appeal contains a judgment against a surety for an undertaking, the trial court administrator shall enter the judgment against the surety in like manner and with like effect as if the judgment was given in the court below."

ORS 701.085(1) requires an applicant for issuance or renewal of a contractor's license to file a surety bond with the state Construction Contractors Board. In any action against a surety based upon the failure of the surety to pay a claim against the contractor's bond required under ORS 701.085(1), or based upon on the denial of the claim by the surety, "the court may award: (a) Costs; (b) Reasonable attorney fees to the prevailing party as part of the costs; and (c) Twice the amount of any damages that the [Construction Contractors Board] ordered the surety to pay on the claim if the surety arbitrarily and capriciously refused to pay upon order of the board." ORS 701.085(12).

In Oregon, prejudgment interest generally cannot be recovered in actions at law unless there is an agreement to pay interest or a statute imposing interest. *Strader v. Grange Mut. Ins. Co.,* 179 Or. App 329, 338, 39 P.3d 903, 908, *rev. denied,* 334 Or. 190, 47 P.3d 485 (2002) (citation omitted). Oregon's general interest statute, ORS 82.010, provides that an interest rate of 9 percent per annum is payable in certain circumstances (*i.e.,* concerning certain prejudgment monetary obligations and regarding judgments for the payment of money).

ORS 82.010(1)(a) provides for an award of prejudgment interest at the statutory rate of 9 percent per year on "[a]ll moneys after they become due * * * ." ORS 82.010(1)(a) applies to breach of contract actions when: (1) the exact amount of damages is either ascertained or readily ascertainable by simple computation or by reference to generally recognized standards such as market price; and (2) the time from which interest should run is easily ascertained. *See Krieg v. Union Pac. Land Resources Corp.,* 269 Or. 221, 234, 525 P.2d 48, 54 (1974). *See also Public Market Co. of Portland v. City of Portland,* 171 Or. 522, 625, 138 P.2d 916, 918 (1943). Prejudgment interest generally is not available in tort actions in Oregon because the damages usually are not ascertainable until judgment is entered. *Erickson Air-Crane Co. v. United*

*Technologies Corp.*, 87 Or. App. 577, 582, 743 P.2d 747, 750, *rev. denied,* 304 Or. 680, 748 P.2d 142 (1987) (citations omitted).

For a discussion of attorney's fee awards, *see infra* § 8.

***Obligations of surety to perform and/or pay***

In the event of the principal's breach, the surety can "either assume the contract and perform it or pay the damages caused by the principal's breach." In either case, the liability of the surety is determined "by construing the bond and the contract together." *Biomass One, L.P. v. S-P Const.*, 103 Or. App. 521, 529, 799 P.2d 152, 157 (1990).

"When a surety, either corporate or individual, in pursuance of the terms of an undertaking, 'assumes' the performance of the principal's contract, such surety, by being subrogated to the rights of the principal thereunder, must necessarily become subject to all his liabilities." *Ausplund v. Aetna Indem. Co.*, 47 Or. 10, 20, 81 P. 577, 580, *reh'g denied*, 47 Or. 10, 82 P. 12 (1905).

"[I]n order to determine whether a guarantor or other surety is discharged by alteration of the underlying contractual obligation, a court must first ask whether the guarantor consented to the modification. If so, the guarantor is not discharged. If not, the court must determine whether the guarantor is an uncompensated or compensated surety. If the guarantor is uncompensated, a change to the guaranteed contract discharges the guarantor if the change is material, as long as the change is not one that could inure only to the guarantor's benefit. [Footnote omitted] If on the other hand, the guarantor is compensated, an alteration to the contract discharges the guarantor only if it materially increases the guarantor's risk on the contract. [Footnote omitted]." *Marc Nelson Oil Products, Inc. v. Grim Logging Co., Inc.*, 199 Or. App. 73, 80, 110 P.3d 120, 124, *opinion adhered to as modified on reconsideration*, 200 Or. App. 239, 115 P.3d 935 (2005).

Restatement (Third) Suretyship & Guaranty § 41 (1996) states that a guarantor is discharged by a contractual modification if the modification "creates a substituted contract or imposes risks on the secondary obligor fundamentally different from those imposed pursuant to the transaction prior to modification." *See Marc Nelson Oil Products, Inc. v. Grim Logging co., Inc.*, 199 Or. App. 73, 80 n5, 110 P.3d 120, 124 n5, *opinion adhered to as modified on reconsideration*, 200 Or. App. 239, 115 P.3d 935 (2005).

"A material change is one that a careful and prudent person undertaking the risk would regard as substantially increasing the chance of loss." *Samuelson v. Promontory Inv. Corp.*, 85 Or. App. 315, 320, 736 P.2d 207, 210 (1987).

"It is a settled rule of law that where a security reserved in a building contract for the benefit of the sureties on the builder's bond is lessened, impaired, or destroyed by a premature payment to the contractors, the sureties will be released and discharged to the extent at least of the amount so paid.... But this doctrine can have no application where such payment is made with the knowledge and by the consent of the sureties." *Enterprise Hotel Co. v. Book*, 48 Or. 58, 62, 85 P. 333, 335 (1906).

***Whether failure to provide insurance transfers burden to surety*** – No Oregon cases directly address this issue.

***Limitations on damages***

"The general rule is: '... (A) surety is liable only for the payment of actual damages caused by the principal, and may not be held for exemplary or punitive damages, in the absence of any statutory provision imposing such liability.'" *Butler v. United Pac. Ins. Co.*, 265 Or. 473, 474-75, 509 P.2d 1184, 1185 (1973) (quoting 11 Appleman, Insurance Law and Practice s 6361, p. 86 (1944)) (other citations omitted).

***Whether obligee may set off bonded contract funds against other principal-obligee debts or obligations***

The surety was responsible to the obligee on a performance bond for $903,280 in damages attributable to the principal contractor's defective performance, but the obligee owed the principal $945,000. The obligee argued that the surety was not entitled to any part of the $945,000 due the contractor and, therefore, was not entitled to have the $903,280 in damages offset against the $945,000 owed by the obligee. The court disagreed, stating that, because the obligee owed the principal more than the amount of damages, no amount was payable by the principal or its surety to the obligee; "In short, there was no *loss* that AIC's [the surety] bond covered." *Westwood Corp., Developers and Contractors v. Bowen*, 108 Or. App. 310, 318, 815 P.2d 1282, 1287 (1991), *rev. dismissed*, 312 Or. 589, 824 P.2d 418 (1992) (emphasis in original).

***Incorporation of specific contract terms by reference***

"The reason for an incorporation by reference is to cause the provisions of one contract or document to apply to another contract or document to which they otherwise would not apply." *Pioneer Resources, LLC v. Lemargie*, 175 Or. App. 202, 209, 27 P.3d 520, 524 (2001), *rev. denied*, 333 Or. 399, 42 P.3d 1243 (2002).

Where a performance bond refers to a particular contract in a way that is sufficient to identify that contract, and there is "no specific limitation on the undertaking, the contract is incorporated into the bond," and the surety is liable for a breach of any the terms of the incorporated contract. *Biomass One, L.P. v. S-P Const.*, 103 Or. App. 521, 528, 799 P.2d 152, 156 (1990) (citing *Ausplund v. Aetna Indem. Co.*, 47 Or. 10, 17, 81 P. 577, *reh'g denied*, 47 Or. 10, 82 P. 12 (1905)).

The contract between an owner and general contractor "must, or is construed to, contain those conditions required by statute." *Wiley Co. v. Home Indem. Co.*, 213 Or. 493, 500, 326 P.2d 123, 126-27 (1958); *State ex rel. Dept. of Administrative Services v. United Pacific Ins. Co.*, 172 Or. App. 435, 442, 18 P.3d 491, 494, *rev. denied*, 332 Or. 431, 30 P.3d 1184 (2001).

**3. Penal Sum Variations**

***Limitations per statute and/or case law*** – "A surety can limit its liability to less than the entire construction contract." *Biomass One, L.P. v. S-P Const.*, 103 Or. App. 521, 529, 799 P.2d 152, 157 (1990).

***Effect of changes in work upon penal sum, if at all***

"[I]n order to determine whether a guarantor or other surety is discharged by alteration of the underlying contractual obligation, a court must first ask whether the guarantor consented to the modification. If so, the guarantor is not discharged. If not, the court must determine whether the guarantor is an uncompensated or compensated surety. If the guarantor is uncompensated, a change to the guaranteed contract discharges the guarantor if the change is material, as long as the change is not one that could inure only to the guarantor's benefit. [Footnote omitted] If on the other hand, the guarantor is compensated, an alteration to the contract discharges the guarantor only if it materially increases the guarantor's risk on the contract. [Footnote omitted]." *Marc Nelson Oil Products, Inc. v. Grim Logging Co., Inc.*, 199 Or. App. 73, 80, 110 P.3d 120, 124, *opinion adhered to as modified on reconsideration*, 200 Or. App. 239, 115 P.3d 935 (2005).

Restatement (Third) Suretyship & Guaranty § 41 (1996) states that a guarantor is discharged by a contractual modification if the modification "creates a substituted contract or imposes risks on the secondary obligor fundamentally different from those imposed pursuant to the transaction prior to modification." *See Marc Nelson Oil Products, Inc. v. Grim Logging co., Inc.*, 199 Or. App. 73, 80 n5, 110 P.3d 120, 124 n5, *opinion adhered to as modified on reconsideration*, 200 Or. App. 239, 115 P.3d 935 (2005).

"A material change is one that a careful and prudent person undertaking the risk would regard as substantially increasing the chance of loss." *Samuelson v. Promontory Inv. Corp.*, 85 Or. App. 315, 320, 736 P.2d 207, 210 (1987).

"It is a settled rule of law that where a security reserved in a building contract for the benefit of the sureties on the builder's bond is lessened, impaired, or destroyed by a premature payment to the contractors, the sureties will be released and discharged to the extent at least of the amount so paid.... But this doctrine can have no application where such payment is made with the knowledge and by the consent of the sureties." *Enterprise Hotel Co. v. Book*, 48 Or. 58, 62, 85 P. 333, 335 (1906).

***Statutory or case law protections or dangers to penal sum***

"We adhere to the doctrine ... to the effect that the surety is liable in the aggregate only to the extent of the penalty named in the bond. 'This of course does not include attorney fees, interest, or costs.'" *U.S. Fidelity & Guaranty Co. v. Zidell-Steinberg Co.*, 151 Or. 538, 555, 50 P.2d 584, 591, *modified*, 151 Or. 538, 51 P.2d 687 (1935) (citations omitted).

"The general rule is that the liability of a surety is limited to the amount of its bond. However, when the principal defaults or fails to perform, the surety may, where permitted by contract or with the acceptance of the other party to the principal contract, assume the role of its principal for purposes of performing the obligation which it has bonded. When the surety does so, it becomes responsible for performance of the principal contract and for all obligations incurred in connection with performance, notwithstanding the limits of liability in the bond." *Copeland Sand and Gravel, Inc. v. Insurance Co. of North America*, 40 Or. App. 831, 834-35, 596 P.2d 623, 625 (1979), *rev'd on other grounds*, 288 Or. 325, 607 P.2d 718 (1980).

In *Copeland Sand and Gravel, Inc. v. Insurance Co. of North America,* in reversing the decision of the court of appeals based on an evaluation of the evidence of record, the Supreme Court of Oregon reasoned:

> The Court of Appeals based its conclusion upon a rule of law that a surety, by assuming the principal's role in the actual performance of the principal's contract '* * * becomes responsible for performance of the principal contract and for all obligations incurred in connection with performance, notwithstanding the limits of liability in the bond.' [Footnote omitted] However correct that rule may be, the record does not show, as a matter of law, that [the surety] assumed the performance of [the principal's] contract.

288 Or. 325, 332, 607 P.2d 718, 721 (1980).

## 4. Parties Covered

### *Statutes and/or case law as to whether only obligees are covered*

ORS 279C.380(1)(a), *as amended*, 2005 Oregon Laws Ch. 103, § 20(1) – "Except as provided in ORS 279C.390" ["Exemption of Contracts from Bid Security and Bonds"], a successful bidder for a public improvement contract must deliver to the contracting agency a performance bond. "The performance bond must be solely for the protection of the contracting agency that awarded the contract and any public agency or agencies for whose benefit the contract was awarded."

A subcontractor on a public contract could not recover on a performance bond provided by the general contractor to the state. The bond expressly named the state, through its Department of Administrative Services, as the sole obligee. The court held that "the key distinguishing feature" of the bond was that the state was the only obligee and therefore only the state had a right to bring an action the bond. The subcontractor had no right to bring a direct claim against the bond. *State ex rel. Dept. of Administrative Services v. United Pacific Ins. Co.*, 172 Or. App. 435, 443, 18 P.3d 491, 494, *rev. denied sub nom State ex rel. Oregon Waste Systems v. United Pacific Ins. Co. and Dept. of Transp.*, 332 Or. 431, 30 P.3d 1184 (2001).

***Coverage for:***

**Third-party beneficiaries** – The Oregon Supreme Court held that an engineering firm that provided services to a bonded contractor on a private contract was a third-party beneficiary on the bond. Plaintiff engineering firm provided construction services on a private project for a contractor that subsequently went bankrupt without paying plaintiff. Plaintiff sought to recover against the contractor's bond, which stated, in part, as "the condition of this obligation is such that if the contractor ... shall (a) Pay all persons, firms and corporations who perform labor ... under the Contract ...; (d) Fully completed the work as provided in the Contract ...; (e) Fully indemnify and save harmless the Owner ... against and from all cost and damage which it may suffer by reason of a default in the performance of any of the foregoing provisions ...." The court held that, although the bond was an "archaic form" using "words of condition," the words at issue were "words of promise." Therefore, under the bond, the surety had "promised" that laborers would paid, and the third-party engineering firm had a right of action against the bond. The court quoted 4 Corbin, Contracts s 800, 153-64 (1951), which states that "the third party has an enforceable right if the surety promises in the bond, either in express words or by reasonable implication, to pay money to him." *Jacobs Assoc. v. Argonaut Ins. Co.*, 282 Or. 551, 553-559, 580 P.2d 529, 529-533 (1978).

A subcontractor attempted to bring a claim for nonpayment under the general contractor's performance bond. The subcontractor argued that it was a third-party obligee under the bond because the bond incorporated the prime contract, which contained a statutory provision requiring prompt payment to subcontractors. The Oregon Court of Appeals held, however, that the subcontractor had no right under the performance bond because the bond specifically stated that the owner was the only obligee under the bond and the only party entitled to bring an action on the bond. *State ex rel. Dept. of Administrative Services v. United Pacific Ins. Co.*, 172 Or. App. 435, 442-43, 18 P.3d 491, 494-95, *rev. denied sub nom State ex rel. Oregon Waste Systems v. United Pacific Ins. Co. and Dept. of Transp.*, 332 Or. 431, 30 P.3d 1184 (2001).

**Assignees** – The owner of certain property executed to plaintiff a bond for a deed, covenanting to convey to plaintiff said property upon payment of $100 plus interest. Plaintiff's husband assigned the bond to a third-party in payment for goods without telling plaintiff. The assignee then assigned the bond to a second assignee, who then attempted to purchase said property. The court held that, because of information available to the second assignee, she was not an innocent purchaser, and, upon plaintiff's payment of the $100 plus interest to the second assignee, the latter was to execute to plaintiff "a good and sufficient deed" to the property. *Hawley v. Hawley*, 43 Or. 352, 353, 356, 73 P. 3, 4, 5 (1903).

**Dual obligees** – Pursuant to an agreement for dissolution of a partnership, the partners' action against the surety accrued when the principal defaulted on his promise to pay the partnerships' creditors at the time those obligations were due. The court held that the partners, as obligees, did not have to pay the creditors before having a cause of action against the surety. *Chada v. Tapp*, 277 Or. 3, 8, 558 P.2d 1225, 1227 (1977).

## 5. Notice or Filing Required

### *Statutory provisions*

**Public Works Bonds** – Former ORS 279.029 required successful bidders on public improvement contracts to "execute and deliver to the public contracting agency a good and sufficient bond ... in a sum equal to the contract price for the faithful performance of the contract." ORS 279.029(4)(b). Under former ORS 279.526(1), "[a] person claiming to have supplied labor or materials for the prosecution of the work provided for in the contract" had a right of action on the contractor's bond provided pursuant to ORS 279.029. Former ORS 270.528 set forth the requirements for notice of a claim brought under ORS 279.526.

Although the above statutory provisions characterized the required bond as one to ensure the contractor's obligations to pay, regulations characterized the bond as ensuring performance obligations. *See* James L. Knoll & Michael R. Seidl, *Oregon*, Ch. 38, 187-88 (in *Fifty State Construction Lien And Bond Law* (Robert F. Cushman, ed., 1992).

The 2003 Oregon Legislature repealed, *inter alia*, ORS 279.029, ORS 279.526, and ORS 279.528, effective March 1, 2005. 2003 Oregon

Laws Ch. 794. The repeal "applie[d] only to public contracts first advertised, but if not advertised then entered into, on or after March 1, 2005." *See* Note preceding ORS 279.005.

The Oregon Legislature replaced ORS 279.029, ORS 279.526, ORS 279.528 and other related statutes with statutes specifically applicable to "public works bonds" or payment bonds for public construction contracts. *See* ORS 279C.600, *as amended* 2005 Oregon Laws Ch. 360, § 3 ("Actions Against Payment Bond of Contractor or Subcontractor"); ORS 279C.605, *as amended* 2005 Oregon Laws Ch. 360, § 4 ("Notice"); ORS 279C.610, *as amended* 2005 Oregon Laws Ch. 360, § 5 ("Action on Contractor's Payment Bond; Time Limitation"); ORS 279C.625, *as amended* 2005 Oregon Laws Ch. 103, §§ 35, 40 ("Payment Bond Execution; Joint Liability").

A "public works bond," as referred to in the amended statutes (ORS 279C.600 – ORS 279C.625, supra) must provide that "the contractor or subcontractor" will pay claims ordered by the Bureau of Labor and Industries to workers performing labor upon public works projects." 2005 Oregon Laws Ch. 360, § 2.

**Claims Filed with the Construction Contractors Board (ORS 701.145)** – ORS 701.145(1) – A person having certain specified claims involving work on a residential structure or an appurtenance thereto or on a large or small commercial structure or an appurtenance thereto must file a statement of the claim with the Construction Contractors Board on a form prescribed by the board.

ORS 701.145(2)-(4). The Construction Contractors Board may suspend processing of the claim under certain conditions, dismiss or close the claim under certain conditions, or accept the claim and "initiate proceedings to determine the validity of the claim."

ORS 701.145(5) – If the Construction Contractors Board cannot resolve the claim, the board "may" issue a contested case notice and issue a proposed default order or refer the matter for hearing.

ORS 701.145(6) – The Construction Contractors Board must send a copy of the notice of a contested case and any proposed order to the contractor's bond surety.

**Claims Not Resolved Under ORS 701.145** – ORS 701.146, *as amended,* 2005 Oregon Laws Ch. 263, pertains to certain large commercial structure claims and certain small claims not resolved under ORS 701.145.

ORS 701.146(1) – For claims not resolved under ORS 701.145, a person must bring an action against the licensed contractor in court or initiate a proceeding to resolve the claim through binding arbitration under ORS 36.600 – ORS 36.740.

ORS 701.146(2) – The claimant must file the claim with the Construction Contractors Board by delivering to the board a copy of the complaint, the demand for arbitration, or such other document necessary to initiate arbitration. "The complaint, demand or other document must be accompanied by a statement of claim in a form prescribed by board rule. The claimant must provide the same information to its surety. Delivery must be "by certified mail, return receipt requested, no later than the earlier of: (a) The 90th day after the complaint, demand or other document was filed or made; (b) The 14th day before the first day of trial or arbitration; or (c) The 30th day before: (A) The court issues a judgment on the complaint; or (B) The arbitrator issues an award on the arbitration."

ORS 701.146(4) – Generally, if the claimant has given proper notice to the surety, a judgment or award against the contractor entered in the court action or the arbitration is binding on the surety.

ORS 701.146(6) – "If a court issues a judgment on an action, or reduces an arbitration award to judgment, against a contractor ..., the claimant must deliver a certified copy of the judgment to the board and to the surety no later than the 30th day after entry of the judgment in order to retain a claim against the bond."

ORS 701.146(7) – "Upon receipt of a timely delivered certified copy of the judgment, the board shall issue a proposed order in the amount of the judgment together with any costs, interest and attorney fees awarded under the judgment, to the extent that the judgment, costs, interest and fees are within the jurisdiction of the board.... The board shall issue the proposed order in a form that indicates the surety's maximum liability to the claimant."

ORS 701.085(9) – The contractor's surety bond "is for the exclusive purpose of payment of final orders and arbitration award of the [Construction Contractors Board]."

ORS 701.085(10) – Once a claim has been determined under ORS 701.145, *supra,* or ORS 701.146, supra, the Construction Contractors Board must notify the contractor's bond surety of the final order. "The notification shall include a list of all claims upon which a final order has been issued."

***Case law rules concerning condition precedent notice***

"The requirement that notice be given timely is a substantive condition precedent to recovery under the Oregon Tort Claims Act that, if not satisfied, deprives a plaintiff of the right to make a claim." *Butterfield v. State*, 163 Or. App. 227, 232, 987 P.2d 569, 571 (1999), *rev. denied*, 330 Or. 252, 6 P.3d 1099 (2000) (internal quotations and citations omitted).

## 6. Time for Suit

***Statutes of limitation particular to performance bonds and other applicable statutes of limitation***

ORS 12.080(1) is the statute of limitations applicable to contracts. ORS 12.080(1) states, in relevant part:

> An action upon a contract or liability, express or implied, excepting those mentioned in ORS 12.070 ["Action on Judgment, Decree, or Sealed Instrument"], 12.110 [tort statute of limitations], 12.135 ["Action Arising from Construction, Alteration or Repair of Improvement to Real Property"] and except as otherwise provided in ORS 72.7250 ["Statute of Limitations in Contracts for Sale"] ... shall be commenced within six years.

Generally, ORS 12.080(1) runs from the date of the breach of the contract; however, the limitations period is tolled if the defendant fraudulently conceals the breach. *Bruns v. Walters*, 175 Or. App. 360, 366 n9, 28 P.3d 646, 650 n9 (2001).

The statute of limitations applicable to the liability of a surety to a third party for the tortious act of the principal is the statute applicable to the surety's contract with the principal, especially where the principal's liability has been reduced to judgment and continues to exist. *United Pac. Ins. Co.*, 486 F.2d 556, 556 (9th Cir. 1973) (Oregon law).

ORS 12.135(1) – "An action against a person, whether in contract, tort or otherwise, arising from such person having performed the construction alteration or repair of any improvement to real property or the supervision or inspection thereof, or from such person having furnished the design planning, surveying, architectural or engineering services for such improvement, shall be commenced within the applicable period of limitation otherwise established by law; but in any event such action shall be commenced within 10 years from substantial completion or abandonment of such construction, alteration or repair of the improvement to real property."

ORS 30.275, as amended, 2005 Oregon Laws, Ch. 684 - Sets forth the requirements for notice of claims in tort actions against public bodies. The claimant must give notice for wrongful death within one year after the alleged loss or injury and for all other claims, within 180 days after the alleged loss or injury. Those time periods do not include the time period, "not exceeding 90 days, during which the person injured is unable to give notice because of the injury or because of minority, incompetency or other incapacity." ORS 30.275(2).

**Timely Filing of Claims – Construction Contractors Board** – ORS 701.139 – The Construction Contractors Board may resolve a dispute against a licensed contractor "only if a claim is made against the contractor's surety bond." See ORS 701.085, supra. To have access to the bond, the person must file a claim as described under ORS 701.143, supra, within the applicable time limits.

ORS 701.143(1) – If the owner of a new structure files the claim, the Construction Contractors Board must receive it no later than the earlier of "(a) One year after the date the structure was first occupied; or (b) Two years after substantial completion of the structure by the contractor filed against."

ORS 701.143(2) – Except as otherwise provided, if the owner of an existing structure files the claim, the Construction Contractors Board must receive it "no later than one year after the date the work was substantially completed by the contractor filed against."

ORS 701.085(11) – A suit or action may not be commenced against a surety on a contractor's bond until 30 days after the date that the surety is notified by the Construction Contractors Board that "payment is due on the claim."

***Case law statements about enforceability of limitations contained in bonds***

A contractor's bond contained a provision stating that "any suits at law or proceedings in equity brought against this bond to recover a claim thereunder must be instituted within six months after the first breach of said contract." The court stated that the parties to a contract "may stipulate that an action for a breach of an agreement must be brought within a certain period, and, if such limitation is reasonable, it will be upheld." *Ausplund v. Aetna Indem. Co.*, 47 Or. 10, 13, 22, 81 P. 577, 578, 581, *reh'g denied*, 47 Or. 10, 82 P. 12 (1905). *See also Fink v. Guardsmark, LLC,* 2004 WL 1857114, *3 - *4 (D. Or. 2004) (applying Oregon law) (unpublished opinion) (citing and discussing the *Ausplund v. Aetna* case decision with approval).

***Varying statutes of limitation by agreement in bond or contract***

Where a subcontract provided for a one-year statute of limitations, the court held that "[t]he limitation on actions arises from the contract and is governed by the language of the contract." *Biomass One, L.P. v. S-P Const.*, 103 Or. App. 521, 526, 799 P.2d 152, 155 (1990).

An insurer is not required to show prejudice before it can assert a suit limitation provision as an affirmative defense. *Herman v. Valley Ins. Co.,* 145 Or. App. 124, 131, 928 P.2d 985, 990 (1996) (ORS 742.240 sets a minimum 24 month contractual limitation period for fire insurance policies), *rev. denied,* 325 Or. 438, 939 P.2d 621 (1997).

## 7. Procedure

***Statutory or procedural rules that may affect handling or administration of lawsuits***

Oregon Rule of Civil Procedure ("ORCP") 7C(2) states "If the summons is served by any manner other than publication, the defendant shall appear and defend within 30 days from the date of service. If the summons is served by publication ..., the defendant shall appear and defend within 30 days from the date stated in the summons. The date so stated in the summons shall be the date of the first publication."

ORCP 15A – "A motion or answer to the complaint or third party complaint and the reply to a counterclaim or answer to a cross-claim shall be filed with the clerk by the time required by Rule 7C(2) [*supra*] to appear and defend. Any other motion or responsive pleading shall be filed not later than 10 days after service of the pleading moved against or to which the responsive pleading is directed."

***Venue requirements and jurisdictional limitations***

ORS 14.030 – "When the court has jurisdiction of the parties, it may exercise it in respect to any cause of action or suit wherever arising, except for the specific recovery of real property situated without the state, or for an injury thereto."

ORS 14.040 – "Actions and suits for the following causes shall be commenced and tried in the county in which the subject of the action or suit, or some part thereof, is situated: (1) Actions for the recovery of real property, or an estate or interest therein, or for injuries to real property .... (3) Suits for the partition of real property. (4) Suits for the foreclosure of a lien or mortgage upon real property. (5) Suits for the determination of an adverse claim, estate, or interest in real property, or the specific performance of an agreement in relation thereto."

ORS 14.050(2) – "Actions for the following causes shall be commenced and tried in the county where the causes, or some part thereof, arose: ... (2) Against a public officer or person specifically appointed to execute the duties of the public officer for an act done by the officer or person in virtue of the office of the public officer; or against a person who, by the command of the public officer, or in aid of the public officer, shall do anything touching the duties of such officer."

ORS 14.080 – "All other actions shall be commenced in the county in which the defendants, or one of them, reside at the commencement of the action or in the county where the cause of action arose. ... (2) For purposes of this section, a corporation incorporated under the laws of this state, a limited partnership or a foreign corporation authorized to do business in this state shall be deemed to be a resident of any county where the corporation or limited partnership conducts regular sustained business activity or has an office for the transaction of business or where any agent authorized to receive process resides. A foreign corporation or foreign limited partnership not authorized to transact business in this state shall be deemed not to be a resident of any county in this state."

ORS 14.110(1)(a) – "The court or judge thereof may change the place of trial, on the motion of either party to an action or suit, when it appears from the affidavit of such party that the motion is not made for the purpose of delay and: (a) That the action or suit has not been commenced in the proper county; ..."

Oregon Rule of Civil Procedure ("ORCP") 4L provides for personal jurisdiction "in any action where prosecution of the action against a defendant in this state is not inconsistent with the Constitution of this state or the Constitution of the United States." ORCP 4L authorizes a trial court to "exercise personal jurisdiction over an out-of-state defendant to the extent permitted by the Due Process Clause." *Shamrock Building Materials, Inc. v. Overseas Building Supply, L.L.C.*, 189 Or. App. 302, 305-06, 76 P.3d 127, 129 (2003). To determine whether a court has personal jurisdiction over a defendant, the court engages in a two-part inquiry: 1) whether the defendant has minimum contacts with the forum state; and 2) whether, even if minimum contacts exist, the exercise of jurisdiction is reasonable. *See State ex rel. Circus Circus Reno, Inc. v. Pope*, 317 Or. 151, 159-60, 854 P.2d 461 (1993).

***Court rules***

*Rules applicable to court proceedings in Oregon include:*

- Oregon Rules of Civil Procedure;
- Oregon Rules of Appellate Procedure;
- Oregon Uniform Trial Court Rules;
- Tax Court Rules; and
- Supplementary Local Rules of the Oregon Trial Courts that are adopted by the respective counties.

The rules for Oregon courts are available at: http://www.ojd.state.or.us.

***Particular agency regulations/rules*** – Not applicable.

***Arbitration requirements and application***

It is the policy of the State of Oregon "to construe arbitration agreements liberally to enhance arbitrability of disputes." *Union county School Dist. No. 1 v. Valley Inland Pacific Constructors, Inc.*, 59 Or. App. 602, 606-07, 652 P.2d 349, 352 (1982).

Oregon's Uniform Arbitration Act is codified at ORS 36.600 – ORS 36.740.

ORS 36.620 sets forth the requirements for a valid arbitration agreement —

ORS 36.620(1) – "An agreement contained in a record to submit to arbitration any existing or subsequent controversy arising between the parties to the agreement is valid, enforceable and irrevocable except upon a ground that exists at law or in equity for the revocation of a contract."

ORS 36.620(2) "... [T]he court shall decide whether an agreement to arbitrate exists or a controversy is subject to an agreement to arbitrate."

ORS 36.620(3) – "An arbitrator shall decide whether a condition precedent to arbitrability has been fulfilled."

ORS 36.620(4) – "If a party to a judicial proceeding challenges the existence of, or claims that a controversy is not subject to, an agreement to arbitrate, the arbitration proceeding may continue pending final resolution of the issue by the court, unless the court otherwise orders."

ORS 36.625(8) – On a petition showing an agreement to arbitrate and alleging another person's refusal to arbitrate pursuant to that agreement, a judge "shall" decide all issues raised under the petition unless there is a constitutional right to a jury trial on a particular issue.

ORS 701.565 sets forth the statutory requirements for arbitration involving construction defects in a residence.

ORS 701.565 (1) – "An owner may not compel arbitration or commence a court action against a contractor, subcontractor or supplier to assert a claim arising out of or relating to any defect in the construction, alteration or repair of a residence or in any system, component or material incorporated into a residence located in this state unless the owner has sent that contractor, subcontractor or supplier a notice of defect ...."

ORS 701.565(2), (3) – Set forth the statutory requirements for the requisite notice.

ORS 701.595 – If an owner compels arbitration, but the owner has not complied with the required statutory procedures, the arbitrator "must" dismiss the arbitration without prejudice. The owner may not commence a new arbitration unless the owner follows the required statutory procedures.

## 8. Attorney's Fees

***Statutes and/or case law limiting or permitting recovery of attorney's fees***

Awards of attorney's fees are potentially available to parties in litigation only when authorized by a statute or by a contract (i.e., express or implied) between the parties. *Stelljes v. State Bd of Parole,* 307 Or. 365, 368, 769 P.2d 177, 178 (1989) (citations omitted). *See also Sands v. Purcell,* 11 Or. App. 614, 615, 504 P.2d 768, 769 (1972).

Oregon Rule of Civil Procedure ("ORCP") 68C governs the procedure for pleading, proof, and award of attorney's fees in all cases, regardless of the source of the right to recovery of the fees. ORCP 68C(1). That is the applicable procedural rule, except when an award of attorney's fees is: (1) claimed as damages arising before the action; or (2) granted by order rather than entered as part of a judgment. *Id.*

**Attorney's fee awards under ORS 742.061** – A successful claimant in an action on a public works bond is eligible for an award of "a reasonable amount to be fixed by the court as attorney fees" to be "taxed as part of the costs of the action and any appeal thereon." ORS 742.061(1). *See State ex rel. Town Concrete Pipe, Inc. v. Andersen,* 264 Or. 565, 572-73, 505 P.2d 1162, 1165-66 (1973) (statute generally authorizing recovery of attorney's fees, if settlement is not made within six months from the date proof of loss is filed with an "insurer" and when the claimant's recovery exceeds the amount of any tender by the insurer, authorizes award of attorney fees in favor of the claimant in an action on a public works bond) (applying predecessor statute to ORS 742.061). *See also Oregon State Highway Commission v. DeLong Corp.,* 9 Or. App. 550, 582-587, 495 P.2d 1215, 1231-33 (1972) (successful claimant on a performance bond was entitled to recover reasonable attorney's fees from the surety under the predecessor statute to ORS 742.061), *cert. denied*, 411 U.S. 965, and *reh'g denied*, 412 U.S. 944 (1973).

Concerning a claimant's right to an award of attorney's fees when prevailing against the surety in an action on a surety bond, ORS 742.061(1) provides in relevant part:

> Except as otherwise provided in subsections (2) [concerning actions to recover personal injury protection benefits] and (3) [concerning actions to recover uninsured or underinsured motorist benefits] of this section, if settlement is not made within six months from the date proof of loss is filed with an insured and an action is brought in any court of this state upon any policy of insurance of any kind or nature, and the plaintiff's recovery exceeds the amount of any tender made by the defendant in such action, a reasonable amount to be fixed by the court as attorney fees shall be taxed as part of the costs of the action and any appeal thereon.

In an action brought on a contractor's bond, if the amount of the claimant's recovery does not exceed the amount of any tender made by the defendant or surety, "a reasonable amount to be fixed by the court as attorney fees shall be taxed and allowed to the defendant as part of the costs of the action and any appeal thereon." ORS 742.061(1). *See*, *Great Western Coatings, Inc. v. Carboline Co.*, 746 F. Supp. 11, 15 (D. Or. 1990) (payment bond surety was "entitled to attorney fees in a reasonable amount to be fixed by the court" under ORS 742.061 when supplier of paint products failed to recover more than the amount of any tender made by the surety). See also Westwood Corp., Developers and Contractors v. Bowen, 108 Or. App. 310, 319, 815 P.2d 1282, 1287 (1991) (performance bond surety and principal were awarded their respective attorney's fees, and no apportionment of services and fees was necessary in light of predominantly common issues among the various claims, pursuant to the predecessor statute to ORS 742.061), *rev. dismissed*, 312 Or. 589, 824 P.2d 418 (1992) (citations omitted).

The right to recover attorney's fees by prevailing contractors and sureties in actions brought on contractors' bonds is codified at ORS 742.061(1), which provides in relevant part:

> If the action is brought upon the bond of a contractor or subcontractor executed and delivered as provided in ORS 279B.055, 279B.060, 279C.380 or 701.430 and the plaintiff's recovery does not exceed the amount of any tender made by the defendant in such action, a reasonable amount to be fixed by the court as attorney fees shall be taxed and allowed to the defendant as part of the costs of the action and any appeal thereon. If in an action brought upon such a bond the surety is allowed attorney fees and costs and the contractor or subcontractor has incurred expenses for attorney fees and costs in defending the

> action, the attorney fees and costs allowed the surety shall be applied first to reimbursing the contractor or subcontractor for such expenses.

As noted above, ORS 742.061 provides that "a reasonable attorney fee[] shall be taxed ..." (emphasis added). That language does not allow the courts any discretion on the question of whether or not to award attorney's fees in the first instance. *Dockins* v. State Farm Ins. Co., 330 Or. 1, 6 n7, 997 P.2d 859, 861 n7 (2000). The amount of the reasonable attorney's fees to award is left to the court's discretion.

**Attorney's fee awards under terms of a contract** – Where the principal agreed to indemnify its surety for any payments made under a performance bond, and the indemnity agreement provided "[i]n any suit on this Agreement, Surety may recover its further expenses and attorney's fees incurred in such suit," the court held that, in a suit on the indemnity agreement, attorney fees were "properly awarded according to the language of the contract." It was unnecessary to determine whether the surety was the "prevailing party" as defined in ORS 20.096(5). City of Portland v. George D. Ward & Assoc., Inc., 89 Or. App. 452, 459-60, 750 P.2d 171, 176, *rev. denied*, 305 Or. 672, 757 P.2d 422 (1988).

***What fees are recoverable, if any***

In determining whether an attorney fee is reasonable, the court's analysis is "largely ... framed" by the opponent's objections to the petitioner's request. The court depends upon the opponent to "raise objections to the petitioner's request with as much particularity as possible and to support those objections with argument and (where appropriate) documentation that will assist this court in its efforts." *Dockins v. State Farm Ins. Co.*, 330 Or. 1, 6, 997 P.2d 859, 862 (2000).

Courts consider a number of factors in determining the reasonableness of an attorney fee award. The Oregon Supreme Court has indicated that the factors listed in Disciplinary Rule ("DR") 2-106(B) of the Code of Professional Responsibility, which bars attorneys from charging fees in excess of a reasonable amount, are "relevant in determining a reasonable attorney fee under ORS 742.061." *Dockins v. State Farm Ins. Co.*, 330 Or. 1, 5 & n6, 997 P.2d 859, 861 & n6 (2000). DR 2-106(B) lists the following factors:

(1) The time and labor required, the novelty and difficulty of the questions involved, and the skill requisite to perform the legal service properly.
(2) The likelihood, if apparent to the client, that the acceptance of the particular employment will preclude other employment by the lawyer.
(3) The fee customarily charged in the locality for similar legal services.
(4) The amount involved and the results obtained.
(5) The time limitations imposed by the client or by the circumstances.
(6) The nature and length of the professional relationship with the client.
(7) The experience, reputation, and ability of the lawyer or lawyers performing the services.
(8) Whether the fee is fixed or contingent.

***Incorporation of specific contract terms by reference***

"A party is not entitled to an award of attorney fees unless there is a statute or a contract providing for fees." *Biomass One, L.P. v. S-P Const.*, 103 Or. App. 521, 527, 799 P.2d 152, 156 (1990).

Where the bond incorporated the subcontract, which provided for attorney fees, and the subcontractor prevailed in the breach of contract action at issue, the subcontractor's surety was entitled to attorney fees incurred in defending its subcontractor. *Biomass One, L.P. v. S-P Const.*, 103 Or. App. 521, 529-30, 799 P.2d 152, 157 (1990).

**9. Special Provisions** – Not applicable.

**10. Remarks** – Not applicable.

**11. Case Annotations**

***Interpretation of AIA bond forms*** – There are no Oregon cases specifically addressing the construction of A311 or A312 forms.

***Cases in which surety steps into shoes of obligee***

"'It is universally recognized that the surety upon paying the creditor is entitled to be substituted to the creditor's position. This right is known as the right of subrogation. It amounts to equitable assignment, in that equity will treat the surety as though he were an assignee of the creditor, standing in his shoes to enforce the debt against the debtor together with any collateral held as security for the debt, entitled to all priorities and immunities enjoyed by the creditor.'" *Reimann v. Hybertsen*, 275 Or. 235, 239, 550 P.2d 436, 437, *opinion modified*, 276 Or. 95, 553 P.2d 1064 (1976) (quoting Simpson on Suretyship 206-07, Ch. 2, § 47, 1950).

Where the subrogee stands in the shoes of the subrogor, "the subrogee's rights rise no higher than the rights of the subrogor, and the person against whom claim is made may assert, as a defense to the subrogation claim, any defenses available to the subrogor." *State, By and Through Healy v. Smither*, 290 Or. 827, 832, 626 P.2d 356, 359 (1981).

"We see no reason why the subrogee, whose derivative rights normally include the benefits of all advantages available to the subrogor as to all persons, should not as well be subject to the limitations on the subrogor's right of recovery as to all persons. We therefore hold that in a receivership proceeding, where a priority dispute exists between creditors of the same class, a judgment creditor whose claim is derived from another by way of subrogation, stands in the same position a[s] would the subrogor and the creditor claiming priority; and the subrogee is subject to any defenses available against the subrogor." *State, By and Through Healy v. Smither*, 290 Or. 827, 837, 626 P.2d 356, 362 (1981).

# PENNSYLVANIA

Samuel J. Arena, Jr., Robert T. Carlton, Jr. and Eric M. Hurwitz[1]

## 1. Requirement for Bond

### *Statutory provisions for projects that are:*

**Public** – The bonding requirements for Pennsylvania public works projects are set forth in the Pennsylvania Public Works Contractors Bond Law of 1967, 8 P.S. §§ 191-202 (the "Bond Law") and in Part I of the Commonwealth Procurement Code, 62 Pa. C.S.A. §§ 101-2311(the "Procurement Code"), which was enacted in 1998.

Prior to the adoption of the Procurement Code in 1998, the Bond Law was the controlling statute with regard to bond requirements for all public bodies in the Commonwealth of Pennsylvania. This changed in a very significant way in 1998.

---

[1] Samuel J. Arena, Jr. is a partner and Eric M. Hurwitz is an associate with:
Stradley, Ronon, Stevens & Young, LLP
2600 One Commerce Square
Philadelphia, Pennsylvania 19103
(215) 564-8000
Robert T. Carlton, Jr. is of-counsel with:
Wolff & Samson, P.C.
Two Penn Center, Suite 1310
1500 John F. Kennedy Boulevard
Philadelphia, Pennsylvania 19102
(215) 567-2878

***The Bond Law***

The Bond Law no longer covers commonwealth agencies, but still covers contracts let by counties, school districts, cities, boroughs, townships and municipal authorities.

Section 3 of the Bond Law (8 P.S. § 193) applies to all public owners (other than commonwealth agencies), counties, school districts, intermediate units (special needs educational facilities), area vocational-technical schools, cities, boroughs, incorporated towns, townships and home-rule municipalities, and provides that before a prime contractor is awarded any contract exceeding $5,000 for "the construction, reconstruction, alteration or repair of any public building or other public work or public improvement, including highway work," the contractor shall furnish to the contracting body a performance bond at 100 percent of the contract amount, conditioned upon the faithful performance of the contract in accordance with the plans, specifications and conditions of the contract.

Surety bonds provided pursuant to Section 3 "shall be executed by one or more surety companies legally authorized to do business in the Commonwealth of Pennsylvania" and must be "filed in the office of the contracting body which awarded the contract for which such bonds were given." 8 P.S. § 193(b), (c).

Section 3.1 of the Bond Law (8 P.S. § 193.1) is applicable to "contracting bodies" defined as "any county, school district, intermediate unit [special needs educational facilities], area vocational-technical school, city, borough, incorporated town, township, home-rule municipality and authority formed under the ... Municipal Authority Act of 1945" and provides that before the award of any contract for the construction, reconstruction, alteration or repair of any public building or other public work or public improvement, including highway work by such a "contracting body," exceeding $10,000, the contractor must furnish financial security, acceptable to and approved by the contracting body. Such "financial security" may include, but is not limited to, federal or commonwealth chartered lending institution irrevocable letters of credit and restrictive or escrow accounts equal to 100 percent of the contract and conditioned upon the prime contractor's faithful performance.

Any bond or other financial security required by Section 3.1 must be executed by one or more surety companies or federal or commonwealth chartered lending institutions, legally authorized to do business in

Pennsylvania. Thus, Section 3.1 of the Bond Law (8 P.S. § 193.1) vests the contracting body in counties, school districts, cities, boroughs, townships and municipal authorities, among others, with considerable discretion as to the form of financial security that it must require so long as the performance security and payment security are each equal to 100 percent of the contract amount.

The Bond Law prohibits any representative of a contracting body, in issuing an invitation for bids, to require that bonds be furnished by any particular surety company or through any particular agent or broker. Any person who violates this prohibition is guilty of a misdemeanor and is subject to a fine not exceeding $5,000, or imprisonment for a term not exceeding five years, or both. 8 P.S. § 198.

Sections 3 and 3.1 each provide that the bond or financial security "shall be solely for the protection of the contracting body which awarded the contract." 8 P.S. § 193(a)(1); 8 P.S. § 193.1(a)(1).

***The Procurement Code***

The Procurement Code applies to bonds issued in connection with public contracts for commonwealth "purchasing agencies." Under the Procurement Code, "purchasing agencies" include commonwealth agencies authorized to enter into contracts for themselves or as the agents of another commonwealth agency. 62 Pa. C.S.A. § 103.

Pursuant to the Procurement Code, for all construction contracts for amounts between $25,000 and $100,000, the purchasing agency "shall require contract performance security, in an amount equal to at least 50 percent of the contract price, as the purchasing agency, in its discretion, determines necessary to protect the interests of the commonwealth." 62 Pa. C.S.A. § 903(a).

When a construction contract is in excess of $100,000, the contractor must obtain "a performance bond, executed by a surety company authorized to do business in the Commonwealth and made payable to the Commonwealth, in an amount equal to 100 percent of the price specified in the contract and conditioned upon the faithful performance of the contract in accordance with the plans, specifications and conditions of the contract." 62 Pa. C.S.A. § 903(a)(1).

Subsection (b) provides that the "performance bond shall be solely for the protection of the purchasing agent which awarded the contract." 62 Pa. C.S.A. § 903(b).

Subsection (c) also provides that section 903 "shall not be construed to limit the authority of the Commonwealth agency to require a performance bond, payment bond or other security in addition to those bonds or in circumstances other than specified in subsection (a)." 62 Pa. C.S.A. § 903(c).

The departments which are subject to the Procurement Code include, among others, the Department of General Services ("DGS"), the Department of Transportation ("PennDOT") and the Department of Environmental Protection ("DEP"). The general conditions of contract promulgated by DGS and DEP, and the standard specifications promulgated by PennDOT, all require that the contractor must provide a performance bond and payment bond, each for 100 percent of the contract amount. DEP's general conditions also require a maintenance bond in 10 percent of the contract amount. DGS has promulgated its own bond form entitled "CONTRACT BOND" which contains the performance bond and payment bond obligations all in a single document. PennDOT and DEP have not promulgated a bond form, but their bid packages usually include the form of performance bond and payment bond that a successful bidder must provide as a condition of being awarded the contract.

**Private** – No statutes in the Commonwealth of Pennsylvania require performance bonds on private projects.

**Department of Transportation** – The Pennsylvania Department of Transportation is considered a "purchasing agency" under the Procurement Code.

***Case law rules that might generally apply***

The Bond Law is similar to the federal Miller Act in its purpose and language. Accordingly, courts interpreting the Bond Law have relied upon decisions interpreting analogous statutory provisions in the Miller Act. *Walters Tire Serv., Inc. v. Nat'l Union Fire Ins. Co.*, 434 Pa. 235, 239-40, 252 A.2d 593, 595 (1969); *Visor Builders, Inc. v. Devon E. Tranter, Inc.*, 470 F. Supp. 911, 920 (M.D. Pa. 1978); *Lite-Air Prod., Inc. v. Fid. & Deposit Co. of Maryland*, 437 F. Supp. 801, 803 (E.D. Pa. 1977).

Because the language of the Bond Law regarding performance bonds is considered to be much broader than the narrower language regarding payment bonds, courts will not rely upon payment bond cases in interpreting performance bonds. *Downingtown Area Sch. Dist. v. Int'l Fid. Ins. Co.*, 671 A.2d 782, 786-87 (Pa. Commw. Ct. 1996).

In interpreting a surety's liability under a performance bond, Pennsylvania courts will look to the actual language of the bond, with due regard for surrounding circumstances. *Downingtown Area Sch. Dist. v. Int'l Fid. Ins. Co.*, 671 A.2d 782, 786 (Pa. Commw. Ct. 1996) (citing *Lite-Air Prod., Inc. v. Fid. & Dep't. Co. of Maryland*, 437 F. Supp. 801, 803 (E.D. Pa. 1977)).

## 2. Damages Covered

***Set forth in any statutes and/or case law***

The statutes require a performance bond conditioned upon the principal's faithful performance of the contract. The statutes are silent on the surety's obligations to take over and complete a contract.

***Obligations of surety to perform and/or pay***

When determining whether a surety is liable for certain types of damages, the bond itself is the "primary determinant." *North American Specialty Ins. Co. v. Chichester Sch. Dist.*, 158 F. Supp. 2d 468, 471 (E.D. Pa. 2001).

As a general principle, where a performance bond surety fails to complete its properly defaulted principal's work, the surety is liable for the loss sustained by the obligee, not exceeding the amount of the bond. *Turner Constr. Co. v. First Indem. of America Ins. Co.*, 829 F. Supp. 752, 759 (E.D. Pa. 1993), *aff'd*, 22 F.3d 303 (3d Cir. 1994) (citing *Purdy v. Massey*, 306 Pa. 288, 159 A. 545, 547 (1932)).

Depending on the language of the performance bond, the surety may be held liable for damages beyond the mere cost of the completion of the project. *Downingtown Area Sch. Dist. v. Int'l Fid. Ins. Co.*, 671 A.2d 782, 786-88 (Pa. Commw. Ct. 1996).

The surety's obligation to complete or pay, are often set forth in the form of the bond for a particular project. For example, in *North American Specialty Ins. Co. v. Chichester Sch. Dist.*, Civ. A. 99-2394,

2000 WL 1052055 (E.D. Pa. July 20, 2000), the bond form (apparently AIA Form A312) delineated the surety's obligations to the obligee and vice versa in the event of the principal's default. In other instances, the performance bond may be silent as to the surety's rights and/or obligations to take over and complete, but will set forth the items of damage for which the surety will be liable.

**Bad faith** – Pennsylvania's so-called "bad faith" statute (42 Pa. C.S.A. § 8371) provides that "In any action arising under an insurance policy, if the court finds that the insurer has acted in bad faith toward the insured, the court may take all of the following actions:[award interest, punitive damages, court costs and attorney fees.]"

The Pennsylvania Supreme Court has not addressed the application of the Pennsylvania "bad faith" statute to claims under surety bonds. Although several early federal decisions applying Pennsylvania law extended the application of the "bad faith" statute to sureties, the more recent, and better reasoned opinions, have declined to do so. *Ferrick Constr. Co. v. One Beacon Ins. Co.*, 2004 WL 3051443 (Philadelphia County Dec. 27, 2004); *M.A. Bruder & Sons, Inc. v. Williams*, 47 Pa. D. & C. 4th 243 (Monroe County C.C.P. 2000); *Collier Dev. Co., Inc. v. Jeffco Constr. Co.*, 25 D. & C. 4th 193, 143 Pgh. L.J. 385 (April 13, 1995); *The Norwood Co. v. RLI Ins. Co.*, 2002 WL 485694 (E.D. Pa. April 1, 2002); *Superior Precast, Inc. v. Safeco Ins. Co. of America*, 71 F. Supp. 2d 438 (E.D. Pa. 1999); *Pullman Power Prod. Corp. v. Fid. and Guar. Ins. Co.*, No. 96-636, 1997 WL 33425288 (W.D. Pa. Feb. 21, 1997); *Allegheny Valley Joint Sewerage Auth. v. The American Ins. Co.*, No. 94-2105, 1995 WL 1944748 (W.D. Pa. Aug. 17, 1995).

***Whether failure to provide insurance transfers burden to surety*** – There are no statutes or cases concerning this topic.

***Limitations on damages*** – There are no statutes or cases concerning this topic.

***Whether obligee may set off bonded contract funds against other principal-obligee debts or obligations*** – There are no statutes or cases concerning this topic.

***Incorporation of specific contract terms by reference***

Where a performance bond incorporates the terms of the underlying construction contract, the surety's liability cannot be extended by the contract beyond the agreed-upon provisions of the performance bond. *North American Specialty Ins. Co. v. Chichester Sch. Dist.*, 158 F. Supp. 2d 468, 472-73 (E.D. Pa. 2001). *But see Downingtown Area Sch. Dist. v. Int'l Fid. Ins. Co.*, 671 A.2d 782, 786-88 (Pa. Commw. Ct. 1996) (finding that even where a performance bond does not explicitly provide for the recovery of delay and liquidated damages, the obligee may recover such damages by virtue of the construction contract which provides for them, if not inconsistent with the bond itself).

## 3. Penal Sum Variations

There are no statutes or cases concerning this topic.

***Limitations per statute*** – Not applicable.

***Effect of changes in work upon penal sum, if at all*** – Not applicable.

***Statutory or case law protections or dangers to penal sum*** – Not applicable.

## 4. Parties Covered

***Statutes and/or case law as to whether only obligees are covered***

Section 3(a) of the Bond Law expressly states that, "Such [performance] bond shall be solely for the protection of the contracting body which awarded the contract." 8 P.S. § 193(a).

A performance bond required by the Procurement Code, "[S]hall be solely for the protection of the purchasing agency which awarded the contract." 62 Pa. C.S.A. § 903(b).

***Coverage for:***

**Third-party beneficiaries** – In *Van Cor, Inc. v. Am. Cas. Co.*, 417 Pa. 408, 208 A.2d 267 (1965), the Pennsylvania Supreme Court held that absent an express grant of third-party beneficiary status, co-prime contractors are not third-party beneficiaries of each prime contractor's performance bond.

**Assignees** – There are no statutes or cases concerning this topic.

**Dual obligees** – The statutes do not contain any provision for dual obliges. Indeed, the Bond Law and the Procurement Code specifically provide that the bond shall be solely for the protection of the agency or contracting body awarding the contract.

## 5. Notice or Filing Required

***Statutory provisions***

Pennsylvania has no statutory provisions regarding notice or filing requirements for a performance bond claim other than the below referenced statute of limitations.

***Case law rules concerning condition precedent notice*** – Not applicable.

## 6. Time for Suit

***Statutes of limitation particular to performance bond and other applicable statutes of limitation*** – In Pennsylvania, the statute of limitations for an action on a performance bond is one year. 42 Pa. C.S.A. § 5523(3).

***Case law statements about enforceability of limitations contained in bonds***

The leading Pennsylvania case holds that the cause of action on a performance bond accrues at the time of the principal's default. *Turner Construction, Inc. v. American States Insurance Co.*, 397 Pa. Super. 29,

579 A.2d 915, *appeal denied*, 527 Pa. 603, 589 A.2d 693 (1990) (where the bond principal is under a contractual obligation to remedy deficient work, the obligee's cause of action under the performance bond accrues, and the one-year period begins to run, when the bond principal refuses to remedy the deficient work).

At least one Pennsylvania court has applied a "discovery rule" in this context. *Altoona Area School Dist. v. Campbell*, 152 Pa. Cmwlth. 131, 143, 618 A.2d 1129, 1135 (1992) (citing Pa. C.S.A. § 5523 and stating "section 5523 is a statute of limitations, not a statute of repose, and is subject to the discovery rule. The discovery rule tolls the running of a statute of limitations until the plaintiff knows or reasonably should know that an injury has occurred.").

Prior to the Pennsylvania Superior Court's decision in *Ash v. Continental Ins. Co.*, 861 A.2d 979 (Pa. Super. Ct. 2004), there was conflicting case law as to applicable period of limitations for a bad faith claim pursuant to 42 Pa. C.S.A. § 8371. In *Ash*, the superior court held that bad faith claims against an insurer pursuant to 42 Pa. C.S.A. § 8371 are subject to a two-year statute of limitations. *Ash*, 861 A.2d at 984. Based upon *Ash*, to the extent that bad faith claims against a surety pursuant to 42 Pa. C.S.A. § 8371 are viable, they likely also are subject to a two-year limitations period.

### *Varying statutes of limitation by agreement in bond or contract*

***Nullum tempus occurit regi*** – The Commonwealth of Pennsylvania and its agencies are immune from the running of the statute of limitation under the doctrine of *nullum tempus occurit regi,* "time does not run against the king." *Commonwealth, Department of Transportation v. J.W. Bishop & Co.*, 497 Pa. 58, 439 A.2d 101 (1981).

*Nullum tempus* is available to political subdivisions such as counties or school districts when they are seeking to enforce strictly public rights, "that is, when the cause of action accrues to them in their governmental capacity and the suit is brought to enforce an obligation imposed by law as distinguished from one arising out of an agreement voluntarily entered into by the defendant." *Altoona Area School Dist. v. Inter-State Tile & Mantel Co, Inc.*, 152 Pa. Cmwlth. 131, 618 A.2d 1129, 1132 (1993) (citing *City of Philadelphia v. Holmes Elec. Protective Co.*, 335 Pa. 273, 6 A.2d 884 (1939) and holding that a school district was not legally obligated to build a library and, therefore, could not invoke the doctrine of *nullum tempus* to defeat the statute of limitations. *Montgomery County v. Microvote Corp.*, 320 F.3d 440 (3d Cir. 2003) (applying *nullum tempus* in suit by county against manufacturer of voting machines and surety, where county was required by law to procure the machines); *Mt. Lebanon School District v. W.R. Grace & Co.*, 414 Pa. Super. 455, 607 A.2d 756 (1992) (applying *nullum tempus* where plaintiff school district was required by constitution and statute to erect schools and contracted with private contractors to that end).

**Waiver of *nullum tempus* by agreement in bond** – In *Wilson Area School District v. Skepton*, 71 Pa. D. & C. 4th 142, 151, 2005 WL 1595430 (C.P. Northampton) the court held that a municipal school district waived the application of *nullum tempus* when it accepted a performance bond with a one year limitation of action provision for a high school construction project.

## 7. Procedure

There is no special statutory procedure for an action against a performance bond surety.

***Venue requirements and jurisdictional limitations***

Pursuant to Pennsylvania Rule of Civil Procedure 2179, an action against a corporation or similar entity may be brought in and only in: (1) the county where its registered office or principal place of business is located; (2) a county where it regularly conducts business; (3) the county where the cause of action arose; (4) a county where a transaction or occurrence took place out of which the cause of action arose; or (5) a county where the property or a part of the property which is the subject matter of the action is located provided that equitable relief is sought with respect to the property. Pa. R. Civ. P. 2179.

***Court rules***

Each Pennsylvania Court of Common Pleas has its own local rules of civil procedure. The United States District Court for the Eastern, Middle and Western Districts each have their own local rules of civil procedure.

### *Particular agency regulations/rules*

There are no agency regulations or rules applicable to performance bonds that may affect the handling or administration of lawsuits under performance bonds in Pennsylvania.

### *Arbitration requirements and application*

Cases in Pennsylvania are subject to mandatory arbitration where the amount in controversy, exclusive of interest and costs, exceeds: (i) $50,000 in judicial districts embracing first, second, second class A or third class counties or home rule counties which but for the adoption of a home rule charter would be a county of one of these classes; or (ii) $35,000 in any other judicial district. 42 Pa. C.S.A. § 7361(b).

Any party may appeal the arbitration decision for a trial de novo before the Court of Common Pleas. 42 Pa. C.S.A. § 7361(d).

## 8. Attorney's Fees

### *Statutes and/or case law limiting or permitting recovery of attorney's fees*

Attorney's fees are not recoverable unless the bond so provides. *Downingtown Area School District v. International Fidelity Ins. Co.*, 769 A.2d 560 (Pa. Cmwlth. 2001). However, attorney's fees were awarded to the obligee in *North American Specialty Ins. Co. v. Chichester Sch. Dist.*, 158 F. Supp. 2d 468, 473-74 (E.D. Pa. 2001). In that case, the performance bond (apparently AIA Form A312) provided in paragraph 6.2:

> To the limit of the amount of this Bond ... the Surety is obligated, without duplication for ... [a]dditional legal, design professional and delay costs resulting from the Contractor's Default, and resulting from the actions or failure to act of the Surety....

A surety will be obligated to pay attorney's fees where the performance bond explicitly provides for such damages. *Dept. of Transp. v. Manor Mines, Inc.*, 117 Pa. Cmwlth. 342, 353, 544 A.2d 538, 543 (1988), *aff'd*, 523 Pa. 112, 565 A.2d 428 (1989).

**9. Special Provisions**

There are no special provisions in the Bond Law or the Procurement Code beyond the plain language of the statutes which require bonds for 100 percent of the contract price and conditioned upon the principal's faithful performance of the contract.

Section 8(a) of the Bond Law, 8 P.S. § 198(a) forbids any representative of a contracting body, in issuing an invitation for bids, to require that bonds be furnished by a particular surety company or through a particular agent or broker.

**10. Remarks** – Not applicable.

**11. Case Annotations**

***Interpretation of AIA bond forms***

*In re Modular Structures, Inc.*, 27 F.3d 72, 74 n.1 (3d Cir. 1994) ("the surety stands in the shoes of other parties to the construction project through the use of the equitable doctrine of subrogation.").

*North American Specialty Ins. Co. v. Chichester Sch. Dist.*, 158 F. Supp. 2d 468, 473-74 (E.D. Pa. 2001) which held that AIA Form A312 made the surety liable for "legal costs" resulting form the principal's default and resulting from the actions or failure to act of the surety under Paragraph 4 of Form A312.

*Department of Transportation v. Manor Mines, Inc.*, 117 Pa. Cmwlth. 342, 544 A.2d 538, 543-44 (1988), *aff'd,* 523 Pa. 112, 565 A.2d 428 (1989) (attorney's fees provision in a performance bond obligated the surety to pay a five percent attorney fee for the Department of Transportation's collection of money due for roadway repair).

*North American Specialty Ins. Co. v. Chichester Sch. Dist.*, Civ. A. 99-2394, 2000 WL 1052055 at *15-*17 (E.D. Pa. July 20, 2000). Paragraph 3.3 of AIA Form A312[2]does not require the obligee to

---

2 Paragraph 3.3 of A312 provides:

> If there is no Owner default, the Surety's obligation under the Bond shall arise after: ....
> 3.3. The Owner has agreed to pay the Balance of the Contract Price to the Surety in accordance with the terms of the Construction

contractually commit to a specified payment to the surety prior to any performance by the surety of the defaulted contract. Paragraph 3.3 only mandates that the obligee agree to pay the balance of the contract price to the surety in accordance with the terms of the contract.

***Cases in which surety steps into shoes of obligee***

**Subrogation** – Pennsylvania recognizes the surety's right to equitable subrogation in and to contract funds held by the obligee. *Jacobs v. Northeastern Corp.,* 416 Pa. 417, 206 A.2d 49 (1965).

---

Contract or to a contractor selected to perform the Construction Contract in accordance with the terms of the contract with the Owner.

# PUERTO RICO

Edward Etcheverry and Raymond Perez-Brayfield, CPCU[1]

## 1. Requirement for Bond

The Commonwealth of Puerto Rico codifies the requirements for, and the rights and liabilities of, sureties and co-sureties issuing bonds in Articles 1721-1752 of the Puerto Rico Civil Code, 31 L.P.R.A. 4871-4957. We address below those sections, which are most applicable to performance bonds.

31 L.P.R.A. § 4871 defines a surety as "a person [who] binds himself to pay or perform for a third person in case the latter should fail to do so." If the surety binds himself jointly with the principal debtor, the provisions of §§ 3101-3112 of this title shall be observed.

31 L.P.R.A. § 4872 defines the types of suretyship (i.e., conventional, legal or judicial, gratuitous, or for valuable consideration). This section also recognizes that suretyship may also be extended to other sureties, either with consent, ignorance or even against the opposition of the latter.

31 L.P.R.A. § 4873 requires a *valid underlying obligation* for a suretyship relationship to exist. If the underlying obligation is null and void, there can be no security.

---

[1] Edward Etcheverry is the Managing Partner, and Raymond Peréz-Brayfield is Of Counsel to:

Etcheverry Harrison LLP
150 South Pine Island Road, Suite 105
Ft. Lauderdale, Florida 33324
(954) 370-1681

31 L.P.R.A. § 4875 *limits the obligation of the surety* to that of the principal debtor and even reduces the obligation irrespective of the surety binding itself for more. "A surety may bind himself to less but not to more than the principal debtor as to quantity as well as to the burden of the conditions. Should he have bound himself for more, his obligation shall be reduced to the limits of that of the debtor."

31 L.P.R.A. § 4876 codifies the suretyship axiom that suretyship "is not presumed; it must be *expressed and cannot be extended* further than that specified therein." This section goes on to state that "[i]f it be simple and indefinite it shall include not only the principal obligation but all its accessories, including the costs of the suit, it being understood, with regard to the latter, that the surety shall only be liable for those incurred after he has been asked to pay."

31 L.P.R.A. § 4877 sets forth the *qualifications for a surety and submits the surety to the jurisdiction of court*, declaring "[a] party who is bound to give security must present a person having capacity to bind himself, and with sufficient property to answer for the obligation which he guarantees. The surety shall be understood as subject to the jurisdiction of the court or judge of the place where this obligation is to be fulfilled."

31 L.P.R.A. § 4898 addresses the *liability of several sureties* of one debtor principal, acknowledging that "[s]hould there be several sureties but only one debtor for the same debt, the liability therefore shall be divided among them all. The creditor can claim from each surety nothing but the proper portion which he may be required to pay, unless the joint liability has been expressly stipulated."

31 L.P.R.A. § 4911 specifically recognizes the *surety's right of indemnification* against the principal debtor. A surety who pays an obligation of the principal debtor is entitled to be indemnified for: (a) the total amount of the debt; (b) legal interest from the day payment was communicated to the principal; (c) expenses incurred by the surety after it has informed the principal that it has been sued for payment; (d) additional losses and damage when proper. This section applies even when the bond may have been given without knowledge of the principal.

31 L.P.R.A. § 4912 codifies the *equitable principle of subrogation*, stating "by virtue of such payment the surety is subrogated in all the rights which the creditor had against the debtor. Should the surety have compromised with the creditor, he cannot demand of the debtor more than that which he has really paid."

31 L.P.R.A. § 4913 allows a principal debtor to raise any defenses that it could have asserted against a creditor, if the surety paid the creditor *without first giving notice* to the principal.

31 L.P.R.A. § 4914 involves a surety's *premature payment*. "If the debt was for a term and the surety paid it before it was due, he cannot require the debtor to reimburse him until the period has expired."

31 L.P.R.A. § 4915 addresses *dual payments* by the surety and the principal to the same creditor. If the surety has paid before notifying the principal, and the principal also pays the claim, the surety has no remedy against the principal and must pursue the creditor.

31 L.P.R.A. § 4916 codifies the *equitable principle of exoneration*, allowing the surety, even before paying, the right to proceed against the principal debtor.

31 L.P.R.A. § 4951 provides that the *obligation of the surety shall expire* at the same time as that of the principal debtor, and for the same causes as all other obligations.

31 L.P.R.A. § 4955 discharges a surety in the event an *extension* is granted to the principal debtor by the creditor, without the consent of the surety. Despite the clear language of the Code, courts generally have not discharged the surety for such extension.

31 L.P.R.A. § 4956 deals with the *impairment of a surety's subrogation rights*. "The sureties... shall be released from their obligation whenever by an act of the creditor they cannot be subrogated to the rights, mortgages and privileges of the same." This section applies only when the creditor's actions have affected a right of the surety against the debtor in a case where the surety intends to be subrogated to the creditor's position.

*See* additional sections cited below.

***Statutory provisions for projects that are:***

**Public** – 22 L.P.R.A. 46, Article 425 of Puerto Rico Political Code requires contractors to obtain performance bonds for *all* public projects. This includes public projects by the Commonwealth of Puerto Rico, its agencies, departments, instrumentalities and municipal governments. Section 46 requires "all contractors ... to give sufficient bond, with penalty, conditioned on the faithful performance of the works in a proper manner and within the time named in the contracts."

Most Puerto Rico government instrumentalities and municipal governments have enacted more specific regulations setting forth the requirements for performance bonds. For example, "[i]n cases of public works and improvements, in addition to what is required under § 4366 of this title, the contractor shall post or produce the corresponding bonds and warranties required by the Board to ensure compliance with the contract, before signing the corresponding agreement." 21 L.P.R.A. § 4506.

**Private** – No statutes in Puerto Rico require performance bonds on private projects.

**Department of Transportation** – 9 L.P.R.A. § 2004a applies to contracts for construction, operation and maintenance, providing that "the Authority and/or the Department of Transportation and Public Works may contract with private entities, and through the use of private funds, the final design, construction, operation and maintenance of new highways, bridges, avenues, expressways and ancillary transit facilities, subject to the following conditions.... The private entity to whom the contract is awarded shall give a bond that guarantees to the Commonwealth of Puerto Rico, faithful compliance with all obligations under the contract, the amount of which bond shall be established by the Authority or the Secretary of Transportation and Public Works, using as a criterion the investment contemplated for the project or the work or stage in question."

***Case law rules that might generally apply***

**Interpretation of bond language** – "Although '[the] prevailing doctrine is that [a surety bond] should be liberally interpreted in favor of its beneficiary,' that principle 'is not a blank check to the judicial power to rule out the pacts and agreements between the parties.'" *Luan Inv. Corp. v. Rexach Construction*, 2000 T.S.P.R. 182.... Rather, the rule of liberal construction applies only where the text of the agreement is ambiguous. '[I]f the text of a bond agreement is clear, or the true meaning of its clauses can be easily discerned, the courts should adhere to its text.... *Caguas Plumbing, Inc. v. Continental Const. Corp.,* 2001 T.S.P.R. 164, 2001 WL 1618390 at *5 (P.R. 2001)." *Citibank v. Grupo*

*Cupey*, 382 F.3d 29 at 31-32 (1st Cir. 2004); *see also, Caribe Lumber v. Inter-American Builder*, 101 D. P.R. 458 (1973).

"The adherence to the clear text of a surety agreement is consistent with the Puerto Rico Civil Code, which provides that 'contracting parties may make the agreement and establish the clauses and conditions which they may deem advisable, provided they are not in contravention of the laws, morals, or public order 31 L.P.R.A. 3372.'" *Id.*

Suretyship is not insurance. *Caribe Lumber v. Inter-American Builder*, 101 D. P.R. 458 (1973).

Clear and precise clauses in text of contract incorporated into performance bond, limiting responsibility of surety, cannot be construed to extend surety's obligations to other clauses of the contract. *See Municipality of San Juan v. Stadium and Coliseum Opers.*, 113 D. P.R. 490 (1982). Doctrine regarding liberal construction of performance bond for its beneficiary cannot be extended to preempt agreements and facts between the parties. *Id.*

## 2. Damages Covered

***Set forth in any statutes and/or case law***

See above 22 L.P.R.A. 46, Article 425.

The purpose of a performance bond is generally to guarantee completion of the project and thus some Puerto Rico courts have limited recovery to completion costs. *Sloan Const. Co. v. American Renov. and Const. Co.*, 313 F. Supp. 2d 24; *United States v. Island Constructors, Inc.*, 179 F. Supp. 133.

"The terms of the bond will govern as to the types of damages recoverable. Puerto Rico courts enforce the parties right to enter into any agreement provided they are not in contravention of the laws, morals, or public order 31 L.P.R.A. 3372." *Citibank v. Grupo Cupey*, 382 F.3d 29 (1st Cir. 2004).

***Obligations of surety to perform and/or pay*** – Subject to the provisions and conditions of the performance bond.

***Whether failure to provide insurance transfers burden to surety*** – Statutes or case law do not transfer the burden to surety.

***Limitations on damages***

31 L.P.R.A. § 4875 *limits the obligation of the surety* to that of the principal debtor and even reduces the obligation should the surety bind itself for more. "A surety may bind himself to less but not to more than the principal debtor as to quantity as well as to the burden of the conditions. Should he have bound himself for more, his obligation shall be reduced to the limits of that of the debtor." *See Luan Inv. Corp. v. Rexach Const. Co., Inc.*, 152 D. P.R. 652 (2000) (surety was not responsible for 10 year warranty period in bonded contract as bond contained two year statute of limitations).

Puerto Rico courts enforce the penal sum limitations on performance bonds. *Demas v. Builders Ins. Co.,* 109 D. P.R. 774 (1980); *Municipality of San Juan v. Stadium and Coliseum Opers.*, 113 D. P.R. 490 (1982).

Liability of surety extends to liquidated damages if these are prescribed for in the construction contract and are validly assessed against the principal. *Olazbal v. United States Fidelity & Guaranty Company*, 103 D. P.R. 448 (1975). "When a liquidated damages clause is included in a construction contract and the terms of said contract are in turn incorporated in a performance bond, the surety must answer for the nonperformance of the contractor, including the liquidated damages agreed to in the penal clause. *See Olazabal v. United States Fid. & Guar. Co.,* 3 P.R. Offic. Trans. 624, 642 (1975); *see also Demas v. Builders Ins. Co.,* 9 P.R. Offic. Trans. 1037, 1048-49 (1980)." *Plaza Athenee, S.E. v. U.S. Fidelity and Guar. Co.,* Slip Copy, 2005 WL 1114368, D. Puerto Rico, 2005.

"Damages in Puerto Rico are compensatory. *Torres v. Castillo Alicea,* 111 D. P.R. 792, 804 & n. 7 (1981) (torts); *Perez v. Sampedro,* 86 D. P.R. 526, 530 (1962) (contracts); *see Marina Industrial v. Brown Boveri,* — D. P.R. —, 83 J.T.S. 31 (March 18, 1983) (punitive damages do not exist in Puerto Rico)." *Noble v. Corporacion Insular de Seguros,* 738 F.2d 51 (Puerto Rico,1984).

A surety is not liable for additional work not contemplated by the bonded contract. *Demas v. Builders Insurance Company*, 109 D. P.R. 774 (1980).

***Whether obligee may set off bonded contract funds against other principal-obligee debts or obligations*** There are no cases in Puerto Rico involving this issue.

***Incorporation of specific contract terms by reference***

A surety can undertake lesser obligations than those contained in the principal's contract. *See* 31 L.P.R.A. § 4875. A surety may pledge himself to specific terms making him potentially responsible to a lesser degree than the debtor. *Luan Invest. v. Rexach Const. Co.*, 152 D. P.R. 652 (2000). The fact that the contract between the principal and the obligee was incorporated by reference does not override the clear and precise language of the bond limiting the surety's obligations. *Id.* at 662.

"Clear and precise clauses in text of contract incorporated to payment and performance bond, limiting responsibility of surety, cannot be construed to extend surety to other clauses of contract." *Municipality of San Juan v. Stadium & Coliseum Operators*, 113 D. P.R. 490 (1982).

### 3. Penal Sum Variations

***Limitations per statute and/or case law*** – Puerto Rico does not have statutory limitations on performance bond penal sums.

***Effect of changes in work upon penal sum, if at all*** – A surety is not liable for additional work not contemplated by the bonded contract. *Demas v. Builders Insurance Company*, 109 D. P.R. 774 (1980).

***Statutory or case law protections or dangers to penal sum***

Puerto Rico courts enforce penal sum limitations on performance bonds. *Demas v. Builders Insurance Co.*, 109 D. P.R. 774 (1980); *Mun. of San Juan v. Stadium & Coliseum Operators*, 113 D. P.R. 490 (1982).

### 4. Parties Covered

***Statutes and/or case law as to whether only obligees are covered***

Subject to bond language. Puerto Rico courts have enforced bond language limiting the persons who can recover under same to the named obligees.

In the case of *Grupo Cupey, infra,* the lender of the obligee, as assignee, filed a claim against the surety alleging to be the beneficiary under the performance bond. The court enforced the terms of the bond which expressly limited the surety's liability to named obligees and thus dismissed the assignee's claim, concluding, "[w]e see no overriding principle that should prevent a surety from bargaining for a contractual provision that prevents parties other than those named in the original transaction from pursuing a cause of action under the bond." *Citibank v. Grupo Cupey,* 382 F.3d 29 (1st Cir. 2004).

"It has been uniformly decided that a condition incorporated into a bond limiting the right to actions against the bond to named beneficiaries clearly establish that the parties did not intend to extend its benefits to unnamed beneficiaries." *Ferrer v. Alliance Company of P.R.*, 93 D. P.R. 1 (1966).

***Coverage for:***

**Third-party beneficiaries** – Puerto Rico does not recognize third-party beneficiaries to a performance bond. *See United States v. Island Constructors, Inc.*, 179 F. Supp. 133 (D.C. P.R. 1959) (Government was not an intended third-party beneficiary of the performance bond for purposes of collecting taxes).

Subcontractor was not a valid claimant under the performance bond. *Caguas Plumbing, Inc. v. Continental Const. Corp.,* 2001 J.T.S. 169 (2001) (distinguishing between obligations under the payment and performance bonds).

**Assignees** – Although subject to the terms of the bond, Puerto Rico does not generally recognize assignments of performance bond. *Citibank v. Grupo Cupey,* 382 F.3d 29 (1st Cir. 2004); *Ferrer v. Alliance Company of P.R.*, 93 D. P.R. 1 (1966).

**Dual obligees** – Subject to the terms of the bond.

## 5. Notice or Filing Required

***Statutory provisions*** – Puerto Rico statutes do not provide for any unusual notice requirements for suit under a performance bond.

***Case law rules concerning condition precedent notice***

Although there are no specific condition precedent notice cases in Puerto Rico involving a performance bond, the Supreme Court of Puerto Rico did recognize the importance of notice to a surety in the payment bond context. The supreme court enforced the language in a payment bond requiring notification of claim within a stated period of time and dismissed the claimant's action against the surety without need of proving prejudice to the surety. *Caribe Lumber v. Inter-American Builder*, 101 D. P.R. 458 (1973); *compare, Industrial Equip. Corp. v. Builders, Inc.*, 108 D. P.R. 290 (1979) (lack of notice under payment bond did not discharge surety in the absence of prejudice).

## 6. Time for Suit

***Statutes of limitation particular to performance bonds and other applicable statutes of limitation*** – Under Puerto Rico law, breach of contract actions have a statute of limitations of 15 years. 31 L.P.R.A. § 5294.

***Case law statements about enforceability of limitations contained in bonds***

Statute of limitations period may be limited by contract. In the context of a payment bond claim the Puerto Rico Supreme Court concluded that "[t]he mention of a specific period to file a claim under the bond is binding for the parties and once the time period passes all obligations of the surety are extinguished if no proper claim is made against the surety." *Caguas Plumbing, Inc. v. Continental Const. Corp.*, 2001 J.T.S. 169; *see also Luan Inv. Corp. v. Rexach Const. Co., Inc.*, 152 D. P.R. 652 (2000).

***Varying statutes of limitation by agreement in bond or contract*** – See above.

## 7. Procedure

***Statutory or procedural rules that may affect handling or administration of lawsuits*** – Not applicable.

***Venue requirements and jurisdictional limitations***

31 L.P.R.A. § 4877 requires a surety to submit itself to the jurisdiction of the court, stating "... [t]he surety shall be understood as subject to the jurisdiction of the court or judge of the place where this obligation is to be fulfilled."

Under Puerto Rico law, surety on subcontractor's performance bond binding surety jointly and severally with principal debtor could be sued independently without joining subcontractor and contractor was not bound by subcontract provision for arbitration or required to comply with statutory conditions precedent to suit against surety. 31 L.P.R.A. §§ 3108, 4891; *see also, McDonough Const. Co. of Fla. v. Maryland Cas. Co.,* 215 F. Supp 488 (D.C. P.R. 1961).

***Court rules*** – Not applicable.

***Particular agency regulations/rules*** – Not applicable.

***Arbitration requirements and application***

**PR Law of Commercial Arbitration** – 32 L.P.R.A 3201 *et seq.* acknowledges the right to arbitrate. "Two or more parties may agree in writing to submit to arbitration, in conformity with the provisions of this chapter, any dispute which may be the object of an existing action between them at the time they agree to the arbitration; or they may include in a written agreement a provision for the settlement by arbitration of any dispute which may in future arise between them from such settlement or in connection therewith. Such an agreement shall be valid and irrevocable except for the grounds prescribed by law for the reversal of an agreement."

The Federal Arbitration Act applies to interstate commerce contracts and provides that arbitration clauses in such contracts are deemed to be valid, irrevocable and mandatory. *PaineWebber, Inc. v. Soc. de Gananciales*, 151 D.P.R. 307 (2000). Under the Miller Act, the federal court must apply the Federal Arbitration Act provisions, where the underlying subcontract came within the ambit of the Act and must stay trial until the arbitration is concluded, as the surety was not a party to the subcontract. *Seaboard Surety Co. v. Electronic & Missile Facilities Inc.*, 206 F. Supp. 790 (D.C. P.R. 1962).

General principles applicable to contractual arbitration are: (a) parties have ample rights to incorporate into arbitration agreement any qualifications they deem appropriate to their case, and arbiter is compelled to fulfill them; (b) arbitration agreement confers upon arbiter authority for award and limits his scope; and (c) any award beyond powers delegated by arbitration compact is null and void. *Rivera v. Samaritano & Co., Inc.*, 108 D. P.R. 604 (1979).

Although in Puerto Rico there is a strong public policy in favor of arbitration, this mechanism will only be used if the parties have agreed to arbitration and to the manner of the arbitration agreed upon. The nature and extension of the powers of the arbitrator are limited by the language and the intention of the parties in the arbitration agreement. Whether a controversy is subject to arbitration must be determined by the courts. Any party may request relief from the court to compel arbitration as agreed upon. *Crufon Construction v. Autoridad de Edificios Públicos*, 2002 JTS 24, Vol. XXV, at 726-7.

A surety on a prime contractor's bond is entitled to stay the bond action until the contractor's right to compel arbitration under the subcontracts was given effect even though sureties were not parties to subcontracts. *Commonwealth Coating Corp. v. Continental Casualty Co.*, 214 F. Supp. 949 (D.C. P.R. 1963).

## 8. Attorney's Fees

***Statutes and/or case law limiting or permitting recovery of attorney's fees***

Attorney's fees are recoverable under certain circumstances as set forth in Rules 41.3 and 44.3 of the Puerto Rico Rules of Civil Procedure, 32 L.P.R.A. App. III.

"To determine whether party or its lawyer was obstinate so as to warrant award of attorney fees under Puerto Rico rule, court must examine whether litigant was unreasonably adamant or stubbornly litigious, beyond the acceptable demands of the litigation, thereby wasting time and causing court and other litigants unnecessary expense and delay, and this determination is dependent on the particular facts of each case and lies within the sound discretion of the court. Puerto Rico Rules Civ. Proc., Rule 44.1(d), 32 L.P.R.A. App. III." *Taber Partners I v. Insurance Co. of North America, Inc.*, 926 F. Supp. 36 (D.C. P.R. 1996).

"Party is 'obstinate' for purposes of Puerto Rico rule governing attorney fees if it engages in actions which make necessary litigation which could have been avoided, prolongs litigation unnecessarily, or requires other party to incur expenses in pursuit of avoidable tasks. *Puerto Rico Rules Civ. Proc., Rule 44.1(d),* 32 L.P.R.A. App. III." *Taber Partners I v. Insurance Co. of North America, Inc.*, 926 F. Supp. 36 (D.C. P.R. 1996).

"Finding of obstinacy under Puerto Rico rule concerning award of attorney fees is not entitlement to prevailing party but is sanction designed to punish the offending party as well as to recompense those victimized by offender's recalcitrance. *Puerto Rico Rules Civ. Proc., Rule 44.1(d),* 32 L.P.R.A. App. III." *Taber Partners I v. Insurance Co. of North America, Inc.*, 926 F. Supp. 36 (D.C. P.R. 1996).

"Puerto Rico rules respecting attorney fees and prejudgment interest are rules of decision that should be applied by federal court sitting in diversity. *Puerto Rico Rules Civ. Proc., Rules 44.1(d), 44.3(b),* 32 L.P.R.A. App. III." *Newell Puerto Rico, Ltd. v. Rubbermaid Inc.,* 20 F.3d 15 (1st Cir. 1994).

*See also*, *Oficina de Etica Gubernamental v. Román González*, 2003 JTS 74, Vol. XXVI, at 973-4; *Domínguez Vargas v. Great American Life Assurance Company of Puerto Rico, Inc.*, 2002 J.T.S 110, Vol. XXVI, at 21-2.

***What fees are recoverable, if any*** – Attorney's fees and prejudgment interest as determined by the court. Rules 41.3 and 44.3 of the Puerto Rico Rules of Civil Procedure 32 L.P.R.A. App. III.

***Incorporation of specific contract terms by reference*** – Not applicable.

**9. Special Provisions** – Not applicable.

**10. Remarks**

**Impairment of suretyship status** – 31 L.P.R.A. § 4956 deals with the *impairment of a surety's subrogation rights*. "The sureties ... shall be released from their obligation whenever by an act of the creditor they cannot be subrogated to the rights, mortgages and privileges of the same." This section applies only when the creditor's actions have affected a right of the surety against the debtor in a case where the surety intends to be subrogated to the creditor's position.

As a general rule, the surety will be released from liability towards the creditor only to the degree where the creditor's actions have prejudiced the interests or rights of the surety. The surety may exercise rights under 31 L.P.R.A. § 4956 only when the creditor's action has produced substantial prejudice to the surety's subrogation rights. If the prejudice is partial, the surety is entitled to a *pro tanto* discharge. The surety has the burden of proof that the creditor's action has barred subrogation against debtor resulting in damage against the surety. *Commonwealth v. Urb. Damiro, Inc.*, 112 D.P.R. 244 (1982).

**Improper payment or overpayment defense** – The obligee failed to perform the following actions as required by the contract: (a) did not request periodical progress reports to the contractor; (b) did not request an estimate report of work performed; (c) did not retain 10 percent of the contract amount; and (d) made unjustified payments to the contractor. As a result, the surety was partially relieved of its obligations to the extent that it was prejudiced by the actions of the obligee. *See Olazabal v. United States Fidelity & Guaranty Co.*, 103 D. P.R. 448 (1975).

**Substantial completion** – "When a project is substantially complete, the contractor has the right to receive the contract balance minus a retention for punch list items. Other effects are: the contract period ends, warranty terms begin; risks for loss of the works transfer to the owner; owner has the burden to prove construction defects; and *resolution of the contract is no longer an option*. The criteria mainly used to determine whether a work is substantially complete is based on the proportion between the cost of completing the work versus total cost." *Master Concrete v. Fraya,* 152 D. P.R. 616 (2000).

"We have no doubt that a certified work, more than 90 percent of which has been paid for by the owner after it has been inspected by an expert, is, for all practical purposes, a 'substantially completed' work ... In other words, one of the main elements to be taken into consideration when deciding when a work is 'substantially completed' is the total amount paid by the owner of the work vis-à-vis the total cost of the work." *Constructora Bauza, Inc. v. Garcia Lopez*, 129 D. P.R. 579 (1991).

## 11. Case Annotations

***Interpretation of AIA bond forms*** – None.

***Cases in which surety steps into shoes of obligee***

31 L.P.R.A. § 4912 codifies the *equitable principle of subrogation*, stating "by virtue of such payment the surety is subrogated in all the rights which the creditor had against the debtor. Should the surety have compromised with the creditor, he cannot demand of the debtor more than that which he has really paid."

Surety having satisfied contractual debt with respect to the contractor would stand in the same legal right by subrogation; therefore, the privilege vested upon the creditors of the contractors would vest by operation of the law in the surety, and the direct action against the owner of the project would correspond and benefit said surety. *Federal Insurance Company v. Constructora Maza, Inc.,* 500 F. Supp. 246 (D.C. P.R. 1979).

"'Subrogation transfers to the subrogated the credits with the corresponding rights, either against the debtor or against third persons, be they sureties or holders of mortgages.' The result of all this is that the privilege vested in these creditors of the contractor would vest by 'operation of law' in the surety. See: 12 Manresa, Comentarios al Codigo Civil, at 304-306 (1950 ed.). The surety's interest would be separate and superior to that of the other creditors. Payment by the surety assures him full indemnification. Article 1737 C.C.P.R., 31 L.P.R.A. § 4911." "By virtue of such payment the surety is subrogated in all the rights which the creditor had against the debtor." Article 1438, C.C.P.R., 31 L.P.R.A. § 4912. Under Article 1166 C.C.P.R., 31 L.P.R.A. § 3250. *Id.*

Surety has the right to recover from the project owner any unpaid amounts for bond premium, which is separate and superior to that of any other creditor of contractor, and labor said surety has paid. *Id.*

Surety who satisfies obligations of contractor fills the shoes of the owner of the project; therefore, if it lacks action to be reimbursed of all payments, said owners would be unjustly enriched by the completion of the project by the surety. *Id.*

# RHODE ISLAND

Richard R. Beretta and Geoffrey W. Millsom[1]

## 1. Requirement for Bond

***Statutory provisions for projects that are:***

**Public** – R.I. Gen. Laws § 37-12-1 requires contractors awarded a contract by the Rhode Island Department of Transportation or the Department of Administration for the construction, improvement, completion or repair of any public road, public building or bridge with a price in excess of $50,000 to provide a performance bond.

R.I. Gen. Laws § 37-13-14 provides that the State of Rhode Island or any city, town, agency or committee therein that awards contracts for public works in excess of $50,000 shall require a performance bond that conforms to the requirements set forth in § 37-12-1.

R.I. Gen. Laws § 37-2-41 extends the performance bond requirements set forth in § 37-12-1 and § 37-13-14 to every construction contract requiring an expenditure of public funds by any state or governmental entity.

---

[1] Richard R. Beretta and Geoffrey W. Millsom are shareholders with:
Adler Pollock & Sheehan P.C.
One Citizens Plaza, 8th Floor
Providence, Rhode Island 02903-2443
(401) 274-7200

**Private** – No statutes in Rhode Island require performance bonds on private projects.

**Department of Transportation** – Construction contracts awarded by the Rhode Island Department of Transportation are covered under R.I. Gen. Laws § 37-12-1 (discussed above).

***Case law rules that might generally apply*** – None.

## 2. Damages Covered

***Set forth in any statutes and/or case law***

R.I. Gen. Laws § 9-21-10 provides that in any civil action in which a verdict is rendered or a decision made for pecuniary damages, there shall be added by the clerk of the court to the amount of damages interest at the rate of 12 percent per annum thereon from the date the cause of action accrued, which shall be included in the judgment entered therein. Post-judgment interest shall be calculated at the rate of 12 percent per annum and accrue on both the principal amount of the judgment and the prejudgment interest entered therein. This section does not apply until entry of judgment or to any bond or other contractual obligation where interest is already provided.

**Case law** – Rhode Island law requires courts to strictly construe performance bonds. *Rhode Island Department of Corrections v. ADP Marshall, Inc.*, No. Civ. A. PB99-4704, 2004 WL 877560 (R.I. Super. March 29, 2004).

***Obligations of surety to perform and/or pay***

The nature and extent of a surety's liability on a performance bond is governed by the terms of the bond. *Narragansett Pier R.R. Co. v. Palmer*, 70 R.I. 298, 302 (1944).

***Whether failure to provide insurance transfers burden to surety*** – No Rhode Island statutes or case law transfers the burden of providing insurance to the surety.

***Limitations on damages***

A performance bond is not intended to compensate for indirect loss or to indemnify against liability to others. *Rhode Island Department of Corrections v. ADP Marshall, Inc.*, No. Civ. A. PB99-4704, 2004 WL 877560, at *8 (R.I. Super March 29, 2004).

A performance bond surety is not under any liability to any of the persons who have furnished labor or materials or both that were used in the performance of the project pursuant to a contract with its principal. *Glens Falls Indem. Co. v. American Awning & Tent Co.,* 180 A. 367 (R.I. 1935).

The consequential damages assessed against a surety on a performance bond may exceed the penal sum to the extent that the damages flow from the surety's own breach of its obligations under the bond. *Marshall Contractors, Inc. v. Peerless Ins. Co.*, 827 F. Supp. 91, 95 (D.R.I. 1993).

In the case of performance bonds, recovery is not limited to the amount of the bond. *Marshall Contractors, Inc. v. Peerless Ins. Co.*, 827 F. Supp. 91, 95 (D.R.I. 1993) (suggesting that surety could be liable for bad faith, consequential damages for economic loss, and, where appropriate, damages for emotional distress and punitive damages).

Whenever the penalty on a bond becomes a debt due and payable as to the surety, he is as much liable for interest thereon as if he had been originally the principal debtor. Under this rule, when the bond is breached, the penalty to the amount of the damages immediately becomes the debt of the surety and bears interest the same as any other debt on contract, if the principal claim bears interest. Generally, this is the rule irrespective of whether demand was made on the surety or surety had notice of the principal's default. *South County Sand & Gravel, Inc. v. National Bonding & Acc. Ins.*, No. C.A. NO. 82-327, 1989 WL 1110278, at *6 (R.I. Super. May 17, 1989).

***Whether obligee may set off bonded contract funds against other principal-obligee debts or obligations*** – Not applicable.

***Incorporation of specific contract terms by reference*** – Not applicable.

### 3. Penal Sum Variations

***Limitations per statute*** – Rhode Island does not have any statutory limitations on performance bond penal sums.

***Effect of changes in work upon penal sum, if at all*** – Rhode Island has no applicable law.

***Statutory or case law protections or dangers to penal sum*** – There is no applicable Rhode Island case law.

### 4. Parties Covered

***Statutes and/or case law as to whether only obligees are covered***

A performance bond surety may only be liable to a named obligee. *Rhode Island Department of Corrections v. ADP Marshall, Inc.*, No. Civ. A. PB99-4704, 2004 WL 877560, at *9 (R.I. Super March 29, 2004).

***Coverage for:***

**Third-party beneficiaries** – Rhode Island courts will not construe a performance bond by implication to extend a surety's liability to unnamed third-party beneficiaries. *Rhode Island Department of Corrections v. ADP Marshall, Inc.*, No. Civ. A. PB99-4704, 2004 WL 877560, at *9 (R.I. Super March 29, 2004).

**Assignees** – The assignee of a performance bond obligee may recover under the bond. *South County Sand & Gravel, Inc. v. National Bonding & Acc. Ins.*, No. C.A. NO. 82-327, 1989 WL 1110278, at *5 (R.I. Super. May 17, 1989).

**Dual obligees** – Rhode Island permits dual obligees. *See Rhode Island Department of Corrections v. ADP Marshall, Inc.*, No. Civ. A. PB99-4704, 2004 WL 877560, at *9 (R.I. Super March 29, 2004).

## 5. Notice or Filing Required

***Statutory provisions***

No Rhode Island statute or case law addresses notice as a condition precedent under a performance bond. Notice requirements under payment bonds, however, have been statutorily abrogated in Rhode Island.

## 6. Time for Suit

***Statutes of limitation particular to performance bonds and other applicable statutes of limitation***

R.I. Gen. Laws § 9-1-13 provides that except as otherwise specially provided, all civil actions, including actions for breach of contract, shall be commenced within 10 years next after the cause of action shall accrue, and not after.

R.I. Gen. Laws § 9-1-17 provides actions on contracts or liabilities under seal shall be commenced and sued within 20 years next after the cause of action shall accrue.

R.I. Gen Laws 37-12-5 provides that no suit under a *payment* bond shall be commenced after the expiration of two years, or under the maximum time limit as contained within any labor or material payment bond required, whichever period is longer, after the day on which the last of the labor was furnished or performed or material or equipment was furnished or supplied by any person claiming under the section.

***Case law statements about enforceability of limitations contained in bonds***

Limitations periods set forth in contracts are generally enforced in Rhode Island. *Hay v. Pawtucket Mut. Ins. Co.*, 824 A.2d 458, 460 (R.I. 2003); *DiIorio v. Abington Mut. Fire Ins. Co.*, 121 R.I. 689, 694, 402 A.2d 745, 747 (R.I. 1979).

***Varying statutes of limitation by agreement in bond or contract*** – Not applicable.

## 7. Procedure

***Statutory or procedural rules that may affect handling or administration of lawsuits***

R.I. Super Ct. R. Civ. P. 12 permits a defendant 20 days to answer or otherwise respond to a complaint.

R.I. Super Ct. R. Civ. P. 38 provides that any party may demand a trial by jury of any issue triable of right by a jury by serving upon the other parties a demand therefor in writing at any time after the commencement of the action and not later than 10 days after the service of the last pleading directed to such issue and filing the demand with the court.

R.I. Gen. Laws § 45-15-5 provides that before filing a claim against any town or city, a party must take the following method to obtain what is due: The person shall present to the town council of the town, or to the city council of the city, a particular account of that person's claim, debt, damages, or demand, and how incurred or contracted; which being done, in case just and due satisfaction is not made to him or her by the town or city treasurer of the town or city within 40 days after the presentment of the claim, debt, damages, or demand, the person may commence his or her action against the treasurer for the recovery of the complaint.

***Venue requirements and jurisdictional limitations***

R.I. Gen. Laws § 8-2-14 provides:

> The superior court shall have original jurisdiction of all actions at law where title to real estate or some right or interest therein is in issue, except actions for possession of tenements let or held at will or by sufferance; and shall have exclusive original jurisdiction of all other actions at law in which the amount in controversy shall exceed the sum of $10,000; and shall also have concurrent original jurisdiction with the district court in all other actions at law in which the amount in controversy exceeds the sum of $5,000 and does not exceed $10,000; provided, that the plaintiff shall not recover costs unless he or she shall recover in such action not less than $5,000 or unless the action is one in which the title to real estate or some right or interest therein is in question, or unless in the discretion of the court, on motion, costs are awarded. If an action is brought in the superior court which is within

the jurisdiction conferred by this section, the superior court shall have jurisdiction of all other actions arising out of the same transaction or occurrence, provided the other actions are joined with the action within the jurisdiction conferred by this section or are subsequently made a part thereof under applicable procedural rules.

R.I. Gen. Laws § 9-4-4 provides:

Personal or transitory actions and suits brought by or against corporations, if brought in the superior court, shall be brought in the court for the county, and if brought in a district court, shall be brought in the division in which the other party or some one of the other parties dwell, or in the court for the county or in the district court for the division in which the defendant or some one of the defendants shall be found, or in which the corporation is located by its charter, or if not located by its charter, in which the annual meetings of the corporation are required to be, or if not required to be, are actually held.

R.I. Gen. Laws § 9-4-5 provides:

If no one of the plaintiffs or defendants dwell within the state, and a corporation established out of the state be a party, personal or transitory actions or suits by or against it may, if brought in the superior court, be brought in the court for any county, or if in the district court, in any division.

R.I. Gen. Laws § 9-4-3 provides:

All other actions and suits, if brought in the superior court, shall be brought in the court for the county, or if brought in the district court, shall be brought in the division in which some one of the plaintiffs or defendants shall dwell, or in the superior court for the county or in the district court for the division in which the defendant or some one of the defendants shall be found; and if no one of the plaintiffs or defendants shall dwell in the state, the action, if brought in the superior court, may be brought in the court for any county, or if in a district court, in any division.

R.I. Gen. Laws § 8-2-27 provides:

Any civil cause or any question of law or fact therein may, by consent of the parties and with approval of the court, be tried and determined in any county. When civil actions involving a common question of law or fact are pending in different counties, the court may in the interest of convenience order any such action transferred to another county for the purpose of consolidating the actions for trial.

***Arbitration requirements and application***

If the construction contract underlying a performance bond contains an arbitration provision, the arbitration provision shall apply to the surety for all disputes involving questions of the claimant's right to recovery against the surety. R.I. Gen. Laws § 10-3-21.

**Public Works Arbitration Act, R.I. Gen. Laws §§ 37-16-1 to 37-16-27** – A performance bond surety on a public works construction project that is subject to arbitration by virtue of either an arbitration provision in the contract or pursuant to R.I. Gen. Laws § 37-16-2(b) is bound to arbitrate any claims under the bond in accordance with the provisions of the Public Works Arbitration Act. R.I. Gen. Laws § 37-16-27.

The superior court has jurisdiction to enforce arbitration provisions and arbitration awards. R.I. Gen. Laws § 37-16-5. The court may conduct a trial on the issue of arbitrability. R.I. Gen. Laws § 37-16-6.

The method for appointing an arbitrator set forth in the contract shall be followed. If none is provided the parties shall agree as to the method. In the event that the parties are unable to agree as to the method for appointing an arbitrator, the court shall appoint one. R.I. Gen. Laws § 37-16-7.

The arbitrator(s) must appoint a time and place for the hearing and provide notice thereof to the parties. R.I. Gen. Laws § 37-16-8

In order to be enforceable, arbitration awards must be written and confirmed by the superior court within one year after the award is made. Upon entry of an order confirming the award, judgment may enter. Judgment so entered shall have the full force and effect as though it had been issued by the court in which it is entered. R.I. Gen. Laws §§ 37-16-14; 37-16-16; 37-16-17; 37-16-22; 37-16-24 .

**Rhode Island Arbitration Act, R.I. Gen. Laws § 10-3-1, *et seq.*** – A party may petition to superior court to enforce an arbitration agreement. R.I. Gen. Laws § 10-3-4. If there is a dispute as to whether the issue is subject to arbitration, it shall be decided by the court and proceed summarily to trial on the issue of arbitrability. R.I. Gen. Laws § 10-3-5.

At any time within one year of the award a party may apply to the superior court for an order confirming the award. R.I. Gen. Laws § 10-3-11. Upon entry of an order confirming the award, judgment may enter. R.I. Gen. Laws § 10-3-16. Judgment so entered shall have the full force and effect as though it had been issued by the court in which it is entered. R.I. Gen. Laws § 10-3-18.

## 8. Attorney's Fees

***Statutes and/or case law limiting or permitting recovery of attorney's fees***

A court may award a reasonable attorney's fee to the prevailing party in any civil action arising from a breach of contract in which the court (1) finds that there was a complete absence of a justiciable issue of either law or fact raised by the losing party; or (2) renders a default judgment against the losing party. R.I. Gen. Laws § 9-1-45.

The Rhode Island Supreme Court is reluctant to affirm a grant of attorney's fees where any justiciable issue is presented. *Rhode Island Promac, Inc. v. Vulcan Associates I*, No. W.C. 99-16, 2005 WL 2077357, at *4 (R.I. Super. Aug 19, 2005).

## 9. Special Provisions – None.

## 10. Remarks

Rhode Island statutory and case law is far better developed in the payment bond context than in the area of performance bonds. While payment bond statutes and case law obviously are not controlling in situations involving performance bonds, a Rhode Island court is likely to be heavily influenced by these statutes and decisions. Accordingly, performance bond sureties and practitioners in Rhode Island are advised to be cognizant of the law regarding payment bonds.

## 11. Case Annotations

Where the parties have failed to expressly designate the governing law, a performance bond is to be construed in accordance with the law governing the principal's obligation, unless some other state has a more significant relationship to the transaction or the parties. *Marshall Contractors, Inc. v. Peerless Ins. Co.*, 827 F. Supp. 91, 94 (D.R.I. 1993).

Surety and agent owed no duty to the principal to correctly classify its construction projects and charge Class A, rather than Class B, premium rates for payment and performance bonds. *Fleet Const. Co., Inc. v. Aetna Life & Cas. Co.,* 746 A.2d 1247 (R.I. 2000).

***Interpretation of AIA bond forms*** – None.

***Cases in which surety steps into shoes of obligee***

The surety, performing the contracts, succeeds by subrogation to all the rights of the obligee. It has performed the contract at a substantial loss and is entitled to the retained funds to the extent necessary to repair that loss. *Glens Falls Indem. Co. v. American Awning & Tent Co.,* 180 A. 367, 376 (R.I. 1935).

# SOUTH CAROLINA

C. Allen Gibson, Jr.[1]

## 1. Requirement for Bond

***Statutory provisions for projects that are:***

**Public** – South Carolina Code § 11-35-3030 requires a performance bond in an amount equal to 100 percent of the price specified in the contract for all public construction contracts valued at more than $100,000. The surety must meet criteria established by the state and the bond must be in a form satisfactory to the state.

**Private** – There are no statutes in South Carolina that require performance bonds on private projects.

**Department of Transportation** – South Carolina Code § 57-5-1660 requires a performance bond on all SCDOT public highway construction contracts exceeding $10,000. The performance bond must be in the full amount of the contract. The surety must be satisfactory to the authority awarding the contract.

---

[1] C. Allen Gibson, Jr. is a shareholder of:
Buist Moore Smythe McGee P.A.
5 Exchange Street
Charleston, South Carolina 29401
(843) 722-3400

***Case law rules that might generally apply***

"The state requires performance bonds for public construction contracts to protect itself from a principal's breach." *Masterclean, Inc. v. Star Insurance Co.*, 347 S.C. 405, 556 S.E.2d 371, 376 (2001).

## 2. Damages Covered

***Set forth in any statutes and/or case law***

South Carolina statutes provide detailed guidance with regard to payment bond claimants and damages but do not specifically address in the statutes the damages covered under a performance bond. Performance bonds will be construed like any contract and the damages that are proximately caused by a breach of the obligation of the bond will be recoverable.

***Obligations of surety to perform and/or pay***

"The bond's primary obligation rests on the principal to perform the contract. When the principal fails, the surety performs according to the terms of the bond." *Masterclean, Inc. v. Star Insurance Co.*, 347 S.C. 405, 556 S.E.2d 371, 376 (2001). The terms of the bond will set forth the specific obligations of the surety. When a surety does undertake to perform the principal's obligation, the surety "must necessarily become subject to all his liabilities." *National Loan and Exchange Bank v. Gustafson*, 157 S.C. 221, 154 S.E. 167, 176 (1930). "A surety's obligation is contractual and cannot extend beyond the terms of the bond and the intent of the parties thereto." *S.C. Public Service Commission v. Colonial Construction*, 274 S.C. 581, 266 S.E.2d 76, 77 (1980).

***Whether failure to provide insurance transfers burden to surety*** – There are no statutes or case law which address this issue.

***Limitations on damages***

"A surety must pay the obligee only if the principal defaults..." *Masterclean, Inc. v. Star Insurance Co.*, 347 S.C. 405, 556 S.E.2d 371, 374 (2001). "The general rule is...that in a suit on an obligation containing the statement of a penal sum the recovery cannot exceed that sum." *Stelts v. Martin*, 90 S.C. 14, 72 S.E. 550, 552 (1911).

***Whether obligee may set off bonded contract funds against other principal-obligee debts or obligations*** – No cases address this issue.

***Incorporation of specific contract terms by reference***

If a bond incorporates an agreement by reference, the two will be read together and construed as a whole. *S.C. Public Service Commission v. Colonial Construction*, 274 S.C. 581, 266 S.E.2d 76, 77 (1980).

### 3. Penal Sum Variations

***Limitations per statute***

A performance bond for construction in the state must be in an amount equal to 100 percent of the price specified in the contract. S.C. Code § 11-35-3030(2)(a)(1) and 57-5-1660(a)(1) (for SCDOT projects).

***Effect of changes in work upon penal sum, if at all***

The statutes both for general construction projects and for SCDOT projects in South Carolina require performance bonds for the full amount of the contract. Although there is no case law interpreting the effect of minor changes, it is reasonable to expect that additive or deductive changes will by necessity increase or decrease the penal sum of the performance bond. However, if the underlying risk assumed by the surety is substantially changed, then the surety will be discharged from its obligation under the bond if it has not received notice of or consented to the additional risk. *Carriage Town, Inc. v. Landco, Inc.*, 998 F. Supp. 646, 648 (D.S.C. 1998) citing *Employers Insurance v. Construction Management Engineers*, 297 S.C. 354, 377 S.E.2d 119, 122 (S.C. App. 1989).

***Statutory or case law protections or dangers to penal sum***

No statutes directly address this issue. In the case of *Aiken County v. BSP Division of Envirotech Corp.*, 657 F. Supp. 1339 (D.S.C. 1986) *aff'd in part and rev'd on other grounds*, 866 F.2d 661 (4th Cir. 1989) the court held that a surety can limit its liability to the penal sum of the bond. 657 F. Supp. at 1368. In addition, the court held that "a surety is not liable for punitive damages absent a showing of active participation in the fraud..." *Id.*

## 4. Parties Covered

***Statutes and/or case law as to whether only obligees are covered***

No statutes or case law directly address this issue. However, courts will generally enforce the specific language of the bond. See *Cullum Mechanical v. S.C. Baptist Hospital*, 336 S.C. 423, 520 S.E.2d 809 (S.C. App. 1999), *rev'd on other grounds*, 344 S.C. 426, 544 S.E.2d 838 (2001).

***Coverage for:***

**Third-party beneficiaries** – The terms of the bond will ordinarily control and the courts will not create an obligation that was not within the intent of the parties. In *Cullum Mechanical*, the South Carolina Court of Appeals held that a surety that issued a bid bond but did not subsequently provide performance and payment bonds for a public project was not liable to the subcontractors for the failure to provide that payment bond. *Cullum Mechanical v. S.C. Baptist Hospital*, 336 S.C. 423, 520 S.E.2d 809, 814 (S.C. App. 1999), *rev'd on other grounds*, 344 S.C. 426, 544 S.E.2d 838 (2001).

**Assignees** – Although there are no specific cases on the assignment of the benefits of a performance bond, the courts will generally enforce the assignment of a contract. "When a contract is assigned, the assignee should have all the same rights and privileges, including the right to sue on the contract, as the assignor." *Twelfth RMA Partners v. National Safe Corporation*, 335 S.C. 635, 518 S.E.2d 44, 46 (S.C. App. 1999).

**Dual obligees** – Although no cases address this specific issue, dual obligees should each equally be entitled to enforce the obligation of the performance bond.

## 5. Notice or Filing Required

### *Statutory provisions*

There is no statutory provision regarding filing of a performance bond. Although the South Carolina statutes have detailed notice provisions regarding payment bonds, there are no statutory notice provisions for a performance bond. The notice requirements will ordinarily be those set forth in the bond.

### *Case law rules concerning condition precedent notice*

A claimant against a surety bond is not required to provide notice to the surety prior to bringing an action against the principal. A judgment against the principal will be conclusive as against the surety even though the surety did not have notice of the underlying suit unless the judgment was obtained by fraud, collusion or the court lacks jurisdiction over the surety. *Cooper v. Beauliau*, 310 S.C. 392, 426 S.E.2d 819, 820 (S.C. App. 1992) citing *Ward v. Federal Insurance Co.*, 233 S.C. 561, 106 S.E.2d 169 (1958).

Of course, "a surety must pay the obligee only if the principal defaults..." *Masterclean, Inc. v. Star Insurance Co.*, 347 S.C. 405, 556 S.E.2d 371, 374 (2001). In addition, the courts will generally enforce the specific conditions which are included in the bond before imposing liability on the surety. See *Lite House, Inc. v. North River Insurance Co.*, 322 S.C. 26, 471 S.E.2d 166 (1996) and *Kennedy v. Henderson*, 289 S.C. 393, 346 S.E.2d 526 (1986).

## 6. Time for Suit

### *Statutes of limitation particular to performance bonds and other applicable statutes of limitation*

South Carolina Code § 15-3-530 provides a general three year statute of limitations for a breach of contract action. However, § 15-3-520 provides for a 20 year statute of limitations on a bond or a sealed instrument. The statutes do not directly address a limitation period for an action against a performance bond. In *S&S Construction, Inc. of Anderson v. Reliance Insurance Co.*, 42 F. Supp. 2d 622 (D.S.C. 1998) the court held that the one year statute of limitations specifically provided for regarding a *payment* bond claim would govern rather than the 20 year statute of limitations for sealed instruments. However, since there is no specific statutory limit for the time within which to bring a performance bond claim, the reasoning of this case will not apply.

***Case law statements about enforceability of limitations contained in bonds***

It has long been held that the provision in a bond which requires suit to be brought within a period of time less than that prescribed by statute is not enforceable. *Barringer v. Fidelity & Deposit Co. of Maryland*, 161 S.C. 4, 159 S.E. 373, 375 (1931). However, where there is a specific state statute dealing with limitation periods for bringing bond claims such as exists with payment bond claims, then the specific statute and the shorter timeframe will be enforced. *S and S Construction, Inc. v. Reliance Insurance Company*, 42 F. Supp. 2d 622 (D.S.C. 1998).

***Varying statutes of limitations by agreement in bond or contract***

South Carolina Code § 15-3-140 specifically prohibits any contract clause that attempts to shorten the statutory period for bringing a cause of action.

**7. Procedure**

***Statutory or procedural rules that may affect handling or administration of lawsuits***

A defendant has 30 days after service of a summons and complaint to file an answer to an action brought in the state courts. Rule 12, South Carolina Rules of Civil Procedure.

***Venue requirements and jurisdictional limitations***

South Carolina's long arm statute is set forth at South Carolina Code § 36-2-803. It is routinely interpreted to extend jurisdiction to the constitutional limits imposed by the due process clause. Venue for a particular action will be governed by South Carolina Code § 15-7-10 *et seq*. A South Carolina resident has the right to have the action tried in the county in which the defendant resides at the time of commencement of the action. S.C. Code § 15-7-30. If none of the parties reside in the state, then the plaintiff may designate the county in the complaint. *Id.* However, venue may be changed pursuant to the requirements of South Carolina Code § 15-7-100.

***Court rules*** – The South Carolina Supreme Court has adopted Rules of Civil Procedure which are modeled after the Federal Rules of Civil Procedure.

***Particular agency regulations/rules***

Each governmental agency, municipality or political subdivision may adopt its own regulations or ordinances. These should be reviewed carefully in the event of a dispute with any particular agency or political subdivision.

***Arbitration requirements and application***

South Carolina has adopted a Uniform Arbitration Act. See S.C. Code § 15-48-10 *et seq*. Although arbitration provisions in a contract are generally enforced, the South Carolina act has a requirement that the contract must include a specific notice on the face of the contract in order to be enforceable pursuant to the South Carolina act. That notice must be in UNDERLINED, ALL CAPITAL LETTERS and must state that the contract is subject to arbitration pursuant to the South Carolina Arbitration Act.

## 8. Attorney's Fees

***Statutes and/or case law limiting or permitting recovery of attorney's fees***

South Carolina Code § 27-1-15 provides for an award of attorney's fees in favor of a payment bond claimant if the surety fails to make a reasonable and fair investigation, but there is no similar statutory provision regarding performance bond claims.

***What fees are recoverable if any*** – Not applicable.

## 9. Special Provisions

There is no affirmative cause of action by a principal against a surety for bad faith refusal to pay a performance bond claim. However, the surety's bad faith may be asserted as a defense to an indemnity action brought by the surety against the principal. *Masterclean v. Star Insurance Co.*, 347 S.C. 405, 566 S.E.2d 371, 376 (2001).

**10. Remarks** – Not applicable.

## 11. Case Annotations

***Interpretation of AIA bond forms*** – South Carolina cases have not specifically addressed AIA bond forms A311 or A312.

***Cases in which surety steps into shoes of obligee***

The terms of the bond will set forth the specific obligations of the surety. When a surety does undertake to perform the principal's obligation, the surety "must necessarily become subject to all his liabilities." *National Loan and Exchange Bank v. Gustafson*, 157 S.C. 221, 154 S.E. 167, 176 (1930). However, "a surety's obligation is contractual and cannot extend beyond the terms of the bond and the intent of the parties thereto." *S.C. Public Service Commission v. Colonial Construction*, 274 S.C. 581, 266 S.E.2d 76, 77 (1980).

# SOUTH DAKOTA

William P. Fuller[1]

## 1. Requirement for Bond

***Statutory provisions for projects that are:***

**Public** – There are several South Dakota statutes that require public performance bonds. SDCL § 5-21-1 provides in part that "when any contract is entered into for the construction of public improvement or the furnishing of any material or labor therefor, the contractor is required, before commencing such work, to furnish surety in an amount not less than the contract price, for the faithful performance of the contract, with the additional obligation that the contractor shall promptly pay all persons supplying him with labor or material in the prosecution of the work provided for in the contract."

SDCL § 5-18-1(3) defines public improvement as "the cost of which is payable from taxes or other funds under the control of the public corporation and also local improvements for which special assessments are to be levied." *See also Midstates Excavating, Inc. v. Farmers and Merchants Bank and Trust*, 410 N.W.2d 190, 194 (S.D. 1987).

1 William P. Fuller is a shareholder of:
Woods, Fuller, Shultz & Smith P.C.
300 South Phillips Avenue, Suite 300
P.O. Box 5027
Sioux Falls, South Dakota 57117-5027
(605) 336-3890

SDCL § 5-21-3 provides in part that "if a contract is entered into for the construction, alteration, or repair of improvements to be located in this state, including public improvements, and the contractor or subcontractor furnishes surety for the faithful performance of the contract, there is hereby imposed an additional obligation upon the surety to the State of South Dakota that the contractor or subcontractor shall promptly pay all taxes which may accrue to the State of South Dakota under the provisions of chapters 10-46, 10-46A, and 10-46B."

SDCL § 5-23-16 provides that "as soon as practicable after the bids have been opened and examined, the Bureau of Administration shall give notice to the successful bidder that his proposal has been accepted. The bidder shall within 10 days thereafter enter into a contract with the state, on such forms as shall be provided, to furnish the same in accordance with the schedule and specifications or in accordance with the bid as accepted. The contract shall be secured by bond, cash, bank cashier's check, bank money order, or approved security. In the case of supplies or equipment especially manufactured according to specifications, the bond, cash, bank cashier's check, bank money order, or security shall be in the total sum of the contract."

SDCL § 7-25-12 provides that "the board must further require a bond from the contractor in a sum equal to the contract price, conditioned that the contractor will execute his contract and complete the building or buildings according to the plans and specifications and to the full satisfaction of the board, and account for all moneys paid to him and pay all bills and claims on account of labor or materials furnished in and about the performance of the contract including all demands of subcontractors, such bond to stand as security for all such bills, claims, and demands and to be a surety bond issued by some surety company authorized to do a surety bonding business in the state or a personal bond with sufficient sureties, to be approved by the board of county commissioners."

SDCL § 9-35-19 provides that "all municipalities may require every person offering a CATV system to furnish any person applying therefor along lines of its wires, cables, or other conduits, with such service and may require performance bonds or expiration dates contingent upon construction or commencement of operations."

SDCL § 11-7-85 provides that "the commission may in its discretion require a purchaser or a lessee to furnish a performance bond as security for its fulfillment of the agreement with the commission. The performance bond shall have such surety and be in such form and amount as the commission may approve."

SDCL § 11-9-43 provides that "as security for its fulfillment of the agreement with the governing body, a purchaser or lessee of redevelopment property shall furnish a performance bond, with such surety and in such form and amount as the governing body may approve or make such other guaranty as the governing body may deem necessary in the public interest."

SDCL § 13-20-7 provides that "when supplies or equipment are to be purchased, a school board advertising pursuant to § 13-20-3 may require a reasonable deposit guaranteeing the execution of contract and the furnishing of a performance bond by the successful bidder in accordance with chapters 5-18 and 5-21. The board may accept an annual bond provided that it meets the requirements of chapters 5-18 and 5-21. The board shall reserve the right to reject any and all bids."

SDCL § 13-20-7.1 provides that "when school facilities are to be built or remodeled or improvements are to be made to school sites, the school board advertising pursuant to § 13-20-3 shall require a reasonable deposit guaranteeing the execution of the contract and the furnishing of a performance bond by the successful bidder in accordance with chapters 5-18 and 5-21. The board shall reserve the right to reject any and all bids."

SDCL § 24-11-42(3) provides that "a contract made under § 24-11-4 shall: ... (3) If the contract includes construction, require a performance bond approved by the governing body that is adequate and appropriate for the proposed construction contract."

SDCL § 31-12-15 provides that "when any bid, as provided for in § 31-12-14 has been accepted, the board of county commissioners, county highway board, or board of township supervisors, as the case may be, shall enter into a contract with the person whose bid has been accepted. The contract shall be in writing specifying the work to be done or the materials to be furnished, or both, the time for completion, and the contract price or rate of payments. The board shall require the person receiving the contract to furnish a bond with approved sureties, and in an amount the board considers sufficient, conditioned upon the faithful performance of the contract according to the plans and specifications."

SDCL § 31-13-7 provides that "contracts let by the board of township supervisors without advertising for bids shall also be in writing specifying the work to be done, the time in which it is to be completed, and the amount to be paid, and the board may require the contractor to furnish a bond with approved sureties in such sum as it shall deem sufficient, conditioned for the faithful performance of the contract according to the plans and specifications."

SDCL § 31-14-13 provides that "at the time of entering into a contract under § 31-14-11, the contractor shall execute to the county a satisfactory bond with sufficient surety, to be approved by the board of county commissioners, or a certified check in the total sum of the contract, conditioned that the contractor will fulfill his contract according to the plans and specifications and account for all moneys paid to him, and pay all bills and claims on account of supplies, materials, or labor used in connection with or consumed in carrying on of any work in connection with such contract including all demands of subcontractors, and such bond or certified check shall stand as security for the faithful performance of said contract and for the payment of all such bills, claims, and demands. Such contract and bond or certified check shall be filed in the office of the county auditor."

SDCL § 31-23-1 provides that "except as provided in § 31-12-15, before any contract is entered into for the construction, repair, or improvement of any public highway by the State of South Dakota, or any public corporation within the State of South Dakota, the person to whom such contract is awarded shall furnish a performance bond running to the State of South Dakota in an amount not less than the contract price for the faithful performance of such contract, in the form and conditioned as required by the statutes of the State of South Dakota."

SDCL § 36-21A-94 provides that "no application may be approved by the commission unless the subdivider offers satisfactory proof of his ability to provide promised public improvements including water, sewer, gas and streets. Satisfactory proof shall be in the form of performance bonds or other security."

SDCL § 45-9-15 provides that "without limiting its general authority, the Board of Minerals and Environment may require, or may delegate to the office of the state geologist, specific authority to require the furnishing of a plugging and performance bond in the amount of $5,000 per well drilled, or $20,000 blanket, with good and sufficient surety, conditioned for the performance of the duty to plug each dry or abandoned well, to restore the premises, insofar as possible, to the condition which existed prior to the filing of the application to drill; and conditioned on the proper performance of all of the requirements of

§§ 45-9-5 to 45-9-18, inclusive. The condition of the bond insofar as it relates to restoration of the surface shall be deemed to have been complied with if the landowner or lessee and the producer or driller adopt a different plan as approved by the board. The board may require additional bond if the circumstances require.

SDCL § 5-21-1.1, however, provides that "the requirement of a performance security may be waived by public corporations when the bid submitted does not exceed $25,000."

SDCL § 5-21-1, further, provides that "the State of South Dakota, acting through the Bureau of Administration, shall waive the requirement of a performance and payment bond, before the bid letting, on state projects if the awarded contract does not exceed $50,000."

SDCL § 5-21-2 provides that "in case any such public corporation shall fail or neglect to require the execution of the surety provided for in § 5-21-1, such public corporation shall be liable to pay any person who shall have performed labor or furnished any material that entered into the erection, alteration, repair or improvement of such building, the value of such work or material and an action may be maintained therefor; provided, that an action brought under the provisions of this section shall be commenced within 90 days from the acceptance of the work for which the same shall be claimed."

SDCL § 5-18-18.2 provides in part that "the governing board of a unit of local government shall be exempted from the provisions of this chapter if it is able to purchase materials, supplies or equipment at a substantial savings at a public sale or auction. Any performance bond required by § 5-21-1 may be waived on items purchased for less than $10,000 at a public sale or auction."

SDCL § 5-18-19 provides that "it shall be unlawful for any public corporation or its officers to enter into any contract in violation of the terms of this chapter or chapter 5-21, and any such contract entered into shall be null and void and of no force and effect."

SDCL § 9-41A-53 provides that "a municipal power agency may contract for planning, acquisition, construction, reconstruction, operation, maintenance, repair, extension, and improvement of generation and transmission facilities outside of the corporate limits of its members, or may contract with other public or private owners of these facilities to perform these functions, without advertising for bids, preparing final plans and specifications in advance of construction, or securing performance and payment bonds as required for other public contracts in § 5-21-1, except to the extent that its governing body determines that these actions are desirable in furtherance of the purposes of this chapter. Except as otherwise provided by this section, no contract shall be invalid or unenforceable by reason of nonperformance of the conditions required by any other law relating to public contracts. If a bond is secured, no lien may be filed under chapter 44-9 for the furnishing of labor, skill, material, or machinery for the improvement covered thereby."

SDCL § 34-20B-96 provides that "the Department of Health shall, in addition to other powers and duties vested in it by this chapter or any other act, enter into contracts for educational and research activities without performance bonds."

**Private** – No statutes in South Dakota require performance bonds on private projects. A private owner may, however, "in contracting with the contractor, ... require the contractor to provide a performance bond or other security assuring the owner that the supplier will be paid and no mechanic's liens will be filed." *Larsons Concrete Co., Inc. v. Stroschein*, 353 N.W.2d 354, 360 n.4 (S.D. 1984) (citing *Albright v. Smith*, 51 N.W. 590, 593 (S.D. 1892).

Private construction projects, moreover, are covered by South Dakota's mechanic's and materialmen's lien laws. *See Farmers State Bank v. Ed Cox and Son*, 132 N.W.2d 282, 292 (S.D. 1965) (Hanson, J., dissenting).

**Department of Transportation** – No performance bond statute in South Dakota applies specifically to the Department of Transportation.

***Case law rules that might generally apply***

"A contractors bond should be construed in connection with the contract with which it was executed and the statute requiring it. However, a bond may be conditioned more broadly than the minimum requirements of the statute." *J.D. Evans Equip. Co., Sioux Road v. Johnson*, 160 N.W.2d 637, 639 (S.D. 1968); *see also Farmers State Bank v. Ed Cox and Son*, 132 N.W.2d 282, 286 (S.D. 1965).

The right of a plaintiff to maintain an action against the public corporation for failure to obtain a performance bond is not predicated on the insolvency of the principal contractor. *Handelan v. Smee Sch. Dist.*, 159 N.W. 888, 890 (S.D. 1916).

Members and officers of public corporations are not personally liable for the public corporations failure to obtain a performance bond. *See Plumbing Supply Co. v. Bd. of Educ. of Indep. Sch. Dist.*, 142 N.W. 1131, 1132-33 (S.D. 1913).

## 2. Damages Covered

***Set forth in any statutes and/or case law***

SDCL § 5-21-7 provides that "if recovery on the bond should be inadequate to pay the amounts found due all such persons, judgment shall be given to each person for his pro rata of the amount of recovery. The surety company may pay into court for distribution among such claimants and creditors the full amount of the penalty named in the bond, less any amount which surety company may have paid to the public corporation by reason of the execution of such bond, and upon so doing the surety company shall be relieved from further liability."

SDCL § 56-2-12 provides that "a surety cannot be held beyond the express terms of his contract, and if such contract prescribes a penalty for its breach, he cannot in any case be liable for more than the penalty."

An item is within the coverage of a bond "if it is such that the cost accountant would charge it as a direct expense item to a particular job and not to plant and equipment." *Margulies v. Ogdie*, 10 N.W.2d 513, 515 (S.D. 1943).

A performance bond covers all such labor and material that "could reasonably be regarded as within the contemplation of the parties" at the time of contracting. *See Finch v. Enke*, 222 N.W. 657, 658 (S.D. 1929).

"In order to create liability on the part of the surety for the purchase price of tools and appliances under these contract bonds, at least the following elements we think must be present: First, the tool or appliance must be purchased specifically and particularly for use in the performance of the particular contract; second, the use of such tool or appliance must be at least proper, if not reasonably necessary, in connection with and about the carrying out of the contract; third, the tool or appliance must be used in or about the performance of the contract; fourth, the tool or appliance must be such that it is reasonably to be expected in the natural course of events that its normal life for the purpose for which it was designed will be practically consumed by its use in and about the performance of the contract, and in this connection the facts of each particular case must be taken into consideration." *Dennis v. Enke*, 224 N.W. 925, 928 (S.D. 1929).

A performance bond "should be construed most strongly in favor of indemnity." *Farmers State Bank v. Ed Cox and Son*, 132 N.W.2d 282, 287 (S.D. 1965); *see also Western Material Co. v. Enke*, 228 N.W. 385, 387 (S.D. 1929).

SDCL § 21-1-11 provides that "every person who is entitled to recover damages certain, or capable of being made certain by calculation, and the right to recover which is vested in him upon a particular day, is entitled also to recover interest thereon from that day, except during such time as the debtor is prevented by law, or by the act of the creditor, from paying the debt."

"The person liable is in default for not paying interest only when he knows or can readily ascertain the exact sum of his indebtedness by computation. Even assuming that the defendants had admitted coverage under their bond they could not have known the extent of their liability until that was determined by the court. Accordingly, there was no error in denying interest prior to judgment." *See Farmers State Bank v. Ed Cox and Son*, 132 N.W.2d 282, 290-91 (S.D. 1965).

### 3. Penal Sum Variation

South Dakota, generally, does not have statutory limits on public improvement contract performance bond penal sums.

### 4. Parties Covered

#### *Statutes and/or case law as to whether only obligees are covered*

SDCL § 5-21-5 provides that "any person who has furnished labor or material used in the construction of any such public improvement as described in § 5-21-1, payment for which has not been made, shall have the right to intervene and be made a party to any action instituted by the public corporation on the surety, and to have his rights and claims adjudicated in such action and judgment rendered thereon, subject, however, to the priority of claim and judgment of such public corporation. If the full amount of liability of the surety company is insufficient to pay the full amount of such claims and demands, then, after paying the full amount due the public corporation, the remainder shall be distributed pro rata among such interveners."

SDCL § 31-23-3 provides in part that "any person having direct contractual relationship with a subcontractor but not contractual relationship express or implied with the contractor furnishing a performance bond under § 31-23-1 shall have a right of action upon the said bond upon giving written notice to said contractor within six months from the date on which such person did or performed the last of the labor or furnished or supplied the last of the material for which such claim is made, stating with substantial accuracy the amount claimed and the name of the party to whom the material was furnished or supplied or for whom the labor was done or performed."

"It is not necessary, however, that the person for whose benefit the contract has been made should be named in the contract; but it must appear by the direct terms of the contract that it was made for his benefit." *Thompson Yards, Inc. v. Van Nice*, 239 N.W. 753, 755 (S.D. 1931).

"If it is sufficiently definite and precise to impose a liability to pay the claims of third parties, the bond furnished to the state or a public agency is an enforceable obligation irrespective of the minimum requirements of the statute and afford a right of action to a person furnishing labor or materials." *J.D. Evans Equip. Co., Sioux Road v. Johnson*, 160 N.W.2d 637, 639 (S.D. 1968).

A performance bond's coverage scope is determined from the instrument. *See Farmers State Bank v. Ed Cox and Son*, 132 N.W.2d 282, 286 (S.D. 1965).

Performance bonds, however, do not cover money loaned by lending institutions. *See Farmers State Bank v. Kuipers Construction Co.*, 190 N.W.2d 769, 774 (S.D. 1971).

## 5. Notice or Filing Required

### *Statutory provisions*

SDCL § 5-21-4 provides that "the surety within 60 days after entering into such performance bond shall send notice of the bond to the secretary of revenue. Six months after the completion of the contract and the acceptance of the improvement by the owner thereof, the additional obligation imposed upon the surety shall cease unless written notice, within such period of time, of unpaid use taxes and contractors' excise taxes, is given to the surety by the secretary of revenue."

SDCL § 5-21-6 provides that "if no suit should be brought by the public corporation within the six months from the completion and final settlement of such contract, the person supplying the contractor with labor or material shall, upon application therefor and furnishing affidavit to the corporation that labor or material for the prosecution of such work has been supplied by him and payment of the same has not been made, be furnished with a certified copy of such contract and surety, upon which he shall have a right of action and shall be authorized to bring suit in the name of the public corporation in the circuit court for the county in which such contract was performed and not elsewhere, for his use and benefit, against such contractor and his surety, and to prosecute the same to final judgment; provided, that where suit is instituted by any such person on the surety of the contractor, it shall not be commenced until six months after the complete performance of such contract and final settlement thereof but must be commenced within one year thereafter; provided, further, that where suit is so instituted by any such person, only one action shall be brought, and any person may file his claim in such action and be made a party thereto within one year from the completion of the work under such contract, and not later; and provided, further, that costs shall not be taxed in such suit against the public corporation."

SDCL § 5-21-8 provides that "in all suits instituted under the provisions of §§ 5-21-5 and 5-21-6, personal notice of the pendency of such suit, informing them of their right to intervene, as the court may order, shall be given to all known creditors, and in addition thereto notice shall be given by publication in some newspaper of general circulation, published in the county where the contract is being performed once each week for at least two successive weeks with the first publication to be made at least three months before the time limited therefor."

SDCL § 5-23-21.3 provides in part that "the Bureau of Administration shall publish notice of its intent to purchase property or liability insurance or performance bonds."

SDCL § 31-23-3 provides in part that "any person having direct contractual relationship with a subcontractor but not contractual relationship express or implied with the contractor furnishing a performance bond under § 31-23-1 shall have a right of action upon the said bond upon giving written notice to said contractor within six months from the date on which such person did or performed the last of the labor or furnished or supplied the last of the material for which such claim is made, stating with substantial accuracy the amount claimed and the name of the party to whom the material was furnished or supplied or for whom the labor was done or performed."

***Case law rules concerning condition precedent notice***

Performance bond notice requirements "merely establish[] a condition precedent which must be met before materialmen may recover against the surety, namely, the materialmen must have given notice that they are owed money on the project. If the materialmen give the appropriate notice under the terms of the bond, they still have one year in which to file their law suit. If the materialmen do not give the appropriate notice, they also have one year to sue but may be met with a defense of failure to give the required notice." *See Northwest Pipe Fittings, Inc. v. St. Paul Fire and Marine Ins. Co.*, 508 N.W.2d 376, 378 (S.D. 1993).

**6. Time for Suit**

***Statutes of limitation particular to performance bonds and other applicable statutes of limitation***

SDCL § 15-2-13(1) provides in part that "an action upon a contract, obligation, or liability, express or implied" may be "commenced only within six years after the cause of action shall have accrued."

SDCL § 5-21-2 provides that "in case any such public corporation shall fail or neglect to require the execution of the surety provided for in § 5-21-1, such public corporation shall be liable to pay any person who shall have performed labor or furnished any material that entered into the erection, alteration, repair or improvement of such building, the value of such work or material and an action may be maintained therefor; provided, that an action brought under the provisions of this section shall be commenced within 90 days from the acceptance of the work for which the same shall be claimed."

SDCL § 5-21-6 provides that "if no suit should be brought by the public corporation within the six months from the completion and final settlement of such contract, the person supplying the contractor with labor or material shall, upon application therefor and furnishing affidavit to the corporation that labor or material for the prosecution of such work has been supplied by him and payment of the same has not been made, be furnished with a certified copy of such contract and surety, upon which he shall have a right of action and shall be authorized to bring suit in the name of the public corporation in the circuit court for the county in which such contract was performed and not elsewhere, for his use and benefit, against such contractor and his surety, and to prosecute the same to final judgment; provided, that where suit is instituted by any such person on the surety of the contractor, it shall not be commenced until six months after the complete performance of such contract and final settlement thereof but must be commenced within one year thereafter; provided, further, that where suit is so instituted by any such person, only one action shall be brought, and any person may file his claim in such action and be made a party thereto within one year from the completion of the work under such contract, and not later; and provided, further, that costs shall not be taxed in such suit against the public corporation."

SDCL § 31-23-4 provides that "every suit instituted under this chapter shall be brought in the name of the State of South Dakota for the use of the person suing, in the circuit court of the State of South Dakota within the circuit in which the contract was to be performed, and not elsewhere, irrespective of the amount in controversy in such suit, but no such suit shall be commenced after the expiration of one year after the date of final settlement of such contract. The State of South Dakota shall not be liable for the payment of any costs or expenses of any such suit."

SDCL § 53-9-6 provides that "every provision in a contract restricting a party from enforcing his rights under it by usual legal proceedings in ordinary tribunals, or limiting his time to do so, is void. However, agreements to submit controversies to arbitration, as authorized by the Uniform Arbitration Act, are valid and enforceable, and any provision in a surety contract which limits the time for enforcement is valid and enforceable if the limitation of time is not less than two years after the cause of action has accrued."

***Case law statements about enforceability of limitations contained in bonds***

"We believe the proper rule is that the law should set the limitation periods, not private contracts." *Sheehan v. Morris Irrigation*, 410 N.W.2d 569, 570 (S.D. 1987).

"A surety can limit the extent of its liability, but not the time for bringing suit." *Sheehan v. Morris Irrigation*, 410 N.W.2d 569, 571 (S.D. 1987).

## 7. Procedure

***Statutory or procedural rules that may affect handling or administration of lawsuits***

DCL § 5-21-6 provides that "if no suit should be brought by the public corporation within the six months from the completion and final settlement of such contract, the person supplying the contractor with labor or material shall, upon application therefor and furnishing affidavit to the corporation that labor or material for the prosecution of such work has been supplied by him and payment of the same has not been made, be furnished with a certified copy of such contract and surety, upon which he shall have a right of action and shall be authorized to bring suit in the name of the public corporation in the circuit court for the county in which such contract was performed and not elsewhere, for his use and benefit, against such contractor and his surety, and to prosecute the same to final judgment; provided, that where suit is instituted by any such person on the surety of the contractor, it shall not be commenced until six months after the complete performance of such contract and final settlement thereof but must be commenced within one year thereafter; provided, further, that where suit is so instituted by any such person, only one action shall be brought, and any person may file his claim in such action and be made a party thereto within one year from the completion of the work under such contract, and not later; and provided, further, that costs shall not be taxed in such suit against the public corporation."

SDCL § 21-25A-1 provides in part that "a written agreement to submit any existing controversy to arbitration or a provision in a written contract to submit to arbitration any controversy thereafter arising between the parties is valid, enforceable and irrevocable, save upon such grounds as exist at law or in equity for the revocation of any contract."

SDCL § 31-23-4 provides that "every suit instituted under this chapter shall be brought in the name of the State of South Dakota for the use of the person suing, in the circuit court of the State of South Dakota within the circuit in which the contract was to be performed, and not elsewhere, irrespective of the amount in controversy in such suit, but no such suit shall be commenced after the expiration of one year after the date of final settlement of such contract. The State of South Dakota shall not be liable for the payment of any costs or expenses of any such suit."

"Where liability exists by contract or otherwise, without any other action of the board [of county commissioners], suit may be brought directly in court, subject only to the requirement ... that before an action is brought claim shall have been presented to the county board and an opportunity given to pay without suit. Plaintiff has complied with this requirement. The measure of recovery would not change the procedure from an original action in the circuit court to an appeal from the board of county commissioners." *Western Material Co. v. Deltener*, 264 N.W. 207, 210 (S.D. 1935).

A court may take judicial notice that "the performance of contracts of this kind requires a plant and equipment suitable therefor, many items of which are expensive and the purchase of which could not be justified by any single contract unless it was extremely large" and that "this kind of work is generally performed by persons who engage therein as a business and who maintain, for the purpose of the general contracting business, a very considerable amount of equipment intended and designed to be used in that business over a period of several years and in the performance of a number of contracts." *Dennis v. Enke*, 224 N.W. 925, 927 (S.D. 1929).

## 8. Attorney's Fees

***Statutes and/or case law limiting or permitting recovery of attorney's fees***

"Ordinarily the terms 'costs' and 'expenses' as used in a statute are not understood to include attorney's fees and the court may allow attorney's fees as costs for or against any party to an action only in cases where specifically provided by statute. ... At common law the right to recover attorney's fees from an opponent in litigation did not exist. In the absence of a statute or rule of court or some agreement expressly authorizing taxing of attorney's fees in addition to ordinary statutory costs, such an item of expense is not allowable." *Tracy v. T & B Constr. Co.*, 182 N.W.2d 320, 323 (S.D. 1970).

SDCL § 58-1-2(8) defines insurance as "a contract whereby one undertakes to indemnify another or to pay or provide a specified or determinable amount or benefit upon determinable contingencies."

SDCL § 58-1-2(10) defines insurer as "every person engaged as indemnitor, surety, or contractor in the business of entering into contracts of insurance."

SDCL § 58-9-31 provides that "surety insurance includes insurance guaranteeing the performance of contracts, other than insurance policies, and guaranteeing and executing bonds, undertakings, and contracts of suretyship."

SDCL § 58-12-3 provides in part that "in all actions or proceedings hereafter commenced against any ... insurance company, ... on any policy or certificate of any type or kind of insurance, if it appears from the evidence that such company or exchange has refused to pay the full amount of such loss, and that such refusal is vexatious or without reasonable cause, the Department of Labor, the trial court and the appellate court, shall, if judgment or an award is rendered for plaintiff, allow the plaintiff a reasonable sum as an attorney's fee to be recovered and collected as a part of the costs, provided, however, that when a tender is made by such insurance company, exchange or self-insurer before the commencement of the action or proceeding in which judgment or an award is rendered and the amount recovered is not in excess of such tender, no such costs shall be allowed. The allowance of attorney fees hereunder shall not be construed to bar any other remedy, whether in tort or contract, that an insured may have against the same insurance company or self-insurer arising out of its refusal to pay such loss."

"The question of whether an insurer's refusal to pay is vexatious or without reasonable cause is necessarily one of fact and whether attorney's fees are to be allowed must depend on the facts and circumstances of each particular case." *Tracy v. T & B Constr. Co.*, 182 N.W.2d 320, 323 (S.D. 1970) (awarding attorney's fees to an obligee named in a contractor's performance bond).

## 9. Special Provisions

SDCL § 31-23-5 provides that "the remedy provided for in this chapter shall be exclusive."

Failure to obtain a performance bond may result in a forfeiture of any bid security a contractor provides. *See Rapid City Area Sch. Dist. No. 51-4 v. Black Hills and Western Tours, Inc.*, 303 N.W.2d 811, 814 (S.D. 1981) (holding that contractor's bid security was forfeited to school district after failing to obtain a performance bond).

"Fraud on the part of the obligee such as will avoid a contract of suretyship is not confined to positive affirmations which are untrue, but may consist in the concealment or withholding by him from the surety, at the time the contract of suretyship is executed, of material facts affecting the risk, which the obligee has the opportunity, and which it is his duty, to disclose." *Wakonda State Bank v. Fairfield*, 220 N.W. 515, 517 (S.D. 1928).

## 10. Remarks – Not applicable.

## 11. Case Annotations

***Interpretation of AIA bond forms*** – Not applicable.

***Cases in which surety steps into shoes of obligee***

"'When it is sought to enforce the right, something more must be shown than that defendant could have been compelled by the original creditor to pay the debt. ... The right to recover from a third person does not stand on the same footing as the right to recover from the principal. As to the latter, the right is absolute—as to the former, it is conditional.' Likewise, ... '[t]hat the surety on one bond has paid the debt does not alone entitle him to step into the creditor's shoes and recover what he has expended from the bondsmen on another obligation. To entitle him to do so, his equities must appear to be superior to those of the sureties on the other bond.'" *American Sur. Co. v. Western Sur. Co.*, 22 N.W.2d 429, 431 (S.D. 1946) (quoting *Northern Trust Co. v. Consolidated Elevator Co.*, 171 N.W. 265, 268 (Minn. 1919); *Fidelity & Deposit Co. v. Bowen*, 98 N.W. 897, 898 (Iowa 1904)).

# TENNESSEE

Joseph T. Getz[1]

## 1. Requirement for Bond

***Statutory provisions for projects that are***

**Public** – Tennessee has several statutes that require performance bonds on state, county, or city authority projects.

T.C.A. § 4-15-102 requires contractors who enter into a contract for a project supervised *by the State Building Commission*, in excess of $100,000, to execute a performance bond in an amount determined by the commission. Such bond shall be sufficient in amount to secure the faithful and satisfactory completion of the state building or improvement project and payment of all labor and materials used by the contractor, or any immediate or remote subcontractor under the contract.

T.C.A. § 12-4-201 requires that no contract be let for *any public work*, by any city, county, or state authority, until the contractor has executed a performance bond for 25 percent of the contract price if the contract is in excess of $100,000.

**Private** – Tennessee does not require performance bonds on private projects.

---

1 Joseph T. Getz is a shareholder of:
Less, Getz & Lipman, LLC
100 Peabody Place Suite 1000
Memphis, Tennessee 38103
(901) 525-8700

**Department of Transportation** – T.C.A. § 54-5-119 requires that all contractors who enter into contracts with the department execute a performance bond in an amount fixed by the department.

***Case law rules that might generally apply***

When the terms of the bond contain the minimum requirements of the code and no more, it is termed a statutory bond. On the other hand, when the bond, according to its terms, extends greater privilege to the claimant than required by statute it is referred to as a common law bond. The surety is required by statute to afford certain protection under certain statutory rules; but if the surety elects by the terms of its bond to extend that protection under less stringent rules, it may do so and is bound by the terms of its bond. *Wal-Board Supply Co., Inc. v. Daniels*, 629 S.W.2d 686, 688 (Tenn. Ct. App. 1981).

Statutory bonds are construed in the light of the statute creating the obligation secured and the purposes for which the bond is required, as disclosed in the statute; the statute which provides for the giving of a bond becomes a part of the bond and imports into the bond any conditions prescribed by the statute which are not in fact included in the bond as written. A court can assume that, when a bond was executed to comply with a statute, absent anything indicating otherwise, the parties intended to comply with the statute and nothing more. *State ex rel. Pope v. U.S. Fire Ins. Co.*, 145 S.W.3d 529 (Tenn. 2004).

In relation to equipment used on a job site, rental payments for equipment used by a contractor in the execution of a state highway contract are recoverable against its surety. Payments which consummate in the actual sale of the equipment to the contractor are not so recoverable. *U.S. Fidelity & Guaranty Co. v. Thompson & Green Machinery Co., Inc.*, 568 S.W.2d 821, 824 (Tenn. 1978).

## 2. Damages Covered

***Set forth in any statutes and/or case law***

T.C.A. § 12-4-707 states that a contractor on a public project who has not paid any subcontractor or supplier within 30 days after the contractor is paid by an agency, shall pay interest at the rate of one and one-half percent per month, unless otherwise provided by contract between the agency and the business, or by contract between the business and the subcontractor or supplier.

T.C.A. § 25-1-102 states that in actions brought on bonds or agreements for the payment of money, or with collateral conditions, and recovery had by the plaintiff, the judgment shall be entered for the stipulated penalty, to be discharged by the payment of the principal and interest due thereon, or the damages assessed by the jury, and execution shall issue accordingly.

T.C.A. § 66-34-302. When a subcontractor, materialman or furnisher has performed in accordance with the provisions of such person's written contract with a contractor, the contractor shall pay to the subcontractor, materialman or furnisher within the time provided in such contract the full amount received by the contractor for such subcontractor's, materialman's, or furnisher's work and materials for which subcontractor, materialman or furnisher has made timely application for payment and such subcontractor's, materialman's or furnisher's pro rata share of any interest provided for in Section 66-34-601 which was actually received by the contractor.

T.C.A. § 66-34-601 provides that any payment not made in accordance with the above section shall accrue interest, from the date due until the date paid at the rate of interest for delinquent payments provided in written contract.

T.C.A. § 66-34-602 allows the prevailing party, in a suit filed under the Prompt Pay Act, to recover reasonable attorneys fees against the non-prevailing party, provided that the non-prevailing party has acted in bad faith.

Where a trial court held a case under advisement for 19 months after trial date until the entry of judgment, the award of prejudgment interest for that period was within the discretion of the court. The award will not disturb such a decision "unless the record reveals a manifest and palpable abuse of discretion." Prejudgment interest is awarded to compensate the party that has been wronged for the loss of the use of the money it should have received earlier and not as punishment to the wrongdoer. There are, however, circumstances which may make the award of prejudgment interest inappropriate, including situations where the party seeking prejudgment interest has been inexcusably dilatory in pursuing a claim or has unreasonably delayed the proceedings after suit was filed or has already been otherwise compensated for the lost time value of its money.

*General Const. Contractors Ass'n, Inc. v. Greater St. Thomas Baptist Church*, 107 S.W.3d 513, 525-526 (Tenn. Ct. App. 2002).

***Obligations of surety to perform and/or pay***

The typical performance bond gives the surety the choice of refusing to perform the contract after the contractor defaults. In that case the surety is liable to the owner for the damages caused by the contractor's default but only up to the penal sum of the bond. On the other hand, the penal sum does not limit the liability of a surety that takes over performance of the contract. The surety who takes over performance has a duty to complete the contract without regard to cost. Furthermore, the penal sum does not limit its liability for damages caused by its own default while performing the contract. *In re Technology for Energy, Corp.*, 123 B.R. 979, 982 -983 (Bankr. E.D. Tenn. 1991).

***Whether failure to provide insurance transfers burden to surety*** – Tennessee statutes do not transfer the burden to the surety.

***Limitations on damages***

T.C.A. § 47-12-101 states that "[w]hen any surety...for the payment of money...other than the surety of a guardian, executor, administrator, or public officer, or guarantor of negotiable paper, apprehends that the principal is likely to become insolvent, or to migrate from the state, without previously discharging the debt or obligation, the surety may, if the debt or security be due, by notice in writing, require the creditor forthwith to put it to suit. Unless, within 30 days thereafter, the creditor commences an action, and proceeds with due diligence in the ordinary course of law to recover judgment for the debt or obligation, and by execution to make the amount due thereon, the creditor shall forfeit the right which the creditor would otherwise have to recover it from the surety."

T.C.A. § 47-12-102 states that the surety shall prove by 2 witnesses the service on the creditor of a copy of the notice required by T.C.A. § 47-12-101.

Generally, a surety's liability is the same as that of principal and cannot be greater than that of principal, either as to the amount or the burdensome character or conditions; however, obligations of principal and surety do not have to be equal. *In re Microwave Products of America, Inc.*, 118 B.R. 566 (Bankr. W.D. Tenn. 1990).

In upholding damage for delay clauses, the Tennessee Court of Appeals found the county not liable for losses suffered by road-building contractor due to unexpected amount of subsurface rock encountered. County did not warrant accuracy of estimates by providing estimates to bidders nor engage in negligent misrepresentation as to the estimates. Parties to a contract are free to allocate risks and burdens as they seem fit. Contract clearly placed risk of delay upon contractor, contractor failed to show that actual losses were greater than those contemplated, and contractor did not allege that county actively interfered with its operations. *Brown Bros., Inc. v. Metropolitan Government of Nashville and Davidson County,* 877 S.W.2d 745 (Tenn. Ct. App. 1993).

In deciding liability of surety, requirements of statute which require bond, and not terms of bond, are controlling, and any provisions of bond which purport to diminish surety's statutory liability are mere surplusage. *Exchange Mut. Ins. Co. v. Olsen*, 655 S.W.2d 938 (Tenn. 1983).

Interest is recoverable on a bond with collateral conditions only after judgment. *People's Bank & Trust Co. v. U.S. Fidelity & Guar. Co.*, 3 S.W.2d 163 (Tenn. 1928).

***Whether obligee may set off bonded contract funds against other principal-obligee debts or obligations***

T.C.A. § 20-6-401 states a comaker or surety, when sued alone, may, with the consent of the comaker's or surety's comaker or principal, use, by way of setoff, any of the debts or demands, held by such comaker or principal against the plaintiff at the commencement of the action, and matured when offered in setoff, but the plaintiff may meet it in the same way as if made by the comaker or principal who originally held the debts or demands.

A provision in a contract requiring the owner to retain a percentage of all payments made during the completion of the contract is not only for the protection of the owner, but is also for the benefit of the surety on the bond. *Central Towers Apartments, Inc. v. Martin*, 453 S.W.2d 789 (Tenn. Ct. App. 1969).

### *Incorporation of specific contract terms by reference*

Other writings, or matters contained therein, which are referred to in a written contract may be regarded as incorporated by reference as a part of the contract and may be considered in the construction of the contract. Where a written contract refers to another instrument and makes the terms and conditions of such other instrument a part of it, the two will be construed together. It is generally held that a contract and a bond given to secure its performance must, where construction of the contract is called for, be construed together. Such a bond is sometimes regarded as a part of the contract. Uncertainty in the contract may be clarified or explained by resorting to the bond. *McCall v. Towne Square, Inc.*, 503 S.W.2d 180, 183 (Tenn. 1973) (citing 17 AM. JUR. 2D, *Contracts*, §§ 263-65).

The true rule is that in the case of subcontracts, a reference by the contracting parties to an extraneous writing for a particular purpose makes it a part of their agreement only for the purpose specified. *Guerini Stone Co. v. P.J. Carlin Constr. Co.*, 240 U.S. 264, 277-278 (1916).

An arbitration provision, which was incorporated by reference in the general conditions of a contract entered into by a contractor and a corporation was part of the binding written contract. Although there was not specific reference to the arbitration clause, the managing partner of the corporation had used the standard form on previous projects, the reference was not hidden, and the contract noted it incorporated general conditions of another contract clearly provided near the top of the contract. *T.R. Mills Contractors, Inc. v. WRH Enterprises, LLC*, 93 S.W.3d (Tenn. Ct. App. 2002).

## 3. Penal Sum Variations

***Limitations per statute*** – Tennessee does not have any statutory limitations on penal sums.

### *Effect of changes in work upon penal sum, if any*

Sureties on a bond of a contractor are released by his being required, without their knowledge, to do a higher and more costly class of work than contracted for. *Southern Bridge Co. v. Bogenshot*, 48 S.W. 97 (Tenn. Ct. App. 1898).

Performance surety may be discharged where extensive changes exhaust building fund if changes are not funded from some other source. *Wagner v. Frazier,* 712 S.W.2d 109 (Tenn. Ct. App. 1986).

A cardinal change in the contract without the surety's consent releases the surety from the bond. *In re Technology for Energy Corp.*, 140 B.R. 214, 227 (Bankr. E.D. Tenn. 1992).

***Statutory or case law protections or dangers to penal sum***

The typical performance bond gives the surety the choice of refusing to perform the contract after the contractor defaults. In that case the surety is liable to the owner for the damages caused by the contractor's default but only up to the penal sum of the bond. On the other hand, the penal sum does not limit the liability of a surety that takes over performance of the contract. The surety who takes over performance has a duty to complete the contract without regard to cost. Furthermore, the penal sum does not limit its liability for damages caused by its own default while performing the contract. *In re Technology for Energy, Corp.*, 123 B.R. 979, 982-983 (Bankr. E.D. Tenn. 1991).

## 4. Parties Covered

***Statutes and/or case law as to whether only obligees are covered***

"The bond in suit contains a provision for amendments of the contract and for the continued liability of the surety after the amendments and after extensions of time of performance by the owner. We held in *Cass v. Smith*, 240 S.W. 781 (Tenn. 1922), that the obligation[s] of the surety to laborers and materialmen were not affected by alterations or amendments of the contract agreed upon between the contractor and the owner. 'They were not parties to the alleged change, and it is well settled that the surety on a bond like this will not be relieved of the obligation to laborers and materialmen who did not participate in such an alteration agreement between the owner and the contractor.'" *City of Knoxville v. Melvin F. Burgess, Inc.*, 175 S.W.2d 548, 551 (Tenn. 1943).

***Coverage for:***

**Third-party beneficiaries** – Prime contractor was not third-party beneficiary of coprime contractor's bonding company's performance or labor and material payment bonds issued to project's owner in that language of bonds specifically limited intended beneficiary to owner. *Moore Const. Co., Inc. v. Clarksville Dept. of Electricity*, 707 S.W.2d 1 (Tenn. Ct. App. 1985).

The dual nature of public contractors' statutory bonds conditioned both for the faithful performance of the contract and for the payment of laborers and materialmen. The rights of laborers and materialmen are independent of the rights of the obligee in the bond, and are the same as though the two undertakings were embraced in separate instruments. In accordance with these principles, it is held that the right of laborers and materialmen to recover against the surety on such a bond cannot be defeated by any act or omission of the obligee named in the instrument, not authorized or participated in by the laborers or materialmen. *City of Knoxville v. Melvin F. Burgess, Inc.*, 175 S.W.2d 548, 551 (Tenn. 1943).

The beneficiary, though not a party to the contract, may maintain an action, directly in his own name against the promisor, where such promise between the promisor and promisee is made upon sufficient consideration for the benefit of the third party. *Title Guar. & Trust Co. v. Bushnell*, 228 S.W. 699 (Tenn. 1921).

Performance bond which operated to require the contractor and its surety to indemnify the state, the Department of Transportation and all of its officers, agents and employees did not place an obligation on the surety to anyone other than the state and, hence, did not create a third-party beneficiary contract for the benefit of owners of a convenience store with respect to their nuisance claim. *Anthony v. Construction Products, Inc.*, 677 S.W.2d 4 (Tenn. Ct. App. 1984).

**Assignees** – There are no Tennessee cases discussing assignment of obligee's right to make a claim against a performance bond.

**Dual obligees** – Where a bond runs to several obligees, only one of whom is injured by a breach thereof, he may sue on the bond in his own name, or in the name of all the obligees to his use. *Renkert v. Elliott*, 79 Tenn. 235 (Tenn. 1883).

## 5. Notice or Filing Required

***Statutory provisions***

T.C.A. § 12-4-205 states that a furnisher of labor or material, or such laborer, shall, after such labor or material is furnished, or such labor is done, within 90 days after the completion of such public work, give written notice by return receipt certified mail, or by personal delivery, either to the contractor who executed the bond, or to the public official who had charge of the awarding of the contract, setting forth the nature, an itemized account of the material furnished or labor done, and the balance due therefor; and a description of the property improved.

***Case law rules concerning condition precedent notice***

Where a person was a surety on a note and the maker of the note paid it by checks and it was turned over to him, but one of the checks went to protests and was never paid, held that the surety could not be held for the payment of this sum unless he has given notice within a reasonable time. *First Nat. Bank of Huntsville, Tenn. v. Ashley*, 10 Tenn. App. 44 (Tenn. Ct. App. 1929).

## 6. Time for Suit

***Statutes of limitation particular to performance bonds and other applicable statutes of limitation***

T.C.A. § 28-3-109 states that actions on contracts not otherwise provided for shall be commenced within six years after the cause of action accrued. Also, the cause of action on demand notes shall be commenced within 10 years after the cause of action accrued.

T.C.A. § 12-4-206. Several persons entitled may join in one suit on such bond, or one of them may file a bill in equity in behalf of all such, who may, upon execution of a bond for costs, by petition assert their rights in the proceeding; provided, that action shall be brought or claims so filed within six months following the completion of such public work, or of the furnishing of such labor or materials.

***Case law statements about enforceability of limitations contained in bonds***

Where the period within which to bring suit is plainly expressed in a surety bond, an action must be brought within the time set, unless the provision is waived and time extended by agreement of the parties. *J.R. Hale & Sons v. R.C. Stone Engineering Co.*, 14 Tenn. App. 461 (Tenn. Ct. App. 1932).

Three-year statute of limitations governing property tort actions did not apply to action brought by state board of regents to recover for defective roof on university building, in absence of express provision making such statute applicable to action by the state, since state, in entering into contract for construction of university building, was acting in its sovereign capacity. *Dunn v. W. F. Jameson & Sons, Inc.*, 569 S.W.2d 799 (Tenn. 1978).

***Varying statutes of limitation by agreement in bond or contract***

Where a highway contractor's performance bond specifically referred to and incorporated a six-month limitations statute, a suit against the surety for rental charges, which was not brought within six months from date of completion of the highway project was barred by limitations, as against contention that complainant had six years in which to sue. *Thompson & Green Machinery Co. v. Travelers Indem. Co.*, 421 S.W.2d 643 (Tenn. Ct. App. 1967).

**7. Procedure**

***Statutory or procedural rules that may affect handling or administration of lawsuits*** – Not applicable.

***Venue requirements and jurisdictional limitations***

T.C.A. § 56-15-112 states that "[a]ny surety company ... may be sued ... in any court which has ... jurisdiction of actions or suits upon such ... bond ... in the county in which such ... bond was made or guaranteed, or in the county in which the principal office of such company is located; and such ... bond shall be treated as made or guaranteed in the county in which the office is located, to which it is returnable or in which it is filed;

or in the county in which the principal in such ... bond resided when it was made or guaranteed."

***Court rules***

Generally, see the Tennessee Rules of Civil Procedure. Additionally, each Tennessee Judicial District has its own local rules regarding the procedure for that district. Look to the individual district to determine any local procedural rules that may apply.

***Particular agency regulations/rules*** – Not applicable.

***Arbitration requirements and application***

In general, see the Uniform Arbitration Act, T.C.A. §§ 29-5-301 through 320.

Surety on performance bond was bound by arbitration clause where performance bond incorporated by reference the terms of subcontract, the subcontract incorporated by reference the general contract and the general contract imposed obligation to submit all unresolved disputes to arbitration, and same was true though it was surety, which did not sign general contract, that sought to avoid arbitration. *Exchange Mutual Ins. Co. v. Haskell Company,* 742 F.2d 274 (6th Cir. 1984).

Construing the scope of a valid agreement to arbitrate in the context of § 2 of the Federal Arbitration Act, the Tennessee Supreme Court noted that while the purpose of the FAA is to insure enforceability of such agreements, parties nonetheless "cannot be forced to arbitrate claims that they did not agree to arbitrate." *Frizzell Constr. Co. v. Gatlinburg, L.L.C.*, 9 S.W.3d 79, 84 (Tenn. 1999).

An arbitration agreement must be in writing to be binding and enforceable. *Merrimack Mut. Fire Ins. Co. v. Batts*, 59 S.W.3d 142 (Tenn. Ct. App. 2001).

A court may not vacate an arbitration award simply because it disagrees with the result. Instead, a court may only vacate or modify an award based upon the specific grounds set forth in T.C.A. §§ 29-5-313, 314. The purpose of arbitration is to avoid the formalities and delay of the courts and to act as an expeditious and final alternative to litigation. *Arnold v. Morgan Keegan Co., Inc.*, 914 S.W.2d 445 (Tenn. 1996).

An agreement to arbitrate does not affect rights and duties of parties; it simply shifts the form of dispute settlement. Parties may structure and limit arbitration agreements as they see fit. *T.R. Mills Contractors, Inc. v. WRH Enterprises, LLC*, 93 S.W.3d (Tenn. Ct. App. 2002).

## 8. Attorney's Fees

***Statutes and/or case law limiting or permitting recovery of attorney's fees***

T.C.A. § 56-7-105 states that anyone conducting insurance or fidelity bonding in this state, in all cases when a loss occurs and they refuse to pay the loss within 60 days after a demand has been made, shall be liable to pay, in addition to the loss and interest thereon, a sum not exceeding 25 percent on the liability for the loss; provided, that the refusal to pay the loss was not in good faith, and that such failure to pay inflicted additional expense, loss, or injury including attorney fees upon the holder of the policy or fidelity bond; and provided further, that such additional liability, within the limit prescribed, shall, in the discretion of the court or jury trying the case, be measured by the additional expense, loss, and injury including attorney fees thus entailed.

When principal and its indemnified surety are sued by obligee under surety's bond, and surety exercises its right under indemnity agreement of principal to hire separate counsel and incur litigation expenses in defense of action, liability of principal for attorney's fees and expenses incurred by surety depends on whether, under all facts, it was reasonably necessary for surety to so act in its own defense, and whether surety acted in good faith toward principal. *Central Towers Apartments, Inc. v. Martin*, 453 S.W.2d 789 (Tenn. Ct. App. 1969).

Tennessee statute barred insureds from recovering from insurers consequential damages for lost profits, loss of lease, and reimbursement of fine in addition to property loss, interest, and 25 percent statutory penalty for refusal to pay insurance claim for fire damages to heavy equipment. *Rice v. Van Wagoner Companies, Inc.*, 738 F. Supp. 252 (M.D. Tenn. 1990).

Before an insured can recover a penalty for an insurer's bad faith in handling a claim: (1) the policy of insurance must, by its terms, have become due and payable; (2) a formal demand for payment must have been made; (3) the insured must have waited 60 days after making his demand before filing suit, unless there was a refusal to pay prior to the expiration of the 60 days; and (4) the refusal to pay must not have been in good faith. *Marlin Financial & Leasing Corp. v. Nationwide Mut. Ins. Co.*, 157 S.W.3d 796 (Tenn. Ct. App. 2004).

***What fees are recoverable, if any***

In the event of a loss which is covered by a policy of insurance and the refusal of the insurer to pay the same within 60 days after a demand has been made by the holder of the policy and a finding has been made that such refusal was in bad faith, the insurer shall be liable to pay such holder, in addition to the loss, not more than 25 percent of the liability of the insurer for the loss and all reasonable attorney's fees for the prosecution of the case against the insurer. *Chandler v. Prudential Ins. Co.*, 715 S.W.2d 615, 620 (Tenn. Ct. App. 1986).

**9. Special Provisions** – Not applicable.

**10. Remarks** – Not applicable.

**11. Case Annotations**

The language of contracts of fidelity insurance is to be construed under the rules of the law of insurance, and, when ambiguous or doubtful, is to be given the strongest interpretation in favor of the person indemnified. *Green v. United States Fidelity & Guaranty Co.*, 185 S.W. 726 (Tenn. 1916).

Where a "word" is omitted in the condition of a bond, without which, the condition is insensible, if it appear from other parts of the bond, what the meaning of the parties was, the court will supply or add the word to the condition. *Kincannon v. Carroll*, 17 Tenn. 11 (Tenn. 1836).

***Interpretation of AIA bond forms*** – Tennessee cases have not specifically addressed AIA forms of bonds A311 or A312.

***Cases in which surety steps into shoes of obligee***

The doctrine of subrogation is an equitable one and it is recognized that payment of an obligation by a surety entitles him to stand in the place of the creditor and be substituted to all of the rights of the creditor against the principal. *Hickory Springs Mfg. Co., Inc. v. Evans*, 541 S.W.2d 97 (Tenn. 1976).

# TEXAS

Laird E. Lawrence and Stacy Blakeley[1]

## 1. Requirements for Bond

***Statutory provisions for projects that are:***

**Public** – Tex. Gov't Code § 2253.021 – requires that a governmental entity that makes a public work contract with a prime contractor require the contractor, before beginning work, to execute a performance bond if the contract is in excess of $100,000.

Tex. Ins. Code Article 7.19 – requires that a government code bond may be executed only by a surety company that is authorized and admitted to write surety bonds in this state. If the amount of the bond exceeds $100,000, the surety must also:

> (1) hold a certificate of authority from the U.S. Secretary of the Treasury to qualify as a surety on obligations permitted under federal law; or
> (2) have obtained reinsurance for any liability in excess of $100,000 from a reinsurer that is authorized to do business in Texas and is the holder of the certificate of authority from the U.S. Secretary of the Treasury to qualify as a surety or reinsurer on obligations permitted under federal law.

---

1 Laird E. Lawrence is a founding partner and Stacy Blakeley is of counsel at:
Kleiman Lawrence Baskind Fitzgerald LLP
8750 N. Central Expressway, Suite 777
Dallas, Texas 75231
(214) 265-7400

Tex. Water Code § 49.275 – The Water Code requires that any person, firm, partnership, or corporation to whom a contract is let must give good and sufficient performance and payment bonds in accordance with Chapter 2253 of the Government Code.

**Private** – A performance bond on a private project will be a common law bond because bonds are not required on private projects. However, an agreement of suretyship is required to be in writing. Tex. Bus. & Com. Code § 26.01.

**Department of Transportation** – "Governmental entity" as defined in Tex. Gov't Code § 2253.001 includes a department, board, or agency of the state, so highway projects must be bonded. Also, Tex. Transp. Code § 223.006 specifically requires a bond from a successful bidder.

***Case law rules that might generally apply***

Statutory provisions governing recovery on performance bond are mandatory as well as exclusive and provide only procedure and remedy for presenting claim against a statutory bond. *City of San Antonio v. Argonaut Ins. Co.,* 644 S.W.2d 90 (Tex. App.-San Antonio 1982, writ ref'd n.r.e.).

## 2. Damages Covered

***Set forth in any statutes and/or case law***

When a surety fails to meet its obligations under a performance bond, the measure of damages is generally the amount it would cost over and above the contract price to complete the project or repair the defects. *New Amsterdam Casualty Co. v. Bettes,* 407 S.W.2d 307 (Tex. Civ. App.–Dallas 1966, writ ref'd n.r.e.).

A performance bond is enforceable only to the extent of the obligee's actual damages. However, when an obligee's actual damages exceed the penal sum of the bond, a surety's liability generally is limited to the penal sum of the bond. *Great American Ins. Co. v. North Austin Municipal Utility Dist. 1,* 908 S.W.2d 415 (Tex. 1995). See *Bill Curphy Co. v. Elliot*, 207 F.2d 103, 108-09 (5th Cir. 1953) (surety not liable for actual damages necessary to complete construction project in excess of face amount of bond because to hold otherwise would make it "futile to state any amount of liability in the bond" and overlook the "well-established rule in Texas and elsewhere that the sole object of stating the penalty in a bond is to fix the limit of liability of the signers.")

Liquidated damages can be recovered against a surety. *Victore Ins. Co. v. City of Bowie,* 23 S.W.3d 499 (Tex. App.-Ft. Worth 2000, no writ); *Fidelity and Deposit Co. v. Stool,* 607 S.W.2d 17, 26 (Tex. Civ. App.-Tyler 1980, no writ). Unless otherwise provided by contract, liquidated damages cease accruing after substantial completion. *Page v. Travis-Williamson County Water & App. District No. 1*, 367 S.W.2d 307 (Tex. 1963).

***Limitations on damages***

Sureties generally are not liable for the deceptive acts of their principals. *Qantel Business Systems, Inc. v. Custom Controls,* 761 S.W.2d 302 (Tex. 1998); *Home Savings Assoc. v. Guerra,* 733 S.W.2d 134, 136 (Tex. 1987) (holding that derivative liability will not be subscribed to a defendant based solely on its participation in an innocent transaction).

Sureties generally are not liable for damages caused by the negligence of the principal unless the bond reflects the intention to assume such damages. *Page v. Schlortt*, 89 S.W.2d 249 (Tex. Civ. App.–Austin 1935); *F & G v. Eubanks*, 126 T.405, 87 S.W.2d 248 (1935).

***Whether obligee may set off bonded contract funds against other principal-obligee debts or obligations***

Tex. Prop. Code § 53.151(b) provides that a surety issuing a payment or performance bond in connection with improvements has a priority claim over other creditors of its principal to contract funds to the extent of any loss it suffers or incurs.

Tex. Gov't Code § 2253.071 provides that the contract balances of a public work contract remaining after cost of completion are paid shall be paid according to the principal's and the surety's interest as may be established by agreement or by judgment of a court. The surety that completes a public work contract or incurs a loss under the government code performance bond has a claim to the proceeds of the contract prior to all other creditors of the principal to the full extent of the surety's loss.

***Incorporation of specific contract terms by reference***

The performance bond required on a public work must be conditioned upon the "faithful performance of the work in accordance with the plans, specifications, and contract documents." Tex. Gov't Code § 2253.021. The bond form typically mandated by public owners specifically incorporates the terms of the contract into the bond, which appears consistent with the language of the government code.

### 3. Penal Sum Variations

The penal limit of the performance bond on a public work must be the amount of the contract. Tex. Gov't Code § 2253.021(b). The penal amount for a common law performance bond is negotiable.

### 4. Parties Covered

***Statutes and/or case law as to whether only obligees are covered***

Tex. Gov't Code § 2253.021(e) – A bond executed for a public work contract with the state or a department, board, or agency of the state must be payable to the state in a form approved by the attorney general. A bond executed for a public work contract with another governmental entity must be payable to and in a form approved by the awarding governmental entity.

***Coverage for:***

**Third-party beneficiaries** – A performance bond is for the benefit of the obligee so subcontractors/suppliers generally do not have the right to make a claim on a performance bond. *Laughlin Environmental, Inc. v. Premier Towers, L.P.*, 126 S.W.3d 668, 671 (Tex. App.-Houston [14th Dist.] 2004, no pet.) (dicta only).

**Assignees** – Absent a prohibition against assignment or limiting language, an obligee may assign its rights under a surety bond if the assignment does not otherwise prejudice the surety's rights. *Travelers Idem. Co. v. Dahlen,* 734 S.W.2d 729 at 732 (Tex. App.-Dallas 1987, writ ref'd n.r.e.); *Augusta Court Co. Owners Assoc. v. Levin, Roth & Kasner, P.C.*, 971 S.W.2d 119 (Tex. App.-Houston [14th Dist. 1998, pet. denied).

**Dual obligees** – The effect of the dual obligee bonds is that the owner agrees that the interest of the lender shall be the amount of the construction money which it shall have advanced and that claims of the lender on the bond shall be prior and superior to that of the owner. The liability of the surety under the bond is in no sense increased because lender is also an obligee. The interest of the lender is only by way of priority to any damages for which the surety would be liable if it were not an obligee. *New Amsterdam Casualty Co. v. Bettes,* 407 S.W.2d 307, 311 (Tex. Civ. App.–Dallas 1966, writ ref'd n.r.e.).

## 5. Notice or Filing Required

***Statutory provisions***

No Texas statute requires a particular type of notice for the assertion of a claim on a government code performance bond. Courts generally look at the facts and circumstances surrounding a claim to determine if reasonable notice was given and whether there was a reasonable opportunity given to the surety to respond. However, since the contract is typically incorporated into the bond, the contract should be reviewed. With common law bonds, the terms of the bond (and incorporated contract) will control.

Tex. Civ. Prac. & Rem. Code § 16.071 provides that a contract stipulation requiring a claimant to give notice of claim for damages as a condition precedent to the right to sue on a contract is not valid unless the stipulation is reasonable. A stipulation that requires notification within less than 90 days is void. This prohibition applies to a contract between a federal prime contractor and a subcontractor, except that the notice period stipulated in the subcontract may be for a period not less than the period stipulated in the prime contract, minus seven days.

***Case law rules concerning condition precedent notice*** – Not applicable.

## 6. Time for Suit

***Statutes of limitation particular to performance bonds and other applicable statutes of limitation***

Tex. Gov't Code § 2253.078 provides that a suit on a public works performance bond may not be brought after the first anniversary of the date of final completion, abandonment, or termination of the public work contract.

Several cases suggest that if "final" completion is the trigger date for limitations, limitations actually begin to run at "substantial" completion because substantial completion is the equivalent of full performance in Texas. *Commercial Union Insurance Company v. LaVilla ISD*, 779 S.W.2d 102, 105 (Tex. App.-Corpus Christi 1989, no writ); *TransAmerica Ins. Co. v. Housing Authority of City of Victoria*, 669 S.W.2d 818, 823 (Tex. App.-Corpus Christi 1984, writ ref'd n.r.e.).

Tex. Civ. Prac. & Rem. Code § 16.051 provides that any action for which there is no express provision on limitations, except for actions involving real property, shall be brought no later than four years after the cause of action accrues.

***Varying statutes of limitation by agreement in bond or contract***

Pursuant to Tex. Gov't Code § 2253.023, the statutory limitations period may not be varied. Section 2253.023 provides that:

> (a) a bond furnished by a prime contractor in an attempt to comply with this chapter shall be construed to comply with this chapter regarding the rights created, limitations on those rights, and remedies provided; and (b) a provision in a bond furnished by a prime contractor in an attempt to comply with this chapter that expands or restricts a right or liability under this chapter shall be disregarded, and this chapter shall apply to that bond.

With respect to a performance bond on a private work, Tex. Civ. Prac. & Rem. Code § 16.070 is relevant. That section provides that a person may not contract for a limit to the time in which to bring suit on a contract to a period shorter than two years. See also *U. S. Fidelity & Guaranty Co. v. Eastern Hills Methodist Church*, 609 S.W.2d 298, 300 (Tex. Civ. App.–Ft. Worth 1980, writ ref'd n.r.e.).

Tex. Civ. Prac. & Rem. Code § 16.061 states that certain provisions listed above (§§ 16.070 and 16.051, among others) are not applicable to the state, any political subdivision of the state, including county, incorporated city or town, a navigation district, a municipal utility district, a port authority, entity acting under Section 52, Article III or Section 59, Article XVI, Texas Constitution.

Prior to the enactment of Government Code § 2253.023 referred to above, a Texas appellate court held that the statutory one-year limitations period could not be changed by the terms of the bond. *TransAmerica Ins. Co. v. Housing Authority of the City of Victoria,* 669 S.W.2d 818 (Tex. App.-Corpus Christi 1984, writ ref'd n.r.e.). In another case, it held that the representations by the contractor did not extend the limitations period for a claim against the surety unless the surety also took affirmative action to toll the statute of limitations. *Commercial Union Ins. Co. v. LaVilla Indep. School District,* 779 S.W.2d 102 (Tex. App.-Corpus Christi 1989, no writ).

## 7. Procedure

***Statutory or procedural rules that may affect handling or administration of lawsuits***

In district and county courts, an answer to a lawsuit is due by 10:00 a.m. on the first Monday following 20 days from the date of service upon the defendant. Tex. R. Civ. P. 99(b). If the 20th day is on a Monday, the answer is due on the following Monday. *Proctor v. Green*, 673 S.W.2d 390, 392 (Tex. App.-Houston [1st Dist.] 1984, no writ). Service on the secretary of state is considered constructive service of the defendant, so the time limit for answering begins running when the secretary of state is served. *Bonewitz v. Bonewitz*, 726 S.W.2d 227, 230 (Tex. App.-Austin 1987, writ ref'd n.r.e.).

Pursuant to Tex. R. Civ. P. 120(a), by filing a special appearance, a defendant may challenge personal jurisdiction without submitting to that jurisdiction. However, the special appearance must be filed within the same time as the answer and must be the first pleading filed.

### *Venue requirements and jurisdictional limitations*

Venue for a suit on a government code performance bond is a county in which any part of the public work is located. Tex. Gov't Code § 2253.077.

Tex. Ins. Code Art. 7.01 provides that suit on a bond should be in the county where the bond is "filed."

Since performance bonds on private works are not required by statute, the venue provisions of Tex. Civ. Prac. & Rem. Code §§ 15.001, *et seq*. control. Under Tex. Civ. Prac. & Rem. Code §§ 15.020 and 15.035, parties to a contract may contractually agree to venue, subject to certain limitations. In an action to recover title or damages to, or remove encumbrances from, real property, venue is in the county where the property is located. If no mandatory or contractual provisions apply, the general venue rules will control. The general venue rule is that suit may be brought in the county (1) where all or a substantial part of the events or omissions giving rise to the claim occurred; (2) where the defendant resides at the time of accrual of a cause of action or, if not an actual person, where it has its principal place of business in Texas; or (3) if (1) and (2) do not apply, where the plaintiff resided at the time the cause of action accrued. Tex. Civ. Prac. & Rem. Code § 15.002.

An objection to improper venue through a motion to transfer venue must be filed prior to or concurrently with the answer or any other motion, except a special appearance, which must come first. Tex. Civ. Prac. & Rem. Code § 86; *Wichita City v. Hart*, 917 S.W.2d 779, 781 (Tex. 1996).

### *Court rules*

In addition to the Texas Rules of Civil Procedure, the courts in each county may have their own local rules of procedure. Local rules for the particular county in which the lawsuit is filed should be referred to early and often to ensure compliance.

Texas Rule of Civil Procedure 30 provides that a surety may be sued jointly with its principal or may be sued alone in cases provided for by statute. Texas Rule of Civil Procedure 31 provides that no surety shall be sued unless its principal is joined with it or unless a judgment has previously been rendered against the principal except where otherwise provided for by law.

Tex. Civ. Prac. & Rem. Code § 17.001 provides that a judgment may not be rendered against a surety unless judgment is also rendered against the principal. However, it further provides that a surety may be sued without suing the principal if the principal is (1) a nonresident or resides in a place where he cannot be reached by ordinary process of law; (2) resides in a place that is unknown or cannot be ascertained by the use of reasonable diligence; (3) dead; or (4) actually or notoriously insolvent. While Tex. Gov't Code § 2253.073 provides that a payment bond beneficiary may sue the principal or the surety, jointly and severally, it contains no such language regarding suit on a performance bond.

**Jury** – A request for a jury must be made in writing and filed with the clerk at least 30 days before trial. Tex. R. Civ. P. 216(a). Additionally, a jury fee must be paid. Under Tex. R. Civ. P. 216(a), the fee is $5 and must be paid at least 30 days before trial. However, Tex. Gov't Code § 51.604 states that the jury fee for district court is $30 and for county court is $22, and that those fees include the $5 Rule 216(a) fee. Additionally, § 51.604 provides that the fee must be paid no later than 10 days before trial. While it might be reasonable to expect that the 10-day statutory deadline would trump the 30-day procedural deadline, at least one Texas court has concluded otherwise. *Universal Printing Co. v. Premier Victorian Homes*, 73 S.W.3d 283, 289 (Tex. App.-Houston [1st Dist.] 2001, pet. denied.). Consequently, to be safe the jury fee should be paid at least 30 days before trial.

***Particular agency regulations/rules***

Tex. Gov't Code § 2260.001, *et seq*. establishes the exclusive procedure for pursuing contract claims where a legislative resolution granting permission to sue the state is needed. *See also* Tex. Civ. Prac. & Rem. Code § 107.001, *et seq*. However, the procedure established in § 2260.001, *et seq*. does not apply to the Texas Department of Transportation. Instead, the Texas Administrative Procedure Act, Tex. Gov't Code § 2001.001, *et seq*., as well as the internal claim procedures of the Texas Department of Transportation apply to disputes involving those contracts.

***Arbitration requirements and application***

Texas has a general arbitration statute. Tex. Civ. Prac. & Rem. Code § 171.001, *et seq.* A written agreement to arbitrate is valid and enforceable if the agreement is to arbitrate a controversy that (1) exists at the time of the agreement; or (2) arises between the parties after the date of the agreement. Every reasonable presumption supporting arbitration will be allowed. *Southwest Health Plan, Inc. v. Sparkman,* 921 S.W.2d 355, 358 (Tex. App.-Fort Worth 1996, no writ). Any doubt concerning the scope of the arbitration agreement should be resolved in favor of arbitration. *Cantella & Co., Inc. v. Goodwin*, 924 S.W.2d 943 (Tex. 1996) (orig. proceeding).

In *Teal Construction Co. v. Darren Casey Interests, Inc.*, 46 S.W.3d 417 (Tex. App.-Austin 2001, pet. denied), a Texas court of appeals stated that an "unsigned paper may be incorporated by reference in the contract signed by the party sought to be charged," concluding that an unsigned arbitration agreement could be made enforceable through incorporation by reference in a signed contract. The case did not involve a surety, but since the sureties typically incorporate the principal's contract with the obligee into the performance bond, it is likely that the surety on a performance bond can be compelled to arbitrate if the incorporated contract contains an otherwise enforceable arbitration provision.

## 8. Attorney's Fees

***Statutes and/or case law limiting or permitting recovery of attorney's fees***

Tex. Gov't Code § 2253.074 provides that a court may award costs and reasonable attorney's fees that are equitable in a proceeding to enforce a claim on a statutory payment bond or to declare that any part of a claim is invalid but does not specifically provide for the recovery of attorney's fees on a suit on a performance bond. However, Tex. Civ. Prac. & Rem. Code § 38.001 permits recovery of reasonable attorney's fees in the prosecution of a valid contract claim. The Texas Supreme Court has concluded that since the obligee has a right to sue the surety on its bond, which bond is a contract, the obligee is entitled to recover attorney's fees under § 38.001 of the Tex. Civ. Prac. & Rem. Code. *Great American Ins. Co. v. North Austin Municipal Utility District*, 908

S.W.2d 415, 427 (Tex. 1995). The court further found that the surety was liable for the fees incurred by the obligee in the prosecution of its bond claim, even if award of the fees against the surety resulted in the total award exceeding the penal limit of the bond. The surety was not liable, however, for attorney's fees assessed against its principal in excess of the penal limit. *Great American*, 908 S.W.2d at 427.

In addition to recovery of attorney's fees based on Tex. Civ. Prac. & Rem. Code § 38.001, if a contract specifically provides for the recovery of attorney's fees, fees can be recoverable by the prevailing party.

Pursuant to Tex. Civ. Prac. & Rem. Code § 38.004, a court may take judicial notice of the usual and customary attorney's fees and of the contents of the case file without receiving further evidence in (1) a proceeding before the court; or (2) a jury case in which the amount of attorney's fees is submitted to the court by agreement. Section 38.004 only applies when the claim for fees is made pursuant to Tex. Civ. Prac. & Rem. Code § 38.001. *Hasty v. Inwood Buckhorn*, 908 S.W.2d 494, 503 (Tex. App.-Dallas 1995, writ denied).

When determining the reasonableness of attorney's fees, the fact finder should consider (1) the time and labor required, the novelty and difficulty of the questions involved, and the skill to perform the legal service properly; (2) the likelihood ... that the acceptance of the particular employment will preclude other employment by the lawyer; (3) the fee customarily charged in the locality for similar legal services; (4) the amount involved and the results obtained; (5) the time limitations imposed by the client by the circumstances; (6) the nature and length of the professional relationship with the client; (7) the experience, reputation, and ability of the lawyer or lawyers performing the services; and (8) whether the fee is fixed or contingent on results obtained or uncertainty of collection before the legal services have been rendered. *Arthur Andersen & Co. v. Perry Equipment Corp.,* 945 S.W.2d 812, 818 (Tex. 1997).

## 9. Special Provisions

Pursuant to Tex. Bus. & Com. Code § 34.02, when a cause of action has accrued on a contract for the payment of money or performance of an act, the surety on the contract may require by written notice that the obligee forthwith sue on the contract. A surety who gives notice under this section is discharged from liability if the obligee is not under legal disability and either (1) fails to sue on the contract during the first term of court after receiving the notice or during the second term showing good cause for a delay; or (2) fails to prosecute the suit to judgment and execution. *Great American Ins. Co. v. North Austin Municipal Utility Dist.*, 908 S.W.2d 415, 419 (Tex. 1995).

Tex. Bus. & Com. Code § 35.52 provides that if a contract is principally for the construction or repair of improvements to real property located in Texas and the contract contains the provision that makes the contract or any conflict arising under it subject to the law of another state or to litigation or arbitration in another state, that provision is voidable by the party obligated to perform the construction or repair.

Tex. Civ. Prac. & Rem. Code § 16.009 provides that a person must bring a suit for damages for injury, damage, or loss to real property against a person who constructs or repairs the improvements not later than 10 years after substantial completion of the improvement in an action arising out of defective or unsafe condition of the property or a deficiency in the construction or repair of the improvement. The period can be extended for up to two years depending on when the claim is made. This section does not bar an action on a written warranty or other guarantee that expressly provides for a longer effective period.

Texas has a trust fund statute that provides that construction payments are trust funds if made to a contractor, subcontractor, or officer, director, or agent of a contractor or subcontractor under a construction contract for the improvement of specific real property. Additionally, loan receipts are trust funds if borrowed by a contractor, subcontractor, or owner for the purpose of improving real property in the state and the loan is secured in whole or in part by a lien on the property. Tex. Prop. Code § 162.001. However, the trust fund statute does not apply to a corporate surety who issues a payment bond covering the contract for the construction or repair of the improvement or to a bank, savings and loan, or other lender. Tex. Prop. Code § 162.004.

Tex. Prop. Code § 53.151 provides that a creditor of an original contractor may not collect, enforce a security interest against, garnish, or levy execution on money due an original contractor or the contractor's surety from an owner. The same prohibition applies to the creditors of a subcontractor seeking collection from the general contractor.

## 10. Remarks

In Texas, a surety does not owe a common law duty of good faith and fair dealing to either the principal, the obligee, third party obligees on the payment bond, or its indemnitors. *See Assoc. Ind. v. CAT Contracting,* 964 S.W.2d 276 (Tex. 1998); *Great American Ins. Co. v. Austin Municipal Utility Dist.*, 908 S.W.2d 415 (Tex. 1995); *TACON Mechanical v. Aetna*, 65 F.3d 486 (5th Cir. 1995); *Fireman's Fund Ins. Co. v. Murchison*, 937 F.2d 204 (5th Cir. 1991).

For the last several years, Texas contractors (and their sureties) have struggled with the doctrine of sovereign immunity as pled by public entities as a defense to contract claims. Though Tex. Gov't Code § 2260.001, *et seq.*, has been amended to broaden the types of damages recoverable by a contractor against a unit of state government, that chapter of the government code still provides the exclusive means of recovery. In other words, a contractor (and presumably its subrogated surety) must still initiate the administrative procedures outlined in Chapter 2260, which ultimately require a legislative resolution to appropriate funds to pay a claim determined by an administrative law judge to be valid. However, effective September 1, 2005, Local Government Code Chapter 271 has been amended to waive immunity and permit the adjudication of a claim for breach of contract against a "local governmental entity, other than a county or a unit of state government," as that term is defined in government code Chapter 2260.001, including a (a) municipality; (b) public school or junior college district; and (c) special purpose district or authority. The damages recoverable are limited to the balance due and owed by the local government entity under the contract, including compensation for increased cost to perform incurred as a direct result of owner caused delay or acceleration; the amount owed for change orders or additional work the contractor is directed to perform by the local governmental entity; and interest as allowed by law. Neither other consequential damages, exemplary damages, or unabsorbed home office overhead damages are recoverable. Similarly, attorney's fees are not recoverable against the local governmental entity unless the contract expressly authorizes the prevailing party to recover those fees by referring specifically to the appropriate section of Chapter 271. It should be noted that Chapter 271 does not apply to units of state government.

The prompt payment provisions of the Texas Insurance Code do not apply to surety bond claims. Tex. Ins. Code § 542.053(4). (Tex. Ins. Code Art. 7.20 establishes a timetable for responding to payment bond claims but does not create a private cause of action for failure to abide by that timetable.) Similarly, the provisions regarding notice of settlement do not apply to surety bond claims. Tex. Ins. Code § 542.152(2).

## 11. Case Annotations

***Interpretation of AIA bond forms*** – Not applicable.

***Cases in which surety steps into shoes of obligee*** – Not applicable.

# UTAH

Brian J. Babcock[1]

## 1. Requirement for Bond

The State of Utah requires performance bonds on all public projects. However, Utah does not have a statute which requires performance bonds to be furnished on private projects.

***Statutory provisions for projects that are:***

**Public** – Utah Code Annotated § 14-1-18 provides for application of the Utah Procurement Code relating to performance bonds. The section states that the Utah Procurement Code which requires performance bonds applies to any "political subdivision" which it defines as "any county, city, town, school district, public transit district, special district, redevelopment agency, public corporation, institution of higher education of the state, public agency of any political subdivision, and, to the extent provided by law, any other entity which expends public funds for construction." U.C.A. § 14-1-18(1)(a).

The section states that the Utah Procurement Code "applies to all contracts for the construction, alteration, or repair of any public building

---

1 Brian J. Babcock is a shareholder of:
Babcock Scott & Babcock, PC
Washington Federal Plaza
505 East 200 South, Suite 300
Salt Lake City, Utah 84102
(801) 531-7000

or public work of the state or a political subdivision of the state." U.C.A. § 14-1-18(2).

The Utah Procurement Code under U.C.A. § 63-56-504 states:

> (1) When a construction contract is awarded under this chapter, the contractor to whom the contract is awarded shall deliver the following bonds or security to the state, which shall become binding on the parties upon the execution of the contract:
>
> (a) a performance bond satisfactory to the state that is in an amount equal to 100 percent of the price specified in the contract and is executed by a surety company authorized to do business in this state or any other form satisfactory to the state; ... U.C.A. § 63-56-504(1) and (1)(a).

A person applying for a public works project or public building improvement must post a performance and payment bond to be eligible to receive the contract as the lowest responsive bidder. Building improvement:

(a) means the construction or repair of a public building or structure; and

(b) does not include construction or repair at an international airport. U.C.A. 1953 § 11-39-101(2).

Public works project:

(a) means the construction of:

(i) a park or recreational facility; or

(ii) a pipeline, culvert, dam, canal, or other system for water, sewage, storm water, or flood control; and

(b) does not include:

(i) the replacement or repair of existing infrastructure on private property;

(ii) construction commenced before June 1, 2003; and

(iii) construction or repair at an international airport. U.C.A. 1953 § 11-39-101(12).

A lowest responsive bidder means a contractor who, among other things, furnishes a payment and performance bond as required by law. U.C.A. 1953 § 11-39-101(10).

**Private** – No statutes in Utah require performance bonds on private projects.

**Department of Transportation –**

***Utah Administrative Code – Transportation:***

R916-1-7(1) – At the time of execution of the contract, the successful bidder shall furnish a performance bond and a payment bond, each in a sum equal to the full amount of the contract. Each bond shall be on the form provided by the department and shall be executed by a surety company or companies licensed by the state of Utah. These companies must be listed on the current United States Department of the Treasury Circular 570 as acceptable sureties on Federal bonds.

R916-3 – Design-Build Contracts – Transportation

R916-3-8 – Acceptable Bid Security; Performance and Payment Bonds.

(1) The Executive Director shall have the right to waive the requirement to provide bid security, or may reduce the amount of such security, if he or she determines that the bid security otherwise required by U.C.A. Sections 63-56-37 through 39 to be unnecessary to protect the State.

(2) The Executive Director shall have the right to reduce the amount of the payment and performance bonds below the 100 percent level required by U.C.A. Sections 63-56-37 through 39, if he or she determines that a 100 percent bond is unnecessary to protect the State.

(3) Bid security, payment bonds and performance bonds must be provided on the forms included in the RFP.

***Case law rules that might generally apply***

A property owner required contractors on a project to obtain performance bonds. The owner hired a management company to oversee the construction of the project, but retained some management functions. A contractor on the project did not obtain a performance bond and when the contractor defaulted on the project, the owner tried to recover the incurred damages from the management company, whom the owner claimed was liable for the management's failure to assure that the contractor obtained a performance bond. The court held that the management company was not liable because the owner retained some management functions and with reasonable care could have discovered the contractor's failure to obtain a bond. *Great Salt Lake Minerals &*

*Chemical Corp. v. Arthur G. McKee & Co.*, 539 P.2d 371, 373 (Utah 1975).

Generally an unlicensed contractor cannot commence or maintain any action in any court of the state for collection of compensation for performing any act for which a license is required by this chapter without alleging and proving that he was properly licensed. However, the court may allow an unlicensed contractor to recover for quantum meruit where the party for whom work is performed has not relied on unlicensed contractor's representations that it was licensed and contractor has posted a performance bond. *A.K. & R. Whipple Plumbing and Heating v. Aspen Const.*, 977 P.2d 518, 523 (Utah 1999).

## 2. Damages Covered

***Set forth in any statutes and/or case law***

A creditor may limit the creditor's ability to recover damages from the surety for the principal's default if the creditor discharges the surety's obligations by dealing directly with the principal, thereby altering the principal's obligation. When a creditor releases a principal of the principal's obligations, the creditor also releases the surety from the surety's obligations. *Horman v. Gordon*, 740 P.2d 1346, 1354 (Utah App. 1987) (citing Restatement of Security § 122); *See also* U.C.A. § 15-4-5.

***Obligations of surety to perform and/or pay***

Although a performance bond agreement stated that the contractor alone, not the surety, remained liable for the contractor's potential default, the court held that the surety was also liable to subcontractors and materialmen, where the contractor fails "to perform undertakings or covenants of [the contractor's] agreement." *De Luxe Glass Co. v. Martin*, 208 P.2d 1127, 1131 (Utah 1949).

***Whether failure to provide insurance transfers burden to surety*** – Utah statutes and cases do not address a shift from the contractor to the surety when the contractor failed to provide insurance.

### *Limitations on damages*

A party suing on a performance bond is limited to recovery of those damages foreseen by the surety when the surety issued the bond. "The rule as to what damages are recoverable for breach of contract is based upon the concept of reasonable foreseeability that loss of such general character would result from the breach. Therefore, to be compensable, the loss must result from the breach in the natural and usual course of events, so that it can fairly and reasonably be said that if the minds of the parties had adverted to breach when the contract was made, loss of such character would have been within their contemplation.

In the Hartford case we held that the loss involved there was the kind of loss that Hartford's bond covered. In applying the rule to this case, however, we must come to the opposite conclusion. Could it reasonably have been foreseen that the natural and usual consequences of the failure to construct the improvements would bring about the foreclosure of the trust deeds and loss of title? Did the loss of plaintiffs' down payment result from the breach of the promise to construct improvements in the natural and usual course of events?" *Fleck v. National Property Management, Inc.*, 590 P.2d 1254, 1255 (Utah 1979).

### *Whether obligee may set off bonded contract funds against other principal-obligee debts or obligations*

Where a performance bond was provided on a project and the project was delayed, the court found that "it is a recognized principle of contract law that a breach of an insubstantial nature, which is severable and does not vitally change the transaction, does not release the other party completely from performing his obligations under the contract, but gives rise to a right for damages for any loss occasioned thereby." The contractor and its surety were allowed an offset on any loss incurred as a result of the delay. *Prudential Federal Sav. and Loan Ass'n v. Hartford Acc. & Indem. Co.*, 325 P.2d 899, 903 (Utah 1958).

### *Incorporation of specific contract terms by reference*

A surety issued performance bonds to a contractor and the contractor signed a supplemental indemnity agreement limiting the liability of the surety. While interpreting the meaning of the words in the agreements, the court stated that "[t]he general rule in Utah is that 'one contract will not merge into another unless it is plainly shown that that was the intent of the parties; and this is usually where the later contract fully covers an earlier one.'" *Horman v. Gordon*, 740 P.2d 1346, 1351 (Utah App. 1987)(quoting *Foote v. Taylor*, 635 P.2d 46, 48 (Utah 1981). The court ascertains the parties' intent by first looking within the four corners of the agreement. *James Constructors, Inc. v. Salt Lake City Corp.*, 888 P.2d 665, 674 (Utah App. 1994).

Courts utilize rules of contract construction to interpret provisions in a bond agreement, thereby promoting "predictability of bond coverage and [minimizing] the impact of luck or chance." *Home Sav. and Loan v. Aetna Cas. and Sur. Co.*, 817 P.2d 341, 351 (Utah App. 1991).

### 3. Penal Sum Variations

***Limitations per statute*** – Utah does not have statutory limitations on performance bond penal sums.

***Effect of changes in work upon penal sum, if at all***

"The real situation is that the waiver provision in the surety bond was to the effect that alterations in the terms or in work done under them or extension of time of performance or any other forbearance on the part of either the Owner or the Principal (Contractor) 'shall not in anyway release the Principal and the Surety or Sureties * * from their liability' under the bond. The provision was to avoid the severity of the common law rule which already has been relaxed by decisions in many states, including ours. The trend of modern decisions which this provision of the contract recognizes is that a departure from the terms of the contract, faithful performance of which the surety guaranteed, should not fully release the surety. The provision does not mean that if the surety is damaged or injured by the departure or alteration, it cannot defend pro tanto for the damage or prejudice suffered by such alteration. A provision that the surety shall not be released in any way from liability cannot be converted into a defense by the owner against a claim for damage which the alteration or change in the work done under the contract may have caused the surety over and above the liability it would have had to pay if the change had not been made. The waiver provision does not include a breach of the contract by the owner; but, as we view the matter, it is not necessary to determine whether the departure of plaintiff and Contractor from the terms of Article 3 of the contract is an alteration by conduct or a breach. We think that even if there was a breach by the Owner in regard to the matter of premature payments or failure to retain the percentages, the Surety would not be totally released, but could defend only to the extent that its liability had been increased by such breach." *Corporation of President of Church of Jesus Christ of Latter-Day Saints v. Hartford Accident & Indemnity Co.*, 95 P.2d 736, 740-41 (Utah 1939).

***Statutory or case law protections or dangers to penal sum*** – There are no cases that require a variation in the penal sum.

## 4. Parties Covered

***Statutes and/or case law as to whether only obligees are covered***

Where construction contract provided under "general conditions" that contractor had to provide and pay for materials, labor, equipment, and other facilities for completion of work, and surety bond provided that surety undertook that principal would perform all terms, conditions and agreements of contracts, and contractor failed to pay for materials purchased from materialman, surety would be liable to owner for amounts paid creditors. *De Luxe Glass Co. v. Martin*, 208 P.2d 1127, 1130-31 (Utah 1949).

***Coverage for:***

**Third-party beneficiaries** – Not applicable.

**Assignees** – The courts allow a surety to become an assignee where a surety furnishes a performance bond to a contractor and the contractor assigns the contractor's rights to pursue any claims or causes of action the contractor may have in connection with a project. *B & A Associates v. L.A. Young Sons Const. Co.*, 796 P.2d 692, 693-94 (Utah 1990).[18]

Assignors can only enforce those rights held by the assignor at the time of assignment. An obligee attempts to assign the obligee's rights against a performance bond. It was later discovered that the obligee did not have any rights against the performance bond because the contractor, who obtained the performance bond for the construction project, finished the project prior to the obligee's assignment. Therefore, the assignor did not have any rights to assign. *Aird Ins. Agency v. Zions First Nat. Bank*, 612 P.2d 341, 344 (Utah 1980).

**Dual obligees** – When there are joint obligees to a bond, both obligees shall be entitled to join in a suit against the bond. *Salt Lake County v. Golding*, 2 Utah 319 (Utah.Terr. 1877).

## 5. Notice or Filing Required

***Statutory provisions*** – There are no statutory provisions requiring an obligee to give notice to a surety of a performance bond.

***Case law rules concerning condition precedent notice***

Courts will enforce provisions in bond agreements that require the indemnitor to be provided adequate notice by the surety concerning the claims against the surety. *American Bonding Co. v. Nelson*, 763 P.2d 814, 816-17 (Utah App. 1988).

## 6. Time for Suit

***Statutes of limitation particular to performance bonds and other applicable statutes of limitation***

Utah statutes provide for a six-year statute of limitations for instrument of writing (U.C.A. 1953 § 78-12-23) and a three year statute of limitations for first party insurance agreements (U.C.A. 1953 § 31A-21-313).

While this case deals specifically with a payment bond, the analysis and ruling may also be applicable to performance bonds. A court dismissed an insurance company's appeal from a lower court's decision that a materialman's suit is not a victim of a lesser one-year statute of limitations described in U.C.A. § 14-2-2. The court reasoned that the subcontractor, not the owner or contractor, obtained the bond, and therefore the U.C.A. § 14-2-2 time limitation does not apply. *Arnold Machinery Co. v. Prince*, 550 P.2d 193, 194 (Utah 1976).

***Case law statements about enforceability of limitations contained in bonds*** – Not applicable.

***Varying statutes of limitation by agreement in bond or contract***

Courts do not enforce a limitation in the agreements based upon principles of public policy and abuses of the judicial system. "[T]the majority of jurisdictions hold an agreement contained in an original obligation never to assert the statute of limitations violates the public policy of the statute and is invalid. Statutes of limitations are not designed exclusively for the benefit of individuals but are also for the public good. These statutes of repose are intended to prevent the revival and enforcement of stale demands; against which it may be difficult to defend, because of lapse of time, fading of memory, and possible loss of documents. If effect were given to a waiver of the statute of limitations contained in a contract, such a stipulation would be inserted in every promissory note and similar instrument as a matter of routine. The door would be open to the very abuses the statute was designed to prevent, and the result would be an annihilation of the statute." *Hirtler v. Hirtler*, 566 P.2d 1231, 1231-32 (Utah 1977).

## 7. Procedure

***Statutory or procedural rules that may affect handling or administration of lawsuits*** – Not applicable.

***Venue requirements and jurisdictional limitations***

Utah courts have personal jurisdiction over a nonresident defendant when the defendant's alleged actions encompass one of the activities enumerated in the Utah long-arm statute, U.C.A. 1953 § 78-27-24, and exercising jurisdiction over the nonresident defendant comports with the federal due process requirements. *Starways, Inc. v. Curry*, 980 P.2d 204, 206 (Utah 1999).

An action on a bond shall be brought in a court of competent jurisdiction where the construction contract was to be performed. U.C.A. 1953 § 63-56-504.

***Court rules*** – Not applicable.

***Particular agency regulations/rules*** – Not applicable.

***Arbitration requirements and application***

The Utah Uniform Arbitration Act found at U.C.A. § 78-31a-107 (1953) *et seq.* provides that:

> (1) An agreement contained in a record to submit to arbitration any existing or subsequent controversy arising between the parties to the agreement is valid, enforceable, and irrevocable except upon a ground that exists at law or in equity for the revocation of a contract.
> (2) The court shall decide whether an agreement to arbitrate exists or a controversy is subject to an agreement to arbitrate.
> (3) An arbitrator shall decide whether a condition precedent to arbitrability has been fulfilled and whether a contract containing a valid agreement to arbitrate is enforceable.
> (4) If a party to a judicial proceeding challenges the existence of, or claims that a controversy is not subject to, an agreement to arbitrate, the arbitration proceeding may continue pending final resolution of the issue by the court, unless the court otherwise orders.

## 8. Attorney's Fees

***Statutes and/or case law limiting or permitting recovery of attorney's fees***

One large distinction in Utah courts is the different treatment of attorney's fees with performance bonds and payment bonds. Statutorily, payment bonds can recover attorneys fees, § 63-56-504(6); however, attorneys fees incurred in a suit against a performance bond surety are not recoverable unless the contract or performance bond provide for payment of prevailing attorneys fees. *Lignell v. Berg*, 593 P.2d 800, 808 (Utah 1979).

**9. Special Provisions** – Not applicable.

**10. Remarks** – Not applicable.

**11. Case Annotations**

***Interpretation of AIA bond forms*** – Utah cases have not specifically addressed AIA forms of bonds A311 and A312.

***Cases in which surety steps into shoes of obligee***

Subrogation of a surety from a principal "began as a rather narrow doctrine borrowed from Roman or civil law and was confined to the case where one secondarily liable was compelled to pay the debt of one primarily liable; thus an indorser on a note was permitted to be subrogated to the payee against the maker where he paid the payee-creditor. The surety or guarantor was permitted to indemnify itself from its principal by succeeding to the rights of the creditor against such principal. It should not be overlooked that in many cases where subrogation is allowed, there exists a direct right against the principal debtor, either by express or implied contract. Thus, in cases of suretyship and guaranty, there is, if not an express contract, as in the instant case, an implied contract that the principal should indemnify the surety if the latter is compelled to pay the creditor." *Beaver County v. Home Indemnity Co.*, 52 P.2d 435, 450 (Utah 1935).

A surety has the choice to either pay or perform on a contract when the principal defaults. When the surety determines to pay rather than perform the creditor must accept payment or risk forfeiting the creditor's rights to claim against the surety. *Lilenquist v. Utah State Nat. Bank*, 100 P.2d 185, 188 (Utah 1940).

A surety's right of subrogation "is bound up in the contract and dates back to the time when it entered into the contract of suretyship and has superior rights to that of an assignee.... Where a surety on a contractor's bond completes work abandoned by a contractor, such surety is entitled to moneys under the contract, sufficient to save him from loss on his suretyship contract, and such right is superior to any assignment made by the contractor." *Salt Lake City v. O'Connor*, 249 P. 810, 815 (Utah 1926).

# VERMONT

Bradford R. Carver and Eric H. Loeffler[1]

## 1. Requirement for Bond

***Statutory provisions for projects that are:***

**Public** – Not applicable.

**Private** – Not applicable.

**Department of Transportation** – ***State Highway Projects*** – 19 V.S.A. § 10(8) provides that the Vermont Agency of Transportation shall, except where otherwise specifically provided by law, "[r]equire any contractor or contractors, employed in any project of the agency for construction of a transportation improvement, to file in the office of the secretary a good and sufficient surety bond to the state of Vermont, executed by a surety company authorized to transact business in this state in such sum as the agency shall direct, conditioned for the compliance by the contractor or contractors and their agents and servants, with all matters and things set forth and specified to be by the principal kept, done and performed at the time and in the manner in the contract between the agency and the contractor or contractors specified, and to

---

1 Bradford R. Carver is a partner and Eric H. Loeffler is an associate with:
Hinshaw & Culbertson LLP
One International Place, Third Floor
Boston, Massachusetts 02110
(617) 213-7000

pay over, make good and reimburse the state of Vermont, for all loss or losses and damage or damages which the state of Vermont may sustain by reason of failure or default on the part of the contractor or contractors. The agency is authorized to require any other condition in the bond that may from time to time be necessary. The secretary at his or her discretion as to the best interest of the state, may accept other good and sufficient surety in lieu of a bond and, in cases involving contracts for $100,000 or less, may waive the requirement of a performance bond."

***Case law rules that might generally apply***

A surety bond must be given a reasonable construction so as to give effect to intention of the parties and to carry out, rather than defeat, the purpose for which it was executed. *See Town of Windsor, to Use and Benefit of Samson Plaster Board Co. v. Standard Acc. Ins. Co.*, 112 Vt. 426, 26 A.2d 83 (1942). "Where the meaning of such a bond is clear and unambiguous, it should be enforced, like other contracts, according to the manifest intention of the parties." *Id.* (citation omitted). "The effect of the rule is to give such contracts of indemnity a reasonable construction, so as to give effect to the intention of the parties and to carry out, rather than defeat, the purpose for which they were executed." *Id.*

**2. Damages Covered**

***Set forth in any statutes and/or case law***

"[W]hen the bond is breached, the penalty to the amount of the damages immediately becomes the debt of the surety and bears interest, the same as any other debt on contract, if the principal claim bears interest." *City of Montpelier v. National Sur. Co.*, 97 Vt. 111, 122 A. 484, 488 (1923).

***Obligations of surety to perform and/or pay*** – Not applicable.

***Whether failure to provide insurance transfers burden to surety*** – Not applicable.

***Limitations on damages*** – Not applicable.

***Whether obligee may set off bonded contract funds against other principal-obligee debts or obligations***

"Subrogation is an equity called into existence for the purpose of enabling a party secondarily liable, but who has paid the debt, to reap the benefit of any securities or remedies which the creditor may hold against the principal debtor and by the use of which the party paying may thus be made whole." *Walker Process Equipment Co. v. Cooley Bldg. Corp.*, 129 Vt. 333, 278 A.2d 714 (1971). "[I]t is well settled that a surety paying the debt, will, in equity, be subrogated to the securities which the creditor holds." *Benton v. Bailey*, 50 Vt. 137 (1877).

"[T]he well-settled doctrine that a surety is entitled to be subrogated to all the rights and remedies of the creditor, including his securities, against the principal whose debt he is compelled to pay, is said to rest not in contract, but upon principles of natural justice and moral obligation." *Clay v. Severance*, 55 Vt. 300 (1883).

Subrogation "arises when one man is compelled to pay a debt for which another is primarily liable and which, in good conscience, should have been discharged by the latter." *Norfolk & Dedham Fire Insurance Co. v. Aetna Casualty & Surety Co.*, 132 Vt. 341, 343, 318 A.2d 659 (1974). "[T]he right of a surety to be subrogated to the rights of the contractor or his creditors, does not attach unless all the principal obligations are discharged." *Walker Process*, 129 Vt. at 340, 278 A.2d at 718.

***Incorporation of specific contract terms by reference***

"[W]here a bond and contract are executed at the same time between the same parties as obligee and principal obligor relative to the same subject matter, they are taken in connection as forming several parts of one agreement." *Westinghouse Elec. Supply Co. v. B. L. Allen, Inc.*, 138 Vt. 84, 91, 413 A.2d 122, 127 (1980) (citations omitted).

**3. Penal Sum Variations**

***Limitations per statute*** – Not applicable.

***Effect of changes in work upon penal sum, if at all*** – Not applicable.

***Statutory case law protections or dangers to penal sum***

"The bond of a compensated surety is not to be so construed as to extend liability beyond the terms of the contract." *Town of Windsor, to Use and Benefit of Samson Plaster Board Co. v. Standard Acc. Ins. Co.*, 112 Vt. 426, 26 A.2d 83 (1942) (citation omitted).

"Nothing can be clearer, both upon principle and authority, than the doctrine that the liability of a surety is not to be extended by implication beyond the terms of his contract." *Stern v. Sawyer*, 78 Vt. 5, 61 A. 36 (1905).

The obligation of a surety is measured by its contract. *Vermont-People's Nat. Bank v. Robbins' Estate*, 166 A. 6 (1933).

## 4. Parties Covered

***Statutes and/or case law as to whether only obligees are covered*** – Not applicable.

***Coverage for:***

**Third-party beneficiaries** – There does not appear to be any case law in Vermont addressing the extent to which a third party may recover on a performance bond. Under general rules of contract interpretation, however, "[t]he determination of whether a party may be classified as a third-party beneficiary, as opposed to an incidental beneficiary, is based on the original contracting parties' intention." *McMurphy v. State*, 171 Vt. 9, 16, 757 A.2d 1043, 1049 (2000).

**Assignees** – Not applicable.

**Dual obligees** – Not applicable.

## 5. Notice or Filing Required

***Statutory provisions*** – Not applicable.

***Case law rules concerning condition precedent notice***

Where a bond provides for the giving of notice of any breach of contract covered by the bond, within a reasonable time after such breach comes to knowledge of obligee, failure of obligee to give such notice will release surety from obligations imposed by bond. *Springfield Co-op. Freeze Locker Plant v. Wiggins*, 115 Vt. 445, 63 A.2d 182 (1949) (holding that where owner failed to give surety notice, as required by surety bond, of default of contractor causing damage to side walls of freeze locker plant built by contractor, surety was not liable for the damage to the side walls).

## 6. Time for Suit

***Statutes of limitation particular to performance bonds and other applicable statutes of limitation***

"A civil action, except one brought upon the judgment or decree of a court of record of the United States or of this or some other state, and except as otherwise provided, shall be commenced within six years after the cause of action accrues and not thereafter." 12 V.S.A. § 511

***Case law statements about enforceability of limitations contained in bonds***

Where bond providing that surety company should indemnify corporation for contractor's failure to perform contract for construction of freeze locker plant, limited bringing of suit by corporation to within 12 months from date fixed in construction contract for completion of plant, and corporation's loss occurred more than 12 months after such date, bond was void as in violation of statute. *Springfield Co-op. Freeze Locker Plant v. Wiggins*, 115 Vt. 445, 448, 63 A.2d 182, 184-185 (1949).

***Varying statutes of limitation by agreement in bond or contract***

"Except as otherwise provided by statute, any provision in a contract which limits the time in which an action may be brought under the contract or which waives the statute of limitations shall be null and void." 12 V.S.A. § 465.

## 7. Procedure

***Statutory or procedural rules that may affect handling or administration of lawsuits*** – Not applicable.

***Venue requirements and jurisdictional limitations***

"An action before a superior court shall be brought in the county in which one of the parties resides, if either resides in the state; otherwise, on motion, the complaint shall be dismissed. If neither party resides in the state, the action may be brought in any county." 12 V.S.A. § 402(a).

***Court rules*** – Not applicable.

***Particular agency regulations/rules*** – Not applicable.

***Arbitration requirements and application***

12 V.S.A. § 5674 provides:

> (a) On application of a party showing an agreement subject to this chapter and the opposing party's refusal to arbitrate, the court shall order the parties to proceed with arbitration. If the opposing party denies the existence of the agreement, the court shall determine the issue summarily. If the court finds for the moving party, it shall order the parties to proceed with arbitration. Otherwise, the application shall be denied.
> (b) On application to compel or stay arbitration, and on a showing that there is no agreement to arbitrate, the court may stay a commenced or threatened arbitration proceeding. When in substantial and bona fide dispute, the issue of whether there is an agreement to arbitrate shall be forthwith and summarily tried. The court shall order the stay if it finds no enforceable agreement to arbitrate. Otherwise, the court shall order the parties to proceed to arbitration.
> (c) When the existence or validity of an agreement to arbitrate or a party's refusal to arbitrate is in substantial and bona fide dispute, the court shall proceed summarily to the determination of the issue.
> (d) Notwithstanding section 5672 of this title relating to venue, if an issue referable to arbitration under an alleged agreement is involved in an action or proceeding pending in a superior court, applications to compel or to stay arbitration shall be made only to that court.

(e) Any action or civil proceeding involving an issue which is subject to arbitration shall be stayed if an order to compel arbitration or an application therefor has been made. If the issue is severable, the stay may be with respect only to that issue. When application to compel arbitration is made to a court other than the one in which the action or proceeding is pending, any order to compel arbitration shall include that stay.
(f) An order to compel arbitration shall not be refused on the ground that the claim in issue lacks merits or bona fides nor because the applicant has failed to show fault or grounds for the claim sought to be arbitrated.

## 8. Attorney's Fees

***Statutes and/or case law limiting or permitting recovery of attorney's fees***

Vermont follows the "American Rule" which requires each party to bear its own costs and attorney fees. *See Imported Car Center, Inc. v. Billings*, 163 Vt. 76, 79, 653 A.2d 765, 768 (1994); *Gramatan Home Investors Corp. v. Starling*, 143 Vt. 527, 535, 470 A.2d 1157, 1162 (1983).

***What fees are recoverable, if any*** – Not applicable.

## 9. Special Provisions – Not applicable.

## 10. Remarks – Not applicable.

## 11. Case Annotations

**Validity of bond** – Delivery is essential to the validity of a bond. *Westinghouse Elec. Supply Co. v. B. L. Allen, Inc.*, 138 Vt. 84, 91, 413 A.2d 122, 127 (1980), *citing In re Moffitt Estate*, 116 Vt. 286, 289, 75 A.2d 698, 699 (1950). However, formal delivery need not be proved by direct evidence, but it may be inferred from the acts of the parties. *Id.*

**Effect of default judgment against principal on surety's obligation** – "It seems a fairly settled rule that a judgment against a principal is not ordinarily binding on his surety." *Pierce Consulting Engineering Co. v.*

*City of Burlington*, 15 F.R.D. 23 (D. Vt. 1953) (citations omitted). The Vermont Supreme Court has held "that a judgment against a principal is never binding on his surety unless the surety has either expressly stipulated, or by reasonable intent, has stipulated to be bound by a judgment or decree against the principal." *Id., citing Ballantine & Sons v. Fenn*, 84 Vt. 117, 78 A. 713 (1911).

**Material alteration of bonded obligation** – "The rule is well settled that a compensated surety is relieved from its obligations for a departure from the contract only when the departure is shown to be material and prejudicial." *City of Montpelier v. National Sur. Co.*, 97 Vt. 111, 122 A. 484, 488 (1923).

***Interpretation of AIA bond forms*** – Not applicable.

***Cases in which surety steps into shoes of obligee*** – Not applicable.

# VIRGINIA

Shannon J. Briglia[1]

## 1. Requirement for Bond

The Virginia Public Procurement Act ("VPPA") requires performance bonds for all public construction contracts, including privately funded projects built on publicly owned land, and transportation projects whose contract value exceeds $100,000.

***Statutory provisions for projects that are:***

**Public** – Except for transportation-related projects, the performance bond must be equivalent to 100 percent of the contract sum. Va. Code Ann. § 2.2-4337(A)(1)(2002). The bond is "conditioned upon the faithful performance of the contract in strict conformity with the plans, specifications and conditions of the contract." *Id.* Public bodies may require performance bonds on construction contracts less than $100,000. Va. Code Ann. § 2.2-4337(E). The surety issuing the performance bond must be legally authorized to do business in Virginia. Va. Code Ann. § 2.2-4337(B). General contractors may require their subcontractors to furnish performance bonds in a penal sum equal to the subcontract. Va. Code Ann. § 2.2-4337(F).

---

[1] Shannon J. Briglia is a shareholder of:
Wickwire Gavin, P.C.
8100 Boone Boulevard, Suite 700
Vienna, Virginia 22182
(703) 790-8750

**Private** – The 2002 change to Va. Code Ann. § 2.2-4337 added language requiring performance bonds on contracts in excess of $100,000 for projects sited on publicly owned lands. This change should apply to privately funded projects located on public land. In addition, under the Public Private Education Facilities & Infrastructure Act of 2002, Va. Code Ann. § 56-575.1, *et seq.* ("PPEA"), performance bonds complying with § 2.2-4337 are required on any education facility, including, but not limited to, (i) a school building, any functionally related and subordinate facility and land to a school building (including any stadium or other facility primarily used for school events), and any depreciable property provided for use in a school facility that is operated as part of the public school system or as an institution of higher education; (ii) any building or facility that meets a public purpose and is developed or operated by or for any public entity; (iii) any improvements, together with equipment, necessary to enhance public safety and security of buildings to be principally used by a public entity; (iv) utility and telecommunications and other communications infrastructure; (v) recreational facilities; (vi) technology infrastructure, including, but not limited to, telecommunications, automated data processing, word processing and management information systems, and related information, equipment, goods and services; or (vii) any improvements necessary or desirable to any unimproved locally- or state-owned real estate.

**Department of Transportation** – For transportation-related projects, the bond shall be in a form and amount satisfactory to the public body. Va. Code Ann. § 2.2-4337(A)(1). Section 103.05 of the Virginia Department of Transportation ("VDOT") Road and Bridge Specifications (2002 ed.) requires the performance bond to be equivalent to the contract sum.

***Case law rules that might generally apply***

Where a surety's liability for the principal's obligation is shown, the surety is liable for the whole debt. *Bd. of Supervisors v. Southern Cross Coal Corp.*, 380 S.E.2d 636 (Va. 1989). The liability of the surety to the obligee is measured by that of the principal and the liability of both is primary. *Id.*; *see also, D.C. McLain, Inc. v. Arlington County*, 452 S.E.2d 659 (Va. 1995).

The obligations of the surety can be no broader or more extensive than those of its principal. *Ranger Constr. Co. v. Prince William County Sch. Bd.*, 605 F.2d 1298 (4th Cir. 1979).

## 2. Damages Covered

***Set forth in any statutes and/or case law***

The performance bond on a public contract is conditioned upon the faithful performance of the contract in strict conformity with the plans, specifications and conditions of the contract. Va. Code Ann. § 2.2-4337.

***Obligations of surety to perform and/or pay***

A performance bond is intended to guarantee completion of the improvements it covers. Thus, the obligee of such a bond need not incur any expense or do any work on the improvements before collecting on the bond. *Bd. of Supervisors v. Safeco,* 310 S.E.2d 445 (Va. 1983).

***Whether failure to provide insurance transfers burden to surety***

Statutes do not transfer the burden of providing insurance to the surety. However, failure to provide certification of required insurance for a Department of Transportation contract within 15 calendar days after being notified of the contract award will justify cancellation of the award and forfeiture of the bid bond. VDOT Road and Bridge Specifications § 103.08.

***Limitations on damages***

Bonds provided pursuant to Va. Code Ann. § 2.2-4337 are performance bonds, not penal sum bonds. The penalty for nonperformance is not automatic forfeiture of the penal sum but the reasonable costs of completing the work. *See, Bd. of County Supervisors v. Sie-Gray Devs., Inc.*, 334 S.E.2d 542 (Va. 1985); *Bd. of Supervisors of Fairfax County v. Ecology One, Inc.*, 245 S.E.2d 425 (Va. 1978).

The maximum amount potentially recoverable by an obligee for breach of a performance bond is the penal sum of the bond. The obligee may also recover statutory interest under Virginia Code § 8.01-382 but not consequential damages. *See, Bd. of Supervisors of Stafford County v. Safeco Ins. Co.*, 310 S.E.2d 445 (Va. 1983).

***Whether obligee may set off bonded contract funds against other principal-obligee debts or obligations***

"The general rule with respect to the right of the surety of a building contractor who completes the contract upon default by the contractor, to moneys in the hands of the contractee, earned by the contractor before default, is that upon the completion of the contract the surety is entitled to be subrogated to the rights which the obligee had to, or could assert against, such funds upon the principal contractor's default to the extent necessary to reimburse itself for the outlay made to complete the contract." *Fidelity & Cas. Co. v. Copenhaver Co.,* 165 S.E. 528 (Va. 1932) (quotation omitted).

***Incorporation of specific contract terms by reference*** – Not applicable.

### 3. Penal Sum Variations

***Limitations per statute***

Va. Code Ann. § 2.2-4337(A)(1) requires the penal sum of the performance bond for all non-transportation-related contracts to be equivalent to 100 percent of the contract sum. Performance bonds for transportation-related contracts may be in "an amount satisfactory to the public body." *Id.* Department of Transportation Specifications require a performance bond equivalent to the contract sum. VDOT Road and Bridge Specifications § 103.05.

***Effect of changes in work upon penal sum, if at all***

If the owner and contractor engage in practices that constitute a material change in the construction contract provisions, and the contractor subsequently defaults on the contract, the surety is discharged of its obligation under the performance bond. *Southwood Builders, Inc. v. Peerless Ins. Co.*, 366 S.E.2d 104, 106-08 (Va. 1998); *Am. Sur. Co. v. Plank & Whitsett, Inc.*, 165 S.E. 660, 663 (Va. 1932) (payments of substantial sums before they are due, or failure to retain the required retainage, are generally held to be such variations in terms to discharge the surety from its obligations to the owner).

A surety can recover amounts improperly paid by the owner to the contractor. *Continental Ins. Co. v. City of Va. Beach*, 908 F. Supp. 341 (E.D. Va. 1995). The surety may recover amounts improperly paid because, "[t]he obligee in the bond is not only required to exercise good faith with the surety at the time the obligations are assumed, but this good faith must be kept inviolate in all subsequent transactions affecting their rights and obligations created by the contract and the bond." *Plank & Whitsett,* 165 S.E. at 666.

***Statutory or case law protections or dangers to penal sum***

The maximum amount the surety can be liable for is the penal sum of the bond. *Bd. of Supervisors of Stafford County*, 310 S.E.2d at 450 (citing to an earlier statute affirming this principle which was repealed because "it merely declared what were 'long standing and clear principles of substantive law.'")

## 4. Parties Covered

***Statutes and/or case law as to whether only obligees are covered*** – There are no statutes or case law confirming the principle that only obligees are covered by a performance bond.

***Coverage for:***

**Third-party beneficiaries** – Persons who are third-party beneficiaries under a written contract may maintain a suit in their own name for breach of any covenant or promise made for their benefit in the contract. Va. Code Ann. § 55-22 (2005); *see also*, *Richmond Shopping Center, Inc. v. Wiley N. Jackson Co.*, 255 S.E.2d 518 (Va. 1979) (landowner could not maintain a suit as a third-party beneficiary to a road construction contract between the Department of Transportation and contractor because the contract contained no promises for the landowner's benefit). The rights of third-party beneficiaries are limited to parties upon whom the contract clearly and definitely intended to confer a benefit. *Valley Landscape Co. v. Rolland*, 237 S.E.2d 120 (Va. 1977).

**Assignees** – A public body may assign its rights under a bond to a developer as consideration for completing the work guaranteed by the bond. *See Transdulles Centre Ltd., P'ship v. USX Corp.*, 761 F. Supp. 430 (E.D. Va. 1991); *Bd. of County Supervisors v. Sie-Gray Developers, Inc.*, 334 S.E.2d at 546; *Bd. of Supervisors of Fairfax County v. Ecology One, Inc.*, 245 S.E.2d at 428.

**Dual obligees** – There are no cases in Virginia involving dual obligees.

## 5. Notice or Filing Required

***Statutory provisions***

A surety may require a creditor, by written notice, to institute suit against the principal upon the debt for which he is surety before proceeding against the surety. VA. CODE ANN. § 49-25. Failure of the creditor to institute suit within 30 days after receiving notice will discharge the surety. Va. Code Ann. § 49-26.

***Case law rules concerning condition precedent notice*** – There are no notice requirements for filing suit upon a performance bond.

## 6. Time for Suit

***Statutes of limitation particular to performance bonds and other applicable statutes of limitation***

Actions brought against the surety on a performance bond provided for a Department of Transportation contract must be brought within five years after completion of the work. Va. Code Ann. § 2.2-4340. On all other public contracts, suit must be brought within one year after "(i) completion of the contract, including the expiration of all warranties and guarantees, or (ii) the discovery of the defect or breach of warranty that gave rise to the action." Va. Code Ann. § 2.2-4340.

The statute of limitations for contracts under seal is five years. Va. Code Ann. § 8.01-246(2). Performance bonds are viewed as sealed instruments. *See, County School Bd. v. Whitlow*, 286 S.E.2d 230 (Va. 1982).

***Case law statements about enforceability of limitations contained in bonds***

Contractual statutes of limitation for a period shorter than that fixed by statute will be enforced when they are not against public policy or unreasonably short. *Bd. of Supervisors. v. Sentry Ins.*, 391 S.E.2d 273 (1990(citing *Bd. of Supervisors. v. Sampson*, 369 S.E.2d 178, 180 (Va. 1988)).

***Varying statutes of limitation by agreement in bond or contract***

A contractual statute of limitation must be clearly and definitively set forth in the contract. *Id.* at 275. Merely setting conditions upon the obligee's mechanism for determining the amount of damages methods or for enforcing the terms of the bond or contract will not be viewed as a limitation period on the right to sue. *Id.*

## 7. Procedure

***Statutory or procedural rules that may affect handling or administration of lawsuits***

The surety is not, by virtue of its status in a tri-partite bond relationship or pursuant to its equitable rights of subrogation, a "contractor" with the Department of Transportation as defined under Va. Code Ann. § 33.1-387. *XL Specialty Ins. Co. v. Commonwealth*, 611 S.E.2d 356 (Va. 2004). However, Va. Code Ann. § 33.1-192.1, which provides that "[n]o suit or action shall be brought against [VDOT] by a contractor or any persons claiming under him... on any contract... unless the claimant shall have exhausted the review process provided by Code § 33.1-386" applies to sureties and requires the surety to exhaust administrative procedures prescribed by that section before suit is brought against the Department of Transportation. *Id.*

***Venue requirements and jurisdictional limitations***

All suits under a performance bond required for a public contract must be filed in the county or city which the public project, or any part of it, is situated. Va. Code Ann. § 8.01-261(1). All other suits against a "fidelity and surety insurer" may be instituted at the place where the surety assumed any obligation or duty or at the place where the principal obligor may be sued. Va. Code Ann. § 38.2-2415. When the commonwealth is a party, the suit shall be in the circuit court for the City of Richmond. *Id.*

***Court rules*** – Not applicable.

***Particular agency regulations/rules*** – Not applicable.

***Arbitration requirements and application***

Section 2.2-4366 of the VPPA permits public bodies to "utilize mediation and other alternative dispute resolution procedures." With regard to the commonwealth, its agencies, and school boards, however, such procedures are nonbinding and specifically subject to the authority of the attorney general under Va. Code Ann. § 21-127 governing the compromise and settlement of disputes involving the interests of the commonwealth.

A surety is not entitled to compel arbitration where the surety bond does not incorporate the construction subcontract which contains an otherwise binding arbitration provision. *Colonial Mech. Corp. v. Seaboard Sur. Co.*, 14 Va. Cir. 178 (Va. Cir. Ct. 1988). Recently, the Fourth Circuit has declined to allow a non-signatory to an arbitration agreement to compel submission of disputes to arbitration unless the contract containing the arbitration provision clearly makes the non-signatory a third-party beneficiary of the arbitration clause. *Brantley v. Republic Mortgage Ins. Co.*, ___ F.3d ___ (4th Cir. Sept. 28, 2005). This case could impair the surety's ability to compel arbitration under the terms of the underlying bonded contract with the obligee which is incorporated by reference.

## 8. Attorney's Fees

***Statutes and/or case law limiting or permitting recovery of attorney's fees***

There is no statutory right to recover attorney's fees under a performance bond.

Virginia adheres to the "American Rule," providing that in the absence of a statutory or contractual provision to the contrary, attorney's fees are generally not recoverable by the prevailing litigant. *Transdulles Ctr. Inc. v. USX Corp., et al.*,, 976 F.2d 219, 228 (4th Cir. 1992).

In an analogous situation, sureties are liable under the provisions of the VPPA and their payment bonds for attorney's fees and interest to the extent that such amounts are owed by the surety's principal pursuant to the terms of subcontracts or purchase orders. *See United States ex rel. Maddux Supply Co. v. St. Paul Fire & Marine Ins. Co.*, 86 F.3d 332 (4th Cir. 1996).

***What fees are recoverable, if any***

In awarding fees against an opposing party, the fact finder is required to determine from the evidence the amount of the reasonable fees under the facts and circumstances of each particular case based upon a "lodestar" fee evaluation. *Greenwald Cassell Assocs. v. Guffey*, 450 S.E.2d 181 (Va. App. 1994).

Expert testimony is ordinarily necessary to assist the fact finder to determine the reasonableness of the fees to be awarded. *Tazewell Oil Co. v. United Va./Crestar Bank*, 413 S.E.2d 611 (Va. 1992).

***Incorporation of specific contract terms by reference*** – Not applicable.

## 9. Special Provisions – Not applicable.

## 10. Remarks

The Virginia Supreme Court rejected a claim that a surety is liable for consequential damages incurred by an obligee, *see Safeco*, 310 S.E.2d at 445. However, the court has not addressed whether a surety is liable in tort for claims of bad faith. Both a federal court sitting in Virginia and a circuit court have implied that a right to sue a surety for bad faith, or, at the least, a right to pursue bad faith as a defense to an indemnity action, may lie. *Bell BCI Co. v. Old Dominion Demolition Corp.*, 294 F. Supp. 2d 807 (E.D. Va. 2003); *Transamerica Premier Ins. Co. v. Turf Specialists of No. Va., Inc.*, et al., 31 Va. Cir. 26 (Va. Cir. Ct. 1993).

## 11. Case Annotations

***Interpretation of AIA bond forms*** – Virginia cases have not specifically addressed AIA forms of bonds A311 or A312.

***Cases in which surety steps into shoes of obligee***

"When a principal defaults on a contract guaranteed by a performance or payment bond and the surety performs on the bond, principles of surety law and the doctrine of equitable subrogation impose certain rights and duties running between the surety, principal, and obligor, and allow the surety to enforce such rights and duties." *XL Specialty Ins. Co. v. Commonwealth*, 611 S.E.2d 356 (Va. 2005). A surety claiming equitable subrogation does not "simply step into the shoes of" the contractor because it may be entitled to enforce claims beyond those the contractor could raise. *Id.* at 370.

A surety defending an obligee's suit stands in the principal's shoes and may assert such defenses as his principal could have asserted in the suit. *Bd. of Supervisors v. Southern Cross Coal Corp.*, 380 S.E.2d at 96; *see also, Bd. of County Supervisors. v. Sie-Gray Developers, Inc.*, 334 S.E.2d at 546 (suggesting that a defense unavailable to a principal would likewise be unavailable to a surety).

# WASHINGTON

Alexander Friedrich[1]

## 1. Requirement for Bond

***Statutory provisions for projects that are:***

**Public** – ***Contractor's Bond Act*** – The general contractor on any state, county, municipal, public body, city or town must execute a performance and labor and material payment bond, in an amount equal to the full contract price.

Chapter 39.08 RCW requires contractors to obtain a bond conditioned that such contractor shall faithfully perform all of the provisions of the public works contract and pay all laborers, mechanics and subcontractors and materialmen, and all persons who supply such person or persons, or subcontractors with provisions and supplies for carrying on of such work.

**Private** – ***Washington Registration of Contractor's Act*** – A construction contractor must file a surety bond with the Department of Labor & Industries as a condition precedent to obtaining registration for the conduct of construction activities in the state of Washington.

---

[1] Alexander Friedrich is a partner of:
Yusen & Friedrich
215 NE 40th Street, Suite C-3
Seattle, Washington 98105
(206) 545-2123

Chapter 18.27 RCW requires all contractors to obtain a bond that shall be conditioned that the applicant will pay all persons performing labor, including employee benefits, for the contractor, will pay all taxes and contributions due the state of Washington, and will pay all persons furnishing labor or material or renting or supplying equipment to the contractor and will pay all amounts that may be adjudged against the contractor by reason of breach of contract including negligent or improper work in the conduct of the contracting business.

***Electrical Contractor's Act*** – Any person, firm, partnership or corporation or other entity that offers to undertake or submit a bid for work of installing or maintaining wires or equipment that conveys electrical current must furnish a bond.

Chapter 19.28 RCW. The bond shall be conditioned that the principal will pay for all labor, including employee benefits, and material furnished, or used upon the work, taxes and contributions due the state of Washington, and all damages that may be sustained by any person, firm, partnership or corporation or other entity due to a failure of the contractor to make any installation or maintenance in accordance with this chapter.

**Department of Transportation** – Not applicable.

***Case law rules that might generally apply***

**Public Works Bond** – A material or equipment supplier will not be able to claim against the Washington Public Works Bond (Ch. 39.08 RCW) unless it supplies to a "subcontractor." There is a two–part test to define who is a "subcontractor." These tests are found in *Farwest Steel Corporation vs. Mainline Metal Works, Inc.*, 48 Wn. App 719 (1987). First test: Does the subcontractor perform work on the project site? If so, then it should be a "subcontractor." Second test: Does the "subcontractors" subcontract with the prime contractor account for at least 10 percent of the owner/prime contractor contract? If so, then the subcontractor status may be established.

**Private** – ***Washington Registration of Contractor's Act*** – Upper-tier contractor cannot reach the proceeds of a contractor's registration bond posted by a lower-tier contractor pursuant to RCW 18.27.040. *Stewart Carpet vs. Contractors Bonding*, 105 Wn.2d 353 (1986).

## 2. Damages Covered

***Set forth in any statutes and/or case law***

**Public Works** – ***Contractor's Bond Act – RCW 39.08*** – Provides that the general contractor shall faithfully perform all provisions of the Public Works Contract and pay all laborers, mechanics and subcontractors and materialmen and all persons who supply such person or persons or subcontractors with provisions and supplies for the carrying on of such work. The bond shall be in an amount equal to the full contract price.

**Private** – ***Washington Registration of Contractor's Act – RCW 18.27*** – Provides that the bond shall be in the penal sum of $12,000 if a general contractor and $6,000 if a specialty contractor (RCW 18.27.040(1)).

***Electrical Contractor's Act – RCW 19.28*** – Provides that the bond shall be in the penal sum of $4,000. (RCW 19.28.041(3)).

***Obligations of surety to perform and/or pay*** – See above.

***Whether failure to provide insurance transfers burden to surety***

**Surety bond** – ***liability limited*** – RCW 19.72.107 specifically provides that:

> (1) A surety bond may not provide any type of insurance coverage. A surety bond shall not be liable for damages based upon or arising out of any tortious injury including death to:
>
> (a) Any person; and
>
> (b) Any real or personal property.
>
> Failure to have any or adequate insurance required by contract does not transfer the burden to the surety.

***Limitations on damages***

The surety's liability is not greater than that of its principal. *Turner vs. Wexler*, 14 Wn. App 143 (1975). A surety cannot be held liable for more than the penal amount of the bond. *In re Davidson* 31 Wn. App 480, 642 P.2d 1259 (1982). These cases simply follow the plain language of the controlling statute, RCW 19.72.180 which prohibits the imposition of liability on a surety in excess of the bond amount.

***Whether obligee may set off bonded contract funds against other principal-obligee debts or obligations*** – Not applicable.

***Incorporation of specific contract terms by reference***

If language of bond is plain and unambiguous, it is interpreted under general contract principles in ascertaining the mutual intentions of the parties, but, if language of bond is ambiguous, it is construed in favor of liability of surety. *Joint Administrative Board of Plumbing and Pipefitting Industry vs. Fallon*, 89 Wn.2d 90 (1977).

**3. Penal Sum Variations**

***Limitations per statute***

Washington does not have statutory limitations on performance bond penalty sums, other than as set forth above.

**Public** – The bond referenced in RCW 39.08.010 (Public Works Bond) shall be in an amount equal to the full contract price agreed to be paid for such work for public improvement.

**Private** – ***Washington Registration of Contractor's Act – RCW 18.27 –*** Provides that the bond shall be in the penal sum of $12,000 for a general contractor and $6,000 if a specialty contractor. Only "residential homeowner" as defined in RCW 18.27.010(8), is entitled to recover the full $12,000 (RCW 18.27.040(5)). Non-residential homeowner claimants are only entitled to recover not more than one-half of the bond amount ($6,000). RCW 18.27.040(5).

***Effect of changes in work upon penal sum, if at all*** – Not applicable.

***Statutory or case law protections or dangers to penal sum*** – RCW 19.72.180 prohibits the imposition of the liability on a surety in excess of the bond amount.

## 4. Parties Covered

***Statutes and/or case law as to whether only obligees are covered***

In Washington, performance bonds do not benefit subcontractors and suppliers because there are no third-party beneficiaries on performance bonds. *Hewson Construction vs. Reintree Corporation*, 101 Wash. 2d 819 (1984). The Washington Supreme Court in *Hewson Construction* held that performance bonds run solely to the named obligee and to no other party.

***Coverage for:***

**Third-party beneficiaries** – *Hewson Construction vs. Reintree Corporation,* 101 Wash. 2d 819 (1984).

**Assignees** – Action on a bond is assignable. *Gilmore vs. Westermen*, 13 Wash. 390 (1896).

**Dual obligees** – Not applicable.

## 5. Notice or Filing Required

***Statutory provisions***

**Public Works** – ***Preclaim Notices*** – Every party furnishing materials, supplies or provisions to any subcontractor must supply the general contractor a notice in writing within 10 days after the date of the first delivery of the materials, supplies or provisions to the subcontractor (does not apply to labor). See RCW 39.080.065.

***Notice of Claim*** – RCW 39.08.010 requires that *every party* including both first tier and second tier subcontractors and suppliers must provide notice in writing to the public body within 30 days of completion and acceptance of the work by the public body.

***Case law rules concerning condition precedent notice***

The Washington Supreme Court held that failure to provide timely preclaim notice pursuant to RCW 39.08.065 by a claimant that provides both materials and labor to a subcontractor is a complete bar to recovery against the performance bond furnished by the general contractor. *LRS Electric vs. Hamre Construction,* 153 Wash. 2d 731 (2005).

Failure to file the notice of claim precludes any lawsuit against the bond. *Fidelity and Deposit Company of Maryland vs. Conway, Inc.*, 14 Wash. 2d 551 (1942).

## 6. Time for Suit

***Statutes of limitation particular to performance bonds and other applicable statutes of limitation***

**Public Works Bond** – The beneficiary on the Public Works Bond must file suit within six years after accrual of the cause of action which can occur no later than 30 days after the project is accepted. *Industrial Coatings vs. Fidelity and Deposit Company of Maryland*, 117 Wash. 2d 511 (1991).

**Private** – ***Contractor's Registration Act Bonds*** – RCW 18.27.040(3) provides in part as follows:

> Actions upon the bond or deposit brought by residential homeowner for breach of contract by a party to a construction contract shall be commenced by filing a complaint within two years from the date the claimed contract work was substantially completed or abandoned. Action upon the bond by any other party authorized by statute shall be commenced by filing the summons and complaint within one year from the date the claimed labor was performed and benefits accrued, taxes and contributions owing the state of Washington came due, materials and equipment were furnished.

***Electrical Contractor's Bond*** – Any action shall be brought within one year from the completion of the work in the performance of which the breach is alleged to have occurred. RCW 19.28.071.

***Case law statements about enforceability of limitations contained in bonds*** – Not applicable.

***Varying statutes of limitation by agreement in bond or contract***

No bond delivered or issued in this state shall contain any condition, stipulation or agreement limiting rights of action against the surety to a period of less than one year from the time when the cause of action accrued. RCW 48.18.200(1)(c).

## 7. Procedure

***Statutory or procedural rules that may affect handling or administration of lawsuits*** – Not applicable.

***Venue requirements and jurisdictional limitations***

Washington does not have jurisdictional limitations that apply to performance bonds.

**Public Works Bonds** – Exclusive venue lies with the superior court of the county where the notice of claim is filed and is governed by laws regulating civil action seeking foreclosure against real property. RCW 60.28.030.

**Contractor's Registration Act Bonds** – Actions upon the bond shall be commenced by filing summons and complaint with the clerk of the superior court. See RCW 18.27.040(3).

**Electrical Contractor's Bond** – Any person, firm or corporation sustaining any damage or injury by reason of the contractor's breach of the conditions of the bond may bring an action against the surety; the action shall be brought in the superior court of any county in which the principal on the bond resides or transacts business or in the county in which the work was performed as a result of which the breach is alleged to have occurred. RCW 19.28.071.

***Court rules*** – Not applicable.

***Particular agency regulations/rules*** – Not applicable.

***Arbitration requirements and application***

All civil actions including claims against a performance bond where the sole relief sought is a money judgment up to $35,000 exclusive of interest and costs, are subject to mandatory arbitration. RCW 7.06.020.

## 8. Attorney's Fees

***Statutes and/or case law limiting or permitting recovery of attorney's fees***

**Public Works Bonds** – Reasonable attorney's fees are recoverable in actions to foreclose upon the bond only if the suit is brought after 30 days have passed since the filing of the notice of claim. RCW 39.08.030. However, the surety is only liable for attorney's fees when it has such an adverse interest that it might use its superior financial position to continue the suit to the disadvantage of the opposing party. *Lakeside Pump and Equipment, Inc. vs. Austin Construction Company* 89 Wash. 2d 839 (1978).

Claimants are entitled to recover attorney's fees and interest on claims against the public works bonds from the date the first notice of claim is filed with the public owner at the statutory rate of 12 percent per-annum. *Keller Supply Company, Inc., vs. Lydig Construction,* 57 Wash. App. 594 (1990).

An obligee who is compelled to assume the burden of legal action to obtain the benefit of its performance bond is entitled to its attorney's fees. *Olympic Steamship vs. Centennial Insurance Company,* 117 Wash. 2d 37 (1991).

**Contractor's Registration Act** – The prevailing party in an action against the contractor and the contractor's bond for breach of contract by a party to the construction contract is entitled to costs, interest and reasonable attorney's fees. The surety upon the bond is not liable in an aggregate amount in excess of the amount named in the bond nor for any monetary penalty assessed. (See RCW 18.27.040(6))

**Electrical Contractor's Bond** – No provisions for the recovery of attorney's fees and costs are provided in RCW 19.28 against surety.

***What fees are recoverable, if any*** – Not applicable.

9. **Special Provisions** – Not applicable.

10. **Remarks** – Not applicable.

11. **Case Annotations**

***Interpretation of AIA bond forms***

Interpreting the AIA Document 311 performance bond, the court specifically held that surety was liable on its bond subject to a single express condition subsequent (the principal's prompt and faithful performance). Failure to declare a default does not relieve the surety of its duty to pay on the bond. *Colorado Structures, Inc., vs. Insurance Company of the West*, 125 Wash. App 907 (2005).

***Cases in which surety steps into shoes of obligee*** – Not applicable.

# WEST VIRGINIA

W. Alan Torrance, Jr. and Robert G. Lovett, Jr.[1]

## 1. Requirement for Bond

***Statutory provisions for projects that are:***

**Public** – The requirement for a performance bond is set forth in the rules governing bidding on public projects known as the West Virginia Fairness in Competitive Bidding Act, as amended in 2004. W. Va. Code § 5-22-1 (2005) The pertinent portion of the act states:

> The state and its subdivisions shall, except as provided in this section, solicit competitive bids for every construction project exceeding $25,000 in total costs: Provided, that a vendor who has been debarred pursuant to the provision of sections thirty-three-f, inclusive, article three, chapter five-a of this code may not bid on or be awarded a contract under this section. All bids submitted pursuant to this chapter shall include a valid bid bond or other surety as approved by the state of West Virginia or its subdivisions.

W. Va. Code § 5-22-1(c) (2005).

---

1 W. Alan Torrance, Jr. is a shareholder and Robert G. Lovett, Jr. is a summer associate of:
Dickie, McCamey & Chilcote, P.C.
Two PPG Place, Suite 400
Pittsburgh, Pennsylvania 15222-5402
(800) 243-5412

Following the solicitation of bids, the construction contract shall be awarded to the lowest qualified responsible bidder who shall furnish a sufficient performance and payment bond: Provided, That the state and its subdivisions may reject all bids and solicit new bids on the project. W. Va. Code § 5-22-1(d) (2005).

Furthermore, per W. Va. Code § 5-22-1(b)(2) (2005), the statute applies to "the State of West Virginia, every political subdivision thereof, every administrative entity that includes such a subdivision, all municipalities and all county boards of education."

Performance bonds are also required on design-build projects. W. VA. CODE § 5-22A-10(9) (2005).

No officer, employee or representative of any public entity is permitted to require that the bond be obtained from any particular surety, agent, broker or producer. W. Va. Code §§ 5-22-1(g); 5-22A-10(9) (2005).

At the time of the execution of the contract, the successful bidder shall execute and deliver to the division a good and sufficient surety or collateral bond payable to the State of West Virginia in the amount of 100 percent of the contract price. W. Va. CSR 157-3-5.5.

**Private** – There is no statutory requirement for performance bonds on private projects.

**Department of Transportation** – A common bond form used by the Division of Highways includes performance and payment bond obligations in a single contract bond. The bond explicitly identifies the surety's indemnity obligations for the negligence of principal and its subcontractors for damages, the release of any and all mechanic's liens (even though none are permitted against public property) and any patent, trademark or copyright infringements.

In addition, final payment to principal and release of the surety are conditioned upon payment of all taxes which must be evidenced by a certificate from state and local officials verifying that all applicable taxes have been paid in full. *W. Va. CSR 157-3-11.6.f.*

## 2. Damages Covered

### *Set forth in any statutes and/or case law*

In general, the liability of the surety is coextensive with that of the principal. However, the liability of the surety is a legal as distinguished from a moral one and is governed by contract. *Gateway Communications, Inc. v. John R. Hess, Inc., et al.,* 541 S.E. 2d 595, 599 (W. Va. 2000).

The reasonable cost of completion includes correction of previously performed work that arises from the default of the principal. Calculation of the cost of completion begins on the date upon which action must be taken by the surety after a declaration of default. *Continental Realty Corp. v. Andrew J. Crevolin Co.*, 380 F. Supp. 246, 256 (S.D. W. Va. 1974). In the absence of an agreement to the contrary, legal expenses and accounting costs are not recoverable. *Id.*

### *Incorporation of specific contract terms by reference*

In general, a compensated surety is not looked upon with favor in regard to its liability. *Continental Realty Corp. v. Andrew J. Crevolin*, 380 F. Supp. 246, 254 (S.D. W. Va. 1974). As a surety for profit, the bond will be construed most strongly in favor of the obligee. *Mills v. Indemnity Ins. Co.,* 171 S.E. 532, 533 (W. Va. 1933).

Notwithstanding, the principles of freedom of contract will be applied to enforce the terms of the principal's contract to the benefit of the surety. In *Wellington Power Corp. v. CNA Surety Corp.*, 614 S.E.2d 680, 687 (W. Va. 2005), a pay-if-paid condition precedent clause in a subcontract form was successfully relied upon by the payment bond surety to deny payment to two subcontractors on a public project. The contract term was held not to be in violation of the public policy of West Virginia or the applicable statute, W. Va. Code § 38-2-39 (2004).

## 3. Penal Sum Variations

### *Limitations per statute and/or case law*

The extent of liability of the surety is limited by the penalty of the bond and is otherwise the same as that of the principal, *Mayle v. Aetna*

*Casualty and Surety Company,* 166 S.E. 2d 133, 135 (W. Va. 1969), provided the surety reasonably complies with the terms of bond. *See, Robinson v. Fidelity & Deposit Company, et. al.*, 383 S.E.2d 95 (W. Va. 1989).

***Statutory or case law protections or dangers to penal sum***

Courts are able, under a breach of contract theory, to order that payments be made to the obligee in excess of the penal sum for surety's failure to abide by the terms of the bond subsequent to the principal's default. *See supra, Continental Realty Corp.,* 380 F. Supp. at 246. To the extent the court determines surety has breached the bond, all foreseeable damages are recoverable including lost profits, finance charges, cost of winterizing and guarding the bonded work. *Id.*

**Department of Transportation** – The penal sum of the bond must be in an amount that is 100 percent of awarded contract. W. Va. CSR 157-3-5.5. However, in certain instances and at any time during the project, the Department of Highways regulations permit the principal to obtain a bond in the amount of 102 percent of the adjusted contract value at any time during the project and thereby delete any provisions for retainage in the contract. W. Va. CSR 157-3-11.6.f.

## 4. Parties Covered

***Statutes and/or case law as to whether only obligees are covered***

The Statute does not identify any parties covered other than the public entity.

The courts will enforce the language of the bond and agreements executed simultaneously with the bond to honor assignments and trust agreements. *See Logan Planning Mill Company v. Fidelity & Casualty Company of New York,* 212 F. Supp. 906 (SD. W. Va. 1962).

## 5. Notice or Filing Required

***Statutory provisions*** – There are no statutory notice requirements.

## 6. Time for Suit

***Statutes of limitation particular to performance bonds and other applicable statutes of limitation***

In the absence of a shorter limitations period in the bond, a performance bond claim arising from a private or public project, including instances when the State of West Virginia is obligee, is considered a breach of contract claim. Accordingly, suit must be filed within 10 years from the date the cause of action accrues. W. Va. Code § 55-2-6 (1923).

***Case law statements about enforceability of limitations contained in bonds***

The statute of limitations accrues on a performance bond claim when the work is completed, unless the bonded contract sets forth a specific event such as substantial completion or final payment. *Gateway Communications, Inc. v. John R. Hess, Inc.*, 541 S.E.2d 595, 599 (W. Va. 2000).

***Varying statutes of limitation by agreement in bond or contract***

The parties may agree to shorten the limitations period provided the change is reasonable. *See, e.g., Hilton v. Norfolk & W. Ry. Co.*, 194 F. Supp. 915 (D.C. W. Va. 1961); *American Surety Co. of New York v. Wheeling Structural Steel Co.*, 26 F. Supp. 395 (D.C. W. Va. 1939) (*rev'd on other grounds*). However, by statute, limitations period for filing suit on a performance bond can be no less than two years. W. Va. Code § 33-6-14 (2005).

## 7. Procedure

***Statutory or procedural rules that may affect handling or administration of lawsuits*** – Not applicable.

***Venue requirements and jurisdictional limitations*** – The terms of the bond govern the forum for the dispute.

***Arbitration requirements and application***

When the bond incorporates by reference a contract that contains an arbitration provision, a finding regarding contractor defenses will be binding on the surety. If identified as a party on a demand for arbitration, the surety will be required to participate. *Rashid v. Schenck Construction Co.*, 438 S.E.2d 543, 547 (W. Va. 1993).

**8. Attorney's Fees**

***Statutes and/or case law limiting or permitting recovery of attorney's fees***

In the absence of an express provision for attorney's fees in either the incorporated contract or the bond itself, the recovery of attorney's fees is unlikely. *Continental Realty Corp. v. Andrew J. Crevolin Co.*, 380 F. Supp. 246, 256 (S.D. W. Va. 1974).

**9. Special Provisions** – Not applicable.

**10. Remarks**

The courts of West Virginia are divided into two levels, the circuit courts, which serve as the trial courts, and the Supreme Court of West Virginia. Because the jurisdiction of the supreme court is discretionary, there is no automatic right to appeal a result in the circuit court. Consequently, case law in West Virginia with respect to performance bonds is limited.

Given that West Virginia is primarily statutory, in the past, some scholars have been led to the mistaken belief that West Virginia law does not require performance bonds on public projects. The genesis of this misunderstanding is based upon a review of the payment bond requirements for public projects which is included in the chapter governing mechanic's liens. This section makes no mention of performance bonds.

## 11. Case Annotations

**Equitable Subrogation** – In general, sureties enjoy super priority to contract funds on a defaulted contract. *See Logan Planning Mill Company v. Fidelity & Casualty Company of New York,* 212 F. Supp. 906 (S.D. W. Va. 1962) in addition to *American States Insurance Company v. Prozzillo,* 1988 U.S. Dist. LEXIS, 17213 (N.D. W. Va. 4/20/88).

***Interpretation of AIA bond forms*** – Not applicable.

***Cases in which surety steps into shoes of obligee*** – Not applicable.

# WISCONSIN

Brian W. Mullins[1]

## 1. Requirement for Bond

Prime contractors in Wisconsin are not required to furnish any bond on private projects. However, there are public works performance bond requirements. Those requirements vary depending upon the amount of the contract and upon whether the public owner is the state or a local governing unit.

***Statutory provisions for projects that are:***

**Public** – The statutory bond requirements for Wisconsin public works are contained in Wis. Stat. § 779.14. The performance bond requirements for state projects are supplemented from time to time by written standards established by the Wisconsin Department of Administration and the Wisconsin Department of Transportation. The Wisconsin Department of Transportation has also included bonding requirements in its standard specifications. Under Wisconsin's public works bond statute, local governmental units may also prepare written standards for performance bonding.

[1] Brian W. Mullins is a shareholder of:
Wickwire Gavin, P.C.
22 East Miffin Street, Suite 800
Madison, Wisconsin 53703
(608) 257-5335

**Private** – Wisconsin does not require performance bonds on private projects. However, if a performance bond is provided on a private project, it will be interpreted as contracts are and the rights and obligations of parties will be controlled by the terms of the bond.

**Department of Transportation** – As noted above, the Wisconsin Department of Transportation has included a bonding requirement in its standard specifications. That requirement specifies that a performance bond is to be provided on all projects. The Department of Transportation provision also specifies that the amount of the bond is to be the full amount of the contract and that the form of the bond shall be as furnished by the Department of Transportation. The Department of Transportation also specifies that the surety must be acceptable to the department, and to the governor when required by law. These requirements are contained in § 103.5, Standard Specifications for Highway and Structure Construction, State of Wisconsin, Department of Transportation (1996 edition).

**Other** – Local professional football stadium districts are exempt from the public performance bond requirements.

***Case law rules that might generally apply*** – See below.

## 2. Damages Covered

### *Set forth in any statutes and/or case law*

The form and terms of the performance bond, as approved by the public owner, will control damages covered by the performance bond and the obligations of the surety to perform and/or pay. For larger projects (state projects above $250,000 and local governmental projects above $100,000, each amount indexed annually by the state) the performance bond must extend to "the faithful performance of the contract." Wis. Stat. § 779.14.

### *Obligations of surety to perform and/or pay*

Under most bonds the surety's liability for damages is co-extensive with that of the principal. Also, in addition to limitations set forth under the terms of the bond, the surety is generally entitled to assert all defenses against claims that are available to the principal. *Waukesha Concrete Products v. Capital Indem. Corp., Inc.*, 127 Wis. 2d 332, 379 N.W.2d 333 (Ct. App. 1985).

***Whether failure to provide insurance transfers burden to surety*** – Not applicable.

***Limitations on damages***

As a general matter, the surety is not liable for any amounts in excess of the penal sum of the performance bond. If the obligee waives its rights against the principal, the obligee also waives its rights against the surety. In Wisconsin punitive damages are not available in connection with a breach-of-contract claim. *White v. Benkowski*, 37 Wis. 2d 285, 155 N.W.2d 74 (1967).

***Whether obligee may set off bonded contract funds against other principal-obligee debts or obligations*** – Not applicable.

***Incorporation of specific contract terms by reference*** – Not applicable.

**3. Penal Sum Variations**

***Limitations per statute and/or case law***

Typically, but not always, bonds on public works in Wisconsin must be in an amount at least equal to the contract price. *Golden Valley Supply v. Amer. Ins. Co.,* 195 Wis. 2d 866, 537 N.W.2d 58 (Ct. App. 1995). (See also revisions to Wis. Stat. § 779.14 subsequent to *Golden Valley*.) The amount of the prime contractor's own contract, not the total amount of all prime contractors together, establish the contract price for purposes of the performance bond requirement. Generally, unless the surety exercises an option to take over the project and complete the work, the surety has no obligation beyond the penal sum. Also, the surety will typically be relieved of liability, at least to the extent that the surety's security (such as the unpaid contract balance) has been compromised, by an owner's failure to conform with the owner's contractual obligations. *City of*

*Wauwatosa v. Volpano*, 224 Wis. 503, 272 N.W. 459 (1937). This would occur, for example, where an owner makes an advance payment to the contractor or fails to maintain contractual retainage, and such failure prejudices the surety. If the surety exercises an option to complete the work, its liability may not be limited to the penal sum of the bond. The terms of the bond must be reviewed to determine the surety's potential obligation.

***Effect of changes in work upon penal sum, if at all*** – Not applicable.

***Statutory or cases law protections or damages to penal sum*** – Not applicable.

## 4. Parties Covered

***Statutes and/or case law as to whether only obligees are covered***

In private projects, the terms of the bond will determine what parties are covered. In Wisconsin public works performance bonds, the statutory bonding requirement extends only to second-tier subcontractors (first-tier subcontractors on transportation projects). However, a public owner has discretion to reduce the scope of the bond, except in large projects (more than $250,000 for state projects and more than $100,000 for local government projects, each amount being indexed annually by the state). The terms of the actual bond provided by a surety are enforceable to the extent those terms go beyond the contractually or statutorily required bonding provisions.

***Coverage for:***

**Third-party beneficiaries** – Not applicable.

**Assignees** – Not applicable.

**Dual obligees** – Not applicable.

## 5. Notice or Filing Required

***Statutory provisions***

In its recent statutory revisions, Wisconsin dropped specific notice requirements for the obligee in connection with bond claims. Wis. Stat. § 779.14(2)(am) requires that subcontractors or suppliers must have notified the prime contractor in writing that the subcontractor or supplier has provided or will provide labor or materials to the public work or improvement in order to maintain an action on a bond. The notice must be provided no later than 60 days after the date on which the subcontractor or supplier first provided the labor or materials. This subcontractor/supplier notice is not required under certain circumstances specified in the statutes. It is unclear whether a subcontractor or supplier has any direct action rights on a performance bond. If, however, a subcontractor or supplier does have rights under a performance bond, this notice provision does appear to apply.

**Private projects** – The terms of the bond will control as to any notice or filing requirements.

***Case law rules concerning condition precedent notice*** – See Case Annotations at § 11 below.

## 6. Time for Suit

***Statutes of limitation particular to performance bonds and other applicable statutes of limitation***

Under the Wisconsin public works bond statute, and depending upon the terms of the bond itself, claimants have one year after completion of work under the contract to commence an action on the bond.

***Case law statements about enforceability of limitations contained in bonds***

The one-year statute of limitations for any action for an action on a performance bond applies, rather than the general six-year statute of limitations for contract actions. *Milwaukee Metro. Sewerage Dist. v. Fidelity & Deposit Co.*, 56 F.3d 821 (7th Cir. 1995).

***Varying statutes of limitation by agreement in bond or contract***

Wisconsin courts will allow an extended period to bring a claim on a bond if the terms of the bond itself provides a longer claim period than the statute.

## 7. Procedure

***Statutory or procedural rules that may affect handling or administration of lawsuits***

The procedure for claims on performance bonds are the same as those which govern general lawsuits. Unless the action is brought in federal court, the initial lawsuit will be filed in a circuit court.

***Venue requirements and jurisdictional limitations*** – The general rules for venue requirements and jurisdictional limitations of Wisconsin courts apply to actions brought on a performance bond.

***Court rules*** – There are no special court rules that apply to actions on performance bonds. General trial court rules will apply.

***Particular agency regulations/rules*** – Not applicable.

***Arbitration requirements and application***

If an arbitration clause is included in a contract, the Wisconsin Arbitration Act will make the clause specifically enforceable. Wis. Stat. § 788.01. There is no clear case law as to whether or not the action brought directly on the surety bond, not involving an owner's claim against the contractor, is subject to an arbitration clause contained in the prime contract. The Wisconsin courts have held that although the State of Wisconsin, as a party, can be required to proceed through arbitration, any award against the state would not be binding unless successfully presented to the State Claims Board for processing. *State v. P.G. Miron Const. Co. Inc.*, 181 Wis. 2d 1045, 512 N.W.2d 499 (1994).

## 8. Attorney's Fees

***Statutes and/or case law limiting or permitting recovery of attorney's fees***

There is no statutory right in Wisconsin to recover attorney's fees under a performance bond. Wisconsin adheres to the general rule providing that in the absence of a statutory or contractual provision to the contrary, attorney's fees are generally not recoverable by the prevailing party.

***What fees are recoverable, if any*** – Not applicable.

## 9. Special Provisions

**Proportional distribution of insufficient bond funds** – If the amount of the performance bond is insufficient to satisfy all claims, then the bond amount must be distributed among the claiming parties proportionally. Wis. Stat. § 779.14(2)(b).

**Effect of assignment, modification, or change of contract** – No assignment, modification, or change of contract, change of the work covered thereby or extension of time to complete the contract will release the surety on a performance bond which is required under Wisconsin's public bonding law. Wis. Stat. § 779.14(1)(e)4.

**Approval of bond by a public official** – A performance bond required under § 779.14 of the Wisconsin statutes must be approved by the presiding officer of the public owner. This includes the state official authorized to enter into the contract for projects with the state; the corporation counsel for county projects; the mayor for city projects; the president for village projects; the chairperson for town projects; and the school district president for school projects.

**Direct purchase contracts exempted** – The requirements set forth in Wisconsin's public bonding law do not apply to a contract for the direct purchase of materials by the state or by a local unit of government. Wis. Stat. § 779.14(1)(f).

**Substitute payment assurances** – The Wisconsin performance bond statute for public works provides that, except on large projects, the public owner (whether it is the state or a local governmental unit) may permit a prime contractor to substitute a different payment assurance for the performance bond. For the State of Wisconsin, Department of Administration projects, the substituted payment and performance assurance must be for an amount at least equal to the contract price and is to be in the form of a bond, an irrevocable letter of credit, or an escrow account acceptable to the Department of Administration.

**Prohibition against public owner specifying surety company or broker** – The Wisconsin performance bond statute for public works expressly precludes the invitation for bids and the public owner from requiring that a performance bond must be furnished by a specified surety company or through a specified agent or broker. Wis. Stat. § 779.14(1)(e)5.

## 10. Remarks

Prior to 1997, Wisconsin's bonding statute for public works generally followed the Miller Act. Recent revisions to the statute which provide a fair amount of discretion to the public owner for projects below a certain dollar amount, have yet to be tested through litigation. Hence, the application of the statutes is somewhat uncertain.

## 11. Case Annotations

Under the Wisconsin performance bond law for public works, the public owner may be liable for damages suffered by subcontractors and suppliers as the result of the public owner's failure to require a prime contractor to obtain a bond required by statute. *Holmen Concrete v. Hardy Const. Co.*, 2004 WI App. 165, 276 Wis. 2d 126, 686 N.W.2d 705. However, the subcontractor/supplier claimant must file notice of claim against the public body as required under the public claim notices of the Wisconsin statutes. *Smith v. Town of Pershing*, 10 Wis. 2d 352, 102 N.W.2d 765 (1960); *Cowin & Co. v. City of Merrill*, 202 Wis. 614, 233 N.W. 561 (1930).

The construction and interpretation of a surety bond are for the court, and a lower court decision may be reviewed independently by an appellate court. *Matter of Wisconsin Sur. Corp.*, 112 Wis. 2d 396, 332 N.W.2d 860 (Ct. App. 1983).

The rules of construction and interpretation that apply to other contracts also apply to bonds. *Waukesha Concrete Products v. Capital Indem. Corp.*, 127 Wis. 2d 332, 379 N.W.2d 333 (Ct. App. 1985).

No state officer, board, or commission has the power to release a surety from liability under a performance bond or to assign claims it may have against a contractor. 12 *Op. Atty. Gen.* 584 (1923).

The delivery of a surety bond constitutes execution thereof; the surety cannot thereafter withdraw from a public contractor's bond or limit the liability. 7 *Op. Atty. Gen.* 569 (1918).

The court interprets, for purposes of the statute of limitations, when work was completed, independent of the parties' contract. *Arbor Vitae-Woodruff School v. Gulf Ins.*, 2002 WI App. 24, 250 Wis. 2d 637, 639 N.W.2d 788.

Generally, the scope of the performance bond surety's liability is defined by the bond itself. The surety's liability on the bond is usually co-extensive with that of the principal. However, the surety generally assumes no liability beyond that set forth in the bond. *Waukesha Concrete Products v. Capital Indem. Corp.*, 127 Wis. 2d 332, 379 N.W.2d 333 (Ct. App. 1985).

***Interpretation of AIA bond forms*** – Not applicable.

***Cases in which surety steps into shoes of obligee*** – Not applicable.

# WYOMING

Dennis J. Bartlett[1]

## 1. Requirement for Bond

Wyoming requires bonding or other security for all public works projects. There are two levels of bonding requirements. Contracts in excess of $25,000 administered by the Wyoming Department of Administration and Information must be bonded. For other public works projects, any contract in excess of $7,500 must be bonded or otherwise guaranteed. The bond amount varies depending on the size of the contract.

***Statutory provisions for projects that are:***

**Public** – For projects administered by the Wyoming Department of Administration and Information, Wyo. Stat. § 9-2-1016(b)(xviii)(C) requires that:

> [b]efore any contract exceeding $25,000 in amount, for the construction, alteration or repair of any public building or public work or improvement of the state is awarded to any person, the person shall furnish to the state a performance and payment bond executed by a surety company authorized to do business in the state of Wyoming or

1 Dennis J. Bartlett is a member of:
Kerr Brosseau Bartlett O'Brien, LLC
1600 Broadway, Suite 1600
Denver, Colorado 80202
(303) 812-1200

> other form of surety satisfactory to the state, in an amount equal to 100 percent of the contract price.

Similarly, on all other public works projects above a certain dollar amount Wyo. Stat. § 16-6-112 mandates a performance bond or other form of guarantee be obtained. Wyo. Stat. § 16-6-112(a)(ii) conditions the bond:

> For the use and benefit of any person performing any work or labor or furnishing any material or goods of any kind which were used in the execution of the contract, conditioned for the performance and completion of the contract according to its terms, compliance with all requirements of law and payment as due of all just claims for work or labor performed, material furnished and taxes, excises, licenses, assessments, contributions, penalties and interest accrued in the execution of the contract.

**Private** – There is no statute in Wyoming requiring bonding on private contracts.

**Department of Transportation** – The Wyoming Department of Transportation ("WYDOT") requires a performance bond executed by a surety and on a form agreeable to WYDOT "for the performance and completion of the terms of the contract as well as to assure payment of taxes, licenses, penalties or assessments associated with the contract." *See* Wyoming Department of Transportation, Bonding Requirements dated 07/19/2005.

***Case law rules that might generally apply***

Like interpretation of other contracts when construing the terms of a bond "the parties' intention is to be secured from the words of the agreement.... When the meaning of the contract is unambiguous, the plain meaning of the terms is used." *Pete Lien & Sons, Inc. v. Ellsworth Peck Constr. Co.,* 896 P.2d 761, 763 (Wyo. 1995) (citations omitted).

Where a bond is given pursuant to a statute, the statutory provisions are incorporated into the bond. *Vaughn Excavating & Constr., Inc. v. P.S. Cook Co.,* 981 P.2d 485, 487 (Wyo. 1999).

"The statutory bond is to secure performance of the contract, and not the performance of any duties outside the contract, though incidentally connected with it." *Franzen v. Southern Sur. Co.,* 246 P. 30, 35 (Wyo. 1926).

## 2. Damages Covered

### *Set forth in any statutes and/or case law*

While the protection of the bonding statute is to be viewed expansively, the surety's liability for payment is limited to those things which were clearly contemplated when the bond was issued. *Vaughn Excavating and Constr., Inc. v. P.S. Cook Co.,* 981 P.2d 485, 488 (Wyo. 1999). Therefore, while the statute, Wyo. Stat. § 16-6-112(a)(ii), provides the bond shall be conditioned upon "payment as due of all just claims for work or labor performed, material furnished and taxes, excises, licenses, assessments, contributions, penalties and interest" the obligation to pay interest and penalties does not extend down to second tier claimants. *Vaughn,* 981 P.2d at 487. This is because the bond is not liable for terms of a contract between and subcontractor and its supplier which "accrue only to the benefit of the supplier and not the project." *Id.* at 488.

Purchases of equipment not used or consumed on the job are not covered by the public works statute or bonds issued in connection therewith. Similarly, significant repair costs which have a useful life beyond the bonded project are not covered by the bond. *Colorado Builders' Supply Co. v. National Fire Ins. Co.,* 423 P.2d 79 (Wyo. 1967).

Delay or liquidated damages are recoverable from the surety if provided for in the contract. *St. Paul Fire & Marine Ins. Co. v. City of Green River,* 93 F. Supp. 2d 1170 (D. Wyo. 2000) *aff'd,* 6 Fed. Appx. 828 (10th Cir. 2001).

### *Obligations of surety to perform and/or pay*

The statute does not define the surety's rights upon the principal's default and the surety's options and rights upon the principal's default will be determined by the language of the performance bond it issued and the indemnity agreement it has with its principal. However, one of the statutory sections states that one option a surety has is "prompt payment of all obligations under the guarantee" but does not state that is the exclusive option. Wyo. Stat. § 16-6-112(c).

In *St. Paul Fire & Marine Ins. Co. v. City of Green River,* 93 F. Supp. 2d 1170 (D. Wyo. 2000) *aff'd,* 6 Fed. Appx. 828 (10th Cir. 2001), the court held a surety proceeding promptly after its principal's termination could not be terminated by the city even if it was not going to meet the completion deadline in the contract. Further, under the bond form in that case the surety could elect to utilize the principal's employees to complete the job. *Id.* The city's actions deprived the surety of the ability to protect itself, was a material breach of the city's obligations and rendered the bond obligation void. *Id.*

***Whether failure to provide insurance transfers burden to surety***

The applicable statutes do not transfer this burden to the performance bond surety. Whether the bonded contract transfers this obligation requires a fact specific analysis.

***Limitations on damages***

Wyoming recognizes contractual provisions that limit recoverable damages. For example, in *Mountain Fuel Supply Co. v. Central Engineering & Equip. Co.,* 611 P.2d 863 (Wyo. 1980), the court recognized the ability of parties in a contract to limit damages recoverable by using a liquidated damages clause. *Mountain Fuel Supply,* 611 P.2d at 866 (*citing* Wyo. Stat. § 34-21-298 (§ 2-719, U.C.C.)).

In *Commercial Union Ins. Co. v. Stamper*, 732 P.2d 534 (Wyo. 1987), the court addressed the issue of whether the public policy of Wyoming prohibits the limitation of damages in certain insurance contracts, more specifically insurance policy limitations in uninsured-motorist and medical benefit provisions. The court rejected the argument that Wyoming law prohibited the contractual limitation of coverage in these contracts. *Commercial Union,* 732 P.2d at 538. In making this decision, the court stated that it adheres to the general rule that insurance companies can include any desired provision in insurance contracts, including limitation of damages clauses, subject only to what is specifically prohibited by statute or public policy. *See McKinney v. McKinney*, 135 P.2d 940 (Wyo. 1943) (such a limitation was not against public policy).

***Whether obligee may set off bonded contract funds against other principal-obligee debts or obligations***

No reported decisions were found. However, an interesting discussion of the surety's equitable subrogation rights is set forth in the dissenting opinion in *Texas W. Oil & Gas Corp. v. Fitzgerald,* 726 P.2d 1056, 1075 (Wyo. 1986), a guarantee case. The guarantor was held liable for interfering with the debtor's contract. The dissent discussed the equitable rights of the surety including recognizing the right to be subrogated to the obligee's rights in any security for the principal's obligations and the right to be indemnified by the principal.

***Incorporation of specific contract terms by reference***

Wyoming recognizes the doctrine that bonds are to be interpreted according to the contracts referenced therein and the statutes under which they were issued.

**3. Penal Sum Variations**

***Limitations per statute***

The bond on public works projects administered by the Department of Administration and Information must be for 100 percent of the original contract price. Wyo. Stat. § 9-2-1016(b)(xviii)(C). On all other public works projects the bond must be "[i]n an amount not less than ... 50 percent of the contract price unless the contract exceeds ... $100,000 in which case the ... governing body may fix a sufficient amount." Wyo. Stat. § 16-6-112(a)(iii).

***Effect of changes in work upon penal sum, if at all*** – No cases found.

***Statutory or case law protections or dangers to penal sum***

A surety's liability is limited to the penal sum of the bond. *Board of County Comm'rs v. Mason,* 264 P. 93 (Wyo. 1928). See also, *Hoiness-La Bar Ins., v. Julien Constr. Co.,* 743 P.2d 1262 (Wyo. 1987) where the producing agent was held liable to the obligee for failing to obtain a separate payment bond and the obligee suffered losses because it did not have separate penal sums available to it when the principal defaulted and left unpaid sub-subcontractors and suppliers.

## 4. Parties Covered

***Provisions in statutes and/or case law as to whether only obligees are covered*** – Third parties have rights against surety bonds under Wyoming law.

***Coverage for:***

**Third-party beneficiaries** – On public works bonds "any person entitled to the protection of a bond or other form of guarantee" may maintain an action for the amount due. Wyo. Stat. § 16-6-113.

In Wyoming, in determining whether a third-party beneficiary has rights under a contractual agreement, the question becomes whether the parties to the contract intended the third party to directly benefit from their deal. *Wyoming Mach. Co. v. United States Fidelity and Guar. Co.*, 614 P.2d 716, 720 (Wyo. 1980). If the parties intended the third party to receive a direct benefit, this third party is a third-party beneficiary and has a right to bring an action on the contract to enforce his rights. *Cordero Mining Co. v. United States Fidelity & Guar. Ins. Co.*, 67 P.3d 616, 623 (Wyo. 2003). Otherwise, the third party is an incidental beneficiary without the power to pursue an action against the parties to the contract to enforce the contract. *Wyoming Mach. Co.*, 614 P.2d at 720.

**Assignees** – Claims against surety bonds are assignable under Wyoming law. *Shoshoni Lumber Co. v. Fidelity & Deposit Co.,* 24 P.2d 690 (Wyo. 1933) (payment bond claim case).

**Dual obligees** – No cases found.

## 5. Notice or Filing Required

***Statutory provisions***

Public works notice requirements regarding suit commenced on public works bonds are contained within Wyo. Stat. § 16-6-113 which provides, in part, claimants "shall notify the obligee named in the bond, or other guarantee of the beginning of the action, giving the names of the parties, describing the guarantee and stating the amount and nature of his claim. No judgment shall be entered in the action within 30 days after giving the notice."

Public works bond notices on contracts in excess of $50,000 require at the start of the project are contained within Wyo. Stat. § 16-6-121. This section requires subcontractors and suppliers to give notice to the prime contractor of their claim to protection under the bond within 60 days of their first furnishing services or materials or their rights are waived.

***Case law rules concerning condition precedent notice***

Notice requirements will be enforced and are a condition precedent to maintaining an action on a surety bond. *National Sur. Co. v. W. H. Holliday Co.,* 295 P. 913 (Wyo. 1931).

In *Pete Lien & Sons, Inc. v. Ellsworth Peck Constr. Co.,* 896 P.2d 761, 763 (Wyo. 1995), the court held a surety on a private project payment bond could require the claimant give notice within 90 days of having supplied work to preserve a claim on the bond—holding the 90-day notice requirement was reasonable.

## 6. Time for Suit

***Statutes of limitation particular to performance bonds and other applicable statutes of limitation***

On public works bonds "No action shall be maintained on any bond or other form of guarantee satisfactory to the state or any political subdivision ... unless commenced within one year after the date of first publication of notice of final payment of the contract." Wyo. Stat. § 16-6-115.

Wyoming's statute of limitation on any written contract is 10 years. Wyo. Stat. § 1-3-105(a)(1). A limitation defense must be raised by a motion to dismiss or as an affirmative defense in the answer or it is waived. W.R.C.P. 8(c).

***Case law statements about enforceability of limitations contained in bonds***

"Such provisions, if reasonable, limiting the time within which actions may be brought on building contract bonds are valid and will be enforced." *Quin Blair Enterprises, Inc. v. Julien Constr. Co.,* 597 P.2d 945, 956 (Wyo. 1979). In this case the court held a two and one-half year delay in the time between filing of the complaint and service on the surety was not reasonable and under a performance bond limitation clause requiring suit "be instituted before the expiration of two years." The claim was held time barred. *Id.*

***Varying statutes of limitation by agreement in bond or contract*** – *See Quin Blair Enterprises, Inc. v. Julien Constr. Co.,* 597 P.2d 945, 956 (Wyo. 1979), discussed above.

## 7. Procedure

***Statutory or procedural rules that may affect handling or administration of lawsuits***

Note the discussion of Wyo. Stat. § 26-15-124 (c) in the attorney fees section, *infra.* Maintaining a defense after discovery of information that leads the surety to conclude the defense is not viable subjects the surety to an award of attorney fees.

***Venue requirements and jurisdictional limitations***

Actions to enforce bond obligations "may be brought in any court of competent jurisdiction by the authorized officer or agency to enforce payment." Wyo. Stat. § 16-6-112(c). Wyoming's general rule of venue is actions are to be brought in the county where the defendant resides or may be served. Wyo. Stat. § 1-5-108.

***Court rules*** – While there are some significant differences, Wyoming's rules of civil procedure are modeled after the Federal Rules.

***Particular agency regulations/rules*** – None located.

***Arbitration requirements and application*** – No cases found.

## 8. Attorney's Fees

***Statutes and/or case law limiting or permitting recovery of attorney's fees***

Wyoming follows the American Rule on the recovery of attorney's fees, which holds each party responsible for his attorney's fees. Nonetheless, if a statute or contractual provision authorizes the recovery of attorney's fees, a party may be reimbursed for his fees. *Forshee v. Delaney*, 118 P.3d 445 (Wyo. 2005).

A Wyoming statute permits the recovery of attorney's fees in a breach of insurance contract action. Wyo. Stat. § 26-15-124 (c) provides that a court may award attorney's fees if the insurer, including sureties, fails to properly pay the full amount of loss covered by the insurance contract. Courts do not permit recovery under Wyo. Stat. § 26-15-124 when the surety did not breach its duties under the performance bond. *St. Paul Fire & Marine Ins. Co. v. City of Green River*, 93 F. Supp. 2d 1170 (Wyo. 2000) *aff'd,* 6 Fed. Appx. 828 (10th Cir. 2001).

In Wyoming attorney's fees are recoverable in breach of contract actions where the contract provides for the recovery of such fees. *Forshee v. Delaney*, 118 P.3d 445 (Wyo. 2005).

## 9. Special Provisions

Wyoming Statutes, Title 38, deal with surety rights and remedies. In appropriate cases these codified rights include: the right to require the claimant bring suit on a written instrument guaranteed by the surety, Wyo. Stat. § 38-1-101; the right of subrogation to the obligee's position, Wyo. Stat. § 38-1-104; the right to sue the principal for exoneration, Wyo. Stat. § 38-1-107; and the right to maintain a *quia timet* action, Wyo. Stat. §§ 38-1-108 & 109.

Wyoming codifies the method of bond execution. Wyo. Stat. § 38-3-101. Bonds issued by sureties that are not qualified to do business in Wyoming are void. Wyo. Stat. § 38-3-103. Issuing or acquiring bonds from an unauthorized surety is a misdemeanor. Wyo. Stat. § 38-3-104.

## 10. Remarks

Wyoming is a state of vast expanses, with a small population of fiercely independent, proud people. The citizens have forged strong ties to each other. If possible, when litigating disputes in Wyoming sureties should seriously consider removal to federal court. If that is not possible, association with established local counsel is highly recommended.

## 11. Case Annotations

***Interpretation of AIA bond forms*** – No reported cases were found that identify the bonds at issue as being AIA form bonds.

***Cases in which surety steps into shoes of obligee***

The dissent in *Texas W. Oil & Gas Corp. v. Fitzgerald,* 726 P.2d 1056, 1075 (Wyo. 1986), a guarantee case, stands for the proposition that a surety paying a loss is equitably subrogated to the obligee's rights in security pledged by the principal and, separately, has an equitable right of indemnification from the principal.